List of Sample Documents and Forms

EDITING AND REVISION SYMBOLS

Symbol	Problem	page
ab	wrong abbreviation	696
acr	unclear acronym	228
agr p	error in pronoun agreement	683
agr sv	error in subject-verb agreement	682
an	analogy needed	231
av	active voice needed	213
bias	biased language	236
ca	wrong pronoun case	687
cap	capital letter needed	696
cl	words add clutter	222
comb	combined sentences	223
cont	faulty contraction	693
coord	faulty coordination	685
cs	comma splice	682
dgl	dangling modifier	683
euph	euphemism	228
frag	sentence fragment	680
it	faulty "it" sentence opener	218
jarg	needless jargon	227
mod	misplaced modifier	212
neg	negative phrasing	221
nom	nominalization	220
offen	offensive language	237
os	overstuffed sentence	216
over	overstatement	229
par	faulty parallelism	684
pct	faulty punctuation	687
./	period	688
?/	question mark	688
!/	exclamation point	688
;/	semicolon	688
:/	colon	689
,/	comma	689
ap/	apostrophe	692
"/"	quotation marks	693

Symbol	Problem	page
[]/	brackets	694
()/	parentheses	695
--/	dash	695
.../	ellipses	694
ital	italics	695
-/	hyphen	696
pref	needless preface	218
prep	needless preposition	220
pv	passive voice needed	215
qual	needless qualifier	222
red	redundant phrase	217
ref	faulty pronoun reference	211
rep	needless repetition	217
ro	run-on sentence	681
sexist	sexist usage	237
short	short sentence needed	225
simple	simpler word needed	226
sp	misspelled word	698
spec	specific word needed	230
st mod	stacked modifying nouns	212
sub	faulty subordination	686
th	faulty "there" sent. opener	218
tone	inappropriate tone	232
trans	transition needed	701
trite	overused expression	228
ts	faulty topic sentence	202
var	sentence variety needed	225
w	wordiness	217
wo	faulty word order	212
wv	weak verb	219
ww	wrong word	230
#	faulty numbering	697
¶	new paragraph needed	201
¶ coh	paragraph lacks coherence	203
¶ lngth	paragraph too long or short	204
¶ un	paragraph lacks unity	202

A Topical List of the GUIDELINES Boxes

A Guide to the CHECKLISTS

THIRTEENTH EDITION

Technical Communication

John M. Lannon
University of Massachusetts, Dartmouth

Laura J. Gurak
University of Minnesota

PEARSON

Boston Columbus Indianapolis New York San Francisco Upper Saddle River
Amsterdam Cape Town Dubai London Madrid Milan Munich Paris Montréal Toronto
Delhi Mexico City São Paulo Sydney Hong Kong Seoul Singapore Taipei Tokyo

Senior Acquisitions Editor: Brad Potthoff
Editorial Assistant: Lauren Cunningham
Development Editor: Bruce Cantley
Executive Market Development Manager: Donna Kenly
Executive Marketing Manager: Joyce Nilsen
Senior Supplements Editor: Donna Campion
Executive Digital Producer: Stefanie A. Snajder
Digital Editor: Sara Gordus
Digital Content Specialist: Erin Reilly
Production Manager: Ellen MacElree
Project Coordination, Text Design, and Electronic Page Makeup: Integra
Cover Designer/Manager: John Callahan
Cover Photos: luxxxam/Shutterstock
Senior Manufacturing Buyer: Roy L. Pickering, Jr.
Printer/Binder: R. R. Donnelley & Sons/Crawfordsville
Cover Printer: R. R. Donnelley & Sons/Crawfordsville

Library of Congress Cataloging-in-Publication Data
Lannon, John M.
Technical communication/John M. Lannon, University of Massachusetts, Dartmouth, Laura J. Gurak, University of Minnesota.—13th edition.
pages cm
Includes index.
ISBN-13: 978-0-321-89997-2 (student)
ISBN-13: 978-0-321-89542-4 (exam copy)
ISBN-10: 0-321-89997-0 (Student)
ISBN-10: 0-321-89542-8 (exam copy)
1. Technical writing. 2. Communication of technical information. I. Gurak, Laura J. II. Title.
T11.L24 2014
808.06'66—dc23
2013011949

Photo Credits: 2, Yuri Arcurs/Shutterstock; 16, Zurijeta/Shutterstock; 35, Jeffrey Greenberg/The Image Works; 61, Coston Stock/Alamy; 82, Tom Merton/Getty Images; 105, Westend61/Getty Images; 124, Andersen Ross/Getty Images; 152, Kutay Tanir/Getty Images; 173, mediaphotos/Getty Images; 192, Anke van Wyk/fotolia; 209, Artifacts Images/Getty Images; 245, kay/Getty Images; 250, (tr) PhotoAlto sas/Alamy; 250, (bl) kay/Getty Images; 274, (l) RGB Ventures LLC dba SuperStock/Alamy; 274, (r) Design Pics Inc.—RM Content/Alamy; 275, YuryZap/Shutterstock; 292, Yuri Arcurs/Shutterstock; 318, Brigette M. Sullivan/PhotoEdit, Inc.; 333, Ian Dagnall/Alamy; 348, Ross Ananai/Getty Images; 379, Ian Shaw/Alamy; 408, Aaron Amat/Shutterstock; 428, BSIP SA/Alamy; 464, Photography 1st/Alamy; 456, Mladen Curakovic/Alamy; 489, Pressmaster/Shutterstock; 510, Pressmaster/Shutterstock; 554, Bill Aron/PhotoEdit, Inc.; 590, Monty Rakusen/cultura/Corbis; 607, (tr) John M.Lannon; 620, NetPhotos2/Alamy; 633, stuwdamdorp/Alamy; 637, Reprinted with permission of Marriott International, Inc.

10 9—DOC—16 15

Student ISBN-13: 978-0-321-89997-2
Student ISBN-10: 0-321-89997-0

Exam Copy ISBN-13: 978-0-321-89542-4
Exam Copy ISBN-10: 0-321-89542-8

A la Carte ISBN-13: 978-0-321-89537-0
A la Carte ISBN-10: 0-321-89537-1

www.pearsonhighered.com

Brief Contents

Detailed Contents

3 Persuading Your Audience 35

4 Weighing the Ethical Issues 61

5 Teamwork and Global Considerations 82

6 An Overview of the Technical Writing Process 105

PART 2 The Research Process 123

7 Thinking Critically about the Research Process 124

8 Evaluating and Interpreting Information 152

18 Technical Definitions 408

19 Technical Descriptions, Specifications, and Marketing Materials 428

20 Instructions and Procedures 456

Preface

Whether digital, face-to-face, handwritten, or printed, workplace communication is more than a value-neutral exercise in "information transfer:" it is a complex social transaction. From reports to proposals, job applications to email messages, video chats to oral presentations, every rhetorical situation has its own specific interpersonal, ethical, legal, and cultural demands. Moreover, today's professional needs to be a skilled communicator and a discriminating consumer of information, skilled in methods of inquiry, retrieval, evaluation, and interpretation essential to informed decision making.

Designed in response to these issues, *Technical Communication*, Thirteenth Edition, addresses a wide range of interests for classes in which students from a variety of majors are enrolled. The text explains, illustrates, and applies rhetorical principles to an array of assignments—from memos, résumés, and email to formal reports and proposals. To help students develop awareness of audience and accountability, exercises incorporate the problem-solving demands typical in college and on the job. Self-contained chapters allow for various course plans and customized assignments.

WHAT'S NEW IN THIS EDITION?

Technical Communication, Thirteenth Edition, has been thoroughly revised to account for the latest innovations in workplace communication and today's technologically sophisticated, diverse, and global workforce. Students will benefit from a variety of new content and features in this edition, including

- **Throughly revised chapter on social media,** with updated coverage of using Facebook on the job, using LinkedIn for networking, using customer review sites such as Yelp! as a form of surveying, and using Twitter feeds on the job.
- **Updated chapter on email,** with a brand new section on using text messaging on the job.
- **Updated technology coverage throughout the book**, including attending virtual meetings, digital brainstorming, using digitized print sources and subject directories in the research process, using Prezi for oral presentations, and citing Facebook and Twitter sources.
- **New Digital and Social Media Projects** throughout the book to emphasize the growing importance of using social media on the job.

- **Expanded coverage of plagiarism** to highlight the ethical importance of avoiding intentional or unintentional plagiarism on the job.
- **New section on style, tone, and email** to help students avoid unprofessional email habits.
- **More logical coverage of usability** now highlighted in the chapters on audience and instructions and procedures.

HALLMARKS OF *TECHNICAL COMMUNICATION*

Technical Communication, Thirteenth Edition, retains—and enhances or expands—the features that have made it a best-selling text for technical communication over twelve editions. These include the following:

- **Complete coverage for any course in technical communication, business communication, or professional writing.** The topics move from basic foundational concepts to chapters on research, visuals, style, document design, and usability, and finally to specific documents and applications. The appendix includes thorough coverage of MLA, APA, and CSE documentation styles, and a handbook of grammar, mechanics, and usage.
- **A reader-friendly writing style that presents all topics clearly and concisely.** Simple, straightforward explanations of concepts and audience/purpose analyses of specific document types help differentiate technical communication from academic writing.
- **The most current and thorough coverage of workplace technologies, ethics, and global considerations in the workplace.** Always prominent in the book, these three topics have been updated and expanded throughout to keep up with the changes in the contemporary workplace.
- **Strong coverage of information literacy.** According to the American Library Association Presidential Committee on Information Literacy, information-literate people "know how knowledge is organized, how to find information, and how to use information in such a way that others can learn from them." Critical thinking—the basis of information literacy—is covered intensively in Part II and integrated throughout the text.
- **A focus on applications beyond the classroom.** Clear ties to the workplace have always been a primary feature of this book. This edition includes examples from everyday on-the-job situations and sample documents, as well as dedicated chapters on ethics and on teamwork and global issues Each chapter opener includes a quote from an on-the-job communicator.
- **Emphasis on the humanistic aspects of technical communication.** Technical communication is ultimately a humanistic endeavor, with broad societal

impact—not just a set of job-related transcription tasks. Accordingly, situations and sample documents in this edition address complex technical and societal issues such as global warming, public health issues, environmental and energy topics, digital technology, and genomics.

- **Plentiful model documents and other useful figures throughout the book.** Descriptions and instructions for creating technical documents are accompanied by clear, annotated examples. Graphic illustrations throughout make abstract concepts easy to understand.
- **Highly praised pedagogical features.** Pedagogical features, including chapter-opening Learning Objectives, summary Guidelines boxes, real-world Consider This boxes, Case studies, annotated figures, summary marginal notes, and end-of-chapter Checklists and Projects reinforce chapter topics. These features are outlined in more detail below.

HOW THIS BOOK IS ORGANIZED

Technical Communication is designed to allow instructors maximum flexibility. Each chapter is self-contained, and each part focuses on a crucial aspect of the communication process. Following are the five major parts of the book:

- **Part I: Communicating in the Workplace** treats job-related communication as a problem-solving process. Students learn to think critically about the informative, persuasive, and ethical dimensions of their communications. They also learn how to adapt to the interpersonal challenges of collaborative work, and to address the various needs and expectations of global audiences.
- **Part II: The Research Process** treats research as a deliberate inquiry process. Students learn to formulate significant research questions; to explore primary and secondary sources in hard copy and electronic form; to evaluate and interpret their findings; and to summarize for economy, accuracy, and emphasis.
- **Part III: Organization, Style, and Visual Design** offers strategies for organizing, composing, and designing messages that readers can follow and understand. Students learn to control their material and develop a readable style. They also learn about the rhetorical implications of graphics and page design—specifically, how to enhance a document's access, appeal, and visual impact for audiences who need to locate, understand, and use the information successfully.
- **Part IV: Specific Documents and Applications** applies earlier concepts and strategies to the preparation of print and electronic documents and oral presentations. Various letters, memos, reports, and proposals offer a balance of examples from the workplace and from student writing. Each sample document has been chosen so that students can emulate it easily. Chapters on

email and text messaging, Web pages, and social media emphasize the important role of digital communication in today's workplace.

- **Part V: Resources for Writers** includes "A Quick Guide to Documentation," which provides general guidance as well as specific style guides and citation models for MLA, APA, and CSE, and "A Quick Guide to Grammar, Usage, and Mechanics," which provides a handy resource for answering questions about the basic building blocks of writing.

LEARNING ENHANCEMENT FEATURES

This book is written and designed to be a highly accessible document, so that readers can "read to learn and learn to do." *Technical Communication*, Thirteenth Edition, includes the following learning enhancement features that will help students access the material easily and use the ideas to become effective technical communicators:

- ***Chapter opening quotations*** demonstrate the real-world applications of each chapter's topic.
- ***Learning Objectives*** at the beginning of each chapter provide a set of learning goals for students to fulfill.
- ***Guidelines* boxes** help students prepare specific documents by synthesizing the chapter's information.
- ***Cases* and sample situations** encourage students to make appropriate choices as they analyze their audience and purpose and then compose their document.
- **Sample documents** model various kinds of technical writing, illustrating for students what they need to do. Captions and annotations identify key features in sample documents.
- ***Consider This* boxes** provide interesting and topical applications of the important issues discussed in various chapters, such as collaboration, technology, and ethics.
- ***Notes* callouts** clarify up-to-the-minute business and technological advances and underscore important advice.
- **Marginal notes** summarize larger chunks of information to reinforce key chapter concepts.
- ***Checklists*** promote careful editing, revision, and collaboration. Students polish their writing by reviewing key criteria for the document and by referring to cross-referenced pages in the text for more information on each point.
- **General, team, global, and digital and social media *Projects*** at each chapter's end help students apply what they have learned.

INSTRUCTIONAL SUPPLEMENTS

A wide array of supplements for both instructors and students accompany *Technical Communication*, Thirteenth Edition:

For Instructors

- **Instructor's Manual, by Daun Daemon, North Carolina State University.** Available both in print and online, the Instructor's Manual includes general and chapter-by-chapter teaching tips, additional chapter exercises, quizzes, and sample syllabi. In addition, it provides guidance on using MyTechCommLab as an online resource for courses. Contact your local Pearson representative for details.
- **PowerPoint slides.** Fully revised to accompany the thirteenth edition, the PowerPoint presentations provide a wealth of chapter-by-chapter slides that can be projected or printed to enhance in-class instruction or simply used for review and class planning.
- **MyTest.** Pearson MyTest is a powerful assessment generation program that helps instructors easily create and print quizzes, study guides, and exams. Questions and tests are authored online, allowing instructors ultimate flexibility and the ability to efficiently manage assessments anytime, anywhere. To access MyTest, go to <www.pearsonhighered.com/mytest/>, log on, and follow the instructions. You must first be registered.

For Students

- **MyTechCommLab.** Instructors who package MyTechCommLab with *Technical Communication* provide their students with a comprehensive resource that offers the very best multimedia support for technical writing in one integrated, easy-to-use site. Features include interactive model documents, case studies, multimedia resources, and more. MyTechCommLab may be packaged with the text for an additional small cost and is available for purchase at <www.mytechcommlab.com>.

MyTechCommLab™

- **Companion Web site.** The companion Web site provides numerous materials to help students get the most out of this course. Resources include topical overviews, multiple choice quizzes, model documents, and other resources.
- **Interactive Pearson eText.** An eBook version of *Technical Communication* is also available on MyTechCommLab. This dynamic, online version of the text

includes marginal icons that link students to additional resources located on MyTechCommLab, such as interactive model documents, instructional videos, and podcasts.

- **CourseSmart eTexbook.** Students can subscribe to *Technical Communication*, Thirteenth Edition, as a CourseSmart eText at <www.CourseSmart.com>. The site includes all of the book's content in a format that enables students to search the text, bookmark passages, integrate their notes, and print reading assignments that incorporate lecture notes.

ACKNOWLEDGMENTS

Many of the refinements in this and earlier editions were inspired by generous and insightful suggestions from the following reviewers: Cindy Allen, James Madison University; Angela Anderson, University of Alaska, Anchorage; Dana Anderson, Indiana University; Mary Beth Bamforth, Wake Technical Community College; Marian G. Barchilon, Arizona State University East; Carl N. Bean, Virginia Polytechnic and State University; Christiana Birchak, University of Houston Downtown; Jeannie Boniecki, Naugatuck Valley Community College; Susan L. Booker, Hampden-Sydney College; Gene Booth, Albuquerque Technical Vocational Institute; Alma Bryant, University of South Florida; Beth Camp, Linn-Benton Community College; John Carlberg, University of Wisconsin-Whitewater; Joanna B. Chrzanowski, Jefferson Community College; Jim Collier, Virginia Tech; Daryl Davis, Northern Michigan University; Charlie Dawkins, Virginia Polytechnical Institute and State University; Charlsye Smith Diaz, University of Maine; Pat Dorazio, SUNY Institute of Technology; Keri Dutkiewicz, Davenport University; Julia Ferganchick-Neufang, University of Arkansas; Madelyn Flammia, University of Central Florida; Regina Clemens Fox, Arizona State University; Clint Gardner, Salt Lake Community College; Mary Frances Gibbons, Richland College; Lucy Graca, Arapahoe Community College; Roger Graves, DePaul University; Baotong Gu, Eastern Washington University; Gil Haroian-Guerin, Syracuse University; Susan Guzman-Trevino, Temple College; Wade Harrell, Howard University; Linda Harris, University of Maryland, Baltimore County; Michael Joseph Hassett, Brigham Young University; Cecilia Hawkins, Texas A & M University; Robert A. Henderson, Southeastern Oklahoma State University; TyAnna K. Herrington, Georgia Institute of Technology; Mary Hocks, Georgia State University; Robert Hogge, Weber State University; Lynn Hublou, South Dakota State University; Glenda A. Hudson, California State University-Bakersfield; Phillip Jacowitz, Embry-Riddle Aeronautical University; Gloria Jaffe, University of Central Florida; Bruce L. Janoff, University of Pittsburgh; Mitchell H. Jarosz, Delta College; Jeanette Jeneault, Syracuse University; Jack

Jobst, Michigan Technical University; Christopher Keller, University of Hawaii at Hilo; Kathleen Kincade, Stephen F. Austin State University; Susan E. Kincaid, Lakeland Community College; JoAnn Kubala, Southwest Texas State University; Karen Kuralt, Louisiana Tech University; Kevin LaGrandeur, New York Institute of Technology; Thomas LaJeunesse, University of Minnesota Duluth; Elizabeth A. Latshaw, University of South Florida; Lindsay Lewan, Arapahoe Community College; Sherry Little, San Diego State University; Linda Loehr, Northeastern University; Tom Long, Thomas Nelson Community College; Rose Marie Mastricola, Northeast Wisconsin Technical College; Lisa J. McClure, Southern Illinois University-Carbondale; Michael McCord, Minnesota State University, Moorhead; Devonee McDonald, Kirkwood Community College; James L. McKenna, San Jacinto College; Lisa McNair, Georgia Institute of Technology; Troy Meyers, California State University Long Beach; Mohsen Mirshafiei, California State University, Fullerton; Roxanne Munch, Joliet Junior College; Thomas Murphy, Mansfield University; Thomas A. Murray, SUNY Institute of Technology; Shirley Nelson, Chattanooga State Technical Community College; Gerald Nix, San Juan College; Megan O'Neill, Creighton University; Celia Patterson, Pittsburgh State University; Don Pierstorff, Orange Coast College; Peter Porosky, Johns Hopkins University; Carol Clark Powell, University of Texas at El Paso; Cindy Raisor, Texas A&M University; Dirk Remley, Kent State University; Don Rhyne, San Joaquin Valley College; Kenneth Risdon, University of Minnesota; Elizabeth Robinson, Texas A&M University; Mark Rollins, Ohio University, Athens; Beverly Sauer, Carnegie Mellon University; Jan Schlegel, Tri-State University; Lauren Sewell Ingraham, University of Tennessee at Chattanooga; Carol M. H. Shehadeh, Florida Institute of Technology; Sharla Shine, Terra Community College; Rick Simmons, Louisiana Technical University; Susan Simon, City College of the City University of New York; Clay Kinchen Smith, Santa Fe Community College; Judy Sneller, South Dakota School of Mines & Technology; Tom Stuckert, University of Findlay; Terry Tannacito, Frostburg State University; Anne Thomas, San Jacinto College; Jessica Trant, University of South Florida; Maxine Turner, Georgia Institute of Technology; Mary Beth VanNess, University of Toledo; Madeleine Vessel, New Mexico State University; Jeff Wedge, Embry-Riddle University; Christian Weisser, Florida Atlantic U. Honors College; Deanna M. White, The University of Texas at San Antonio; Nicole Wilson, Bowie State University; Kristin Woolever, Northeastern University; Carolyn Young, University of Wyoming; Stephanee Zerkel, Westark College; Beverly Zimmerman, Brigham Young University; Don Zimmerman, Colorado State University.

For this edition, we are grateful for the comments of the following reviewers: Dana Anderson, Indiana University; Jeanelle Barrett, Tarleton State University; Michael Creeden, Florida International University; Madelyn Flammia, University of Central Florida; Ian Granville, University of Florida; Ava Lunsford, San Jacinto

College; Manuel Martinez, Santa Fe College; William Matter, Richland College; Nancy Riecken, Ivy Technical Community College; and Nicole Wilson, Bowie State University.

We thank our colleagues and students at the University of Massachusetts and the University of Minnesota, respectively, for their ongoing inspiration. This edition is the product of much guidance and support. From Brad Potthoff, Joe Opiela, Mary Ellen Curley, and Ellen MacElree we received outstanding editorial guidance and support. Many thanks to Bruce Cantley for his generous and unflagging development help and valuable ideas, and to Martha Beyerlein for managing the production process with such thoughtfulness and precision.

From John M. Lannon, special thanks to those who help me keep going: Chega, Daniel, Sarah, Patrick, and Zorro. From Laura J. Gurak, thanks greatly to Nancy, to my friends and family, and to my four-legged companions for the ongoing support and friendship.

—John M. Lannon and Laura J. Gurak

PART 1

Communicating in the Workplace

1 Introduction to Technical Communication

"Writing is essential to my work. Everything we do at my company results in a written product of some kind—a formal technical report, a summary of key findings, recommendations and submissions to academic journals or professional associations. We also write proposals to help secure new contracts. Writing is the most important skill we seek in potential employees and nurture and reward in current employees. It is very hard to find people with strong writing skills, regardless of their academic background."

—Paul Harder, President, mid-sized consulting firm

LEARNING OBJECTIVES FOR THIS CHAPTER

- Define technical communication
- Understand that technical communication has a global reach
- Appreciate the role of technical communication in most careers
- Identify the main features and aims of technical communication
- Recognize a typical technical document
- Observe the challenges facing one communicator at work

WHAT IS TECHNICAL COMMUNICATION?

Technical communication is the exchange of information that helps people interact with technology and solve complex problems. Almost every day, we make decisions or take actions that depend on technical information. When we install any new device, from a microwave oven to a new printer, it's the setup information that we look for as soon as we open the box. Before we opt for the latest high-tech medical treatment, we learn all we can about its benefits and risks. From banking systems to online courses to business negotiations, countless aspects of daily life are affected by technology. To interact with technology in so many ways, we need information that is not only technically accurate but also easy to understand and use.

Technical communication helps us interact with technology in our daily lives

Technical communication serves various needs in various settings. People may need to perform a task (say, assemble a new exercise machine), answer a question (say, about the safety of a flu shot), or make a decision (say, about suspending offshore oil drilling). In the workplace, we are not only consumers of technical communication, but producers as well. Any document or presentation we prepare (memo, letter, report, Web page, PowerPoint) must advance the goals of our readers, viewers, or listeners.

Technical communication helps us solve complex problems

Figure 1.1 shows a sampling of the kinds of technical communication you might encounter or prepare, either on the job or in the community.

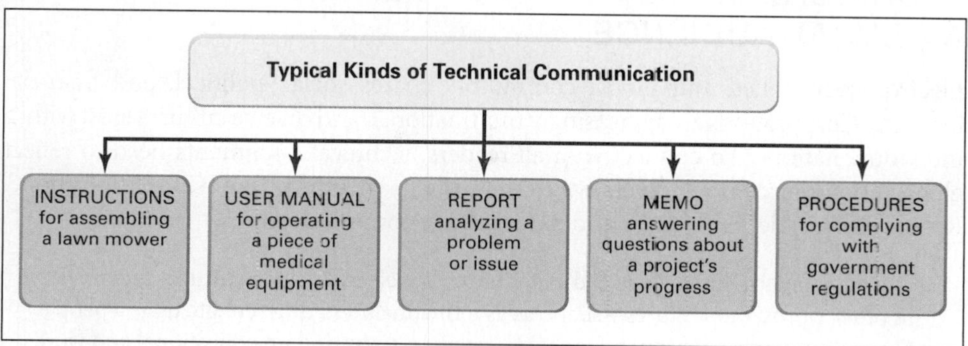

FIGURE 1.1 Technical Communication Serves Various Needs

TECHNICAL COMMUNICATION IS A DIGITAL *AND* A HUMAN ACTIVITY

In today's world of digital tools, we write and communicate more than ever: texting, emailing, using social networking sites, looking up research and news information on the Web, video conferencing with colleagues, and so forth. We do all this with such speed that we often forget to pay attention to basic professional standards for workplace communication.

Digital communication requires attention to style and tone

For instance, we sometimes use an informal, chatty tone—appropriate for friends but not for the office—when sending a workplace email. Or we might be in a hurry and fail to notice our use of humor, which may be welcomed in person but could be misunderstood in an email. An unclear or inaccurate email could easily cause a legal conflict or a safety error; a tone that seems inappropriate could result in wasted hours spent resolving the interpersonal situation instead of working on the project.

Digital technology is no substitute for human interaction

Despite the power of digital technology, only humans can give meaning to all the information that we convey and receive. Information technology is no substitute for human interaction. People make information meaningful by thinking critically and addressing questions that no computer can answer:

Questions that only a person can answer

- Which information is relevant to this situation?
- Can I verify the accuracy of this source?
- What does this information mean?
- What action does it suggest?
- How does this information affect me or my colleagues?
- With whom should I share it?
- How might others interpret this information?

With so much information available via the Web and other sources, no one can afford to "let the data speak for themselves."

TECHNICAL COMMUNICATION REACHES A GLOBAL AUDIENCE

Write to a diverse audience

Electronically linked, our global community shares social, political, and financial interests. Corporations are increasingly multinational, and diverse cultures exist within individual nations. To connect with all readers, technical documents need to reflect global and intercultural diversity. In his article, "Culture and Communication," Robert G. Hein defines culture and its impact on communication:

How cultures shape communication styles

> Our accumulated knowledge and experiences, beliefs and values, attitudes and roles—in other words, our cultures—shape us as individuals and differentiate us as a people. Our cultures, inbred through family life, religious training, and educational and work

> experiences . . . manifest themselves . . . in our thoughts and feelings, our actions and reactions, and our views of the world.
>
> Most important for communicators, our cultures manifest themselves in our information needs and our styles of communication . . . our expectations as to how information should be organized, what should be included in its content, and how it should be expressed. (125)

Cultures differ over which behaviors seem appropriate for social interaction, business relationships, contract negotiation, and communication practices. An effective communication style in one culture may be offensive elsewhere. For example, one survey of top international executives reveals the following attitudes toward U.S. communication style (Wandycz 22–23):

How various cultures view U.S. communication style

- Latin America: "Americans are too straightforward, too direct."
- Eastern Europe: "An imperial tone . . . It's always about how [Americans] know best."
- Southeast Asia: "To get my respect, American business [people] should know something about [our culture]. But they don't."
- Western Europe: "Americans miss the small points."
- Central Europe: "Americans tend to oversell themselves."

In addition to being broadly accessible, any document prepared for a global audience must reflect sensitivity to cultural differences. For more on cross-cultural communication, see Chapters 3 and 5.

TECHNICAL COMMUNICATION IS PART OF MOST CAREERS

Whatever your job description, expect to be evaluated, at least in part, on your communication skills. At one IBM subsidiary, for example, 25 percent of an employee's evaluation is based on how effectively that person shares information (Davenport 99). Even if you don't anticipate a "writing" career, expect to be a part-time technical communicator, who will routinely face situations such as these:

Most professionals serve as part-time technical communicators

- As a medical professional, psychologist, social worker, or accountant, you will keep precise records that are, increasingly, a basis for legal action.
- As a scientist, you will report on your research and explain its significance.
- As a manager, you will write memos, personnel evaluations, inspection reports, and give oral presentations.
- As a lab or service technician, you will keep daily activity records and help train coworkers in installing, using, or servicing equipment.
- As an attorney, you will research and interpret the law for clients.

- As an engineer or architect, you will collaborate with colleagues as well as experts in related fields before presenting a proposal to your client. (For example, an architect's plans are reviewed by a structural engineer who certifies that the design is sound.)
- As an employee or intern in the nonprofit sector (an environmental group or a government agency), you will research important topics and write brochures, press releases, or handbooks for clients.

The more you advance in your field, the more you will need to share information and establish contacts. Managers and executives spend much of their time negotiating, setting policies, and promoting their ideas—often among diverse cultures around the globe.

In addition, most people can expect to work for multiple different employers throughout their career. Each employer will have questions such as the following:

Employers seek portable skills

- Can you write and speak effectively?
- Can you research information, verify its accuracy, figure out what it means, and shape it for the reader's specific purposes?
- Can you work on a team, with people from diverse backgrounds?
- Can you get along with, listen to, and motivate others?
- Are you flexible enough to adapt to rapid changes in business conditions and technology?
- Can you market yourself and your ideas persuasively?
- Are you ready to pursue lifelong learning and constant improvement?

These are among the portable skills employers seek in today's college graduates—skills all related to communication.

TECHNICAL COMMUNICATORS PLAY MANY ROLES

What technical communicators do

Full-time technical communicators serve many roles. Trade and professional organizations employ technical communicators to produce newsletters, pamphlets, journals, and public relations material. Many work in business and industry, preparing instructional material, reports, proposals, and scripts for industrial films. They also prepare sales literature, publicity releases, handbooks, catalogs, brochures, Web pages, intranet content, articles, speeches, and oral and multimedia presentations.

Related career paths

Technical communicators also do other work. For example, they edit reports for punctuation, grammar, style, and logical organization. They may also oversee publishing projects, coordinating the efforts of writers, visual artists, graphic designers, content experts, and lawyers to produce a complex manual or proposal. Given their broad range of skills, technical communicators often enter related fields such as publishing, magazine editing, Web site management, television, and college teaching.

MAIN FEATURES OF TECHNICAL COMMUNICATION

Almost any form of technical communication displays certain shared features: The communication is reader-centered, accessible and efficient, often produced by teams, and delivered in both paper and digital versions.

Reader-Centered

Focus on the reader, not the writer

Unlike poetry, fiction, or college essays, a technical document rarely focuses on the writer's personal thoughts and feelings. This doesn't mean that your document should have no personality (or voice), but it does mean that the needs of your readers come first.

What readers expect

Workplace readers typically are interested in "who you are" only to the extent that they want to know what you have done, what you recommend, or how you speak for your company. Reader-centered documents focus on what people need to learn, do, or decide.

Accessible and Efficient

Make documents easy to navigate and understand

Readers expect to find the information they need and to get questions answered clearly. For instance, the document shown in Figure 1.2 (see page 9) is written and designed so that a nontechnical audience can find and follow the information. Instead of long technical passages, the content is presented in short chunks, in the form of questions that readers might ask.

An accessible and efficient technical document includes elements such as those displayed in Figure 1.2 and listed below.

Elements that make a document accessible and efficient

- **worthwhile content**—includes all (and only) the information readers need
- **sensible organization**—guides the reader and emphasizes important material
- **readable style**—promotes fluid reading and accurate understanding
- **effective visuals**—clarify concepts and relationships, and substitute for words whenever possible
- **effective page design**—provides heads, lists, type styles, white space, and other aids to navigation
- **supplements (abstract, appendix, glossary, linked pages, and so on)**—allow readers to focus on the specific parts of a long document that are relevant to their purpose

Recognize your legal accountability

Accessible, efficient communication is no mere abstract notion: In the event of a lawsuit, faulty writing is treated like any other faulty product. If your inaccurate, unclear, or incomplete information leads to injury, damage, or loss, you and your company or organization can be held responsible.

> **NOTE** *Make sure your message is clear and straightforward—but do not oversimplify. Information designer Nathan Shedroff reminds us that, while clarity makes information easier to understand, simplicity is "often responsible for the 'dumbing down' of information rather than the illumination of it" (280). The "sound bytes" that often masquerade as network news reports serve as a good case in point.*

Often Produced by Teams

Prepare for teamwork

Technical documents are often complex. Instead of being produced by a lone writer, complex documents usually are created by teams composed of writers, Web designers, engineers or scientists, managers, legal experts, and other professionals. The teams might be situated at one site or location or distributed across different job sites, time zones, and countries.

Delivered in Paper and Digital Versions

Select the appropriate medium or combination of media

Technical documents can be delivered in a variety of media such as print (hard copy), CDs, Web pages, PDF documents, ebooks, podcasts, and online videos. In fact, distinctions between print and digital communication are becoming blurred. Figure 1.2 is a good example: The document is in PDF format and can be read on the Web, downloaded to your own computer for future reading, or printed on paper. Technical communicators must write well but must also be able to think about page design and media choices.

> **NOTE** *In many cases, print documents are still the basis for much of a company's communication. Despite continued advances in electronic communication, paper is not going away.*

PURPOSES OF TECHNICAL COMMUNICATION

What purpose or combination of purposes will your document serve?

Most forms of technical communication address one of three primary purposes: (1) to anticipate and answer questions (inform your readers); (2) to enable people to perform a task or follow a procedure (instruct your readers); or (3) to influence people's thinking (persuade your readers). Often, as in Figure 1.2, these purposes will overlap.

Documents that Inform

Anticipate and answer your readers' questions

Informational documents are designed to inform—to provide information that answers readers' questions clearly and efficiently. Figure 1.2 is primarily informational. It is designed for a wide audience of readers who may know little about the topic.

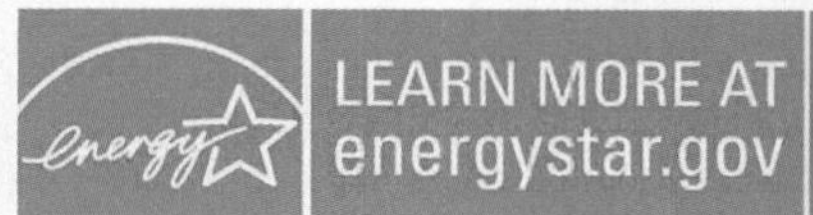

ENERGY STAR®, a U.S. Environmental Protection Agency and U.S. Department of Energy program, helps us all save money and protect our environment through energy efficient products and practices. For more information, visit www.energystar.gov.

Frequently Asked Questions
Information on Compact Fluorescent Light Bulbs (CFLs) and Mercury
July 2008

Why should people use CFLs?
Switching from traditional light bulbs (called incandescent) to CFLs is an effective, simple change everyone in America can make right now. Making this change will help to use less electricity at home and prevent greenhouse gas emissions that lead to global climate change. Lighting accounts for close to 20 percent of the average home's electric bill. ENERGY STAR qualified CFLs use up to 75 percent less energy (electricity) than incandescent light bulbs, last up to 10 times longer, cost little up front, and provide a quick return on investment.

If every home in America replaced just one incandescent light bulb with an ENERGY STAR qualified CFL, in one year it would save enough energy to light more than 3 million homes. That would prevent the release of greenhouse gas emissions equal to that of about 800,000 cars.

Do CFLs contain mercury?
CFLs contain a very small amount of mercury sealed within the glass tubing – an average of 4 milligrams. By comparison, older thermometers contain about 500 milligrams of mercury – an amount equal to the mercury in 125 CFLs. Mercury is an essential part of CFLs; it allows the bulb to be an efficient light source. No mercury is released when the bulbs are intact (not broken) or in use.

Most makers of light bulbs have reduced mercury in their fluorescent lighting products. Thanks to technology advances and a commitment from members of the National Electrical Manufacturers Association, the average mercury content in CFLs has dropped at least 20 percent in the past year. Some manufacturers have even made further reductions, dropping mercury content to 1.4 – 2.5 milligrams per light bulb.

What are mercury emissions caused by humans?
EPA estimates the U.S. is responsible for the release of 104 metric tons of mercury emissions each year. Most of these emissions come from coal-fired electrical power. Mercury released into the air is the main way that mercury gets into water and bio-accumulates in fish. (Eating fish contaminated with mercury is the main way for humans to be exposed.)

Most mercury vapor inside fluorescent light bulbs becomes bound to the inside of the light bulb as it is used. EPA estimates that the rest of the mercury within a CFL – about 14 percent – s released into air or water when it is sent to a landfill, assuming the light bulb is broken. Therefore, if all 290 million CFLs sold in 2007 were sent to a landfill (versus recycled, as a worst case) – they would add 0.16 metric tons, or 0.16 percent, to U.S. mercury emissions caused by humans.

How do CFLs result in less mercury in the environment compared to traditional light bulbs?
Electricity use is the main source of mercury emissions in the U.S. CFLs use less electricity than incandescent lights, meaning CFLs reduce the amount of mercury into the environment. As shown in the table below, a 13-watt, 8,000-rated-hour-life CFL (60-watt equivalent; a common light bulb type) will save 376 kWh over its lifetime, thus avoiding 4.5 mg of mercury. If the bulb goes to a landfill, overall emissions savings would drop a little, to 4.0 mg. EPA recommends that CFLs are recycled where possible, to maximize mercury savings.

Table 1

Light Bulb Type	Watts	Hours of Use	kWh Use	National Average Mercury Emissions (mg/kWh)	Mercury from Electricity Use (mg)	Mercury From Landfilling (mg)	Total Mercury (mg)
CFL	13	8,000	104	0.012	1.2	0.6	1.8
Incandescent	60	8,000	480	0.012	5.8	0	5.8

Headings are phrased in the form of questions readers will ask

Statistics are persuasive as well as informative

Paragraphs and sentences are short

Additional technical information is included in parentheses

White space allows the eye to move around the page

Table provides easy-to-read comparative data

FIGURE 1.2 An Effective Technical Document Language, visuals, and layout make the information easy for everyday readers to understand.

Source: U.S. Environmental Protection Agency <www.energystar.gov/ia/partners/promotions/change_light/downloads/Fact_Sheet_Mercury.pdf> Energy Star, a joint program of the U.S. Environmental Protection Agency and the U.S. Department of Energy.

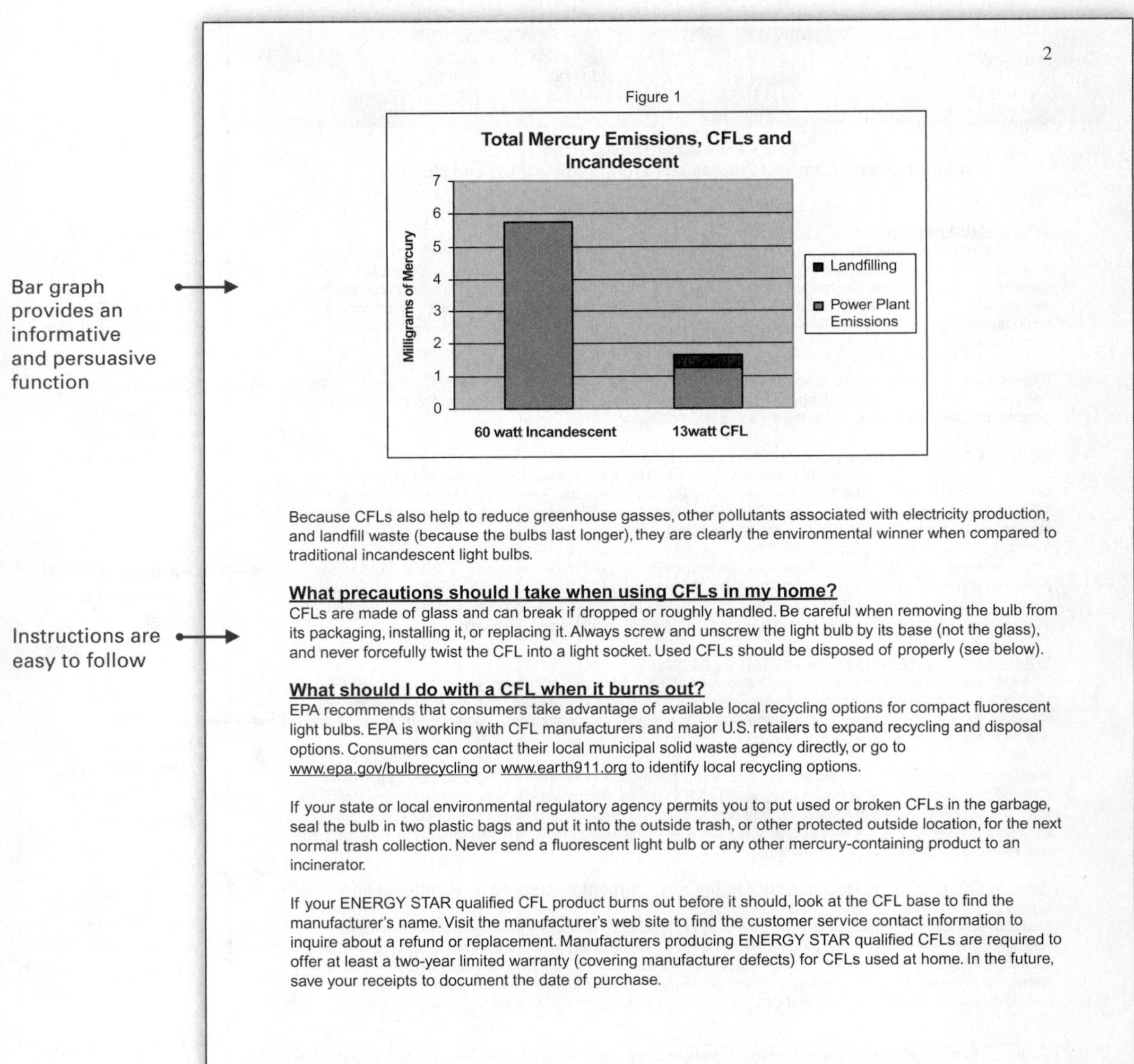

2

Figure 1

Because CFLs also help to reduce greenhouse gasses, other pollutants associated with electricity production, and landfill waste (because the bulbs last longer), they are clearly the environmental winner when compared to traditional incandescent light bulbs.

What precautions should I take when using CFLs in my home?
CFLs are made of glass and can break if dropped or roughly handled. Be careful when removing the bulb from its packaging, installing it, or replacing it. Always screw and unscrew the light bulb by its base (not the glass), and never forcefully twist the CFL into a light socket. Used CFLs should be disposed of properly (see below).

What should I do with a CFL when it burns out?
EPA recommends that consumers take advantage of available local recycling options for compact fluorescent light bulbs. EPA is working with CFL manufacturers and major U.S. retailers to expand recycling and disposal options. Consumers can contact their local municipal solid waste agency directly, or go to www.epa.gov/bulbrecycling or www.earth911.org to identify local recycling options.

If your state or local environmental regulatory agency permits you to put used or broken CFLs in the garbage, seal the bulb in two plastic bags and put it into the outside trash, or other protected outside location, for the next normal trash collection. Never send a fluorescent light bulb or any other mercury-containing product to an incinerator.

If your ENERGY STAR qualified CFL product burns out before it should, look at the CFL base to find the manufacturer's name. Visit the manufacturer's web site to find the customer service contact information to inquire about a refund or replacement. Manufacturers producing ENERGY STAR qualified CFLs are required to offer at least a two-year limited warranty (covering manufacturer defects) for CFLs used at home. In the future, save your receipts to document the date of purchase.

Bar graph provides an informative and persuasive function

Instructions are easy to follow

FIGURE 1.2 *(Continued)*

Documents that Instruct

Enable your readers to perform certain tasks

Instructional documents help people do something: assemble a new computer, perform CPR, or, in the case of Figure 1.2, install and then dispose of a fluorescent light bulb safely. On page 2 of that document the steps are grouped under specific headings and written using action verbs ("unscrew the light bulb by its base"; "seal the bulb in two plastic bags"). Cautions about what *not* to do appear as needed ("Never send a fluorescent light bulb . . . to an incinerator.").

Documents that Persuade

Persuasion encourages people to take a desired action. While some documents (such as a sales letter) are explicitly persuasive, even the most technical of documents can have an implicitly persuasive purpose. The bar graph in Figure 1.2, for example, encourages readers to use compact fluorescent bulbs by showing their low amount of mercury emissions relative to traditional light bulbs.

Motivate your readers

PREPARING EFFECTIVE TECHNICAL DOCUMENTS

Whether you are a full-time communication professional or an engineer, nurse, scientist, technician, legal expert, or anyone whose job requires writing and communicating, the main question you face is this: "How do I prepare the right document for this group of readers and this particular situation?"

A main question you must answer

Other chapters in this book break down the process in more detail. In Chapter 2, for example, you will learn about analyzing the audience and purpose for any document and situation. Later, you will see examples of document types typically used in workplace environments. But regardless of the type, producing an effective document typically requires that you complete the four basic tasks depicted in Figure 1.3 and described on page 12.

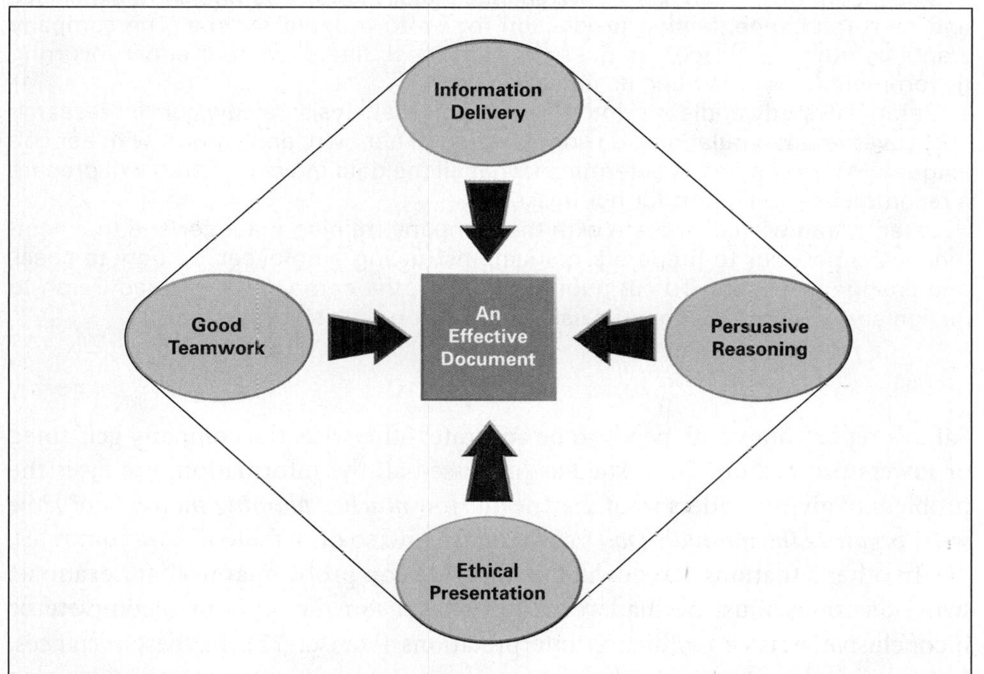

FIGURE 1.3 How an Effective Document Is Produced

A workplace communicator's four basic tasks

- **Deliver information readers can use**—because different people in different situations have different information needs. (Chapter 2)
- **Use persuasive reasoning**—because people often disagree about what the information means and what action should be taken. (Chapter 3)
- **Weigh the ethical issues**—because unethical communication lacks credibility and could alienate readers. (Chapter 4)
- **Practice good teamwork**—because working in teams is how roughly 90 percent of U.S. workers spend some part of their day ("People" 57). (Chapter 5)

The short cases that follow illustrate how a typical professional confronts these tasks in her own day-to-day communication on the job.

CASE Providing Information Readers Can Use

"Can I provide exactly what readers need?"

Sarah Burnes was hired two months ago as a chemical engineer for Millisun, a leading maker of cameras, multipurpose film, and photographic equipment. Sarah's first major assignment is to evaluate the plant's incoming and outgoing water. (Waterborne contaminants can taint film during production, and the production process itself can pollute outgoing water.) Management wants an answer to this question: How often should we change water filters? The filters are expensive and hard to change, halting production for up to a day at a time. The company wants as much "mileage" as possible from these filters, without either incurring government fines or tainting its film production.

Sarah will study endless printouts of chemical analysis, review current research and government regulations, do some testing of her own, and consult with her colleagues. When she finally determines what all the data indicate, Sarah will prepare a recommendation report for her bosses.

Later, Sarah will collaborate with the company training manager and the maintenance supervisor to prepare a manual, instructing employees on how to check and change the filters. To cut publishing costs, the company has asked Sarah to design and produce this manual using its desktop publishing system.

Sarah's report, above all, needs to be accurate; otherwise, the company gets fined or lowers production. Once she has processed all the information, she faces the problem of giving readers what they need: *How much explaining should I do? How will I organize the manual? Do I need visuals?* And so on.

In other situations, Sarah will face a persuasion problem as well, for example, when decisions must be made or actions taken on the basis of incomplete or inconclusive facts or conflicting interpretations (Hauser 72). In these instances, Sarah will seek consensus for *her* view.

CASE Being Persuasive

"Can I influence people to see things my way?"

Millisun and other electronics producers are located on the shores of a small harbor, the port for a major fishing fleet. For twenty years, these companies have discharged effluents containing metal compounds, PCBs, and other toxins directly into the harbor. Sarah is on a multicompany team, assigned to work with the Environmental Protection Agency to clean up the harbor. Much of the team's collaboration occurs via email.

Enraged local citizens are demanding immediate action, and the companies themselves are anxious to end this public relations nightmare. But the team's analysis reveals that any type of cleanup would stir up harbor sediment, possibly dispersing the solution into surrounding waters and the atmosphere. (Many of the contaminants can be airborne.) Premature action might actually increase danger, but team members disagree on the degree of risk and on how to proceed.

Sarah's communication here takes on a persuasive dimension: She and her team members first have to resolve their own disagreements and produce an environmental impact report that reflects the team's consensus. If the report recommends further study, Sarah will have to justify the delays to her bosses and the public relations office. She will have to make other people understand the dangers as well as she does.

In the preceding case, the facts are neither complete nor conclusive, and views differ about what these facts mean. Sarah will have to balance the various political pressures and make a case for her interpretation. Also, as company spokesperson, Sarah will be expected to protect her company's interests. Some elements of Sarah's persuasion problem: *Are other interpretations possible? Is there a better way? Can I expect political or legal fallout?*

CASE Considering the Ethical Issues

"Can I be honest and still keep my job?"

To ensure compliance with OSHA[1] standards for worker safety, Sarah is assigned to test the air purification system in Millisun's chemical division. After finding the filters hopelessly clogged, she decides to test the air quality and discovers dangerous levels of benzene (a potent carcinogen). She reports these findings in a memo to the production manager, with an urgent recommendation that all employees be tested for benzene poisoning. The manager phones and tells Sarah to "have the filters replaced," but says nothing at all about her recommendation to test for benzene poisoning. Now Sarah has to decide what to do about this lack of response: Assume the test is being handled, and bury the memo in some file cabinet? Raise the issue again, and risk alienating her boss? Send copies of her original memo to someone else who might take action?

[1] Occupational Safety and Health Administration.

As the preceding case illustrates, Sarah also will have to reckon with the ethical implications of her writing, with the question of "doing the right thing." For instance, Sarah might feel pressured to overlook, sugarcoat, or suppress facts that would be costly or embarrassing to her company.

Situations that compromise truth and fairness present the hardest choices of all: remain silent and look the other way, or speak out and risk being fired. Some elements of Sarah's ethics problem: *Is this fair? Who might benefit or suffer? What other consequences could this have?*

In addition to solving these various problems, Sarah has to work in a team setting: Much of her writing will be produced in collaboration with others (editors, managers, graphic artists), and her audience will extend beyond readers from her own culture.

CASE Working on a Team and Thinking Globally

"Can I connect with all these different colleagues?"

Recent mergers have transformed Millisun into a multinational corporation with branches in eleven countries, all connected by an intranet. Sarah can expect to collaborate with coworkers from diverse cultures on research and development and with government agencies of the host countries on safety issues, patents and licensing rights, product liability laws, and environmental concerns. Also, she can expect to confront the challenges of addressing the unique needs and expectations of people from various cultures across the globe. She will need to be careful about how she writes her daily email status reports, for example, so that these reports convey respect for cultural differences.

In order to standardize the sensitive management of the toxic, volatile, and even explosive chemicals used in film production, Millisun is developing automated procedures for quality control, troubleshooting, and emergency response to chemical leakage. Sarah has been assigned to a team that is preparing computer-based training packages and instructional videos for all personnel involved in Millisun's chemical management worldwide.

As a further complication, Sarah will have to develop working relationships with people she has never met face-to-face, people from other cultures, and people she knows only via an electronic medium.

For Sarah Burnes, or any of us, writing is a process of discovering what we want to say, "a way to end up thinking something [we] couldn't have started out thinking" (Elbow 15). Throughout this process in the workplace, we rarely work alone but instead collaborate with others for information, help in writing, and feedback.

Projects

GENERAL

1. Write a memo to your boss, justifying reimbursement for this course. Explain how the course will help you become more effective on the job. (See Chapter 14 for memo elements and format.)
2. Locate a Web site for an organization that hires graduates in your major. In addition to technical knowledge, what writing and communication skills does this organization seek in job candidates? Discuss your findings in class and write a short memo to other students, explaining what communication skills they require in order to find a job in this or a similar organization.

TEAM

Introducing a Classmate

Class members will work together often this semester. To help everyone become acquainted, your task is to introduce to the class the person seated next to you. (That person, in turn, will introduce you.) Follow this procedure:

a. Exchange with your neighbor whatever personal information you think the class needs: background, major, career plans, communication needs of your intended profession, and so on. Each person gets five minutes to tell her or his story.
b. Take careful notes; ask questions if you need to.
c. Take your notes home and select only the information you think the class will find useful.
d. Prepare a one-page memo telling your classmates who this person is. (See Chapter 14 for memo elements and format.)
e. Ask your neighbor to review the memo for accuracy; revise as needed.
f. Present the class with a two-minute oral paraphrase of your memo, and submit a copy of the memo to your instructor.

DIGITAL AND SOCIAL MEDIA

With a team of 2–3 other students, visit a government Web site, such as the Food and Drug Administration <www.fda.gov>, the Centers for Disease Control <www.cdc.gov>, NASA <www.nasa.gov>, or the Environmental Protection Agency <www.epa.gov>. Locate documents that are similar in purpose to Figure 1.1 in this chapter. Analyze these documents, noting whether they are available in PDF and whether they conform to one of the three purposes (informative, instructional, persuasive) described in this chapter or whether they are a blend of these purposes. Also, locate the Facebook page for NASA and compare it with NASA's Web site. How is content presented differently on each site? Does the Facebook page appear to have a different purpose from the Web site? If so, what are the differences?

GLOBAL

Look back at the Sarah Burnes case in this chapter. Assume that you are about to join a team at work, a team that has members from Ireland, India, China, and the United States. Use the Internet to learn what you can about patterns of communication; issues to look for include politeness, turn-taking, use of first names or titles, and gender roles. Describe your findings in a short memo to your instructor.

2 Meeting the Needs of Specific Audiences

"Audience makes all the difference. I write for students, small groups of scholars, and general readers. I pitch grant proposals to larger groups of scholars, either nationally (as for the National Endowment for the Humanities) or locally (among colleagues throughout the disciplines at my university). I assume my audiences are happy enough to listen to me at first, but that to keep them reading I need to supply varying degrees of background and explanation pitched to their background and familiarity with the subject matter."

—John Bryant, Professor

LEARNING OBJECTIVES FOR THIS CHAPTER

- Understand the key concepts of "audience" and "purpose"
- Picture exactly who will use your document and why
- Consider your audience's technical background
- Consider the audience's cultural background
- Pinpoint the needs and goals of your audience
- Identify the length, format, tone, and other qualities your audience prefers
- Understand the concept of usability in relation to audience and purpose

All technical communication is intended for people who will use and react to the information. These people are considered to be the *audience* for your document: people who are reading the material in order to do something or learn something.

Before you start writing, you need to identify precisely who will be reading the document and to understand how that particular audience will use your material. For example, you might need to *define* something—as in explaining to insurance clients what the term "variable annuity" means. You might need to *describe* something—as in showing an architectural client what a new office building will look like. You might need to *explain* something—as in instructing an auto repair technician how to reprogram the car's electronic ignition. Or you might need to *propose* something—as in arguing for change in your company's sick-leave policy. Preparing an effective document requires systematic analysis of your audience and the ways in which they will use your document (Figure 2.1).

Because people's basic requirements vary, every audience expects a message tailored to its own specific interests, social conventions, ways of understanding problems, and information needs.

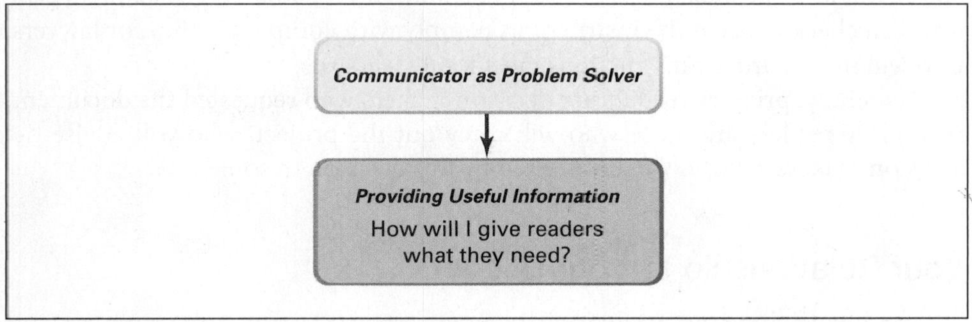

FIGURE 2.1 Communicators Begin by Considering Their Audience

ANALYZE YOUR DOCUMENT'S AUDIENCE AND PURPOSE

Explore all you can about who will use your document, why they will use it, and how they will use it. Begin by analyzing your audience and the background, needs, and preferences of these readers. Among the questions you must answer are these:

Questions for analyzing a document's audience

- Who is the main audience for this document?
- Who else is likely to read it?
- What is your relationship with the audience?
- Are multiple types of relationships involved?
- What information does this audience need?
- How familiar might the audience be with technical details?
- Do these readers have varying levels of expertise?
- What culture or cultures does your audience represent?
- How might cultural differences shape readers' expectations and interpretations?

Answer these questions by considering the suggestions that follow.

Primary and Secondary Audiences

"Who is the main audience for this document?"

When writing a technical document, keep two audiences in mind. Most documents are geared to an immediate audience of readers. This is your primary audience. For instance, a set of instructions for installing new email software for an office network might be directed primarily toward the computer support staff who would be doing the installing.

"Who else is likely to read it?"

But most documents also have a secondary audience, those individuals outside the immediate circle of people who will be needing the information directly. For example, a secondary audience for software instructions might be managers, who will check to see if the instructions comply with company policy, or lawyers, who will make sure the instructions meet legal standards.

Generally, primary readers are decision makers who requested the document. Secondary readers are those who will carry out the project, who will advise the decision makers, or who will be affected by this decision in some way.

Your Relationship to Your Readers

"What is my relationship with this audience?"

Besides identifying your audience in a general way, you also need to understand your relationship with everyone involved. In your situation, will the readers be superiors, colleagues, or subordinates? Your answer will help you determine the level of formality and authority to use in the document. Are the readers from inside or outside your organization? Answering this question will help you decide how confidential you need to be. Do you know the readers personally? If so, perhaps you can adopt a more informal tone. Are they likely to welcome or to resist your information? Knowing the answer will help you decide how persuasive you need to be. Are they a combination of people from various levels, both inside and outside the company? The answer will help you tailor your document for various readers.

Purpose of Your Document

Spell out precisely what you want your document to accomplish and how you expect readers to use it. In other words, determine your purpose. Ask these questions:

Questions for deciding on the purpose of your document

- What is the main purpose of the document?
- What other purpose or purposes does the document serve?
- What will readers do with this information?

Answer these questions by considering the suggestions in the sections that follow.

Primary and Secondary Purposes

Most forms of technical communication fulfill a specific primary purpose. As discussed in Chapter 1, the primary purpose (to inform, to instruct, or to persuade) will affect the document's overall shape and substance.

Many documents have one or more secondary purposes. For example, the primary purpose in a typical instruction manual is to instruct, that is, to teach an audience how to assemble or use the product. But for ethical and legal reasons, companies also want people to use the product safely. A manual for a power tool or a lawnmower, for instance, almost always begins with a page that spells out safety hazards and precautions, before instructing readers about how to proceed with the mechanism.

Write a clear audience and purpose statement

In planning your document, work from a clear statement that identifies the target audience as well as the document's primary and secondary purposes. For example [italics added], "The purpose of my document is *to inform* company employees of the new absentee policy and *to instruct* them on how to follow the procedures properly," or "The purpose of my document is *to inform* my division's programmers about the new antivirus software, as well as *to instruct* them on how to install the software and *to persuade* them of the importance of running weekly virus scans."

Intended Use of the Document

"How will readers use this document?"

In addition to determining purposes of a document from your own perspective, also consider how and why it will be used by others. As you plan your document, answer these questions:

Questions for anticipating how your document will be used

- Do my readers simply want to learn facts or understand concepts?
- Will they use my information in making some type of decision?
- Will people act immediately on the information?
- Do they need step-by-step instructions?
- In my audience's view, what is most important about this document?

Besides answering these questions, try asking members of your audience directly, so you can verify what they want to know.

ASSESS THE AUDIENCE'S TECHNICAL BACKGROUND

"How much expertise does this audience possess?"

When you write for a close acquaintance (coworker, engineering colleague, chemistry professor who reads your lab reports, or supervisor), you adapt your report to that person's knowledge, interests, and needs. But some audiences are larger and less defined (say, for a journal article, a computer manual, a set of first-aid procedures, or an accident report). When you have only a general notion about your audience's background, decide whether your document should be *highly technical, semitechnical,* or *nontechnical,* as depicted in Figure 2.2.

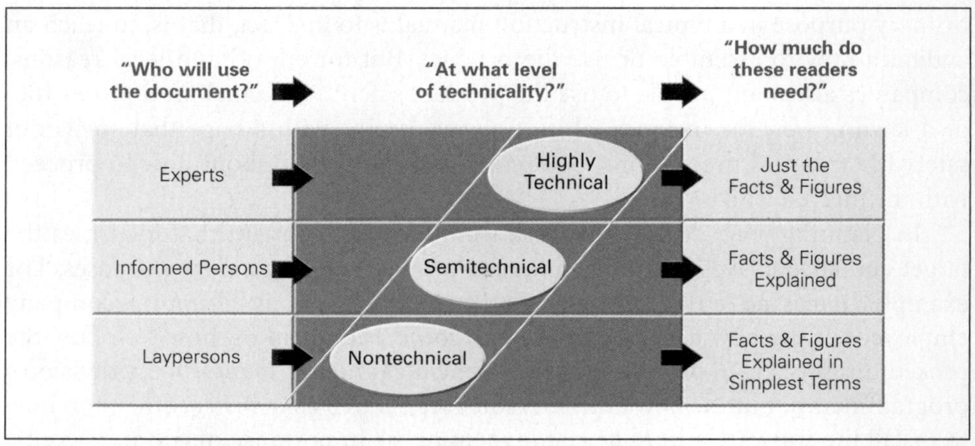

FIGURE 2.2 Deciding on a Document's Level of Technicality

Highly Technical Audience

Readers at a specialized level expect to be presented the facts and figures they need—without long explanations. In Figure 2.3, an emergency-room physician reports to the patient's doctor, who needs an exact record of symptoms, treatment, and results.

For her expert colleague, this physician doesn't need to define the technical terms (*pulmonary edema, sinus rhythm*). Nor does she need to interpret lab findings (*4+ protein, elevated serum transaminase*). She uses abbreviations that her colleague clearly understands (*wbc, BUN, 5% D & W*). Because her colleague knows all about specific treatments and medications (*defibrillation, Xylocaine drip*), she does not explain their scientific bases. Her report answers concisely the main questions she can anticipate from this particular reader: *What was the problem? What was the treatment? What were the results?*

The patient was brought to the ER by ambulance at 1:00 A.M., September 27, 2010. The patient complained of severe chest pains, dyspnea, and vertigo. Auscultation and EKG revealed a massive cardiac infarction and pulmonary edema marked by pronounced cyanosis. Vital signs: blood pressure, 80/40; pulse, 140/min; respiration, 35/min. Lab: wbc, 20,000; elevated serum transaminase; urea nitrogen, 60 mg%. Urinalysis showed 4+ protein and 4+ granular casts/field, indicating acute renal failure secondary to the hypotension.

The patient received 10 mg of morphine stat, subcutaneously, followed by nasal oxygen and 5% D & W intravenously. At 1:25 A.M. the cardiac monitor recorded an irregular sinus rhythm, indicating left ventricular fibrillation. The patient was defibrillated stat and given a 50 mg bolus of Xylocaine intravenously. A Xylocaine drip was started, and sodium bicarbonate administered until a normal heartbeat was established. By 3:00 A.M., the oscilloscope was recording a normal sinus rhythm.

As the heartbeat stabilized and cyanosis diminished, the patient received 5 cc of Heparin intravenously, to be repeated every six hours. By 5:00 A.M. the BUN had fallen to 20 mg% and vital signs had stabilized: blood pressure, 110/60; pulse, 105/min; respiration, 22/min. The patient was now conscious and responsive.

Expert readers need facts and figures, which they can interpret for themselves

FIGURE 2.3 A Technical Version of an Emergency Treatment Report This version is written for medical experts.

Semitechnical Audience

In certain cases, readers will have some technical background, but not as much as the experts. For instance, first-year medical students have specialized knowledge, but less than advanced students. Yet all medical students could be considered semitechnical. Therefore, when you write for a semitechnical audience, identify the *lowest* level of understanding in the group, and write to that level. Too much explanation is better than too little.

The partial version of the medical report in Figure 2.4 might appear in a textbook for medical or nursing students, in a report for a medical social worker, or in a monthly report for the hospital administration.

This version explains the raw data (highlighted in yellow). Exact dosages are omitted because no one in this audience actually will be treating this patient. Normal values of lab tests and vital signs, however, help readers interpret the report results.

Informed but nonexpert readers need enough explanation to understand what the data mean

Examination by stethoscope and electrocardiogram revealed a massive failure of the heart muscle along with fluid buildup in the lungs, which produced a cyanotic discoloration of the lips and fingertips from lack of oxygen.

The patient's blood pressure at 80 mm Hg (systolic)/40 mm Hg (diastolic) was dangerously below its normal measure of 130/70. A pulse rate of 140/minute was almost twice the normal rate of 60–80. Respiration at 35/minute was more than twice the normal rate of 12–16.

Laboratory blood tests yielded a white blood cell count of 20,000/cu mm (normal value: 5,000–10,000), indicating a severe inflammatory response by the heart muscle. The elevated serum transaminase enzymes (produced in quantity only when the heart muscle fail) confirmed thes earlier diagnosis. A blood urea nitrogen level of 60 mg% (normal value: 12–16 mg%) indicated that the kidneys had ceased to filter out metabolic waste products. The 4+ protein and casts reported from the urinalysis (normal value: 0) revealed that the kidney tubules were degenerating as a result of the lowered blood pressure.

The patient immediately received morphine to ease the chest pain, followed by oxygen to relieve strain on the cardiopulmonary system, and an intravenous solution of dextrose and water to prevent shock.

FIGURE 2.4 **A Semitechnical Version of an Emergency Treatment Report** This version is written for readers who are not experts but who have some medical background.

(Experts know the normal values.) Knowing what medications the patient received would be especially important in answering this audience's central question: *How is a typical heart attack treated?*

Nontechnical Audience

People with no specialized training (laypersons) look for the big picture instead of complex details. They expect technical data to be translated into words most people understand. Laypersons are impatient with abstract theories, but they want enough background to help them make the right decision or take the right action. They are bored or confused by excessive detail, but frustrated by raw facts left unexplained or uninterpreted. They expect to understand the document after reading it only once.

The nontechnical version of the medical report shown in Figure 2.5 might be written for the patient's spouse who is overseas on business, or as part of a script for a documentary about emergency-room treatment. Nearly all interpretation (highlighted in yellow), this version mentions no specific medications, lab tests, or normal values. It merely summarizes events and briefly explains what they mean and why these particular treatments were given.

Heart sounds and electrical impulses were both abnormal, indicating a massive heart attack caused by failure of a large part of the heart muscle. The lungs were swollen with fluid and the lips and fingertips showed a bluish discoloration from lack of oxygen.

Blood pressure was dangerously low, creating the risk of shock. Pulse and respiration were almost twice the normal rate, indicating that the heart and lungs were being overworked in keeping oxygenated blood circulating freely.

Blood tests confirmed the heart attack diagnosis and indicated that waste products usually filtered out by the kidneys were building up in the bloodstream. Urine tests showed that the kidneys were failing as a result of the lowered blood pressure.

The patient was given medication to ease the chest pain, oxygen to ease the strain on the heart and lungs, and intravenous solution to prevent the blood vessels from collapsing and causing irreversible shock.

Laypersons need everything translated into terms they understand

FIGURE 2.5 A Nontechnical Version of an Emergency Treatment Report This version is written for readers who have no medical background.

In a different situation, however (say, a malpractice trial), the layperson jury would require detailed technical information about medication and treatment. Such a report would naturally be much longer—basically a short course in emergency coronary treatment.

Audiences with Varying Technical Backgrounds

The technical background of large and diverse audiences can be variable and hard to pin down. When you must write for audiences at different levels, follow these suggestions:

How to tailor a document to address different technical backgrounds

- If the document is short (a letter, memo, or anything less than two pages), rewrite it at different levels for different backgrounds.
- If the document exceeds two pages, address the primary readers. Then provide appendices for secondary readers. Transmittal letters, informative abstracts, and glossaries can also help nonexperts understand a highly technical report. (See Chapter 22 for use and preparation of appendices and other supplements.)

For an illustration of these differences, consider the following case.

CASE Tailoring a Single Document for Multiple Audiences

Different readers have differing information needs

You are a metallurgical engineer in an automotive consulting firm. Your supervisor has asked you to test the fractured rear axle of a 2009 Delphi pickup truck recently involved in a fatal accident. Your assignment is to determine whether the fractured axle *caused* or *resulted from* the accident.

After testing the hardness and chemical composition of the metal and examining microscopic photographs of the fractured surfaces (fractographs), you conclude that the fracture resulted from stress that developed *during* the accident. Now you must report your procedure and your findings to a variety of readers.

"What do these findings mean?"

Because your report may serve as courtroom evidence, you must explain your findings in meticulous detail. But your primary readers (the decision makers) will be nonspecialists (the attorneys who have requested the report, insurance representatives, possibly a judge and a jury), so you must translate your report, explaining the principles behind the various tests, defining specialized terms such as "chevron marks," "shrinkage cavities," and "dimpled core," and showing the significance of these features as evidence.

"How did you arrive at these conclusions?"

Secondary readers will include your supervisor and outside consulting engineers who will be evaluating your test procedures and assessing the validity of your findings. Consultants will be focusing on various parts of your report, to verify that your procedure has been exact and faultless. For this group, you will have to include appendices spelling out the technical details of your analysis: *how* hardness testing of the axle's case and core indicated that the axle had been properly carburized; *how* chemical analysis ruled out the possibility that the manufacturer had used inferior alloys; *how* light-microscopic fractographs revealed that the origin of the fracture, its direction of propagation, and the point of final rupture indicated a ductile fast fracture, not one caused by torsional fatigue.

In the previous scenario, primary readers need to know *what your findings mean,* whereas secondary readers need to know *how you arrived at your conclusions.* Unless it serves the needs of each group independently, your information will be worthless.

Web-Based Documents for Multiple Audiences

Web pages are ideal for displaying and linking various levels of information. Figure 2.6 accommodates different levels of interest and expertise.

IDENTIFY THE AUDIENCE'S CULTURAL BACKGROUND

"What cultural differences exist in this audience, and how can I bridge those differences?"

Within North America and beyond, information needs and preferences often are culturally determined. For example, certain cultures value thoroughness and complexity in their documents, with lists of data and every detail included and explained. Some cultures place high value on a formal, businesslike tone. Other cultures prefer multiple perspectives on the material, lots of graphics, and a friendly, encouraging tone (Hein 125–26).

North American business culture is accustomed to "plain talk" that gets right to the point, but Eastern cultures tend to consider this rude, preferring indirect, more ambiguous messages, which leave interpretation up to the reader (Leki 151; Martin and Chaney 276–77). To avoid seeming impolite, some people might hesitate to ask for clarification or additional information. In certain cultures, even disagreement or refusal might be expressed as "We will do our best" or "This is very difficult" instead of "No"—to avoid offending and to preserve harmony (Rowland 47).

Consider how cultural differences might create misunderstanding in your situation, and seek an approach that bridges these differences.

ANTICIPATE YOUR AUDIENCE'S PREFERENCES

Readers approach any document with certain preferences: its desired length and details, the format and medium in which it should be presented, and the appropriate tone, as well as deadline and budget expectations.

Length and Details

Give readers only what they need and want

The length and amount of detail in your document depends on what you can learn about your audience's needs. Were you asked to "keep it short" or to "be comprehensive"? Are people more interested in conclusions and recommendations, or do they want everything spelled out?

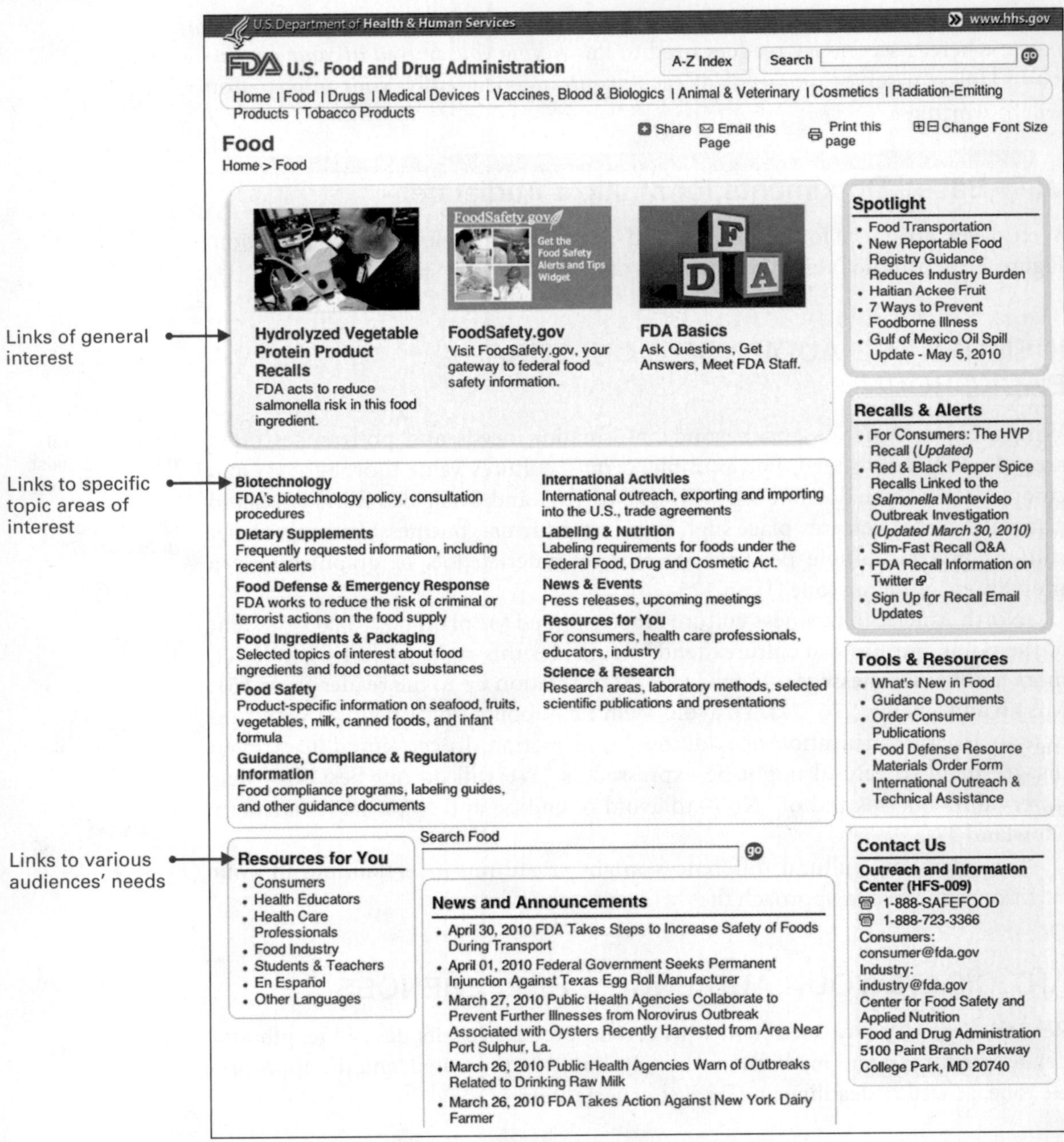

FIGURE 2.6 **A Web Page Designed for Multiple Audiences** This page addresses diverse groups including non-English speakers (links listed under *Resources For You*). For science professionals and other specialized readers, links include *Biotechnology* and *Science and Research*.

Source: U.S. Food and Drug Administration <www.fda.gov/food>.

Format and Medium

Decide how your document will look and will be distributed

Does your audience expect a letter, a memo, a short report, or a long, formal report with supplements (title page, table of contents, appendixes, and so on—see pages 533–36)? Can visuals and page layout (charts, graphs, drawings, headings, lists) make the material more accessible? In this instance, is the proper distribution medium via hard copy, email or attachment, Web posting, or other means?

Tone

Decide on the appropriate tone for your situation

The tone of your writing conveys an image of who you are: your *persona*—the image that comes through between the lines. Tone can range from formal (as in a business letter to a client) to semiformal (as in a memo announcing a change in company dress policy) to informal (as in a quick email to colleagues announcing the upcoming company picnic). Workplace readers expect a tone that reflects both the importance or urgency of the topic and the relationship between writer and reader. For example, the letter to a client that begins with "We are pleased to forward your annual investment statement" is probably appropriate. But a similar tone used in the memo about the company picnic would seem stuffy and pretentious ("I am pleased to announce…").

At the same time, the tone of your writing can range from friendly and encouraging to distant and hostile. For example, a bossy tone in a memo to your employees ("It would behoove you to…") would make them feel demeaned and resentful. In short, your tone is effective when you sound like a likable person talking to people in a workplace setting. The notion of *workplace setting* is key here: Always avoid the kind of free-for-all tone that is common in tweets, text messages, and emails among casual friends outside of work.

Due Date and Timing

Know when to submit the document

Does your document have a deadline? Workplace documents almost always do. Is there a best time to submit it? Do you need to break down the deadline into a schedule of milestones? Will any of your information become outdated if you wait too long to complete the document?

Budget

Calculate the financial costs

Does your document have a production budget? If so, how much? Where can you save money? How much time can your company afford to allot you for creating the document or Web page? How much money can you spend obtaining permission to use materials from other sources? How much can you spend on printing, binding, and distributing your document?

NOTE *Although a detailed analysis can tell you a great deal, rarely is it possible to pin down an audience with certainty—especially when the audience is large and diverse. Before submitting a final document, examine every aspect, trying to anticipate specific audience questions or objections. Better yet, ask selected readers for feedback on early drafts.*

GUIDELINES for Analyzing Your Audience and Its Use of the Document

- **Picture exactly what these readers need and how they expect to use your document.** Whether it's the company president or the person next to you in class, that person has specific concerns and information needs. Your readers may need to complete a task, solve a problem, make a decision, evaluate your performance, or take a stand on an issue. Think carefully about exactly what you want your readers to be able to do.
- **Learn all you can about who will use your document.** Are your primary readers superiors, colleagues, or subordinates? Are they inside or outside your organization? Who else might be interested or affected? What do readers already know about this topic? How much do they care? Are they likely to welcome or reject your information?
- **In planning your document, work from a clear statement of audience and purpose.** For example, "The purpose of my document is to [describe using verbs: *persuade, instruct, inform*] the target audience [identify precisely: *colleagues, superiors, clients*]."
- **Consider your audience's technical background.** Colleagues who speak your technical language will understand raw data. Managers who have limited technical knowledge expect interpretations and explanations. Clients with little or no technical background want to know what this information means to them, personally (to their health, pocketbook, safety). However, none of these generalizations might apply to your situation. When in doubt, aim for low technicality.
- **When you don't know exactly who will be reading your document, picture the "general reader."** A nontechnical audience will expect complex information to be explained in ways that have meaning for them, personally, and insofar as possible in everyday language. (For example, refer to "heart and lungs" instead of "cardiopulmonary system." Instead of "A diesel engine generates 10 BTUs per gallon of fuel compared with 8 BTUs generated by a conventional gasoline engine," write "A diesel engine yields 25 percent better gas mileage than its gas-burning counterpart.")
- **Consider readers' cultural backgrounds.** Identify as closely as possible your audience's specific customs and values. How might cultural differences play a role in readers' interpretation of your presentation?

- **Anticipate your audience's reactions.** If the topic is controversial or the news is bad, will some people resist your message? Will some feel threatened or offended? Should you be bold and outspoken or tread lightly? No matter how accurate your information or how sensible your ideas, an alienated audience will reject them out of hand.
- **Anticipate your audience's questions.** Based on their needs and concerns, readers have questions such as these: What is the purpose of this document? Why should I read it? What happened, and why? Who was involved? How do I perform this task? How did you perform it? What action should be taken, and why? How much will it cost? What are the risks? Give readers what they need to know, instead of what they already know. Give them enough material to understand your position and to react appropriately.
- **Anticipate your audience's preferences.** Try to pinpoint the length, detail, format, medium, tone, timing, and budget preferred by this audience. As the situation allows, adjust your document accordingly.

DEVELOP AN AUDIENCE AND USE PROFILE

In order to focus sharply on your audience, purpose, and the many factors discussed in this chapter, develop your own version of the Audience and Use Profile Sheet shown in Figure 2.7 (page 31) for any document you prepare. Modify this sheet as needed to suit your own situation, as shown in the following case.

CASE Developing an Audience and Use Profile

Assume that you face this situation: First-year students increasingly are dropping out of your major because of low grades or stress or inability to keep up with the work load. As part of your work-study duties, your department chairperson asks you to prepare a "Survival Guide" for next year's incoming students to the major. This one- or two-page memo should focus on the challenges and the pitfalls of the major and should include a brief motivational section along with whatever additional information you decide readers need.

Adapt Figure 2.7 (page 31) to develop your audience and use profile. Here are some possible responses:

Audience and Use Profile

Audience and Purpose

- *Who is my primary audience?* Incoming students to the major
- *Any secondary audiences?* Department faculty

- *What is my relationship with everyone involved?* Primary audience: student colleagues who don't know me very well; secondary audience: major faculty, who must approve the final document.
- *What is the purpose of the document?* This document has multiple purposes: to inform, instruct, and persuade.
- *Audience and purpose statement:* The purpose of this document is to explain to incoming students the challenges and pitfalls of year 1 of our major. I will show how the number of dropouts has increased, describe what seems to go wrong and explain why, suggest steps for avoiding common mistakes, and emphasize the benefits of enduring the first year.
- *Intended use of this document:* To enable students to craft their own survival plan based on the information, advice, and encouragement provided in the document.
- *Information needs:* Incoming students know very little about this topic. They need everything spelled out.
- *Technical background:* In regard to this topic, the primary audience can be considered laypersons.
- *Cultural considerations:* The document will refer readers from other countries and cultures (exchange students, nonnative speakers of English, and so on) to designated advisors for additional assistance.
- *Probable questions (along with others you anticipate):* "How big is the problem?" "How can this problem affect me personally?" "How much time will I need to devote to homework?" "How should I budget my time?" "Can I squeeze in a part-time job?" "Why do so many students drop out?" "Whom should I see if I'm having a problem?"
- *Probable reaction to document:* Most readers should welcome this information and take it seriously. However, some students who don't know the meaning of failure might feel patronized or offended. Some faculty might resent any suggestions that courses are too demanding.

Audience Preferences about the Document

- *Length and detail:* Because the document was requested by the department and not by the primary audience, I can't expect students to tolerate more than a page or two.
- *Format and medium:* Paper memo mailed to each student (along with a brief, welcoming cover letter), and a PDF version posted to the department Web site.
- *Tone:* Since we students are all in this situation together, a friendly, informal, and positive (to avoid panic) but serious tone seems best.
- *Due date and timing:* This document must be available before students arrive next fall—but not so early that it gets forgotten or overshadowed by other registration paperwork.
- *Budget:* This document will be sent as a PDF via email. No printing costs are involved.

Audience and Purpose

Primary audience: ______________________ *(name, title)*

Secondary audience(s): ______________________ *(technicians, managers, other)*

Relationship with audience: ______________________ *(colleague, employer, other)*

Purpose of document: ______________________ *(inform, instruct, persuade)*

Audience and purpose statement: ______________________

____

____

Intended use of document: ______________________ *(perform tasks, solve a problem, other)*

Information needs: ______________________ *(background, basic facts, other)*

Technical background: ______________________ *(layperson, expert, other)*

Cultural considerations: ______________________ *(level of detail or directness, other)*

Probable questions: ______________________ *?*

______________________ *?*

______________________ *?*

______________________ *?*

Probable reaction: ______________________ *(resistance, approval, anger, other)*

Audience Preferences about the Document

Length and detail: ______________________ *(comprehensive, concise, other)*

Format and medium: ______________________ *(letter, memo, Web posting, other)*

Tone: ______________________ *(businesslike, confident, informal, other)*

Due date and timing: ______________________ *(meet deadline, wait for the best time, other)*

Budget: ______________________ *(what can be spent on what)*

FIGURE 2.7 **Audience and Use Profile** Depending on your situation, you can adapt this sheet, as shown in the case that begins on page 29. For a completed profile in a persuasive situation, see Figure 3.5, page 58.

CHECK YOUR DOCUMENT FOR USABILITY

A *usable* document is safe, dependable, and easy to read and navigate. Regardless of the type or format (print or digital) of the document, a usable document allows people to do three things (Coe, *Human Factors* 93; Spencer 74):

- easily locate the information they need
- understand the information immediately
- use the information safely and successfully

For more on usability see pages 482–86 in Chapter 20.

To guide your writing and revision, consult the following Usability Checklist. This checklist identifies broad usability standards that apply to virtually any document. In addition, specific elements (visuals, page layout) and specific documents (proposals, memos, instructions) have their own standards as well. These standards are detailed in the individual checklists for usability throughout this book.

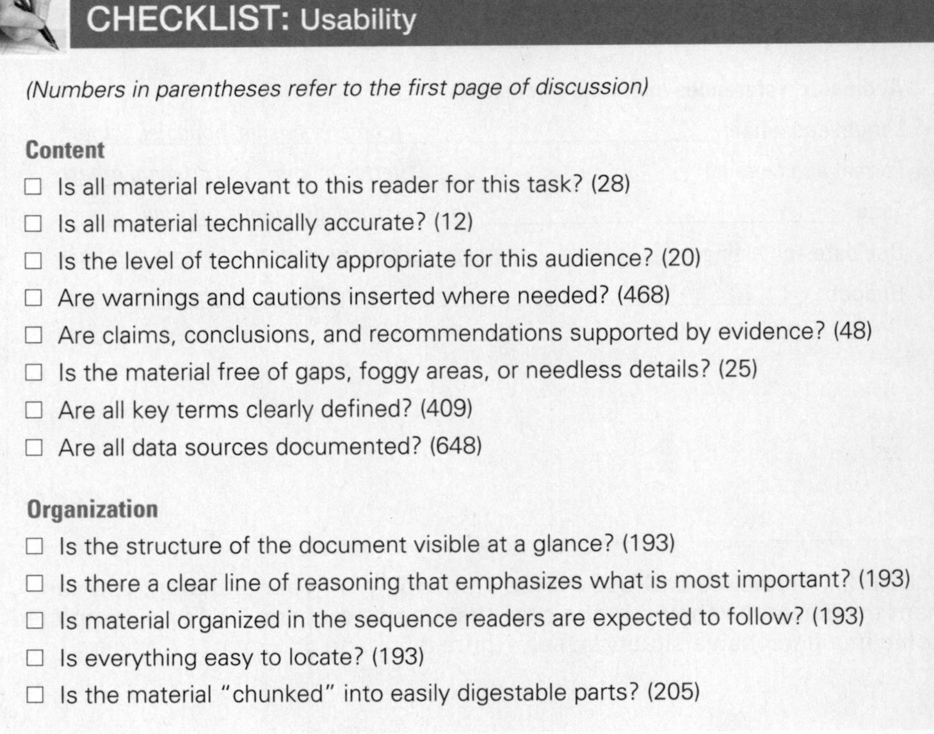

CHECKLIST: Usability

(Numbers in parentheses refer to the first page of discussion)

Content

- ☐ Is all material relevant to this reader for this task? (28)
- ☐ Is all material technically accurate? (12)
- ☐ Is the level of technicality appropriate for this audience? (20)
- ☐ Are warnings and cautions inserted where needed? (468)
- ☐ Are claims, conclusions, and recommendations supported by evidence? (48)
- ☐ Is the material free of gaps, foggy areas, or needless details? (25)
- ☐ Are all key terms clearly defined? (409)
- ☐ Are all data sources documented? (648)

Organization

- ☐ Is the structure of the document visible at a glance? (193)
- ☐ Is there a clear line of reasoning that emphasizes what is most important? (193)
- ☐ Is material organized in the sequence readers are expected to follow? (193)
- ☐ Is everything easy to locate? (193)
- ☐ Is the material "chunked" into easily digestable parts? (205)

Style

- ☐ Is each sentence understandable the first time it is read? (211)
- ☐ Is rich information expressed in the fewest words possible? (216)
- ☐ Are sentences put together with enough variety? (225)
- ☐ Are words chosen for exactness, and not for camouflage? (225)
- ☐ Is the tone appropriate for the situation and audience? (232)

Page Design

- ☐ Is page design inviting, accessible, and appropriate for the readers' needs? (293)
- ☐ Are there adequate aids to navigation (heads, lists, type styles)? (297)
- ☐ Are adequate visuals used to clarify, emphasize, or summarize? (246)
- ☐ Do supplements (front and end matter) accommodate the needs of a diverse audience? (533)

Ethical, Legal, and Cultural Considerations

- ☐ Does the document reflect sound ethical judgment? (63)
- ☐ Does the document comply with copyright law and other legal standards? (73)
- ☐ Does the document respect readers' cultural diversity? (51)

Projects

GENERAL

1. Find a short article from your field (or part of a long article or a selection from your textbook for an advanced course). Choose a piece written at the highest level of technicality you can understand and then translate that piece for a layperson, as in the example on page 23. Exchange translations with a classmate from a different major. Read your neighbor's translation and write a paragraph evaluating its level of technicality. Submit to your instructor a copy of the original, your translated version, and your evaluation of your neighbor's translation.
2. Assume that a new employee is taking over your job because you have been promoted. Identify a specific problem in the job that could cause difficulty for the new employee. Assume that you will need to write instructions for the employee to help him or her avoid or cope with the problem. Create an audience and use profile based on Figure 2.7 (page 31). Use the page 29 Case as a model for your responses.

TEAM

Form teams of 3–6 people. Teammates should be of the same or similar majors (electrical engineering, biology, graphic design, etc.). Research the job market for graduates in your major, including specific types of skills that employers seek beyond those courses in your specialty (such as technical communication, public speaking, oral presentations, Web design, or the like). The final document will be posted to the department's Web site.

Before you can prepare this document, you need a thorough analysis of your audience and purpose. Complete your audience and use profile using the worksheet on page 31 or a modified version of this worksheet. Include a clear and specific audience and purpose statement.

Appoint a team member to present the complete Audience and Use Profile for class evaluation, comparison, and response.

DIGITAL AND SOCIAL MEDIA

Locate a Web site that accommodates various readers at different levels of technicality. Sites for government agencies such as those listed below are good sources of both general and specialized information.

- Environmental Protection Agency (EPA) <www.epa.gov>
- Nuclear Regulatory Commission (NRC) <www.nrc.gov>
- National Institutes of Health (NIH) <www.nih.gov>
- Food and Drug Administration (FDA) <www.fda.gov>

Examine one of these sites and find an example of (a) material aimed at a general audience, and (b) material on the same topic aimed at a specialized or expert audience. First, list the specific features that enabled you to identify each piece's level of technicality. Next, using the Audience and Use Profile Sheet (p. 31), record the assumptions about the audience made by the author of the nontechnical version. Finally, evaluate how well that piece addresses a nontechnical reader's information needs. (*Hint:* Check out, for instance, the MEDLINE link at the NIH site.)

Be prepared to discuss your evaluation in class.

GLOBAL

The U.S. Immigration and Naturalization Service's Web site, at <www.ins.gov>, is designed for a truly global audience. After visiting the site, answer these questions:

- Would this site be easy for virtually any English speaker to navigate? List the features that accommodate readers from diverse areas of the globe.
- Could improvements be made in the site's ease of use? What changes would you recommend?

Print out relevant site pages and be prepared to discuss your conclusions in class.

3 Persuading Your Audience

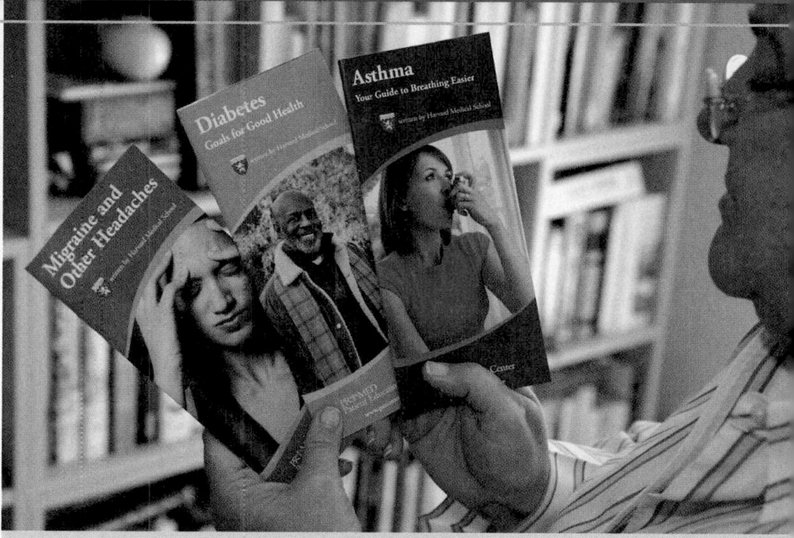

"For me, persuasion is mostly about getting along with coworkers. What I didn't understand when I started working after college is the whole idea of organizational behavior. I assumed that, as long as I worked hard and did a good job, I would get my raises and promotions. But it's not that simple. I had to leave my first job because I didn't learn soon enough how people react in certain situations, for instance, that 'constructive' suggestions from the new person are not always appreciated.

My advice: Learn about the people you're working for and with. Spend a lot of time observing, listening, and asking questions about how the organization works at the person-to-person level."

—Ryan Donavan, Programmer

LEARNING OBJECTIVES FOR THIS CHAPTER

- Appreciate the role of persuasion in technical communication
- Identify a specific persuasive goal for your document
- Anticipate how audiences may react to your argument
- Respect any limitations such as company rules or legal constraints
- Support your argument using evidence and reason
- Understand that cultural differences may influence audience reactions
- Prepare a convincing argument

Why persuasion is difficult

Persuasion means trying to influence someone's actions, opinions, or decisions (Figure 3.1). In the workplace, we rely on persuasion daily: to win coworker support, to attract clients and customers, to request funding. But changing someone's mind is never easy, and sometimes impossible. Your success will depend on what you are requesting, whom you are trying to persuade, and how entrenched those people are in their own views.

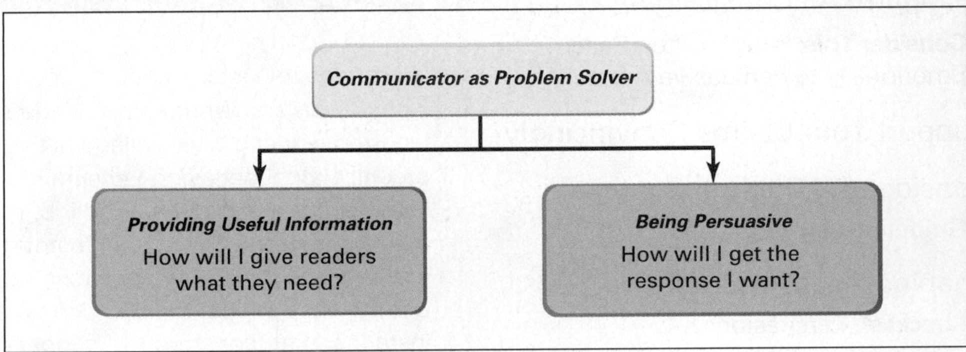

FIGURE 3.1 Informing and Persuading Require Audience Awareness

Implicit versus explicit persuasion

Almost all workplace documents, to some extent, have an *implicitly* persuasive goal: namely, to assure readers that the information is accurate, the facts are correct, and the writer is fluent, competent, and knowledgeable. But the types of documents featured in this chapter have an *explicitly* persuasive goal: namely, to win readers over to a particular point of view about an issue that is in some way controversial.

Explicit persuasion is required whenever you tackle an issue about which people disagree. Assume, for example, that you are Manager of Employee Relations at Softbyte, a software developer whose recent sales have plunged. To avoid layoffs, the company is trying to persuade employees to accept a temporary cut in salary.

As you plan various memos and presentations on this volatile issue, you must first identify your major *claims*. (A claim is a statement of the point you are trying to prove.) For instance, in the Softbyte situation, you might first want employees to recognize and acknowledge facts they've ignored:

> Because of the global recession, our software sales in two recent quarters have fallen nearly 30 percent, and earnings should remain flat all year.

A claim about what the facts are

Even when a fact is obvious, people often disagree about what it means or what should be done about it. And so you might want to influence their interpretation of the facts:

> Reduced earnings mean temporary layoffs for roughly 25 percent of our staff. But we could avoid layoffs entirely if each of us at Softbyte would accept a 10 percent salary cut until the market improves.

A claim about what the facts mean

And eventually you might want to ask for direct action:

> Our labor contract stipulates that such an across-the-board salary cut would require a two-thirds majority vote. Once you've had time to examine the facts, we hope you'll vote "yes" on next Tuesday's secret ballot.

A claim about what should be done

As you present your case, you will offer support for your claims before you finally ask readers to take the action you favor. Whenever people disagree about what the facts are or what the facts mean or what should be done, you need to make the best case for your own view.

On the job, your memos, letters, reports, and proposals advance claims like these (Gilsdorf, "Executives' and Academics' Perception" 59–62):

> We can't possibly meet this production deadline without sacrificing quality.
>
> We're doing all we can to correct your software problem.
>
> Our equipment is exactly what you need.
>
> I deserve a raise.

Claims require support

Such claims, of course, are likely to be rejected—unless they are backed up by a convincing argument.

NOTE *"Argument," in this context, means "a process of careful reasoning in support of a particular claim"—it does not mean "a quarrel or dispute." People who "argue skillfully" are able to connect with others in a rational, sensible way, without causing animosity. But people who are merely "argumentative," on the other hand, simply make others defensive.*

IDENTIFY YOUR SPECIFIC PERSUASIVE GOAL

What do you want people to be doing or thinking? Arguments differ considerably in the level of involvement they ask from people.

Types of persuasive goals

- **Arguing to influence people's opinions.** Some arguments ask for minimal audience involvement. Maybe you want people to agree that the benefits of bioengineered foods outweigh the risks, or that your company's monitoring of employee email is hurting morale. The goal here is merely to move readers to change their thinking, to say "I agree."
- **Arguing to enlist people's support.** Some arguments ask people to take a definite stand. Maybe you want readers to support a referendum that would restrict cloning experiments, or to lobby for a daycare center where you work. The goal is to get people actively involved, to get them to ask "How can I help?"
- **Submitting a proposal.** Proposals offer plans for solving problems. The proposals we examine in Chapter 23 typically ask audiences to take—or to approve—some form of direct action (say, a plan for improving your firm's computer security or a Web-based orientation program for new employees). Your proposal goal is achieved when people say "Okay, let's do this project."
- **Arguing to change people's behavior.** Getting people to change their behavior is a huge challenge. Maybe you want a coworker to stop dominating your staff meetings, or to be more open about sharing information that you need to do your job. People naturally take such arguments personally. And the more personal the issue, the greater people's resistance. After all, you're trying to get them to admit, "I was wrong. From now on, I'll do it differently."

The above goals can and often do overlap, depending on the situation. But never launch an argument without a clear view of exactly what you want to see happen.

TRY TO PREDICT AUDIENCE REACTION

Any document can evoke different reactions depending on a reader's temperament, interests, fears, biases, ambitions, or assumptions. Whenever peoples' views are challenged, they react with defensive questions such as these:

Audience questions about your attempts to persuade

- Says who?
- So what?
- Why should I?
- What's in this for me?
- What will it cost?
- What are the risks?
- What are you up to?
- What's in it for you?
- Will it mean more work for me?
- Will it make me look bad?

Reactions to persuasive messages can differ greatly

People read between the lines. Some might be impressed and pleased by your suggestions for increasing productivity or cutting expenses; some might feel offended or threatened. Some might suspect you of trying to undermine your boss. Such are the "political realities" in any organization (Hays 19).

No one wants bad news; some people prefer to ignore it. If you know something is wrong, that a product or project is unsafe, inefficient, or worthless, you have to decide whether "to try to change company plans, to keep silent, to 'blow the whistle,' or to quit" (19). Does your organization encourage outspokenness and constructive criticism? Is bad news allowed to travel upward, from subordinates to superiors (say, senior management), and if so, is the news likely to be accepted or suppressed? Find out—preferably before you take the job. For more on conveying bad-news messages, see pages 324, 362.

EXPECT AUDIENCE RESISTANCE

People who haven't made up their minds about what to do or think are more likely to be receptive to persuasive influence.

People rely on persuasion to make up their minds

> We need others' arguments and evidence. We're busy. We can't and don't want to discover and reason out everything for ourselves. We look for help, for short cuts, in making up our minds. (Gilsdorf, "Write Me" 12)

People who *have* decided what to think, however, naturally assume they're right, and they often refuse to budge. Whenever you question people's stance on an issue or try to change their behavior, expect resistance:

Once their minds are made up, people tend to hold stubbornly to their views

> By its nature, informing "works" more often than persuading does. While most people do not mind taking in some new facts, many people do resist efforts to change their opinions, attitudes, or behaviors. (Gilsdorf, "Executives" 61)

Getting people to admit you might be right means getting them to admit they might be wrong. The more strongly they identify with their position, the more resistance you can expect.

When people do yield to persuasion, they may respond grudgingly, willingly, or enthusiastically (Figure 3.2). Researchers categorize these responses as compliance, identification, or internalization (Kelman 51–60):

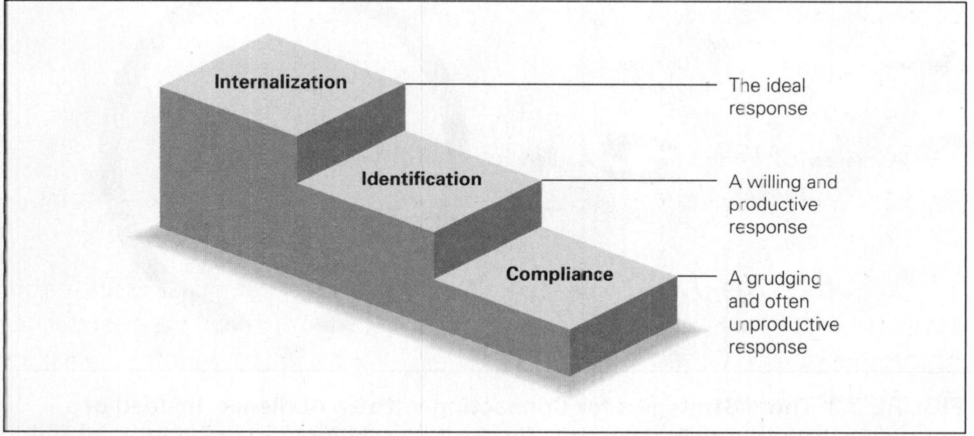

FIGURE 3.2 The Levels of Response to Persuasion

Some ways of yielding to persuasion are more productive than others

- **Compliance:** "I'm yielding to your demand in order to get a reward or to avoid punishment. I really don't accept it, but I feel pressured, and so I'll go along to get along."
- **Identification:** "I'm going along with your appeal because I like and believe you, I want you to like me, and I feel we have something in common."
- **Internalization:** "I'm yielding because what you're suggesting makes good sense and it fits my goals and values."

Although achieving compliance is sometimes necessary (as in military orders or workplace safety regulations), nobody likes to be coerced. If readers merely comply because they feel they have no choice, you probably have lost their loyalty and goodwill—and as soon as the threat or reward disappears, you will lose their compliance as well.

KNOW HOW TO CONNECT WITH THE AUDIENCE

Choosing the best connections

Persuasive people know when to simply declare what they want, when to reach out and create a relationship, when to appeal to reason and common sense, or when to employ some combination of these strategies (Kipnis and Schmidt 40–46). These three strategies, respectively, can be labeled the *power connection*, the *relationship connection*, and the *rational connection* (Figure 3.3). To get a better understanding of these three different strategies, picture the scenario on page 41.

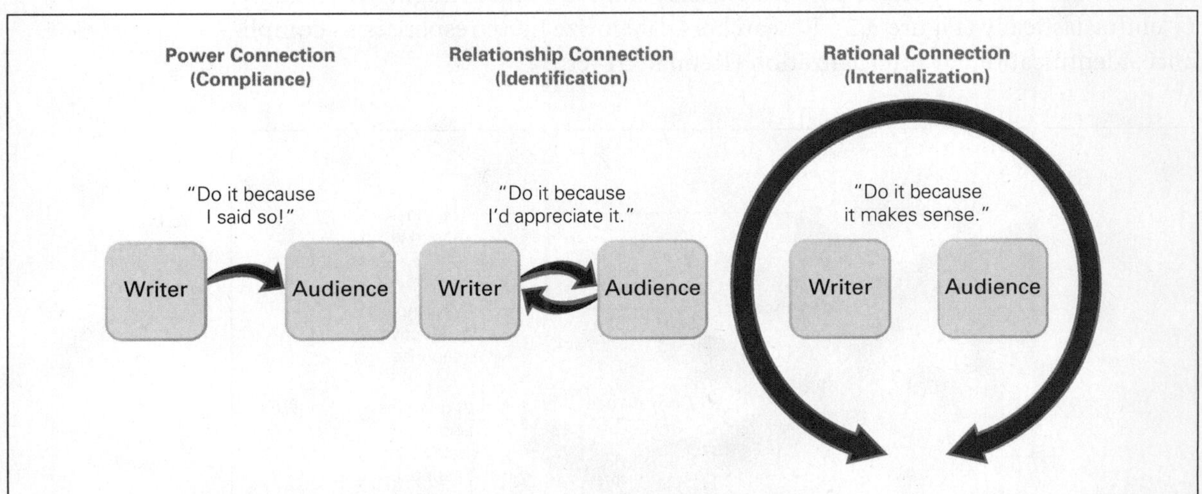

FIGURE 3.3 Three Strategies for Connecting with an Audience Instead of intimidating your audience, try to appeal to the relationship or—better yet—appeal to people's intelligence as well.

CASE Connecting with the Audience

Your Company, XYZ Engineering, has just developed a fitness program, based on findings that healthy employees work better, take fewer sick days, and cost less to insure. This program offers clinics for smoking, stress reduction, and weight loss, along with group exercise. In your second month on the job you read this notice in your email:

> TO: Employees at XYZ.com
> FROM: GMaximus@XYZ.com
> DATE: June 6, 20XX
> SUBJECT: *Physical Fitness*
>
> On Monday, June 10, all employees will report to the company gymnasium at 8:00 A.M. for the purpose of choosing a walking or jogging group. Each group will meet for 30 minutes three times weekly during lunch time.

Power connection: Orders readers to show up

How would you react to the previous notice? Despite the reference to "choosing," the recipients of the memo are given no real choice. They are simply ordered to show up at the gym. Typically used by bosses and other authority figures, this type of *power connection* does get people to comply but it almost always alienates them as well!

Suppose, instead, that you receive this next version of the memo. How would you react in this instance?

> TO: Employees at XYZ.com
> FROM: GMaximus@XYZ.com
> DATE: June 6, 20XX
> SUBJECT: *An Invitation to Physical Fitness*
>
> I realize most of you spend lunch hour playing cards, reading, or just enjoying a bit of well-earned relaxation in the middle of a hectic day. But I'd like to invite you to join our lunchtime walking/jogging club.
>
> We're starting this club in hopes that it will be a great way for us all to feel more healthy. Why not give it a try?

Relationship connection: Invites readers to participate

Leaves choice to readers

This second version conveys the sense that "we're all in this together." Instead of being commanded, readers are invited to participate. Someone who seems likable and considerate is offering readers a real choice.

Often the biggest variable in a persuasive message is the reader's perception of the writer. Readers are more open to people they like and trust. The *relationship connection* often works for this reason and it is especially vital in cross-cultural communication, as long as it does not sound too "chummy" and informal to carry any real authority. (For more on tone, see pages 232–38.)

Of course, you would be unethical in appealing to—or faking—the relationship merely to hide the fact that you have no evidence to support your claim (R. Ross 28). People need to find the claim believable ("Exercise will help me feel more healthy") and relevant ("I personally need this kind of exercise").

Here is a third version of the memo. As you read, think about the ways in which its approach differs from those of the first two examples.

TO: Employees at XYZ.com
FROM: GMaximus@XYZ.com
DATE: June 6, 20XX
SUBJECT: *Invitation to Join One of Our Jogging or Walking Groups*

Rational connection: Presents authoritative evidence

I want to share a recent study from the *New England Journal of Medicine,* which reports that adults who walk two miles a day could increase their life expectancy by three years.

Other research shows that 30 minutes of moderate aerobic exercise, at least three times weekly, has a significant and long-term effect in reducing stress, lowering blood pressure, and improving job performance.

Offers alternatives

As a first step in our exercise program, XYZ Engineering is offering a variety of daily jogging groups: The One-Milers, Three-Milers, and Five-Milers. All groups will≈meet at designated times on our brand new, quarter-mile, rubberized clay track.

For beginners or skeptics, we're offering daily two-mile walking groups. For the truly resistant, we offer the option of a Monday–Wednesday–Friday two-mile walk.

Offers a compromise

Coffee and lunch breaks can be rearranged to accommodate whichever group you select.

Leaves choice to readers

Offers incentives

Why not take advantage of our hot new track? As small incentives, XYZ will reimburse anyone who signs up as much as $100 for running or walking shoes, and will even throw in an extra fifteen minutes for lunch breaks. And with a consistent turnout of 90 percent or better, our company insurer may be able to eliminate everyone's $200 yearly deductible in medical costs.

This version conveys respect for the reader's intelligence and for the relationship. With any reasonable audience, the rational connection stands the best chance of success.

NOTE *Keep in mind that no cookbook formula exists, and in many situations, even the best persuasive attempts may be rejected.*

ALLOW FOR GIVE-AND-TAKE

Reasonable people expect a balanced argument, with both sides of the issue considered evenly and fairly. Persuasion requires flexibility on your part. Instead of merely pushing your own case forward, consider other viewpoints. In advocating your position, for example, you need to do these things (Senge 8):

How to promote your view

- explain the reasoning and evidence behind your stance
- invite people to find weak spots in your case, and to improve on it
- invite people to challenge your ideas (say, with alternative reasoning or data)

When others offer an opposing view, you need to do these things:

How to respond to opposing views

- try to see the issue their way, instead of insisting on your way
- rephrase an opposing position in your own words, to be sure you understand it accurately
- try reaching agreement on what to do next, to resolve any insurmountable differences
- explore possible compromises others might accept

Perhaps some XYZ employees (see the previous case), for example, have better ideas for making the exercise program work for everyone.

ASK FOR A SPECIFIC RESPONSE

Unless you are giving an order, diplomacy is essential in persuasion. But don't be afraid to ask for what you want:

Spell out what you want

> The moment of decision is made easier for people when we show them what the desired action is, rather than leaving it up to them. . . . No one likes to make decisions: there is always a risk involved. But if the writer asks for the action, and makes it look easy and urgent, the decision itself looks less risky. (Cross 3)

Let people know what you want them to do or think.

NOTE *Overly direct communication can offend audiences from other cultures. Don't mistake bluntness for clarity.*

NEVER ASK FOR TOO MUCH

People never accept anything they consider unreasonable. And the definition of "reasonable" varies with the individual. Employees at XYZ Engineering (see page 41 case), for example, differ as to which walking/jogging option they might accept. To the runner writing the memo, a daily five-mile jog might seem perfectly reasonable, but to most people this would seem outrageous. XYZ's program, therefore, has to

Stick with what is achievable

offer something most of its audience (except, say, couch potatoes and those in poor health) accept as reasonable.

Any request that exceeds its audience's "latitude of acceptance" (Sherif 39–59) is doomed.

RECOGNIZE ALL CONSTRAINTS

Constraints are limits or restrictions imposed by the situation:

Communication constraints in persuasive situations

- What can I say around here, to whom, and how?
- Should I say it in person, by phone, in print, online?
- Could I be creating any ethical or legal problems?
- Is this the best time to say it?
- What is my relationship with the audience?
- Who are the personalities involved?
- Is there any peer pressure to overcome?
- How big an issue is this?

Organizational Constraints

Constraints based on company rules

Organizations announce their own official constraints: deadlines; budgets; guidelines for organizing, formatting, and distributing documents; and so on. But communicators also face *unofficial* constraints:

Decide carefully when to say what to whom

> Most organizations have clear rules for interpreting and acting on statements made by colleagues. Even if the rules are unstated, we know who can initiate interaction, who can be approached, who can propose a delay, what topics can or cannot be discussed, who can interrupt or be interrupted, who can order or be ordered, who can terminate interaction, and how long interaction should last. (Littlejohn and Jabusch 143)

The exact rules vary among organizations, but anyone who ignores those rules (say, by going over a supervisor's head with a complaint or suggestion) invites disaster.

Airing even a legitimate gripe in the wrong way through the wrong medium to the wrong person can be fatal to your work relationships. The following email, for instance, is likely to be interpreted by the executive officer as petty and whining behavior, and by the maintenance director as a public attack.

> TO: CEO@XYZ.com
> CC: MaintenanceDirector@XYZ.com
> FROM: Middle Manager@XYZ.com
> DATE: May 13, 20XX
> RE: *Trash Problem*

> Please ask the Maintenance Director to get his people to do their job for a change. I realize we're all understaffed, but I've gotten dozens of complaints this week about the filthy restrooms and overflowing wastebaskets in my department. If he wants us to empty our own wastebaskets, why doesn't he let us know?

Wrong way to the wrong person

Instead, why not address the message directly to the key person—or better yet, phone the person?

> TO: MaintenanceDirector@XYZ.com
> FROM: MiddleManager@XYZ.com
> DATE: May 13, 20XX
> RE: *Staffing Shortage*
>
> I wonder if we could meet to exchange some ideas about how our departments might be able to help one another during these staff shortages.

A better way to the right person

Can you identify the unspoken rules in companies where you have worked? What happens when such rules are ignored?

Legal Constraints

What you are allowed to say may be limited by contract or by laws protecting confidentiality or customers' rights or laws affecting product liability:

Constraints based on the law

Major legal constraints on communication

- In a collection letter for nonpayment, you can threaten to take legal action, but you cannot threaten to publicize the refusal to pay, nor pretend to be an attorney (Varner and Varner 31–40).
- If someone requests information on one of your employees, you can "respond only to specific requests that have been approved by the employee. Further, your comments should relate only to job performance which is documented" (Harcourt 64).
- When writing sales literature or manuals, you and your company are liable for faulty information that leads to injury or damage.

Whenever you prepare a document, be aware of possible legal problems. For instance, suppose an employee of XYZ Engineering (case on page 41) is injured or dies during the new exercise program you've marketed so persuasively. Could you and your company be liable? Should you require physical exams and stress tests (at company expense) for participants? When in doubt, always consult an attorney.

Public relations and legal liabilities

Ethical Constraints

While legal constraints are defined by federal and state law, ethical constraints are defined by honesty and fair play. For example, it may be perfectly legal to promote a new pesticide by emphasizing its effectiveness, while downplaying its carcinogenic

Constraints based on honesty and fair play

effects; whether such action is *ethical,* however, is another issue entirely. To earn people's trust, you will find that "saying the right thing" involves more than legal considerations. (See Chapter 4 for more on ethics.)

NOTE *Persuasive skills carry tremendous potential for abuse. "Presenting your best case" does not mean deceiving others—even if the dishonest answer is the one people want to hear.*

Time Constraints

Constraints based on the right timing

Persuasion often depends on good timing. Should you wait for an opening, release the message immediately, or what? Let's assume that you're trying to "bring out the vote" among members of your professional society on some hotly debated issue, say, whether to refuse to work on any project related to biological warfare. You might prefer to wait until you have all the information you need or until you've analyzed the situation and planned a strategy. But if you delay, rumors or paranoia could cause people to harden their positions—and their resistance.

Social and Psychological Constraints

Constraints based on audience

Too often, what we say can be misunderstood or misinterpreted because of constraints such as these:

"What is our relationship?"

- **Relationship with the audience:** Is your reader a superior, a subordinate, a peer? (Try not to dictate to subordinates nor to shield superiors from bad news.) How well do you know each other? Can you joke around or should you be serious? Do you get along or have a history of conflict or mistrust? What you say and how you say it—and how it is interpreted—will be influenced by the relationship.

"How receptive is this audience?"

- **Audience's personality:** Willingness to be persuaded depends largely on personality (Stonecipher 188–89). Does this person tend to be more open- or closed-minded, more skeptical or trusting, more bold or cautious, more of a conformist or a rugged individual? The less persuadable your audience, the harder you have to work. For a totally resistant audience, you may want to back off or give up altogether.

"How unified is this audience?"

- **Audience's sense of identity and affiliation as a group:** Does the group have a strong sense of identity (union members, conservationists, engineers)? Will group loyalty or pressure to conform prevent certain appeals from working? Address the group's collective concerns.

"Where are most people coming from on this issue?"

- **Perceived size and urgency of the issue:** Does the audience see this as a cause for fear or for hope? Is trouble looming or has a great opportunity emerged? Has the issue been understated or overstated? Big problems often cause people to exaggerate their fears, loyalties, and resistance to change—or to seek quick solutions. Assess the problem realistically. Don't downplay a serious problem, but don't cause panic, either.

CONSIDER THIS: People Often React Emotionally to Persuasive Appeals

We've all been on the receiving end of attempts to influence our thinking:

- *You need this product!*
- *This candidate is the one to vote for!*
- *Try doing things this way!*

How do we decide which appeals to accept or reject? One way is by evaluating the argument itself, by asking *Does it make good sense? Is it balanced and fair?* But arguments rarely succeed or fail merely on their own merits. Emotions play a major role.

Why We Say No

Management expert Edgar Schein outlines various fears that prevent people from trying or learning something new (34–39):

- **Fear of the unknown:** *Why rock the boat?* (Change can be scary, and so we cling to old, familiar ways of doing things, even when those ways aren't working.)
- **Fear of disruption:** *Who needs these headaches?* (We resist change if it seems too complicated or troublesome.)
- **Fear of failure:** *Suppose I screw up?* (We worry about the shame or punishment that might result from making errors.)

To overcome these basic fears, Schein explains, people need to feel "psychologically safe":

> They have to see a manageable path forward, a direction that will not be catastrophic. They have to feel that a change will not jeopardize their current sense of identity and wholeness. They must feel that . . . they can . . . try out new things without fear of punishment. (59)

Why We Say Yes

Social psychologist Robert Cialdini pinpoints six subjective criteria that move people to accept a persuasive appeal (76–81):

- **Reciprocation:** *Do I owe this person a favor?* (We feel obligated—and we look for the chance—to reciprocate, or return, a good deed.)
- **Consistency:** *Have I made an earlier commitment along these lines?* (We like to perceive ourselves as behaving consistently. People who have declared even minor support for a particular position [say by signing a petition], will tend to accept requests for major support of that position [say, a financial contribution].)
- **Social validation:** *Are other people agreeing or disagreeing?* (We often feel reassured by going along with our peers.)
- **Liking:** *Do I like the person making the argument?* (We are far more receptive to people we like—and often more willing to accept a bad argument from a likable person than a good one from an unlikable person!)
- **Authority:** *How knowledgeable does this person seem about the issue?* (We place confidence in experts and authorities.)
- **Scarcity:** *Does this person know (or have) something that others don't?* (The scarcer something seems, the more we value it [say, a hot tip about the stock market].)

A typical sales pitch, for example, might include a "free sample of our most popular brand, which is nearly sold out" offered by a chummy salesperson full of "expert" details about the item itself.

Cross-Cultural Differences

Different cultures can weigh these criteria differently: Cialdini cites a survey of Citibank employees in four countries by researchers Morris, Podolny, and Ariel. When asked by a coworker for help with a task, U.S. bank employees felt

▶▶

CONSIDER THIS *(continued)*

obligated to comply, or reciprocate, if they owed that person a favor. Chinese employees were influenced mostly by the requester's status, or authority, while Spanish employees based their decision mainly on liking and friendship, regardless of the requester's status. German employees were motivated mainly by a sense of consistency in following the bank's official rules: If the rules stipulated they should help coworkers, they felt compelled to do so (81).

SUPPORT YOUR CLAIMS CONVINCINGLY

Persuasive claims are backed up by reasons that have meaning for the audience

The most persuasive argument will be the one that presents the strongest case—from the audience's perspective:

> When we seek a project extension, argue for a raise, interview for a job . . . we are involved in acts that require good reasons. Good reasons allow our audience and ourselves to find a shared basis for cooperating . . . . [Y]ou can use marvelous language, tell great stories, provide exciting metaphors, speak in enthralling tones, and even use your reputation to advantage, but what it comes down to is that you must speak to your audience with reasons they understand. (Hauser 71)

Imagine yourself in the following situation: As documentation manager for Bemis Lawn and Garden Equipment, a rapidly growing company, you supervise preparation and production of all user manuals. The present system for producing manuals is inefficient because three respective departments are involved in (1) assembling the material, (2) word processing and designing, and (3) publishing the manuals in hard copy, PDF, and hyperlinked versions. Much time and energy are wasted as a manual goes back and forth among engineering and product-testing specialists, communication specialists, and the art and printing department. After studying the problem and calling in a consultant, you decide that greater efficiency would result if content management software were installed on the company server. This way, all employees involved could contribute to all three phases of the process. To sell this plan to supervisors and coworkers you will need good reasons, in the form of *evidence* and *appeals to readers' needs and values* (Rottenberg 104–06).

Offer Convincing Evidence

Evidence (factual support from an outside source) is a powerful persuader—as long as it measures up to readers' standards. Discerning readers evaluate evidence by using these criteria (Perloff 157–58):

Criteria for worthwhile evidence

- **The evidence has quality.** Instead of sheer quantity, people expect evidence that is strong, specific, new, different, and verifiable (provable).

- **The sources are credible.** People want to know where the evidence comes from, how it was collected, and who collected it.
- **The evidence is considered reasonable.** It falls within the audience's "latitude of acceptance" (discussed on page 44).

Common types of evidence include factual statements, statistics, examples, and expert testimony.

Factual Statements. A *fact* is something that can be demonstrated by observation, experience, research, or measurement—and that your audience is willing to recognize.

> Most of our competitors already have content management systems in place.

Offer the facts

Be selective. Decide which facts best support your case.

Statistics. Numbers can be highly convincing. Many readers focus on the "bottom line": costs, savings, losses, profits.

> After a cost/benefit analysis, our accounting office estimates that an integrated content management network will save Bemis 30 percent in production costs and 25 percent in production time—savings that will enable the system to pay for itself within one year.

Cite the numbers

But numbers can mislead. Your statistics must be accurate, trustworthy, and easy to understand and verify (see pages 163–67). Always cite your source.

Examples. Examples help people visualize and remember the point. For example, the best way to explain what you mean by "inefficiency" in your company is to show "inefficiency" occurring:

> The figure illustrates the inefficiency of Bemis's present system for producing manuals:

Show what you mean

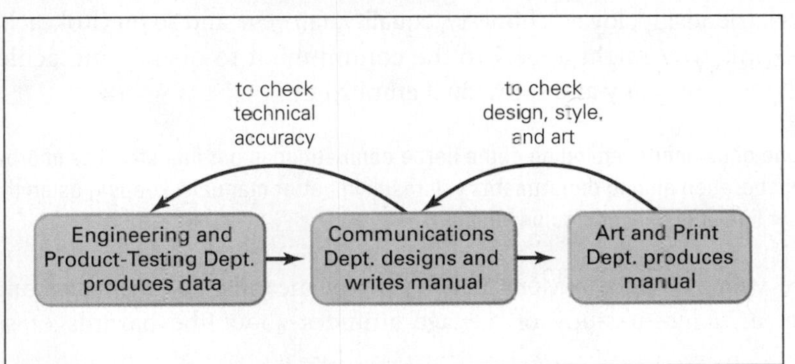

> A manual typically goes back and forth through this cycle three or four times, wasting time and effort in all three departments.

Always explain how each example fits the point it is designed to illustrate.

Expert Testimony. Expert opinion—if it is unbiased and if people recognize the expert—lends authority and credibility to any claim.

Cite the experts

> Ron Catabia, nationally recognized networking consultant, has studied our needs and strongly recommends we move ahead with a content management system.

NOTE *Finding evidence to support a claim often requires that we go beyond our own experience by doing some type of research. (See Part 2, "The Research Process")*

Appeal to Common Goals and Values

Evidence alone may not be enough to change a person's mind. At Bemis, for example, the bottom line might be very persuasive for company executives, but managers and employees will be asking: Does this threaten my authority? Will I have to work harder? Will I fall behind? Is my job in danger? These readers will have to perceive some benefit beyond company profit.

"What makes these people tick?"

If you hope to create any kind of consensus, you have to identify at least one goal you and your audience have in common: "What do we all want most?" Bemis employees, like most people, share these goals: job security and control over their jobs and destinies. Any persuasive recommendation will have to take these goals into account:

Appeal to shared goals

> I'd like to show how content management skills, instead of threatening anyone's job, would only increase career mobility for all of us.

People's goals are shaped by their values (qualities they believe in, ideals they stand for): friendship, loyalty, honesty, equality, fairness, and so on (Rokeach 57–58).

At Bemis, you might appeal to the commitment to quality and achievement shared by the company and individual employees:

Appeal to shared values

> None of us needs reminding of the fierce competition in our industry. The improved collaboration among departments will result in better manuals, keeping us on the front line of quality and achievement.

Give your audience reasons that have real meaning for *them* personally. For example, in a recent study of teenage attitudes about the hazards of smoking, respondents listed these reasons for not smoking: bad breath, difficulty concentrating, loss of friends, and trouble with adults. No respondents listed dying of cancer—presumably because this last reason carries little meaning for young people personally (Baumann et al. 510–30).

NOTE *We are often tempted to emphasize anything that advances our case and to ignore anything that impedes it. But any message that prevents readers from making their best decision is unethical, as discussed in Chapter 4.*

CONSIDER THE CULTURAL CONTEXT

How cultural differences govern a persuasive situation

Reaction to persuasive appeals can be influenced by a culture's customs and values[1]: Cultures might differ in their willingness to debate, criticize, or express disagreement or emotion. They might differ in their definitions of "convincing support," or they might observe special formalities in communicating. Expressions of feelings and concern for one's family might be valued more than logic, fact, statistics, research findings, or expert testimony. Some cultures consider the *source* of a message as important as its content, or they trust oral more than written communication. Establishing rapport and building a relationship might weigh more heavily than proof and might be an essential prelude to getting down to business. Some cultures take indirect, roundabout approaches to an issue, viewing it from all angles before declaring a position.

Cultures differ in their attitudes toward big business, technology, competition, or women in the workplace. They might value delayed gratification more than immediate reward, stability more than progress, time more than profit, politeness more than candor, age more than youth. Cultures respond differently to different emotional pressures, such as feeling obliged to return favors or following the lead of their peers. (See Consider This, page 47.)

Face saving is every person's priority

One key value in all cultures is the primacy of *face saving*: "the act of preserving one's prestige or outward dignity" (Victor 159–61). People lose face in situations such as the following:

How people lose face

- **When they are offended or embarrassed by blatant criticism:** A U.S. businessperson in China decides to "tell it like it is," and proceeds to criticize the Tiananmen Square massacre and China's illegal contributions to American political parties (Stepanek 4).

[1] Adapted from Beamer 293–95; Gesteland 24; Hulbert, "Overcoming" 42; Jameson 9–11; Kohl et al. 65; Martin and Chaney 271–77; Nydell 61; Thatcher 193–94; Thrush 276–77; Victor 159–66.

- **When their customs are ignored:** An American female arrives to negotiate with older, Japanese males; Silicon Valley businesspeople show up in T-shirts and baseball caps to meet with hosts wearing suits.
- **When their values are trivialized:** An American in Paris greets his French host as "Pierre," slaps him on the back, and jokes that the "rich French food" on the flight had him "throwing up all the way over" (Isaacs 43).

Whenever people feel insulted, meaningful interaction is over

Roughly 60 percent of business ventures between the United States and other countries fail (Isaacs 43), often, arguably, because of cultural differences.

Show respect for a culture's heritage by learning all you can about its history, landmarks, famous people, and especially its customs and values (Isaacs 43). The following questions can get you started.

Questions for analyzing cultural differences

What is accepted behavior?

- Preferred form for greetings or introductions (first or family names, titles)
- Casual versus formal interaction
- Directness and plain talk versus indirectness and ambiguity
- Rapid decision making versus extensive analysis and discussion
- Willingness to request clarification
- Willingness to argue, criticize, or disagree
- Willingness to be contradicted
- Willingness to express emotion

What are the values and attitudes?

- Big business, competition, and U.S. culture
- Youth versus age
- Rugged individualism versus group loyalty
- Status of women in the workplace
- Feelings versus logic
- Candor versus face saving
- Progress and risk taking versus stability
- Importance of trust and relationship building
- Importance of time ("Time is money!" or "Never rush!")
- Preference for oral versus written communication

Take the time to know your audience, to appreciate their frame of reference, and to establish common ground. (For more on cultural considerations, see Chapter 5.)

NOTE *Violating a person's cultural frame of reference is offensive, but so is reducing individual complexity to a laundry list of cultural stereotypes. Any generalization about a group presents a limited picture and in no way accurately characterizes even one much less all members of the group.*

GUIDELINES for Persuasion

Later chapters offer specific guidelines for various persuasive documents such as sales letters and proposals. But beyond attending to the unique requirements of a particular document, remember this principle:

No matter how brilliant, any argument rejected by its audience is a failed argument.

If readers find cause to dislike you or conclude that your argument has no meaning for them personally, they usually reject *anything* you say. Connecting with an audience means being able to see things from their perspective. The following guidelines can help you make that connection.

Analyze the Situation

- **Assess the political climate.** Who will be affected by your document? How will they react? How will they interpret your motives? Can you be outspoken? Could the argument cause legal problems? The better you assess readers' political feelings, the less likely your document will backfire. Do what you can to earn confidence and goodwill:
  - Be aware of your status in the organization; don't overstep.
  - Do not expect anyone to be perfect—including yourself.
  - Never overstate your certainty or make promises you cannot keep.
  - Be diplomatic; don't make anyone look bad or lose face.
  - Ask directly for support: "Is this idea worthy of your commitment?"
  - Ask your intended readers to review early drafts.

  When reporting company negligence, dishonesty, incompetence, or anything else that others do not want to hear, expect fallout. Decide beforehand whether you want to keep your job (or status) or your dignity (more in Chapter 4).
- **Learn the unspoken rules.** Know the constraints on what you can say, to whom you can say it, and how and when you can say it. Consider the cultural context.
- **Decide on a connection (or combination of connections).** Does the situation call for you to merely declare your position, appeal to the relationship, or appeal to common sense and reason?
- **Anticipate your audience's reaction.** Will people be surprised, annoyed, angry? Try to address their biggest objections beforehand. Express your judgments ("We could do better") without making people defensive ("It's all your fault").

Develop a Clear and Credible Plan

- **Define your precise goal.** Develop the clearest possible view of what you want to see happen.

GUIDELINES *continued*

- **Do your homework.** Be sure your facts are straight, your figures are accurate, and that the evidence supports your claim.
- **Think your idea through.** Are there holes in this argument? Will it stand up under scrutiny?
- **Never make a claim or ask for something that people will reject outright.** Consider how much is *achievable* in this situation by asking what people are thinking. Invite them to share in decision making. Offer real choices.
- **Consider the cultural context.** Will some audience members feel that your message ignores their customs? Will they be offended by a direct approach or by too many facts and figures without a relationship connection? Remember that, beyond racial and ethnic distinctions, cultural groups also consist of people who share religious or spiritual views, sexual orientations, political affiliations, and so on.

Prepare Your Argument

- **Be clear about what you want.** Diplomacy is always important, but people won't like having to guess about your purpose.
- **Avoid an extreme persona.** Persona is the image or impression of the writer's personality suggested by the document's tone. Resist the urge to "sound off" no matter how strongly you feel, because audiences tune out aggressive people no matter how sensible the argument. Admit the imperfections in your case. Invite people to respond. A little humility never hurts. Don't hesitate to offer praise when it's deserved.
- **Find points of agreement with your audience.** "What do we *all* want?" Focus early on a shared value, goal, or experience. Emphasize your similarities.
- **Never distort the opponent's position.** A sure way to alienate people is to cast the opponent in a more negative light than the facts warrant.
- **Try to concede something to the opponent.** Reasonable people respect an argument that is fair and balanced. Admit the merits of the opposing case before arguing for your own. Show empathy and willingness to compromise. Encourage people to air their own views.
- **Do not merely criticize.** If you're arguing that something is wrong, be sure you can offer realistic suggestions for making it right.
- **Stick to claims you can support.** Show people what's in it for them—but never distort the facts just to please the audience. Be honest about the risks.
- **Stick to your best material.** Not all points are equal. Decide which material—from your audience's view—best advances your case.

Present Your Argument

- **Before releasing the document, seek a second opinion.** Ask someone you trust and who has no stake in the issue at hand. If possible, have your company's legal department review the document.
- **Get the timing right.** When will your case most likely fly—or crash and burn? What else is going on that could influence people's reactions? Look for a good opening in the situation.
- **Decide on the proper format.** Does this audience and topic call for a letter, a memo, or some type of report? Your decision will affect how positively your message is received. Can visuals and page layout (charts, graphs, drawings, headings, lists) make the material more accessible?
- **Decide on the appropriate medium.** Given the specific issue and audience, should you communicate in person, in print, by phone, email, fax, newsletter, bulletin board? (See also page 344.) Should all recipients receive your message via the same medium? If your document is likely to surprise readers, try to warn them.
- **Be sure everyone involved receives a copy.** People hate being left out of the loop—especially when any change that affects them is being discussed.
- **Invite responses.** After people have had a chance to consider your argument, gauge their reactions by asking them directly.
- **Do not be defensive about negative reactions.** Admit mistakes, invite people to improve on your ideas, and try to build support.
- **Know when to back off.** If you seem to be "hitting the wall," don't push. Try again later or drop the whole effort. People who feel they have been bullied or deceived will likely become your enemies.

SHAPING YOUR ARGUMENT

To understand how our guidelines are employed in an actual persuasive situation, see Figure 3.4. The letter is from Rosemary Garrido of Energy Empowerment, Inc., a consulting firm that works with contractors to maximize the energy efficiency of offices and retail locations. Garrido's letter is a persuasive answer to her potential customer's main question: "Is it worthwhile to make energy efficient changes to the storefront we've bought?" As you read the letter, notice the evidence and appeals Rosemary uses to support her opening claim and how she focuses on her reader's needs. Rosemary used the Audience and Use Profile Sheet (Figure 3.5) to help formulate her approach to the letter.

Energy Empowerment, Inc.
2568 Sheridan Avenue
Suite 9
St. Paul MN 55106

May 14, 20XX

Mr. Dean Winfield, President
XPressMart, Inc.
1720 St. James Avenue
Minneapolis, MN 55405

Dear Mr. Winfield:

The writer states her claim clearly, directly, and politely →

I applaud XPressMart's recent commitment to energy efficiency and sustainability in the retail sector, beginning with your newly-purchased storefront in the Cedar-Riverside area. In our meeting last week, you asked me to follow-up with a detailed explanation as to why we feel energy efficiency is the right decision—both for the environment and your company's bottom line. Below I outline Energy Empowerment's three-point rationale.

Offers first reason →

Backs up reason with evidence →

First, you and your contractor, Jeff Manko, will find that the process of "going green" is actually quite straightforward, rather than another level of complication to an already complicated renovation process. As you can see from the enclosed chart, we have adapted the guidelines from the EPA's EnergyStar program to make both reconstruction decisions and the purchase of new HVAC systems, insulation, and doors and windows a straightforward process. We will work with Jeff every step of the way to ensure the seamless renovation of the store.

Offers second reason →

Appeals to shared value (environment) and goal (success) →

Second, by demonstrating XPressMart's commitment to the environment, you are not only helping reduce your company's carbon footprint, but also attracting today's environmentally-conscious customers. The Cedar-Riverside location, being adjacent to two college campuses, is the perfect place to begin.

1-800-555-3984 www.energyempowerment.com

FIGURE 3.4 Supporting a Claim with Good Reasons Give your audience a clear and logical path.

Dean Winfield, May 14, 20XX, page 2

Currently the storefront rates only a 42 on EnergyStar's performance scale. By improving that rating to 75 or above, this location will qualify for an EnergyStar display sticker, which, according to the EPA's Annual Report last year, increases retails sales in urban areas. Between the EnergyStar rating and your focus on sustainable products, expect to attract the interest of all residents of this forward-thinking community.

Finally, and perhaps most importantly, rest assured that the costs you put into reconstruction, systems, and other materials will pay for themselves in less than two years. Jeff and I have assembled a preliminary proposal itemizing costs, to which I will add my estimates regarding cost recuperation. However, know that in Energy Empowerment's 12-year history, every store and office renovation project has paid for itself remarkably quickly. As a recent example, consider our recent small office renovation in Columbia Heights, which recouped its costs in only 14 months.

If I can answer any further questions, please do not hesitate to email me at rgarrido@esi.com or call me (extension 646). Again, we applaud your commitment to the environment and look forward to working with you and Jeff.

Best regards,

Rosemary Garrido

Rosemary Garrido

Executive Manager

cc: Jeff Manko, Manko Construction
Encl. Energy Star's performance chart

Cites statistics

Closes with best reason

Appeals to shared goal (cost)

Offers example

FIGURE 3.4 *(Continued)*

Audience and Purpose

Primary audience: *Dean Winfield, President, XPressMart, Inc.*

Secondary audience(s): *Jeff Manko, Owner, Manko Construction*

Relationship with audience: *A possible customer for an energy-efficient renovation*

Purpose of document: *To help in gaining an important consulting project*

Audience and purpose statement: *To pave the way for a potential customer to hire us for our consulting services*

Intended use of document: *To provide information/rationale for a hiring decision*

Technical background: *Novice to moderate*

Prior knowledge about this topic: *Is new to the process of energy-efficiency renovation costs and results*

Information needs: *Needs, costs, benefits and statistics before proceeding*

Cultural considerations: *None in particular*

Probable questions: *How complicated is this process going to be?*
Will these green renovations impact business in any real way?
Will the cost of making these major renovations pay for themselves?

Audience's Probable Attitude and Personality

Attitude toward topic: *Highly interested but somewhat skeptical*

Probable objections: *These renovations may be too expensive for our bottom line*

Probable attitude toward this writer: *Receptive but cautious*

Organizational climate: *Open and flexible*

Persons most affected by this document: *Winfield and other decision makers*

Temperament: *Winfield takes a conservative approach to untested innovations*

Probable reaction to document: *Readers should feel somewhat reassured*

Audience Expectations about the Document

Material important to this audience: *Evidence that the renovations will be cost effective*

Potential problems: *Readers may have further questions I haven't anticipated*

Length and detail: *A concise argument that gets right to the point*

Format and medium: *A formal letter delivered via overnight mail*

Tone: *Encouraging, friendly, and confident*

Due date and timing: *ASAP—to illustrate our responsiveness to customer concerns*

FIGURE 3.5 **Audience and Use Profile Sheet** Notice how this profile sheet expands on the one shown in Figure 2.7 (page 31), to account for specific considerations in preparing an explicitly persuasive document.

NOTE *People rarely change their minds quickly or without good reason. A truly resistant audience will dismiss even the best arguments and may end up feeling threatened and resentful. Even with a receptive audience, attempts at persuasion can fail. Often, the best you can do is avoid disaster and allow people to ponder the merits of the argument.*

CHECKLIST: Persuasion

(Numbers in parentheses refer to the first page of discussion.)

Planning and Preparing Your Document

- ☐ Have I identified my precise goal in this situation? (37)
- ☐ Am I accounting for the political realities involved? (38)
- ☐ Can I elicit more than mere audience compliance in this situation? (39)
- ☐ Have I chosen the approach most likely to connect with this audience? (40)
- ☐ Am I constructing a balanced and reasonable argument? (43)
- ☐ Have I spelled out what I want this audience to do or think? (43)
- ☐ Am I seeking an outcome that is achievable in this situation? (43)
- ☐ Have I considered the various constraints in this situation? (44)
- ☐ Do I provide convincing evidence to support my claims? (48)
- ☐ Will my appeals have personal meaning for this audience? (50)
- ☐ Overall, do I argue skillfully without being "argumentative"? (37)
- ☐ Have I anticipated my audience's reaction? (38)

Cultural Considerations*

- ☐ Is the document sensitive to the culture's customs and values? (51)
- ☐ Have I avoided stereotyping of different cultures and groups of people? (52)
- ☐ Does the document conform to the country's safety and regulatory standards? (73)
- ☐ Does the document provide the expected level of detail? (25)
- ☐ Does the document avoid possible misinterpretation? (25)
- ☐ Does the document enable everyone to save face? (51)
- ☐ Is the document organized in a way that readers will consider appropriate? (209)
- ☐ Does the document observe accepted interpersonal conventions? (98)
- ☐ Does the tone reflect the appropriate level of formality or casualness? (52)
- ☐ Is the document's style appropriately direct or indirect? (5)
- ☐ Is the document's format consistent with the culture's expectations? (316)
- ☐ Does the document embody universal standards for ethical communication? (69)
- ☐ Should the document be supplemented by a more personal medium? (52)

**Source:* Adapted from Caswell-Coward 265; Weymouth 144; Beamer 293–95; Martin and Chaney 271–77; Thatcher 193–94; Victor 159–61.

Projects

GENERAL

1. Find an effective persuasive letter. In a memo (Chapter 14) to your instructor, explain how the message succeeds. Base your evaluation on the persuasion guidelines pages (53–55) and the checklist (page 59). Attach the letter to your memo. Now, evaluate an ineffective document, explaining how and why it fails.
2. Think about some change you would like to see on your campus or at work. Perhaps you would like to promote something new, such as a campus-wide policy on plagiarism, changes in course offerings or requirements, an off-campus shuttle service, or a daycare center. Or perhaps you would like to improve something, such as the grading system, campus lighting, the system for student evaluation of teachers, or the promotion system at work. Or perhaps you would like to stop something from happening, such as noise in the library or conflict at work.

   Decide whom you want to persuade and write a memo (Chapter 14) to that audience. Anticipate your audience's questions, such as:

   - Do we really have a problem or need?
   - If so, should we care enough about it to do anything?
   - Can the problem be solved?
   - What are some possible solutions?
   - What benefits can we anticipate? What liabilities?

   Can you think of additional audience questions? Do an audience and use analysis based on the profile sheet, page 58.

   Don't think of this memo as the final word but as a consciousness-raising introduction that gets the reader to acknowledge that the issue deserves attention. At this early stage, highly specific recommendations would be premature and inappropriate.

TEAM

As a class, select a topic that involves persuasion. Topics might include childhood obesity, climate change, nutritional supplements, or other. In teams of 2–3 students, find a document (online or print) that makes a persuasive case about the topic. Write a short summary of what techniques these documents use to make a persuasive case. Are you able to identify the document's specific persuasive goal (page 37)?

DIGITAL AND SOCIAL MEDIA

Digital information, such as Web sites, Facebook pages, or YouTube videos, uses a mix of media formats (text, images, color, sounds) and a focus on particular audiences to make a persuasive case. Using the same topic your class selected for the Team project, work in teams of 2–3 students to identify ways in which digital media was used to target the audience's sense of identity and affiliation as a group (page 46). Present your findings to class.

GLOBAL

1. Effective persuasive techniques in one culture may not work in another culture. Do a Web search on "intercultural communication" and locate a topic that is important for technical communication. For instance, you might locate information about the different ways in which certain types of visuals that are persuasive in one culture are not effective in another. Write a short summary of your findings, cite your sources, and present your information in class.
2. Use the questions on page 52 as a basis for interviewing a student from another country or culture. Be prepared to share your findings with the class.

4 Weighing the Ethical Issues

"Most of my writing is for clients who will make investment decisions based on their understanding of complex financial data, presented in a concise, *nontechnical* way. These people are not in any way experts. They want to know, 'What do I do next?' While I can never guarantee the certainty of any stock or mutual fund investment, my advice has to be based on an accurate and honest assessment of all the facts involved."

—Roger Fernandez,
Certified Financial Planner

LEARNING OBJECTIVES FOR THIS CHAPTER

- Appreciate the role of ethics in technical communication
- Identify workplace pressures that lead to unethical communication
- Recognize common workplace examples of hiding the truth
- Use critical thinking to help solve ethical dilemmas
- Differentiate between ethical practices and legal guidelines
- Avoid plagiarism—either intentional or unintentional
- Determine when and how to report ethical violations on the job

Arguments can "win" without being ethical if they "win" at any cost. For instance, advertisers effectively win customers with an implied argument that "our product is just what you need!" Some of their more specific claims can be: "Our artificial sweetener is composed of proteins that occur naturally in the human body [amino acids]" or "Our Krunchy Cookies contain no cholesterol!" Such claims are technically accurate but misleading: amino acids in certain sweeteners can alter body chemistry to cause headaches, seizures, and possibly brain tumors; processed food snacks often contain saturated fat and trans fats, from which the liver produces cholesterol.

We are often tempted to emphasize anything that advances our case and to ignore anything that impedes it. But communication is unethical if it leaves recipients at a disadvantage or prevents them from making their best decision (Figure 4.1). To help insure that your writing is ethical, keep it accurate, honest, and fair (Johannesen 1).

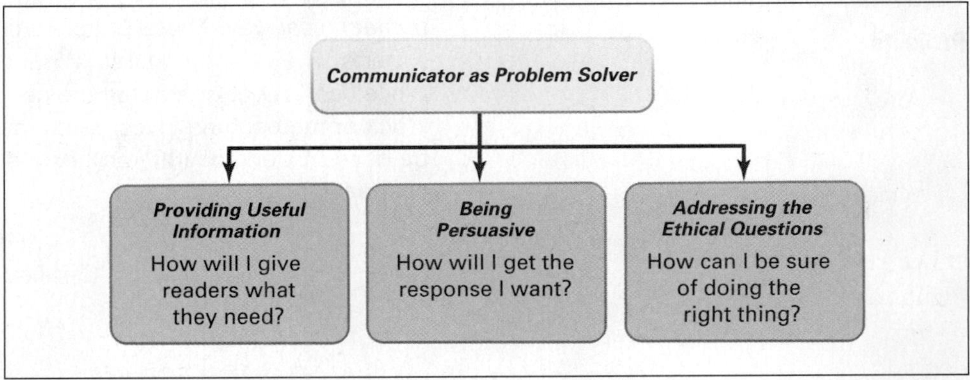

FIGURE 4.1 In Addition to Being Informative and Persuasive, Communicators Must Be Ethical

RECOGNIZE UNETHICAL COMMUNICATION IN THE WORKPLACE

Recent financial scandals reveal a growing list of corporations accused of boosting the value of company stock by overstating profits and understating debt. As inevitable bankruptcy loomed, executives hid behind deceptive accounting practices; company officers quietly unloaded personal shares of inflated stock while employees and investors were kept in the dark and ended up losing billions. Small wonder that "opinion polls now place business people in lower esteem than politicians" (Merritt, "For MBAs" 64).

Unethical communication in the workplace is all too common

NOTE *Among the 84 percent of college students surveyed who claim to be "disturbed" by corporate dishonesty, "59 percent admit to cheating on a test... and only 19 percent say they would report a classmate who cheated" (Merritt, "You Mean" 8).*

Corporate scandals make for dramatic headlines, but more routine examples of deliberate miscommunication rarely are publicized:

Routine instances of unethical communication

- A person lands a great job by exaggerating his credentials, experience, or expertise.
- A marketing specialist for a chemical company negotiates a huge bulk sale of its powerful new pesticide by downplaying its carcinogenic hazards.
- A manager writes a strong recommendation to get a friend promoted, while overlooking someone more deserving.

Business Week reports that 20 percent of employees surveyed claim to have witnessed fraud on the job. Common abuses range from falsifying expense accounts to overstating hours worked ("Crime Spree" 8).

Other instances of unethical communication, however, are less black and white. Here is one engineer's description of the gray area in which issues of product safety and quality often are decided:

> The company must be able to produce its products at a cost low enough to be competitive.... To design a product that is of the highest quality and consequently has a high and uncompetitive price may mean that the company will not be able to remain profitable, and be forced out of business. (Burghardt 92)

Ethical decisions are not always "black and white"

Do you emphasize to a customer the need for extra careful maintenance of a highly sensitive computer, and risk losing the sale? Or do you downplay maintenance requirements, focusing instead on the computer's positive features? The decisions we make in these situations are often influenced by the pressures we feel.

KNOW THE MAJOR CAUSES OF UNETHICAL COMMUNICATION

Ethics are often compromised because of outside pressure

Well over 50 percent of managers surveyed nationwide feel "pressure to compromise personal ethics for company goals" (Golen et al. 75). To save face, escape blame, or get ahead, anyone might be tempted to say what people want to hear or to suppress or downplay bad news. But normally honest people usually break the rules only when compelled by an employer, coworkers, or their own bad judgment. Figure 4.2 depicts how workplace pressures to "succeed at any cost" can influence ethical values.

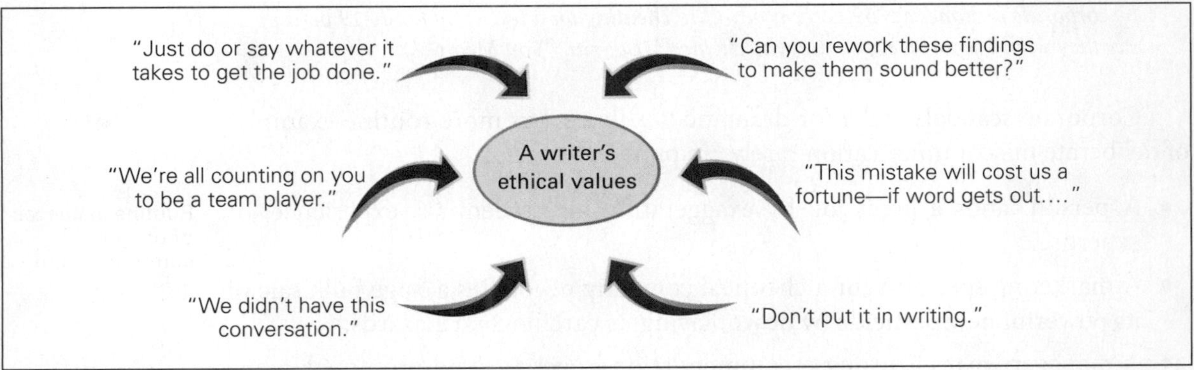

FIGURE 4.2 How Workplace Pressures Can Influence Ethical Values A decision that is more efficient, profitable, or better for the company might overshadow a person's sense of what is right.

Yielding to Social Pressure

Sometimes, you may have to choose between doing what you know is right and doing what your employer or organization expects, as in this next example:

Looking the other way

> Just as your automobile company is about to unveil its new pickup truck, your safety engineering team discovers that the reserve gas tanks (installed beneath the truck but outside the frame) may, in rare circumstances, explode on impact from a side collision. You know that this information should be included in the owner's manual or, at a minimum, in a letter to the truck dealers, but the company has spent a fortune building this truck and does not want to hear about this problem.

Companies often face the contradictory goals of *production* (producing a product and making money on it) and *safety* (producing a product but spending money to avoid accidents that may or may not happen). When production receives first priority, safety concerns may suffer (Wickens 434–36). In these circumstances, you need to rely on your own ethical standards. In the case of the reserve gas tanks, if you decide to publicize the problem, expect to be fired for taking on the company.

Mistaking Groupthink for Teamwork

Organizations rely on teamwork and collaboration to get a job done; technical communicators often work as part of a larger team of writers, editors, designers, engineers, and production specialists. Teamwork is important in these situations, but teamwork should not be confused with *groupthink*, which occurs when group pressure prevents individuals from questioning, criticizing, reporting bad news, or "making waves" (Janis 9). Group members may feel a need to be accepted by the team, often at the expense of making the right decision. Anyone who has ever given in to adolescent peer pressure has experienced a version of groupthink.

Blindly following the group

Groupthink also can provide a handy excuse for individuals to deny responsibility (see Figure 4.3). For example, because countless people work on a complex project (say, a new airplane), identifying those responsible for an error is often impossible—especially in errors of omission, that is, when something that should have been done was overlooked (Unger 137).

My job is to put together a persuasive ad for this brand of diet pill. It is someone else's job to make sure the claims are accurate and cause the customer no harm. It was someone else's job to make sure the stuff was safe. My job is only to promote the product. If someone does get hurt, it won't be my problem!

FIGURE 4.3 Hiding behind Groupthink
(*Source:* Judith Kaufman)

One source offers this observation:

> People commit unethical acts inside corporations that they never would commit as individuals representing only themselves. (Bryan 86)

Once their assigned task has been completed, employees might mistakenly assume that their responsibility has been fulfilled.

UNDERSTAND THE POTENTIAL FOR COMMUNICATION ABUSE

Telling the truth versus meeting workplace expectations

On the job, you write in the service of your employer. Your effectiveness is judged by how well your documents speak for the company and advance its interests and agendas (Ornatowski 100–01). You walk the proverbial line between telling the truth and doing what your employer expects (Dombrowski 79).

Workplace communication influences the thinking, actions, and welfare of numerous people—customers, investors, coworkers, the public, policymakers—to name a few. These people are victims of communication abuse whenever we give them information that is less than the truth as we know it, as in the following situations.

Suppressing Knowledge the Public Needs

Pressures to downplay the dangers of technology can result in censorship:

Examples of suppressed information

- The biotech industry continues to resist any food labeling that would identify genetically modified ingredients (Raeburn 78).
- Some prestigious science journals have refused to publish studies linking chlorine and fluoride in drinking water with cancer risk, and fluorescent lights with childhood leukemia (Begley, "Is Science" 63).
- MIT's Arnold Barnett has found that information about airline safety lapses and near-accidents is often suppressed by air traffic controllers because of "a natural tendency not to call attention to events in which their own performance was not exemplary" or their hesitation to "squeal" about pilot error (qtd. in Ball 13).

Hiding Conflicts of Interest

Can scientists and other experts who have a financial stake in a particular issue or experiment provide fair and impartial information about the topic?

Hidden conflicts of interest

- In one analysis of 800 scientific papers, Tufts University's Sheldon Krimsky found that 34 percent of authors had "research-related financial ties," but none had been disclosed (King B1).
- *Los Angeles Times* medical writer Terence Monmaney investigated 36 drug review pieces in a prestigious medical journal and found "eight articles by researchers with undisclosed financial links to drug companies that market treatments evaluated in the articles" (qtd. in Rosman 100).
- Analysts on a popular TV financial program have recommended certain company stocks (thus potentially inflating the price of that stock) without disclosing that their investment firms hold stock in these companies (Oxfeld 105).

Exaggerating Claims about Technology

Organizations that have a stake in a particular technology (say, bioengineered foods) may be especially tempted to exaggerate its benefits, potential, or safety and to downplay the technology's risks. If your organization depends on outside funding (as in the defense or space industry), you might find yourself pressured to make unrealistic promises.

Falsifying or Fabricating Data

Research data might be manipulated or invented to support specific agendas (say, by a scientist seeking grant money). Sometimes it's a matter of timing; developments in fields such as biotechnology often occur too rapidly to allow for adequate peer review of articles before they are published ("Misconduct Scandal" 2).

Using Visual Images That Conceal the Truth

Pictures are generally more powerful than words and can easily distort the real meaning of a message. For example, as required by law, TV commercials for prescription medications must identify a drug's side effects—which can often be serious. But the typical drug commercial lists the side effects while showing images of smiling, healthy people. The happy images eclipse the sobering verbal message.

Stealing or Divulging Proprietary Information

Information that originates in a specific company is the exclusive intellectual property of that company. Proprietary information includes company records, product formulas, test and experiment results, surveys financed by clients, market research, plans, specifications, and minutes of meetings (Lavin 5). In theory, such information is legally protected, but it remains vulnerable to sabotage, theft, or leaks to the press. Fierce competition among rival companies for the very latest intelligence gives rise to measures like these:

Examples of corporate espionage

> Companies have been known to use business school students to garner information on competitors under the guise of conducting "research." Even more commonplace is interviewing employees for slots that don't exist and wringing them dry about their current employer. (Gilbert 24)

Misusing Electronic Information

Ever-increasing amounts of personal information are stored in databases (by schools, governments, credit card companies, insurance companies, pharmacies), and of course all employers keep data about their employees. So how we combine, use, and share that information raises questions about privacy (Finkelstein 471). Also, a database is easy to alter; one simple command can change the facts or wipe them out. Private or inaccurate information can be sent from one database to countless others.

The proliferation of Web transactions creates broad opportunities for communication abuse, as in these examples:

Web-based communication abuses

- Plagiarizing or republishing electronic sources without giving proper credit or obtaining permission
- Copying digital files—music CDs, for example—without consent of the copyright holders
- Failing to safeguard the privacy of personal information about a Web site visitor's health, finances, buying habits, or affiliations
- Publishing anonymous attacks, or smear campaigns, against people, products, or organizations
- Selling prescription medications online without adequate patient screening or physician consultation
- Offering inaccurate medical advice or information

Withholding Information People Need for Their Jobs

Nowhere is the adage that "information is power" more true than among coworkers. One sure way to sabotage a colleague is to deprive that person of information about the task at hand. Studies show that employees withhold information for more benign reasons as well, such as fear that someone else might take credit for their work or might "shoot them down" (Davenport 90).

Exploiting Cultural Differences

Based on its level of business experience or its particular social values or financial need, a given culture might be especially vulnerable to manipulation or deception. Some cultures, for example, place greater reliance on interpersonal trust than on lawyers or legal wording, and a handshake can be worth more than the fine print of a legal contract. Other cultures may tolerate abuse or destruction of their natural resources in order to generate much-needed income. If you know something about a culture's habits or business practices and then use this information unfairly to get a sale or make a profit, you are behaving unethically.

Consider this recent attempt to use cultural differences as a basis for violating personal privacy: In a program of library surveillance, the FBI asked librarians to compile lists of materials being read by any "foreign national patron" or anyone with a "foreign sounding name." The librarians refused (Crumpton 8).

For more on cultural considerations, see Chapters 3 and 5.

RELY ON CRITICAL THINKING FOR ETHICAL DECISIONS

Because of their effects on people and on your career, ethical decisions challenge your critical thinking skills:

Ethical decisions require critical thinking

- How can I know the "right action" in this situation?
- What are my obligations, and to whom, in this situation?
- What values or ideals do I want to represent in this situation?
- What is likely to happen if I do X—or Y?

Ethical issues resist simple formulas, but the following criteria offer a limited form of guidance.

Reasonable Criteria for Ethical Judgment

Reasonable criteria (standards that most people consider acceptable) take the form of *obligations, ideals,* and *consequences* (Christians et al. 17–18; Ruggiero, 3rd ed. 33–34). *Obligations* are the responsibilities you have to everyone involved:

Our obligations are varied and often conflicting

- **Obligation to yourself,** to act in your own self-interest and according to good conscience
- **Obligation to clients and customers,** to stand by the people to whom you are bound by contract—and who pay the bills
- **Obligation to your company,** to advance its goals, respect its policies, protect confidential information, and expose misconduct that would harm the organization
- **Obligation to coworkers,** to promote their safety and well-being
- **Obligation to the community,** to preserve the local economy, welfare, and quality of life
- **Obligation to society,** to consider the national and global impact of your actions and choices

When the interests of these parties conflict—as they often do—you have to decide where your primary obligations lie.

Ideals are the values that you believe in or stand for: loyalty, friendship, compassion, dignity, fairness, and whatever qualities make you who you are. *Consequences* are the beneficial or harmful results of your actions. Consequences may be immediate or delayed, intentional or unintentional, obvious or subtle. Some consequences are easy to predict; some are difficult; some are impossible. Figure 4.4 depicts the relations among these three criteria.

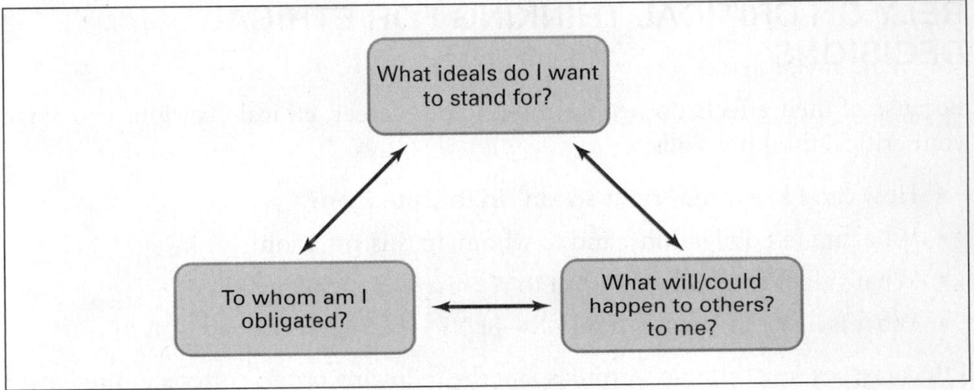

FIGURE 4.4 Reasonable Criteria for Ethical Judgment

The criteria on page 69 help us understand why even good intentions can produce bad judgments, as in the following situation.

What seems like the "right action" might be the wrong one

> Someone observes... that waste from the local mill is seeping into the water table and polluting the water supply.... But before [a remedy] can be found, extremists condemn the mill for lack of conscience and for exploiting the community. People get upset and clamor for the mill to be shut down and its management tried on criminal charges. The next thing you know, the plant does close, 500 workers are without jobs, and no solution has been found for the pollution problem. (Hauser 96)

Because of their zealous dedication to the *ideal* of a pollution-free environment, the extremist protestors failed to anticipate the *consequences* of their protest or to respect their *obligation* to the community's economic welfare.

Ethical Dilemmas

Ethical questions often resist easy answers

Ethics decisions are especially frustrating when no single choice seems acceptable (Ruggiero, 3rd ed. 35). For example, the proclaimed goal of "welfare reform" is to free people from lifelong economic dependence. One could argue that dedication to this *consequence* would violate our *obligations* (to the poor and the sick) and our *ideals* (of compassion or fairness). On the basis of our three criteria, how else might the welfare-reform issue be considered?

ANTICIPATE SOME HARD CHOICES

Communicators' ethical choices basically are concerned with honesty in choosing to reveal or conceal information:

What to reveal and what to conceal is at the root of every hard choice

- What exactly do I report and to whom?
- How much do I reveal or conceal?

- How do I say what I have to say?
- Could misplaced obligation to one party be causing me to deceive others?

The following case illustrates the difficulty of making sound ethical decisions.

CASE A Hard Choice

You are an assistant structural engineer working on the construction of a nuclear power plant in a developing country. After years of construction delays and cost overruns, the plant finally has received its limited operating license from the country's Nuclear Regulatory Commission (NRC).

During your final inspection of the nuclear core containment unit, on February 15, you discover a ten-foot-long hairline crack in a section of the reinforced concrete floor, within 20 feet of the area where the cooling pipes enter the containment unit. (The especially cold and snowless winter likely has caused a frost heave under a small part of the foundation.) The crack has either just appeared or was overlooked by NRC inspectors on February 10.

The crack could be perfectly harmless, caused by normal settling of the structure; and this is, after all, a "redundant" containment system (a shell within a shell). But, then again, the crack might also signal some kind of serious stress on the entire containment unit, which ultimately could damage the entry and exit cooling pipes or other vital structures.

You phone your boss, who is just about to leave on vacation, and who tells you, "Forget it; no problem," and hangs up.

You know that if the crack is reported, the whole start-up process scheduled for February 16 will be delayed indefinitely. More money will be lost; excavation, reinforcement, and further testing will be required—and many people with a stake in this project (from company executives to construction officials to shareholders) will be furious—especially if your report turns out to be a false alarm. All segments of plant management are geared up for the final big moment. Media coverage will be widespread. As the bearer of bad news—and bad publicity—you suspect that, even if you turn out to be right, your own career could be damaged by your apparent overreaction.

You may have to choose between the goals of your organization and what you know is right

On the other hand, ignoring the crack could compromise the system's safety, with unforeseeable consequences. Of course, no one would ever be able to implicate you. The NRC has already inspected and approved the containment unit—leaving you, your boss, and your company in the clear. You have very little time to decide. Start-up is scheduled for tomorrow, at which time the containment system will become intensely radioactive.

What would you do? Justify your decision on the basis of the obligations, ideals, and consequences involved.

Working professionals commonly face choices similar to the one depicted above. They must often make these choices alone or on the spur of the moment, without the luxury of contemplation or consultation.

NEVER DEPEND ONLY ON LEGAL GUIDELINES

Communication can be legal without being ethical

Can the law tell you how to communicate ethically? Sometimes. If you stay within the law, are you being ethical? Not always—as illustrated in this chapter's earlier section on communication abuses. In fact, even threatening statements made on the Web are considered legal by the Supreme Court as long as they are not likely to cause "imminent lawless action" (Gibbs 34).

Legal standards "sometimes do no more than delineate minimally acceptable behavior." In contrast, ethical standards "often attempt to describe ideal behavior, to define the best possible practices for corporations" (Porter 183).

Except for the instances listed below, lying is rarely illegal. Common types of legal lies are depicted in Figure 4.5. Later chapters cover other kinds of lying that are often legal, such as page design that distorts the real emphasis of the content or words that are deliberately unclear, misleading, or ambiguous.

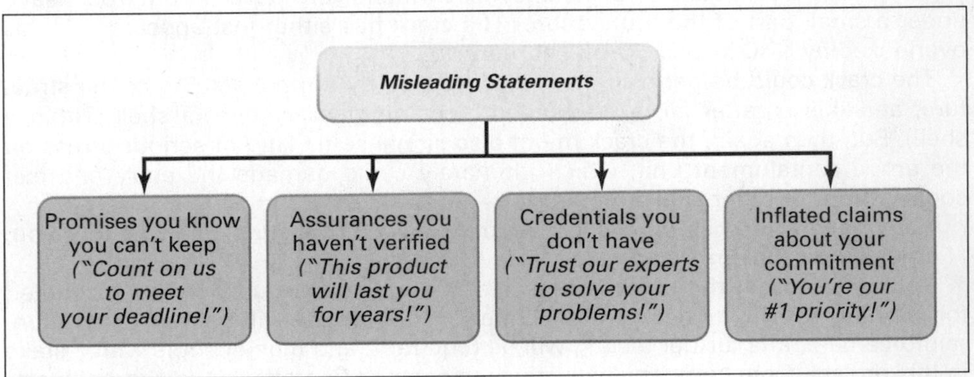

FIGURE 4.5 Statements That Are Misleading but May Be Legal

What, then, are a communicator's legal guidelines? Workplace communication is regulated by the types of laws described below.

Laws that govern workplace communication

- **Laws against deception** prohibit lying under oath, lying to a federal agent, lying about a product so as to cause injury, or breaking a contractual promise.
- **Laws against libel** prohibit any false written statement that attacks or ridicules anyone. A statement is considered libelous when it damages someone's reputation, character, career, or livelihood or when it causes humiliation or mental suffering. Material that is damaging but *truthful* would not be considered libelous unless it were used intentionally to cause harm. In the event of a libel suit, a writer's ignorance is no defense; even when the damaging material has been obtained from a source presumed reliable, the writer (and publisher) are accountable.[1]

[1] Thanks to colleague Peter Owens for the material on libel.

- **Laws protecting employee privacy** impose strict limits on information employers are allowed to give out about an employee. (See page 240 for more on this topic.)
- **Copyright laws** (pages 148–50) protect the ownership rights of authors—or of their employers, in cases where the writing was done as part of their employment.
- **Laws against software theft** prohibit unauthorized duplication of copyrighted software. A first offense carries up to five years in prison and fines up to $250,000. Piracy is estimated to cost the software industry more than $2 billion yearly ("On Line" A29).
- **Laws against electronic theft** prohibit unauthorized distribution of copyrighted material via the Internet as well as possession of ten or more electronic copies of any material worth $2,500 or more (Evans 22).
- **Laws against stealing or revealing trade secrets.** The FBI estimates that roughly $25 billion of proprietary information (trade secrets and other intellectual property) is stolen yearly. The Economic Espionage Act makes such theft a federal crime; this law classifies as "trade secret" not only items such as computer source code or the recipe for our favorite cola, but even a listing of clients and contacts brought from a previous employer (Farnham 114, 116).
- **Laws against deceptive or fraudulent advertising** prohibit false claims or suggestions, for example, implying that a product or treatment will cure disease, or representing a used product as new. Fraud is defined as lying that causes another person monetary damage (Harcourt 64). Even a factual statement such as "our cigarettes have fewer additives" is considered deceptive because it implies that a cigarette with fewer additives is safer than other cigarettes (Savan 63).
- **Liability laws** define the responsibilities of authors, editors, and publishers for damages resulting from incomplete, unclear, misleading, or otherwise defective information. The misinformation might be about a product (such as failure to warn about the toxic fumes from a spray-on oven cleaner) or a procedure (such as misleading instructions in an owner's manual for using a tire jack). Even if misinformation is given out of ignorance, the writer is liable (Walter and Marsteller 164–65).

Legal standards for product literature vary from country to country. A document must satisfy the legal standards for safety, health, accuracy, or language for the country in which it will be distributed. For example, instructions for any product requiring assembly or operation have to carry warnings as stipulated by the country in which the product will be sold. Inadequate documentation, as judged by that country's standards, can result in a lawsuit (Caswell-Coward 264–66; Weymouth 145).

NOTE *Large companies have legal departments to consult about various documents. Most professions have ethics guidelines (as on page 79). If your field has its own formal code, obtain a copy.*

LEARN TO RECOGNIZE PLAGIARISM

What is plagiarism?

Ethical communication includes giving proper credit to the work of others. In both workplace and academic settings, plagiarism (representing the words, ideas, or perspectives of others as your own) is a serious breach of ethics. Even when your use of a source may be perfectly legal, you will still be violating ethical standards if you fail to cite the information source or fail to identify material that is being directly quoted. Figure 4.6 shows some ways in which plagiarism can occur.

Blatant versus Unintentional Plagiarism

Blatant cases of plagiarism occur when a writer consciously lifts passages from another work (print or online) and incorporates them into his or her own work without quoting or documenting the original source. As most students know, this can result in a failing grade and potential disciplinary action. More often, writers will simply fail to cite a source being quoted or paraphrased, often because they misplaced the original source and publication information, or forgot to note it during their research (Anson and Schwegler 633–36). Whereas this more subtle, sometimes unconscious, form of misrepresentation is less blatant, it still constitutes plagiarism and can undermine the offender's credibility, or worse. Whether the infraction is intentional or unintentional, people accused of plagiarism can lose their reputation and be sued or fired.

Plagiarism and the Internet

The rapid development of Internet resources has spawned a wide array of misconceptions about plagiarism. Some people mistakenly assume that because material posted on a Web site, Facebook page, Twitter feed, or blog is free, it can be paraphrased or copied without citation. Despite the ease of cutting and pasting digital information, the fact remains: Any time you borrow someone else's words, ideas, perspectives, or images—regardless of the medium used in the original source—you need to document the original source accurately.

Plagiarism and Your Career

Whatever your career plans, learning to gather, incorporate, and document authoritative source material is an absolutely essential job skill. By properly citing a range of sources in your work, you bolster your own credibility and demonstrate your skills as a researcher and a writer. (For more on incorporating and documenting sources and on avoiding plagiarism, see A Quick Guide to Documentation,

Original Source. To begin with, language is a system of communication. I make this rather obvious point because to some people nowadays it isn't obvious: they see language as above all a means of "self-expression." Of course, language is one way that we express our personal feelings and thoughts—but so, if it comes to that, are dancing, cooking, and making music. Language does much more: it enables us to convey to others what we think, feel, and want. Language-as-communication is the prime means of organizing the cooperative activities that enable us to accomplish as groups things we could not possibly do as individuals. Some other species also engage in cooperative activities, but these are either quite simple (as among baboons and wolves) or exceedingly stereotyped (as among bees, ants, and termites). Not surprisingly, the communicative systems used by these animals are also simple or stereotypes. Language, our uniquely flexible and intricate system of communication, makes possible our equally flexible and intricate ways of coping with the world around us: In a very real sense, it is what makes us human (Claiborne 8).

Plagiarism Example 1 One commentator makes a distinction between language used as a means of self-expression and language-as-communication. It is the latter that distinguishes human interaction from that of other species and allows humans to work cooperatively on complex tasks (8).

What's wrong? The source's name is not given, and there are no quotation marks around words taken directly from the source (highlighted in yellow in the example).

Plagiarism Example 2 Claiborne notes that language "is the prime means of organizing the cooperative activities." Without language, we would, consequently, not have civilization.

What's wrong? The page number of the source is missing. Parenthetical references should immediately follow the material being quoted, paraphrased, or summarized. You may omit a parenthetical reference only if the information that you have included in your attribution is sufficient to identify the source in your Works Cited list and no page number is needed.

Plagiarism Example 3 Other animals also engage in cooperative activities. However, these actions are not very complex. Rather they are either the very simple activities of, for example, baboons and wolves or the stereotyped activities of animals such as bees, ants, and termites (Claiborne 8).

What's wrong? A paraphrase should capture a specific idea from a source but must not duplicate the writer's phrases and words (highlighted in yellow in the example). In the example, the wording and sentence structure follow the source too closely.

FIGURE 4.6 A Few Examples of Plagiarism Can you spot the plagiarism in the examples above that follow the original source?

pages 644–79. For more on recognizing plagiarism, go to <www.indiana.edu/~wts/pamphlets/plagiarism.shtml>.)

NOTE *Plagiarism and copyright infringement are not the same. You can plagiarize someone else's work without actually infringing copyright. These two issues are frequently confused, but plagiarism is primarily an ethical issue, whereas copyright infringement is a legal and economic issue. (For more on copyright and related legal issues, see Chapter 7.)*

CONSIDER THIS: Ethical Standards Are Good for Business

To earn public trust, companies increasingly are hiring "professional ethical advisors" to help them "sort out right from wrong when it comes to developing, marketing, and talking about new technology" (Brower 25). Here are instances of good standards that pay off.

By Telling Investors the Truth, a Company Can Increase Its Stock Value

Publicly traded companies that tell the truth about profits and losses are tracked by more securities analysts than companies that use "accounting smoke screens" to hide bad economic news. "All it takes is the inferential leap that more analysts touting your stock means a higher stock price" (Fox 303).

High Standards Earn Customer Trust

Wetherill Associates, Inc., a car parts supply company, was founded on the principle of honesty and "taking the right action." Among Wetherill's policies:

- *Employees are given no sales quotas, so that no one will be tempted to camouflage disappointing sales figures.*
- *Employees are required to be honest in all business practices.*
- *Lies (including "legal lies") to colleagues or customers are grounds for being fired.*
- *Gossip or backbiting are penalized.*

From a $50,000 start-up budget and 45 people who shared this ethical philosophy in 1978, the company has grown to 480 employees and $160 million in yearly sales and $16 million in profit—and continues growing at 25 percent annually (Burger 200–01; Courtesy of Wetherill Associates, Inc.).

Sharing Information with Coworkers Leads to a Huge Invention

Information expert Keith Devlin describes how one company's "strong culture of sharing ideas paid a handsome dividend":

> The invention of Post-it Notes by 3M's Art Fry came about as a result of a memo from another 3M scientist who described the new glue he had developed. The new glue had the unusual property of providing firm but very temporary adhesion. As a traditional bonding agent, it was a failure. But Fry was able to see a novel use for it, and within a short time, Post-it Notes could be seen adorning every refrigerator door in the land. (179–80)

For more on the problem of information hoarding among employees, see page 97.

DECIDE WHEN AND HOW TO REPORT ETHICAL ABUSES

What is whistle-blowing?

Suppose your employer asks you to cover up fraudulent Medicare charges or a violation of federal pollution standards. If you decide to resist, your choices seem limited: resign or go public (i.e., blow the whistle).

Walking away from a job isn't easy, and whistle-blowing can spell career disaster. Many organizations refuse to hire anyone blacklisted as a whistle-blower. Even if you do not end up being fired, expect your job to become hellish. Consider, for example, the Research Triangle Institute's study of consequences for whistle-blowers in 68 different instances. Following is an excerpt:

> More than two-thirds of all whistle-blowers reported experiencing at least one negative outcome.... Those most likely to experience adverse consequences were "lower ranking [personnel]." Negative consequences included pressure to drop their allegations, [ostracism] by colleagues, reduced research support, and threatened or actual legal action. Interestingly... three-fourths of these whistle-blowers experiencing "severe negative consequences" said they would definitely or probably blow the whistle again. (qtd. in "Consequences of Whistle Blowing" 2)

Consequences of whistle-blowing

Despite the retaliation they suffered, few people surveyed regretted their decision to go public.

Employers are generally immune from lawsuits by employees who have been dismissed unfairly but who have no contract or union agreement specifying length of employment (Unger 94). Current law, however, offers some protection for whistle-blowers.

Limited legal protections for whistle-blowers

- The Federal False Claims Act allows an employee to sue, in the government's name, a contractor who defrauds the government (say, by overcharging for military parts). The employee receives up to 25 percent of money recovered by the suit. Also, this law allows employees of government contractors to sue when they are punished for whistle-blowing (Stevenson A7).
- Anyone punished for reporting employer violations to a regulatory agency (Federal Aviation Administration, Nuclear Regulatory Commission, Occupational Health and Safety Administration, and so on) can request a Labor Department investigation. A claim ruled valid leads to reinstatement and reimbursement for back pay and legal expenses.[2]
- Laws in some states protect employees who report discrimination or harassment on the basis of sexual orientation (Fisher, "Can I Stop" 205).
- Beyond requiring greater accuracy and clarity in the financial reports of publicly traded companies, The Sarbanes-Oxley Act of 2002 imposes criminal penalties for executives who retaliate against employees who blow the whistle on corporate misconduct. This legislation also requires companies to establish confidential hotlines for reporting ethical violations.
- One Web-based service, <www.Ethicspoint.com>, allows employees to file their reports anonymously and then forwards this information to the company's ethics committee.

Even with such protections, an employee who takes on a company without the backing of a labor union or other powerful group can expect lengthy court battles, high legal fees (which may or may not be recouped), and disruption of life and career.

Before accepting a job offer, do some discreet research about the company's reputation. (Of course you can learn only so much before actually working there.)

---

[2]Although employees are legally entitled to speak confidentially with OSHA inspectors about health and safety violations, one survey reveals that inspectors themselves believe such laws offer little protection against company retribution (Kraft 5).

Learn whether the company has *ombudspersons*, who help employees file complaints, or hotlines for advice on ethics problems or for reporting misconduct. Ask whether the company or organization has a formal code for personal and organizational behavior (Figure 4.7). Finally, assume that no employer, no matter how ethical, will tolerate any public statement that makes the company look bad.

NOTE *Sometimes the right choice is obvious, but often it is not. No one has any sure way of always knowing what to do. This chapter is only an introduction to the inevitable hard choices that, throughout your career, will be yours to make and to live with. For further guidance and case examples, go to The Online Ethics Center for Engineering and Science at <www.onlineethics.org>.*

CHECKLIST: Ethical Communication

Use this checklist for any document you prepare or for which you are responsible. (Numbers in parentheses refer to the first page of discussion.)

Accuracy

- ☐ Have I explored all sides of the issue and all possible alternatives? (43)
- ☐ Do I provide enough information and interpretation for recipients to understand the facts as I know them? (80)
- ☐ Do I avoid exaggeration, understatement, sugarcoating, or any distortion or omission that would leave readers at a disadvantage? (66)
- ☐ Do I state the case clearly instead of hiding behind jargon and euphemism? (227)

Honesty

- ☐ Do I make a clear distinction between "certainty" and "probability"? (157)
- ☐ Are my information sources valid, reliable, and relatively unbiased? (154)
- ☐ Do I actually believe what I'm saying, instead of being a mouthpiece for groupthink or advancing some hidden agenda? (65)
- ☐ Would I still advocate this position if I were held publicly accountable for it? (64)
- ☐ Do I inform people of all the consequences or risks (as I am able to predict) of what I am advocating? (66)
- ☐ Do I give candid feedback or criticism, if it is warranted? (68)

Fairness

- ☐ Am I reasonably sure this document will harm no innocent persons or damage their reputations? (72)
- ☐ Am I respecting all legitimate rights to privacy and confidentiality? (68)
- ☐ Am I distributing copies of this document to every person who has the right to know about it? (69)
- ☐ Do I credit all contributors and sources of ideas and information? (74)

Source: Adapted from Brownell and Fitzgerald 18; Bryan 87; Johannesen 21–22; Larson 39; Unger 39–46; Yoos 50–55.

IEEE CODE OF ETHICS

WE, THE MEMBERS OF THE IEEE, in recognition of the importance of our technologies in affecting the quality of life throughout the world and in accepting a personal obligation to our profession, its members and the communities we serve, do hereby commit ourselves to the highest ethical and professional conduct and agree:

1. to accept responsibility in making decisions consistent with the safety, health and welfare of the public, and to disclose promptly factors that might endanger the public or the environment;

2. to avoid real or perceived conflicts of interest whenever possible, and to disclose them to affected parties when they do exist;

3. to be honest and realistic in stating claims or estimates based on available data;

4. to reject bribery in all its forms;

5. to improve the understanding of technology, its appropriate application, and potential consequences;

6. to maintain and improve our technical competence and to undertake technological tasks for others only if qualified by training or experience, or after full disclosure of pertinent limitations;

7. to seek, accept, and offer honest criticism of technical work, to acknowledge and correct errors, and to credit properly the contributions of others;

8. to treat fairly all persons regardless of such factors as race, religion, gender, disability, age, or national origin;

9. to avoid injuring others, their property, reputation, or employment by false or malicious action;

10. to assist colleagues and co-workers in their professional development and to support them in following this code of ethics.

Approved by the IEEE Board of Directors | February 2006

FIGURE 4.7 **A Sample Code of Ethics** Notice the many references to ethical communication in this engineering association's code of professional conduct.

Source: The Institute of Electrical and Electronics Engineers, Inc., <www.ieee.org>. © 2007 IEEE. Reprinted with permission from the IEEE.

GUIDELINES for Ethical Communication

How do we balance self-interest with the interests of others—our employers, the public, our customers? Listed below are guidelines:

Satisfying the Audience's Information Needs

1. **Give the audience everything it needs to know.** To accurately see things as you do, your audience needs more than just a partial view. Don't bury readers in needless details, but do make sure they get all of the facts and get them straight. If you're at fault, admit it and apologize immediately.
2. **Give people a clear understanding of what the information means.** Even when all the facts are known, they can be misinterpreted. Do all you can to ensure that your readers understand the facts as you do. If you're not certain about your own understanding, say so.

Taking a Stand versus the Company

1. **Get your facts straight, and get them on paper.** Don't blow matters out of proportion, but do keep a paper (and digital) trail in case of possible legal proceedings.
2. **Appeal your case in terms of the company's interests.** Instead of being pious and judgmental ("This is a racist and sexist policy, and you'd better get your act together"), focus on what the company stands to gain or lose ("Promoting too few women and minorities makes us vulnerable to legal action").
3. **Aim your appeal toward the right person.** If you have to go to the top, find someone who knows enough to appreciate the problem and who has enough clout to make something happen.
4. **Get legal advice.** Contact a lawyer and your professional society.

Leaving the Job

1. **Make no waves before departure.** Discuss your departure only with people "who need to know." Say nothing negative about your employer to clients, coworkers, or anyone else.
2. **Leave all proprietary information behind.** Take no hard-copy documents or digital files prepared on the job—except for those records tracing the process of your resignation or termination.

The ethics checklist (page 78) incorporates additional guidelines from other chapters. For additional advice, go to "Online Science Ethics Resources" at <www.chem.vt.edu/ethics/vinny/ethxonline.html>.

Source: Adapted from G. Clark 194; Lenzer and Shook 102; Unger 127–30.

Projects

GENERAL

1. Visit a Web site for a professional association in your field (American Psychological Association, Society for Technical Communication, American Nursing Association) and locate its code of ethics. How often are communication-related issues mentioned? Print a copy of the code for a class discussion of the role of ethical communication in different fields.
2. Prepare a brief presentation for classmates or coworkers in which you answer these questions: *What is plagiarism? How do I avoid it?* Start by exploring the following sites:
   - *Plagiarism: What It Is and How to Recognize and Avoid It,* from Writing Tutorial Services at <www.indiana.edu/~wts/pamphlets/plagiarism.html>
   - *Avoiding Plagiarism,* from the Writing Lab at <www.gervaseprograms.georgetown.edu/hc/plagiarism.html>

Find at least one additional Web source.

In one page or less, summarize a practical, working definition of plagiarism, and a list of strategies for avoiding it. (See page 176 for guidelines for summarizing.) Attach a copy of relevant Web pages to your presentation. Be sure to credit each source of information (page 646).

TEAM

Assume that you are a training manager for ABC Corporation, which is in the process of overhauling its policies on company ethics. Developing the company's official Code of Ethics will require months of research and collaboration with attorneys, ethics consultants, editors, and company officers. Meanwhile, your boss has asked you to develop a brief but practical set of "Guidelines for Ethical Communication," as a quick and easy reference for all employees until the official code is finalized. Using the material in this chapter, prepare a two-page memo (Chapter 14) for employees, explaining how to avoid ethical pitfalls in corporate communication.

DIGITAL AND SOCIAL MEDIA

Examine Web sites that make competing claims about a controversial topic such as bioengineered foods and crops, nuclear power, or alternative medicine. For example, compare claims about nuclear energy from the Nuclear Energy Institute <www.nei.org> with claims from the Sierra Club <www.sierraclub.org>, the American Council on Science and Health <www.acsh.org>, and the Nuclear Regulatory Commission <www.nrc.gov>. Do you find possible examples of unethical communication, such as conflicts of interest or exaggerated claims? Refer to page 66 and the Checklist for Ethical Communication (page 78) as a basis for evaluating the various claims. Report your findings in a memo (Chapter 14) to your instructor and classmates.

GLOBAL

Find an example of a document designed to "sell" an item, an idea, or a viewpoint (a sales brochure for a new automobile, a pharmaceutical brochure for some popular prescription medication, a Web page for an environmental or political organization, or something similar). Write a brief description of places in the document where you think the writers considered (or ignored) the importance of writing for a cross-cultural audience. For each item you describe, explain why this is an important ethical consideration.

5 Teamwork and Global Considerations

"My work in preparing user manuals is almost entirely collaborative. The actual process of writing takes maybe 30 percent of my time. I spend more time consulting with my information sources such as the software designers and field support people. I then meet with the publication and graphics departments to plan the manual's structure and format. As I prepare various drafts, I have to keep track of which reviewer has which draft. Because I rely on others' feedback, I circulate materials often. And so I write email memos on a regular basis. One major challenge is getting everyone involved to agree on a specific plan of action and then to stay on schedule so we can meet our publication deadline."

—Pam Herbert,
Technical Writer, software firm

LEARNING OBJECTIVES FOR THIS CHAPTER

- Manage a team project and run a successful meeting
- Help team members overcome personal differences
- Use listening skills and creative thinking in group settings
- Brainstorm using face-to-face and digital methods
- Review and edit the work of your peers
- Avoid unethical behavior as a team member
- Understand how to work productively on a global team

Complex documents (especially long reports, proposals, and manuals) are rarely produced by one person working alone. An instruction manual for a medical device (say a cardiac pacemaker), for instance, is typically produced by a team of writers, engineers, graphic artists, editors, reviewers, marketing personnel, and lawyers. Other team members might research, edit, and proofread.

Technical writers often collaborate

How a collaborative document is produced

Traditionally composed of people from one location, teams are increasingly distributed across different job sites, time zones, and countries. The Internet—via email, videoconferencing, instant messaging, blogs, and other communication tools—offers the primary means for distributed (or virtual) teams to interact. In addition, Internet conferencing and other software allow distributed teams to collaborate. But whether the team is on-site or distributed, members have to find ways of expressing their views persuasively, of accepting constructive criticism, and of getting along and reaching agreement with others who hold different views.

TEAMWORK AND PROJECT MANAGEMENT

Teamwork is successful only when there is strong cooperation, a recognized team structure, and clear communication. The following guidelines explain how to manage a team project in a systematic way.

GUIDELINES for Managing a Collaborative Project

- **Appoint a group manager.** The manager assigns tasks, enforces deadlines, conducts meetings, consults with supervisors, and "runs the show."
- **Define a clear and definite goal.** Compose an audience and purpose statement (page 19) that spells out the project's goal and the plan for achieving the goal. Be sure each member understands the goal.

GUIDELINES *continued*

- **Identify the type of document required.** Is this a report, a proposal, a manual, a brochure? Are visuals and supplements (abstract, appendices, and other front and end matter) needed? Will the document be in hard copy or digital form or both?
- **Divide the tasks.** Who will be responsible for which parts of the document or which phases of the project? Who is best at doing what (writing, editing, layout and graphics, oral presentation)? Which tasks will be done individually and which collectively?

  NOTE *Spell out—in writing—clear expectations for each team member. Also keep in mind that the final version should display one consistent style throughout, as if written by one person only.*

- **Establish a timetable.** Gantt and PERT charts (see pages 266–68) help the team visualize the whole project as well as each part, along with start-up and completion dates for each phase.
- **Decide on a meeting schedule.** How often will the group meet, and where and for how long?
- **Establish a procedure for responding to the work of other members.** Will reviewing and editing of draft documents be done in writing, face-to-face, as a group, one-on-one, or online?
- **Develop a file-naming system for various drafts.** It's too easy to save over a previous version and lose something important.
- **Establish procedures for dealing with interpersonal problems.** How will gripes and disputes be aired and resolved (by vote, by the manager, or by some other means)? How will irrelevant discussion be curtailed?
- **Select a group decision-making style.** Will decisions be made alone by the group manager, or by group input or majority vote?
- **Decide how to evaluate each member's contribution.** Will the manager assess each member's performance and in turn be evaluated by each member? Will members evaluate each other? What are the criteria? Figure 5.1 shows one possible form for a manager's evaluation of members. Members might keep a journal of personal observations for overall evaluation of the project.
- **Prepare a project management plan.** Figure 5.2 shows a sample planning form. Distribute completed copies to members.
- **Submit regular progress reports.** These reports (pages 517–20) track activities, problems, and rate of progress.

Source: Adapted from Debs, "Collaborative Writing" 38–41; Hill-Duin 45–50; Hulbert, "Developing" 53–54; McGuire 467–68; Morgan 540–41.

Performance Appraisal for *J. Fishkill*

(Rate each element as [superior], [acceptable], or [unacceptable] and use the "Comment" section to explain each rating briefly.)

- *Cooperation:* [*superior*]

  Comment: *works extremely well with others; always willing to help out; responds positively to constructive criticism*

- *Dependability:* [*acceptable*]

  Comment: *arrives on time for meetings; completes all assigned work*

- *Effort:* [*acceptable*]

  Comment: *does fair share of work; needs no prodding*

- *Quality of work produced:* [*superior*]

  Comment: *produces work that is carefully researched, well documented, and clearly written*

- *Ability to meet deadlines:* [*superior*]

  Comment: *delivers all assigned work on or before the deadline; helps other team members with last-minute tasks*

R.P. Ketchum

Project manager's signature

FIGURE 5.1 Form for Evaluating Team Members Any evaluation of strengths and weaknesses should be backed up by comments that explain the ratings. Decide as a team beforehand what constitutes "effort," "cooperation," and so on. Equivalent criteria for evaluating the manager might include open-mindedness, ability to organize the team, fairness in assigning tasks, and ability to resolve conflicts and to motivate.

Project Planning Form

Project title:
Audience:
Project manager:
Team members:
Purpose of the project:
Type of document required:

Specific Assignments	**Due Dates**	**Person(s) Responsible**
Research:		
Planning:		
Drafting:		
Revising:		
Preparing progress report:		
Preparing oral briefing for the team:		
Final document first draft:		
Final document:		

Work Schedule

Team meetings:	*Date*	*Place*	*Time*	*Note taker*
#1				
#2				
#3				
etc.				
Mtgs. w/instructor				
#1				
#2				
etc.				

Miscellaneous

How will disputes and grievances be resolved?
How will performances be evaluated?
Other matters (use of technology: email, Google Drive, etc.)?

FIGURE 5.2 **Project Planning Form for Managing a Collaborative Project** To manage a team project you need to (a) spell out the project goal, (b) break the entire task down into manageable steps, (c) create a climate in which people work well together, and (d) keep each phase of the project under control.

VIRTUAL MEETINGS

Technologies that enable virtual teamwork

With employees situated around the globe, most organizations recognize the need for teams to meet virtually. Students working on team projects may also need to meet online, due to different class and work schedules. Some of the technologies available for virtual meetings include the following:

- **Email**: Although the most popular tool for general workplace communication, email is the least effective way to hold a virtual meeting. Email does not allow for facial expressions, voice, or other social cues (see page 97). But because email is so easily accessible (on a smartphone, tablet, or computer without any special set-up), a specific, defined issue can be discussed on email, using attachments with track changes (see Figure 5.3).
- **Blogs**: Similar to email, blogs do not provide for social cues or the give-and-take that make meetings so effective. Yet blogs offer a single location to keep track of ideas. Instead of sorting through old emails, team members can go to the blog site and read through a chronological discussion.
- **Conference call**: Phone calls provide more cues than written text, allowing for the give-and-take that is necessary to come to consensus on complex issues. There are many conference call services available. Participants dial in and join the discussion.
- **Internet conferencing**: In these live virtual meetings, participants meet and discuss in real time. Skype can be useful for small groups, but for larger groups, programs such as GoToMeeting, WebEx, or Adobe Connect create a more meeting-like experience, with windows that display each participant and also allow people to share presentations and word-processing files, video, and other documents.
- **Webinars**: A particular kind of video conference, Webinars are Web-based seminars for giving presentations, conducting trainings, and the like via the Internet. For more on Webinars, see Chapter 25, page 616.
- **Digital whiteboard**: Useful as part of an Internet video conference, Webinar, or conference call, digital whiteboards offer a large screen that allows participants to write, sketch, and revise in real time, on their own computers.
- **Collaborative writing software**: Programs such as Google Drive allow teams to "meet in the document" (log in to the document at the same time), view each others' writing and revising in real time, and use a chat window to discuss ideas. As with email, collaborative writing programs are useful for focusing on a specific item or task. See Chapter 6, page 119 for more on digital technology and the writing process.
- **Project management software**: To keep track of tasks, due dates, and responsibilities, software such as Microsoft Project, or even a simple spreadsheet, can ensure that after the meeting, everyone knows his or her role and what's due when.

FACE-TO-FACE MEETINGS

Face-to-face meetings remain vital in the workplace

Despite many digital tools for collaboration, face-to-face meetings are still a fact of life because they provide vital *personal contact.* Meetings are usually scheduled for two purposes: to convey or exchange information, or to make decisions. Informational meetings tend to run smoothly because there is less cause for disagreement. But decision-making meetings often fail to reach clear resolution about various debatable issues. Such meetings often end in frustration because the leader has never managed to take charge.

Taking charge doesn't mean imposing one's views or stifling opposing views. Taking charge *does* mean moving the discussion along and keeping it centered on the issue, as explained in the guidelines below.

GUIDELINES for Running a Meeting

- **Set an agenda.** Distribute copies to members beforehand: "Our 10 A.M. Monday meeting will cover the following items:..." Spell out each item and set a strict time limit for discussion, and stick to this plan.
- **Ask each person to prepare as needed.** A meeting works best when each member prepares a specific contribution.
- **Appoint a different "observer" for each meeting.** At Charles Schwab & Co., the designated observer keeps a list of what worked well during the meeting and what didn't. The list is added to that meeting's minutes (Matson, "The Seven Sins" 31).
- **Begin by summarizing the minutes of the last meeting.**
- **Give all members a chance to speak.** Don't allow anyone to monopolize.
- **Stick to the issue.** Curb irrelevant discussion. Politely nudge members back to the original topic.
- **Keep things moving.** Don't get hung up on a single issue; work toward a consensus by highlighting points of agreement; push for a resolution.
- **Observe, guide, and listen.** Don't lecture or dictate.
- **Summarize major points before calling for a vote.**
- **End the meeting on schedule.** This is not a hard-and-fast rule. If you feel the issue is about to be resolved, continue.

NOTE *For detailed advice on motions, debate, and voting, consult Robert's Rules of Order, the classic guide to meetings, at <www.robertsrules.org>.*

Someone should take minutes at each meeting. This can be done by assigning one person to be the minute-taker for all meetings, or by doing a round-robin approach (everyone takes a turn). Meeting minutes can be brief and should be distributed by email right after the meeting, with opportunities for other team members to make corrections. Minutes help ensure that everyone has the same understanding of the meeting goals and outcomes. For more on meeting minutes, see Chapter 21.

Importance of meeting minutes

SOURCES OF CONFLICT IN COLLABORATIVE GROUPS

Workplace surveys show that people view meetings as "their biggest waste of time" (Schrage 232). This fact alone accounts for the boredom, impatience, or irritability that might crop up in any meeting. But even the most dynamic group setting can produce conflict because of differences such as the following.[1]

Interpersonal Differences

How personality influences communication

People might clash because of differences in personality, working style, commitment, standards, or ability to take criticism. Some might disagree about exactly what or how much the group should accomplish, who should do what, or who should have the final say. Some might feel intimidated or hesitant to speak out. These interpersonal conflicts can actually worsen when the group interacts exclusively online: Lack of personal contact makes it hard for trust to develop.

Gender Differences

Collaboration involves working with peers—those of equal status, rank, and expertise. But gender differences can create perceptions of inequality. Research on ways women and men communicate in meetings indicates a definite gender gap. Communication specialist Kathleen Kelley-Reardon offers this assessment of how gender can influence communication behavior:

How gender codes influence communication

> Women and men operate according to communication rules for their gender, what experts call "gender codes." They learn, for example, to show gratitude, ask for help, take control, and express emotion, deference, and commitment in different ways. (88–89)

Kelley-Reardon explains how women tend to communicate during meetings: Women are more likely than men to take as much time as needed to explore an issue, build consensus and relationship among members, use tact in expressing views, use care in choosing their words, consider the listener's feelings, speak softly, allow interruptions, make requests instead of giving commands (*Could I*

[1]Adapted from Bogert and Butt 51; Debs, "Collaborative Writing" 38; Hill-Duin 45–46; Nelson and Smith 61.

have the report by Friday? versus *Have this ready by Friday.*), and preface assertions in ways that avoid offending (*I don't want to seem disagreeable here, but…*).

One study of mixed-gender interaction among peers indicates that women tend to be agreeable, solicit and admit the merits of other opinions, ask questions, and admit uncertainty (say, with qualifiers such as *maybe, probably, it seems as if*) more often than men (Wojahn 747).

None of these traits, of course, is gender specific. People of either gender can be soft-spoken and reflective. But such traits most often are attributed to the "feminine" stereotype.

Any woman who breaches the gender code, say, by being assertive, may be perceived as "too controlling" (Kelley-Reardon 6). In fact, studies suggest that women have less freedom than male peers to alter their communication strategies: Less assertive males often are still considered persuasive, whereas more assertive females often are not (Perloff 273).

Cultural Differences

How culture influences communication

Another source of conflict in collaborative groups is the potential for misunderstandings based on cultural differences. Issues such as the use of humor, ways of expressing politeness, or cultural references (to sports or television shows, for example) could cause members of the group to understand ideas and meanings differently. See "Global Considerations When Working in Teams" in this chapter (page 98) for more on this topic.

MANAGING GROUP CONFLICT

No team will agree about everything. Before any group can reach final agreement, conflicts must be addressed openly. Management expert David House has this advice for overcoming personal differences (Warshaw 48):

How to manage group conflict

- Give everyone a chance to be heard.
- Take everyone's feelings and opinions seriously.
- Don't be afraid to disagree.
- Offer and accept constructive criticism.
- Find points of agreement with others who hold different views.
- When the group does make a decision, support it fully.

Business etiquette expert Ann Marie Sabath offers the following suggestions for reducing animosity (108–10):

How to reduce animosity

- If someone is overly aggressive or keeps wandering off track, try to politely acknowledge valid reasons for such behavior: "I understand your concern about this, and it's probably something we should look at more closely." If you think the point has value, suggest a later meeting: "Why don't we take some time to think about this and schedule another meeting to discuss it?"

- Never attack or point the finger by using "aggressive 'you' talk": "You should," "You haven't," or "You need to realize." See page 215 for ways to avoid a blaming tone.

Ultimately, collaboration requires compromise and consensus: Each person must give a little. Before your meeting, review the persuasion guidelines on pages 53–55; also, try really *listening* to what other people have to say.

OVERCOMING DIFFERENCES BY ACTIVE LISTENING

Listen actively to avoid conflict

Listening is key to getting along, building relationships, and learning. Information expert Keith Devlin points out that "managers get around two-thirds of their knowledge from face-to-face meetings or telephone conversations and only one-third from documents and computers" (163). In one manager survey, the ability to listen was ranked second (after the ability to follow instructions) among thirteen communication skills sought in entry-level graduates (cited in Goby and Lewis 42).

Many of us seem more inclined to speak, to say what's on our minds, than to listen. We often hope someone else will do the listening. Effective listening requires *active* involvement instead of merely passive reception, as explained in the following guidelines.

GUIDELINES for Active Listening

- **Don't dictate.** If you are the group moderator, don't express your view until everyone else has had a chance.
- **Be receptive.** Instead of resisting different views, develop a "learner's" mind-set: take it all in first, and evaluate it later.
- **Keep an open mind.** Judgment stops thought (Hayakawa 42). Reserve judgment until everyone has had their say.
- **Be courteous.** Don't smirk, roll your eyes, whisper, fidget, or wisecrack.
- **Show genuine interest.** Eye contact is vital, and so is body language (nodding, smiling, leaning toward the speaker). Make it a point to remember everyone's name.
- **Hear the speaker out.** Instead of "tuning out" a message you find disagreeable, allow the speaker to continue without interruption (except to ask for clarification). Delay your own questions, comments, and rebuttals until the speaker has

GUIDELINES *continued*

finished. Instead of blurting out a question or comment, raise your hand and wait to be recognized.

- **Focus on the message.** Instead of thinking about what you want to say or email next, try to get a clear understanding of the speaker's position.
- **Ask for clarification.** If anything is unclear, say so: "Can you run that by me again?" To ensure accuracy, paraphrase the message: "So what you're saying is.... Did I understand you accurately?" Whenever you respond, try repeating a word or phrase that the other person has just used.
- **Observe the 90/10 rule.** You rarely go wrong spending 90 percent of your time listening, and 10 percent speaking. President Calvin Coolidge claimed that "Nobody ever listened himself out of a job." Some historians would argue that "Silent Cal" listened himself right into the White House.

Source: Adapted from Armstrong 24+; Cooper 78–84; Pearce, Johnson, and Barker 28–32; Sittenfeld 88; Smith 29.

THINKING CREATIVELY

Today's rapidly changing workplace demands new and better ways of doing things:

Creativity is a vital asset

> More than one-fourth of U.S. companies employing more than 100 people offer some kind of creativity training to employees. (Kiely 33)

Creative thinking is especially productive in group settings, using one or more of the following techniques.

Brainstorm as a Way of Getting Started

The more ideas the better

When we begin working with a problem, we search for useful material—insights, facts, statistics, opinions, images—anything that sharpens our view of the audience ("Who here needs what?"), the problem ("How can we increase market share for Zappo software?"), and potential solutions ("Which of these ideas might work best?"). *Brainstorming* is a technique for coming up with useful material. Its aim is to produce as many ideas as possible (on paper, screen, whiteboard, or the like) from our personal inventory.

A procedure for brainstorming

1. **Choose a quiet setting and agree on a time limit.**
2. **Decide on a clear and specific goal for the session.** For instance, "We need at least five good ideas about why we are losing top employees to other companies."

3. **Focus on the issue or problem.**
4. **As ideas begin to flow, record every one.** Don't stop to judge relevance or worth, and don't worry about spelling or grammar.
5. **If ideas are still flowing at session's end, keep going.**
6. **Take a break.**
7. **Now confront your list.** Strike out what is useless and sort the remainder into categories. Include any new ideas that crop up.

Brainstorming with Digital Technologies

Brainstorming is most effective in group settings. Face-to-face groups work best, but with team members often scattered across different time zones and countries, digital technologies provide a range of options for brainstorming virtually. Shared documents (such as Google Drive) allow writers to contribute to the same document and use a chat window to discuss ideas at the same time. You can see ideas as they are being typed by others, comment on these ideas, and use the chat window to keep up a conversation. Tools such as Google Hangouts allow video conferencing and uploading and real-time editing of documents. Track changes (see Figure 5.3), a feature available in most word-processing programs, also allows for a back-and-forth brainstorming of ideas. See page 87 for more information on virtual meetings.

Mind-Mapping

A more structured version of brainstorming, *mind-mapping* (Figure 5.4A) helps group members visualize relationships. They begin by drawing a circle around the main issue or concept, centered on the paper or whiteboard. Related ideas are then added, each in its own box, connected to the circle by a ruled line (or "branch"). Other branches are then added, as lines to some other distinct geometric shape containing supporting ideas. Unlike a traditional outline, a mind-map does not require sequential thinking: as each idea pops up, it is connected to related ideas by its own branch. Mind-mapping software such as *Mindjet* automates this process of visual thinking.

A simplified form of mind-mapping is the *tree diagram* (Figure 5.4B), in which major topic, minor topics, and subtopics are connected by branches that indicate their relationships. Page 95 shows a sample tree diagram for a research project.

Storyboarding

A technique for visualizing the shape of an entire process (or a document) is *storyboarding* (Figure 5.4C). Group members write each idea and sketch each visual on a large index card. Cards are then displayed on a wall or bulletin board so that others can comment on or add, delete, refine, or reshuffle ideas, topics, and visuals (Kiely 35–36). Page 200 shows a final storyboard for a long report.

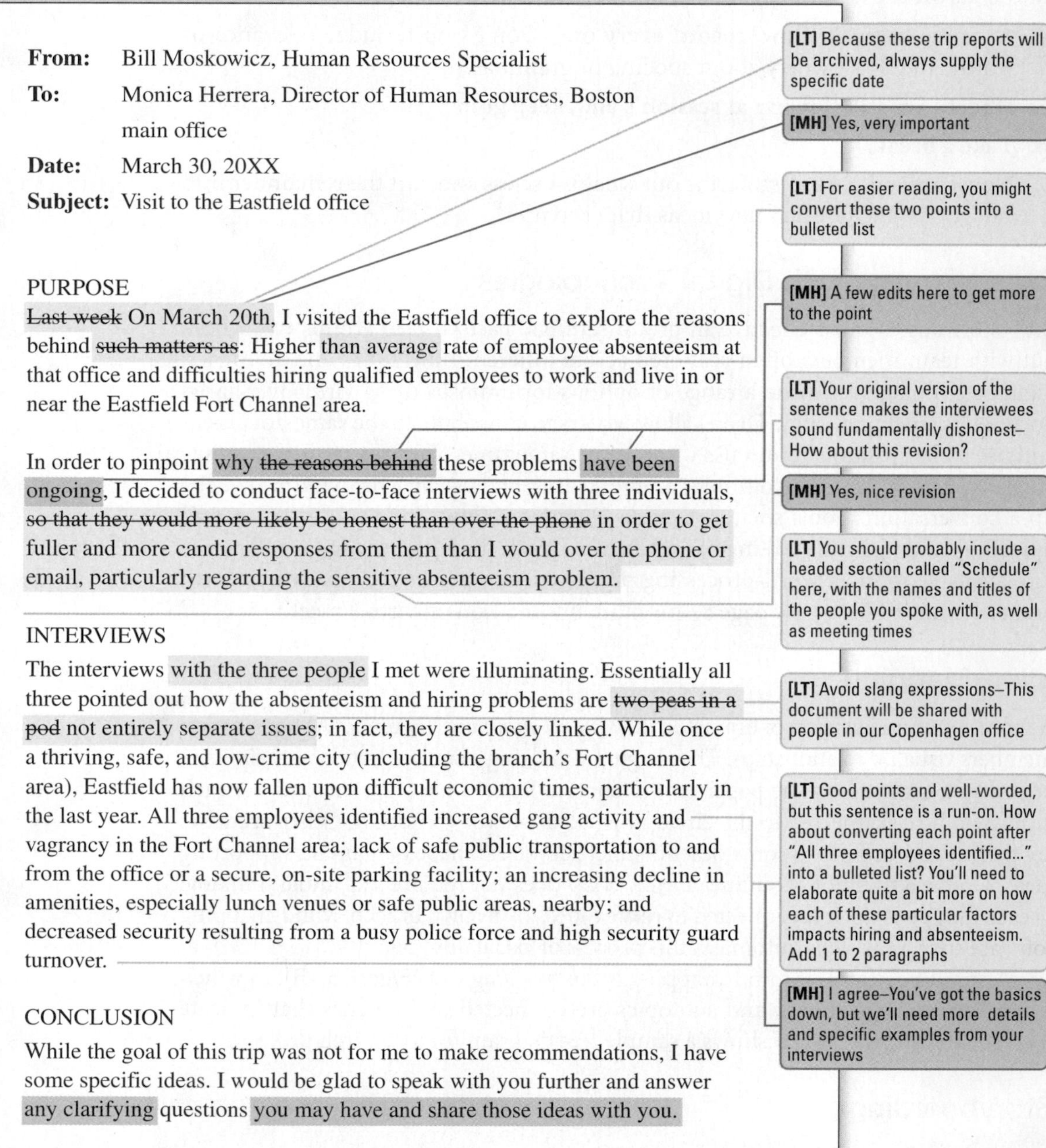
From: Bill Moskowicz, Human Resources Specialist
To: Monica Herrera, Director of Human Resources, Boston main office
Date: March 30, 20XX
Subject: Visit to the Eastfield office

PURPOSE

~~Last week~~ On March 20th, I visited the Eastfield office to explore the reasons behind ~~such matters as~~: Higher than average rate of employee absenteeism at that office and difficulties hiring qualified employees to work and live in or near the Eastfield Fort Channel area.

In order to pinpoint why ~~the reasons behind~~ these problems have been ongoing, I decided to conduct face-to-face interviews with three individuals, ~~so that they would more likely be honest than over the phone~~ in order to get fuller and more candid responses from them than I would over the phone or email, particularly regarding the sensitive absenteeism problem.

INTERVIEWS

The interviews with the three people I met were illuminating. Essentially all three pointed out how the absenteeism and hiring problems are ~~two peas in a pod~~ not entirely separate issues; in fact, they are closely linked. While once a thriving, safe, and low-crime city (including the branch's Fort Channel area), Eastfield has now fallen upon difficult economic times, particularly in the last year. All three employees identified increased gang activity and vagrancy in the Fort Channel area; lack of safe public transportation to and from the office or a secure, on-site parking facility; an increasing decline in amenities, especially lunch venues or safe public areas, nearby; and decreased security resulting from a busy police force and high security guard turnover.

CONCLUSION

While the goal of this trip was not for me to make recommendations, I have some specific ideas. I would be glad to speak with you further and answer any clarifying questions you may have and share those ideas with you.

[LT] Because these trip reports will be archived, always supply the specific date
[MH] Yes, very important
[LT] For easier reading, you might convert these two points into a bulleted list
[MH] A few edits here to get more to the point
[LT] Your original version of the sentence makes the interviewees sound fundamentally dishonest–How about this revision?
[MH] Yes, nice revision
[LT] You should probably include a headed section called "Schedule" here, with the names and titles of the people you spoke with, as well as meeting times
[LT] Avoid slang expressions–This document will be shared with people in our Copenhagen office
[LT] Good points and well-worded, but this sentence is a run-on. How about converting each point after "All three employees identified..." into a bulleted list? You'll need to elaborate quite a bit more on how each of these particular factors impacts hiring and absenteeism. Add 1 to 2 paragraphs
[MH] I agree–You've got the basics down, but we'll need more details and specific examples from your interviews

FIGURE 5.3 A Document That Has Been Edited Using a Track Changes System Notice how two different people, signified by their initials and different text colors, have read and edited Bill Moskowicz's first draft of a trip report. Compare this edited draft with the final version in Chapter 21 (page 497).

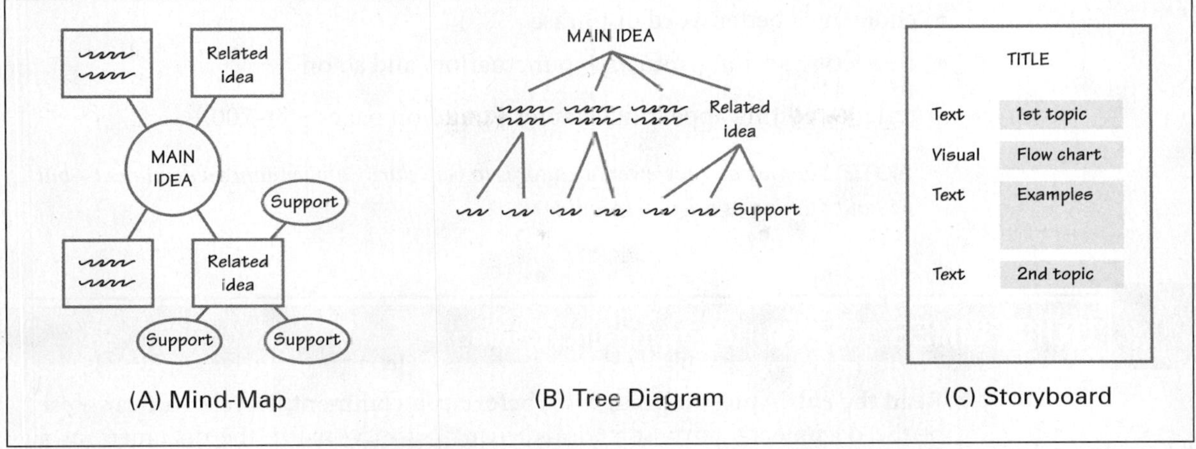

FIGURE 5.4 **Visual Techniques for Thinking Creatively** Each of these techniques produces a concrete mental image of an otherwise abstract process (i.e., the thinking process).

Many digital technologies are available to help you with storyboarding. Presentation software (such as *Microsoft PowerPoint* or *Apple Keynote*) allows you to arrange images and ideas in a linear sequence that can be viewed and edited by the entire team. You can also use movie software, such as *Apple*'s *iMovie*, to create a storyboard that can be played in real time.

REVIEWING AND EDITING OTHERS' WORK

Documents produced collaboratively are reviewed and edited extensively. *Reviewing* means evaluating how well a document connects with its audience and meets its purpose. Reviewers typically examine a document to make sure it includes these features:

What reviewers look for

- accurate, appropriate, useful, and legal content
- material organized for the reader's understanding
- clear, easy-to-read, and engaging style
- effective visuals and page design

In reviewing, you explain to the writer how you respond as a reader; you point out what works or doesn't work. This commentary helps a writer think about ways of revising. (Criteria for reviewing various documents appear in checklists throughout this book.)

Editing means actually "fixing" the piece by making it more precise and readable. Editors typically suggest improvements like these:

Ways in which editors "fix" writing

- rephrasing or reorganizing sentences
- clarifying a topic sentence

- choosing a better word or phrase
- correcting spelling, usage, or punctuation, and so on

(Criteria for editing appear in Chapter 11 and on pages 680–700.)

NOTE *Your job as a reviewer or editor is to help clarify and enhance a document—but without altering its original meaning.*

GUIDELINES for Peer Reviewing and Editing

- **Read the entire piece at least twice before you comment.** Develop a clear sense of the document's purpose and audience. Try to visualize the document as a whole before you evaluate specific parts.
- **Remember that mere mechanical correctness does not guarantee effectiveness.** Poor usage, punctuation, or mechanics distract readers and harm the writer's credibility. However, a "correct" piece of writing might still contain faulty rhetorical elements (inferior content, confusing organization, or unsuitable style).
- **Understand the acceptable limits of editing.** In the workplace, editing can range from fine-tuning to an in-depth rewrite (in which case editors are cited prominently as consulting editors or coauthors). In school, however, rewriting a piece to the extent that it ceases to belong to its author may constitute plagiarism. (See pages 74–75, 97.)
- **Be honest but diplomatic.** Begin with something positive before moving to suggested improvements. Be supportive instead of judgmental.
- **Focus first on the big picture.** Begin with the content and the shape of the document. Is the document appropriate for its audience and purpose? Is the supporting material relevant and convincing? Is the discussion easy to follow? Does each paragraph do its job? Then discuss specifics of style and correctness (tone, word choice, sentence structure, and so on).
- **Always explain why something doesn't work.** Instead of "this paragraph is confusing," say "because this paragraph lacks a clear topic sentence, I had trouble discovering the main idea." (See pages 32–33 for sample criteria.) Help the writer identify the cause of the problem.
- **Make specific recommendations for improvements.** Write out suggestions in enough detail for the writer to know what to do. Provide brief reasons for your suggestions.
- **Be aware that not all feedback has equal value.** Even professional editors can disagree. If different readers offer conflicting opinions of your own work, seek your instructor's advice.

ETHICAL ABUSES IN WORKPLACE COLLABORATION

Teamwork versus survival of the fittest

Our "lean" and "downsized" corporate world sends coworkers a conflicting message, encouraging teamwork while "rewarding individual stars, so that nobody has any real incentive to share the glory" (Fisher, "My Team Leader" 291). The resulting mistrust promotes unethical behavior such as the following.

Intimidating One's Peers

A dominant personality may intimidate peers into silence or agreement (Matson, "The Seven Sins" 30). Intimidated employees resort to "mimicking"—merely repeating what the boss says (Haskin, "Meetings without Walls" 55).

Claiming Credit for Others' Work

Workplace plagiarism occurs when the team or project leader claims all the credit. Even with good intentions, "the person who speaks for a team often gets the credit, not the people who had the ideas or did the work" (Nakache 287–88). Team expert James Stern describes one strategy for avoiding plagiarism among coworkers:

How to ensure that the deserving get the credit

> Some companies list "core" and "contributing" team members, to distinguish those who did most of the heavy lifting from those who were less involved. (qtd. in Fisher, "My Team Leader" 291)

Stern advises groups to decide beforehand—and in writing—exactly who will be given what credit.

Hoarding Information

Surveys reveal that the biggest obstacle to workplace collaboration is people's "tendency to hoard their own know-how" (Cole-Gomolski 6) when confronted with questions like these:

Information people need to do their jobs

- Whom do we contact for what?
- Where do we get the best price, the quickest repair, the best service?
- What's the best way to do X?

People hoard information when they think it gives them power or self-importance, or when having exclusive knowledge might provide job security (Devlin 179). In a worse case, they withhold information when they want to sabotage peers.

GLOBAL CONSIDERATIONS WHEN WORKING IN TEAMS

Teamwork is an increasingly global activity

In today's global environment, teams are often composed of people from many different cultures and countries who are spread throughout different time zones and different continents. Cultures and countries have different norms of communication, and all members of any team need to understand the cultures and personalities of other team members.

NOTE *Each team member is an individual person, not a stereotype, and so both the culture and the person need to be taken into consideration.*

In many global organizations, teams meet virtually, using a variety of technologies.

Interpersonal Issues in Global Teams

Whether working virtually or face-to-face, teams often experience unique interpersonal issues when members are from different countries and cultures. Many cultures value the social (or relationship) function of communication as much as the informative function (Archee 41). Some of these issues are discussed below.

Virtual meetings may lack important social cues

Social Cues. Virtual meetings (see page 87) are often the only option for teams working globally. Yet digital communication often leaves out important social cues that would otherwise be visible in face-to-face settings. Such cues include age, gender, appearance, ethnicity, team status, facial features, seating position, and more (Sproull and Kiesler 40–54; Wojahn 747–48). These cues normally provide important information, such as who is sitting at the head of the table, how people are reacting to what one is saying, and whether the team is made up of international members.

On email, people may adopt a writing style that sounds friendly and conversational, to make up for lack of eye contact and speaking tone. But excessive informality may be interpreted differently by people in different cultures. See Chapter 15, page 363, for more on global considerations when using email.

Be aware of cultural codes

Misunderstanding Cultural Codes. International business expert David A. Victor describes cultural codes that influence group interactions: Some cultures value silence more than speech, intuition and ambiguity more than hard evidence or data, and politeness and personal relations more than business relationships. Cultures also differ in their perceptions of time. Some are "all business" and in a big rush; others take as long as needed to weigh the issues, engage in small talk and digressions, and chat about family, health, and other personal

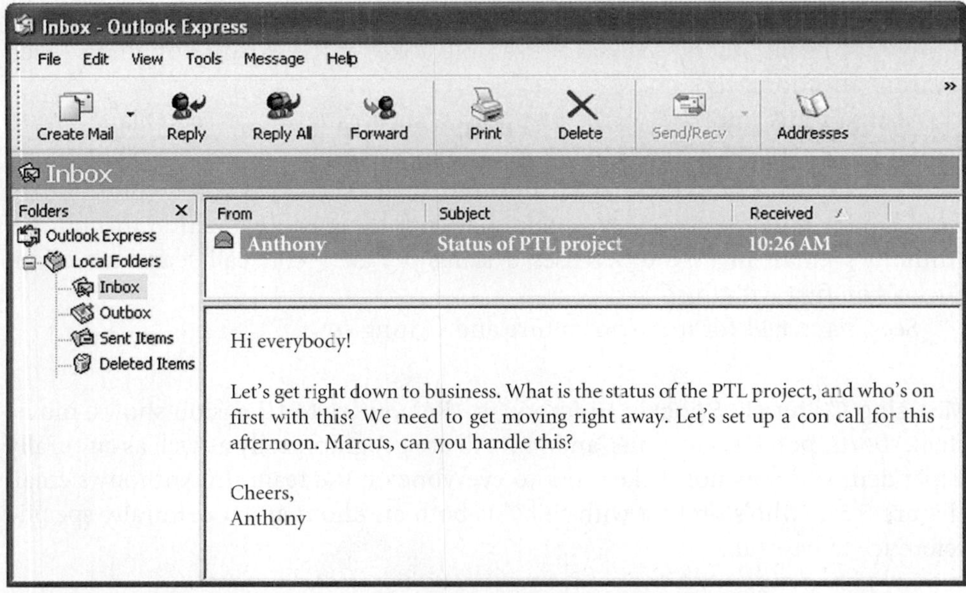

FIGURE 5.5 An Inappropriate Email Message for a Global Audience Notice the variety of ways in which Anthony's email fails to successfully address international and culturally diverse readers.
Source: Outlook Express template used with permission from Microsoft.

matters (233). In Anthony's email (Figure 5.5), the writer's hurried approach ("Let's get right down to business"; "We need to get moving right away") and directness ("Marcus, can you handle this?") might be offensive in cultures that value a more personal and subtle approach.

Individuals from various cultures differ in their willingness to express disagreement; to question or be questioned; to leave things unstated; or to touch, shake hands, kiss, hug, or backslap. Also, direct eye contact is not always a good indicator of listening; some cultures find it offensive. Other eye movements, such as squinting, closing the eyes, staring away, staring at legs or other body parts, are acceptable in some cultures but insulting in others (206). Finally, some cultures value formality over informality. Anthony's email (Figure 5.5) might be perceived as impolite and overly informal by members of some cultures.

Be careful with humor, slang, and idioms

Misusing Humor, Slang, and Idioms. Humor often can relieve tension, especially in a team meeting where tempers might flair or personalities might clash. But humor is culturally dependent. Its timing and use differ greatly among cultures; moreover, the examples used in a joke are often specific to one culture. For instance, a joke that references a sport such as U.S. football may fall flat for people from countries where soccer is "football." Also what some people consider funny may insult others. Avoid, for example, jokes at the expense of others (even if meant affectionately).

Slang means informal words or phrases, such as *bogus* or *cool*. Slang makes sense to those inside the culture but not to those outside. Idioms are phrases that have a meaning beyond their literal meaning, such as "all bark and no bite," which would make no sense to anyone unfamiliar with the meaning behind this phrase. Anthony's email in Figure 5.5 uses a slang phrase ("con call") and an idiom ("who's on first with this?").

See Chapter 11 for more on culture and writing style.

Avoid culturally dependent references

Misusing Culturally Specific References. References to television shows, movie stars, sports, politics, locations, and so forth are geographically as well as culturally dependent and may not make sense to everyone on the team. In Anthony's email (Figure 5.5), "who's on first with this?" is both an idiom and a culturally specific reference to baseball.

Use language that can be translated easily

Failing to Allow for Easy Translation. Often, the documents that your team produces will need to be translated into a number of different languages. Be careful to use English that is easy to translate. Idioms, humor, and analogies are often difficult for translators. Also, certain grammatical elements are important for translation. The lack of an article (*a, the*) or of the word *that* in certain crucial places can cause a sentence to be translated inaccurately. Consider the following examples (Kohl 151):

> Programs **that are** currently running in the system are indicated by icons in the lower part of the screen.

> Programs currently running in the system are indicated by icons in the lower part of the screen.

The first sentence contains the phrase "that are," which might ordinarily be left out by native English writers, as in the second sentence. This second sentence is harder to translate because the phrase "that are" provides the translator with important clues about the relationship of the words *programs, currently*, and *running*.

Active "listening" occurs virtually as well as face-to-face

Failing to Listen. Active listening, described earlier in this chapter, is an excellent way to learn more about your colleagues. Active "listening" can also occur when you read email or text messages; instead of responding with your usual style and tone, take note of the approach of each team member, tuning your eye and ear to that person's particular way of analyzing problems, presenting information, and persuading.

GUIDELINES for Communicating on a Global Team

- **Use the right technology for the situation.** Email and blogs are great for keeping track of discussions and the project's status, but video or phone conferencing as well as instant messaging are the right choices for communicating in real time.
- **Remember that social cues are not conveyed well in digital communication.** Email and other text-based systems leave out crucial information such as body language, facial expressions, and gender.
- **Consider how cultural codes might influence team dynamics.** Some team members may want to get right down to business, whereas others may value small talk or forms of politeness before getting started.
- **Avoid humor, slang, idioms, and cultural references.** These items are not understood identically by people from different cultures and countries, especially if different languages are involved.
- **Write with translation in mind.** Keep your writing simple, with short sentences and nothing too complex in structure that might confuse a translator.
- **Create a glossary so that everyone is using identical vocabulary.** Team members likely will be using specific terminology and abbreviations. A glossary (which can be kept updated on a wiki) ensures that everyone understands and uses terms identically. (For more on glossaries, see page 423.)
- **Agree in advance on technical standards.** For instance, will your team use the metric system (meters, liters) or the Imperial unit system (feet, gallons)? Remember that dates and times are expressed differently in different countries (e.g., 12-20-2013 in the United States would be written as 20-12-2013 in many European countries).
- **Be polite and professional.** All around the globe, respectful behavior and professional communication is always appreciated. Phrases such as *thank you*, *I appreciate it*, and *you're welcome* are always valued.
- **Be respectful of the rank and status of all team members, even if you are the team leader.** Many cultures are quite sensitive to rank.
- **Be an active listener.** Remember that listening, and learning about others, can occur in a meeting or over email.
- **Show respect for differences by choosing words carefully.** *Third world country* is disrespectful because the phrase implies inequality; instead, say "emerging markets" or "developing nations." Spell the names of people and their countries and cities using the correct accent marks and other symbols. Learn to pronounce the names of all team members.
- **Use visual information carefully.** Not all symbols have the same meaning across cultures. When possible, use internationally identifiable symbols such as those endorsed by the International Standards Organization (ISO). See Chapter 12 for more information.

CHECKLIST: Teamwork and Global Considerations

Numbers in parentheses refer to the first page of discussion.)

Teamwork

- ☐ Have we appointed a team manager? (83)
- ☐ Does the team agree on the type of document required? (84)
- ☐ Do we have a plan for how to divide the tasks? (84)
- ☐ Have we established a timetable and decided on a meeting schedule? (84)
- ☐ Do we have an agenda for our first meeting? (88)
- ☐ Do we have a clear understanding of how we will share drafts of the document and how we will name the files? (84)
- ☐ Have we decided what technology to use (track changes, wiki, blog)? (93)
- ☐ Are we using the Project Planning Form? (84)

Running a Meeting

- ☐ Has the team manager created an agenda and circulated it in advance? (88)
- ☐ Do members understand their individual roles on the team so they can be prepared for the meeting? (84)
- ☐ Has someone been appointed to take meeting minutes? (88)
- ☐ Are all members given the opportunity to speak? (88)
- ☐ Does the team manager keep discussion focused on agenda items? (92)
- ☐ Does the meeting end on schedule? (88)

Active Listening

- ☐ Are team members receptive to each other's viewpoints? (91)
- ☐ Does everyone communicate with courtesy and respect? (91)
- ☐ In face-to-face settings, are all team members allowed to speak freely? (88)
- ☐ Are people able to listen to all ideas with an open mind? (91)
- ☐ Are interruptions discouraged? (91)
- ☐ On email, do people take time to reflect on ideas before responding? (336)
- ☐ Do people observe the 90/10 rule (listen 90 percent of the time; speak 10 percent of the time)? (92)

Peer Review and Editing

- ☐ Have I read the entire document twice before I make comments? (96)
- ☐ Have I focused on content, style, and logical flow of ideas before looking at grammar, spelling, and punctuation? (96)
- ☐ Do I know what level of review and editing is expected of me (focus only on the content, or focus on style, layout, and other factors)? (96)

- ☐ Am I being honest but polite and diplomatic in my response? (96)
- ☐ Do I explain exactly why something doesn't work? (96)
- ☐ Do I make specific recommendations for improvements? (96)

Global Considerations

- ☐ Do I understand the communication customs of the international audience for my document? (90)
- ☐ Is my document clear and direct, so that it is easy to translate? (100)
- ☐ Have I avoided humor, idioms, and slang? (99)
- ☐ Have I avoided stereotyping of different cultures and groups of people? (98)
- ☐ Does my document avoid cultural references (such as TV shows and sports), which may not make sense to a global audience? (90)

Projects

GENERAL

Describe the role of collaboration in a company, organization, or campus group where you have worked or volunteered. Among the questions: What types of projects require collaboration? How are teams organized? Who manages the projects? How are meetings conducted? Who runs the meetings? How is conflict managed? Summarize your findings in a one- or two-page memo.

Hint: If you have no direct experience, interview a group representative, say a school administrator or faculty member or editor of the campus newspaper. (See page 142 for interview guidelines.)

TEAM

1. Gender Differences: Divide into small groups of mixed genders. Review pages 89–90. Then test the hypothesis that women and men communicate differently in the workplace.

Each member prepares the following brief messages—without consulting other members:

- A thank-you note to a coworker who has done you a favor.
- A note asking a coworker for help with a problem or project.
- A note asking a team member to be more cooperative or stop interrupting or complaining.
- A note expressing impatience, frustration, confusion, or disapproval to members of your group.
- A recommendation for a friend who is applying for a position with your company.
- A note offering support to a coworker who is having a health problem.
- A note to a new colleague, welcoming this person to the company.
- A request for a raise, based on your hard work.
- The meeting is out of hand, so you decide to take control. Write what you would say.
- Some group members are procrastinating on a project. Write what you would say.

As a group, compare messages, draw conclusions about the original hypothesis, and appoint one member to present findings to the class.

2. Listening Competence: Use the Guidelines on page 91 to:
   a. assess the listening behaviors of one member in your group during collaborative work,
   b. have another member assess your behaviors, and
   c. do a self-assessment.

   Record the findings and compare each self-assessment with the corresponding outside assessment. Discuss findings with the class.

3. Use email or instant messaging to confer on all phases of a collaborative project, including peer review (page 96).

   When your project is complete, write an explanation telling how electronic conferencing eased or hampered the group's efforts and how it improved or detracted from the overall quality of your document.

DIGITAL AND SOCIAL MEDIA

In teams of 2-4 students, discuss (in class) the virtual meeting technologies described on page 87. Which technologies would be most useful for students projects? For workplace meetings? Do you currently use technologies that are not listed here (for example, do you use Facebook for connecting with other students for class projects? Texting? Anything else?) Using Google Drive or a track changes document and email, exchange your ideas and write a memo for your instructor on the pros and cons of virtual meetings.

GLOBAL

On the Web, examine the role of global collaboration in building the International Space Station. Summarize your findings in a memo to share in class.

6 An Overview of the Technical Writing Process

"Deadlines affect how our team approaches the writing process. With plenty of time, we can afford the luxury of the whole process: careful decisions about audience, purpose, content, organization, and style—and plenty of revisions. With limited time, we have limited revisions—so we have to think on our feet. But even when we have to take shortcuts, we try to understand how our audience thinks: 'How can we make this logical to our audience? Will they understand what we want them to understand?'"

—Blair Cordasco,
Training Specialist for an international bank

LEARNING OBJECTIVES FOR THIS CHAPTER

- Identify unique aspects of the technical writing process
- Appreciate the role of critical thinking during that process
- Follow one working writer through an everyday writing situation
- Observe the steps in planning, drafting, and revising a document
- Understand why proofreading is an important final step
- Appreciate the advantages and drawbacks of digital writing tools

Although the writing process (researching, planning, drafting, and revising) is similar across all disciplines, the process for technical writing differs from, say, the process for essay writing in ways such as the following:

Factors that influence the technical writing process

- Research often involves discussions with technical experts.
- Analysis of audience needs and expectations is critical.
- Complex organizational settings and "office politics" play an important role.
- Colleagues frequently collaborate in preparing a document.
- Many workplace documents are carefully reviewed before being released.
- Proper format (letter, memo, report, brochure, and so on) for a document is essential.
- Proper distribution medium (hard copy or digital) is essential.
- Deadlines often limit the amount of time that can be spent preparing a document.

In order to navigate these types of complex decisions, technical communicators rely on the critical thinking strategies discussed and illustrated throughout this chapter.

In *critical thinking*, you test the strength of your ideas or the quality of your information. Instead of accepting an idea at face value, you examine, evaluate, verify, analyze, weigh alternatives, and consider consequences—at every stage of that idea's development. You use critical thinking to examine your evidence and your reasoning, to discover new connections and new possibilities, and to test the effectiveness and the limits of our solutions.

CRITICAL THINKING IN THE WRITING PROCESS

Whether you are working alone or as part of a team, you apply critical thinking throughout the four stages in the technical writing process:

Stages in the writing process

1. Gather and evaluate ideas and information.
2. Plan the document.
3. Draft the document.
4. Revise the document.

As the arrows in Figure 6.1 indicate, no single stage of the writing process is complete until all stages are complete.

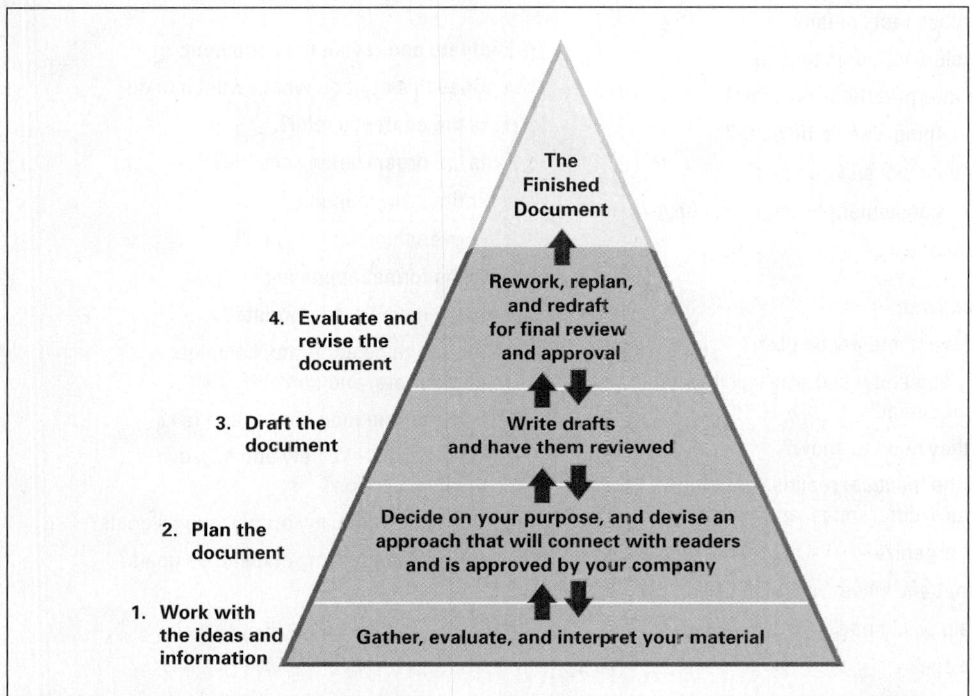
The Finished Document
Rework, replan, and redraft for final review and approval
4. Evaluate and revise the document
Write drafts and have them reviewed
3. Draft the document
Decide on your purpose, and devise an approach that will connect with readers and is approved by your company
2. Plan the document
Gather, evaluate, and interpret your material
1. Work with the ideas and information

FIGURE 6.1 The Writing Process for Technical Documents Like the exposed tip of an iceberg, the finished document provides the only visible evidence of your (or your team's) labor in preparing it.

Figure 6.2 lists the kinds of questions you answer at various stages. On the job, you must often complete these stages under deadline pressure.

This next section will follow one working writer through an everyday writing situation. You will see how he approaches his unique informational, persuasive, and ethical considerations and how he collaborates to design a useful and efficient document.

1. Work with the ideas and information:

- Have I defined the issue accurately?
- Is the information I've gathered complete, accurate, reliable, and unbiased?
- Can it be verified?
- How much of it is useful?
- Is a balance of viewpoints represented?
- What do these facts mean?
- What conclusions seem to emerge?
- Are other interpretations possible?
- What, if anything, should be done?
- What are the risks and benefits?
- What other consequences might this have?
- Should I reconsider?

2. Plan the document:

- What do I want it to accomplish?
- Who is my audience, and why will they use this document?
- What do they need to know?
- What are the "political realities" (feelings, egos, cultural differences, and so on)?
- How will I organize?
- What format and visuals should I use?
- Whose help will I need?
- When is it due?

3. Draft the document:

- How do I begin, and what comes next?
- How much is enough?
- What can I leave out?
- Am I forgetting anything?
- How will I end?
- Who needs to review my drafts?

4. Evaluate and revise the document:

- Does this draft do what I want it to do?
- Is the content useful?
- Is the organization sensible?
- Is the style readable?
- Is everything easy to find?
- Is the format appealing?
- Is the medium appropriate?
- Is everything accurate, complete, appropriate, and correct?
- Is the information honest and fair?
- Who needs to review and approve the final version?
- Does it advance my organization's goals?
- Does it advance my audience's goals?

FIGURE 6.2 Critical Thinking in the Technical Writing Process The actual "writing" (putting words on the page) is only a small part of the overall process.

A SAMPLE WRITING SITUATION

The setting

The company is Microbyte, developer of security software. The writer is Glenn Tarullo (BS, Management; Minor: Computer Science). Glenn has been on the job three months as Assistant Training Manager for Microbyte's Marketing and Customer Service Division.

The assignment

For three years, Glenn's boss, Marvin Long, has periodically offered a training program for new managers. Long's program combines an introduction to the company with instruction in management skills (time management, motivation, communication). Long seems satisfied with his two-week program but has asked Glenn to evaluate it and write a report as part of a company move to upgrade training procedures.

The audience

Glenn knows his report will be read by Long's boss, George Hopkins (Assistant Vice President, Personnel), and Charlotte Black (Vice President, Marketing, the person who devised the upgrading plan). Copies will go to other division heads, to the division's chief executive, and to Long's personnel file.

This writer's problem

Glenn spends two weeks (Monday, October 3 to Friday, October 14) attending and taking notes in Long's classes. On October 14, the trainees evaluate the program. After reading these evaluations and reviewing his notes, Glenn concludes that the program was successful but could stand improvement. How can he be candid without harming or offending anyone (instructors, his boss, or guest speakers)? Figure 6.3 depicts Glenn's problem.

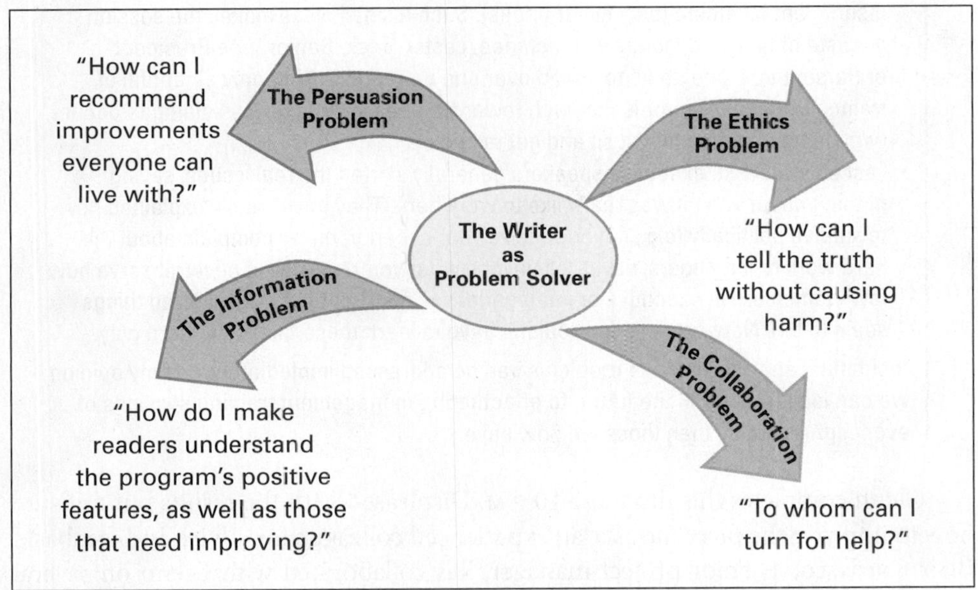

FIGURE 6.3 Glenn's Fourfold Problem Everyday writing situations typically pose similar problems.

The deadline

Glenn is scheduled to present his report in conference with Long, Black, and Hopkins on Wednesday, October 19. Right after the final class (1 P.M., Friday, the 14th), Glenn begins work on his report.

Working with the Information

Getting started

Glenn spends half of Friday afternoon fretting over the details of his situation, the readers and other people involved, the political realities, constraints, and consequences. (He knows no love is lost between Long and Black, and he wants to steer clear of their ongoing conflict.) By 3 P.M., Glenn hasn't written a word. Desperate, he decides to write whatever comes to mind:

Glenn's first draft

> Although the October Management Training Session was deemed quite successful, several problems have emerged that require our immediate attention.
>
> - Too many of the instructors had poor presentation skills. A few never arrived on time. One didn't stick to the topic but rambled incessantly. Jones and Wells seemed poorly prepared. Instructors in general seemed to lack any clear objectives. Also, because too few visual aids were used, many presentations seemed colorless and apparently bored the trainees.
> - The trainees (all new people) were not at all cognizant of how the company was organized or functioned, so the majority of them often couldn't relate to what the speakers were talking about.
> - It is my impression that this was a weak session due to the fact that there were insufficient members (only five trainees). Such a small class makes the session a waste of time and money. For instance, Lester Beck, Senior Vice President of Personnel, came down to spend over one hour addressing only a handful of trainees. Another factor is that with fewer trainees in a class, less dialogue occurs, with people tending to just sit and get talked at.
> - Last but not least, executive speakers generally skirted the real issues, saying nothing about what it was really like to work here. They never really explained how to survive politically (e.g., never criticize your superior; never complain about the hard work or long hours; never tell anyone what you *really* think; never observe how few women are in executive or managerial positions, or how disorganized things seem to be). New employees shouldn't have to learn these things the hard way.
>
> In the final analysis, if these problems can be addressed immediately, it is my opinion we can look forward in the future to effectuating management training sessions of even higher quality than those we now have.

The request for help

Glenn completes this draft at 5:10 P.M. Displeased with the results but not sure how to improve the piece, he asks an experienced colleague for advice and feedback. Blair Cordasco, a senior project manager, has collaborated with Glenn on several earlier projects. Blair agrees to study Glenn's draft over the weekend. Because of this document's sensitive nature, they agree to a phone call to discuss the document on Monday morning.

The colleague's peer review

At 8:05 A.M. Monday, Blair reviews the document with Glenn, looking over some ideas that Blair inserted using track changes. First, she points out obvious style problems: wordiness ("due to the fact that"), jargon ("effectuating"), triteness ("in the final analysis"), implied bias ("weak presentation," "skirted"), among others.

NOTE: *See Chapter 5, Figure 5.3 for an example of how tracking is used to share comments. Another option would be to use a shared document, such as Google document, shared only between Glenn and Blair.*

Blair points out other problems. The piece is disorganized, and even though Glenn is being honest, he isn't being particularly fair. The emphasis is too critical (making Glenn's boss look bad to his superiors), and the views are too subjective (no one is interested in hearing Glenn gripe about the company's political problems). Moreover, the report lacks persuasive force because it contains little useful advice for solving the problems he identifies. The tone is bossy and judgmental. Glenn is in no position to make this kind of *power connection* (see page 40). In its current form, the report will only alienate people and harm Glenn's career. He needs to be more fair, diplomatic, and reasonable.

Planning the Document

Glenn realizes he needs to begin by focusing on his writing situation. His audience and use analysis goes like this[1]:

I'd better decide *exactly* what my primary reader wants.

Long requested the report, but only because Black developed the scheme for division-wide improvements. So I really have two primary readers: my boss and the big boss.

My major question here: Am I including enough detail for all the bosses? The answer to this question will require answers to more specific questions:

Anticipated readers' questions

What are we doing right, and how can we do it better?

What are we doing wrong, and does it cost us money?

Have we left anything out, and does it matter?

How, specifically, can we improve the program, and how will those improvements help the company?

Because all readers have participated in these sessions (as trainees, instructors, or guest speakers), they don't need background explanations.

I should begin with the *positive* features of the last session. Then I can discuss the problems and make recommendations. Maybe I can eliminate the bossy and judgmental tone by *suggesting improvements* instead of *criticizing weaknesses.* Also, I could be more persuasive by describing the *benefits* of my suggestions.

Glenn realizes that if he wants successful future programs, he can't afford to alienate anyone. After all, he wants to be seen as a loyal member of the company, yet preserve his self-esteem and demonstrate he is capable of making objective recommendations.

[1] Throughout this section, Glenn's analysis will address the areas illustrated in the Audience and Use Profile Sheet (Figure 3.5, page 58).

Now, I have a clear enough sense of what to do.

Audience and purpose statement

The purpose of my document is to provide my supervisor and interested executives with an evaluation of the workshop by describing its strengths, suggesting improvements, and explaining the benefits of these changes.

From this plan, I should be able to revise my first draft, but that first draft lacks important details. I should brainstorm to get *all* the details (including the *positive* ones) I want to include.

Glenn's first draft touched on several topics. Incorporating them into his brainstorming (see page 92), he comes up with the following list.

Glenn's brainstorming list

1. better-prepared instructors and more visuals
2. on-the-job orientation *before* the training session
3. more members in training sessions
4. executive speakers should spell out qualities needed for success
5. beneficial emphasis on interpersonal communication
6. need follow-up evaluation (in six months?)
7. four types of training evaluations:
   a. trainees' reactions
   b. testing of classroom learning
   c. transference of skills to the job
   d. effect of training on the organization (high sales, more promotions, better-written reports)
8. videotaping and critiquing of trainee speeches worked well
9. acknowledge the positive features of the session
10. ongoing improvement ensures quality training
11. division of class topics into two areas was a good idea
12. additional trainees would increase classroom dialogue
13. the more trainees in a session, the less time and money wasted
14. instructors shouldn't drift from the topic
15. on-the-job training to give a broad view of the division
16. clear course objectives to increase audience interest and to measure the program's success
17. Marvin Long has done a great job with these sessions over the years

By 9:05 A.M., the office is hectic. Glenn puts his list aside to spend the day on work that has been piling up. Not until 4 P.M. does he return to his report.

Now what? I should delete whatever my audience already knows or doesn't need, or whatever seems unfair or insincere: 7 can go (this audience needs no lecture in training theory); 14 is too negative and critical—besides, the same idea is stated more positively in 4; 17 is obvious brown-nosing, and I'm in no position to make such grand judgments.

Maybe I can unscramble this list by arranging items within categories (strengths, suggested changes, and benefits) from my statement of purpose.

Notice here how Glenn discovers additional *content* (see italic type) while he's deciding about *organization.*

Glenn's brainstorming list rearranged

Strengths of the Workshop

- division of class topics into two areas was useful
- emphasis on interpersonal communication
- videotaping of trainees' oral reports, followed by critiques

Well, that's one category done. Maybe I should combine *suggested changes* with *benefits,* since I'll want to cover them together in the report.

Suggested Changes/Benefits

- more members per session would increase dialogue and use resources more efficiently
- varied on-the-job experiences before the training sessions would give each member a broad view of the marketing division
- executive speakers should spell out qualities required for success and *future sessions should cover professional behavior, to provide trainees with a clear guide*
- follow-up evaluation in six months *by both supervisors and trainees would reveal the effectiveness of this training and suggest future improvements*
- clear course objectives and more visual aids would increase *instructor efficiency* and audience interest

Now that he has a fairly sensible arrangement, Glenn can get this list into report form, even though he will probably think of more material to add as he works. Since this is *internal* correspondence, he uses a memo format.

Drafting the Document

Glenn produces a usable draft—one containing just about everything he wants to cover. (Sentences are numbered for our later reference.)

A later draft

[1]In my opinion, the Management Training Session for the month of October was somewhat successful. [2]This success was evidenced when most participants rated their training as "very good." [3]But improvements are still needed.

[4]First and foremost, a number of innovative aspects in this October session proved especially useful. [5]Class topics were divided into two distinct areas. [6]These topics created a general-to-specific focus. [7]An emphasis on interpersonal communication skills was the most dramatic innovation. [8]This helped class

members develop a better attitude toward things in general. [9]Videotaping of trainees' oral reports, followed by critiques, helped clarify strengths and weaknesses.

[10]A detailed summary of the trainees' evaluations is attached. [11]Based on these and on my past observations, I have several suggestions.

- [12]All management training sessions should have a minimum of ten to fifteen members. [13]This would better utilize the larger number of managers involved and the time expended in the implementation of the training. [14]The quality of class interaction with the speakers would also be improved with a larger group.
- [15]There should be several brief on-the-job training experiences in different sales and service areas. [16]These should be developed prior to the training session. [17]This would provide each member with a broad view of the duties and responsibilities in all areas of the marketing division.
- [18]Executive speakers should take a few minutes to spell out the personal and professional qualities essential for success with our company. [19]This would provide trainees with a concrete guide to both general company and individual supervisors' expectations. [20]Additionally, by the next training session we should develop a presentation dealing with appropriate attitudes, manners, and behavior in the business environment.
- [21]Do a six-month follow-up. [22]Get feedback from supervisors as well as trainees. [23]Ask for any new recommendations. [24]This would provide a clear assessment of the long-range impact of this training on an individual's job performance.
- [25]We need to demand clearer course objectives. [26]Instructors should be required to use more visual aids and improve their course structure based on these objectives. [27]This would increase instructor quality and audience interest.
- [28]These changes are bound to help. [29]Please contact me if you have further questions.

Although now developed and organized, this version still is not near the finished document. Glenn has to make further decisions about his style, content, arrangement, audience, and purpose.

Blair Cordasco offers to review the piece once again and to work with Glenn on a thorough edit.

Revising the Document

At 8:15 A.M. Tuesday, Blair and Glenn begin a sentence-by-sentence revision for worthwhile content, sensible organization, and readable style. Their discussion goes something like this:

> Sentence 1 begins with a needless qualifier, has a redundant phrase, and sounds insulting ("somewhat successful"). Sentence 2 should be in the passive voice, to emphasize the training—not the participants. Also, 1 and 2 are choppy and repetitious, and should be combined.

In my opinion, the Management Training Session for the month of October was somewhat successful. This success was evidenced when most participants rated their training as "very good." (28 words) — Original

The October Management Training Session was successful, with training rated "very good" by most participants. (15 words) — Revised

Sentence 3 is too blunt. An orienting sentence should forecast content diplomatically. This statement can be candid without being so negative.

But improvements are still needed. — Original

A few changes—beyond the recent innovations—should result in even greater training efficiency. — Revised

In sentence 4, "First and foremost" is trite, "aspects" only adds clutter, and word order needs changing to improve the emphasis (on innovations) and to lead into the examples.

First and foremost, a number of innovative aspects in this October session proved especially useful. — Original

Especially useful in this session were several program innovations. — Revised

The final version

In collaboration with his colleague, Glenn continues this editing and revising process on his report. Wednesday morning, after much revising and proofreading, Glenn prints out the final draft, shown in Figure 6.4.

Glenn's final report is both informative and persuasive. But this document did not appear magically. Glenn made deliberate decisions about purpose, audience, content, organization, and style. He sought advice and feedback on every aspect of the document. Most importantly, he *spent time revising and then proofreading.*[2]

NOTE *Writers work in different ways. Some begin by brainstorming. Some begin with an outline. Others simply write and rewrite. Some sketch a quick draft before thinking through their writing situation. Introductions and titles are often written last. Whether you write alone or collaborate in preparing a document, whether you are receiving feedback or providing it, no one step in the process is complete until the whole is complete. Notice, for instance, how Glenn sharpens his content and style while he organizes. Every document you write will require all these decisions, but you rarely will make them in the same sequence.*

No matter what the sequence, revision is a fact of life. It is the one constant in the writing process. When you've finished a draft, you have in a sense only begun. Sometimes you will have more time to submit a document than Glenn did, sometimes much less. Whenever your deadline allows, leave time to revise.

NOTE *Revising a draft doesn't always guarantee that you will improve it. Save each draft and then compare them to select the best material from each one.*

[2] A special thanks to Glenn Tarullo for his perseverance. We made his task doubly difficult by having him explain each of his decisions during this writing process.

MICRO**BYTE**

October 19, 20XX

To: Marvin Long
From: Glenn Tarullo GT
Subject: *October Management Training Program: Evaluation and Recommendations*

Begins on a positive note, and cites evidence

States his claim

The October Management Training Session was successful, with training rated as "very good" by most participants. A few changes, beyond the recent innovations, should result in even greater training efficiency.

Workshop Strengths

Especially useful in this session were several program innovations:

Gives clear examples of "innovations"

—Dividing class topics into two areas created a general-to-specific focus: The first week's coverage of company structure and functions created a context for the second week's coverage of management skills.

—Videotaping and critiquing trainees' oral reports clarified their speaking strengths and weaknesses.

—Emphasizing interpersonal communication skills (listening, showing empathy, and reading nonverbal feedback) created a sense of ease about the group, the training, and the company.

Innovations like these ensure high-quality training. And future sessions could provide other innovative ideas.

Suggested Changes/Benefits

Cites the basis for his recommendations

Based on the trainees' evaluation of the October session (summary attached) and my observations, I recommend these additional changes:

—We should develop several brief (one-day) on-the-job rotations in different sales and service areas before the training session. These rotations would give each member a real-life view of duties and responsibilities throughout the company.

FIGURE 6.4 Glenn's Final Draft Note how this seemingly routine document is the product of a complex—but vital—process. (For a vivid example of how critical thinking pays off, compare this final draft with Glenn's first draft, on page 110.)

Long, Oct. 19, 20XX, page 2

—All training sessions should have at least ten to fifteen members. Larger classes would make more efficient use of resources and improve class–speaker interaction.

—We should ask instructors to follow a standard format (based on definite course objectives) for their presentations, and to use visuals liberally. These enhancements would ensure the greatest possible instructor efficiency and audience interest.

Supports each recommendation with convincing reasons

—Executive speakers should spell out personal and professional traits that are essential to success in our company. Such advice would give trainees a concrete guide to both general company and individual supervisor expectations. Also, by the next training session, we should assemble a presentation dealing with appropriate attitudes, manners, and behavior in the business environment.

—We should do a six-month follow-up of trainees (with feedback from supervisors as well as ex-trainees) to gain long-term insights, to measure the influence of this training on job performance, and to help design advanced training.

Inexpensive and easy to implement, these changes should produce more efficient training.

Closes by appealing to shared goals (economy and efficiency)

Copies: B. Hull, C. Black, G. Hopkins, J. Capilona, P. Maxwell, R. Sanders, L. Hunter

FIGURE 6.4 (*Continued*)

MAKE PROOFREADING YOUR FINAL STEP

No matter how engaging and informative the document, basic errors distract the reader and make the writer look bad (including on various drafts being reviewed by colleagues). In Glenn Tarullo's situation, all of his careful planning, drafting, and revising could be lost on his readers if the final document contained spelling or other mechanical errors. Proofreading detects easily correctable errors such as these:

Errors we look for during proofreading

- **Sentence errors,** such as fragments, comma splices, or run-ons
- **Punctuation errors**, such as missing apostrophes or excessive commas
- **Usage errors**, such as "it's" for "its," "lay" for "lie," or "their" for "there"
- **Mechanical errors**, such as misspelled words, inaccurate dates, or incorrect abbreviations
- **Format errors**, such as missing page numbers, inconsistent spacing, or incorrect form of documenting sources
- **Typographical errors** (typos), such as repeated or missing words or letters, missing word endings (say, *-s* or *-ed* or *-ing*), or a left-out quotation mark

GUIDELINES for Proofreading

- **Save it for the final draft.** Proofreading earlier drafts might cause writer's block and distract you from the document's "rhetorical features" (content, organization, style, and design).
- **Take a break before proofreading your final document.**
- **Work from hard copy.** Research indicates that people read more perceptively (and with less fatigue) from a printed page than from a computer screen.
- **Keep it slow.** Read each word—don't skim. Slide a ruler under each line or move backward through the document, sentence by sentence. For a long document, read only small chunks at one time.
- **Be especially alert for problem areas in your writing.** Do you have trouble spelling? Do you get commas confused with semicolons? Do you make a lot of typos? Make one final pass to check on any problem areas.
- **Proofread more than once.** The more often you do it, the better.
- **Never rely only on the computer.** A synonym found in an electronic thesaurus may distort your meaning. The spell checker cannot differentiate among correctly spelled words such as "their," "they're," and "there" or "it's" versus "its." In the end, nothing can replace your own careful proofreading. (Page 241 summarizes the limitations of computerized aids.)

DIGITAL TECHNOLOGY AND THE WRITING PROCESS

A variety of digital tools and programs exist that provide support for the technical writing process (consult this book's index). For instance:

Digital tools for the technical writing process

- the outline feature, in *Microsoft Word* and similar programs, which allows you to outline
- brainstorming and storyboarding software, which lets you and team members collaborate on the early stages of the writing process
- social media such as Facebook, LinkedIn, and Twitter, which let you research your topic and connect with other experts (see Chapter 26)
- programs such as *PowerPoint* and *Microsoft Word* (or similar programs), which provide attractive formats for your presentations and document
- software such as *Visio* and other similar programs, which allows flowcharting and mapping
- programs that turn word processing documents into Web pages, PDF documents, and more
- wikis or tools such as *Google Drive*, which let you and others contribute to a common document
- tracking systems (track changes), available in most word processing programs, which record all suggested edits and comments from team members
- email, text messaging, and instant messaging, which provide quick turn-arounds needed during the writing process

In Glenn Tarullo's situation, some of these resources helped him with certain parts of the project such as brainstorming, outlining, word processing, and document formatting. Glenn and Blair Cordasco used track changes to share and discuss comments to his draft (see pages 110–11), although due to the document's sensitive content, they shared the document only with each other via a secure server at work, not via email.

But no matter how efficient the writing tools are and how varied the media, effective communication still needs to rely on a deliberate process of the sort that Glenn Tarullo's situation illustrates.

Granted, a quick text message to a friend may not require great effort or planning. But for most types of writing—from an email report to the boss to a research paper for an instructor—we continue to rely on the proven strategies that comprise the writing process. In the end, the *human brain* remains our ultimate tool for navigating the critical thinking decisions that produce effective writing.

CHECKLIST: Proofreading

(Numbers in parentheses refer to the first page of discussion.)

Sentences

- ☐ Are all sentences complete (no unacceptable fragments)? (680)
- ☐ Is the document free of comma splices and run-on sentences? (681)
- ☐ Does each verb agree with its subject? (682)
- ☐ Does each pronoun refer to and agree with a specific noun? (683)
- ☐ Are ideas of equal importance coordinated? (685)
- ☐ Are ideas of lesser importance subordinated? (686)
- ☐ Is each pronoun in the correct case (nominative, objective, possessive)? (687)
- ☐ Is each modifier positioned to reflect the intended meaning? (683)
- ☐ Are items of equal importance expressed in equal (parallel) grammatical form? (684)

Punctuation

- ☐ Does each sentence conclude with appropriate end punctuation? (688)
- ☐ Are semicolons and colons used correctly as a *break* between items? (688)
- ☐ Are commas used correctly as a *pause* between items? (689)
- ☐ Do apostrophes signal possessives, contractions, and certain plurals? (692)
- ☐ Do quotation marks set off direct quotes and certain titles? (693)
- ☐ Is each quotation punctuated correctly? (694)
- ☐ Do ellipses indicate material omitted from a quotation? (694)
- ☐ Do italics indicate certain titles or names, or emphasis or special use of a word? (695)
- ☐ Are brackets, parentheses, and dashes used correctly and as needed? (694)

Mechanics

- ☐ Are abbreviations used correctly and without confusing the reader? (696)
- ☐ Are hyphens used correctly? (696)
- ☐ Are words capitalized correctly? (696)
- ☐ Are numbers written out or expressed as numerals as needed? (697)
- ☐ Has electronic spell checking been supplemented by actual proofreading for words spelled correctly but used incorrectly (as in *there* for *their*)? (698)

Format, Usage, and Keyboarding

- ☐ Are commonly confused words used accurately? (698)
- ☐ Are pages numbered correctly? (298)
- ☐ Are sources cited in a standard form of documentation? (644)
- ☐ Have typographical errors been corrected? (118)

Projects

GENERAL

Compare Glenn's second draft (page 113) with his final draft (page 116). Identify all improvements in content, arrangement, and style besides those already discussed.

TEAM

Working in groups, assume that you are a training team for XYZ Corporation. After completing the first section of this text and the course, what advice about the writing process would you have for a beginning writer who will frequently need to write reports on the job? In a one- or two-page memo to new employees, explain the writing process briefly, and give a list of guidelines these beginning writers can follow. Include a suggestion that new employees explore the company's policy on using email and other digital communication technologies within the company and with clients/customers.

DIGITAL AND SOCIAL MEDIA

In teams of 3-4 students, imagine that as a team you have been asked to create a job description for an entry-level job at your company. (Use your past experience or an internship you've had to think of a job that would be suitable for this exercise.) Before writing the ad, you need to generate some ideas, similar to the process involved with Glenn's first draft on page 110. Using a shared Google document or a word processing document with track changes, share ideas and comments and see if you can come to an agreement about the job description. Write a memo to your instructor discussing your experience with the writing process using digital technology.

GLOBAL

Does the writing process in an Eastern culture (such as Japan, China, or India) differ from that in Western cultures? Use the Internet to research this question. Be prepared to discuss your findings in class.

PART 2

The Research Process

7 Thinking Critically about the Research Process

8 Evaluating and Interpreting Information

9 Summarizing Research Findings and Other Information

7 Thinking Critically about the Research Process

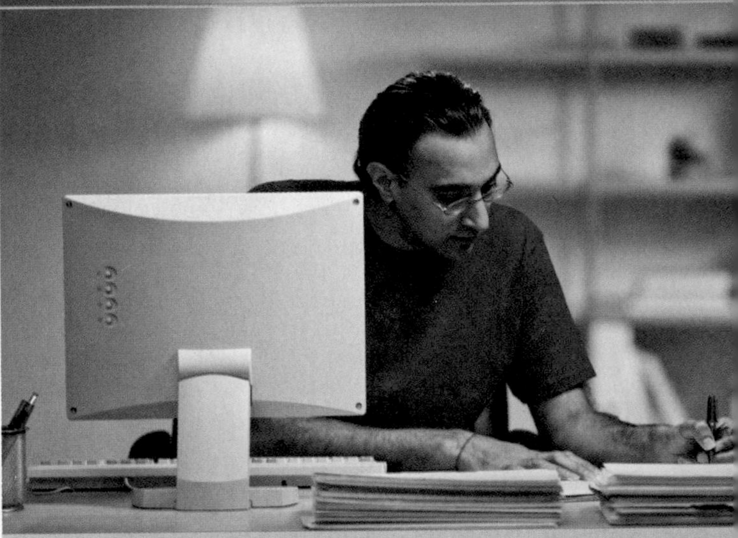

"As a freelance researcher, I search online databases and Web sites for any type of specialized information needed by my clients. For example, yesterday I did a search for a corporate attorney who needed the latest information on some specific product-liability issues, plus any laws or court decisions involving specific products. For the legal research I accessed LEXIS, the legal database that offers full-text copies of articles and cases. For the liability issue I began with Dow-Jones News/Retrieval and then double-checked by going into the Dialog database."

—Mark Casamonte,
Freelance Researcher

LEARNING OBJECTIVES FOR THIS CHAPTER

- Think critically about the research process
- Differentiate between procedural stages and inquiry stages of research
- Differentiate between primary and secondary research
- Explore online secondary sources using various search technologies
- Explore traditional secondary sources (books, periodicals, reference works)
- Explore primary sources (inquiries, interviews, surveys)
- Understand copyright in relation to research practices

Major decisions in the workplace are based on careful research, with the findings recorded in a written report. Some parts of the research process follow a recognizable sequence (Figure 7.1A). But research is not merely a numbered set of procedures. The procedural stages depend on the many decisions that accompany any legitimate inquiry (Figure 7.1B).[1] These decisions require you to *think critically* about each step of the process and about the information you gather for your research.

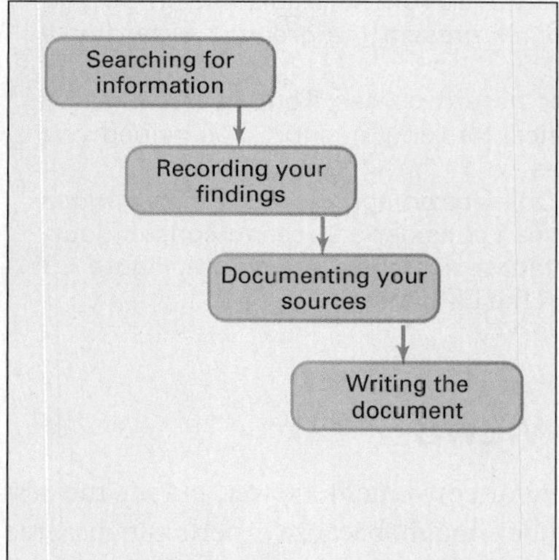

FIGURE 7.1A The Procedural Stages of the Research Process

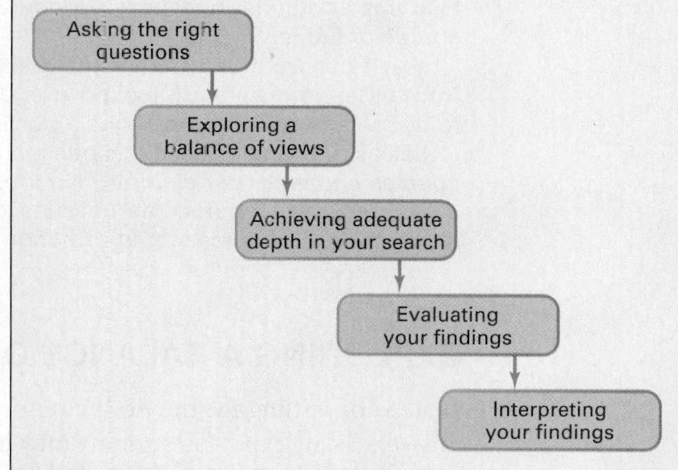

FIGURE 7.1B Stages of Critical Thinking in the Research Process

[1] Our thanks to University of Massachusetts Dartmouth librarian Shaleen Barnes for inspiring this chapter.

ASKING THE RIGHT QUESTIONS

The answers you uncover will only be as good as the questions you ask. Suppose, for instance, you face the following scenario:

CASE Defining and Refining a Research Question

You are the public health manager for a small, New England town in which high-tension power lines run within one hundred feet of the elementary school. Parents are concerned about danger from electromagnetic radiation (EMR) emitted by these power lines in energy waves known as electromagnetic fields (EMFs). Town officials ask you to research the issue and prepare a report to be distributed at the next town meeting in six weeks.

First, you need to identify your exact question or questions. Initially, the major question might be: *Do the power lines pose any real danger to our children?* After phone calls around town and discussions at the coffee shop, you discover that townspeople actually have three main questions about electromagnetic fields: *What are they? Do they endanger our children? If so, then what can be done?*

To answer these questions, you need to consider a range of subordinate questions, like those in the Figure 7.2 tree chart. Any *one* of those questions could serve as subject of a worthwhile research report on such a complex topic. As research progresses, this chart will grow. For instance, after some preliminary reading, you learn that electromagnetic fields radiate not only from power lines but from *all* electrical equipment, and even from the Earth itself. So you face this additional question: *Do power lines present the greatest hazard as a source of EMFs?*

You now wonder whether the greater hazard comes from power lines or from other sources of EMF exposure. Critical thinking, in short, has helped you to define and refine the essential questions.

Let's say you've chosen this question: *Do electromagnetic fields from various sources endanger our children?* Now you can consider sources to consult (journals, interviews, reports, Internet sites, database searches, and so on). Figure 7.3 illustrates likely sources for information on the EMF topic.

EXPLORING A BALANCE OF VIEWS

Instead of settling for the most comforting or convenient answer, pursue the *best* answer. Even "expert" testimony may not be enough, because experts can disagree or be mistaken. To answer fairly and accurately, consider a balance of perspectives from up-to-date and reputable sources:

Try to consider all the angles

- What do informed sources have to say about this topic?
- On which points do sources agree?
- On which points do sources disagree?

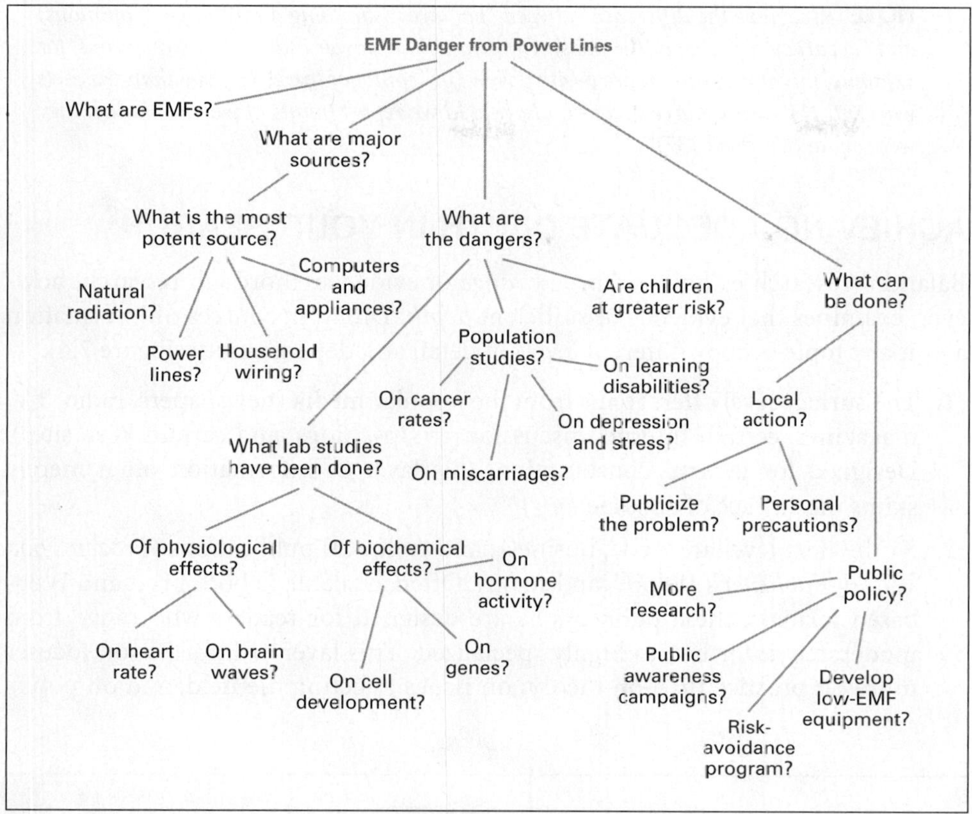

FIGURE 7.2 **How the Right Questions Help Define a Research Problem** You cannot begin to solve a problem until you have defined it clearly.

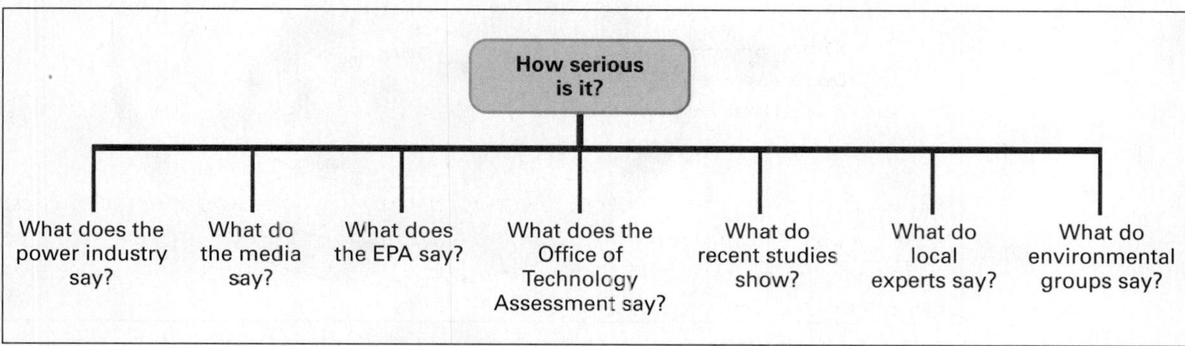

FIGURE 7.3 **A Range of Essential Viewpoints** No single source is likely to offer "the final word." Ethical researchers rely on evidence that represents a fair balance of views.

NOTE *Recognize the difference between "balance" (sampling a full range of opinions) and "accuracy" (getting at the facts). Government or power industry spokespersons, for example, might present a more positive view (or "spin") of the EMF issue than the facts warrant. Not every source is equal, nor should we report points of view as though they were equal (Trafford 137).*

ACHIEVING ADEQUATE DEPTH IN YOUR SEARCH[2]

Balanced research examines a broad *range* of evidence; thorough research, however, examines that evidence in sufficient *depth*. Different sources of information about any topic occupy different levels of detail and dependability (Figure 7.4).

The depth of a source often determines its quality

1. The surface level offers items from the popular media (newspapers, radio, TV, magazines, certain Internet discussion groups, blogs, and certain Web sites). Designed for general consumption, this layer of information often merely skims the surface of an issue.
2. At the next level are trade, business, and technical publications (*Frozen Food World, Publisher's Weekly,* and so on). Often available in both print and Web-based formats, these publications are designed for readers who range from moderately informed to highly specialized. This layer of information focuses more on practice than on theory, on issues affecting the field, and on public

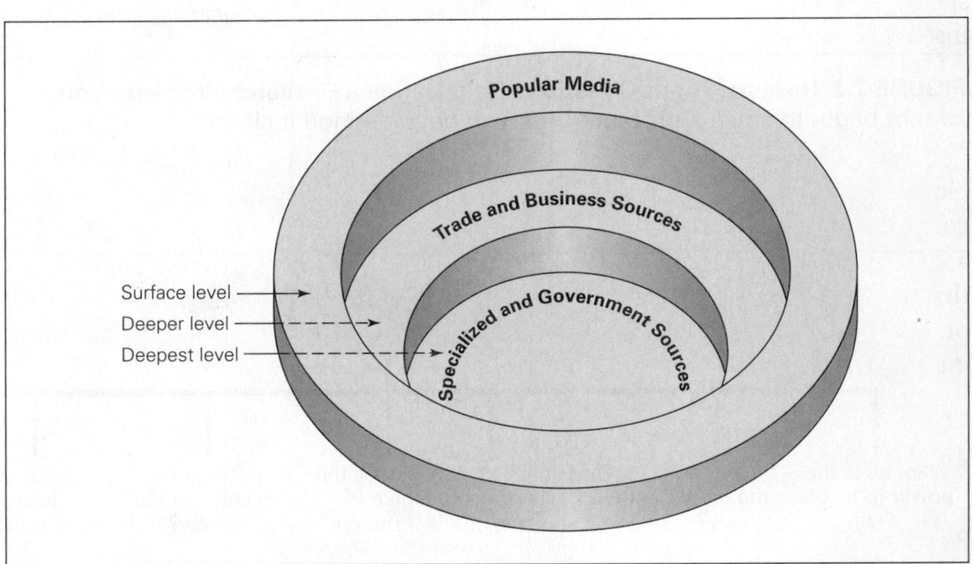

FIGURE 7.4 Effective Research Achieves Adequate Depth

[2] Our thanks to UMass Dartmouth librarian Ross LaBaugh for inspiring this section.

relations. While the information is usually accurate, the general viewpoints tend to reflect a field's particular biases.

3. At a deeper level is the specialized literature (journals from professional associations—academic, medical, legal, engineering). Designed for practicing professionals, this layer of information focuses on theory as well as on practice, on descriptions of the latest studies (written by the researchers themselves and scrutinized by peers for accuracy and objectivity), on debates among scholars and researchers, and on reviews, critiques, and refutations of prior studies and publications.

Also at this deepest level are government sources and corporate documents available through the Freedom of Information Act. Designed for anyone willing to investigate its complex resources, this information layer offers hard facts and detailed discussion, and (in many instances) *relatively* impartial views.

NOTE *Web pages, of course, offer links to increasingly specific levels of detail. But the actual "depth" and quality of a Web site's information depend on the sponsorship and reliability of that site (see page 136).*

How deep is deep enough? This depends on your purpose, your audience, and your topic. But the real story most likely resides at deeper levels. Research on the EMF issue, for example, would need to look beneath media headlines and biased special interests (say, electrical industry or environmental groups), focusing instead on studies by a wide range of experts.

EVALUATING YOUR FINDINGS

Not all findings have equal value. Some information might be distorted, incomplete, or misleading. Information might be tainted by *source bias,* in which a source understates or overstates certain facts, depending on whose interests that source represents (say, power company, government agency, parent group, or a reporter seeking headlines). To evaluate a particular finding, ask these questions:

Questions for evaluating a particular finding

- Is this information accurate, reliable, and relatively unbiased?
- Do the facts verify the claim?
- How much of the information is useful?
- Is this the whole or the real story?
- Do I need more information?

Instead of merely emphasizing findings that support their own biases or assumptions, ethical researchers seek out and report the most *accurate* answer.

INTERPRETING YOUR FINDINGS

Once you have decided which of your findings seem legitimate, you need to decide what they all mean by asking these questions:

Questions for interpreting your findings

- What are my conclusions and do they address my original research question?
- Do any findings conflict?
- Are other interpretations possible?
- Should I reconsider the evidence?
- What, if anything, should be done?

For more advice on evaluating and interpreting data, see Chapter 8.

> **NOTE** *Never force a simplistic conclusion on a complex issue. Sometimes the best you can offer is an indefinite conclusion: "Although controversy continues over the extent of EMF hazards, we all can take simple precautions to reduce our exposure." A wrong conclusion is far worse than no definite conclusion at all.*

PRIMARY VERSUS SECONDARY SOURCES

How primary and secondary research differ

Primary research means getting information directly from the source by conducting interviews and surveys and by observing people, events, or processes in action. *Secondary research* is information obtained second hand by reading what other researchers have compiled in books and articles in print or online. Most information found on the Internet would be considered a secondary source. Some Web-based information is more accurate than others; for instance, a Web page created by a high school student might be interesting but not overly reliable, whereas a Web site that is the equivalent of a traditional secondary source (encyclopedia, research index, newspaper, journal) would be more reliable for your research.

Why you should combine primary and secondary research

Whenever possible, combine primary and secondary research. Typically, you would start by using secondary sources, because they are readily available and can help you get a full background understanding of your topic. However, don't neglect to add your own findings to existing ones by doing primary research.

Working with primary sources can help you expand upon what other people have already learned and add considerable credibility to your work. For instance, assume that your boss asks you to write a report about how well your company's new product is being received in the marketplace: You might consult sales reports and published print and online reviews of the product (secondary research), but you might also survey people who use the product and interview some of them individually (primary research).

EXPLORING SECONDARY SOURCES

Secondary sources include some Web sites; online news outlets and magazines; blogs and wikis; books in the library; journal, magazine, and newspaper articles; government publications; and other public records. Research assignments begin more effectively when you first uncover and sort through what is already known about your topic before adding to that knowledge yourself.

Web-Based Secondary Sources

To find various sites on the Web, use two basic tools: *subject directories* and *search engines.*

- **Subject Directories.** Subject directories are indexes compiled by editors and others who sift through Web sites and compile the most useful links. The *World Wide Web Virtual Library* <www.vlib.org> is one of the oldest and continues to be a comprehensive directory. Popular general subject directories include *Yahoo! Directory* <dir.yahoo.com>, *About.com* <www.about.com>, and the *Open Directory Project* <www.dmoz.org>. More academic directories include *Infomine* <infomine.ucr.edu> and the *Library of Congress's Virtual Reference Shelf* <www.loc.gov/rr/askalib/virtualref.html>. Within Google, you can click on Google Scholar to narrow your search to academic articles only.

Subject directories are maintained by editors

- **Search Engines.** Search engines, such as Yahoo <www.yahoo.com> and Google <www.google.com>, scan for Web sites containing key words. Even though search engines yield a lot more information than subject directories, much of it can be irrelevant. Some search engines, however, are more selective than others, and some focus on specialized topics.

Most search engines are maintained by computers, not people

Locating Secondary Sources Using Google

Most people today, from students to professionals, begin their research of secondary sources by doing a Google search. Google, the most popular of the search engines, searches Web pages, government documents, online news sites, and other sources. Google also has a large collection of books and journal articles that it makes available through agreements with publishers or by digitizing works that either are in the public domain or are out of copyright.

Refine your Google searches

It's fine to start with a Google search just to brainstorm ideas and develop approaches to get started. But you quickly will need to narrow down your findings and do some deeper digging. For instance, a search on "electromagnetic radiation" will yield thousands or even millions of results. You should stick with sites from reliable sources such as universities or government research labs.

Locating Secondary Sources Using Wikipedia

Use Wikipedia as a starting point

The first two Web links in many Google searches are to Wikipedia, the popular online encyclopedia. Wikipedia's content is provided and edited by countless people worldwide. Although these pages can provide a good starting point, the content may not be completely accurate. Use a Wikipedia entry to get an overview of the topic, and to help you locate other sources.

The Wikipedia page on electromagnetic radiation contains footnotes to other sources. You can track down these sources at the library or over the Internet. Think of Wikipedia as a place to get your research started, but not as your final destination.

Other Web-Based Secondary Sources

Google and Wikipedia can help you get started with your research. But the more intensively you investigate the sources you find on the Internet, the more you will need to pay attention to what you are finding. Following are the principal categories of information sources on the Internet.

General Commercial, Organizational, and Academic Web Sites. Search engines pull up a wide variety of hits, most of which will be commercial (.com), organizational (.org), and academic (.edu) Web sites. If a commercial site looks relevant to your search, by all means use it, as long as you think critically about the information presented. Does the company's effort to sell you something affect the content? Be careful also of organizational Web sites, which are likely to be well-researched, but may have a particular social or political agenda. Academic Web sites tend to be credible. However, some academics may also have biases, so never stop thinking critically about what you find on the Web.

Government Web Sites. Search engines will also pull up government Web sites, but your best access route is through the United States government's Web portal at <www.usa.gov>. Most government organizations (local, state, and federal) offer online access to research and reports (Figure 7.5). Examples include the Food and Drug Administration's site at <www.fda.gov>, for information on food recalls, clinical drug trials, and countless related items; and the Federal Bureau of Investigation's site at <www.fbi.gov>, for information about fugitives, crime statistics, and much more. State and local sites provide information on auto licenses, state tax laws, and local property issues. From some of these sites you can link to specific government-sponsored research projects.

> **NOTE** *Be sure to check the dates of reports or data you locate on a government Web site, and find out how often the site is updated.*

Online News Outlets and Magazines. Most major news organizations offer online versions of their broadcasts and print publications. Examples include the *New York Times,* the *Wall Street Journal,* CNN, and National Public Radio. Magazines such as *Time, Newsweek,* and *Forbes* also offer Web versions. Some news is available online only, as in the online magazines *Slate* and *Salon.*

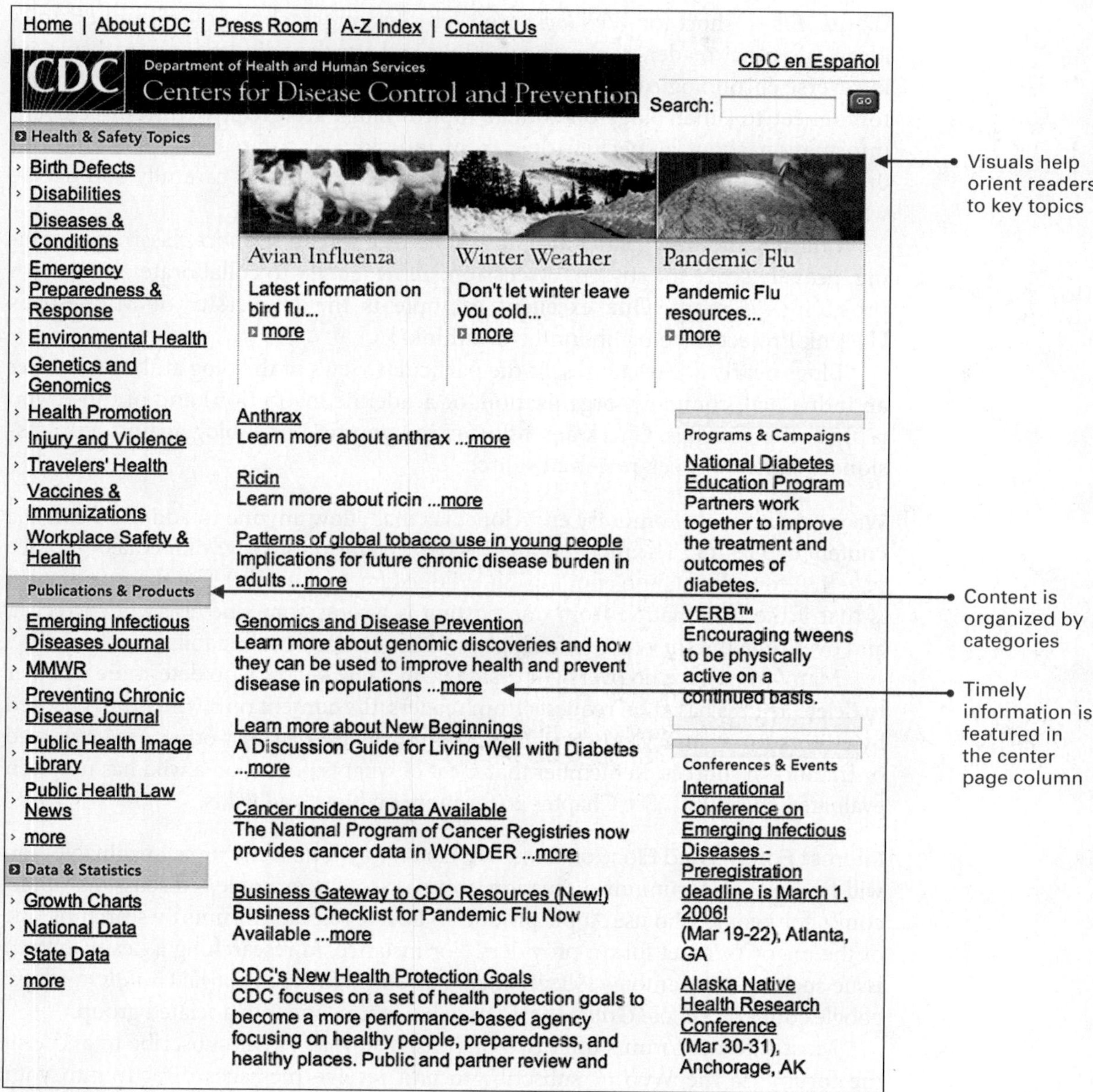

FIGURE 7.5 Centers for Disease Control Home Page The CDC home page provides Health & Safety Topics, disease information, and much more.
Source: Centers for Disease Control and Prevention home page, www.cdc.gov.

NOTE *Make sure you understand how the publication obtains and reviews information. Is it a major news site, such as CNN, or is it a smaller site run by a special-interest group? Each can be useful, but you must evaluate the source. Also keep in mind that many online magazines have a political bias.*

Blogs. *Blogs* (short for *Web logs*) are Web sites on which the blog's author posts ideas, and other readers reply. The postings and attached discussions are displayed in reverse chronological order. Links that the owner has selected also supply ways to connect to other blogs on similar topics. Blogs are great for finding current information about a specific topic from individuals, companies, and nonprofit organizations. Evaluate the information on individual blogs carefully and decide which ones are most relevant and reliable.

Colleges and universities also host blogs as a way to support classroom teaching, provide space for student discussion, allow faculty to collaborate on research projects, and more. One excellent example is the University of Minnesota's UThink Project at <blog.lib.umn.edu/uthink/>.

Blogs nearly always represent the particular views of the blog author (whether an individual, company, organization, or academic institution) and of those who reply to the postings. Check any information you find on a blog against a professionally edited or peer-reviewed source.

Wikis. *Wikis* are community encyclopedias that allow anyone to add to or edit the content of a listing. The most popular wiki is *Wikipedia* <www.wikipedia.org>. (See page 132 for information about using Wikipedia for research.) The theory of a wiki is that if the information from one posting is wrong, someone else will correct it, and over time the site will reach a high level of accuracy and reliability.

Many wikis have no oversight. Aside from a few people who determine whether to delete articles based on requests from readers, the content on a wiki is not checked by editors for accuracy. Always check the information against other peer-reviewed or traditional sources. Remember that most of what is posted on a wiki has not been evaluated objectively. See Chapter 26 for more on blogs and wikis.

Internet Forums and Electronic Mailing Lists. For almost any topic imaginable, you will find a Web forum, or discussion group. (See, for example, <discussions.apple.com>, for people who use Apple products.) Locate relevant forums by searching one of the major Internet forum providers. For instance, in researching a health-related issue such as stress among college students, you might visit *Google Groups* <groups.google.com> or *Yahoo! Groups* <groups.yahoo.com> and join a related group.

Most Internet forums offer two options: You may either subscribe to and visit the forum via the Web or subscribe to and receive messages directly into your email in-box. (Electronic mailing lists, or e-lists, are essentially the same as Internet forums.) Messages may be sent to the entire group or to individual participants.

Material from these sources may be insightful but biased. Visit a variety of forums and/or subscribe to multiple e-lists to get a broad perspective on the issue. Some information posted on forums or sent to e-list subscribers is not moderated (approved by a reviewer prior to being posted). Unmoderated material is usually less reliable.

E-Libraries. Entirely searchable via the Internet, e-libraries are excellent research tools. Aside from the online sites sponsored by public libraries, the most notable and reliable e-library is the Internet Public Library at <www.ipl.org>. E-libraries include links to online books, magazines, newspapers, periodical databases, and other resources including "live" librarians.

Although e-libraries can be efficient stand-ins for traditional, physical libraries, they can never replace such libraries. Resources available in electronic form will not include current books under copyright or a wide range of magazine and news articles and other publications. Supplement what you discover at an e-library with hard-copy materials from a traditional library.

Periodical Databases. Virtually all libraries have their own Web site where a library cardholder or student can access periodical databases. These are electronic collections of articles from newspapers, magazines, journals, and other publications. You can search by title, author, keyword, and so on.

Some of the most popular general periodical databases include *InfoTrac, NewsBank, ProQuest,* and *EBSCOHost.* Your library may also subscribe to specialized databases in a variety of subject areas.

Before initiating a periodical database search, meet with your reference librarian for a tour of the various databases and instructions for searching effectively. Also be aware that some databases may not be accessible from school or home—you may need to visit your library in person.

GUIDELINES for Researching on the Internet

- **Expect limited results from any one search engine or subject directory.** No single search engine can index more than a fraction of the material available on the Web. No subject directory will list the same Web sites as another.
- **When using a search engine, select keywords or search phrases that are varied and technical rather than general.** Some search terms generate more useful hits than others. In addition to "electromagnetic radiation," for example, try "electromagnetic fields," "power lines and health," or "electrical fields." Specialized terms (say, "vertigo" versus "dizziness") offer the best access to reliable sites. However, if you are not able to locate much by using a specialized term, widen your search somewhat.
- **When using Wikipedia or other online encyclopedias, check out the footnotes and other citations.** These references can direct you to other sources, such as government documents, books in the library, or published journal articles.

GUIDELINES *continued*

- **Consider the domain type (where the site originates).** Standard domain types in the United States include .com (commercial organization), .edu (educational institution), .gov or .mil (government or military organization), .net (general usage), and .org (nonprofit organization).
- **Identify the site's purpose and sponsor.** Is the intent merely to relay information, to sell something, or to promote an ideology or agenda? The domain type might alert you to bias or a hidden agenda. A .com site might provide accurate information but also some type of sales pitch. An .org site might reflect a political or ideological bias. Looking for a site's sponsor can also help you evaluate its postings. For example, a Web site about the dangers of bioengineered foods that is sponsored by an advocacy organization may be biased. Figure 8.2 (page 155) shows a Web site that advocates a particular perspective.
- **Look beyond the style of a site.** Sometimes the most reliable material resides in less attractive, text-only sites. The fact that a Web site may look professional doesn't always mean that its content is reliable.
- **Assess the currency of the site's materials.** When was the material created, posted, and updated? Many sites have not been updated in months or years.
- **Assess the author's credentials and assertions.** Check the author's reputation, expertise, and institutional affiliation (university, company, environmental group). Do not confuse the *author* (the person who wrote the material) with the *Webmaster* (the person who created and maintains the site). Follow links to other sites that mention the author. Where, on the spectrum of expert opinion and accepted theory, does this author fall? Is each assertion supported by solid evidence? Verify any extreme claim through other sources, such as a professor or expert in the field. Consider whether your own biases might predispose you to accept certain ideas.
- **Use bookmarks and hotlists for quick access to favorite Web sites.** It is always frustrating when you can't find a helpful Web site that you accessed earlier but didn't bookmark.
- **Save or print what you need before it changes or disappears.** Web sites often change their content or "go dead." Always record the Web address and your access date.
- **Download only what you need; use it ethically; obtain permission; and credit your sources.** Unless they are crucial to your research, omit graphics, sound, and video files. Do not use material created by others in a way that harms the material's creator. For any type of commercial use of material from the Web, obtain written permission from the material's owner and credit the source exactly as directed by its owner. For more information on copyright, see pages 148–50.

Traditional Secondary Sources

As noted earlier, traditional secondary research tools are still of great value. Most hard-copy secondary sources are carefully reviewed and edited before they are published. Every day, more and more hard-copy material is being digitized. See Google books <books.google.com> as well as the Internet Archive <archive.org>. Yet only a fraction of print sources are available on the Internet. It is still important to use hard-copy sources for research.

Locate hard-copy sources by using your library's online public access catalog (OPAC). This catalog can be accessed through the Internet or at terminals in the library. You can search a library's holdings by subject, author, title, or keyword. Visit the library's Web site, or ask a librarian for help. To search catalogs from libraries worldwide, go to the *Library of Congress Gateway* at <www.loc.gov/z3950> or *LibrarySpot* at <www.libraryspot.com>.

Locate hard-copy secondary sources using your library's OPAC

Following are the principal categories of hard-copy sources found at libraries, as well as one type of source material (gray literature) that you will need to track down on your own.

Books and Periodicals. The larger or more specialized the library you visit, the more likely you are to find books by specialist publishers and periodicals that delve into more specific subject areas. When consulting books and periodicals, always check the copyright date and supplement the source with additional information from more recent sources, if necessary.

Reference Works. Reference works are general information sources that provide background and can lead to more specific information.

- **Bibliographies.** Bibliographies are lists of books and/or articles categorized by subject. To locate bibliographies in your field, begin by consulting the *Bibliographic Index Plus,* a list (by subject) of major bibliographies, which indexes over 500,000 bibliographies worldwide. You can also consult such general bibliographies as *Books in Print* or the *Readers' Guide to Periodical Literature.* Or, examine subject area bibliographies, such as *Bibliography of World War II History,* or highly focused bibliographies, such as *Health Hazards of Video Display Terminals: An Annotated Bibliography.*
- **Indexes.** Book and article bibliographies may also be referred to as "indexes." Yet there are other types of indexes that collect information not likely found in standard bibliographies. Examples include the *Index to Scientific and Technical Proceedings,* which indexes conference proceedings in the sciences and engineering. While limited versions of some of these indexes may be available for

free on the Internet, most are only available via a library subscription. Other indexes that may be useful for your research include the following:

- *Newspaper indexes.* Most major newspapers, such as the *New York Times,* have an index covering almost the entire span of the paper's publication.
- *Periodical indexes.* These indexes list articles from magazines and journals. The most commonly known periodical index is the *Readers' Guide to Periodical Literature.*
- *Citation indexes.* Using a citation index, you can track down the publications in which original material has been cited, quoted, or verified.
- *Technical report indexes.* These indexes allow you to look for government and private sector reports. One example would be the *Scientific and Technical Aerospace Reports* index.
- *Patent indexes.* Patents are issued to protect rights to new inventions, products, or processes. You can search for patents by using the *Index of Patents Issued from the United States Patent and Trademark Office* or other similar indexes that cover both U.S. and international patents.

- **Encyclopedias.** Encyclopedias are alphabetically arranged collections of articles. You may want to start by consulting a general encyclopedia, such as *Encyclopedia Britannica* or the *Columbia Encyclopedia,* but then examine more subject-focused encyclopedias, such as *Encyclopedia of Nutritional Supplements, Encyclopedia of Business and Finance,* or *Illustrated Encyclopedia of Aircraft.*
- **Dictionaries.** Dictionaries are alphabetically arranged lists of words, including definitions, pronunciations, and word origins. If you can't locate a particular word in a general dictionary (e.g., a highly specialized term or jargon specific to a certain field), consult a specialized dictionary, such as *Dictionary of Engineering and Technology, Dictionary of Psychology,* or *Dictionary of Media and Communication Studies.*
- **Handbooks.** Handbooks offer condensed facts (formulas, tables, advice, examples) about particular fields. Examples include the *Civil Engineering Handbook* and *The McGraw-Hill Computer Handbook.*
- **Almanacs.** Almanacs are collections of factual and statistical data, usually arranged by subject area and published annually. Examples include general almanacs, such as the *World Almanac and Book of Facts,* or subject-specific almanacs, such as the *Almanac for Computers* or *Baer's Agricultural Almanac.*
- **Directories.** Directories provide updated information about organizations, companies, people, products, services, or careers, often listing addresses and phone numbers. Examples include *The Career Guide: Dun's Employment*

Opportunities Directory and the *Directory of American Firms Operating in Foreign Countries.* For electronic versions, ask your librarian about *Hoover's Company Capsules* (for basic information on thousands of companies) and *Hoover's Company Profiles* (for detailed information).

- **Abstracts.** Abstracts are collected summaries of books and/or articles. Reading abstracts can help you decide whether to read or skip an article and can save you from having to track down a journal you may not need. Abstracts usually are titled by discipline: *Biological Abstracts, Computer Abstracts,* and so on. For some current research, you might consult abstracts of doctoral dissertations in *Dissertation Abstracts International.*

Although the reference works mentioned here are available mainly as print documents, some are available on the Internet. Go to the Internet Public Library at <www.ipl.org> for links to many online reference works. When using a reference work, check the copyright date to make sure you are accessing the most current information available.

Access Tools for Government Publications. The federal government publishes maps, periodicals, books, pamphlets, manuals, research reports, and other information. An example would be the *Journal of Research of the National Bureau of Standards.* These publications may be available in digital as well as hard-copy formats. To help you find what you are looking for, you will need to use an access tool such as the following. (A librarian can teach you to use these tools.)

- The *Monthly Catalog of the United States Government* is the major pathway to government publications and reports.
- The *Government Reports Announcements and Index* is a listing (with summaries) of more than one million federally sponsored published research reports and patents issued since 1964.
- The *Statistical Abstract of the United States,* updated yearly, offers statistics on population, health, employment, and many other areas. It can be accessed via the Web. CD-ROM versions are now available.

Gray Literature. Some useful printed information may be unavailable at any library. This is known as "gray literature," or materials that are unpublished or not typically catalogued. Examples include pamphlets published by organizations or companies (such as medical pamphlets or company marketing materials), unpublished government documents (available under the Freedom of Information Act), dissertations by graduate students, papers presented at professional conferences, or self-published works.

The only way to track down gray literature is to contact those who produce such literature and request anything available in your subject area. For instance, you could contact a professional organization and request any papers on your topic that were delivered at their recent annual conference, or contact a government agency for statistics relevant to your topic. Before doing so, be knowledgeable about your topic and know specifically whom to contact. Don't make vague, general requests.

Keep in mind that gray literature, like much material found on the Web, is often not carefully scrutinized for content by editors. Therefore, it may be unreliable and should be backed up by information from other sources.

EXPLORING PRIMARY SOURCES

Types of primary sources

Once you have explored your research topic in depth by finding out what others have uncovered, supplement that knowledge with information you discover yourself by doing primary research. Primary sources include unsolicited inquiries, informational interviews, surveys, and observations or experiments.

Unsolicited Inquiries

Unsolicited inquiries uncover basic but important information

The most basic form of primary research is a simple, unsolicited inquiry. Letters, phone calls, or email inquiries to experts listed in Web pages or to people you identify in other ways can clarify or supplement information you already have. Try to contact the right individual instead of a company or department. Also, ask specific questions that cannot be answered elsewhere. Be sure what you ask about is not confidential or otherwise sensitive information.

Unsolicited inquiries, especially by phone or email, can be intrusive or even offensive. Therefore, limit yourself to a few questions that don't require extensive research or thought on the part of the person you contact.

Informational Interviews

Informational interviews can lead to original, unpublished material

An excellent primary source of information is the informational interview. Much of what an expert knows may never be published. Therefore, you can uncover highly original information by spending time with your respondent and asking pertinent questions. In addition, an interviewee might refer you to other experts or sources of information.

Expert opinion is not always reliable

Of course, an expert's opinion can be just as mistaken or biased as anyone else's. Like patients who seek second opinions about medical conditions, researchers must seek a balanced range of expert opinions about complex problems or controversial issues. In researching the effects of electromagnetic fields (EMFs), for example, you would seek opinions not only from a company engineer and environmentalist, but also from presumably more objective third parties such as a professor or journalist who has studied the issue. Figure 7.6 provides a partial text of an interview about persuasive challenges faced by a corporation's manager.

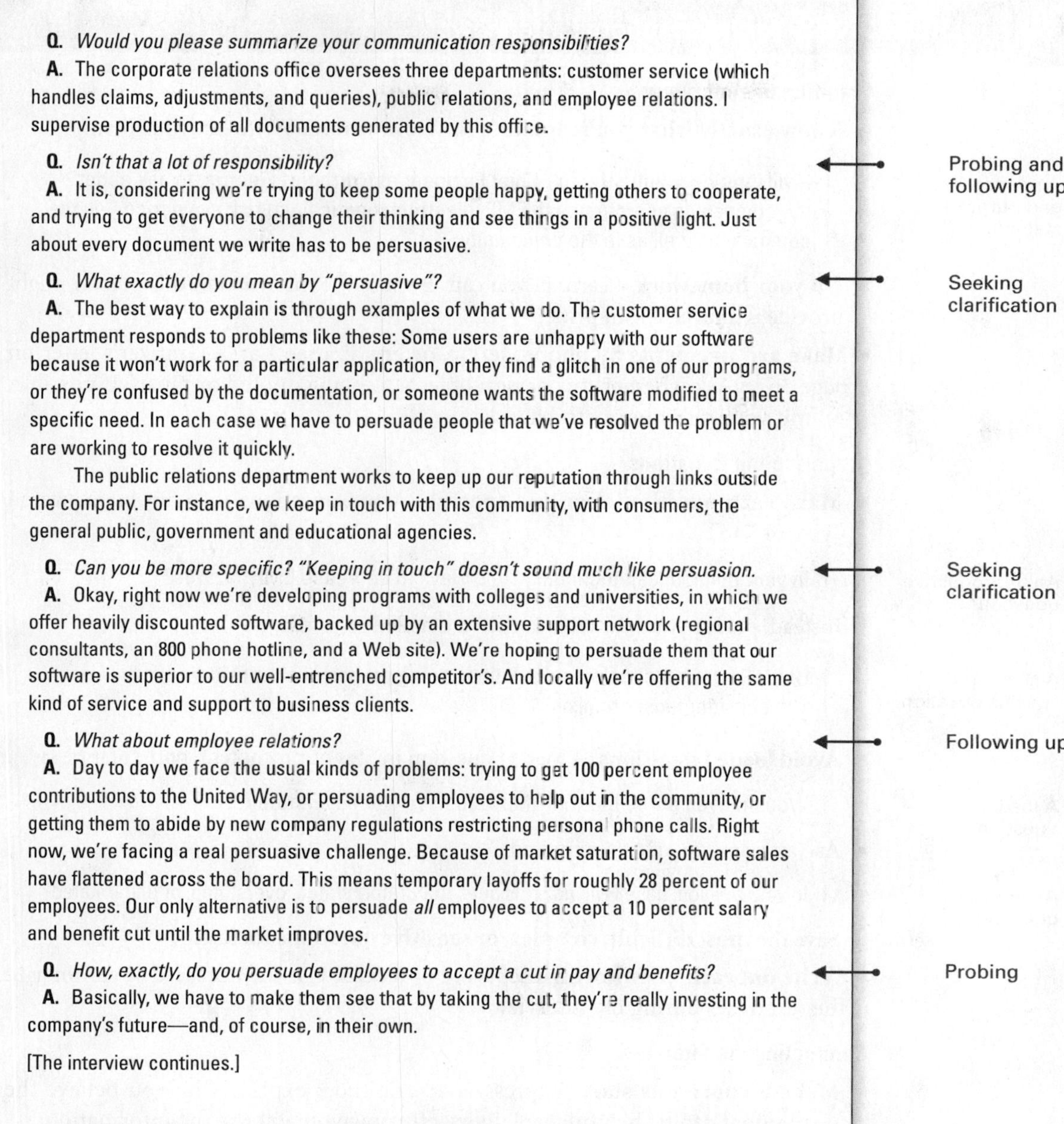

Q. *Would you please summarize your communication responsibilities?*

A. The corporate relations office oversees three departments: customer service (which handles claims, adjustments, and queries), public relations, and employee relations. I supervise production of all documents generated by this office.

Q. *Isn't that a lot of responsibility?*

A. It is, considering we're trying to keep some people happy, getting others to cooperate, and trying to get everyone to change their thinking and see things in a positive light. Just about every document we write has to be persuasive.

Q. *What exactly do you mean by "persuasive"?*

A. The best way to explain is through examples of what we do. The customer service department responds to problems like these: Some users are unhappy with our software because it won't work for a particular application, or they find a glitch in one of our programs, or they're confused by the documentation, or someone wants the software modified to meet a specific need. In each case we have to persuade people that we've resolved the problem or are working to resolve it quickly.

The public relations department works to keep up our reputation through links outside the company. For instance, we keep in touch with this community, with consumers, the general public, government and educational agencies.

Q. *Can you be more specific? "Keeping in touch" doesn't sound much like persuasion.*

A. Okay, right now we're developing programs with colleges and universities, in which we offer heavily discounted software, backed up by an extensive support network (regional consultants, an 800 phone hotline, and a Web site). We're hoping to persuade them that our software is superior to our well-entrenched competitor's. And locally we're offering the same kind of service and support to business clients.

Q. *What about employee relations?*

A. Day to day we face the usual kinds of problems: trying to get 100 percent employee contributions to the United Way, or persuading employees to help out in the community, or getting them to abide by new company regulations restricting personal phone calls. Right now, we're facing a real persuasive challenge. Because of market saturation, software sales have flattened across the board. This means temporary layoffs for roughly 28 percent of our employees. Our only alternative is to persuade *all* employees to accept a 10 percent salary and benefit cut until the market improves.

Q. *How, exactly, do you persuade employees to accept a cut in pay and benefits?*

A. Basically, we have to make them see that by taking the cut, they're really investing in the company's future—and, of course, in their own.

[The interview continues.]

FIGURE 7.6 Partial Text of an Informational Interview This page from an informational interview shows you how to use clear, specific questions and how to follow up and seek clarification to answers.

GUIDELINES for Informational Interviews

Planning the Interview

▶ **Know exactly what you're looking for from whom.** Write out your plan.

Audience and purpose statement

> I will interview Anne Hector, Chief Engineer at Northport Electric, to ask about the company's approaches to EMF (electromagnetic field) risk avoidance—in the company as well as in the community.

▶ **Do your homework.** Learn all you can. Be sure the information this person might provide is unavailable in print.

▶ **Make arrangements by phone, letter, or email.** (See Karen Granger's letter on page 367.) Ask whether this person objects to being quoted or taped. If possible, submit your questions beforehand.

Preparing the Questions

▶ **Make each question clear and specific.** Avoid questions that can be answered "yes" or "no":

An unproductive question

> In your opinion, can technology find ways to decrease EMF hazards?

Instead, phrase your question to elicit a detailed response:

A clear and specific question

> Of the various technological solutions being proposed or considered, which do you consider most promising?

▶ **Avoid loaded questions.** A loaded question invites or promotes a particular bias:

A loaded question

> Wouldn't you agree that EMF hazards have been overstated?

▶ Ask an impartial question instead:

An impartial question

> In your opinion, have EMF hazards been accurately stated, overstated, or understated?

▶ **Save the most difficult, complex, or sensitive questions for last.**

▶ **Write out each question on a separate notecard.** Use the notecard to summarize the responses during the interview.

Conducting the Interview

▶ **Make a courteous start.** Express your gratitude; explain why you believe the respondent can be helpful; explain exactly how you will use the information.

▶ **Respect cultural differences.** Consider the level of formality, politeness, directness, and other behaviors appropriate in the given culture. (See Chapters 3 and 5.)

▶ **Let the respondent do most of the talking.**

▶ **Be a good listener.** For listening advice, see pages 91–92.

- **Stick to your interview plan.** If the conversation wanders, politely nudge it back on track (unless the peripheral information is useful).
- **Ask for clarification if needed.** Keep asking until you understand.

  - —Could you go over that again?
  - —What did you mean by [*word*]?

  Clarifying questions

- **Repeat major points in your own words and ask if your interpretation is correct.** But do not put words into the respondent's mouth.
- **Be ready with follow-up questions.**

  - —Why is it like that?
  - —Could you say something more about that?
  - —What more needs to be done?

  Follow-up questions

- **Keep note taking to a minimum.** Record statistics, dates, names, and other precise data, but don't record every word. Jot key terms or phrases that can refresh your memory later.

Concluding the Interview

- **Ask for closing comments.** Perhaps these can point to additional information.

  - —Would you care to add anything?
  - —Is there anyone else I should talk to?
  - —Can you suggest other sources that might help me better understand this issue?

  Concluding questions

- **Request permission to contact your respondent again, if new questions arise.**
- **Invite the respondent to review your version for accuracy.** If the interview is to be published, ask for the respondent's approval of your final draft. Offer to provide copies of any document in which this information appears.
- **Thank your respondent and leave promptly.**
- **As soon as possible, write a complete summary (or record one verbally).**

Surveys

Surveys help you form impressions of the concerns, preferences, attitudes, beliefs, or perceptions of a large, identifiable group (a *target population*) by studying representatives of that group (a *sample*). While interviews allow for greater clarity and depth, surveys offer an inexpensive way to get the viewpoints of a large group. Respondents can answer privately and anonymously—and often more candidly than in an interview.

Surveys provide multiple, fresh viewpoints on a topic

The tool for conducting surveys is the questionnaire. See Figures 7.7 and 7.8 for a sample questionnaire cover letter and questionnaire.

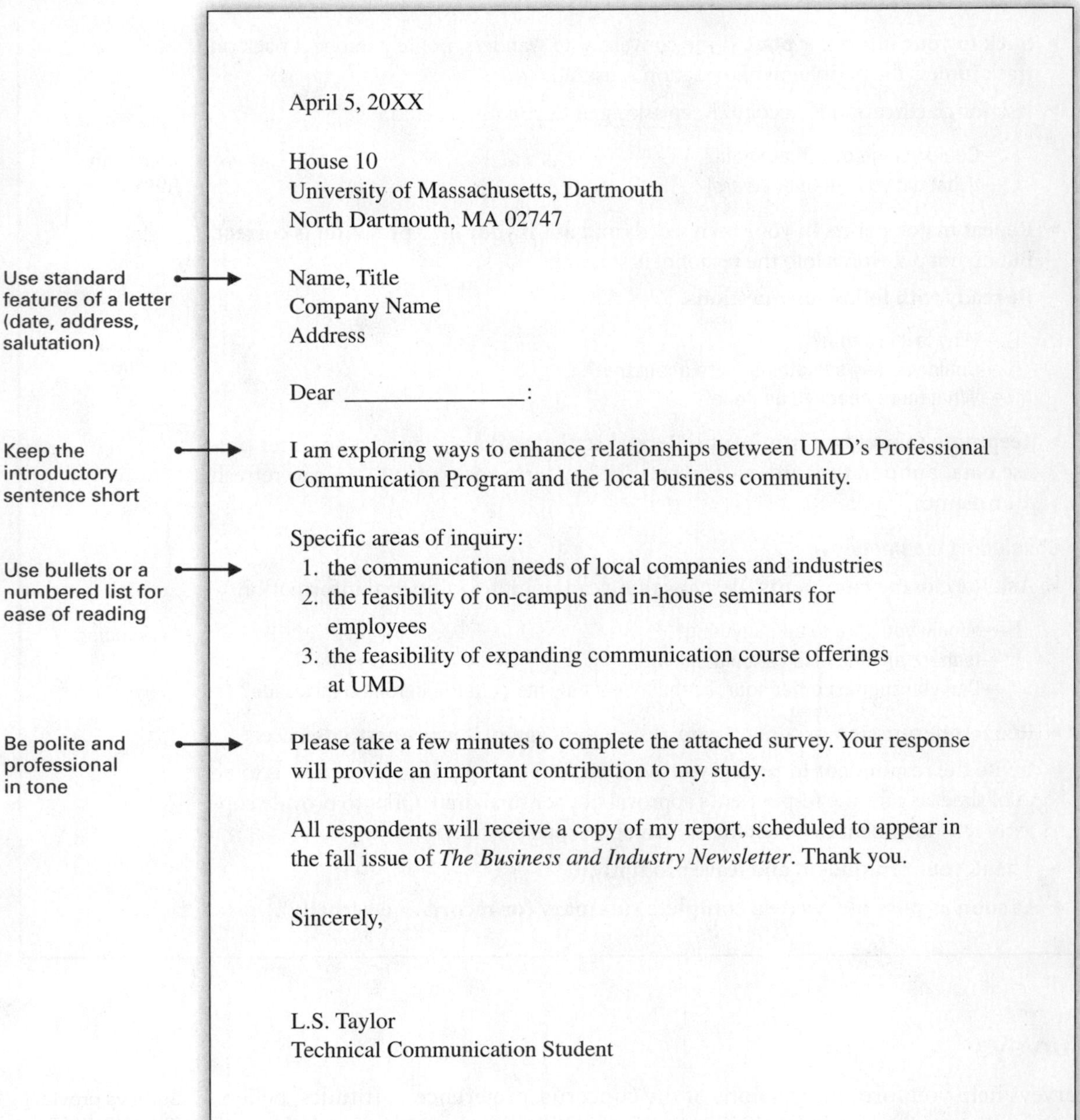
Use standard features of a letter (date, address, salutation)
Keep the introductory sentence short
Use bullets or a numbered list for ease of reading
Be polite and professional in tone

April 5, 20XX

House 10
University of Massachusetts, Dartmouth
North Dartmouth, MA 02747

Name, Title
Company Name
Address

Dear _______________:

I am exploring ways to enhance relationships between UMD's Professional Communication Program and the local business community.

Specific areas of inquiry:

1. the communication needs of local companies and industries
2. the feasibility of on-campus and in-house seminars for employees
3. the feasibility of expanding communication course offerings at UMD

Please take a few minutes to complete the attached survey. Your response will provide an important contribution to my study.

All respondents will receive a copy of my report, scheduled to appear in the fall issue of *The Business and Industry Newsletter*. Thank you.

Sincerely,

L.S. Taylor
Technical Communication Student

FIGURE 7.7 A Questionnaire Cover Letter Use a cover letter when you send out a questionnaire. If the questionnaire will be sent electronically, you can use email to write and send the cover letter.

Communication Questionnaire

1. Describe your type of company (e.g., manufacturing, high tech) ______________________

2. Number of employees (Please check one.)

_____ 0–4 _____ 26–50 _____ 101–150 _____ 301–450
_____ 5–25 _____ 51–100 _____ 151–300 _____ 451+

3. What types of written communication occur in your company? (Label by frequency: daily, weekly, monthly, never.)

_____ memos _____ letters _____ advertising
_____ manuals _____ reports _____ newsletters
_____ procedures _____ proposals _____ other (Specify.)
_____ email _____ catalogs ______________________

4. Who does most of the writing? (Pls. give titles.) ______________________

5. Please characterize your employees' writing effectiveness.

_____ good _____ fair _____ poor

6. Does your company have formal guidelines for writing?

_____ no _____ yes (Pls. describe briefly.) ______________________

7. Do you offer in-house communication training?

_____ no _____ yes (Pls. describe briefly.)

8. Please rank the usefulness of the following areas in communication training (from 1–10, 1 being most important).

_____ organizing information _____ audience awareness
_____ summarizing information _____ persuasive writing
_____ editing for style _____ grammar
_____ document design _____ researching
_____ email etiquette _____ Web page design
_____ other (Pls. specify.) ______________________

9. Please rank these skills in order of importance (from 1–6, 1 being most important).

_____ reading _____ listening _____ speaking to groups
_____ writing _____ collaborating _____ speaking face-to-face

10. Do you provide tuition reimbursement for employees?

_____ no _____ yes

11. Would you consider having UMD communication interns work for you part-time?

_____ no _____ yes

12. Should UMD offer Saturday seminars in communication?

_____ no _____ yes

Additional comments/suggestions: ______________________

____

Open-ended question (allows people to respond as they choose)

Closed-ended question (provides a limited choice of responses)

Questions and sentences are short and to the point

Page layout is clean and easy to read

FIGURE 7.8 **A Questionnaire** A questionnaire will help you gather answers to specific questions and topics.

GUIDELINES for Surveys

- **Define the survey's purpose and target population.** Ask yourself, "Why is this survey being performed?" "What, exactly, is it measuring?" "How much background research do I need?" "How will the survey findings be used?" and "Who is the exact population being studied?"
- **Identify the sample group.** Determine how many respondents you need. Generally, the larger the sample surveyed the more dependable the results (assuming a well-chosen and representative sample). Also determine how the sample will be chosen. Will they be randomly chosen? In the statistical sense, *random* does not mean "haphazard": A random sample means that each member of the target population stands an equal chance of being in the sample group.
- **Define the survey method.** How will the survey be administered—by phone, by mail, or online? Each method has benefits and drawbacks: Phone surveys yield fast results and high response rates; however, they take longer than written surveys. Also, many people find them annoying and tend to be less candid when responding in person. Mail surveys promote candid responses, but many people won't bother returning the survey, and results can arrive slowly. Surveys via the Web or email yield quick results, but computer connections can fail, and (with Web surveys) you have less control over how often the same person responds.
- **Decide on types of questions.** Questions can be *open-* or *closed-ended.* Open-ended questions allow respondents to answer in any way they choose. Measuring the data gathered from such questions is more time-consuming, but they do provide a rich source of information. An open-ended question is worded like this:

Open-ended question

> How much do you know about electromagnetic radiation at our school?

Closed-ended questions give people a limited number of choices, and the data gathered are easier to measure. Here are some types of closed-ended questions:

Closed-ended questions

> Are you interested in joining a group of concerned parents?
>
> YES ____ NO ______

> Rate your degree of concern about EMFs at our school.
>
> HIGH_____ MODERATE_____ LOW_____ NO CONCERN _____

> Circle the number that indicates your view about the town's proposal to spend $20,000 to hire its own EMF consultant.
>
> 1 . . . . 2 . . . . 3 . . . . 4 . . . . 5 . . . . 6 7
>
> Strongly Disapprove   No Opinion   Strongly Approve

> How often do you . . . ?
>
> ALWAYS_____ OFTEN _____ SOMETIMES _____ RARELY _____ NEVER_____

To measure exactly where people stand on an issue, choose closed-ended questions.

▸ **Develop an engaging introduction and provide appropriate information.** Persuade respondents that the questionnaire relates to their concerns, that their answers matter, and that their anonymity is ensured:

> Your answers will help our school board to speak accurately for your views at our next town meeting. All answers will be kept confidential. Thank you.

A survey introduction

Researchers often include a cover letter with the questionnaire, as in Figure 7.7.

Begin with the easiest questions, usually the closed-ended ones. Respondents who commit to these are likely to answer later, more difficult questions.

▸ **Make each question unambiguous.** All respondents should be able to interpret identical questions identically. An ambiguous question allows for misinterpretation:

> Do you favor weapons for campus police? YES______ NO______

An ambiguous question

"Weapons" might mean tear gas, clubs, handguns, tasers, or some combination of these. The limited "yes/no" format reduces an array of possible opinions to an either/or choice. Here is an unambiguous version:

> ______ **Do you favor** (check all that apply):
> ______ Having campus police carry mace and a club?
> ______ Having campus police carry nonlethal "stun guns"?
> ______ Having campus police store handguns in their cruisers?
> ______ Having campus police carry handguns?
> ______ Having campus police carry large-caliber handguns?
> ______ Having campus police carry no weapons?
> ______ Don't know

A clear and incisive question

To account for all possible responses, include options such as "Other," "Don't know," or an "Additional Comments" section.

▸ **Avoid biased questions:**

> Should our campus tolerate the needless endangerment of innocent students by lethal weapons? YES______ NO______

A loaded question

Avoid emotionally loaded and judgmental words ("endangerment," "innocent," "needless"), which can influence a person's response (Hayakawa 40).

▸ **Make it brief, simple, and inviting.** Long questionnaires usually get few replies. And people who do reply tend to give less thought to their answers. Limit the number and types of questions. Include a stamped, return-addressed envelope, and stipulate a return date.

▸ **Have an expert review your questionnaire before use, whenever possible.**

Observations and Experiments

Observations and experiments offer proof to back up assumptions about a topic

Observations or experiments should be your final step, because you now know exactly what to look for.

When you make observations, have a plan in place. Know how, where, and when to look, and jot down or record your observations immediately. You might even take photos or draw sketches of what you observe.

Experiments are controlled forms of observations designed to verify assumptions (e.g., the role of fish oil in preventing heart disease) or to test something untried (e.g., the relationship between background music and productivity). Each field has its own guidelines for conducting experiments (e.g., you must use certain equipment, scrutinize your results in a certain way); follow those guidelines to the letter when conducting your own experiments.

Remember that observations and experiments are not foolproof. During observation or experimentation, you may be biased about what you see (focusing on the wrong events, ignoring something important). In addition, if you are observing people or experimenting with human subjects, they may be conscious of being observed and may alter their normal behaviors.

CONSIDER THIS: Frequently Asked Questions about Copyright

Research often involves working with copyrighted materials. Copyright laws have an ethical purpose: to balance the reward for intellectual labors with the public's right to use information freely.

1. *What is a copyright?*

   A copyright is the exclusive legal right to reproduce, publish, and sell a literary, dramatic, musical, or artistic work that is fixed in a tangible medium (digital or print). Written permission must be obtained to use all copyrighted material except where fair use applies or in cases where the copyright holder has stated other terms of use. For example, a musician might use a Creative Commons "attribution" license as part of a song released on the Internet. This license allows others to copy, display, and perform the work without permission, but only if credit is given. For more about Creative Commons and types of licenses, see <creativecommons.org/licenses>.

2. *What are the limits of copyright protection?*

   Copyright protection covers the exact wording of the original, but not the ideas or information it conveys. For example, Einstein's theory of relativity has no protection but his exact wording does (Abelman 33; Elias 3). Also, paraphrasing Einstein's ideas but failing to cite him as the source would constitute plagiarism.

3. *How long does copyright protection last?*

   Works published before January 1, 1978 are protected for 95 years. Works published on or after January 1, 1978 are copyrighted for the author's life plus 70 years.

4. *Must a copyright be officially registered in order to protect a work?*

   No. Protection begins as soon as a work is created.

5. *Must a work be published in order to receive copyright protection?*

   No.

6. *What is "fair use"?*

   "Fair use" is the legal and limited use of copyrighted material without permission. The source should, of course, be acknowleged. Fair use does not ordinarily apply to case studies, charts and graphs, author's notes, or private letters ("Copyright Protection" 30).

7. *How is fair use determined?*

   In determining fair use, the courts ask these questions:

   - *Is the material being used for commercial or for nonprofit purposes?* For example, nonprofit educational use is viewed more favorably than for-profit use.
   - *Is the copyrighted work published or unpublished?* Use of published work is viewed more favorably than use of unpublished essays, correspondence, and so on.
   - *How much, and which part, of the original work is being used?* The smaller the part, the more favorably its use will be viewed. Never considered fair, however, is the use of a part that "forms the core, distinguishable, creative effort of the work being cited" (*Author's Guide* 30).
   - *How will the economic value of the original work be affected?* Any use that reduces the potential market value of the original will be viewed unfavorably.

8. *What is the exact difference between copyright infringement and fair use?*

   Although using ideas from an original work is considered fair, a paraphrase that incorporates too much of the original expression can be infringement—even when the source is cited (Abelman 41). Reproduction of a government document that includes material previously protected by copyright (graphs, images, company logos, slogans) is considered infringement. The United States Copyright Office offers this caution:

   > There is no specific number of words, lines, or notes that may safely be taken without permission.
   >
   > Acknowledging the source of the copyrighted material does not substitute for obtaining permission. ("Fair Use" 1–2)

   When in doubt, obtain written permission.

9. *What is material in the "public domain"?*

   "Public domain" refers to material not protected by copyright or material on which copyright has expired. Works published in the United States 95 years before the current year are in the public domain. Most government publications and commonplace information, such as height and weight charts or a metric conversion table, are in the public domain. These works might contain copyrighted material (used

CONSIDER THIS (*continued*)

with permission and properly acknowledged). If you are not sure whether an item is in the public domain, request permission ("Copyright Protection" 31).

10. *What about international copyright?*

Copyright protection varies among individual countries, and some countries offer little or no protection for foreign works:

> There is no such thing as an "international copyright" that will automatically protect an author's writings throughout the world. ("International Copyright" 1–2)
>
> In the United States all foreign works that meet certain requirements are protected by copyright (Abelman 36).

11. *Who owns the copyright to a work prepared as part of one's employment?*

A work prepared in the service of one's employer or under written contract for a client is a "work made for hire." The employer or client is legally considered the author and therefore holds the copyright (Abelman 33–34). For example, a manual researched, designed, and written as part of one's employment would be a work made for hire.

For latest developments, visit the United States Copyright Office <www.copyright.gov>.

Projects

GENERAL

Begin researching for the analytical report (Chapter 22) due at semester's end.

Phase One: Preliminary Steps

a. Choose a topic that affects you, your workplace, or your community directly.

b. Develop a tree chart (page 127) to help you ask the right questions.

c. Complete an audience and use profile (page 31).

d. Narrow your topic, checking with your instructor for approval and advice.

e. Make a working bibliography to ensure sufficient primary and secondary sources.

f. List what you already know about your topic.

g. Write an audience and purpose statement (page 19) and submit it in a research proposal (page 559).

h. Make a working outline.

Phase Two: Collecting, Evaluating, and Interpreting Data (Read Chapters 8–9 in preparation for this phase.)

a. In your research, begin with general works for an overview, and then consult more specific sources.

b. Skim the sources, looking for high points.

c. Take notes selectively (page 644), summarize (page 173), and record each source.

d. Plan and administer questionnaires, interviews, and inquiries.

e. Try to conclude your research with direct observation.

f. Evaluate each finding for accuracy, reliability, fairness, and completeness.

g. Decide what your findings mean.

h. Use the checklist on page 171 to reassess your methods, interpretation, and reasoning.

Phase Three: Organizing Your Data and Writing the Report

a. Revise your working outline as needed.

b. Document each source of information (page 648).

c. Write your final draft according to the checklist on page 171.

d. Proofread carefully. Add front and end matter supplements (Chapter 22).

Due Dates: To Be Assigned by Your Instructor

List of possible topics due:

Final topic due:

Proposal memo due:

Working bibliography and working outline due:

Notecards (or note files) due:

Copies of questionnaires, interview questions, and inquiry letters due:

Revised outline due:

First draft of report due:

Final version with supplements and full documentation due:

TEAM

Divide into groups according to majors. Assume that several employers in your field are holding a job fair on campus next month and will be interviewing entry-level candidates. Each member of your group is assigned to develop a profile of *one* of these companies or organizations by researching its history, record of mergers and stock value, management style, financial condition, price/earnings ratio of its stock, growth prospects, products and services, multinational affiliations, ethical record, environmental record, employee relations, pension plan, employee stock options or profit-sharing plans, commitment to affirmative action, number of women and minorities in upper management, or any other features important to a prospective employee. The entire group will then edit each profile and assemble them in one single document to be used as a reference for students in your major.

DIGITAL AND SOCIAL MEDIA

Using Wikipedia as a starting point, research a topic for this class or another class. Select a topic that is "big" (for example, global warming). Use the footnotes in the Wikipedia article to help you narrow your focus. (For instance, you might discover a footnote to an article about global warming and biodiversity.) Use your college library or the Internet, or both, to locate the articles, reports, and other publications cited in these footnotes. Write a short report (3–4 pages) describing your research process.

GLOBAL

Using the Guidelines for Informational Interviews on pages 142–43, write an email to an interviewee who speaks fluent English but comes from another country. How might you approach the request for an interview differently? In addition to research about your topic and your respondent's background prior to the interview, what other research might you do? How might you compose your interview questions with your interviewee's nationality and/or culture in mind? (For more on global considerations, see Chapters 3 and 5.) Compare approaches in class.

8 Evaluating and Interpreting Information

"Our clients make investment decisions based on feasibility and strategy for marketing new products. Our job is to research consumer interest in these potential products (say, a new brand of low-calorie chocolate). In designing surveys, I have to translate the client's information needs into precise questions. I have to be certain that the respondents are answering *exactly* the question I had in mind, and not inventing their own version of the question. Then I have to take these data and translate them into accurate interpretations and recommendations for our clients."

—Jessica North, Senior Project Manager, market research firm

LEARNING OBJECTIVES FOR THIS CHAPTER

- Appreciate the role of critical thinking in evaluating research findings
- Assess the dependability of information sources (print and digital)
- Assess the quality of your evidence
- Interpret your findings accurately and without bias
- Understand that "certainty" in research is an elusive goal
- Recognize common errors in reasoning and statistical analysis
- Understand that research carries the potential for error

Not all information is equal. Not all interpretations are equal either. For instance, if you really want to know how well the latest innovation in robotic surgery works, you need to check with other sources besides, say, the device's designer (from whom you could expect an overly optimistic or insufficiently critical assessment).

Determine if your research sources are valid and reliable

Whether you work with your own findings or the findings of other researchers, you need to decide if the information is valid and reliable. Then you need to decide what your information means. Figure 8.1 outlines your critical thinking decisions, and the potential for error at any stage in this process.

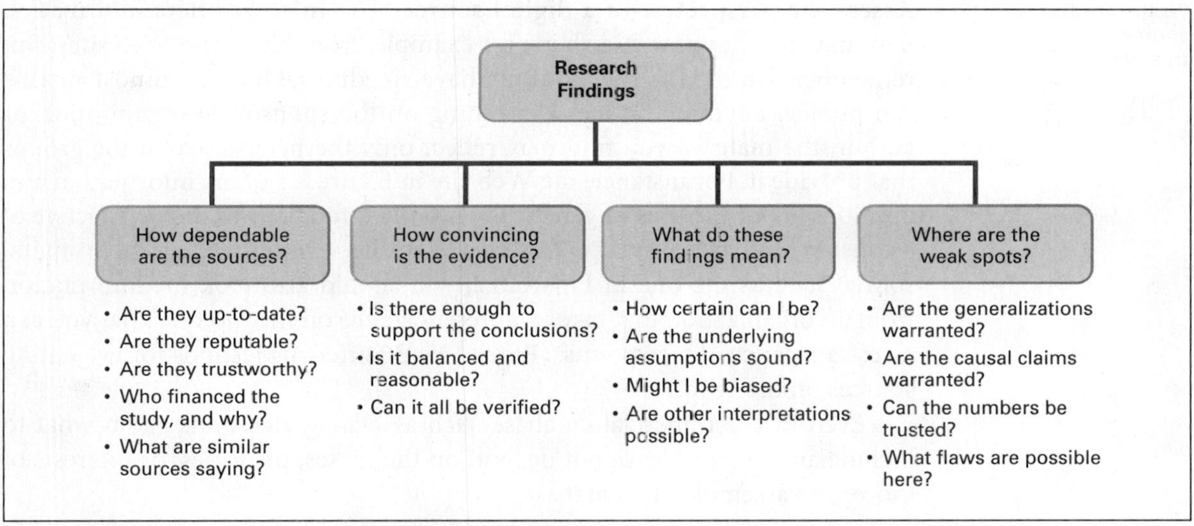

FIGURE 8.1 Critical Thinking Decisions in Evaluating and Interpreting Information Collecting information is often the easiest part of the research process. Your larger challenge is in getting the exact information you need, making sure it's accurate, figuring out what it means, and then double-checking for possible errors along the way.

EVALUATE THE SOURCES

Not all sources are equally dependable. A source might offer information that is out-of-date, inaccurate, incomplete, mistaken, or biased.

"Is the source up-to-date?"

- **Determine the currency of the source.** Even newly published books contain information that can be more than a year old, and journal articles typically undergo a lengthy process of peer review before they are published.

  NOTE *The most recent information is not always the most reliable—especially in scientific research, a process of ongoing inquiry in which what seems true today may be proven false tomorrow. Consider, for example, the recent discoveries of fatal side effects from some of the latest "miracle" drugs.*

"Is the printed source reputable?"

- **Assess the reputation of a printed source.** Check the publication's copyright page. Is the work published by a university, professional society, museum, or respected news organization? Is the publication *refereed* (all submissions reviewed by experts before acceptance)? Does the bibliography or list of references indicate how thoroughly the author has researched the issue (Barnes)? Also check citation indexes (page 138) to see what other experts have said about this particular source. Many periodicals also provide brief biographies or descriptions of authors' earlier publications and achievements.

"Is the electronic source trustworthy?"

- **Assess the perspective of a digital source.** The Internet offers information that may never appear elsewhere, for example, from blogs and Web sites. But remember that the Internet does not have an editorial board—almost anyone can publish anything online. Depending on the sponsoring organization or author, the material you find may reflect only the perspective of the groups that provide it. For instance, the Web site in Figure 8.2 offers information and opinions about the uses of genetically modified foods from the perspective of a consumer advocacy group. If using a Web site, Twitter feed, or other digital source such as the one in Figure 8.2, you should also look for information from an organization that takes a different stance on the topic, so that you can assess a balance of viewpoints. (Pages 135–36 offer suggestions for evaluating sources on the Web.)

  Even in a commercial database such as *Dialog,* decisions about what to include and what to leave out depend on the biases, priorities, or interests of those who assemble that database.

  NOTE *Because a special-interest Web site, Twitter feed, or Facebook page may advocate only one particular point of view, these sources can also provide you with useful clues about the ideas and opinions of their sponsors. Balance this information with information from a variety of sources, including peer reviewed publications, government sites, and special-interest sites that offer differing perspectives.*

- **Consider the possible motives of those who have funded the study.** Much of today's research is paid for by private companies or special-interest groups that have their own agendas (Crossen 14, 19). Medical research may be financed by drug or tobacco companies; nutritional research, by food manufacturers; environmental research, by oil or chemical companies. Instead of a neutral and balanced inquiry, this kind of "strategic research" is designed to support one special interest or another (132–34). Research financed by opposing groups can produce opposing results. Try to determine exactly what those who have funded a particular study stand to gain or lose from the results (234).

"Who financed the study, and why?"

FIGURE 8.2 **A Web Site That Offers a Particular Perspective** This information seems convincing, but it still needs to be balanced with research from sources that take a different view or from sources that are neutral on the issue.

Source: Reprinted with the permission of Institute for Responsible Technology.

NOTE *Keep in mind that any research ultimately stands on its own merits. Thus, funding by a special interest should not automatically discredit an otherwise valid and reliable study. Also, financing from a private company often sets the stage for beneficial research that might otherwise be unaffordable, as when research funded by Quaker Oats led to other studies proving that oats can lower cholesterol (Raloff 189).*

"What are similar sources saying?"

- **Cross-check the source against other, similar sources.** Most studies have some type of flaw or limitation (see page 168). Instead of relying on a single source or study, you should seek a consensus among various respected sources.

EVALUATE THE EVIDENCE

Evidence is any finding used to support or refute a particular claim. Although evidence can serve the truth, it can also distort, misinform, and deceive. For example:

Questions that invite distorted evidence

- How much money, material, or energy does recycling really save?
- How well are public schools educating children?
- Which investments or automobiles are safest?
- How safe and effective are herbal medications?

Competing answers to such questions often rest on evidence that has been chosen to support a particular view or agenda.

"Is there enough evidence?"

- **Determine the sufficiency of the evidence.** Evidence is sufficient when nothing more is needed to reach an accurate judgment or conclusion. Say you are researching the stress-reducing benefits of low-impact aerobics among employees at a fireworks factory. You would need to interview or survey a broad sample: people who have practiced aerobics for a long time; people of both genders, different ages, different occupations, different lifestyles before they began aerobics; and so on. But responses even from hundreds of practitioners might be insufficient unless those responses were supported by laboratory measurements of metabolic and heart rates, blood pressure, and so on.

  NOTE *Although anecdotal evidence ("This worked great for me!") may offer a starting point, personal experience rarely provides enough evidence from which to generalize.*

"Can the evidence be verified?"

- **Differentiate hard from soft evidence.** "Hard evidence" consists of facts, expert opinions, or statistics that can be verified. "Soft evidence" consists of uninformed opinions or speculations, data that were obtained or analyzed unscientifically, and findings that have not been replicated or reviewed by experts.

"Is this claim too good to be true?"

- **Decide whether the presentation of evidence is balanced and reasonable.** Evidence may be overstated, such as when overzealous researchers exaggerate their achievements without revealing the limitations of their study. Or vital facts may be omitted, as when acetaminophen pain relievers are promoted as "safe," even though acetaminophen is the leading cause of U.S. drug fatalities (Easton and Herrara 42–44).

- **Consider how the facts are being framed.** A *frame of reference* is a set of ideas, beliefs, or views that influences our interpretation or acceptance of other ideas. In medical terms, for example, is a "90 percent survival rate" more acceptable than a "10 percent mortality rate"? Framing sways our perception (Lang and Secic 239–40). For instance, what we now call a financial "recession" used to be a "depression"—a term that was coined as a euphemism for "panic" (Bernstein 183). For more on euphemisms, see page 228.

  Whether the language is provocative ("rape of the environment," "soft on terrorism"), euphemistic ("teachable moment" versus "mistake"), or demeaning to opponents ("bureaucrats," "tree huggers"), deceptive framing—all too common in political "spin" strategies—obscures the real issues.

Is the glass "half full" or "half empty"?

INTERPRET YOUR FINDINGS

Interpreting means trying to reach the truth of the matter: an overall judgment about what the findings mean and what conclusion or action they suggest.

"What does this all mean?"

Unfortunately, research does not always yield answers that are clear or conclusive. Instead of settling for the most *convenient* answer, we must pursue the most *reasonable* answer by critically examining a full range of possible meanings.

Identify Your Level of Certainty

Research can yield three distinct and very different levels of certainty:

1. The ultimate truth—the *conclusive answer:*

> Truth is *what is so* about something, as distinguished from what people wish, believe, or assert to be so. In the words of Harvard philosopher Israel Scheffler, truth is the view "which is fated to be ultimately agreed to by all who investigate."[1] The word *ultimately* is important. Investigation may produce a wrong answer for years, even for centuries. For example, in the second century A.D., Ptolemy's view of the universe placed the earth at its center—and though untrue, this judgment was based on the best information available at that time. And Ptolemy's view survived for 13 centuries, even after new information had discredited this belief. When Galileo proposed a more truthful view in the fifteenth century, he was labeled a heretic.
>
> One way to spare yourself further confusion about truth is to reserve the word *truth* for the final answer to an issue. Get in the habit of using the words *belief, theory,* and *present understanding* more often. (Ruggiero, 3rd ed. 21–22)

A practical definition of "truth"

Conclusive answers are the research outcome we seek, but often we have to settle for answers that are less than certain.

---

[1]From *Reason and Teaching.* New York: Bobbs-Merrill, 1973.

2. The *probable answer:* the answer that stands the best chance of being true or accurate, given the most we can know at this particular time. Probable answers are subject to revision in light of new information. This is especially the case with *emergent science,* such as gene therapy or food irradiation.
3. The *inconclusive answer:* the realization that the truth of the matter is more elusive, ambiguous, or complex than we expected.

"Exactly how certain are we?"

We need to decide what level of certainty our findings warrant. For example, we are *certain* about the perils of smoking and sunburn, *reasonably certain* about the health benefits of fruits and vegetables, but *less certain* about the perils of genetically modified food or the benefits of vitamin supplements.

Examine the Underlying Assumptions

Assumptions are notions we take for granted, ideas we often accept without proof. The research process rests on assumptions such as these: that a sample group accurately represents a larger target group, that survey respondents remember facts accurately, that mice and humans share many biological similarities. For a study to be valid, the underlying assumptions have to be accurate.

How underlying assumptions affect research validity

Consider this example: You are an education consultant evaluating the accuracy of IQ testing as a predictor of academic performance. Reviewing the evidence, you perceive an association between low IQ scores and low achievers. You then verify your statistics by examining a cross section of reliable sources. Can you justifiably conclude that IQ tests do predict performance accurately? This conclusion might be invalid unless you verify the following assumptions:

1. That no one—parents, teachers, or children—had seen individual test scores, which could produce biased expectations.
2. That, regardless of score, each child had completed an identical curriculum, instead of being "tracked" on the basis of his or her score.

NOTE *Assumptions can be easier to identify in someone else's thinking than our own. During team discussions, ask members to help you identify your own assumptions.*

Be Alert for Personal Bias

Personal bias is a fact of life

To support a particular version of the truth, our own bias might cause us to overestimate (or deny) the certainty of our findings.

> Unless you are perfectly neutral about the issue, an unlikely circumstance, at the very outset . . . you will believe one side of the issue to be right, and that belief will incline you to . . . present more and better arguments for the side of the issue you prefer. (Ruggiero 134)

Because personal bias is hard to transcend, *rationalizing* often becomes a substitute for *reasoning*:

Reasoning versus rationalizing

> You are reasoning if your belief follows the evidence—that is, if you examine the evidence first and then make up your mind. You are rationalizing if the evidence follows your belief—if you first decide what you'll believe and then select and interpret evidence to justify it. (Ruggiero 44)

Personal bias is often unconscious until we examine our attitudes long held but never analyzed, assumptions we've inherited from our backgrounds, and so on. Recognizing our own biases is a crucial first step in managing them.

Consider Other Possible Interpretations

"What else could this mean?"

Settling on a final meaning can be difficult—and sometimes impossible. For example, issues such as the need for defense spending or the causes of inflation are always controversial and will never be resolved. Although we can get verifiable data and can reason persuasively on many subjects, no close reasoning by any expert and no supporting statistical analysis will "prove" anything about a controversial subject. Some problems are simply more resistant to solution than others, no matter how dependable the sources.

NOTE *Not all interpretations are equally valid. Never assume that any interpretation that is possible is also allowable—especially in terms of its ethical consequences.*

CONSIDER THIS: Standards of Proof Vary for Different Audiences

How much evidence is enough to "prove" a particular claim? This often depends on who is making the inquiry:

- **The scientist** demands at least 95 percent certainty. A scientific finding must be evaluated and replicated by other experts. Good science looks at the entire picture. Findings are reviewed before they are reported. Even then, answers in science are never "final," but open-ended and ongoing.
- **The juror** demands evidence that indicates only 51 percent certainty (a "preponderance of the evidence"). Jurors are not scientists. Instead of the entire picture, jurors get only the information revealed by lawyers and witnesses. A jury bases its verdict on evidence that exceeds "reasonable doubt" (Monastersky 249; Powell 32+). Based on such evidence, courts must make final decisions.
- **The executive** demands immediate (even if insufficient) evidence. In a global business climate of overnight developments (in world markets, political strife, natural disasters), business decisions are often made on the spur of the moment. On the basis of incomplete or unverified information—or even hunches—executives must react to crises and try to seize opportunities (Seglin 54).
- **Specific cultures** have their own standards for evidence. "For example, African cultures rely on storytelling for authenticity. Arabic persuasion is dependent on universally accepted truths. And Chinese value ancient authorities over recent empiricism" (Byrd and Reid 109).

AVOID DISTORTED OR UNETHICAL REASONING

Finding the truth, especially in a complex issue or problem, often is a process of elimination, of ruling out or avoiding errors in reasoning. As we interpret, we make *inferences:* We derive conclusions about what we don't know by reasoning from what we do know (Hayakawa 37). For example, we might infer that a drug that boosts immunity in laboratory mice will boost immunity in humans, or that a rise in campus crime statistics is caused by the fact that young people have become more violent. Whether a particular inference is on target or dead wrong depends largely on our answers to one or more of these questions:

Questions for testing inferences

- To what extent can these findings be generalized?
- Is *Y* really caused by *X*?
- To what extent can the numbers be trusted, and what do they mean?

Three major reasoning errors that can distort our interpretations are faulty generalization, faulty causal reasoning, and faulty statistical analysis.

Faulty Generalization

The temptation to generalize on the basis of limited evidence can be hard to resist. Consider, for example, the highly controversial war in Iraq. Our political leaders initially justified this war by citing limited and often inaccurate evidence to support the conclusion that Iraq possessed weapons of mass destruction and had collaborated with al-Qaeda in planning the 9/11 attacks on New York City and Washington, D.C.

We engage in faulty generalization when we jump from a limited observation to a sweeping conclusion. Even "proven" facts can invite mistaken conclusions, as in the following examples:

Factual observations

1. "Some studies have shown that gingko [an herb] improves mental functioning in people with dementia [mental deterioration caused by maladies such as Alzheimer's Disease]" (Stix 30).
2. "For the period 1992–2005, two thirds of the fastest-growing occupations [called] for no more than a high-school degree" (Harrison 62).
3. "Adult female brains are significantly smaller than male brains—about 8% smaller, on average" (Seligman 74).

Invalid conclusions

1. Gingko is food for the brain!
2. Higher education... Who needs it?!
3. Women are the less intelligent gender.

"How much can we generalize from these findings?"

When we accept findings uncritically and jump to conclusions about their meaning (as in points 1 and 2, above) we commit the error of *hasty generalization.* When we overestimate the extent to which the findings reveal some larger truth (as in point 3, above) we commit the error of *overstated generalization.*

> **NOTE** *We often need to generalize, and we should. For example, countless studies support the generalization that fruits and vegetables help lower cancer risk. But we ordinarily limit general claims by inserting qualifiers such as "usually," "often," "sometimes," "probably," "possibly," or "some."*

Faulty Causal Reasoning

Causal reasoning tries to explain why something happened or what will happen, often in very complex situations. Sometimes a *definite cause is apparent* ("The engine's overheating is caused by a faulty radiator cap"). We reason about definite causes when we explain why the combustion in a car engine causes the wheels to move, or why the moon's orbit makes the tides rise and fall. However, causal reasoning often explores *causes that are not so obvious, but only possible or probable.* In these cases, much analysis is needed to isolate a specific cause.

Suppose you ask: "Why are there no children's daycare facilities on our college campus?" Brainstorming yields these possible causes:

"Did *X* possibly, probably, or definitely cause *Y*?"

> lack of need among students
>
> lack of interest among students, faculty, and staff
>
> high cost of liability insurance
>
> lack of space and facilities on campus
>
> lack of trained personnel
>
> prohibition by state law
>
> lack of government funding for such a project

Assume that you proceed with interviews, surveys, and research into state laws, insurance rates, and availability of personnel. As you rule out some items, others appear as probable causes. Specifically, you find a need among students, high campus interest, an abundance of qualified people for staffing, and no state laws prohibiting such a project. Three probable causes remain: high insurance rates, lack of funding, and lack of space. Further inquiry shows that high insurance rates and lack of funding *are* issues. You think, however, that these obstacles could be eliminated through new sources of revenue such as charging a modest fee per child, soliciting donations, and diverting funds from other campus organizations. Finally, after examining available campus space and speaking with school officials, you conclude that one definite cause is lack of space and facilities. In reporting your findings, you would follow the sequence shown in Figure 8.3.

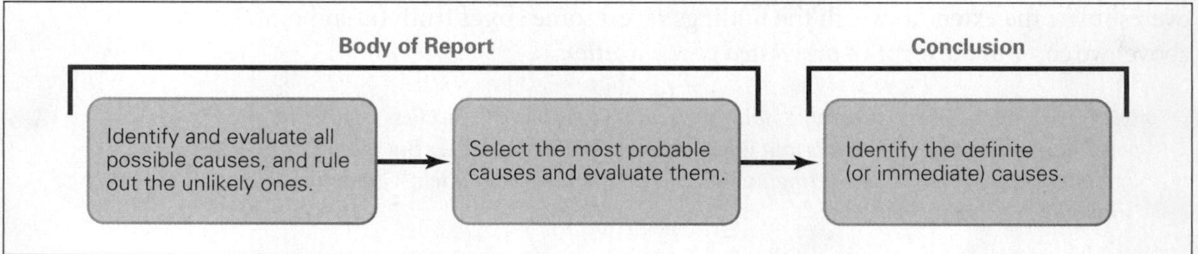

FIGURE 8.3 **The Reporting Sequence in a Causal Analysis** Be sure readers can draw conclusions identical to your own on the basis of the reasoning you present.

The persuasiveness of your causal argument will depend on the quality of evidence you bring to bear, as well as on your ability to explain the links in the chain of your reasoning. Also, you must convince audiences that you haven't overlooked important alternative causes.

NOTE *Any complex effect is likely to have more than one cause. You have to make sure that the cause you have isolated is the right one. In the daycare scenario, for example, you might argue that lack of space and facilities somehow is related to funding. And the college's inability to find funds or space might be related to student need or interest, which is not high enough to exert real pressure. Lack of space and facilities, however, does seem to be the immediate cause.*

Here are common errors that distort or oversimplify cause-effect relationships:

Ignoring other causes

Investment builds wealth. [*Ignores the roles of knowledge, wisdom, timing, and luck in successful investing.*]

Ignoring other effects

Running improves health. [*Ignores the fact that many runners get injured and that some even drop dead while running.*]

Inventing a causal sequence

Right after buying a rabbit's foot, Felix won the state lottery. [*Posits an unwarranted causal relationship merely because one event follows another.*]

Confusing correlation with causation

Women in Scandinavian countries drink a lot of milk. Women in Scandinavian countries have a high incidence of breast cancer. Therefore, milk must be a cause of breast cancer. [*The association between these two variables might be mere coincidence and might obscure other possible causes, such as environment, fish diet, and genetic predisposition* (Lemonick 85).]

Rationalizing

My grades were poor because my exams were unfair. [*Denies the real causes of one's failures.*]

Media researcher Robert Griffin identifies three criteria for demonstrating a causal relationship:

> Along with showing correlation [say, an association between smoking and cancer], evidence of causality requires that the alleged causal agent occurs prior to the condition it causes (e.g., that smoking precedes the development of cancers) and—the most difficult task—that other explanations are discounted or accounted for (240).

For example, epidemiological studies found this correlation: People who eat lots of broccoli, cauliflower, and other cruciferous vegetables have lower rates of some cancers. But other explanations (say, that big veggie eaters might have many other healthful habits as well) could not be ruled out until lab studies showed how a special protein in these vegetables actually protects human cells (Wang 182).

Faulty Statistical Analysis

How numbers can mislead

The purpose of statistical analysis is to determine the meaning of a collected set of numbers. In primary research, our surveys and questionnaires often lead to some kind of numerical interpretation ("What percentage of respondents prefer X?" "How often does Y happen?"). In secondary research, we rely on numbers collected by survey researchers.

Numbers seem more precise, more objective, more scientific, and less ambiguous than words. They are easier to summarize, measure, compare, and analyze. But numbers can be totally misleading. For example, radio or television phone-in surveys often produce distorted data: Although "90 percent of callers" might express support for a particular viewpoint, people who bother to respond tend to have the greatest anger or extreme feelings—representing only a fraction of overall attitudes (Fineman 24). Mail-in or Internet surveys can produce similar distortion. Before relying on any set of numbers, we need to know exactly where they come from, how they were collected, and how they were analyzed.

Common statistical fallacies

Faulty statistical reasoning produces conclusions that are unwarranted, inaccurate, or deceptive. Following are typical fallacies.

"Exactly how well are we doing?"

The Sanitized Statistic. Numbers can be manipulated (or "cleaned up") to obscure the facts. For instance, the College Board's 1996 "recentering" of SAT scores has raised the "average" math score from 478 to 500 and the average verbal score from 424 to 500 (boosts of almost 5 and 18 percent, respectively), although actual student performance remains unchanged (Samuelson, "Merchants" 44).

"How many rats was that?"

The Meaningless Statistic. Exact numbers can be used to quantify something so inexact or vaguely defined that it should only be approximated (Huff 247; Lavin 278): "Boston has 3,247,561 rats." "Zappo detergent makes laundry 10 percent brighter." An exact number looks impressive, but it can hide the fact that certain subjects (child abuse, cheating in college, drug and alcohol abuse, eating habits) cannot be quantified exactly because respondents don't always tell the truth (on account of denial or embarrassment or guessing). Or they respond in ways they think the researcher expects.

Three ways of reporting an "average"

The Undefined Average. The mean, median, and mode can be confused in representing an "average" (Huff 244; Lavin 279): (1) The *mean* is the result of adding up the values of items in a set of numbers, and then dividing that total by the number of items in the set. (2) The *median* is the result of ranking all the values from high to low, then identifying the middle value (or the 50th percentile, as in calculating SAT scores). (3) The *mode* is the value that occurs most often in a set of numbers.

Each of these three measurements represents some kind of average. But unless we know which "average" (mean, median, or mode) is being presented, we cannot possibly interpret the figures accurately.

Assume, for instance, that we want to determine the average salary among female managers at XYZ Corporation (ranked from high to low):

Manager	Salary
"A"	$90,000
"B"	$90,000
"C"	$80,000
"D"	$65,000
"E"	$60,000
"F"	$55,000
"G"	$50,000

In the above example, the *mean* salary (total salaries divided by number of salaries) is $70,000; the *median* salary (middle value) is $65,000; the *mode* (most frequent value) is $90,000. Each is, legitimately, an "average," and each could be used to support or refute a particular assertion (for example, "Women managers are paid too little" or "Women managers are paid too much").

"Why is everybody griping?"

Research expert Michael R. Lavin sums up the potential for bias in the reporting of averages:

> Depending on the circumstances, any one of these measurements may describe a group of numbers better than the other two.... [But] people typically choose the value which best presents their case, whether or not it is the most appropriate to use. (279)

Although the mean is the most commonly computed average, this measurement is misleading when one or more values on either end of the scale (*outliers*) are extremely high or low. Suppose, for instance, that manager "A" (above) was paid a $200,000 salary. Because this figure deviates so far from the normal range of salary figures for "B" through "G," it distorts the average for the whole group, increasing the mean salary by more than 20 percent (Plumb and Spyridakis 636).

The Distorted Percentage Figure. Percentages are often reported without explanation of the original numbers used in the calculation (Adams and Schvaneveldt 359; Lavin 280): "Seventy-five percent of respondents prefer our brand over the competing brand"—without mention that, say, only four people were surveyed.

"Is 51 percent really a majority?"

> **NOTE** *In small samples, percentages can mislead because the percentage size can dwarf the number it represents: "In this experiment, 33% of the rats lived, 33% died, and the third rat got away" (Lang and Secic 41). When your sample is small, report the actual numbers: "Five out of ten respondents agreed. . . ."*

Another fallacy in reporting percentages occurs when the *margin of error* is ignored. This is the margin within which the true figure lies, based on estimated sampling errors in a survey. For example, a claim that "most people surveyed prefer Brand X" might be based on the fact that 51 percent of respondents expressed this preference; but if the survey carried a 2 percent margin of error, the real figure could be as low as 49 percent or as high as 53 percent. In a survey with a high margin of error, the true figure may be so uncertain that no definite conclusion can be drawn.

"How large is the margin of error?"

The Bogus Ranking. This distortion occurs when items are compared on the basis of ill-defined criteria (Adams and Schvaneveldt 212; Lavin 284). For example, the statement "Last year, the Batmobile was the number-one selling car in America" does not mention that some competing car makers actually sold *more* cars to private individuals and that the Batmobile figures were inflated by hefty sales—at huge discounts—to rental-car companies and corporate fleets. Unless we know how the ranked items were chosen and how they were compared (the *criteria*), a ranking can produce a seemingly scientific number based on a completely unscientific method.

"Which car should we buy?"

Confusion of Correlation with Causation. *Correlation* is a numerical measure of the strength of the relationship between two variables (say smoking and increased lung cancer risk, or education and income). *Causation* is the demonstrable production of a specific effect (smoking causes lung cancer). Correlations between smoking and lung cancer or between education and income signal a causal relationship that has been demonstrated by many studies. But not every correlation implies causation. For instance, a recently discovered correlation between moderate alcohol consumption and decreased heart disease risk offers no sufficient proof that moderate drinking *causes* less heart disease.

"Does *X* actually cause *Y*?"

In any type of causal analysis, be on the lookout for *confounding factors*, which are other possible reasons or explanations for a particular outcome. For instance, studies indicating that regular exercise improves health might be overlooking the confounding factor that healthy people tend to exercise more than those who are unhealthy ("Walking" 3–4).

"Could something else have caused *Y*?"

Many highly publicized correlations are the product of *data mining:* In this process, computers randomly compare one set of variables (say, eating habits) with another set (say, range of diseases). From these countless comparisons, certain relationships or associations are revealed (say, between coffee drinking and pancreatic cancer risk). As dramatic as such isolated correlations may be, they constitute no proof of causation and often lead to hasty conclusions (Ross, "Lies" 135).

> **NOTE** *Despite its limitations, data mining is invaluable for "uncovering correlations that require computers to perceive but that thinking humans can evaluate and research further" (Maeglin).*

"Who selected which studies to include?"

The Biased Meta-Analysis. In a meta-analysis, researchers examine a whole range of studies that have been done on one topic (say, high-fat diets and cancer risk). The purpose of this "study of studies" is to decide the overall meaning of the collected findings. Because results ultimately depend on which studies have been included and which omitted, a meta-analysis can reflect the biases of the researchers who select the material. Also, because small studies have less chance of being published than large ones, they may get overlooked (Lang and Secic 174–76).

"How have assumptions influenced this computer model?"

The Fallible Computer Model. Computer models process complex *assumptions* (see page 158) to predict or estimate costs, benefits, risks, and probable outcomes. But answers produced by any computer model depend on the assumptions (and data) programmed in. Assumptions might be influenced by researcher bias or the sponsors' agenda. For example, a prediction of human fatalities from a nuclear reactor meltdown might rest on assumptions about the availability of safe shelter, evacuation routes, time of day, season, wind direction, and the structural integrity of the containment unit. But these assumptions could be manipulated to overstate or understate the risk (Barbour 228). For computer-modeled estimates of accident risk (oil spill, plane crash) or of the costs and benefits of a proposed project or policy (international space station, health care reform), consumers rarely know the assumptions behind the numbers.

"Do we all agree on what these terms mean?"

Misleading Terminology. The terms used to interpret statistics sometimes hide their real meaning. For instance, the widely publicized figure that people treated for cancer have a "50 percent survival rate" is misleading in two ways; (1) *Survival* to laypersons means "staying alive," but to medical experts, staying alive for only five years after diagnosis qualifies as survival; (2) the "50 percent" survival figure covers *all* cancers, including certain skin or thyroid cancers that have extremely high *cure rates,* as well as other cancers (such as lung or ovarian) that are rarely curable and have extremely low *survival rates* ("Are We" 6).

Even the most valid and reliable statistics require that we interpret the reality behind the numbers. For instance, the overall cancer rate today is "higher" than it was in 1910. What this may mean is that people are living longer and thus are more likely to die of cancer and that cancer today rarely is misdiagnosed—or mislabeled because of stigma ("Are We" 4). The finding that rates for certain cancers "double" after prolonged exposure to electromagnetic waves may really mean that cancer risk actually increases from 1 in 10,000 to 2 in 10,000.

"Is this news good, bad, or insignificant?"

The numbers may be "technically accurate" and may seem highly persuasive in the interpretations they suggest. But the actual "truth" behind these numbers is far more elusive. Any interpretation of statistical data carries the possibility that other, more accurate interpretations have been overlooked or deliberately excluded (Barnett 45).

ACKNOWLEDGE THE LIMITS OF RESEARCH

Legitimate researchers live with uncertainty. They expect to be wrong far more often than right. Following is a brief list of things that go wrong with research and interpretation.

Obstacles to Validity and Reliability

What makes a survey valid

Validity and *reliability* determine the dependability of any research (Adams and Schvaneveldt 79–97; Crossen 22–24). *Valid research* produces correct findings. A survey, for example, is valid when (1) it measures what you want it to measure, (2) it measures accurately and precisely, and (3) its findings can be generalized to the target population. Valid survey questions enable each respondent to interpret each question exactly as the researcher intended; valid questions also ask for information respondents are qualified to provide.

Why survey responses can't always be trusted

Survey validity depends largely on trustworthy responses. Even clear, precise, and neutral questions can produce mistaken, inaccurate, or dishonest answers. People often see themselves as more informed, responsible, or competent than they really are. Respondents are likely to suppress information that reflects poorly on their behavior, attitudes, or will power when answering such leading questions as "How often do you take needless sick days?" "Would you lie to get ahead?" "How much TV do you watch?" They might exaggerate or invent facts or opinions that reveal a more admirable picture when answering the following types of questions: "How much do you give to charity?" "How many books do you read?" "How often do you hug your children?" Even when respondents don't know, don't remember, or have no opinion, they often tend to guess in ways designed to win the researcher's approval.

What makes a survey reliable

Reliable research produces findings that can be replicated. A survey is reliable when its results are consistent; for instance, when a respondent gives identical answers to the same survey given twice or to different versions of the same questions. Reliable survey questions can be interpreted identically by all respondents.

Much of your communication will be based on the findings of other researchers, so you will need to assess the validity and reliability of their research as well as your own.

Flaws in Research Studies

Although some types of studies are more reliable than others, each type has limitations (Cohn 106; Harris, Richard 170–72; Lang and Secic 8–9; Murphy 143):

Common flaws in epidemiologic studies

- **Epidemiological studies.** Epidemiologists study various populations (human, animal, or plant) to find correlations (say, between computer use and cataracts). Conducted via observations, interviews, surveys, or records review, these studies are subject to faulty sampling techniques (page 146) and observer bias (seeing what one wants to see). Even with a correlation that is 99 percent certain, an epidemiological study alone doesn't "prove" anything. (The larger the study, however, the more credible.)

Common flaws in laboratory studies

- **Laboratory studies.** Although a laboratory offers controlled conditions, these studies also carry limitations. For example, the reactions of experimental mice to a specific treatment or drug often are not generalizable to humans. Also, the reaction of an isolated group of cells does not always predict the reaction of the entire organism.

Common flaws in clinical trials

- **Human exposure studies** *(clinical trials).* These studies compare one group of people receiving medication or treatment with an untreated group, the *control group.* Limitations include the possibility that the study group may be non-representative or too different from the general population in overall health, age, or ethnic background. (For example, even though gingko may slow memory loss in sick people, that doesn't mean it will boost the memory of healthy people.) Also, anecdotal reports are unreliable. Respondents often invent answers to questions such as "How often do you eat ice cream?" or "Do you sometimes forget to take your medication?"

Deceptive Reporting

"Has bad or embarrassing news been suppressed?"

One problem in reviewing scientific findings is "getting the story straight." Intentionally or not, the public often is given a distorted picture. For instance, although twice as many people in the United States are killed by medications as by auto accidents—and countless others harmed—doctors rarely report adverse drug reactions. For example, one Rhode Island study identified roughly 26,000 adverse reactions noted in doctors' files, of which only 11 had been reported to the Food and Drug Administration (Freundlich 14).

"Is the topic 'too weird' for researchers?"

Some promising but unconventional topics, such as herbal remedies, are rarely the topics of intensive research "partly because few 'respectable' scientists are willing to risk their reputations to do the testing required, and partly because few firms would be willing to pay for it if they were." Drug companies have little interest because "herbal medicines, not being new inventions, cannot be patented" ("Any Alternative?" 83).

Even bad science makes good news

Spectacular claims that are even remotely possible are more appealing than spectacular claims that have been disproven. Examples include "Giant Comet Headed for Earth!" and "Insects may carry the AIDS virus!"

NOTE *All this potential for error doesn't mean we should believe nothing. But we need to be discerning about what we do choose to believe. Critical thinking is essential.*

GUIDELINES for Evaluating and Interpreting Information

Evaluate the Sources

- **Check the posting or publication date.** The latest information is not always the best, but keeping up with recent developments is vital.
- **Assess the reputation of each printed source.** Check the copyright page for background on the publisher, the bibliography for the quality of research, and (if available) the author's brief biography.
- **Assess the quality of your source material.** If using material from the Internet, including Web sites, Twitter feeds, or Wikipedia, see pages 154–56 in this chapter (and pages 132 and 134 in Chapter 7 for more about using Wikipedia for research).
- **Don't let looks deceive you.** Several studies have found that people judge Web sites based in large part on the look of the page. Professional formatting can disguise a special-interest or biased point of view.
- **Identify the study's sponsor.** If a study proclaiming the crashworthiness of the Batmobile has been sponsored by the Batmobile Auto Company, be skeptical about the study's findings.
- **Look for corroborating sources.** A single study rarely produces definitive findings. Learn what other sources say, why they agree or disagree, and where most experts stand.

Evaluate the Evidence

- **Decide whether the evidence is sufficient.** Evidence should surpass personal experience, anecdote, or media reports. Reasonable and informed observers should be able to agree on its credibility.
- **Look for a fair and balanced presentation.** Suspect any claims about "breakthroughs" or "miracle cures" or the like.
- **Try to verify the evidence.** Examine the facts that support the claims. Look for replication of findings.

GUIDELINES *continued*

Interpret Your Findings

- **Don't expect "certainty."** Complex questions are mostly open-ended, and a mere accumulation of facts doesn't "prove" anything. Even so, the weight of evidence usually suggests some reasonable conclusion.
- **Examine the underlying assumptions.** As opinions taken for granted, assumptions are easily mistaken for facts.
- **Identify your personal biases.** Examine your own assumptions. Don't ignore evidence simply because it contradicts your original assumptions.
- **Consider alternative interpretations.** What else might this evidence mean?

Check for Weak Spots

- **Scrutinize all generalizations.** Decide whether the evidence supports the generalization. Suspect any general claim not limited by a qualifier such as "often," "sometimes," or "rarely."
- **Treat causal claims skeptically.** Differentiate correlation from causation, as well as possible from probable or definite causes. Consider confounding factors (other explanations for the reported outcome).
- **Look for statistical fallacies.** Determine where the numbers come from, and how they were collected and analyzed—information that legitimate researchers routinely provide. Note the margin of error.
- **Consider the limits of computer analysis.** Data mining often produces intriguing but random correlations; a meta-analysis might be biased; a computer model is only as accurate as the assumptions and data that were programmed in.
- **Look for misleading terminology.** Examine terms that beg for precise definition in their specific context: "survival rate," "success rate," and so on.
- **Interpret the reality behind the numbers.** Consider the possibility of alternative, more accurate, interpretations of the data.
- **Consider the study's possible limitations.** Small, brief studies are less reliable than large, extended ones; epidemiological studies are less reliable than laboratory studies (which have their own flaws); and animal exposure studies are often not generalizable to human populations.
- **Look for the whole story.** Consider whether bad news may be underreported; good news, exaggerated; bad science, camouflaged and sensationalized; or promising but unconventional topics (say, alternative energy sources) ignored.

CHECKLIST: The Research Process

(Numbers in parentheses refer to the first page of discussion.)

Methods

- ☐ Did I ask the right questions? (126)
- ☐ Is each source appropriately up to date, reputable, trustworthy, relatively unbiased, and borne out by other, similar sources? (154)
- ☐ For digital sources, do I have a clear idea of the author or organization behind the information? (172)
- ☐ Does the evidence clearly support all of the conclusions? (130)
- ☐ Is a fair balance of viewpoints represented? (126)
- ☐ Can all the evidence be verified? (156)
- ☐ Has my research achieved adequate depth? (128)
- ☐ Has the entire research process been valid and reliable? (167)

Interpretation and Reasoning

- ☐ Am I reasonably certain about the meaning of these findings? (157)
- ☐ Can I discern assumption from fact and reasoning from rationalizing? (158)
- ☐ Can I discern correlation from causation? (165)
- ☐ Can I rule out other possible interpretations or conclusions? (159)
- ☐ Have I accounted for all sources of bias, including my own? (158)
- ☐ Are my generalizations warranted by the evidence? (160)
- ☐ Am I confident that my causal reasoning is accurate? (161)
- ☐ Can I rule out confounding factors? (165)
- ☐ Can all of the numbers, statistics, and interpretations be trusted? (163)
- ☐ Have I resolved (or at least acknowledged) any conflicts among my findings? (130)
- ☐ Can I rule out any possible error or distortion in a given study? (168)
- ☐ Am I getting the whole story, and getting it straight? (170)

Documentation

- ☐ Is my documentation consistent, complete, and correct? (644)
- ☐ Is all quoted material clearly marked throughout the text? (645)
- ☐ Are direct quotations used sparingly and appropriately? (645)
- ☐ Are all quotations accurate and integrated grammatically? (647)
- ☐ Are all paraphrases accurate and clear? (647)
- ☐ Have I documented all sources not considered common knowledge? (648)

Projects

GENERAL

From media, personal experience, or the Internet, identify an example of each of the following sources of distortion or of interpretive error:

- a study with questionable sponsorship or motives
- reliance on insufficient evidence
- unbalanced presentation
- deceptive framing of facts
- overestimating the level of certainty
- biased interpretation
- rationalizing
- unexamined assumptions
- faulty causal reasoning
- hasty generalization
- overstated generalization
- sanitized statistic
- meaningless statistic
- undefined average
- distorted percentage figure
- bogus ranking
- fallible computer model
- misinterpreted statistic
- deceptive reporting

Hint: For examples of faulty (as well as correct) statistical reasoning in the news, check out Dartmouth College's *Chance Project* at <www.dartmouth.edu/~chance>.

Submit your examples to your instructor along with a memo explaining each error, and be prepared to discuss your material in class.

TEAM

Projects from the previous or following section may be done as team projects.

DIGITAL AND SOCIAL MEDIA

Uninformed opinions are usually based on assumptions we've never really examined. Examples of popular assumptions that are largely unexamined:

- "Bottled water is safer and better for us than tap water."
- "Forest fires should always be prevented or suppressed immediately."
- "The fewer germs in their environment, the healthier the children."
- "The more soy we eat, the better."

Identify and examine one popular assumption for accuracy. For example, you might tackle the bottled water assumption by visiting the FDA Web site <www.fda.gov> and the Sierra Club site <www.sierra.org>, for starters. Also take a look at the Sierra Club's Twitter feed: <www.twitter.com/Sierra_Club>. (Unless you get stuck, work with an assumption not listed above.) Trace the sites and links you followed to get your information, and write up your findings in a memo to be shared with the class.

GLOBAL

As indicated in the Consider This box on page 159, specific cultures have their own standards for credible evidence. In other words, different cultures reason differently. Using Google, research this phenomenon by conducting a search on "cultural differences in reasoning." Learn how at least two cultures may reason differently from North Americans of European descent, and report your findings.

9 Summarizing Research Findings and Other Information

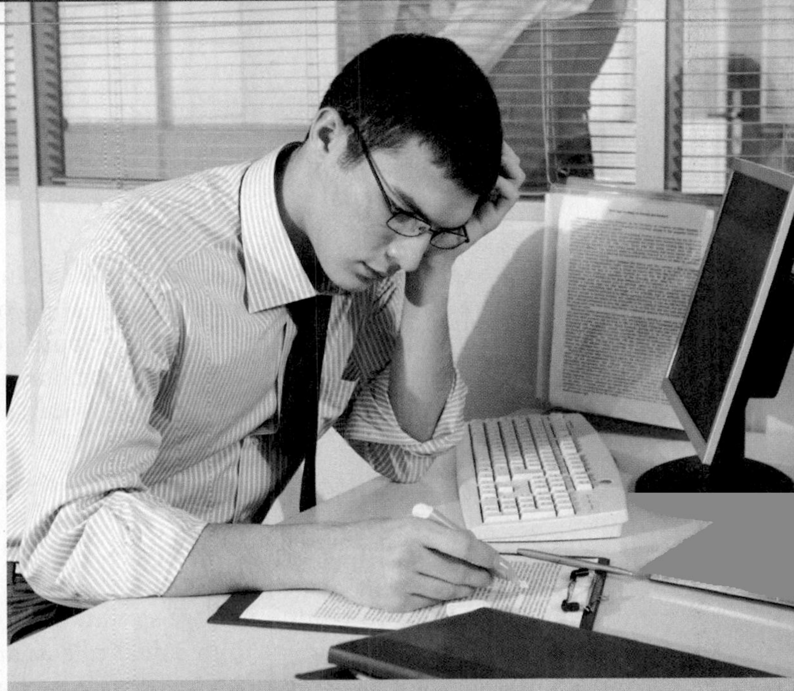

"Every time I run a training session in corporate communication, participants tell horror stories about working weeks or months on a report, only to have it disappear somewhere up the management chain. We use copies of those 'invisible' reports as case studies, and invariably, the summary turns out to have been poorly written, providing readers few or no clues as to the report's significance. I'll bet companies lose millions because new ideas and recommendations get relegated to that stockpile of reports unread yearly in corporate America."

—Frank Sousa,
Communications Consultant

LEARNING OBJECTIVES FOR THIS CHAPTER

- Understand the role of summaries in workplace communication
- Differentiate among four special types of summaries: closing summaries, informative abstracts, descriptive abstracts, and executive abstracts
- Consider ethical issues when writing summaries
- Understand the role digital media plays in the length and content of a summary
- Plan, write, and evaluate a summary of a long document

A *summary* is a restatement of the main ideas in a longer document. Summaries are used to convey the general meaning of the ideas in the original source without all the details or examples that may appear in the original. When you write a summary, provide only the essential information clearly and concisely in your own words, leaving out anything that isn't central to an understanding of the original.

CONSIDERING AUDIENCE AND PURPOSE

Summaries as a research aid

Chapter 7 shows how abstracts (a type of summary) aid our research by providing an encapsulated glimpse of an article or other long document. Also, as we record our research findings, we summarize to capture the main ideas in a compressed form. In addition to this dual role as a research aid, summarized information is vital in day-to-day workplace transactions.

Summaries in the workplace

On the job, you have to write concisely about your work. You might report on meetings or conferences, describe your progress on a project, or propose a money-saving idea. A routine assignment for many new employees is to provide superiors (decision makers) with summaries of the latest developments in their field.

Audience considerations

Formal reports and proposals (discussed in Chapters 22 and 23) and other long documents are typically submitted to busy people: researchers, developers, managers, vice presidents, customers, and so on. For readers who must act quickly or who only need to know the "big picture," reading an entire long report may not only be too time-consuming but also irrelevant. As a result, most long reports, proposals, and other complex documents are commonly preceded by a summary.

Purpose of summaries

The purpose of summaries, then, is to provide only an overview and the essential facts. Whether you summarize your own writing or someone else's, your summary should do three things for readers: (1) describe, in short form, what the original document is all about; (2) help readers decide whether to read the entire document, parts of it, or none of it; and (3) give readers a framework for understanding the full document that will follow if they do plan to read it.

An effective summary communicates the *essential message* accurately and in the fewest possible words. To get a basic idea of how summaries fulfill audience needs, consider the examples in Figures 9.1 and 9.2.

> Scientists know with virtual certainty that human activities are changing the composition of Earth's atmosphere. Increasing levels of greenhouse gases like carbon dioxide (CO_2) since pre-industrial times are well-documented and understood. The atmospheric buildup of CO_2 and other greenhouse gases is largely the result of human activities such as the burning of fossil fuels. Increasing greenhouse gas concentrations tend to warm the planet. A warming trend of about 0.7 to 1.5°F occurred during the 20th century in both the Northern and Southern Hemispheres and over the oceans. The major greenhouse gases remain in the atmosphere for periods ranging from decades to centuries. It is therefore virtually certain that atmospheric concentrations of greenhouse gases will continue to rise over the next few decades.

FIGURE 9.1 A Passage to Be Summarized
Source: Adapted from *State of Knowledge,* U.S. Environmental Protection Agency.

In the previous passage, three ideas make up the essential message: (1) scientists are virtually certain that greenhouse gases largely produced by human activities are warming the planet; (2) rising temperatures worldwide during the 20th century have been demonstrated; and (3) this warming trend almost certainly will continue.

Figure 9.2 shows a summary of the complex passage in Figure 9.1. Note how it captures the original's main ideas, but in a compressed and less technical form that busy readers and general audiences would appreciate. The summary does not, however, change the essential meaning of the original—it merely boils the original down to its basic message.

> Scientists are virtually certain that greenhouse gases largely produced by human activities are warming the planet. Temperatures have risen worldwide during the 20th century and undoubtedly will continue.
>
> *Source:* From *State of Knowledge,* U.S. Environmental Protection Agency.

FIGURE 9.2 A Summarized Version of Figure 9.1

NOTE *For letters, memos, or other short documents that can be read quickly, the only summary needed is usually an opening thesis or topic sentence that previews the contents.*

WHAT READERS EXPECT FROM A SUMMARY

Whether you summarize your own documents (like the sample on page 541) or someone else's, readers will have these expectations:

Elements of a usable summary

- **Accuracy:** Readers expect a precise sketch of the content, emphasis, and line of reasoning from the original.
- **Completeness:** Readers expect to consult the original document only to find more detail—but not to have to make sense of the main ideas and their relationships as these appear in the summary.
- **Readability:** Readers expect a summary to be clear and straightforward—easy to follow and understand.
- **Conciseness:** Readers expect a summary to be informative yet brief, and they may stipulate a word limit (say, two hundred words).
- **Nontechnical style:** Unless they are all experts on this particular subject, readers prefer a document that uses nontechnical terms and simplifies complex ideas—without distorting those ideas.

Although the summary is written last, it is what readers of a long document turn to first. Take the time to do a good job.

GUIDELINES for Summarizing Information

- **Read the entire original.** When summarizing someone else's work, get a complete picture before writing a word.
- **Reread the original, underlining essential material.** Focus on the essential message: thesis and topic sentences, findings, conclusions, and recommendations.
- **Edit the underlined information.** Omit technical details, examples, explanations, or anything readers won't need for grasping the basics.
- **Rewrite in your own words.** Even if this first draft is too long, include everything essential for it to stand alone; you can trim later. In summarizing another's work, avoid direct quotations; if you must quote a crucial word or phrase, use quotation marks around the author's own words. Add no personal comments or other material, except for brief definitions, if needed.
- **Edit your own version.** When you have everything readers will need, edit for conciseness (see page 216).

  a. Cross out needless words—but keep sentences clear and grammatical:

  ~~As far as~~ artificial intelligence ~~is concerned, the~~ technology is ~~only~~ in its infancy.

b. Cross out needless prefaces such as

- The writer argues . . .
- Also discussed is . . .

c. Use numerals for numbers, except to begin a sentence.

d. Combine related ideas in order to emphasize relationships. (See page 269.)

- **Check your version against the original.** Verify that you have preserved the essential message and have added no comments—unless you are preparing an executive abstract (as on page 185).
- **Rewrite your edited version.** Add transitional expressions (see page 701) to emphasize the connections. Respect any stipulated word limit.
- **Document your source.** Cite the exact source below any summary that is not accompanied by its original. (See Appendix A for documentation formats.)

A SITUATION REQUIRING A SUMMARY

The following situation illustrates how the previous Guidelines for Summarizing Information can be applied.

Creating a Summary

The Situation. Assume that you work in the information office of your state's Department of Environmental Management (DEM). In the coming election, citizens will vote on a referendum proposal for constructing the state's first nuclear power plant. Supporters argue that nuclear power would help solve the growing problem of acid rain and global warming from burning fossil fuels. Opponents argue that nuclear power is expensive and unsafe.

To clarify the issues, the DEM will mail a newsletter to each registered voter. You have been assigned to research the recent data and summarize your findings for inclusion in the newsletter. One of the articles appears in Figure 9.3. You have underlined key phrases and noted your critical thinking responses in the margins.

Audience and Use Profile. Because potential readers in this situation represent a broad cross section of interests and backgrounds, the summary has to be accessible to a general audience. However, the document must be sufficiently informative to enable people to weigh both sides of this controversial issue and to make an informed decision in voting on the upcoming referendum. Readers here need a balanced and accurate representation of the original article—without any hint of bias on the writer's part.

1

U.S. Nuclear Power Industry: Background and Current Status

Combine as orienting statement (controlling idea)

Omit background details

Include causes of problem

The U.S. nuclear power industry, while currently generating more than 20 percent of the Nation's electricity, faces an uncertain future. No nuclear power plants have been ordered since 1978, and more than 100 reactors have been cancelled, including all ordered after 1973. No units are currently under active construction; the Tennessee Valley Authority's Watts Bar I reactor, ordered in 1970 and licensed to operate in 1996, was the last U.S. nuclear unit to be completed. The nuclear power industry's troubles include a slowdown in the rate of growth of electricity demand, high nuclear power plant construction costs, public concern about nuclear safety and waste disposal, and a changing regulatory environment.

Obstacles to Expansion

Include major cause

Omit nonvital details

Include key comparison

High construction costs are perhaps the most serious obstacle to nuclear power expansion. Construction costs for reactors completed within the last decade have ranged from $2 billion to $6 billion, averaging about $3,000 per kilowatt of electric generating capacity (in 1995 dollars). The nuclear industry predicts that new plant designs could be built for about half that amount, but construction costs would still substantially exceed the projected costs of coal-and gas-fired plants.

Omit speculation

Include key facts

Of more immediate concern to the nuclear power industry is the outlook for existing nuclear reactors in a deregulated electricity market. Electric utility restructuring, which is currently under way in several states, could increase the competition faced by existing nuclear plants. High operating costs and the need for costly improvements and equipment replacements have resulted in the permanent shutdown during the past decade of 10 U.S. commercial reactors before completion of their 40-year licensed operating periods. Several more reactors are currently being considered for early shutdown.

Include key facts and comparisons

Nevertheless, all is not bleak for the U.S. nuclear power industry, which currently comprises 109 licensed reactors at 68 plant sites in 38 states. Electricity production from U.S. nuclear power plants is greater than that from oil, natural gas, and hydropower, and behind only coal, which accounts for approximately 55 percent of U.S. electricity generation. Nuclear plants generate more than half the electricity in six states.

Include key fact
Omit nonvital details

Average operating costs of U.S. nuclear plants have dropped during the 1990s, and costly downtime has been steadily reduced. Licensed commercial

FIGURE 9.3 **Article to Be Summarized**

Source: Adapted from *Congressional Digest* Jan. 1998: 7+.

U.S. Nuclear Power Industry: Background and Current Status 2

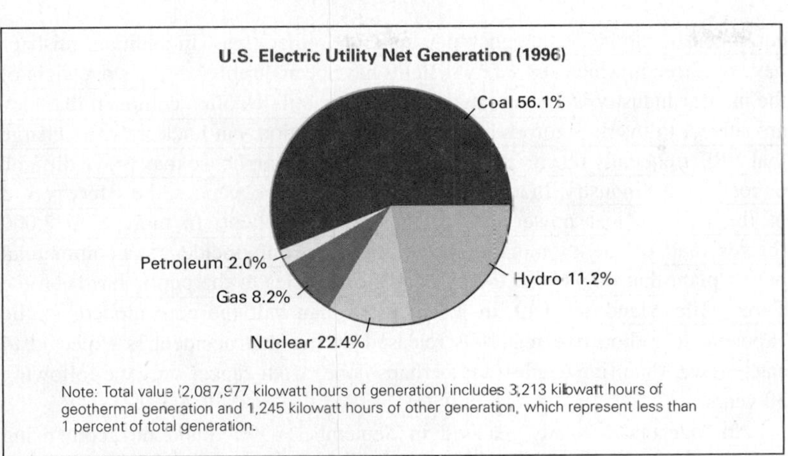

Source: U.S. Department of Energy, Energy Information Administration

reactors generated electricity at an average of 75 percent of their total capacity in 1996, slightly below the previous year's record.

Global warming that may be caused by fossil fuels—the "greenhouse effect"—is cited by nuclear power supporters as an important reason to develop a new generation of reactors. But the large obstacles noted above must still be overcome before electric utilities will order new nuclear units.

Reactor manufacturers are working on designs for safer, less expensive nuclear plants, and the Nuclear Regulatory Commission (NRC) has approved new regulations to speed up the nuclear licensing process, consistent with the Energy Policy Act of 1992. Even so, the Energy Information Administration forecasts that no new U.S. reactors will become operational for a decade or more, if any are ordered at all.

Safety Concerns

Controversy over safety has dogged nuclear power throughout its development, particularly following the Three Mile Island accident in Pennsylvania and the April 1986 Chernobyl disaster in the former Soviet Union. In the United States, safety-related shortcomings have been identified in the construction quality of some plants, plant operation and maintenance

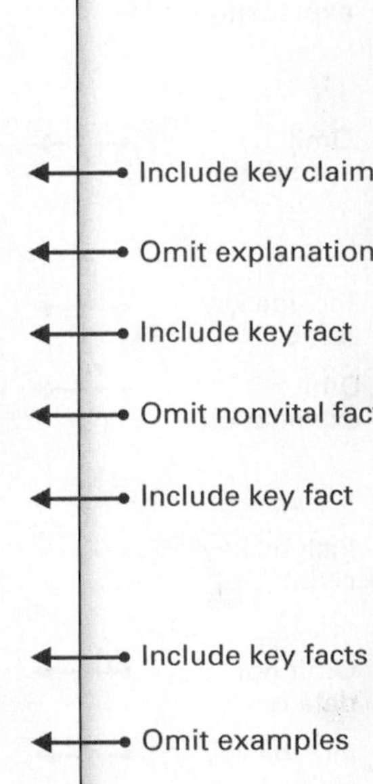

FIGURE 9.3 *(Continued)*

Include key claims →

Include key fact →

Include striking exception →

Omit long explanation →

Omit speculation →

Include key issue →

Omit explanation →

Include key claim →

Omit nonvital details →

Include key claim →

equipment reliability, emergency planning, and other areas. In addition, mishaps have occurred in which key safety systems have been disabled. NRC's oversight of the nuclear industry is an ongoing issue: nuclear utilities often complain that they are subject to overly rigorous and inflexible regulation, but nuclear critics charge that NRC frequently relaxes safety standards when compliance may prove difficult or costly to the industry. In terms of public health consequences, the safety record of the U.S. nuclear power industry has been excellent. In more than 2,000 reactor-years of operation in the United States, the only incident at a commercial power plant that might lead to any deaths or injuries to the public has been the Three Mile Island accident, in which more than half the core melted. Public exposure to radioactive materials released during that accident is expected to cause fewer than five deaths (and perhaps none) from cancer over the following 30 years.

An independent study released in September 1990 found no "convincing evidence" that the Three Mile Island accident had affected cancer rates in the area around the plant. However, a study released in February 1997 concluded that much higher levels of radiation may have been released during the accident than was previously believed.

The relatively small amounts of radioactivity released by nuclear plants during normal operation are not generally believed to pose significant hazards. Documented public exposure to radioactivity from nuclear power plant waste has also been minimal, although the potential long-term hazard of waste disposal remains controversial. There is substantial scientific uncertainty about the level of risk posed by low levels of radiation exposure; as with many carcinogens and other hazardous substances, health effects can be clearly measured only at relatively high exposure levels. In the case of radiation, the assumed risk of low-level exposure has been extrapolated mostly from health effects documented among persons exposed to high levels of radiation, particularly Japanese survivors of nuclear bombing.

The consensus among most safety experts is that a severe nuclear power plant accident in the United States is likely to occur less frequently than one every 10,000 reactor-years of operation. These experts believe that most severe accidents would have small public health impacts and that accidents causing as many as 100 deaths would be much rarer than once every 10,000 reactor-years. On the other hand, some experts challenge the complex calculations that go into predicting such accident frequencies, contending that accidents with serious public health consequences may be more frequent.

FIGURE 9.3 *(Continued)*

U.S. Nuclear Power Industry: Background and Current Status 4

Regulation

A fundamental concern in the nuclear regulatory debate is the performance of NRC in issuing and enforcing nuclear safety regulations. The nuclear industry and its supporters have regularly complained that unnecessarily stringent and inflexibly enforced nuclear safety regulations have burdened nuclear utilities and their customers with excessive costs. But many environmentalists, nuclear opponents, and other groups charge NRC with being too close to the nuclear industry, a situation that they say has resulted in lax oversight of nuclear power plants and routine exemptions from safety requirements.

Primary responsibility for nuclear safety compliance lies with nuclear utilities, which are required to find any problems with their plants and report them to NRC. Compliance is monitored directly by NRC, which maintains at least two resident inspectors at each nuclear power plant. The resident inspectors routinely examine plant systems, observe the performance of reactor personnel, and prepare regular inspection reports. For serious safety violations, NRC often dispatches special inspection teams to plant sites.

Decommissioning and Life Extension

When nuclear power plants end their useful lives, they must be safely removed from service, a process called decommissioning. NRC requires nuclear utilities to make regular contributions to special trust funds to ensure that money is available to remove all radioactive material from reactors after they close. Because no full-sized U.S. commercial reactor has yet been completely decommissioned, which can take several decades, the cost of the process can only be estimated. Decommissioning cost estimates cited by a 1996 Department of Energy report, for one full-sized commercial reactor, ranged from about $150 million to $600 million in 1995 dollars.

It is assumed that U.S. commercial reactors could be decommissioned at the end of their 40-year operating licenses, although several plants have been retired before their licenses expired and others could seek license renewals to operate longer. NRC rules allow plants to apply for a 20-year license extension, for a total operating time of 60 years. Assuming a 40-year lifespan, more than half of today's 109 licensed reactors could be decommissioned by 2016.

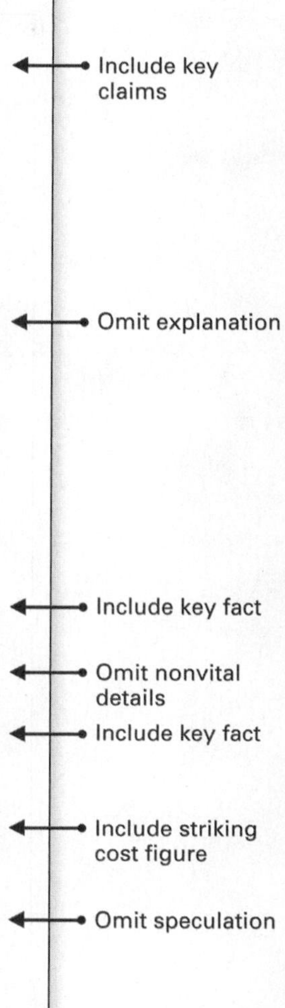

FIGURE 9.3 *(Continued)*

Assume that you rewrote and edited two early drafts of your summary; for coherence and emphasis, you inserted transitions and combined related ideas. Figure 9.4 shows your final draft.

U.S. Nuclear Power Industry: Background and Current Status

Although nuclear power generates more than 20 percent of U.S. electricity, no plants have been ordered since 1978, orders dating to 1973 are cancelled, and no units are now being built. Cost, safety, and regulatory concerns have led to zero growth in the industry.

Nuclear plant construction costs far exceed those for coal- and gas-fired plants. Also, high operating and equipment costs have forced permanent, early shutdown of 10 reactors, and the anticipated shutdown of several more.

On the positive side, the 109 licensed reactors in 38 states produce roughly 22 percent of the nation's electricity—more than oil, natural gas, and hydropower combined, and second only to coal, which produces roughly 55 percent. Also, nuclear power is cleaner than fossil fuels. Yet, despite declining costs and safer, less expensive designs, no new reactors could come online for at least a decade—even if any had been ordered.

Safety concerns persist about plant construction, operation, and maintenance, as well as equipment reliability, emergency planning, and Nuclear Regulatory Commission's (NRC) oversight of the industry. Scientists disagree over the extent of long-term hazards from low-level emissions during plant operation and from waste disposal.

Except for the 1979 partial meltdown at Three Mile Island, however, the U.S. nuclear power industry has an excellent safety record for more than 2,000 reactor-years of operation. Most experts estimate that a severe nuclear accident in the United States will occur less than once every 10,000 reactor-years, but other experts are less optimistic.

Central to the nuclear power controversy is the NRC's role in policing the industry and enforcing safety regulations. Industry supporters claim that overregulation has created excessive costs. But opponents charge the NRC with lax oversight and enforcement.

One final unknown involves "decommissioning": safely closing down an aging power plant at the end of its 40-year operating life, a lengthy process expected to cost $150 million to $600 million per reactor.

Source: Adapted from *Congressional Digest* Jan. 1998: 7+.

FIGURE 9.4 **A Summary of Figure 9.3** Word count in this version has been reduced to roughly 20 percent of the original.

The version in Figure 9.4 is trimmed, tightened, and edited: The word count is reduced to roughly 20 percent of the original length. A summary this long serves well in many situations, but other audiences might want a briefer and more compressed summary—say roughly 15 percent of the original—like the one in Figure 9.5.

U.S. Nuclear Power Industry: Background and Current Status

Although nuclear power generates more than 20 percent of U.S. electricity, cost, safety, and regulatory concerns have led to zero growth in the industry. Moreover, operating and equipment costs are forcing many permanent, early shutdowns.

On the positive side, nuclear reactors generate more of the nation's electricity than all other fossil fuels except coal—and with far less pollution. Yet, despite declining operating costs and safer, less expensive designs, no new reactors could come online for at least a decade—even if any had been ordered.

Safety concerns persist about plant construction, operation, and maintenance as well as equipment reliability, emergency planning, and Nuclear Regulatory Commission's (NRC) oversight. Scientists disagree over the probability of a severe accident and the long-term hazards from normal, low-level emissions or from waste disposal. Except for the 1979 partial meltdown at Three Mile Island, however, the U.S. industry's safety record remains excellent.

Also controversial is the NRC's role in policing and enforcement. Industry supporters claim that excessive regulation has created excessive costs. But opponents charge the NRC with lax oversight and enforcement.

Finally, "decommissioning," safely closing down an aging power plant at the end of its operating life, is a lengthy and expensive process.

Source: Adapted from *Congressional Digest* Jan. 1998: 7+.

FIGURE 9.5 **A More Compressed Summary of Figure 9.3** Word count is roughly 15 percent of the original.

Notice that the essential message remains intact; related ideas are again combined and fewer supporting details are included. Clearly, length in a summary is adjustable according to your audience and purpose.

SPECIAL TYPES OF SUMMARIES

In preparing a report, proposal, or other document, you might summarize works of others as part of your presentation. But you will often summarize your own material as well. For instance, depending on its length, purpose, and audience, your document might include different forms of summarized information, in different locations, with different levels of detail: *closing summary, informative abstract, descriptive abstract*, or *executive abstract.** Figure 9.6 illustrates each of these types of summaries, their placement, and their purpose.

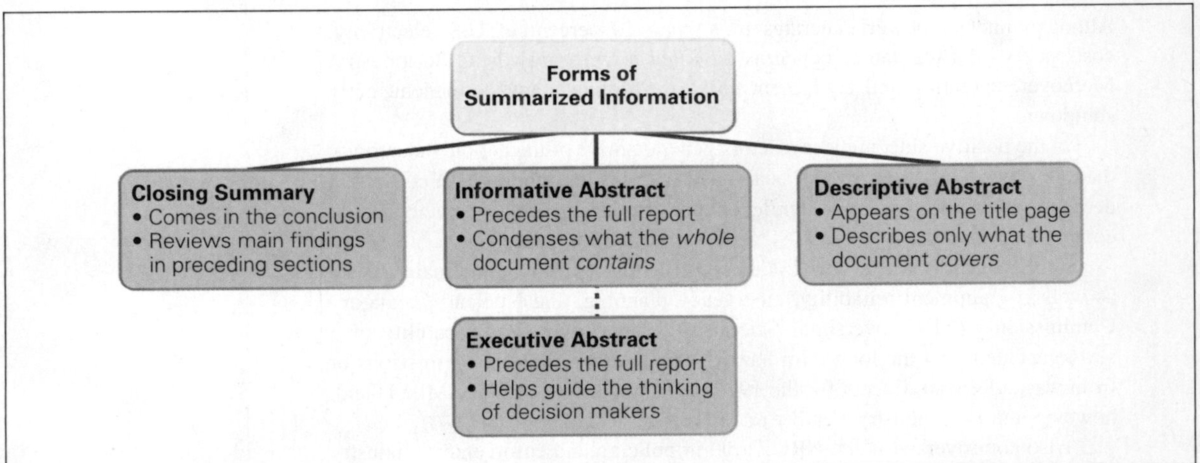

FIGURE 9.6 Summarized Information Assumes Various Forms

Closing Summary

Purpose and placement of closing summaries

A *closing summary* appears at the beginning of a long report's conclusion section. It helps readers review and remember the preceding major findings. This look back at "the big picture" also helps readers appreciate the conclusions and recommendations that typically follow the closing summary. (See pages 532 and 549 for examples.)

Informative Abstract ("Summary")

Purpose and placement of informative abstracts

Readers often appreciate condensed versions of long reports or proposals. Some readers like to see a capsule version before reading the complete document; others simply want to know the basics without having to read the whole document.

*Adapted from David Vaughan. Although we take liberties with his classification, Vaughan helped clarify our thinking about the overlapping terminology that blurs these distinctions.

To meet reader needs, the *informative abstract* appears just after the title page. This type of summary encapsulates what the full version says: It identifies the need or issue that prompted the report; it describes the research methods used; it reviews the main facts and findings; and it condenses the conclusions and recommendations. (See page 541 for an example.)

NOTE *Actually, the title "Informative Abstract" is not used much these days. You are more likely to encounter the title "Summary."*

The heading "Executive Summary" (or "Executive Abstract") is used for material summarized for managers who may not understand all the technical jargon a report might contain. (See below.) By contrast, a "Technical Summary" (or "Technical Abstract") is aimed at readers at the same technical level as the report's author. In short, you may need two or three levels of summary for report readers who have different levels of technical expertise.

(See page 535 for more on the Summary section in a report.)

Descriptive Abstract ("Abstract")

Purpose and placement of descriptive abstracts

A *descriptive abstract* (usually one to three sentences on a report's title page) is another, more compressed form of summarized information. This type of abstract merely describes a report; it doesn't give the report's main points. Such an abstract helps people decide whether to read the report. Thus a descriptive abstract conveys only the nature and extent of a document. It presents the broadest view and offers no major facts from the original. Compare, for example, the abstract that follows with the article summaries in Figures 9.4 and 9.5.

> The track record of the U.S. nuclear power industry is examined and reasons for its lack of growth are identified and assessed.

Because they tend to focus on methodology rather than results, descriptive abstracts are used most often in the sciences and social sciences.*

On the job, you might prepare informative abstracts for a boss who needs the information but who has no time to read the original. Or you might write descriptive abstracts to accompany a bibliography of works you are recommending to colleagues or clients (an annotated bibliography).

Executive Abstract

Purpose and placement of executive abstracts

A special type of informative abstract, the *executive abstract* (or "executive summary") essentially falls at the beginning and "replaces" the entire report. Aimed at

*Our thanks to Daryl Davis for this clarifying distinction.

decision makers rather than technical audiences, an executive abstract generally has more of a persuasive emphasis: Its purpose is to motivate readers to act on the information. Executive abstracts are crucial in cases where readers have no time to read the entire original document and they expect the writer to help guide their thinking. ("Tell me how to think about this," instead of, "Help me understand this.") Unless the reader stipulates a specific format, organize your executive abstract to answer these questions:

Questions to answer in an executive abstract

- What is the issue?
- What was found?
- What does it mean?
- What should be done?

The executive abstract in Figure 9.7 addresses the problem of falling sales for a leading company in the breakfast cereal industry (Grant 223+).

ETHICAL AND GLOBAL CONSIDERATIONS IN SUMMARIZING INFORMATION

Summaries in the Information Age

Information in a summary format is increasingly attractive to today's readers, who often feel bombarded by more information than they can handle. Consider, for example, the popularity of the *USA Today* newspaper, with its countless news items offered in brief snippets for overtaxed readers. In contrast, the *New York Times* offers lengthy text that is information rich but more time-consuming to digest.

Summaries are especially suitable to reading online. Instead of long blocks of text, readers of Web pages expect concise modules, or "chunks," of information that stand alone, are easy to scan, and require little or no scrolling. (See Chapters 13 and 25 for more on Web design.) Magazine Web sites such as *Forbes* or *The Economist* offer email article summaries as well as even shorter summaries via Twitter feeds.

Although chunks of information are an efficient way to stay abreast of new developments, the abbreviated presentation carries potential pitfalls, as media critic Ilan Greenberg points out (650):

Ethical pitfalls of summaries

- A condensed version of a complicated document may provide a useful overview, but this superficial treatment often fails to communicate the document's full complexity—that is, the complete story.
- Whoever summarizes a lengthy piece makes decisions about what to leave out and what to leave in, what to emphasize, and what to ignore. During this selection process, the original message could very well be distorted.
- In a summary of someone else's writing, the tone or "voice" of the original author often disappears—along with that writer's viewpoint or intent. Any distortion of the original writer's intent can be a form of plagiarism.

Status Report: Market Share for Goldilocks Breakfast Cereals (GBC)

In response to a request from GBC's Board of Directors, the accounting division analyzed recent trends in the company's sales volume and profitability.

Findings

- Even though GBC is the cereal industry leader, its sales for the past four years increased at a mere average of 2.5 percent annually, to $5.2 billion, and net income decreased 12 percent overall, to $459 million.
- This weak sales growth apparently results from consumer resistance to retail price increases for cereal, totaling 91 percent in slightly more than a decade, the highest increase of any processed-food product.
- GBC traditionally offers discount coupons to offset price increases, but consumers seem to prefer a lower everyday price.
- GBC introduces an average of two new cereal products annually (most recently, "Coconut Whammos" and "Spinach Crunchies"), but such innovations do little to increase consumer interest.
- A growing array of generic cereal brands have been underselling GBC's products by more than $1 per box, especially in giant retail outlets.
- This past June, GBC dropped its cereal prices by roughly 20 percent, but by this time the brand had lost substantial market share to generic cereal brands.

"What did you find?"

Conclusions

- Slow but progressive loss of market share threatens GBC's dominance as industry leader.
- GBC must regain consumer loyalty to reinvigorate its market base.
- Not only have discount coupon promotions proven ineffective, but the manufacturer's cost for such promotions can total as much as 20 percent of sales revenue.
- Our new cereal products have done more to erode than to enhance GBC's brand image.

"What does it mean?"

FIGURE 9.7 **An Executive Abstract** This document might be the only section of the complete, 40-page report that will be read by many in its intended audience.

"What should be done?"

Recommendations

To regain lost market share and ensure continued dominance, GBC should implement the following recommendations:

1. Eliminate coupon promotions immediately.
2. Curtail development of new cereal products, and invest in improving the taste and nutritional value of GBC's traditional products.
3. Capitalize on GBC's brand recognition with an advertising campaign to promote GBC's "best-sellers" as an "all-day" food (say, as a healthful snack or lunch or an inexpensive alternative to microwave dinners).
4. Examine the possibility of high-volume sales at discounted prices through giant retail chains.

FIGURE 9.7 *(Continued)*

Global considerations

Consider also that when summarizing information you may be tempted to leave out material highly relevant to global or diverse readers. Don't assume that certain facts are always "common knowledge" and leave them out of summaries you know will be read by a global audience.

Although summaries do have their place in our busy world, the more complex the topic, the more readers need the whole story.

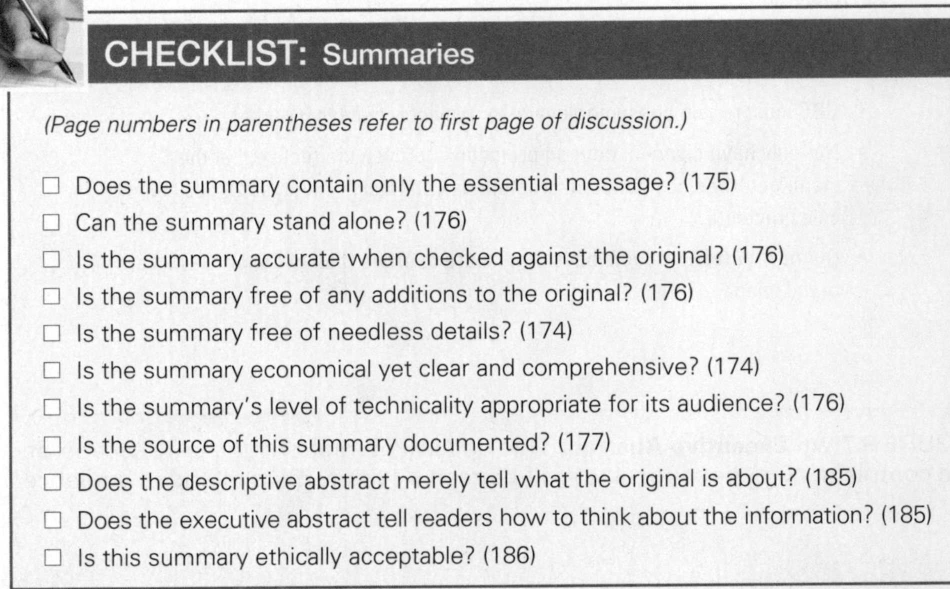

CHECKLIST: Summaries

(Page numbers in parentheses refer to first page of discussion.)

- ☐ Does the summary contain only the essential message? (175)
- ☐ Can the summary stand alone? (176)
- ☐ Is the summary accurate when checked against the original? (176)
- ☐ Is the summary free of any additions to the original? (176)
- ☐ Is the summary free of needless details? (174)
- ☐ Is the summary economical yet clear and comprehensive? (174)
- ☐ Is the summary's level of technicality appropriate for its audience? (176)
- ☐ Is the source of this summary documented? (177)
- ☐ Does the descriptive abstract merely tell what the original is about? (185)
- ☐ Does the executive abstract tell readers how to think about the information? (185)
- ☐ Is this summary ethically acceptable? (186)

Projects

GENERAL

1. Find an article about your major field or area of interest and write both an informative abstract and a descriptive abstract for that article.
2. Find a long article (at least five pages) and summarize it, following the step-by-step process described in this chapter, and keeping accuracy, completeness, conciseness, and nontechnical language always in mind. Capture the essence and main points of the original article in no more than one-fourth the length. Use your own words, and do not distort the original. Submit a copy of the original along with your summary.

TEAM

In small groups, choose a topic for discussion: an employment problem, a campus problem, plans for an event, suggestions for energy conservation, or the like. (A possible topic: Should employers have the right to require lie detector tests, drug tests, or HIV tests for their employees?) Discuss the topic for one class period, taking notes on significant points and conclusions. Afterward, organize and edit your notes according to the directions for writing summaries. Write a summary of the group discussion in no more than 200 words. As a group, compare your individual summaries for accuracy, emphasis, conciseness, and clarity.

DIGITAL AND SOCIAL MEDIA

In class, form teams whose members have similar majors or interests. Decide on a related topic currently in the news. Compare the news coverage of the same topic in different media formats. For example, find the print copy of a newspaper story, then an online version of the same story, and, if available, a Twitter posting (tweet) from the newspaper's Twitter site.

Each team member should compare the benefits and drawbacks of the story's shorter and longer versions, making a copy of each. Are there instances in which the shorter version simply is ethically inadequate as a sole source of information? Using your sample documents, explain and illustrate. As a full team, assemble and discuss the collected findings, and select one member to present the findings to the class.

GLOBAL

Find a long article (longer than five pages) from a technical, scientific, financial, or similar publication that deals with an issue that is global in scope (for instance, an article about the use of pesticides in different countries or one that discusses the ways in which financial decisions have worldwide impacts). Summarize this article for an audience comprising two different groups of nonspecialists: one group of United States citizens and another group of citizens in a different country. Learn what you can about the other country by looking on the Internet and determining key scientific, political, or financial issues. Or bring knowledge you have from your own travel (such as a study abroad experience) or background, or from a class that you took. What will you highlight in the summary for the U.S. readers, and what will you highlight in the article for the non-U.S. readers, and why? Bring both copies to class to discuss with others.

PART 3

Organization, Style, and Visual Design

10 Organizing for Readers

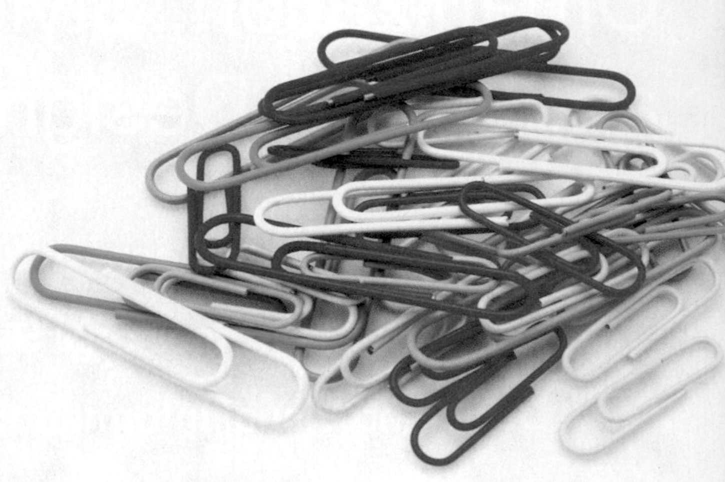

"I have to make sure that whatever I'm writing is clear *to me* first, and that the way I've organized it makes sense *to me*. Then I take that material and become more objective. I try to understand how my audience thinks: 'How can I make this logical to my audience? Will they understand what I want them to understand?'

Organizing is the key. Develop the type of outlining or listing or brainstorming tool that works best for you, but *find* one that works, and use it consistently. Then you'll be comfortable with that general strategy whenever you sit down to write, especially under a rigid deadline."

—Anne Brill,
Environmental Engineer

LEARNING OBJECTIVES FOR THIS CHAPTER

- Work from an introduction-body-conclusion structure
- Create informal and formal outlines
- Prepare a storyboard for a long document
- Shape effective paragraphs
- Chunk information into discrete units
- Provide overviews of longer documents

In order to comprehend your thinking, readers need information organized in a way that makes sense to *them*. But data rarely materializes or thinking rarely occurs in neat, predictable sequences. Instead of forcing readers to make sense of unstructured information, we shape this material for their understanding. As we organize a document, we face questions such as these:

Questions in organizing for readers

- What relationships do the collected data suggest?
- What should I emphasize?
- In which sequence will readers approach this material?
- What belongs where?
- What do I say first? Why?
- What comes next?
- How do I end the presentation?

To answer these questions, we rely on a variety of organizing strategies.

THE TYPICAL SHAPE OF WORKPLACE DOCUMENTS

Standard introduction/body/conclusion pattern

Organize your material to make the document logical from the reader's point of view. Begin with the basics: Useful documents of any length (memo, letter, long report, and so on) typically follow the pattern shown in Figure 10.1: *introduction, body*, and *conclusion*. The introduction attracts the reader's attention, announces the writer's viewpoint, and previews what will follow. The body delivers on the promise implied in the introduction. The body explains and supports the writer's viewpoint, achieving *unity* by remaining focused on that viewpoint and *coherence* by carrying a line of thought from sentence to sentence in a logical order. Finally, the conclusion has various purposes: it might reemphasize key points, take a position, predict an outcome, offer a solution, or suggest further study. Good conclusions give readers a clear perspective on what they have just read.

MEMORANDUM

To: Department Managers
From: Jill McCreary, General Manager J.M.
Date: December 8, 20XX
Subject: *Diversity training initiative*

Introduction announces the topic and provides an overview of what will follow

As part of our ongoing efforts to highlight the company's commitment to diversity, we recently conducted two surveys—one directed to company employees and one to our retail buyers. We have just received the survey results from our outside analysts. The employee survey indicates that the members of all departments appreciate our efforts to create a diverse and comfortable work environment. The customer survey indicates that our company is well regarded for marketing products in ways that appeal to diverse buyers. However, both surveys also illuminate areas in which we could do even better. As a result, we will be initiating a new series of diversity training workshops early next year. Let me explain the survey findings that have led to this initiative.

Body provides the evidence and data to support the claims made in the introduction

First, the employee survey indicates that our workforce is rated "highly diverse" in terms of gender, with nearly equal representation of male and female employees in both managerial and nonmanagerial positions; however, we could do better in terms of minority representation at the managerial level. Meanwhile, the customer survey demonstrates that our customers are "very satisfied" with the diversity of our marketing materials, but that we fail to provide enough materials for our native Spanish-speaking buyers.

Conclusion summarizes by taking a position and making recommendations

Those are the survey highlights—see the attached analysis for a more detailed picture. Again, we are doing well, but could do better. We feel that the best solution to address our weaker areas is to conduct a second series of diversity training workshops in the upcoming 12 months. We hope that these workshops—which are often illuminating to both new employees and those who have attended diversity trainings earlier—will help keep the word "diversity" at the forefront of everyone's thoughts when hiring and mentoring employees and creating marketing materials. More information will follow, but for now please emphasize to your department employees the importance and value of these workshops.

FIGURE 10.1 Document with a Standard Introduction/Body/Conclusion Structure

A nonstandard structure also can be effective in certain cases

There are many ways of adapting this standard structure. For example, Figure 10.2 provides visual features (columns, colors), headings, and an engaging layout. Although organized differently from the previous document, Figure 10.2 does provide an introduction, a body, and a conclusion. The

JUST THE FACTS FOR CONSUMERS

ARSENIC IN YOUR DRINKING WATER

Use of visuals, color, and columns makes the organization clear

What is arsenic?

Arsenic is a toxic chemical element that is unevenly distributed in the Earth's crust in soil, rocks, and minerals.

"What is arsenic?" paragraph is placed above subsequent sections, indicating that it is the introduction

How does arsenic get into my drinking water?

Arsenic occurs naturally in the environment and as a by-product of some agricultural and industrial activities. It can enter drinking water through the ground or as runoff into surface water sources.

How is arsenic in drinking water regulated?

In 1974, Congress passed the Safe Drinking Water Act. This law directs EPA to issue non-enforceable health goals and enforceable drinking water regulations for contaminants that may cause health problems. The goals, which reflect the level at which no adverse health effects are expected, are called maximum contaminant level goals (MCLGs). The MCLG for arsenic is 0 parts per billion (ppb).

The enforceable standard for arsenic is a maximum contaminant level (MCL). MCLs are set as close to the health goals as possible, considering cost, benefits, and the ability of public water systems to detect and remove contaminants using suitable treatment technologies.

Why should I be concerned about arsenic in my drinking water?

Although short-term exposures to high doses (about a thousand times higher than the drinking water standard) cause adverse effects in people, such exposures do not occur from public water supplies in the U.S. that comply with the arsenic MCL.

Some people who drink water containing arsenic in excess of EPA's standard over many years could experience skin damage or problems with their circulatory system, and may have an increased risk of getting cancer. Health effects might include:

- Thickening and discoloration of the skin, stomach pain, nausea, vomiting, diarrhea, and liver effects;
- Cardiovascular, pulmonary, immunological, neurological (e.g., numbness and partial paralysis), reproductive, and endocrine (e.g., diabetes) effects;
- Cancer of the bladder, lungs, skin, kidney, nasal passages, liver, and prostate.

These lengthier sections are balanced in the middle of the page to indicate the body

What is EPA's standard for arsenic in drinking water?

To protect consumers served by public water systems from the health risks of long-term (chronic) arsenic exposure, EPA recently lowered the arsenic MCL from 50 ppb to 10 ppb.

"What is EPA's standard?" section is placed at the bottom of the page, indicating that it is a conclusion

FIGURE 10.2 **Document with a Nonstandard, But Well-Organized Structure**

Source: Environmental Protection Agency <www.epa.gov>

heading "What is arsenic?" represents a form of introduction. The next several headings answer the question posed in the introduction, forming, in essence, the body of the document. The final heading, asking about EPA standards, represents a form of conclusion, moving beyond data and description to the topic of policy and use.

In organizing any document, we typically begin with the time-tested strategy known as *outlining*.

OUTLINING

Outlining is essential

Even basic documents require at least an introduction-body-conclusion outline done in your head and/or a few ideas jotted down in list form. Longer documents require a more detailed outline so that you can visualize your document overall and ensure that ideas flow logically from point to point.

An Outlining Strategy

Start by searching through the information you have gathered and creating a random list of key topics your document should include. For instance, in preparing the drinking water document in Figure 10.2, you might start by simply listing all the types of information you think readers need or expect:

Start by creating a list of essential information

- explain what the EPA is doing about arsenic in drinking water
- define what arsenic is
- explain how arsenic gets into drinking water
- list some of the effects of arsenic (stomach, heart, cancer)
- include specific data
- mention/explain the Safe Water Drinking Act
- refer to/define MCLGs

Now you can reorganize this list, as shown below.

A simple list like the one above usually suffices for organizing a short document like the memo in Figure 10.1. However, for a more complex document, transform your list into a deliberate map that will guide readers from point to point. Create an introduction, body, and conclusion and then decide how you will divide each of these parts into subtopics. An outline for Figure 10.2 might look like this:

Then organize the information into an outline

I. Introduction—Define arsenic.

II. Body

   A. Explain how arsenic gets into drinking water.

   B. Explain how it is regulated (1974 Safe Drinking Water Act/MCLGs, Maximum Contaminant Level Goals).

   C. List some of the health effects of arsenic (visible effects, diseases, cancers).

III. Conclusion—Describe the EPA's standards.

The Formal Outline

In planning a long document, an author or team rarely begins with a formal outline. But eventually in the writing process, a long or complex document calls for much more than a simple list. Figure 10.3 shows a formal outline for the report examining the health effects of electromagnetic fields, on pages 523–33.

Long documents call for formal outlines

NOTE *Long reports often begin directly with a statement of purpose. For the intended audience (i.e., generalists) of the report outlined in Figure 10.3, however, the technical topic must first be defined so that readers understand the context. Also, each level of division yields at least two items. If you cannot divide a major item into at least two subordinate items, retain only your major heading.*

A formal outline easily converts to a table of contents for the finished document, as shown in Chapter 22.

NOTE *Because they serve mainly to guide the writer, minor outline headings (such as items [a] and [b] under II.A.2 in Figure 10.3) may be omitted from the table of contents or the report itself. Excessive headings make a document seem fragmented.*

In technical documents, alphanumeric notation often is replaced by decimal notation. Compare the following with part "A" of the DATA SECTION from Figure 10.3.

Part of a formal outline using decimal notation

2.0 DATA SECTION
- 2.1 Sources of EMF Exposure
  - 2.1.1 power lines
  - 2.1.2 home and office
    - 2.1.2.1 kitchen
    - 2.1.2.2 workshop [and so on]
  - 2.1.3 natural radiation
  - 2.1.4 risk factors
    - 2.1.4.1 current intensity
    - 2.1.4.2 source proximity [and so on]

The decimal outline makes it easier to refer readers to specifically numbered sections ("See section 2.1.2"). Decimal notation is usually preferred in the workplace.

You may wish to expand your *topic outline* into a *sentence outline*, in which each sentence serves as a topic sentence for a paragraph in the document:

A sentence outline

2.0 DATA SECTION
- 2.1 Although the 2 million miles of power lines crisscrossing the United States have been the focus of the EMF controversy, potentially harmful waves also are emitted by household wiring, appliances, electric blankets, and computer terminals.

Sentence outlines are used mainly in collaborative projects in which various team members prepare different sections of a long document.

Children Exposed to EMFs: A Risk Assessment

I. INTRODUCTION
    A. Definition of electromagnetic fields
    B. Background on the health issues
    C. Description of the local power line configuration
    D. Purpose of this report
    E. Brief description of data sources
    F. Scope of this inquiry

II. DATA SECTION [Body]
    A. Sources of EMF exposure
        1. power lines
        2. home and office
            a. kitchen
            b. workshop [and so on]
        3. natural radiation
        4. risk factors
            a. current intensity
            b. source proximity
            c. duration of exposure
    B. Studies of health effects
        1. population surveys
        2. laboratory measurements
        3. workplace links
    C. Conflicting views of studies
        1. criticism of methodology in population studies
        2. criticism of overgeneralized lab findings
    D. Power industry views
        1. uncertainty about risk
        2. confusion about risk avoidance
    E. Risk-avoidance measures
        1. nationally
        2. locally

III. CONCLUSION
    A. Summary and overall interpretation of findings
    B. Recommendations

FIGURE 10.3 **A Formal Outline Using Alphanumeric Notation** In an outline, *alphanumeric notation* refers to the use of letters and numbers.

NOTE *The neat and ordered outlines in this book show the final* ***products*** *of writing and organizing, not the* ***process,*** *which is often initially messy and chaotic. Many writers don't start out with an outline at all! Instead, they scratch and scribble with pencil and paper or click away at the keyboard, making lots of false starts as they hammer out some kind of acceptable draft; only then do they outline to get their thinking straight.*

Not until you finish the final draft of a long document do you compose the finished outline. This outline serves as a model for your table of contents, as a check on your reasoning, and as a way of revealing to readers a clear line of thinking.

NOTE *No single form of outline should be followed slavishly. The organization of any document ultimately is determined by the reader's needs and expectations. In many cases, specific requirements about a document's organization and style are spelled out in a company's style guide (see page 297).*

GUIDELINES for Outlining

- **List key topics and subtopics to be included in your document.** Determine what information is important to include.
- **Set up a standard outline.** Start with a typical introduction, body, and conclusion structure, even if you plan to vary the structure later.
- **Place key topics and subtopics where they fit within your standard outline.** Keep your introduction brief, setting the stage for the rest of your document. Include your specific data in the body section, to back up what you promised in your introduction. Do not introduce new data in the conclusion.
- **Use alphanumeric or decimal notation consistently throughout the outline.**
- **Avoid excessive subtopics.** If you find that your outline is getting into multiple levels of detail too often, think of ways to combine information. Do not go to another level unless there are at least two distinct subtopics at that level.
- **Refine your outline as you write your document.** Continue revising the outline until you complete the document.

STORYBOARDING

Visualize each section of your outline

As you prepare a long document, one useful organizing tool is the *storyboard,* a sketch of the finished document.

Figure 10.4 displays one storyboard module based on Section II A of the outline on page 198. Much more specific and visual than an outline, a storyboard

section title	**Sources of EMF Exposure**
text	Discuss milligauss measurements as indicators of cancer risk
text	Brief lead-in to power line emissions
visual	EPS table comparing power line emissions at various distances
text	Discuss EMF sources in home and office
visual	Table comparing EMF emissions from common sources
text	Discuss major risk factors: Voltage versus current; proximity versus duration of exposure; sporadic, high-level exposure versus constant, low-level exposure
visual	Line graph showing strength of exposure in relation to distance from electrical appliances
text	Focus on the key role of proximity to the EMF source in risk assessment

Special considerations:

- *Define all specialized terms (current, voltage, milligauss, and so on) for a general audience.*
- *Emphasize that no "safe" level of EMF exposure has been established.*
- *Emphasize that even the earth's magnetic field emits significant electromagnetic radiation.*

FIGURE 10.4 One Module from a Storyboard Notice how the module begins with the section title, describes each text block and each visual, and includes suggestions about special considerations. (To see this section of the document in its final form, go to page 524).

maps out each section (or module) of your outline, topic by topic, to help you see the shape and appearance of the entire document in its final form. Working from a storyboard, you can rearrange, delete, and insert material as needed—without having to wrestle with a draft of the entire document.

Storyboarding is especially helpful when people collaborate to prepare various parts of a document and then get together to edit and assemble their material. In such cases, storyboard modules may be displayed on whiteboards, posterboards, flip charts, or computer screens.

NOTE *Try creating a storyboard after writing a full draft, for a bird's-eye view of the document's organization.*

PARAGRAPHING

¶

Readers look for orientation, for shapes they can recognize. But a document's larger design (introduction, body, conclusion) depends on the smaller design of each paragraph.

Shape information into paragraphs

Paragraphs have various shapes and purposes (introduction, conclusion, or transition), but the focus here is on standard *support paragraphs*. Although part of the document's larger design, each support paragraph can usually stand alone in meaning.

The Support Paragraph

All the sentences in a standard support paragraph relate to the main point, which is expressed as the *topic sentence:*

Topic sentences

- As sea levels rise, New York City faces increasing risk of hurricane storm surge.
- A video display terminal can endanger the operator's health.
- Chemical pesticides and herbicides are both ineffective and hazardous.

Each topic sentence introduces an idea, judgment, or opinion. But in order to grasp the writer's exact meaning, people need explanation. Consider the third statement:

- Chemical pesticides and herbicides are both ineffective and hazardous.

Imagine that you are a researcher for the Epson Electric Light Company, assigned this question: Should the company (1) begin spraying pesticides and herbicides under its power lines, or (2) continue with its manual (and nonpolluting) ways of minimizing foliage and insect damage to lines and poles? If you simply responded with the preceding assertion, your employer would have further questions:

- Why, exactly, are these methods ineffective and hazardous?
- What are the problems? Can you explain?

To answer the previous questions and to support your assertion, you need a fully developed paragraph:

Introduction (1-topic sentence)
Body (2–6)
Conclusion (7–8)

> [1]**Chemical pesticides and herbicides are both ineffective and hazardous.** [2]Because none of these chemicals has permanent effects, pest populations invariably recover and need to be resprayed. [3]Repeated applications cause pests to develop immunity to the chemicals. [4]Furthermore, most of these products attack species other than the intended pest, killing off its natural predators, thus actually increasing the pest population. [5]Above all, chemical residues survive in the environment (and living tissue) for years, often carried hundreds of miles by wind and water. [6]This toxic legacy includes such biological effects as birth deformities, reproductive failures, brain damage, and cancer. [7]Although intended to control pest populations, these chemicals ironically threaten to make the human population their ultimate victims. [8]I therefore recommend continuing our manual control methods.

Most standard support paragraphs in technical writing have an introduction-body-conclusion structure. They begin with a clear topic (or orienting) sentence stating a generalization. Details in the body support the generalization.

ts The Topic Sentence

Readers look to a paragraph's opening sentences for the main idea. The topic sentence should appear *first* (or early) in the paragraph, unless you have good reason to place it elsewhere. Think of your topic sentence as "the one sentence you would keep if you could keep only one" (U.S. Air Force Academy 11). In some instances, a main idea may require a "topic statement" consisting of two or more sentences, as in this example:

A topic statement can have two or more sentences

> The most common strip-mining methods are open-pit mining, contour mining, and auger mining. The specific method employed will depend on the type of terrain that covers the coal.

The topic sentence or topic statement should focus and forecast. Don't write *Some pesticides are less hazardous and often more effective than others* when you mean *Organic pesticides are less hazardous and often more effective than their chemical counterparts.* The first version is vague; the second helps us focus and tells us what to expect from the paragraph.

¶un Paragraph Unity

A paragraph is unified when all its content belongs—when every word, phrase, and sentence directly expands on the topic sentence.

A unified paragraph

> **Solar power offers an efficient, economical, and safe solution to the Northeast's energy problems.** To begin with, solar power is highly efficient. Solar collectors installed on fewer than 30 percent of roofs in the Northeast would provide more than 70 percent of the area's heating and air-conditioning needs. Moreover, solar heat collectors are economical, operating for up to twenty years with little or no maintenance. These savings recoup the initial cost of installation within only ten years. Most important, solar power is safe. It can be transformed into electricity through photovoltaic cells (a type of storage battery) in a noiseless process that produces no air pollution—unlike coal, oil, and wood combustion. In contrast to its nuclear counterpart, solar power produces no toxic waste and poses no catastrophic danger of meltdown. Thus, massive conversion to solar power would ensure abundant energy and a safe, clean environment for future generations.

One way to damage unity in the paragraph above would be to veer from the focus on *efficient*, *economical*, and *safe* toward material about the differences between active and passive solar heating or the advantages of solar power over wind power.

Every topic sentence has a key word or phrase that carries the meaning. In the pesticide-herbicide paragraph (page 202), the key words are *ineffective* and *hazardous*. Anything that fails to advance their meaning throws the paragraph—and the readers—off track.

Paragraph Coherence

¶coh

In a coherent paragraph, everything not only belongs, but also sticks together: Topic sentence and support form a *connected line of thought*, like links in a chain.

Paragraph coherence can be damaged by (1) short, choppy sentences; (2) sentences in the wrong order; (3) insufficient transitions and connectors for linking related ideas; or (4) an inaccessible line of reasoning. Here is how the solar energy paragraph might become incoherent:

An incoherent paragraph

> Solar power offers an efficient, economical, and safe solution to the Northeast's energy problems. Unlike nuclear power, solar power produces no toxic waste and poses no danger of meltdown. Solar power is efficient. Solar collectors could be installed on fewer than 30 percent of roofs in the Northeast. These collectors would provide more than 70 percent of the area's heating and air-conditioning needs. Solar power is safe. It can be transformed into electricity. This transformation is made possible by photovoltaic cells (a type of storage battery). Solar heat collectors are economical. The photovoltaic process produces no air pollution.

In the above paragraph, the second sentence, about safety, belongs near the end. Also, because of short, choppy sentences and insufficient links between ideas, the paragraph reads more like a list than a flowing discussion. Finally, a concluding sentence is needed to complete the chain of reasoning and to give readers a clear perspective on what they've just read.

Here, in contrast, is the original, coherent paragraph with sentences numbered for later discussion; transitions and connectors are shown in boldface. Notice how this version reveals a clear line of thought:

A coherent paragraph

> [1]Solar power offers an efficient, economical, and safe solution to the Northeast's energy problems. [2]**To begin with**, solar power is highly efficient. [3]Solar collectors installed on fewer than 30 percent of roofs in the Northeast would provide more than 70 percent of the area's heating and air-conditioning needs. [4]**Moreover**, solar heat collectors are economical, operating for up to twenty years with little or no maintenance. [5]**These savings** recoup the initial cost of installation within only ten years. [6]**Most important**, solar power is safe. [7]**It** can be transformed into electricity through photovoltaic cells (a type of storage battery) in a noiseless process that produces no air pollution—unlike coal, oil, and wood combustion.[8]**In contrast** to its nuclear counterpart, solar power produces no toxic waste and poses no danger of catastrophic meltdown. [9]**Thus**, massive conversion to solar power would ensure abundant energy and a safe, clean environment for future generations.

We can easily trace the sequence of thoughts in the previous paragraph:

1. The topic sentence establishes a clear direction.
2–3. The first reason is given and then explained.
4–5. The second reason is given and explained.
6–8. The third and major reason is given and explained.
9. The conclusion reemphasizes the main point.

To reinforce the logical sequence, related ideas are combined in individual sentences, and transitions and connectors signal clear relationships. The whole paragraph sticks together. For more on transitions and other connectors, see page 701.

¶lgth

Paragraph Length

Paragraph length depends on the writer's purpose and the reader's capacity for understanding. Writing that contains highly technical information or complex instructions may use short paragraphs or perhaps a list. In writing that explains concepts, attitudes, or viewpoints, support paragraphs generally run from 100 to 300 words. But word count really means very little. What matters is *how thoroughly the paragraph makes your point.*

Try to avoid too much of anything. A clump of short paragraphs can make some writing seem choppy and poorly organized, but a stretch of long paragraphs can be tiring. A well-placed short paragraph—sometimes just one sentence—can highlight an important idea.

> **NOTE** *In writing displayed on computer screens, short paragraphs and lists are especially useful because they allow for easy scanning and navigation.*

CHUNKING

Each organizing technique discussed in this chapter is a way of *chunking* information: breaking it down into discrete, digestible units, based on the readers' needs and the document's purpose. Well-chunked material generally is easier to follow and is more visually appealing.

Break information down into smaller units

Chunking enables us to show which pieces of information belong together and how the various pieces are connected. For example, a discussion about research in technical communication might be divided into two chunks:

- Procedural Stages
- Inquiry Stages

A major topic chunked into subtopics

Each of these units then divides into smaller chunks:

- Procedural Stages
  - Searching for Information
  - Recording Your Findings
  - Documenting Your Sources
  - Writing the Document
- Inquiry Stages
  - Asking the Right Questions
  - Exploring a Balance of Views
  - Achieving Adequate Depth in Your Search
  - Evaluating Your Findings
  - Interpreting Your Findings

Subtopics chunked into smaller topics

Any of these segments that become too long might be subdivided again.

> **NOTE** *Chunking requires careful decisions about exactly how much is enough and what constitutes sensible proportions among the parts. Don't overdo it by creating such tiny segments that your document ends up looking fragmented and disconnected.*

In addition to chunking information verbally, we can chunk it visually. Notice how the visual display on page 125 of Chapter 7 (Figures 7.1A and 7.1B) makes relationships immediately apparent. (For more on visual design, see Chapter 12.)

Using visuals for chunking

Finally, we can chunk information by using white space, headings, or other forms of page design. A well-designed page provides immediate cues about where to look and how to proceed. (For more on page design, see Chapter 13.)

When you write for the Web, you chunk information differently than when you write for print. On Web pages, readers expect information in very short chunks because they don't like reading large blocks of text on a computer screen. Also, readers want the option of zeroing in on various parts of the page and of moving from link to link. In printed documents, however, readers tolerate longer

Chunking on the Web versus chunking on a printed page

Using page design for chunking

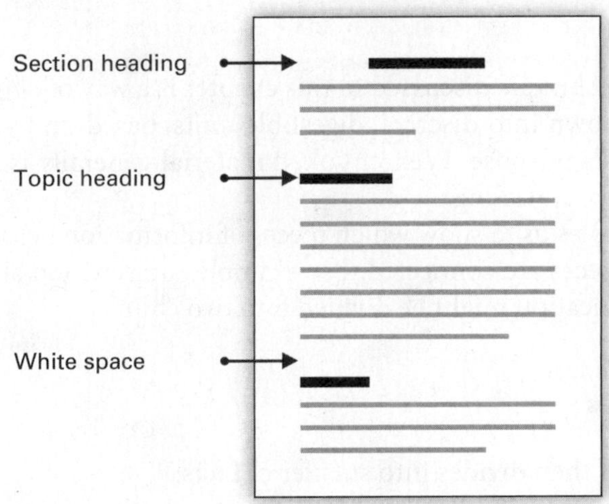

passages of text because the printed page is easier on the eyes. Also, readers expect to *scan* a printed page sequentially rather than navigate a linked network.

PROVIDING AN OVERVIEW

Show the big picture

Once you've settled on a final organization for your document, give readers an immediate preview of its contents by answering their initial questions:

What readers want to know immediately

- What is the purpose of this document?
- Why should I read it?
- What information can I expect to find here?

Readers will have additional, more specific questions as well, but first they want to know what the document is all about and how it relates to them.

An overview should be placed near the beginning of a document, but you may also want to provide section overviews at the beginning of each section in a long document. The following is an overview of a long report on groundwater contamination.

A report overview

> **About This Report**
> This report contains five sections. Section One describes the scope and scale of groundwater contamination in Jackson county. Section Two offers background on previous legislation related to groundwater. Section Three shows the most recent data from the Jackson County Groundwater Project, and Section Four compares that data to national averages. Section Five offers recommendations and ideas for next steps.

Overviews come in various shapes and sizes. The overview for this book, for example, appears on page xxiii, under the heading "How This Book is Organized." An informative abstract of a long document also provides an overview, as on page 541. An overview for an oral presentation appears on page 600 as an introduction to that presentation. Whatever its shape or size a good overview gives readers the "big picture" to help them navigate the document or presentation and understand its details.

ORGANIZING FOR GLOBAL AUDIENCES

Different cultures have varying expectations as to how information should be organized. For instance, a paragraph in English typically begins with a topic sentence, followed by related supporting sentences; any digression from this main idea is considered harmful to the paragraph's *unity*. But some cultures consider digression a sign of intelligence or politeness. To native readers of English, the long introductions and digressions in certain Spanish or Russian documents might seem tedious and confusing, but a Spanish or Russian reader might view the more direct organization of English as abrupt and simplistic (Leki 151).

Expectations differ even among same-language cultures. British correspondence, for instance, typically expresses the bad news directly up front, instead of taking the indirect approach preferred in the United States. A bad news letter or memo appropriate for a U.S. audience could be considered evasive by British readers (Scott and Green 19).

CHECKLIST: Organizing Information

(Numbers in parentheses refer to the first page of discussion.)

- ☐ Does the document employ a standard or varied introduction/body/conclusion structure? (193)
- ☐ Will the outline allow me to include all the necessary data for the document? (196)
- ☐ Is this outline organized using alphanumeric or decimal notation? (197)
- ☐ Have I created a storyboard to supplement my formal outline? (199)
- ☐ Is the information chunked into discrete, digestible units for the proper medium (print or Web)? (205)
- ☐ Does each paragraph include these features? (201)
    - **topic sentence (introduction)**
    - **unity (body that supports the topic sentence)**
    - **coherence (connected line of thought leading to a conclusion)**
- ☐ If appropriate, does the document include an overview, offering a larger picture of what will follow? (206)
- ☐ Have I considered my audience's specific cultural expectations? (207)

Projects

GENERAL

1. For each document below, use the outlining strategy described on page 196 to list the topics that need to be covered. Then, organize your list into a formal outline (page 197) most suited to readers of this particular type of document.
   - instructions for operating a power tool
   - a campaign report describing your progress in political fund-raising
   - a report analyzing the weakest parts in a piece of industrial machinery
   - a report analyzing the desirability of a proposed nuclear power plant in your area
   - a detailed breakdown of your monthly budget to trim excess spending
   - a report evaluating the effects of the ban on DDT in insect control
   - a report investigating the success of a no-grade policy at other colleges

TEAM

Assume your group is preparing a report titled "The Negative Effects of Strip Mining on the Cumberland Plateau Region of Kentucky." After brainstorming and researching, you all settle on four major topics:

- economic and social effects of strip mining
- description of the strip-mining process
- environmental effects of strip mining
- description of the Cumberland Plateau

Assume that subsequent research and further brainstorming produce this list of subtopics:

- strip mining method used in this region
- location of the region
- permanent land damage
- water pollution
- lack of educational progress
- geological formation of the region
- open-pit mining
- unemployment
- increased erosion
- auger mining
- natural resources of the region
- types of strip mining
- increased flood hazards
- depopulation
- contour mining

Arrange these subtopics under appropriate topic headings. Use decimal notation to create the body of a formal outline. Appoint one group member to present the outline in class.

Hint: Assume that your thesis is: "Decades of strip mining have devastated the Cumberland Plateau's environment, economy, and social structure."

DIGITAL AND SOCIAL MEDIA

Locate a Web page and a print document (brochure, user guide) about the same product. Compare these, looking for different ways in which material is organized on the Web versus in print. Compare, for example, the use of headings in each. In class, give a short presentation on these differences.

GLOBAL

Find a document that presents the same information in several languages (assembly instructions, for example). Even without being able to understand all of the languages used, see if you can spot any changes made in the use of headings, the length of paragraphs, or the extent to which information is chunked. Interview a language professor on campus to find out why these choices may have been made.

11 Editing for a Professional Style and Tone

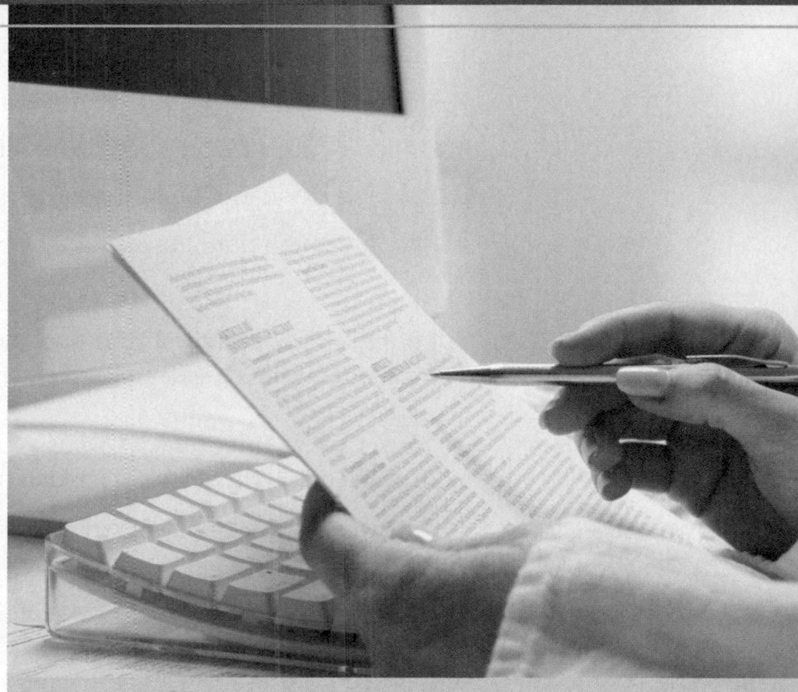

"The amount of time I spend on revision depends on the document. Internal emails and memos get at least one careful review before being distributed. All letters and other documents to outside readers get detailed attention, to make sure that what is being said is actually what was intended. There's the issue of contractual obligations here—and also the issue of liability, if someone, say, were to misinterpret a set of instructions and were injured as a result. Also there's the issue of customer relations: Most people want to transact with businesses that display 'likability' on the interpersonal front. So, getting the style just right is always a priority."

—Andy Wallin,
Communications Manager for a maker of power tools

LEARNING OBJECTIVES FOR THIS CHAPTER

- Appreciate the role of style in any document
- Write clear, concise, and fluent sentences
- Use precise language
- Achieve a tone that connects with your audience
- Understand that various cultures have various style preferences
- Understand that words can have unintended legal and ethical consequences
- Consider tone and style when writing email messages.
- Recognize the benefits and drawbacks of digital editing tools

No matter how technical your document, your audience will not understand the content unless the style is *readable,* with sentences easy to understand and words chosen precisely.

A definition of style

Every bit as important as *what* you have to say is *how* you decide to say it. Your particular writing style is a blend of these elements:

What determines your style

- the way in which you construct each sentence
- the length of your sentences
- the way in which you connect sentences
- the words and phrases you choose
- the tone you convey

Style is more than mechanical correctness

Readable style, of course, requires correct grammar, punctuation, and spelling. But correctness alone is no guarantee of readability. For example, the following response to a job application is mechanically correct but hard to read:

Inefficient style

> We are in receipt of your recent correspondence indicating your interest in securing the advertised position. Your correspondence has been duly forwarded for consideration by the personnel office, which has employment candidate selection responsibility. You may expect to hear from us relative to your application as the selection process progresses. Your interest in the position is appreciated.

Notice how hard you had to work to extract information from the previous paragraph when it could have been expressed this simply:

Readable style

> Your application for the advertised position has been forwarded to our personnel office. As the selection process moves forward, we will be in touch. Thank you for your interest.

Inefficient style makes readers work harder than they should.

Style can be inefficient for many reasons, but especially when it does the following:

Ways in which style goes wrong

- makes the writing impossible to interpret
- takes too long to make the point
- reads like a story from primary school
- uses imprecise or needlessly big words
- sounds stuffy and impersonal

Regardless of the cause, inefficient style results in writing that is less informative and less persuasive than it should be. Also, inefficient style can be unethical when it confuses or misleads the audience, whether intentionally or unintentionally.

To help your audience spend less time reading, you must spend more time revising for a style that is *clear*, *concise*, *fluent*, *exact*, and *likable*.

EDITING FOR CLARITY

Clear writing enables people to read each sentence only once in order to fully grasp its meaning. The following suggestions will help you edit for clarity.

Avoid Ambiguous Pronoun References

ref

Pronouns (*he*, *she*, *it*, *their*, and so on) must clearly refer to the noun they replace.

Ambiguous referent

❙ Our patients enjoy the warm days while **they** last.

(Are the patients or the warm days on their way out?)

Depending on whether the referent (or antecedent) for *they* is *patients* or *warm days*, the sentence can be clarified.

Clear referent

❙ While these warm days last, our patients enjoy them.

or

❙ Our terminal patients enjoy the warm days.

Ambiguous referent

❙ Jack resents his assistant because **he** is competitive.

(Who's the competitive one—Jack or his assistant?)

Clear referent

❙ Because his assistant is competitive, Jack resents him.

or

❙ Because Jack is competitive, he resents his assistant.

(See page 683 for more on pronoun references, and page 237 for avoiding sexist bias in pronoun use.)

mod

Avoid Ambiguous Modifiers

A modifier is a word (usually an adjective or an adverb) or a group of words (usually a phrase or a clause) that provides information about other words or groups of words. If a modifier is too far from the words it modifies, the message can be ambiguous. Position modifiers to reflect your meaning.

Ambiguous modifier

Only press the red button in an emergency.

(Does ***only*** modify ***press*** or ***emergency***?)

Clear modifiers

Press **only** the red button in an emergency.

or

Press the red button in an emergency **only**.

(See page 683 for more on modifiers.)

EXERCISE 1

Edit each sentence below to eliminate ambiguities in pronoun reference or to clarify ambiguous modifiers.

a. Janice dislikes working with Claire because she's impatient.
b. Bill told Fred that he was mistaken.
c. Only use this phone in a red alert.
d. Just place the dishes back in the cabinets after 8 P.M.

st mod

Unstack Modifying Nouns

Too many nouns in a row can create confusion and reading difficulty. One noun can modify another (as in "software development"). But when two or more nouns modify a noun, the string of words becomes hard to read and ambiguous.

Ambiguous use of stacked nouns

Be sure to leave enough time for a **training session participant** evaluation.

(Evaluation of the session or of the participants?)

With no articles, prepositions, or verbs, readers cannot sort out the relationships among the nouns.

Clear sentences with nouns unstacked

Be sure to leave enough time **for** participants **to evaluate** the training session.

or

Be sure to leave enough time **to evaluate** participants in **the** training session.

wo

Arrange Word Order for Coherence and Emphasis

In coherent writing, everything sticks together; each sentence builds on the preceding sentence and looks ahead to the one that follows. In similar fashion, sentences generally work best when the beginning looks back at familiar information and the end provides the new (or unfamiliar) information:

Familiar		Unfamiliar
My dog	has	fleas.
Our boss	just won	the lottery.
This company	is planning	a merger.

The above pattern also emphasizes the new information. Every sentence has a key word or phrase that sums up the new information and that usually is emphasized best at the end of the sentence.

- We expect a **refund** because of your error in our shipment. — Faulty emphasis
- Because of your error in our shipment, we expect a **refund.** — Correct emphasis
- In a business relationship, **trust** is a vital element. — Faulty emphasis
- A business relationship depends on **trust.** — Correct emphasis

One exception to placing key words last occurs with an imperative statement (a command, an order, an instruction), with the subject [*you*] understood. For instance, each step in a list of instructions should begin with an action verb (*insert, open, close, turn, remove, press*).

- **Disable** the alarm before activating the system. — Correct emphasis
- **Remove** the protective seal.

With the opening key word, readers know immediately what action to take.

EXERCISE 2

Edit to unstack modifying nouns or to rearrange word order for coherence and emphasis.

a. Develop online editing system documentation.
b. I recommend these management performance improvement incentives.
c. Our profits have doubled since we automated our assembly line.
d. Education enables us to recognize excellence and to achieve it.
e. In all writing, revision is required.
f. Sarah's job involves fault analysis systems troubleshooting handbook preparation.

Use Active Voice Whenever Possible

av

In general, readers grasp the meaning more quickly and clearly when the writer uses the active voice ("I did it") rather than the passive voice ("It was done by me"). In active voice sentences, a clear agent performs a clear action on a recipient:

Agent	*Action*	*Recipient*	
Joe	lost	your report.	Active voice

Passive voice, in contrast, reverses this pattern, placing the recipient of the action in the subject slot.

	Recipient	***Action***	***Agent***
Passive voice	Your report	was lost	by Joe.

Sometimes the passive eliminates the agent altogether:

Passive voice — Your report was lost.
(Who lost it?)

Passive voice is unethical if it obscures the person or other agent when that person or agent responsible should be identified.

Some writers mistakenly rely on the passive voice because they think it sounds more objective and important—whereas it often makes writing wordy and evasive.

Concise and direct (active) — **I underestimated** labor costs for this project. (7 words)

Wordy and indirect (passive) — Labor costs for this project **were underestimated by me.** (9 words)

Evasive (passive) — Labor costs for this project were underestimated.

A **mistake was made** in your shipment. (By whom?)

In reporting errors or bad news, use the active voice, for clarity and sincerity.

The passive voice creates a weak and impersonal tone.

Weak and impersonal — An offer **will be made** by us next week.

Strong and personal — **We will make** an offer next week.

Use the active voice when you want action. Otherwise, your statement will have no power.

Weak passive — If my claim is not settled by May 15, the Better Business Bureau **will be contacted,** and their advice on legal action **will be taken.**

Strong active — If you do not settle my claim by May 15, **I will contact** the Better Business Bureau for advice on legal action.

Notice above how the second, active version emphasizes the new and significant information by placing it at the end.

Ordinarily, use the active voice for giving instructions.

Passive — The bid **should be sealed.**

Care **should be taken** with the dynamite.

Active — **Seal** the bid.

Be careful with the dynamite.

Avoid shifts from active to passive voice in the same sentence.

During the meeting, project members **spoke** and **presentations were given.**	Faulty shift
During the meeting, project members **spoke** and **gave** presentations.	Correct

EXERCISE 3

Convert these passive voice sentences to concise, forceful, and direct expressions in the active voice.

a. The evaluation was performed by us.
b. Unless you pay me within three days, my lawyer will be contacted.
c. Hard hats should be worn at all times.
d. It was decided to reject your offer.
e. Our test results will be sent to you as soon as verification is completed.

Use Passive Voice Selectively

pv

Use the passive voice when your audience has no need to know the agent.

Mr. Jones **was brought** to the emergency room. The bank failure **was publicized** statewide.	Correct passive

Use the passive voice when the agent is not known or when the object is more important than the subject.

Fred's article **was published** last week. All policy claims **are kept** confidential.	Correct passive

Prefer the passive when you want to be indirect or inoffensive (as in requesting the customer's payment or the employee's cooperation, or to avoid blaming someone—such as your supervisor) (Ornatowski 94).

You have not paid your bill. **You need to overhaul** our filing system.	Blunt use of active voice
This bill **has not been paid.** Our filing system **needs to be overhauled.**	Appropriate (indirect) use of passive voice

Use the passive voice if the person behind the action needs to be protected.

The criminal **was identified.** The embezzlement scheme **was exposed.**	Correct passive

EXERCISE 4

The sentences below lack proper emphasis because of inappropriate use of the active voice. Convert each to passive voice.

a. Joe's company fired him.
b. A power surge destroyed more than two thousand lines of our new applications program.
c. You are paying inadequate attention to worker safety.
d. You are checking temperatures too infrequently.
e. You did a poor job editing this report.

OS

Avoid Overstuffed Sentences

Give no more information in one sentence than readers can retain and process.

Overstuffed

> Publicizing the records of a private meeting that took place three weeks ago to reveal the identity of a manager who criticized our company's promotion policy would be unethical.

Clear things up by sorting out the relationships.

Revised

> In a private meeting three weeks ago, a manager criticized our company's policy on promotion. It would be unethical to reveal the manager's identity by publicizing the records of that meeting.

(Other versions are possible, depending on the intended meaning.)

Even short sentences can be hard to interpret if they have too many details.

Overstuffed

> Send three copies of Form 17-e to all six departments, unless Departments A or B or both request Form 16-w instead.

EXERCISE 5

Unscramble this overstuffed sentence by making shorter, clearer sentences.

A smoke-filled room causes not only teary eyes and runny noses but also can alter people's hearing and vision, as well as creating dangerous levels of carbon monoxide, especially for people with heart and lung ailments, whose health is particularly threatened by secondhand smoke.

EDITING FOR CONCISENESS

Concise writing conveys the most information in the fewest words. But it does not omit those details necessary for clarity. Use fewer words whenever fewer will do.

But remember the difference between *clear writing* and *compressed writing* that is impossible to decipher.

> Send new vehicle air conditioner compression cut-off system specifications to engineering manager advising immediate action. — Compressed

> The cut-off system for the air conditioner compressor on our new vehicles is faulty. Send the system specifications to our engineering manager so they can be modified. — Clear

First drafts rarely are concise. Trim the fat.

Avoid Wordy Phrases

w

Each phrase below can be reduced to one word.

Wordy phrases and their substitutes

due to the fact that	=	because
the majority of	=	most
readily apparent	=	obvious
a large number	=	many
aware of the fact that	=	know

Eliminate Redundancy

red

A redundant expression says the same thing twice, in different words, as in *fellow colleagues.*

Redundant phrases

completely eliminate	**end** result
enter **into**	consensus **of opinion**
mental awareness	**utter** devastation
mutual cooperation	**the month of** August

Avoid Needless Repetition

rep

Unnecessary repetition clutters writing and dilutes meaning.

> In trauma victims, breathing is restored by **artificial respiration.** Techniques of **artificial respiration** include mouth-to-mouth **respiration** and mouth-to-nose **respiration** — Needlessly repetitious

Repetition in the above passage disappears when sentences are combined.

> In trauma victims, breathing is restored by artificial respiration, either mouth-to-mouth or mouth-to-nose. — Concise

NOTE *Don't hesitate to repeat, or at least rephrase, material (even whole paragraphs in a longer document) if you feel that readers need reminders. Effective repetition helps avoid cross-references like these: "See page 23" or "Review page 10."*

EXERCISE 6

Make these sentences more concise by eliminating wordy phrases, redundancy, and needless repetition.

a. I have admiration for Professor Jones.
b. Due to the fact that we made the lowest bid, we won the contract.
c. On previous occasions we have worked together.
d. We have completely eliminated the bugs from this program.
e. This report is the most informative report on the project.
f. This offer is the most attractive offer I've received.

---

th

Avoid *There* Sentence Openers

Many *There is* or *There are* sentence openers can be eliminated.

Needless *There* — **There is** a danger of explosion in Number 2 mineshaft.

Revised — Number 2 mineshaft is in danger of exploding.

Dropping such openers places the key words at the end of the sentence, where they are best emphasized.

NOTE *Of course, in some contexts, proper emphasis would call for a There opener.*

Appropriate *There* opener — People have often wondered about the rationale behind Boris's sudden decision. There were several good reasons for his dropping out of the program.

It

Avoid Some *It* Sentence Openers

Avoid beginning a sentence with *It*—unless the *It* clearly points to a specific referent in the preceding sentence: "This document is excellent. It deserves special recognition."

Needless *It* opener — **It** is necessary to complete both sides of the form.

Revised — Please complete both sides of the form.

pref

Delete Needless Prefaces

Instead of delaying the new information in your sentence, get right to the point.

Wordy preface — **I am writing this letter because** I wish to apply for the position of copy editor.

Concise — Please consider me for the position of copy editor.

As far as artificial intelligence is concerned, the technology is only in its infancy.	Wordy preface
Artificial intelligence technology is only in its infancy.	Concise

EXERCISE 7

Make these sentences more concise by eliminating *There* and *It* openers and needless prefaces.

a. There was severe fire damage to the reactor.
b. There are several reasons why Jane left the company.
c. It is essential that we act immediately.
d. It has been reported by Bill that several safety violations have occurred.
e. This letter is to inform you that I am pleased to accept your job offer.
f. The purpose of this report is to update our research findings.

Avoid Weak Verbs

wv

Prefer verbs that express a definite action: *open, close, move, continue, begin.* Avoid weak verbs that express no specific action: *is, was, are, has, give, make, come, take.*

NOTE *In some cases, such verbs are essential to your meaning: "Dr. Phillips is operating at 7 A.M." "Take me to the laboratory."*

All forms of *to be* (*am, are, is, was, were, will, have been, might have been*) are weak. Substitute a strong verb for conciseness.

My recommendation **is** for a larger budget.	Weak verb
I **recommend** a larger budget.	Strong verb

Don't disappear behind weak verbs and their baggage of needless nouns and prepositions.

Please **take into consideration** my offer.	Wordy verb phrase
Please **consider** my offer.	Concise verb

Strong verbs, or action verbs, suggest an assertive, positive, and confident writer. Here are examples of weak verbs converted to strong verbs:

Weak verbs and their replacements

has the ability to	=	can
give a summary of	=	summarize
make an assumption	=	assume
come to the conclusion	=	conclude
make a decision	=	decide

EXERCISE 8

Edit each of these wordy and vague sentences to eliminate weak verbs.

a. Our disposal procedure is in conformity with federal standards.
b. Please make a decision today.
c. We need to have a discussion about the problem.
d. I have just come to the realization that I was mistaken.
e. Your conclusion is in agreement with mine.

---

prep

Avoid Excessive Prepositions

Excessive prepositions

The recommendation first appeared **in** the report written **by** the supervisor in January **about** that month's productivity.

Appropriate prepositions

The recommendation first appeared in the supervisor's productivity report for January.

Each prepositional phrase here can be reduced.

Prepositional phrases and their replacements

with the exception of	=	except for
in the near future	=	soon
at the present time	=	now
in the course of	=	during
in the process of	=	during (*or* while)

nom

Avoid Nominalizations

Nouns manufactured from verbs (nominalizations) are harder to understand than the verbs themselves.

Nominalization — We ask for the **cooperation** of all employees.
Clear verb form — We ask that all employees **cooperate.**
Nominalization — Give **consideration** to the possibility of a career change.
Clear verb form — **Consider** a career change.

Besides causing wordiness, nominalizations can be vague—by hiding the agent of an action. Verbs are generally easier to read because they signal action.

Nominalization — A **valid requirement** for immediate action exists.

(Who should take the action? We can't tell.)

Precise verb form — We **must act** immediately.

Here are nominalizations restored to their action verb forms:

Nouns traded for verbs

conduct an investigation of	=	investigate
provide a description of	=	describe
conduct a test of	=	test

Nominalizations drain the life from your style. In cheering for your favorite team, you wouldn't say "Blocking of that kick is a necessity!" instead of "Block that kick!"

NOTE *Avoid excessive economy. For example, "Employees must cooperate" would not be an acceptable alternative to the first example in this section. But, for the final example, "Block that kick," would be.*

EXERCISE 9

Make these sentences more concise by eliminating needless prepositions, *to be* constructions, and nominalizations.

a. In the event of system failure, your sounding of the alarm is essential.
b. These are the recommendations of the chairperson of the committee.
c. Our acceptance of the offer is a necessity.
d. Please perform an analysis and make an evaluation of our new system.
e. A need for your caution exists.
f. Power surges are associated, in a causative way, with malfunctions of computers.

Make Negatives Positive

neg

A positive expression is easier to understand than a negative one.

- Please do not be late in submitting your report. — Indirect and wordy
- Please submit your report on time. — Direct and concise

Sentences with multiple negative expressions are even harder to translate.

- Do **not** distribute this memo to employees who have **not** received a security clearance. — Confusing and wordy
- Distribute this memo only to employees who have received a security clearance. — Clear and concise

Besides directly negative words (*no, not, never*), some indirectly negative words (*except, forget, mistake, lose, uncooperative*) also force readers to translate.

Confusing and wordy

- **Do not neglect** to activate the alarm system.
- My diagnosis was **not inaccurate.**

Clear and concise

- **Be sure** to activate the alarm system.
- My diagnosis was **accurate.**

Some negative expressions, of course, are perfectly correct, as in expressing disagreement.

Correct negatives

- This is **not** the best plan.
- Your offer is **unacceptable.**

Prefer positives to negatives, though, whenever your meaning allows:

Trading negatives for positives

did not succeed	=	failed
does not have	=	lacks
did not prevent	=	allowed
not unless	=	only if

cl Clean Out Clutter Words

Clutter words stretch a message without adding meaning. Here are some of the most common: *very, definitely, quite, extremely, rather, somewhat, really, actually, currently, situation, aspect, factor.*

Cluttered

Actually, one **aspect** of a business **situation** that could **definitely** make me **quite** happy would be to have a **somewhat** adventurous partner who **really** shared my **extreme** attraction to risks.

Concise

I seek an adventurous business partner who enjoys risks.

qual Delete Needless Qualifiers

Qualifiers such as *I feel, it seems, I believe, in my opinion,* and *I think* express uncertainty or soften the tone and force of a statement.

Appropriate qualifiers

Despite Frank's poor grades last year he will, **I think,** do well in college.

Your product **seems** to meet our needs.

But when you are certain, eliminate the qualifier so as not to seem tentative or evasive.

Needless qualifiers

It seems that I've made an error.

We **appear to** have exceeded our budget.

NOTE *In communicating across cultures, keep in mind that a direct, forceful style might be considered offensive.*

EXERCISE 10

Make these sentences more concise by changing negatives to positives and by clearing out clutter words and needless qualifiers.

a. Our design must avoid nonconformity with building codes.
b. Never fail to wear protective clothing.
c. We are currently in the situation of completing our investigation of all aspects of the accident.
d. I appear to have misplaced the contract.
e. Do not accept bids that are not signed.
f. It seems as if I have just wrecked a company car.

EDITING FOR FLUENCY

Fluent sentences are easy to read because they provide clear connections, variety, and emphasis. Their varied length and word order eliminate choppiness and monotony. Fluent sentences enhance *clarity*, emphasizing the most important ideas. Fluent sentences also enhance *conciseness*, often replacing several short, repetitious sentences with one longer, more economical sentence. To write fluently, use the following strategies.

Combine Related Ideas

comb

A series of short, disconnected sentences is not only choppy and wordy but also unclear; readers are forced to insert transitions between ideas and decide which points are most important.

> Jogging can be healthful. You need the right equipment. Most necessary are well-fitting shoes. Without this equipment you take the chance of injuring your legs. Your knees are especially prone to injury. (5 sentences)

Disconnected series of ideas

> Jogging can be healthful if you have the right equipment. Shoes that fit well are most necessary because they prevent injury to your legs, especially your knees. (2 sentences)

Clear, concise, and fluent combination of ideas

Most sets of information can be combined to form different relationships, depending on what you want to emphasize. Imagine that this set of facts describes an applicant for a junior management position with your company.

> - Roy James graduated from an excellent management school.
> - He has no experience.
> - He is highly recommended.

Assume that you are a personnel director, conveying your impression of this candidate to upper management. To convey a negative impression, you might combine the information in this way:

> Although Roy James graduated from an excellent management school and is highly recommended, **he has no experience.**

Strongly negative emphasis

The *independent clause* (in boldface) receives the emphasis. (See also page 686, on subordination.) But if you are undecided yet leaning in a negative direction, you might write:

> Roy James graduated from an excellent management school and is highly recommended, **but** he has no experience.

Slightly negative emphasis

In this sentence, the information both before and after *but* appears in independent clauses. Joining them with the coordinating word *but* suggests that both sides of the issue are equally important (or "coordinate"). Placing the negative idea last, however, gives it a slight emphasis. (See also page 685, on coordination.)

Finally, to emphasize strong support for the candidate, you could say this:

Positive emphasis

Although Roy James has no experience, **he graduated from an excellent management school and is highly recommended.**

In the preceding example, the initial information is subordinated by *although*, giving the final information the weight of an independent clause.

NOTE *Combine sentences only to simplify the reader's task. Overstuffed sentences with too much information and too many connections can be hard for readers to sort out.* *(See page 216.)*

EXERCISE 11

Combine each set of sentences below into one fluent sentence that provides the requested emphasis.

Examples:

SENTENCE SET	John is a loyal employee. John is a motivated employee. John is short-tempered with his colleagues.
COMBINED FOR POSITIVE EMPHASIS	Even though John is short-tempered with his colleagues, he is a loyal and motivated employee.

a. The job offers an attractive salary.
It demands long work hours.
Promotions are rapid.
(*Combine for negative emphasis.*)

b. The job offers an attractive salary.
It demands long work hours.
Promotions are rapid.
(*Combine for positive emphasis.*)

c. Company X gave us the lowest bid.
Company Y has an excellent reputation.
(*Combine to emphasize Company Y.*)

d. Superinsulated homes are energy efficient.
Superinsulated homes create a danger of indoor air pollution.
The toxic substances include radon gas and urea formaldehyde.
(*Combine for a negative emphasis.*)

e. Computers cannot *think* for the writer.
Computers eliminate many mechanical writing tasks.
They speed the flow of information.
(*Combine to emphasize the first assertion.*)

Vary Sentence Construction and Length

var

Related ideas often need to be linked in one sentence, so that readers can grasp the connections:

> The nuclear core reached critical temperature. The loss-of-coolant alarm was triggered. The operator shut down the reactor.

Disconnected ideas

> As the nuclear core reached critical temperature, triggering the loss-of-coolant alarm, the operator shut down the reactor.

Connected ideas

But an idea that should stand alone for emphasis needs a whole sentence of its own:

> Core meltdown seemed inevitable.

Correct

However, an unbroken string of long or short sentences can bore and confuse readers, as can a series with identical openings:

> There are a number of drawbacks about diesel engines. **They** are noisy. **They** are difficult to start in cold weather. **They** cause vibration. **They** also give off an unpleasant odor. **They** cause sulfur dioxide pollution.

Boring and repetitive

> Diesel engines have a number of drawbacks including noisiness, cold-weather starting difficulties, vibrations and odor. Most seriously they cause sulfur dioxide pollution.

Varied

Similarly, when you write in the first person, overusing *I* makes you appear self-centered. (Some organizations require use of the third person, avoiding the first person completely, for all manuals, lab reports, specifications, product descriptions, and so on.)

Do not, however, avoid personal pronouns if they make the writing more readable (say, by eliminating passive constructions).

Use Short Sentences for Special Emphasis

short

All this talk about combining ideas might suggest that short sentences have no place in good writing. Wrong. Short sentences (even one-word sentences) provide vivid emphasis. They stick in a reader's mind.

FINDING THE EXACT WORDS

Too often, language can *camouflage* rather than communicate. People see many reasons to hide behind language, as when they do the following:

Situations in which people often hide behind language

- speak for their company but not for themselves
- fear the consequences of giving bad news
- are afraid to disagree with company policy

- make a recommendation some readers will resent
- worry about making a bad impression
- worry about being wrong
- pretend to know more than they do
- avoid admitting a mistake, or ignorance

Poor word choices produce inefficient and often unethical writing that resists interpretation and frustrates the audience. Use the following strategies to find words that are *convincing*, *precise*, and *informative*.

simple

Prefer Simple and Familiar Wording

Don't replace technically precise words with nontechnical words that are vague or imprecise. Don't write *a part that makes the computer run* when you mean *central processing unit*. Use the precise term, and then define it in a glossary for nontechnical readers:

Simple and familiar wording

> **Central processing unit**: the part of the computer that controls information transfer and carries out arithmetic and logical instructions.

In certain contexts, specific technical words are indispensable, but the nontechnical words usually can be simplified. For example, instead of *accoustically attenuating the food consumption area*, try *soundproofing the cafeteria*.

Besides being annoying, needlessly big or unfamiliar words can be ambiguous.

Ambiguous wording

> Make an improvement in the clerical situation.

(Does this mean we should hire more clerical personnel or better personnel or train the personnel we have?)

Whenever possible, choose words you use and hear in everyday speaking:

Trading multiple syllables for fewer

demonstrate	=	show
endeavor	=	effort, try
frequently	=	often
subsequent to	=	after
utilize	=	use

Of course, now and then the complex or more elaborate word best expresses your meaning. For instance, we would not substitute *end* for *terminate* in referring to something with an established time limit.

Precise wording

> Our trade agreement **terminates** this month.

If a complex word can replace a handful of simpler words—and can sharpen your meaning—use it.

| Six rectangular grooves **around the outside edge** of the steel plate **are needed for** the pressure clamps **to fit into.** — Weak

| Six rectangular grooves on the steel plate **perimeter accommodate** the pressure clamps. — Informative and precise

EXERCISE 12

Edit these sentences for straightforward and familiar language.

a. May you find luck and success in all endeavors.
b. I suggest you reduce the number of cigarettes you consume.
c. Within the copier, a magnetic reed switch is utilized as a mode of replacement for the conventional microswitches that were in use on previous models.
d. A good writer is cognizant of how to utilize grammar in a correct fashion.
e. I wish to upgrade my present employment situation.

Avoid Useless Jargon

jarg

When jargon is appropriate

Every profession has its own shorthand and accepted phrases and terms. For example, *stat* (from the Latin "statim" or "immediately") is medical jargon for *Drop everything and deal with this emergency*. For computer buffs, a *glitch* is a momentary power surge that can erase the contents of internal memory; a *bug* is an error that causes a program to run incorrectly. Among specialists these terms are an economical way to communicate.

When jargon is inappropriate

But some jargon is useless in any context. In the world of useless jargon, people don't *cooperate* on a project; instead, they *interface* or *contiguously optimize their efforts.* Rather than *designing a model,* they *formulate a paradigm.*

A popular form of useless jargon is adding *-wise* to nouns, as shorthand for *in reference to* or *in terms of.*

| **Expensewise** and **schedulewise,** this plan is unacceptable. — Useless jargon

| In terms of expense and scheduling, this plan is unacceptable. — Jargon free

Writers create another form of useless jargon when they invent verbs by adding an *-ize* ending to a noun or an adjective: Don't invent *prioritize* from *priority;* instead use *to rank priorities.*

Useless jargon's worst fault is that it makes the person using it seem stuffy and pretentious or like someone with something to hide:

| Unless all parties interface synchronously within given parameters, the project will be rendered inoperative. — Pretentious use of jargon

| Unless we coordinate our efforts, the project will fail. — Jargon free

Before using any jargon, think about your specific audience and ask yourself: "Can I find an easier way to say exactly what I mean?" Only use jargon that improves your communication.

acr

Use Acronyms Selectively

Acronyms are words formed from the initial letter of each word in a phrase (as in *LOCA* from *l*oss *o*f *c*oolant *a*ccident) or from a combination of initial letters and parts of words (as in *bit* from *b*inary dig*it* or *pixel* from *pic*ture *el*ement). Acronyms *can* communicate concisely—but only when the audience knows their meaning, and only when you use the term often in your document. The first time you use an acronym, spell out the words from which it is derived.

An acronym defined

Modem ("modulator + demodulator"): a device that converts, or "modulates," computer data in electronic form into a sound signal that can be transmitted and then reconverted, or "demodulated," into electronic form for the receiving computer.

trite

Avoid Triteness

Worn-out phrases (clichés) make writers seem too lazy or too careless to find exact, unique ways of saying what they mean.

Worn out phrases

make the grade	the chips are down
in the final analysis	not by a long shot
close the deal	last but not least
hard as a rock	welcome aboard
water under the bridge	over the hill

EXERCISE 13

Edit these sentences to eliminate useless jargon and triteness.

a. To optimize your financial return, prioritize your investment goals.
b. The use of this product engenders a 50 percent repeat consumer encounter.
c. We'll have to swallow our pride and admit our mistake.
d. Managers who make the grade are those who can take daily pressures in stride.

euph

Avoid Misleading Euphemisms

A form of understatement, a euphemism is an expression aimed at politeness or at making unpleasant subjects seem less offensive. Thus, *we powder our noses* or *use the boys' room* instead of *using the bathroom;* we *pass away* or *meet our Maker* instead of *dying.*

When euphemisms avoid offending or embarrassing people, they are perfectly legitimate. Instead of telling a job applicant he or she is *unqualified,* we might say, *Your background doesn't meet our needs*. In addition, there are times when friendliness and interoffice harmony are more likely to be preserved with writing that is not too abrupt, bold, blunt, or emphatic (MacKenzie 2).

When a euphemism is appropriate

Euphemisms, however, are unethical if they understate the truth when only the truth will serve. In the sugarcoated world of misleading euphemisms, bad news disappears:

When a euphemism is deceptive

Examples of euphemisms that mislead

- Instead of being *laid off* or *fired,* workers are *surplused* or *deselected,* or the company is *downsized.*
- Instead of *lying* to the public, the government *engages in a policy of disinformation.*
- Instead of *wars* and *civilian casualties,* we have *conflicts* and *collateral damage.*

Plain talk is always better than deception. If someone offers you a job *with limited opportunity for promotion,* expect a *dead-end job.*

Avoid Overstatement

over

Exaggeration sounds phony. Be cautious when using superlatives such as *best*, *biggest*, *brightest*, *most*, and *worst*. Recognize the differences among *always*, *usually*, *often*, *sometimes,* and *rarely*; among *all*, *most*, *many*, *some*, and *few*.

Overstatements

- You never listen to my ideas.
- This product will last forever.
- Assembly-line employees are doing shabby work.

Unless you mean *all employees,* qualify your generalization with *some,* or *most*—or even better, specify *20 percent.*

EXERCISE 14

Edit these sentences to eliminate euphemism, overstatement, or unsupported generalizations.

a. I finally must admit that I am an abuser of intoxicating beverages.
b. I was less than candid.
c. This employee is poorly motivated.
d. Most entry-level jobs are boring and dehumanizing.
e. Clerical jobs offer no opportunity for advancement.
f. Because of your absence of candor, we can no longer offer you employment.

ww

Avoid Imprecise Wording

Words listed as synonyms usually carry different shades of meaning. Do you mean to say *I'm slender, You're slim, She's lean,* or *He's scrawny*? The wrong choice could be disastrous.

Imprecision can create ambiguity. For instance, is *send us more personal information* a request for more information that is personal or for information that is more personal? Does your client expect *fewer* or *less* technical details in your report? See page 699 for a list of words that are commonly confused.

spec

Be Specific and Concrete

General words name broad classes of things, such as *job, computer,* or *person.* Such terms usually need to be clarified by more specific ones.

General terms traded for specific terms

| job | = | senior accountant for Softbyte Press |
| person | = | Sarah Jones, production manager |

The more specific your words, the more a reader can visualize your meaning.

Abstract words name qualities, concepts, or feelings (*beauty, luxury, depression*) whose exact meaning has to be nailed down by *concrete* words—words that name things we can visualize.

Abstract terms traded for concrete terms

| a **beautiful** view | = | snowcapped mountains, a wilderness lake, pink ledge, ninety-foot birch trees |
| a **depressed** worker | = | suicidal urge, insomnia, feelings of worthlessness, no hope for improvement |

Informative writing *tells* and *shows.*

General — One of our **workers** was **injured** by a **piece of equipment recently.**

Specific — **Alan Hill** suffered a **broken thumb** while working on a **lathe yesterday**.

Don't write *thing* when you mean *lever, switch, micrometer,* or *scalpel.*

> **NOTE** *In some instances, of course, you may wish to generalize for the sake of diplomacy. Instead of writing "Bill, Mary, and Sam have been surfing the Web instead of working," you might prefer to generalize: "Some employees. . . ."*
>
> *Most good writing offers both general and specific information. The most general material appears in the topic statement and sometimes in the conclusion because these parts, respectively, set the paragraph's direction and summarize its content.*

EXERCISE 15

Edit these sentences to make them more precise and informative.

a. Anaerobic fermentation is used in this report.
b. Your crew damaged a piece of office equipment.
c. His performance was admirable.
d. This thing bothers me.

Use Analogies to Sharpen the Image

an

Analogy versus comparison

Ordinary comparison shows similarities between two things *of the same class* (two computer keyboards, two methods of cleaning dioxin-contaminated sites). Analogy, on the other hand, shows some essential similarity between two things of *different classes* (writing and computer programming, computer memory and post office boxes).

Analogies are good for emphasizing a point (*Some rain is now as acidic as vinegar*). They are especially useful in translating something abstract, complex, or unfamiliar, as long as the easier subject is broadly familiar to readers. Analogy therefore calls for particularly careful analyses of audience.

Analogies can save words and convey vivid images. *Collier's Encyclopedia* describes the tail of an eagle in flight as "spread like a fan." The following sentence from a description of a trout feeder mechanism uses an analogy to clarify the positional relationship between two working parts:

Analogy

> The metal rod is inserted (and centered, crosslike) between the inner and outer sections of the clip.

Without the analogy *crosslike,* we would need something like this to visualize the relationship:

Missing analogy

> The metal rod is inserted, perpendicular to the long plane and parallel to the flat plane, between the inner and outer sections of the clip.

Besides naming things, analogies help *explain* things. This next analogy helps clarify an unfamiliar concept (dangerous levels of a toxic chemical) by comparing it to something more familiar (human hair).

Analogy

> A dioxin concentration of 500 parts per trillion is lethal to guinea pigs. One part per trillion is roughly equal to the thickness of a human hair compared to the distance across the United States. (*Congressional Research Report 15*)

tone

ADJUSTING YOUR TONE

How tone is created

Your tone is your personal trademark—the personality that takes shape between the lines. The tone you create depends on (1) the distance you impose between yourself and the reader, and (2) the attitude you show toward the subject.

Assume, for example, that a friend is going to take over a job you've held. You're writing your friend instructions for parts of the job. Here is your first sentence:

Informal tone

> Now that you've arrived in the glamorous world of office work, put on your running shoes; this is no ordinary manager-trainee job.

The example sentence imposes little distance between you and the reader (it uses the direct address, *you,* and the humorous suggestion to *put on your running shoes*). The ironic use of *glamorous* suggests just the opposite: that the job holds little glamor.

For a different reader (say, the recipient of a company training manual), you would choose some other opening:

Semiformal tone

> As a manager trainee at GlobalTech, you will work for many managers. In short, you will spend little of your day seated at your desk.

The tone now is serious, no longer intimate, and you express no distinct attitude toward the job. For yet another audience (clients or investors who will read an annual report), you might alter the tone again:

Formal tone

> Manager trainees at GlobalTech are responsible for duties that extend far beyond desk work.

Here the businesslike shift from second- to third-person address makes the tone too impersonal for any writing addressed to the trainees themselves.

We already know how tone works in speaking. When you meet someone new, for example, you respond in a tone that defines your relationship:

Tone announces interpersonal distance

> Honored to make your acquaintance. [formal tone—greatest distance]
> How do you do? [formal]
> Nice to meet you. [semiformal—medium distance]
> Hello. [semiformal]
> Hi. [informal—least distance]
> What's happening? [informal—slang]

Each of these greetings is appropriate in some situations and inappropriate in others.

Whichever tone you decide on, be consistent throughout your document.

Inconsistent tone

- My office isn't fit for a pig. [too informal]
- It is ungraciously unattractive. [too formal]

Consistent tone

- My office is so shabby that it's an awful place to work.

In general, lean toward an informal tone without using slang.

Tone announces attitude

Besides setting the distance between writer and reader, your tone implies your *attitude* toward the subject *and* the reader.

> We dine at seven.
> Dinner is at seven.
> Let's eat at seven.
> Let's chow down at seven.
> Let's strap on the feedbag at seven.
> Let's pig out at seven.

The words you choose tell readers a great deal about where you stand. For instance, in announcing a meeting to review your employee's job evaluation, would you invite this person to *discuss* the evaluation, *talk it over*, *have a chat*, or *chew the fat*? Decide how casual or serious your attitude should be.

GUIDELINES for Deciding about Tone

- **Use a formal or semiformal tone** in writing for superiors, professionals, or academics (depending on what you think the reader expects).
- **Use a semiformal or informal tone** in writing for colleagues and subordinates (depending on how close you feel to your reader).
- **Use an informal tone** when you want your writing to be conversational, or when you want it to sound like a person talking.
- **Avoid a negative tone** when conveying unpleasant information.
- **Above all, find out what tone your particular readers prefer.** When in doubt, do not be too casual!

Consider Using an Occasional Contraction

Unless you have reason to be formal, use (but *do not* overuse) contractions. Balance an *I am* with an *I'm*, a *you are* with a *you're*, and an *it is* with an *it's*. Keep in mind that contractions rarely are acceptable in formal business writing.

NOTE *The contracted version often sounds less emphatic than the two-word version—for example, "**Don't** handle this material without protective clothing" versus "**Do not** handle this material without protective clothing." If your message requires emphasis, do not use a contraction.*

Address Readers Directly

Use the personal pronouns *you* and *your* to connect with readers. Readers often relate better to something addressed to them directly.

Impersonal tone
- Students at this college will find the faculty always willing to help.

Personal tone
- As a student at this college, **you** will find the faculty always willing to help.

NOTE *Use* **you** *and* **your** *only in letters, memos, instructions, and other documents intended to correspond directly with a reader. By using* **you** *and* **your** *in situations that call for first or third person, such as description or narration, you might end up writing something awkward like this: "When you are in northern Ontario, you can see wilderness and lakes everywhere around you."*

EXERCISE 16

The sentences below suffer from pretentious language, unclear expression of attitude, missing contractions, or indirect address. Adjust the tone.

a. Further interviews are a necessity to our ascertaining the most viable candidate.
b. All employees are hereby invited to the company picnic.
c. Employees must submit travel vouchers by May 1.
d. Persons taking this test should use the HELP option whenever they need it.
e. I am not unappreciative of your help.
f. My disapproval is far more than negligible.

Use *I* and *We* When Appropriate

Instead of disappearing behind your writing, use *I* or *We* when referring to yourself or your organization.

Distant tone
- The writer of this letter would like a refund.

Appropriate distance
- **I** would like a refund.

A message becomes doubly impersonal when both writer and reader disappear.

| The requested report will be sent next week. — Impersonal tone

| **We** will send the report **you** requested next week. — Personal tone

Prefer the Active Voice

Because the active voice is more direct and economical than the passive voice, it generally creates a less formal tone. (Review pages 213–16 for use of active and passive voice.)

EXERCISE 17

These sentences have too few *I* or *We* constructions or too many passive constructions. Adjust the tone.

a. Payment will be made as soon as an itemized bill is received.
b. You will be notified.
c. Your help is appreciated.
d. Our reply to your bid will be sent next week.
e. Your request will be given consideration.
f. This writer would like to be considered for your opening.

Emphasize the Positive

Whenever you offer advice, suggestions, or recommendations, try to emphasize benefits rather than flaws. (For more on delivering bad news, see Chapter 16.)

| Because of your division's lagging productivity, a management review may be needed. — Critical tone

| A management review might help boost productivity in your division. — Encouraging tone

Avoid an Overly Informal Tone

How tone can be too informal

Achieving a conversational tone does not mean writing in the same way we would speak to friends at a favorite hangout. *Substandard usage* ("He ain't got none," "I seen it today") is unacceptable in workplace writing; and so is *slang* ("hurling," "bogus," "bummed"). *Profanity* ("This idea sucks," "pissed off," "What the hell") not only conveys contempt for the audience but also triggers contempt for the person using it. *Colloquialisms* ("O.K.," "a lot," "snooze") tend to appear more in speaking than in writing.

How tone can offend

Tone is offensive when it violates the reader's expectations: when it seems disrespectful, tasteless, distant and aloof, too "chummy," casual, or otherwise inappropriate for the topic, the reader, and the situation.

When to use an academic tone

A formal or academic tone is appropriate in countless writing situations: a research paper, a job application, a report for the company president. In a history essay, for example, you would not refer to George Washington and Abraham Lincoln as "those dudes, George and Abe." Whenever you begin with rough drafting or brainstorming, your initial tone might be overly informal and is likely to require some adjustment during subsequent drafts.

bias

Avoid Personal Bias

If people expect an impartial report, try to keep your own biases out of it. Imagine, for example, that you have been assigned to investigate the causes of an employee-management confrontation at your company's Omaha branch. Your initial report, written for the New York central office, is intended simply to describe what happened. Here is how an unbiased description might begin:

A factual account

> At 9:00 A.M. on Tuesday, January 21, eighty female employees set up picket lines around the executive offices of our Omaha branch, bringing business to a halt. The group issued a formal protest, claiming that their working conditions were repressive, their salary scale unfair, and their promotional opportunities limited.

Note the absence of implied judgments; the facts are presented objectively. A biased version of events, from a protestor's point of view, might read like this:

A biased version

> Last Tuesday, sisters struck another blow against male supremacy when eighty women employees paralyzed the company's repressive and sexist administration for more than six hours. The timely and articulate protest was aimed against degrading working conditions, unfair salary scales, and lack of promotional opportunities for women.

Judgmental words (*male supremacy*, *repressive*, *degrading*, *paralyzed*, *articulate*) inject the writer's attitude about events, even though it isn't called for. In contrast to this bias, the following version patronizingly defends the status quo:

A biased version

> Our Omaha branch was the scene of an amusing battle of the sexes last Tuesday, when a group of irate feminists, eighty strong, set up picket lines for six hours at the company's executive offices. The protest was lodged against alleged inequities in hiring, wages, working conditions, and promotion for women in our company.

(For more on how framing of the facts can influence reader judgments, see page 157.)

NOTE *Being unbiased doesn't mean remaining "neutral" about something you know to be wrong or dangerous (Kremers 59). If, for instance, you conclude that the Omaha protest was clearly justified, say so.*

Avoid Sexist Usage

sexist

Language that makes unwarranted assumptions will offend readers. Avoid sexist usage such as referring to doctors, lawyers, and other professionals as *he* or *him*, while referring to nurses, secretaries, and homemakers as *she* or *her*. Words such as *foreman* or *fireman* automatically exclude women; terms such as *supervisor* or *firefighter* are more inclusive.

GUIDELINES for Nonsexist Usage

- **Use neutral expressions** such as *chair* or *chairperson* rather than *chairman* and *postal worker* rather than *postman*.
- **Rephrase to eliminate the pronoun,** but only if you can do so without altering your original meaning. For instance, change *A writer will succeed if he revises* to *A writer who revises succeeds.*
- **Use plural forms** such as *Writers will succeed if they revise* (but not *A writer will succeed if they revise*). For pronoun-referent agreement, see page 683
- **Use occasional paired pronouns** (*him or her, she or he, his or hers*): *A writer will succeed if she or he revises.*
- **Drop condescending diminutive endings** such as *-ess* and *-ette* used to denote females (*poetess, drum majorette, actress*).
- **Use *Ms.* instead of *Mrs.* or *Miss*,** unless you know that person prefers a traditional title. Or omit titles: *Roger Smith and Jane Kelly; Smith and Kelly.*
- In quoting sources that ignore nonsexist standards, consider these options:

  a. Insert [*sic*] ("thus" or "so") following the first instance of sexist usage.
  b. Use ellipses (see page 694) to omit sexist phrasing.
  c. Paraphrase instead of quoting.
  d. Substitute or insert nonsexist words between brackets.

Avoid Offensive Usage of All Types

offen

The words you choose should respect all people regardless of cultural, racial, ethnic, or national background; sexual and religious orientation; age or physical condition. References to individuals and groups should be as neutral as possible.

GUIDELINES for Inoffensive Usage

- **Be as specific as possible when referring to a person's cultural/national identity.** Instead of *Latin American* or *Asian* or *Hispanic* prefer *Cuban American* or *Korean* or *Nicaraguan.* Use *United States* or *U.S.*, rather than *American.*
- **Avoid potentially judgmental expressions.** Instead of *third-world* or *undeveloped nations* or the *Far East,* use *developing* or *newly industrialized nations* or *East Asia.* Instead of *nonwhites,* use *people of color.*
- **Use person-first language** for people with disabilities or medical conditions. Avoid terms that could be considered either pitying or overly euphemistic, such as *victim* or *differently abled.* Focus on the individual instead of the disability: *person who is blind* rather than *blind person,* or *person who has lost an arm* rather than *amputee.*
- **Avoid expressions that demean** those who have medical conditions: *retard, mental midget, insane idea, the blind leading the blind,* or *able-bodied workers.*
- **Use age-appropriate designations** for both genders: *girl* or *boy* for people age fourteen or under; *young person, young adult, young man,* or *young woman* for those of high-school age; and *woman* or *man* for those of college age. (*Teenager* or *juvenile* carries certain negative connotations.) Instead of *elderly* or *old,* use *older persons* or *senior.*

Source: Adapted from the *Publication Manual of the American Psychological Association,* and Schwartz, Marilyn.

EXERCISE 18

The sentences below suffer from negative emphasis, excessive informality, biased expressions, or offensive usage. Adjust the tone.

a. If you want your workers to like you, show sensitivity to their needs.
b. The union has won its struggle for a decent wage.
c. The group's spokesman demanded salary increases.
d. Each employee should submit his vacation preferences this week.
e. While the girls played football, the men waved pom-poms to cheer them on.
f. The explosion left me blind as a bat for nearly an hour.
g. This dude would be an excellent employee if only he could learn to chill out.
h. No way am I going to approve this dog of a proposal.

EXERCISE 19

Find examples of overly euphemistic language (such as "chronologically challenged") or of insensitive language (such as "lame excuse"). Discuss examples in class.

CONSIDERING THE GLOBAL CONTEXT

Cultures differ in their style preferences

The style guidelines in this chapter apply specifically to standard English in North America. But technical communication is a global process: Practices and preferences differ widely in various cultural contexts. For example, some cultures prefer long sentences and elaborate language to convey an idea's full complexity. Others value expressions of respect, politeness, praise, and gratitude more than clarity or directness (Hein 125–26; Mackin 349–50).

Writing in non-English languages tends to be more formal than in English, and some languages rely heavily on passive voice (Weymouth 144). French readers, for example, may prefer an elaborate style that reflects sophisticated and complex modes of thinking. In contrast, our "plain English," conversational style might connote simplemindedness, disrespect, or incompetence (Thrush 277).

Challenges in writing for translation

Documents to be translated into other languages pose special challenges. In translation or in a different cultural context, some words have insulting or negative connotations; for example, in certain cultures, "male" and "female" refer only to animals (Coe, "Writing for Other Cultures" 17). Notable translation disasters include the Chevrolet *Nova*—*no va* means "doesn't go" in Spanish—and the Finnish beer *Koff* for an English-speaking market (Gesteland 20; Victor 44). Many U.S. idioms (*breaking the bank*, *cutthroat competition*, *sticking your neck out*) and cultural references (*the crash of '29*, *Beantown*) make no sense outside of U.S. culture (Coe "Writing" 17–19). Slang (*bogus*, *fat city*) and colloquialisms (*You bet*, *Gotcha*) can seem too informal and crude.

In short, offensive writing (including inappropriate humor) can alienate audiences—from both you *and* your culture (Sturges 32).

LEGAL AND ETHICAL IMPLICATIONS OF WORD CHOICE

Chapter 4 (pages 72–73) discusses how workplace writing is regulated by laws against libel, deceptive advertising, and defective information. One common denominator among these violations is poor word choice. We are each accountable for the words we use—intentionally or not—in framing the audience's perception and understanding. Imprecise or inappropriate word choice can spell big trouble, as seen in the following examples.

Situations in which word choice has ethical or legal consequences

- **Assessing risk.** Is the investment you are advocating "a sure thing" or merely "a good bet," or even "risky"? Are you announcing a "caution," a "warning," or a "danger"? Should methane levels in mineshaft #3 "be evaluated" or do "they pose a definite explosion risk"? Never downplay risks.
- **Offering a service or product.** Are you proposing to "study the problem," to "explore solutions to the problem," or to "eliminate the problem"? Do you "stand behind" your product or do you "guarantee" it? Never promise more than you can deliver.
- **Giving instructions.** Before inserting the widget between the grinder blades, should I "switch off the grinder" or "disconnect the grinder from its power source" or "trip the circuit breaker," or do all three? Always triple-check the clarity of your instructions.
- **Comparing your product with competing products.** Instead of referring to a competitor's product as "inferior," "second-rate," or "substandard," talk about your own "first-rate product" that "exceeds (or meets) standards." Never run down the competition.
- **Evaluating an employee** (T. Clark, "Teaching Students" 75–76). In a personnel evaluation, do not refer to the employee as a "troublemaker" or "unprofessional," or as "too abrasive," "too uncooperative," "incompetent," or "too old" for the job. Focus on the specific requirements of this job, and offer *factual* instances in which these requirements have been violated: "Our monitoring software recorded five visits by this employee to X-rated Web sites during working hours." Or "This employee arrives late for work on average twice weekly, has failed to complete assigned projects on three occasions, and has difficulty working with others." Instead of expressing personal judgments, offer the facts. Be sure everyone involved knows exactly what the standards are well beforehand. Otherwise, you risk violating federal laws against discrimination and libel (damaging someone's reputation) and you may face a lawsuit.

STYLE, TONE, AND EMAIL

Email is the most common form of day-to-day writing in workplace settings, used for everything from quick correspondence (touching base with a coworker about a meeting time or due date) to official communication (a memo or report from the company president). We all know how much time it takes to stay ahead of the email that floods your in-box.

Appropriate style and tone are also important in email

Yet despite so much writing taking place in this format, people often pay little attention to the style and tone of a message. Even with autocorrect and other tools, email can be fraught with spelling errors. Humor and sarcasm, which might be an appropriate tone when writing to a friend, are typically not appropriate in the workplace. The speed of email messages combined with a lack of interpersonal cues (facial expressions, voice) cause many a workplace writer to inadvertently create frustration and even legal problems (see previous section) due to an inappropriately worded message. In general, keep the tone and style of workplace email brief, professional, and polite. See Chapter 15 for a thorough discussion of email in the workplace (pay special attention to "Email, Style, Tone, and Etiquette" on page 336 and to Figures 15.1, 15.2, and 15.3 for examples). See also Chapter 26 for related discussion on writing for blogs, wikis, and social media.

USING DIGITAL EDITING TOOLS EFFECTIVELY

Many of the strategies in this chapter happen automatically with word processing, email, text messaging, and other digital writing tools. For instance, grammar checkers search for ambiguous pronoun references, overuse of passive voice, *to be* verbs, *There* and *It* sentence openers, negative constructions, clutter words, needless prefaces and qualifiers, overly technical language, jargon, sexist language, and so on. Autocorrect and spell check tools look for words judged to be incorrect and suggest or insert replacements. But these digital editing tools can be extremely imprecise and should be used with caution.

The limits of spell check, autocorrect, and other editing tools

These tools do not solve all grammar and spelling problems. For example, both *its* and *it's* are spelled correctly, but only one of them means "it is." The same is true for *their* and *there* (*their* is a possessive pronoun, as in "their books," while *there* is an adverb, as in "There is my dog"). Spell check and autocorrect are great for finding words that are spelled incorrectly, but don't count on them to find words that are *used* incorrectly or for typos that create the wrong word but are correctly spelled words on their own, such as *howl* instead of *how*. Grammar checkers work well to help you locate possible problems, but do not rely solely on what the program tells you. For example, not every sentence that the grammar checker flags as "long" should be shortened. Use these tools wisely and with common sense. Slow down before you press "send" and read the message carefully. If the document is longer than an email message or text, ask someone to proofread it. Many companies employ technical editors who are happy to look over your writing.

NOTE *None of the rules offered in this chapter applies universally. Ultimately, your own sensitivity to meaning, emphasis, and tone—the human contact—will determine the effectiveness of your writing style.*

CHECKLIST: Style

(Numbers in parentheses refer to the first page of the relevant section.)

Clarity

- ☐ Does each pronoun clearly refer to the noun it replaces? (211)
- ☐ Is each modifier close enough to the word or words it defines or explains? (212)
- ☐ Are modifying nouns unstacked? (212)
- ☐ Do most sentences begin with the familiar information and end with new information? (212)
- ☐ Are sentences in active rather than passive voice, unless the agent is immaterial? (213)
- ☐ Does each sentence provide only as much information as readers are able to process easily? (216)

Conciseness

- ☐ Is the piece free of wordiness, redundancy, or needless repetition? (217)
- ☐ Is it free of needless sentence openers and prefaces? (218)
- ☐ Have unnecessary weak verbs been converted to verbs that express a definite action? (219)
- ☐ Have excessive prepositions been removed and nominalizations restored to their verb forms? (220)
- ☐ Have negative constructions been converted to positive ones, as needed? (221)
- ☐ Is the piece free of clutter words and needless qualifiers? (222)

Fluency

- ☐ Are related ideas subordinated or coordinated and combined appropriately? (223)
- ☐ Are sentences varied in construction and length? (225)
- ☐ Does an idea that should stand alone for emphasis get a sentence of its own? (225)
- ☐ Are short sentences used for special emphasis? (225)

Word Choice

- ☐ Is the wording simple, familiar, unambiguous, and free of useless jargon? (226)
- ☐ Is each acronym spelled out upon first use? (228)
- ☐ Is the piece free of triteness, misleading euphemisms, and overstatement? (228)

- ☐ Does the wording precisely convey the intended meaning? (230)
- ☐ Are general or abstract terms clarified by more specific or concrete terms? (230)
- ☐ Are analogies used to clarify and explain? (231)
- ☐ Have I reviewed the spelling, grammar, and word choice to be sure spell check or autocorrect didn't insert any errors? (241)

Tone

- ☐ Is the tone appropriate and consistent for the situation and audience? (232)
- ☐ Is the level of formality what the intended audience would expect? (233)
- ☐ Is the piece free of implied bias, sexist language, or potentially offensive usage? (236)
- ☐ Does the piece display sensitivity to cultural differences? (239)
- ☐ Is the word choice ethically and legally acceptable? (239)

Projects

GENERAL

Using the Checklist for Style, revise the following selections. (*Hint*: use the brief example on page 210 as a model for revision.)

a. Letter to a local newspaper.

In the absence of definitive studies regarding the optimum length of the school day, I can only state my personal opinion based upon observations made by me and upon teacher observations that have been conveyed to me. Considering the length of the present school day, it is my opinion that the day is excessive length-wise for most elementary pupils, certainly for almost all of the primary children.

To find the answer to the problem requires consideration of two ways in which the problem may be viewed. One way focuses upon the needs of the children, while the other focuses upon logistics, transportation, scheduling, and other limits imposed by the educational system. If it is necessary to prioritize these two ideas, it would seem most reasonable to give the first consideration to the primary reason for the very existence of the system, i.e., to meet the educational needs of the children the system is trying to serve.

b. Memo to employees.

We are presently awaiting an on-site inspection of the designated professional library location by corporate representatives relative to electrical adaptations necessary for the computer installation. Meanwhile, all staff members are asked to respect the off-limits designation of the aforementioned location, as requested, due to the liability insurance provisions in regard to the computers.

c. Memo to employees.

The new phone system has proven to be particularly interruptive to the administration office assistants. It is highly imperative that you take particular note to ensure beyond the shadow of a doubt that all calls are of a business nature as far as possible. We are on a message unit cost system which is probationary at best, and the number of phones in our offices is considerably greater than any of our immediate office neighbors have. N.B.: The internal problem has been particularly vexing with phones not being properly replaced in cradles, constituting an additional dimension to an already perplexing internal telephone system dilemma of the greatest magnitude.

TEAM

Use a document written for the course. In small groups, look for problems of clarity, conciseness, and fluency. Mark any grammatical errors. Then ask students with different word-processing programs to run the paper through the grammar and style check programs available to them. Compare the changes your group made with those suggested by the various programs. If the computer suggests changes that appear ungrammatical or incorrect, consult a good handbook for confirmation.

In your group, prepare a list of the advantages and disadvantages of the grammar and style checker programs. Note any topics covered in this chapter that your software programs miss. Are these programs always reliable? What conclusions can you draw from this exercise?

DIGITAL AND SOCIAL MEDIA

In teams of 3-4 students, use a laptop computer OR a smartphone (pick one or the other, one per team) to write an email message to your instructor, asking a question about next week's assignment. First, discuss the word choice, tone, and style most appropriate for this message. Then, as you type, notice which words and sentences are being changed by autocorrect or spell check. Share your results with the rest of class.

GLOBAL

Search the Internet using the keywords "international business culture" to learn about the style preferences of one particular culture. Then, in a one-page memo to your instructor and classmates, describe the style preferences of that culture and give examples of how these preferences differ from the style guidelines presented (i.e., for North American English) in this chapter.

12 Designing Visual Information

"Every presentation, report, or specification I create is heavily dependent on visuals. Among my fellow scientists, charts and graphs help condense large sets of data into patterns and trends that we can grasp quickly. And even when I write a document for lawyers or other non-scientists at the company, I use visuals to make complicated scientific information easy for them to understand. Managers, for example, appreciate charts that illustrate the various pieces of the puzzle that go into researching a new product. Presentation and spreadsheet software make it easy to create professional looking visuals—but I always check the visual carefully before using it in my presentation or document because, as we all know, computers don't catch everything."

—Nanette Bauer,
Research Scientist at a large biotechnology company

LEARNING OBJECTIVES FOR THIS CHAPTER

- Understand the role of visuals in technical communication
- Determine when to use visuals
- Select the right visuals for your readers
- Create tables, graphs, charts, illustrations, photographs, and videos
- Increase visual appeal by using color appropriately
- Identify ethical issues when using visuals
- Understand how cultural considerations affect your choice of visuals

In printed or online documents, in oral presentations or multimedia programs, visuals are a staple of communication. Because they focus and organize information, visuals make data easier to interpret and remember. By offering powerful new ways of looking at data, visuals also reveal meanings that might otherwise remain buried in lists of facts and figures.

WHY VISUALS MATTER

Readers want more than just raw information; they want this material shaped and enhanced so they can understand the message at a glance. Visuals help us answer questions posed by readers as they process information:

Typical audience questions in processing information

- Which information is most important?
- Where, exactly, should I focus?
- What do these numbers mean?
- What should I be thinking or doing?
- What should I remember about this?
- What does it look like?
- How is it organized?
- How is it done?
- How does it work?

When people look at a visual pattern, such as a graph, they see it as one large pattern—the Big Picture that conveys information quickly and efficiently. For instance, the following line graph has no verbal information. The axes are not labeled, nor is the topic identified. But one quick glance, without the help of any words or numbers, tells you that the trend, after a period of gradual rise, has risen sharply. The graph conveys information in a way plain text never could.

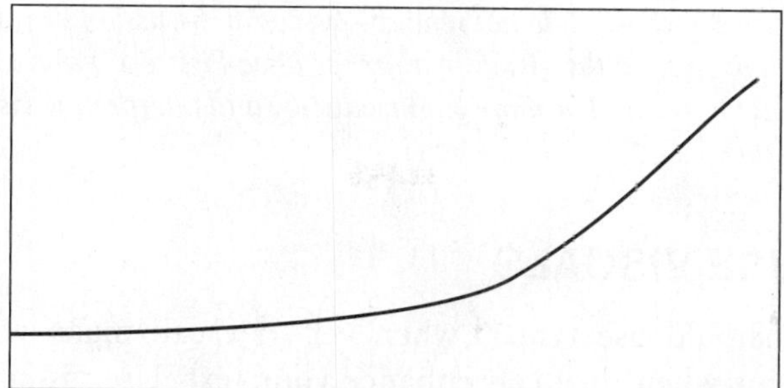

The trend depicted in the above graph would be hard for readers to visualize by just reading the long list of numbers in the following passage:

> The time required for global population to grow from 5 to 6 billion was shorter than the interval between any of the previous billions. It took just 12 years for this to occur, just slightly less than the 13 years between the fourth and fifth billion, but much less time than the 118 years between the first and second billion....

Technical data in prose form can be hard to interpret

When all this information is added to the original graph, as in Figure 12.1, the numbers become much easier to comprehend and compare.

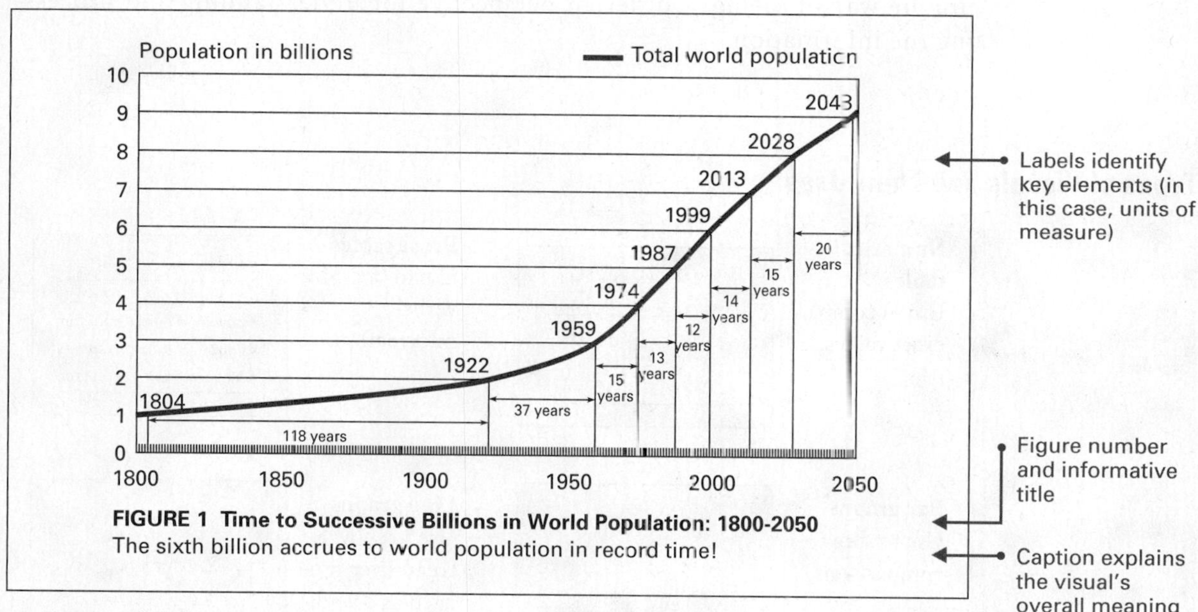

FIGURE 1 Time to Successive Billions in World Population: 1800-2050
The sixth billion accrues to world population in record time!

FIGURE 12.1 **A Graph that Conveys the Big Picture**
Source: United Nations (1995b); U.S. Census Bureau, International Programs Center International Database and Unpublished Tables.

NOTE *Visuals enhance—but do not replace—essential discussion in your written text. In your document refer to the visual by number ("see Figure 1") and explain what to look for and what it means. For more on introducing and interpreting visuals in a document, see page 287.*

WHEN TO USE VISUALS

Use visuals in situations like these

In general, you should use visuals whenever they can make your point more clearly than text or when they can enhance your text. Use visuals to clarify and support your discussion, not just to decorate your document. Use visuals to direct the audience's focus or help them remember something. There may be organizational reasons for using visuals; for example, some companies may always expect a chart or graph as part of their annual report. Certain industries, such as the financial sector, routinely use graphs and charts (such as the graph of the daily Dow Jones Industrial Average).

TYPES OF VISUALS TO CONSIDER

The following overview sorts visual displays into four categories: tables, graphs, charts, and graphic illustrations. Common examples within each category are shown in the table below. Note how each type of visual offers a unique way of seeing, a different perspective for understanding and processing the information.

Types of Visuals and Their Uses

TABLES display organized data across columns and rows for easy comparison.

Numerical tables
Use to compare exact values.

TABLE 1 Charting the Lesson

Lesson	Page	Page	Page
A	1	3	6
B	2	2	5
C	3	1	4

Prose tables
Use to organize verbal information.

TROUBLESHOOTING

Problem	Cause	Solution
• power	• cord	• plug-in
• light	• bulb	• replace
• flicker	• tube	• replace

GRAPHS translate numbers into shapes, shades, and patterns.

Bar graphs
Use to show comparisons.

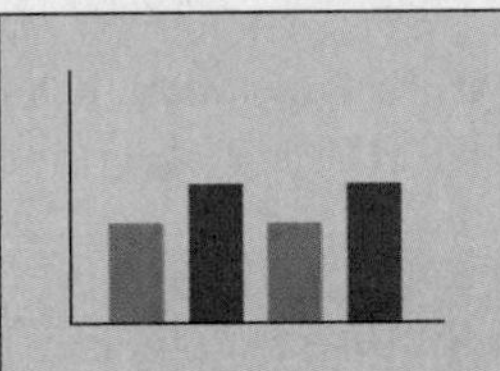

Line graphs
Use to show a trend over time, such as cost or other variables.

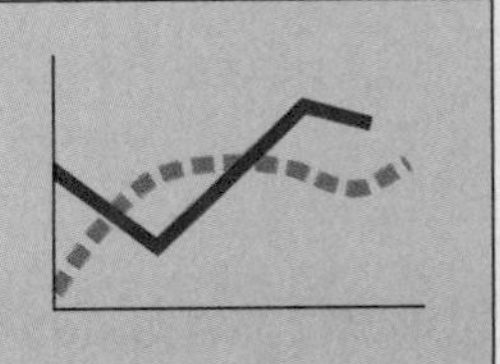

CHARTS depict relationships via geometric, arrows, lines, and other design elements.

Pie charts
Use to relate parts or percentages to the whole.

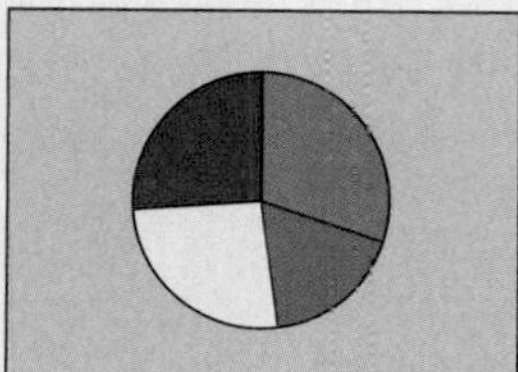

Organization charts
Use to show the hierarchy in a company.

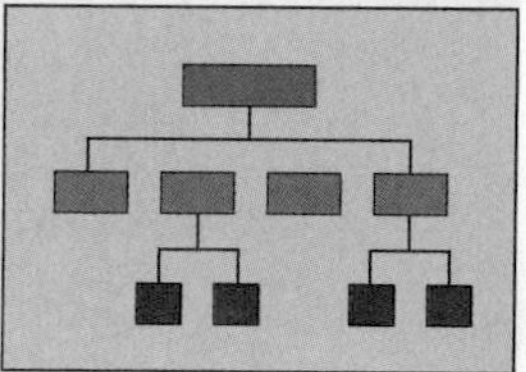

Flowcharts
Use to trace the steps (or decisions) in a procedure or process.

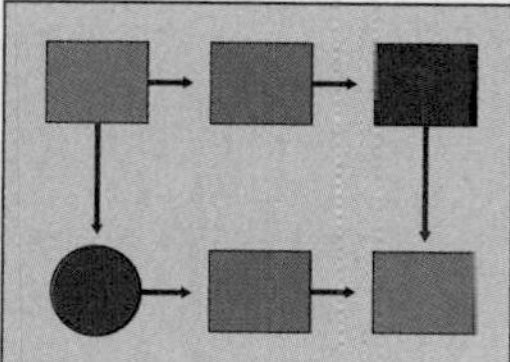

Gantt and PERT charts
Use to depict how the phases of a project relate.

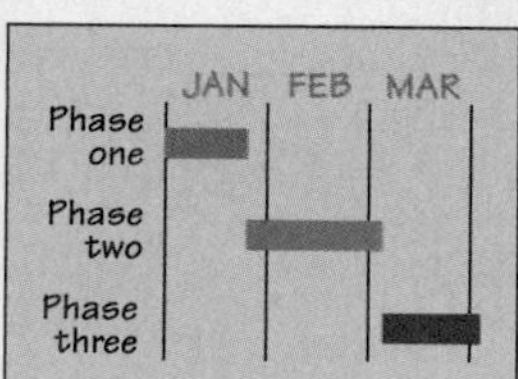

Tree charts
Use to show how the parts of an idea or concept relate.

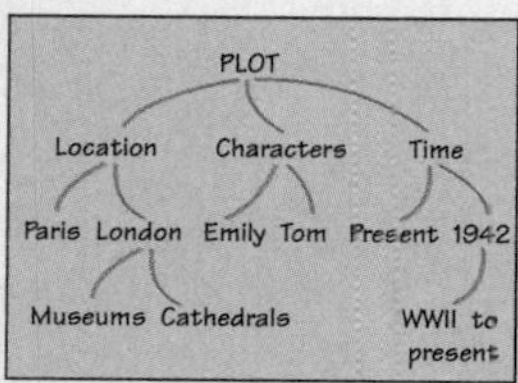

Pictograms
Use icons or other graphic devices that represent the displayed items.

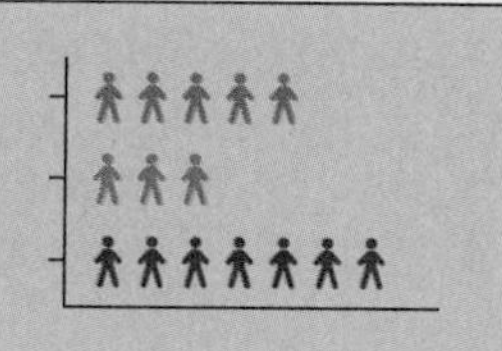

GRAPHIC ILLUSTRATIONS rely on pictures rather than on data or words.

Illustrations
Use to present a realistic but simplified view.

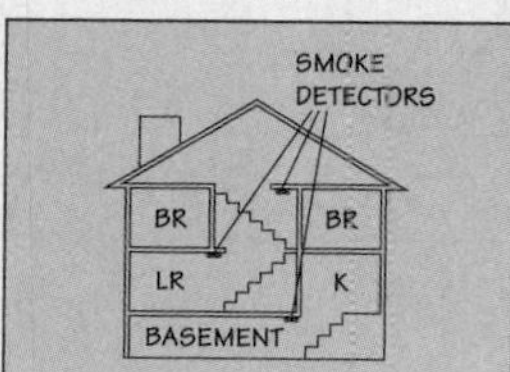

Cutaway diagrams
Use to show what is inside of a device or to help explain how a device works.

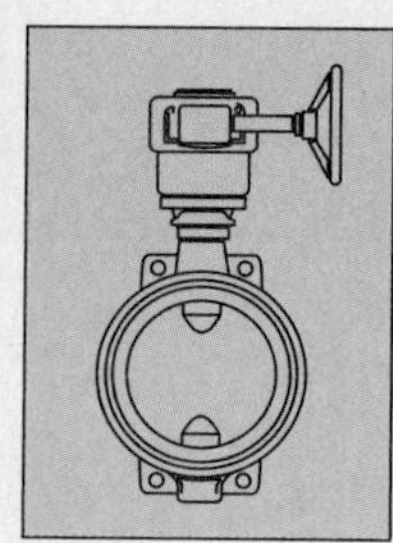

Exploded diagrams
Use to explain how an item is put together or how a reader should assemble a product.

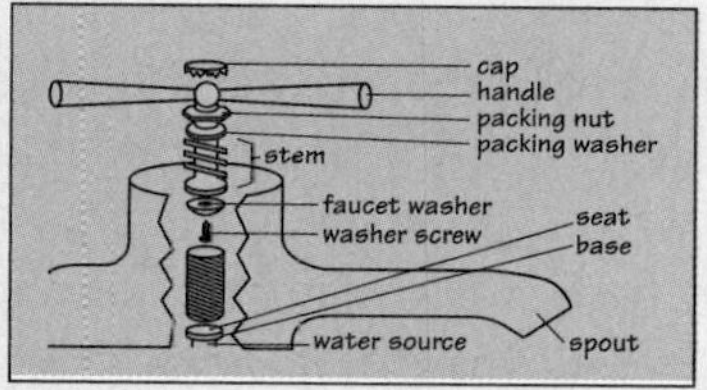

Block diagrams
Use to present the conceptual elements of a process or system—in depicting function instead of appearance.

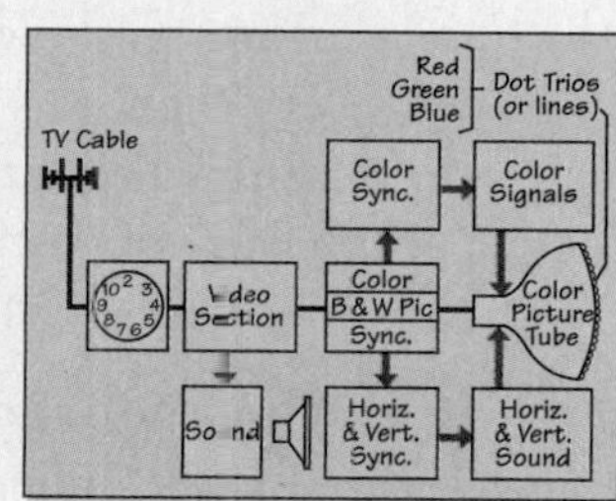

Maps
Use to help readers visualize the position, location, and interrelationship of various data.

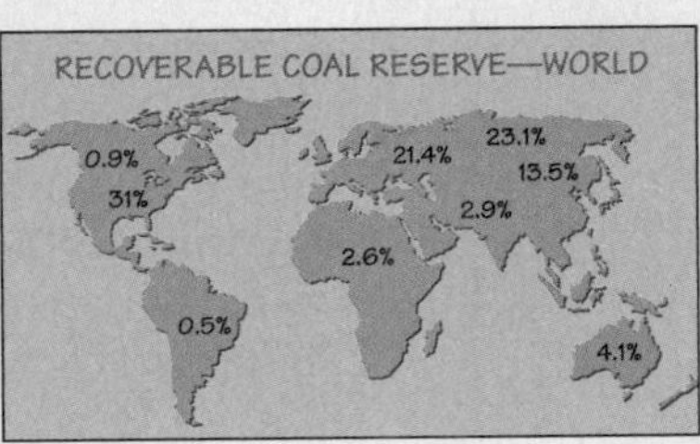

Videos
Use to show a procedure.

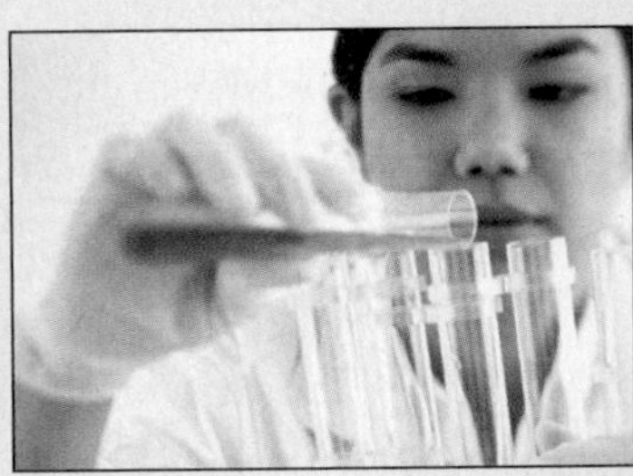

Photographs
Use to show exactly what something looks like.

Symbols and icons
Use to make concepts understandable to broad audiences, including international audiences and people who may have difficulty reading.

HOW TO CHOOSE THE RIGHT VISUALS

To select the most effective display, answer these questions:

Questions about a visual's purpose and audience

- **What is the purpose for using this visual?**
  - To convey facts and figures alone, a table may be the best choice. But if I want my audience to draw conclusions from that data, I may use a graph or chart to show comparisons.
  - To show parts of a mechanism, I probably want to use an exploded or cutaway diagram, perhaps together with a labeled photograph.
  - To give directions, I may want to use a diagram.
  - To show relationships, my best choice may be a flowchart or graph.
- **Who is my audience for these visuals?**
  - Expert audiences tend to prefer numerical tables, flowcharts, schematics, and complex graphs or diagrams that they can interpret for themselves.

- General audiences tend to prefer basic tables, graphs, diagrams, and other visuals that direct their focus and interpret key points extracted from the data.
- Cultural differences might come into play in the selection of appropriate visuals.

NOTE *Although visual communication has global appeal, certain displays might be inappropriate in certain cultures. For more on cultural considerations in selecting visuals, see page 286.*

- **What form of information will best achieve my purpose for this audience?**
  - Is my message best conveyed by numbers, shapes, words, pictures, or symbols?
  - Will my audience most readily understand a particular type of display?

Although several alternatives might work, one particular type of visual (or a combination) usually is superior. The best option, however, may not be available. Your audience or organization may express its own preferences, or choices may be limited by lack of equipment (software, scanners, digitizers), insufficient personnel (graphic designers, technical illustrators), or budget. Regardless of the limitations, your basic task is to enable the audience to interpret the visual correctly.

The many kinds of visuals you can use in your documents are described throughout this chapter. Regardless of type, certain requirements apply to all visuals. These requirements include

Features required in any visual

- using a title and number for each visual
- keeping the design of the visual clean and easy to read
- labeling all parts of the visual and providing legends as needed.
- placing the visual near the text it is helping to describe
- citing the sources of your visual material (both the source of the data and, when appropriate, the source of the actual visual—for instance, the creator of the bar chart or the person who took the photograph)

See the Guidelines boxes throughout this chapter for more information about using specific types of visuals.

NOTE *If you fail to cite the source or creator of a visual, you may be plagiarizing.*

TABLES

A table is a powerful way to display dense textual information such as specifications or comparisons. Numerical tables such as Table 12.1 present *quantitative information* (data that can be measured). Prose tables present

Title explains the table's purpose

Each column has a clear heading

Numbers are aligned properly for ease of reading

Where helpful, data are tallied

Caption explains the numeric relationships

Death Rates for Heart Disease and Cancer 1970–2010

	Number of Deaths (per 100,000)			
	Heart Disease		Cancer	
Year	Male	Female	Male	Female
1970	419	309	248	163
1980	369	305	272	167
1990	298	282	280	176
2000	256	260	257	206
2010	235	236	233	161
% change, 1970–2010	–43.9	–23.6	–6.0	–1.2

Both male and female death rates from heart disease decreased between 1970 to 2010, but males had nearly twice the rate of decrease. After increasing between 1970 and 1990, cancer death rates for both groups decreased to slightly below their 1970 levels.

TABLE 12.1 Data Displayed in a Table Organizes data into columns and rows for easy comparison.
Source: Adapted from *Statistical Abstract of the United States: 2010 (129th ed.)*. Washington: GPO. Tables 113, 115.

Column headings lead into the information

Phrases are brief and aligned for ease of reading

Numbers enhance the verbal information

Note provides more detail

Radon Risk if You Smoke

Radon level	If 1,000 people who smoked were exposed to this level over a lifetime . . .	The risk of cancer from radon exposure compares to . . .	WHAT TO DO: Stop smoking and . . .
20 pCi/L[a]	About 135 people could get lung cancer	←100 times the risk of drowning	Fix your home
10 pCi/L	About 71 people could get lung cancer	←100 times the risk of dying in a home fire	Fix your home
8 pCi/L	About 57 people could get lung cancer		Fix your home
4 pCi/L	About 29 people could get lung cancer	←100 times the risk of dying in an airplane crash	Fix your home
2 pCi/L	About 15 people could get lung cancer	←2 times the risk of dying in a car crash	Consider fixing between 2 and 4 pCi/L
1.3 pCi/L	About 9 people could get lung cancer	(Average indoor radon level)	(Reducing radon levels below 2 pCi/L is difficult)
0.4 pCi/L	About 3 people could get lung cancer	(Average outdoor radon level)	

Note: If you are a former smoker, your risk may be lower.
[a]picocuries per liter

TABLE 12.2 A Prose Table Displays numerical and verbal information.
Source: Home Buyer's and Seller's Guide to Radon. Washington: GPO, 1993.

qualitative information (prose descriptions, explanations, or instructions). Table 12.2 combines numerical data, probability estimates, comparisons, and instructions.

NOTE *Including a caption with your visual enables you to analyze or interpret the trends or key points you want readers to recognize (as in Table 12.1).*

No table should be overly complex for its audience. Table 12.3, designed for expert readers, is hard for nonspecialists to interpret because it presents too much

Toxic Chemical Releases by Industry: 2010

[In millions of pounds (4,438.7 represents 4,438,700,000), except as indicated.]

Industry	2010 SIC[1] code	Total on- and off-site releases	On-site release			Off-site releases/ transfers to disposal
			Total[2]	Point source air emissions	Surface water discharges	
Total[3]	**(X)**	**4,438.7**	**3,920.7**	**1,381.3**	**222.6**	**518.0**
Metal mining	10	1,245.7	1,244.7	1.8	0.7	1.0
Coal mining	12	12.9	12.9	0.1	0.2	-
Food and kindred products	20	153.2	145.8	35.1	83.1	7.3
Tobacco products	21	3.2	2.8	2.4	0.1	0.4
Textile mill products	22	7.4	6.5	4.8	0.3	0.9
Apparel and other textile products	23	0.7	0.5	0.4	-	0.2
Lumber and wood products	24	33.0	31.0	27.0	0.1	2.0
Furniture and fixtures	25	6.2	6.1	5.4	0.0	0.1
Paper and allied products	26	215.0	209.6	146.2	18.7	5.3
Printing and publishing	27	15.0	14.7	7.4	-	0.3
Chemical and allied products	28	544.7	500.3	168.6	44.5	44.4
Petroleum and coal products	29	75.0	71.9	34.6	17.1	3.1
Rubber and misc. plastic products	30	75.3	65.8	51.3	0.1	9.5
Leather and leather products	31	2.1	1.0	0.7	0.0	1.1
Stone, clay, glass products	32	51.2	45.8	38.1	2.1	5.5
Primary metal industries	33	477.5	198.1	35.9	39.4	279.4
Fabricated metals products	34	58.6	38.8	23.7	2.3	19.8
Industrial machinery and equipment	35	14.3	10.7	4.1	0.2	3.6
Electronic, electric equipment	36	20.3	13.8	6.5	3.6	6.4
Transportation equipment	37	74.8	63.5	51.1	0.2	11.2
Instruments and related products	38	8.7	7.9	5.1	1.0	0.8
Miscellaneous	39	7.1	4.9	3.9	0.1	2.2

Can cause information overload for nontechnical audiences

X Not applicable. [1]Standard Industrial Classification, see text, Section 12. Labor Force. [2]Includes on-site disposal to underground injection for Class I wells, Class II to V wells, other surface impoundments, land releases, and other releases, not shown separately. [3]Includes industries with no specific industry identified not shown separately.

TABLE 12.3 A Complex Table Causes Information Overload This table is too complex for anyone but experts.

Source: Environmental Protection Agency, *Annual Toxics Release Inventory.*

information at once. An unethical writer might use a complex table to bury numbers that are questionable or embarrassing (Williams 12). For laypersons, use fewer tables and keep them as simple as possible.

Audience and purpose

Like all other parts of a document, visuals are designed with audience and purpose in mind (Journet 3). An accountant doing an audit might need a table listing exact amounts, whereas the average public stockholder reading an annual report would prefer the "big picture" in an easily grasped bar graph or pie chart (Van Pelt 1). Similarly, scientists might find the complexity of data shown in Table 12.3 perfectly appropriate, but a nonexpert audience (say, environmental groups) might prefer the clarity and simplicity of a chart.

Tables work well for displaying exact values, but often graphs or charts are easier to interpret. Geometric shapes (bars, curves, circles) are generally easier to remember than lists of numbers (Cochran et al. 25).

For specific information about creating tables, see How to Construct a Table on page 256.

NOTE *Any visual other than a table is usually categorized as a figure, and so titled ("Figure 1 Aerial View of the Panhandle Mine Site").*

GRAPHS

Graphs show comparisons and trends

Graphs translate numbers into shapes, shades, and patterns. Graphs display, at a glance, the approximate values, the point being made about those values, and the relationship being emphasized. Graphs are especially useful for depicting comparisons, changes over time, patterns, or trends.

A graph's horizontal axis shows categories (the independent variables) to be compared, such as years within a period (1990, 2000, 2010). The vertical axis shows the range of values (the dependent variables) for comparing the categories, such as the number of deaths from heart failure in a given year. A dependent variable changes according to activity in the independent variable (say, a decrease in quantity over a set time, as in Figure 12.2).

Bar Graphs

Generally easy to understand, bar graphs show discrete comparisons, such as year-by-year or month-by-month. Each bar represents a specific quantity. You can use bar graphs to focus on one value or to compare values over time.

Simple Bar Graph A simple bar graph displays one trend or theme. The graph in Figure 12.2 shows one trend extracted from Table 12.1, male deaths from heart disease. If the audience needs exact numbers, you can record exact values above each bar.

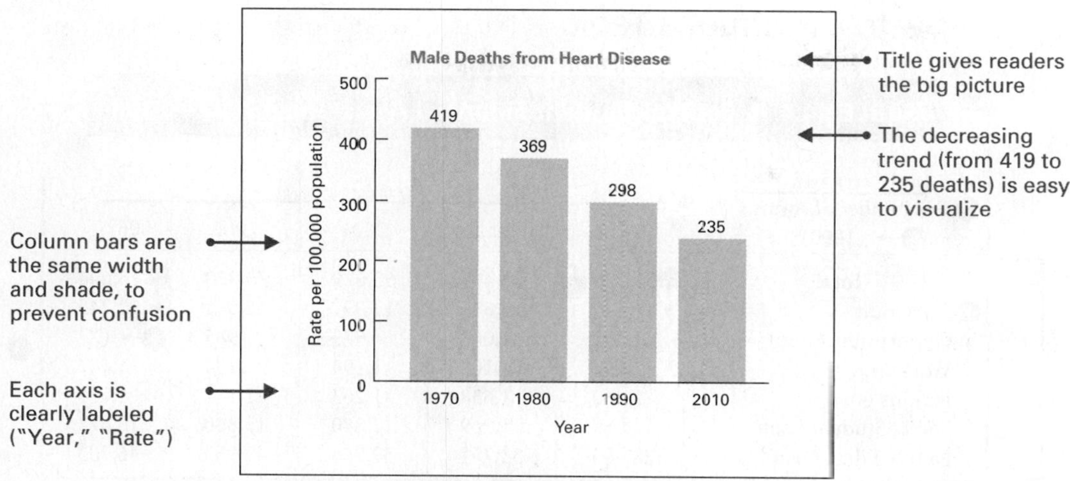

FIGURE 12.2 A Simple Bar Graph Shows a single relationship in the data.

Multiple-Bar Graph A bar graph can display two or three relationships simultaneously. Figure 12.3 contrasts two sets of data, to show comparative trends. Be sure to use a different pattern or color for each data set, and include a key (or *legend*) so that viewers will know which color or pattern corresponds with which data set. The more relationships you include, the more complex the graph becomes, so try to include no more than three on any one graph.

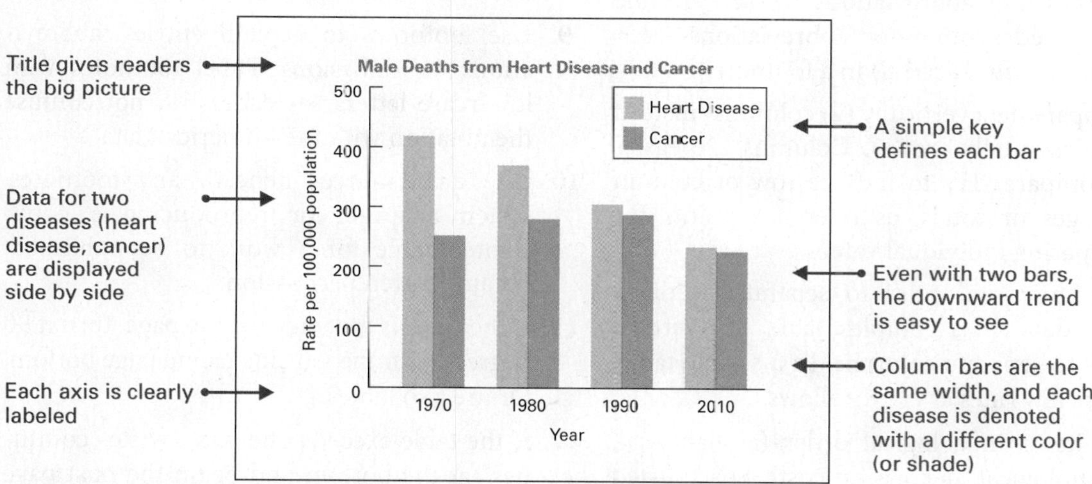

FIGURE 12.3 A Multiple-Bar Graph Shows two or more relationships.

How to Construct a Table

1 → **TABLE 14.4 ■ Federal Student Financial Assistance: 2002 – 2006**

STUB HEAD 2 → Number of Awards 3 → (1000)[a]	COLUMN HEADS 2002	2003	2004	2005	2006[b]
Total	4 **55,525** 5	**62,249**	**68,629**	**73,020**	7 **76,604**
6 Pell Grant	11,640	12,681	13,091	12,901	12,745
Opportunity Grant	1,033	1,064	975	985	8 → (X)
Work-Study	1,097	1,106	1,194	1,184	1,172
Perkins Loan	1,460	1,638	1,263	1,137	1,135
Direct Student Loan	11,689	11,969	12,840	13,860	13,874
Family Educ. Loan	28,606	33,791	39,266	42,953	46,703

ROW HEADS 11

NOTE 9 → [a]As of June 30. [b]Estimate. (X) Not available.

SRC 10 → *Source:* U.S. Department of Education, Office of Postsecondary Education, unpublished data. *Statistical Abstract of the United States: 2007* (126th Edition). Washington: GPO. Table 279.

12

1. Number the table in its order of appearance and provide a title that describes exactly what is being measured.
2. Label stub, column, and row heads (*Number of Awards*; *2006*; *Pell Grant*) to orient readers.
3. Specify units of measurement or use familiar symbols and abbreviations (*$, hr.*). Define specialized symbols or abbreviations (*Å = angstrom, db = decibel*) in a footnote.
4. Compare data vertically (in columns) instead of horizontally (rows). Columns are easier to compare. Try to include row or column averages or totals, as reference points for comparing individual values.
5. Use horizontal rules to separate headings from data. In a complex table, use vertical rules to separate columns. In a simple table, use as few rules as clarity allows.
6. List items in a logical order (alphabetical, chronological, decreasing cost). Space listed items for easy comparison. Keep prose entries as brief as clarity allows.
7. Convert fractions to decimals. Align decimals and all numbers vertically. Keep decimal places for all numbers equal. Round insignificant decimals to whole numbers.
8. Use *x*, *NA*, or a dash to signify any omitted entry, and explain the omission in a footnote (*Not available, Not applicable*).
9. Use footnotes to explain entries, abbreviations, or omissions. Label footnotes with lowercase letters so readers do not confuse the notation with the numerical data.
10. Cite data sources beneath any footnotes. When adapting or reproducing a copyrighted table for a work to be published, obtain written permission.
11. If the table is too wide for the page, turn it 90 degrees with the left side facing page bottom. Or use two tables.
12. If the table exceeds one page, write "continues" at the bottom and begin the next page with the full title, "continued," and the original column headings.

Horizontal-Bar Graph Horizontal-bar graphs are good for displaying a large series of bars arranged in order of increasing or decreasing value, as in Figure 12.4. This format leaves room for labeling the categories horizontally (*Doctorate*, and so on).

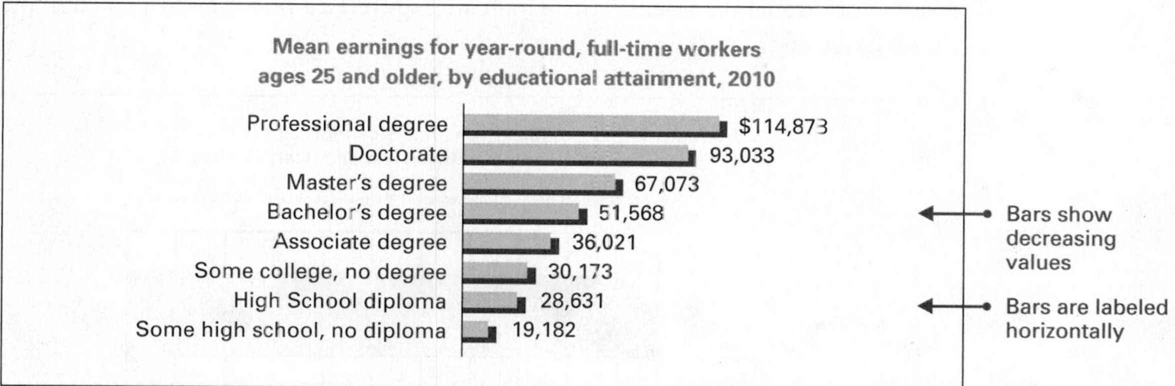

FIGURE 12.4 A Horizontal-Bar Graph Accommodates lengthy labels
Source: Bureau of Labor Statistics.

Stacked-Bar Graph Instead of displaying bars side-by-side, you can stack them. Stacked-bar graphs show how much each data set contributes to the whole.

Figure 12.5 displays other comparisons from Table 12.1. To avoid confusion, don't display more than four or five sets of data in a single bar.

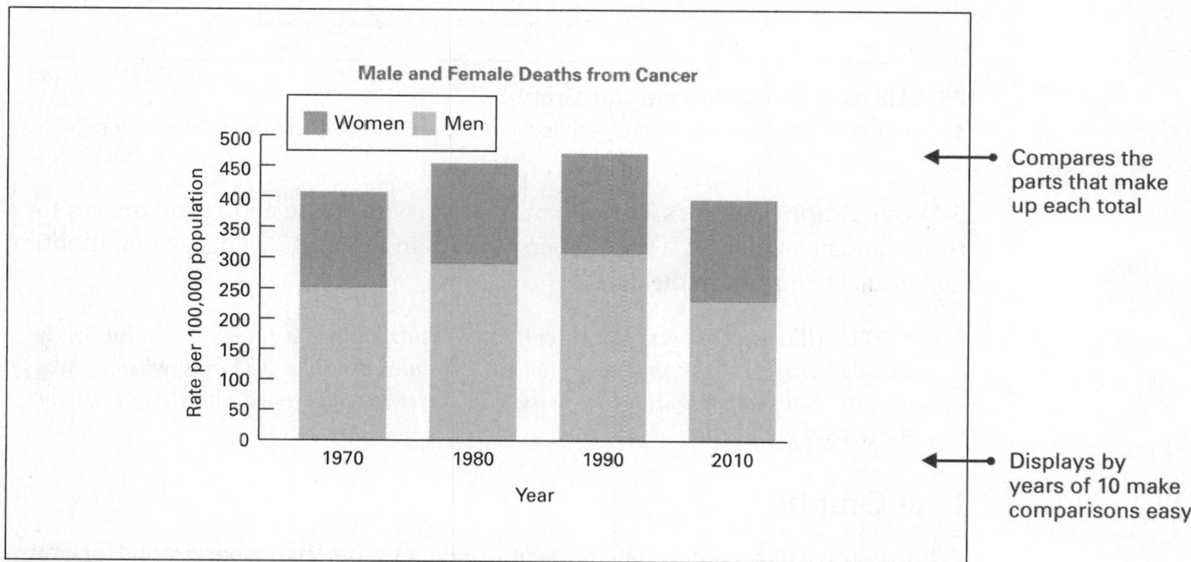

FIGURE 12.5 A Stacked-Bar Graph Displays of 10 make comparisons easy.

100 Percent Bar Graph A type of stacked-bar graph, the 100 percent bar graph shows the value of each part that makes up the 100 percent value, as in Figure 12.6. Like any bar graph, the 100 percent graph can have either horizontal or vertical bars.

Notice how bar graphs become harder to interpret as bars and patterns increase. For a general audience, the data from Figure 12.6 might be displayed in pie charts (page 264).

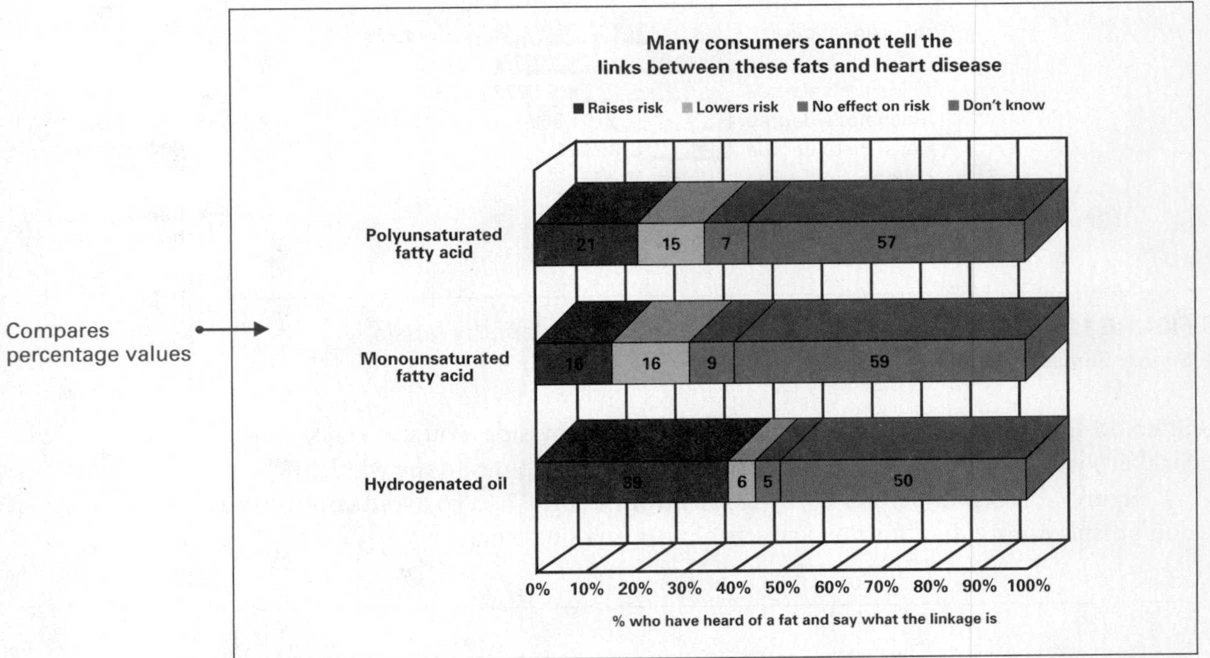

FIGURE 12.6 A 100 Percent Bar Graph
Source: Center for Food Safety and Applied Nutrition, U.S. Food and Drug Administration.

3-D Bar Graph Graphics software makes it easy to shade and rotate images for a three-dimensional view. The 3-D perspectives in Figure 12.7 engage our attention and visually emphasize the data.

> **NOTE** *Although 3-D graphs can enhance and dramatize a presentation, an overly complex graph can be misleading or hard to interpret. Use 3-D only when a two-dimensional version will not serve as well. Never sacrifice clarity and simplicity for the sake of visual effect.*

Line Graphs

A line graph can accommodate many more data points than a bar graph (for example, a twelve-month trend, measured monthly). Line graphs help readers synthesize large bodies of information in which exact quantities don't need to be emphasized.

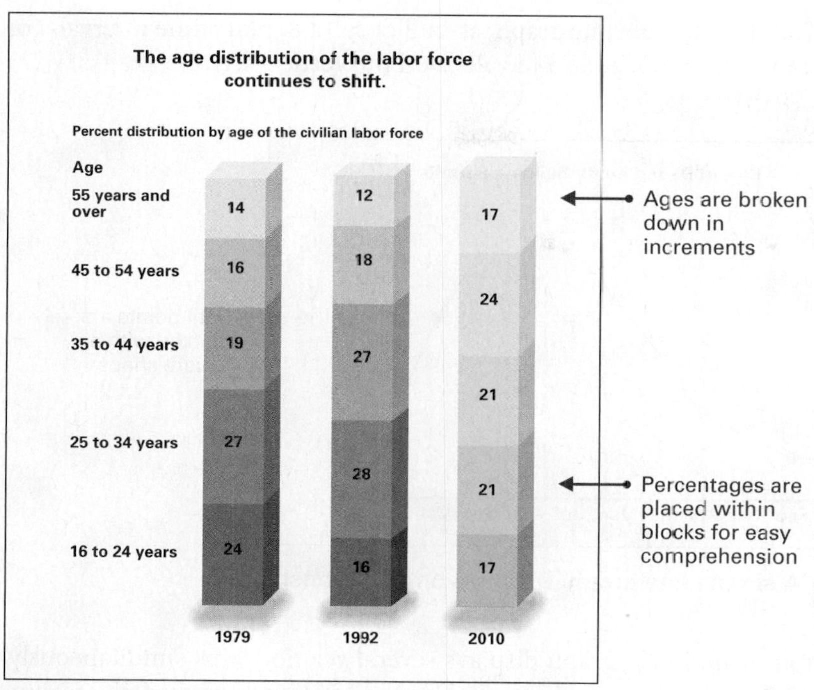

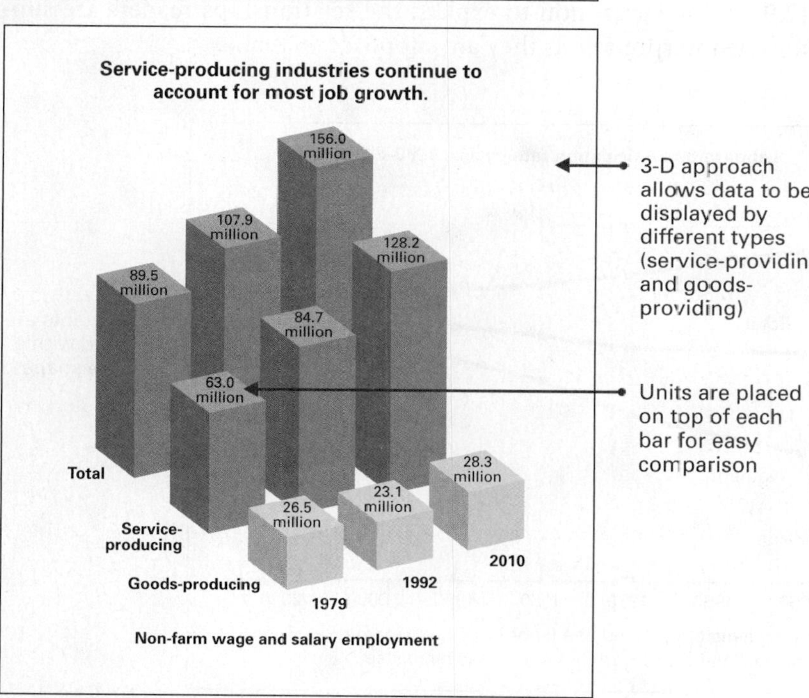

FIGURE 12.7 3-D Bar Graphs Adding a third axis creates the appearance of depth.

Source: Bureau of Labor Statistics.

Simple Line Graph A simple line graph, as in Figure 12.8, plots time intervals (or categories) on the horizontal scale and values on the vertical scale.

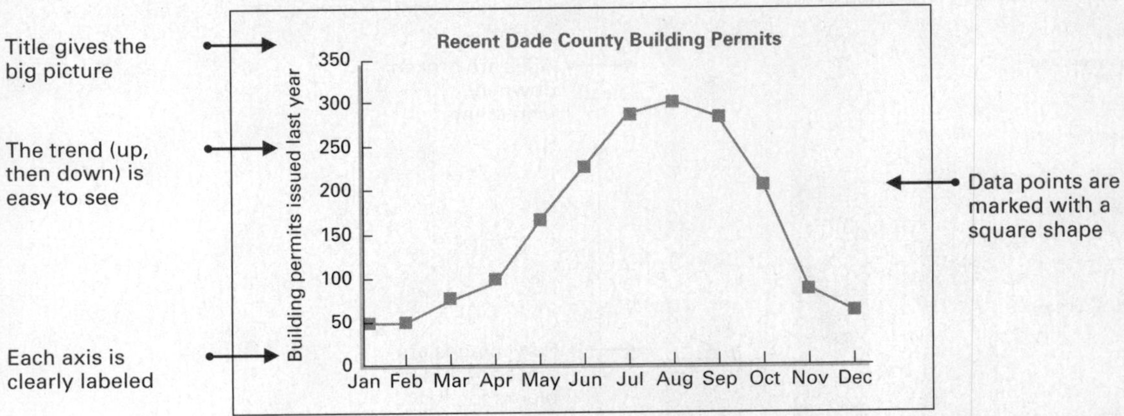

FIGURE 12.8 A simple line graph Displays one relationship.

Multiline Graph A multiline graph displays several relationships simultaneously, as in Figure 12.9. Include a caption to explain the relationships readers are supposed to see and the interpretations they are supposed to make.

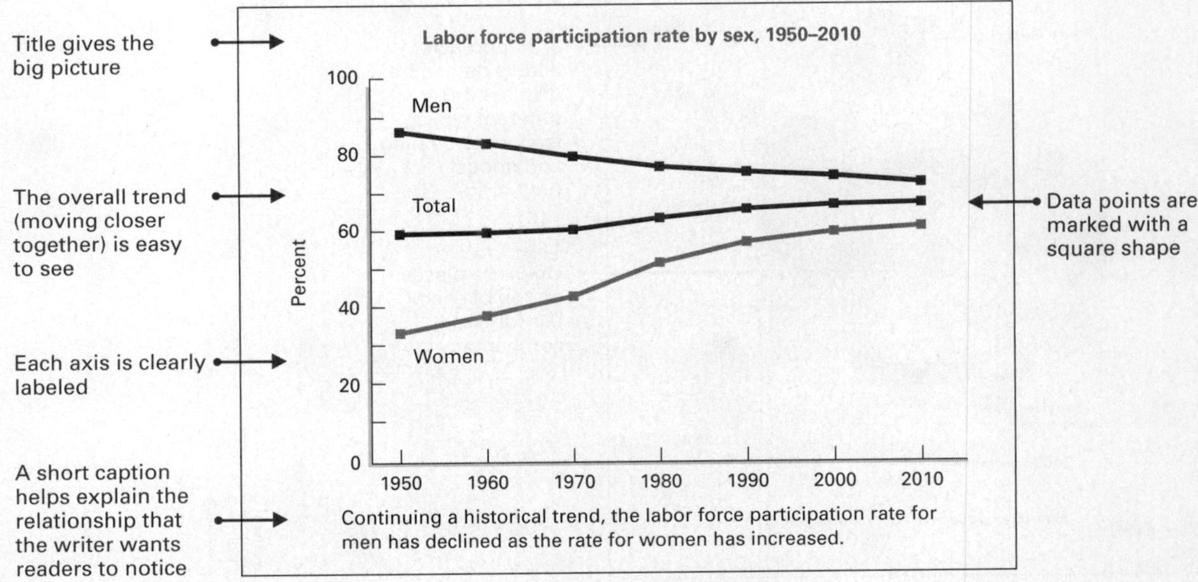

Continuing a historical trend, the labor force participation rate for men has declined as the rate for women has increased.

FIGURE 12.9 A Multiline graph Displays multiple relationships.
Source: Bureau of Labor Statistics.

Deviation Line Graph Extend your vertical scale below the zero baseline to display positive and negative values in one graph, as in Figure 12.10. Mark values below the baseline in intervals parallel to those above it.

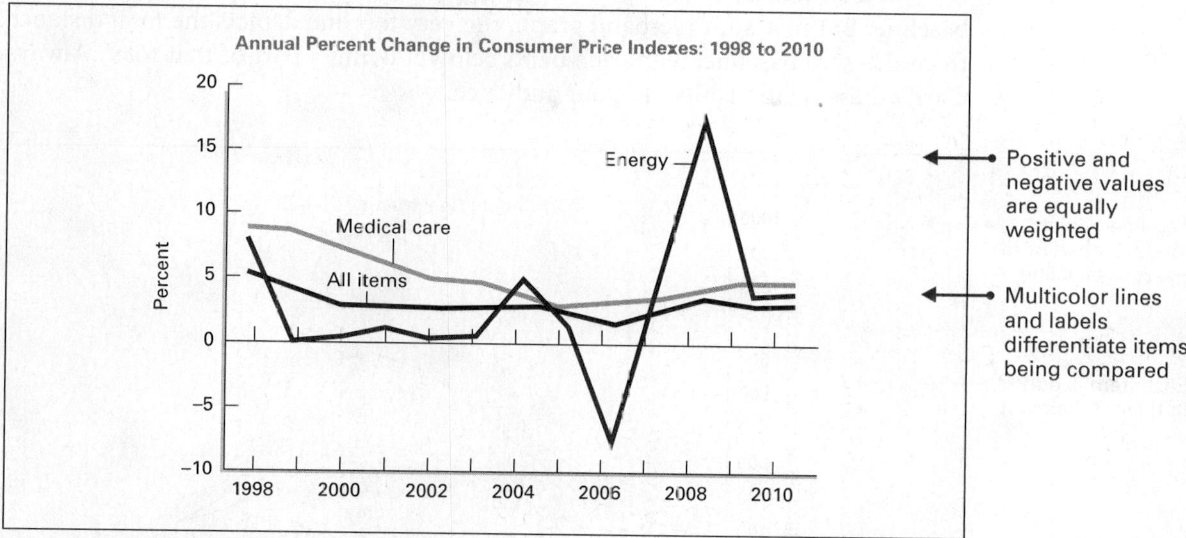

FIGURE 12.10 A Deviation Line Graph Displays negative and positive values.
Source: Chart prepared by U.S. Bureau of the Census.

Band or Area Graph By shading in the area beneath the main plot lines, you can highlight specific information. Figure 12.11 is another version of the Figure 12.8 line graph.

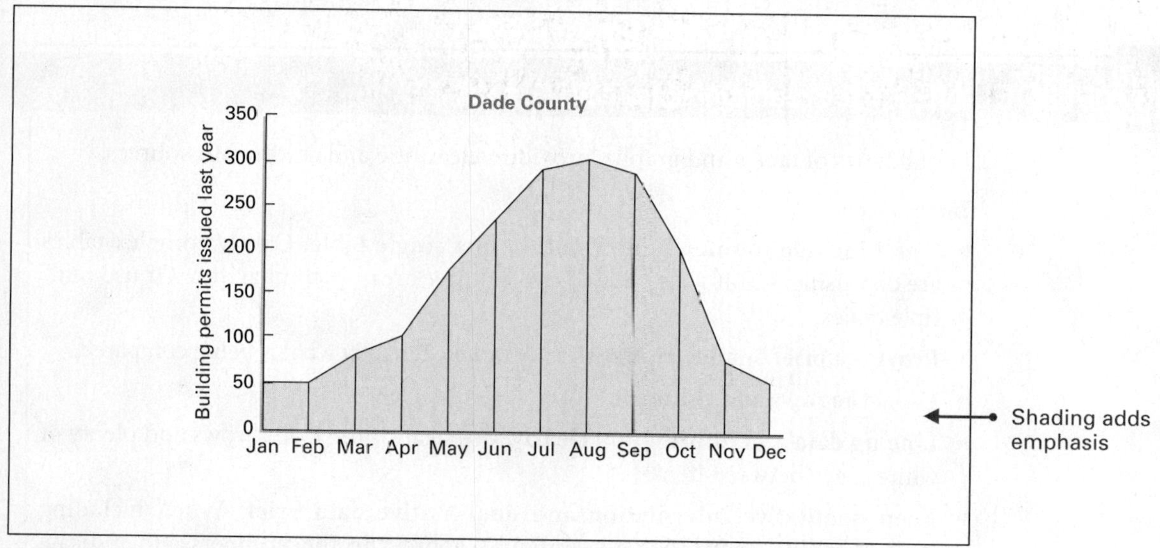

FIGURE 12.11 A Simple Band Graph Uses shading to highlight information.

Multiple-Band Graph The multiple bands in Figure 12.12 depict relationships among sums instead of the direct comparisons depicted in the Figure 12.9 multiline graph. Despite their visual appeal, multiple-band graphs are easy to misinterpret: In a multiline graph, each line depicts its own distance from the zero baseline. But in a multiple-band graph, the very top line depicts the *total* distance from the zero baseline, with each band below it being a part of that total. Always clarify these relationships for your audience.

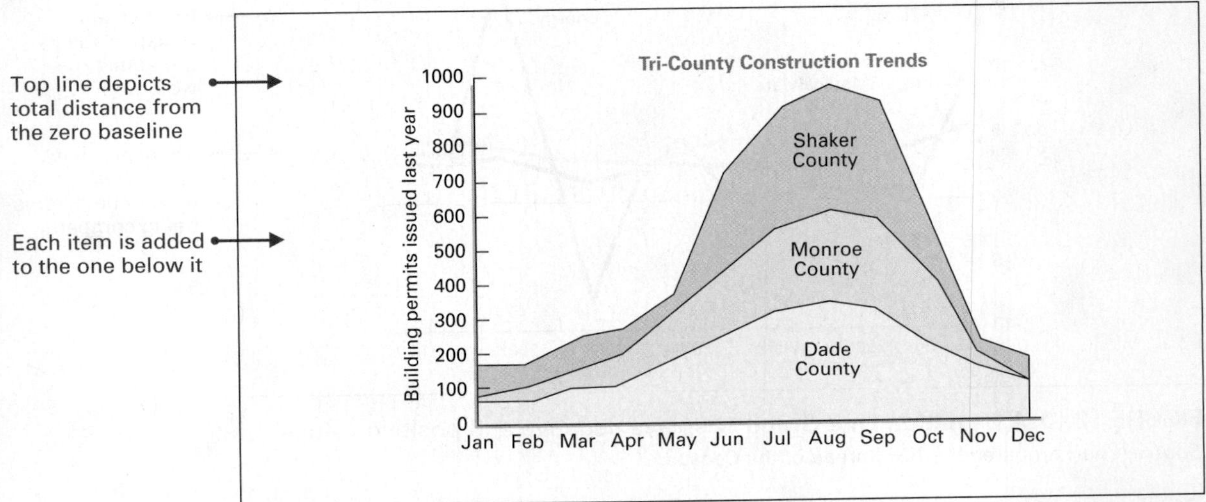

FIGURE 12.12 **A Multiple-Band Graph** Depicts relationships among sums instead of direct comparisons.

GUIDELINES for Creating Tables and Graphs

For all types of tables and graphs, provide a clear title and credit your sources.

Tables

- **Don't include too much information in a single table.** Overly complex tables are confusing. Limit your table to two or three areas of comparison. Or use multiple tables.
- **Provide a brief but descriptive title.** Announce exactly what is being compared.
- **Label the rows and columns.**
- **Line up data and information clearly.** Use neat columns and rows and plenty of white space between items.
- **Keep qualitative information and quantitative data brief.** When including high numbers (more than three digits), abbreviate the numbers and indicate

"in thousands," "in millions," and so on. When using text in a table, limit the number of words.

- **Provide additional information, if necessary.** Add footnotes or a caption at the bottom of the table to explain anything readers may not understand at first glance.

Bar Graphs

- **Use a bar graph only to compare values that are noticeably different.** Small value differences will yield bars that look too similar to compare.
- **Keep the graph simple and easy-to-read.** Don't plot more than three types of bars in each cluster. Avoid needless visual details.
- **Number your scales in units familiar to the audience.** Units of 1 or multiples of 2, 5, or 10 are best.
- **Label both scales to show what is being measured or compared.** If space allows, keep all labels horizontal for easier reading.
- **Use tick marks to show the points of division on your scale.** If the graph has many bars, extend the tick marks into *grid lines* to help readers relate bars to values.

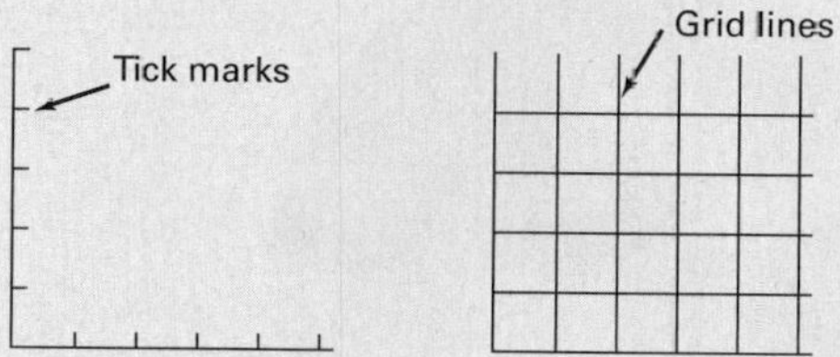

- **Make all bars the same width** (unless you are overlapping them).
- **In a multiple-bar graph, use a different pattern, color, or shade for each bar in a cluster.** Provide a key, or legend, identifying each pattern, color, or shade.
- **Refer to the graph by number ("Figure 1") in your text, and explain what the reader should look for.** Or include a prose caption with the graph.

Line Graphs

Follow the guidelines above for bar graphs, with these additions:

- **Display no more than three or four lines on one graph.**
- **Mark each individual data point used in plotting each line.**
- **Make each line visually distinct (using color, symbols, and so on).**
- **Label each line so readers know what the given line represents.**
- **Avoid grid lines that readers could mistake for plotted lines.**

CHARTS

The terms *chart* and *graph* often are used interchangeably. Technically, a chart displays relationships (quantitative or cause-and-effect) that are *not* plotted on a coordinate system (x and y axes).

Pie Charts

Easy for most people to understand, a pie chart displays the relationship of parts or percentages to the whole. Readers can compare the parts to each other as well as to the whole (to show how much was spent on what, how much income comes from which sources, and so on). Figure 12.13 shows a simple pie chart. Figure 12.14 is an exploded pie chart. Exploded pie charts highlight various pieces of the pie.

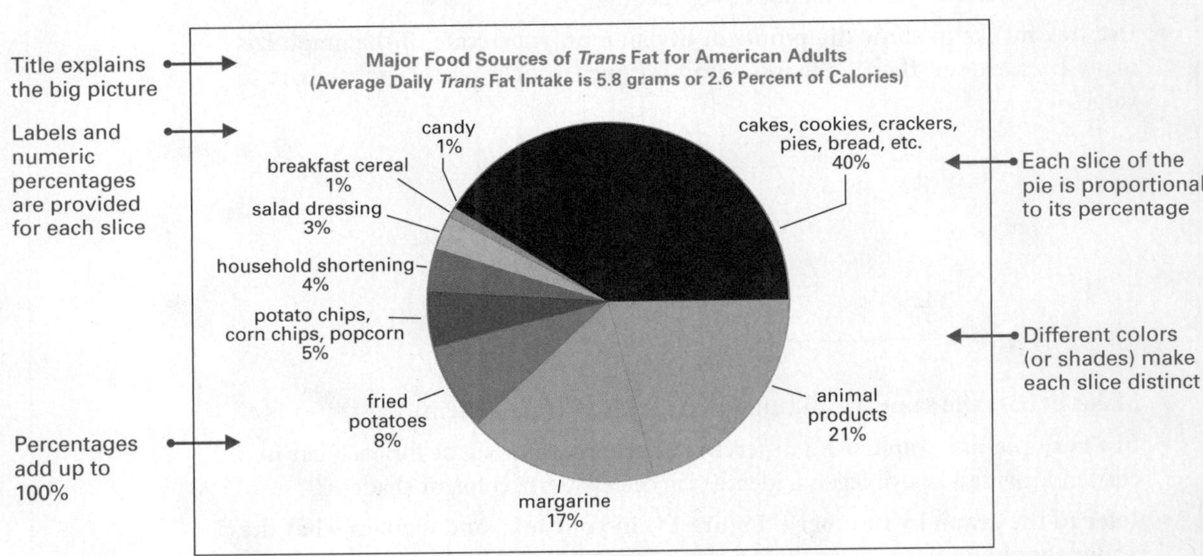

FIGURE 12.13 A Simple Pie Chart Shows the relationships of parts or percentages to the whole.
Source: U.S. Food and Drug Administration.

Organization Charts

An organization chart shows the hierarchy and relationships between different departments and other units in an organization, as in Figure 12.15.

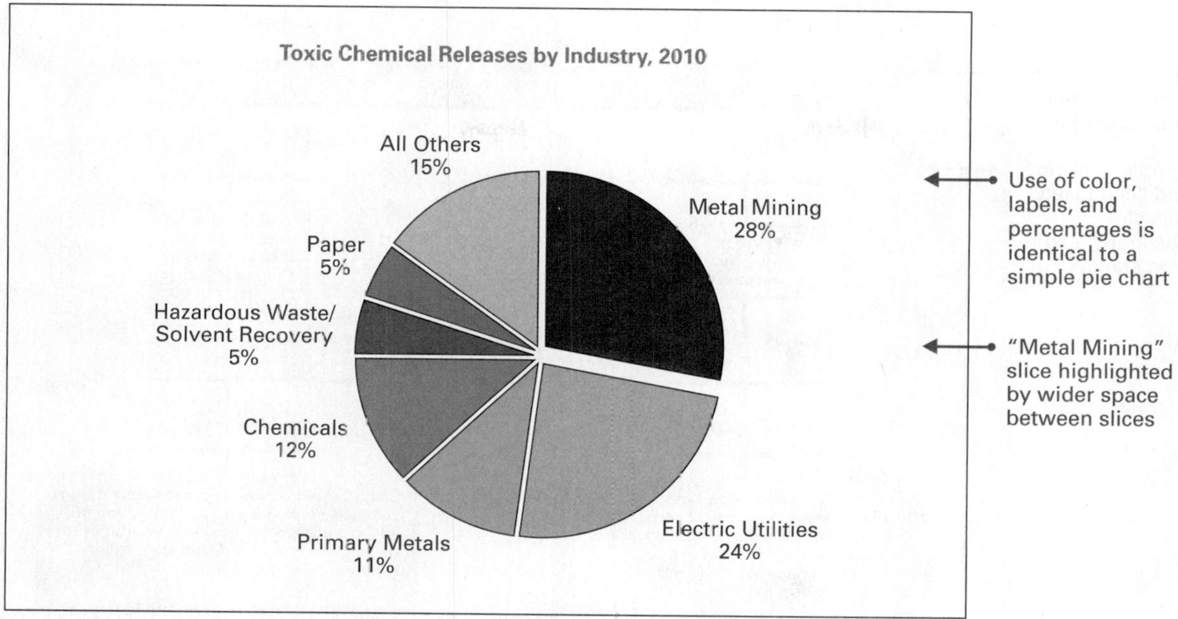

FIGURE 12.14 An Exploded Pie Chart Highlights various slices.
Source: U.S. Environmental Protection Agency. (See Table 12.3, page 253, for data.)

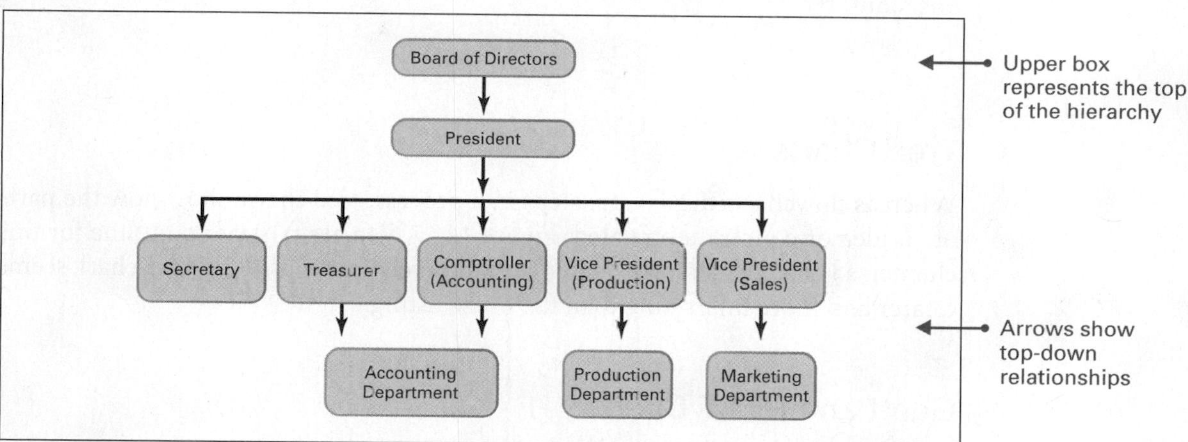

FIGURE 12.15 An Organization Chart Shows how different people or departments are ranked and related.

Flowcharts

A flowchart traces a procedure or process from beginning to end. Figure 12.16 illustrates the procedure for helping an adult choking victim.

Chart is designed to be read quickly in an emergency

Simple "yes/no" and "collapsed/conscious" questions lead to next steps

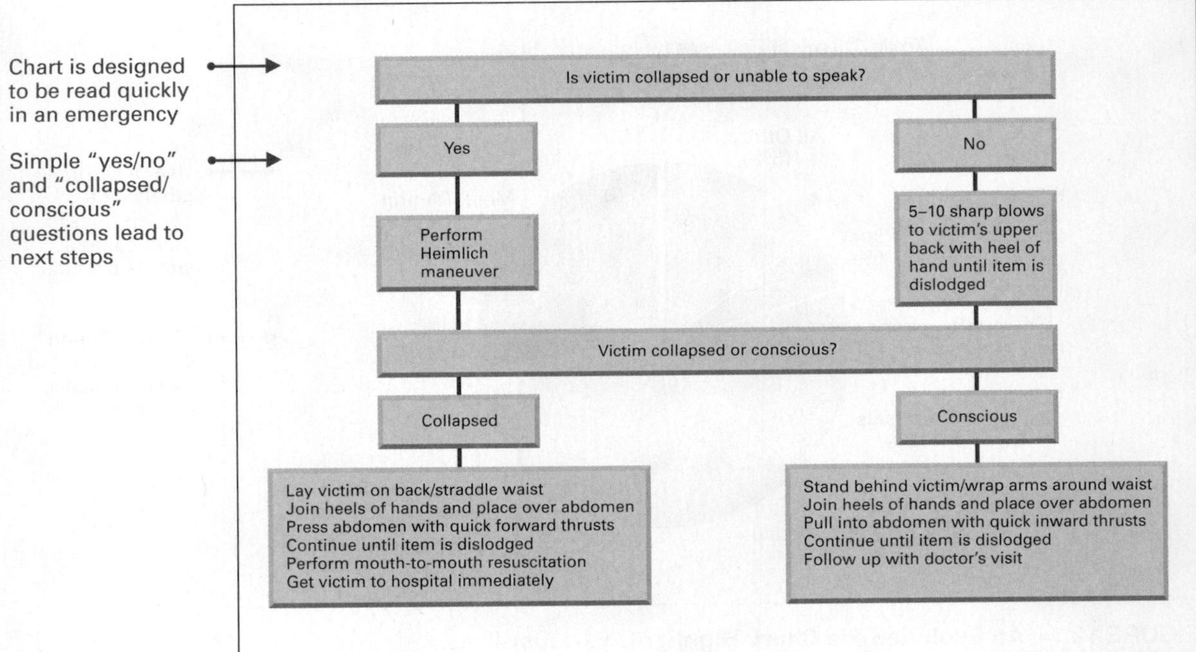

FIGURE 12.16 A Flowchart Depicts a sequence of events, activities, steps, or decisions.

Tree Charts

Whereas flowcharts display the steps in a process, tree charts show how the parts of an idea or concept are related. Figure 12.17 displays part of an outline for this chapter so that readers can better visualize relationships. The tree chart seems clearer and more interesting than the prose listing.

Gantt and PERT Charts

Gantt and PERT charts are useful for project planning

Named for engineer H. L. Gantt (1861–1919), Gantt charts depict how the parts of an idea or concept relate. A series of bars or lines (time lines) indicates start-up and completion dates for each phase or task in a project. Gantt charts are useful for planning and tracking a project. The Gantt chart in Figure 12.18 illustrates the schedule for a manufacturing project. A PERT (Program Evaluation and Review Technique) chart uses shapes and arrows to outline a project's main activities and events (Figure 12.19). Both types of charts can be created with project management software such as *Microsoft Project*.

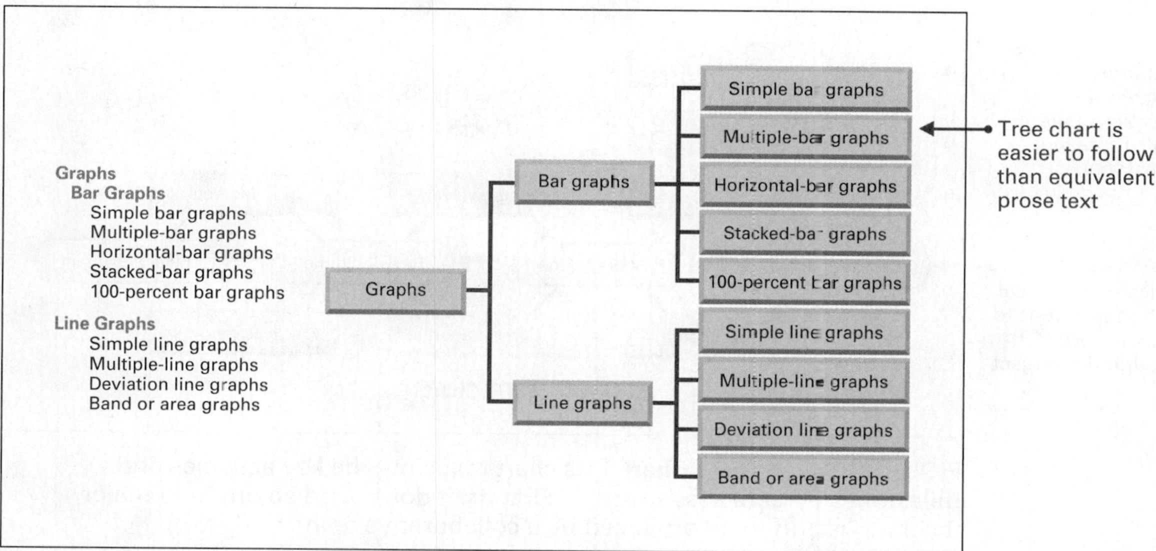

FIGURE 12.17 An Outline Converted to a Tree Chart Shows which items belong together and how they are connected.

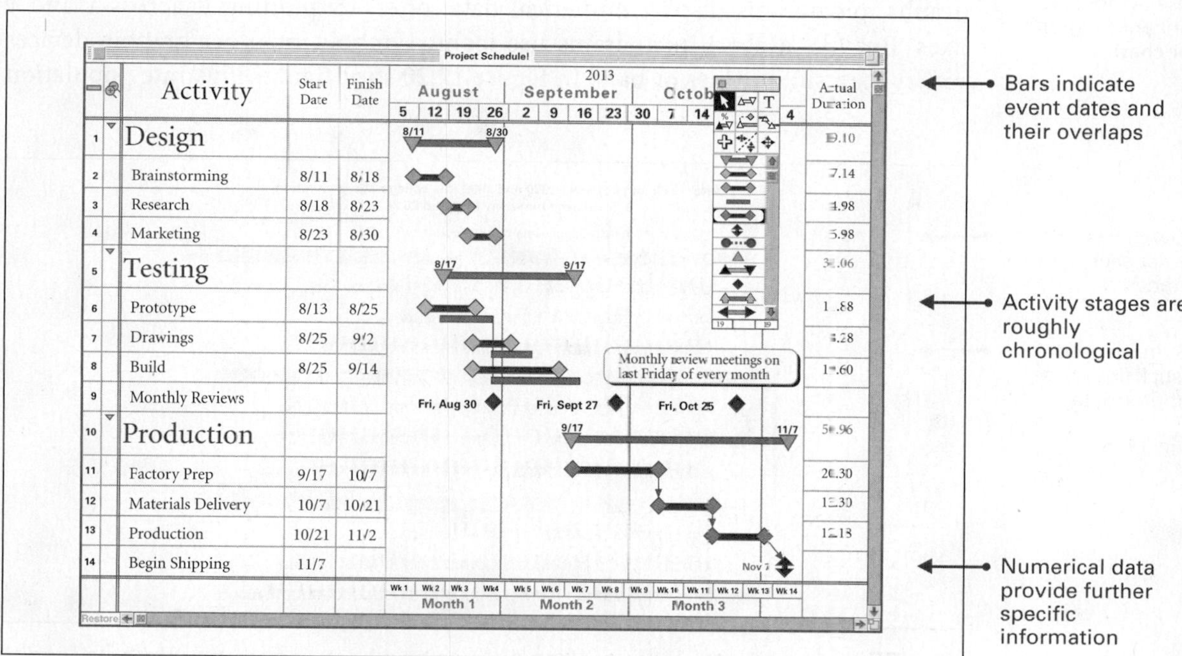

FIGURE 12.18 A Gantt Chart Depicts how the phases of a project interrelate.
Source: Chart created in *FastTrack Schedule™*. Reprinted by permission from AEC Software.

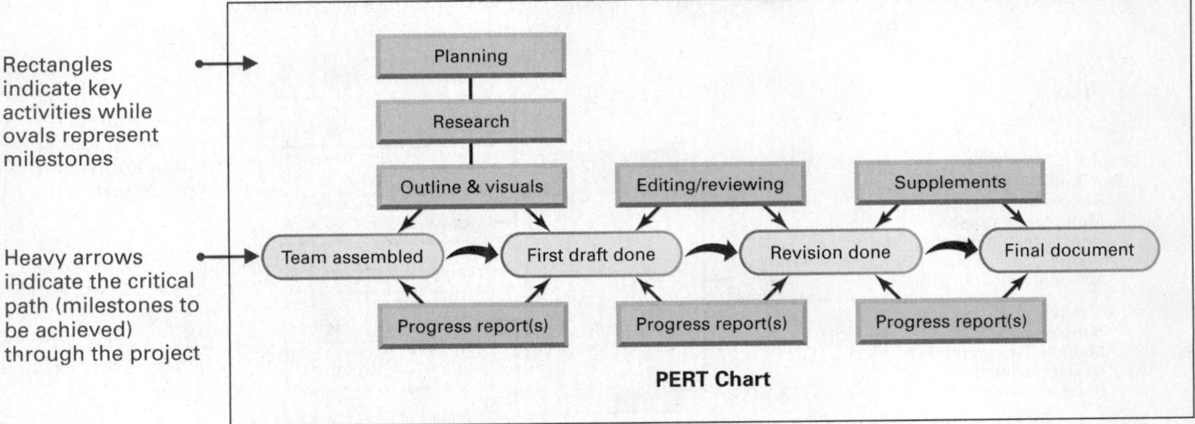

FIGURE 12.19 **A PERT Chart** This chart maps out the key activities and milestones ("Team assembled," "First draft done" and so on) for a major technical report to be produced by a collaborative team.

Pictograms

Pictograms use symbols to enhance a graph or chart

Pictograms are something of a cross between a line graph and a chart. Like line graphs, pictograms display numerical data, often by plotting it across *x* and *y* axes. But like a chart, pictograms use icons, symbols, or other graphic devices rather than simple lines or bars. In Figure 12.20 stick figures illustrate population

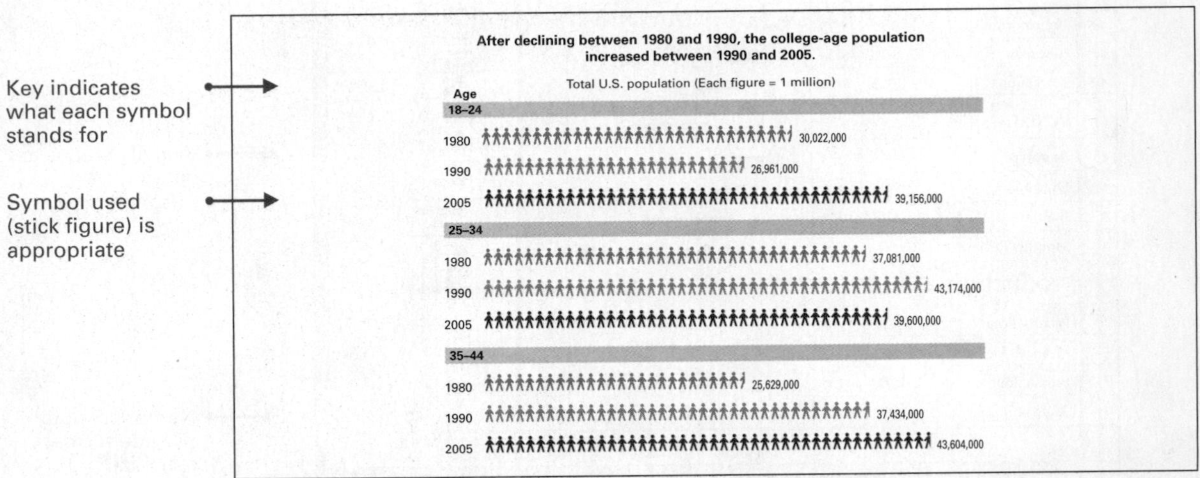

FIGURE 12.20 **A Pictogram** In place of lines and bars, icons and symbols lend appeal and clarity.

Source: U.S. Bureau of the Census.

changes during a given period. Pictograms are visually appealing and can be especially useful for nontechnical or multicultural audiences.

GUIDELINES for Creating Charts

Pie Charts

- **Make sure the parts of the pie add up to 100 percent.**
- **Differentiate and label each slice clearly.** Use different colors or shades for each slice, and label the category and percentage of each slice.
- **Keep all labels horizontal.** Make the chart easy to read.
- **Combine very small pie slices.** Group categories with very small percentages under "other."

Organization Charts

- **Move from top to bottom or left to right.** Place the highest level of hierarchy at the top (top-to-bottom chart) or at the left (left-to-right chart).
- **Use downward- or rightward-pointing arrows.** Arrows show the flow of hierarchy from highest to lowest.
- **Keep boxes uniform and text brief.** Shape may vary slightly according to how much text is in each box. Maintain a uniform look. Avoid too much text in any box.

Flowcharts, Tree Charts, and Gantt Charts

- **Move from top to bottom or left to right.** The process must start at the top (top-to-bottom chart) or left (left-to-right chart).
- **Use connector lines.** Show relationships between the parts.
- **Keep boxes uniform and text brief.** See the tips for organization charts above.

Pictograms

- **Follow the guidelines for bar graphs (page 263).**
- **Use symbols that are universally recognized.**
- **Keep the pictogram clean and simple (avoid too much visual clutter).**

GRAPHIC ILLUSTRATIONS

Illustrations can be diagrams, maps, drawings, icons, photographs, or any other visual that relies mainly on pictures rather than on data or words. For example, the diagram of a safety-belt locking mechanism in Figure 12.21 accomplishes what the verbal text alone cannot: it portrays the mechanism in operation.

Verbal text that requires a visual supplement

> The safety-belt apparatus includes a tiny pendulum attached to a lever, or locking mechanism. Upon sudden deceleration, the pendulum swings forward, activating the locking device to keep passengers from pitching into the dashboard.

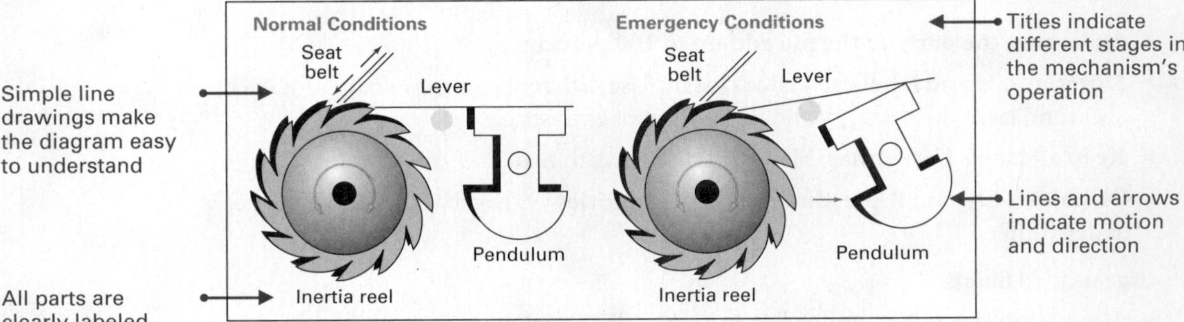

FIGURE 12.21 A Diagram of a Safety-Belt Locking Mechanism
Shows how the basic parts work together.
Source: U.S. Department of Transportation.

Illustrations are invaluable when you need to convey spatial relationships or help your audience see what something actually looks like. Drawings can often illustrate more effectively than photographs because a drawing can simplify the view, omit unnecessary features, and focus on what is important.

Diagrams

Diagrams show how items function or are assembled

Diagrams are especially effective for presenting views that could not be captured by photographing or actually observing the item.

Exploded diagrams show how the parts of an item are assembled, as in Figure 12.22. These often appear in repair or maintenance manuals. Notice how parts are numbered for easy reference to the written instructions.

Cutaway diagrams show the item with its exterior layers removed to reveal interior sections, as in Figure 12.23. Unless the specific viewing perspective is immediately recognizable (as in Figure 12.23), name the angle of vision: "top view," "side view," and so on.

Block diagrams are simplified sketches that represent the relationship between the parts of an item, principle, system, or process. Because block diagrams are designed to illustrate *concepts* (such as current flow in a circuit), the parts are

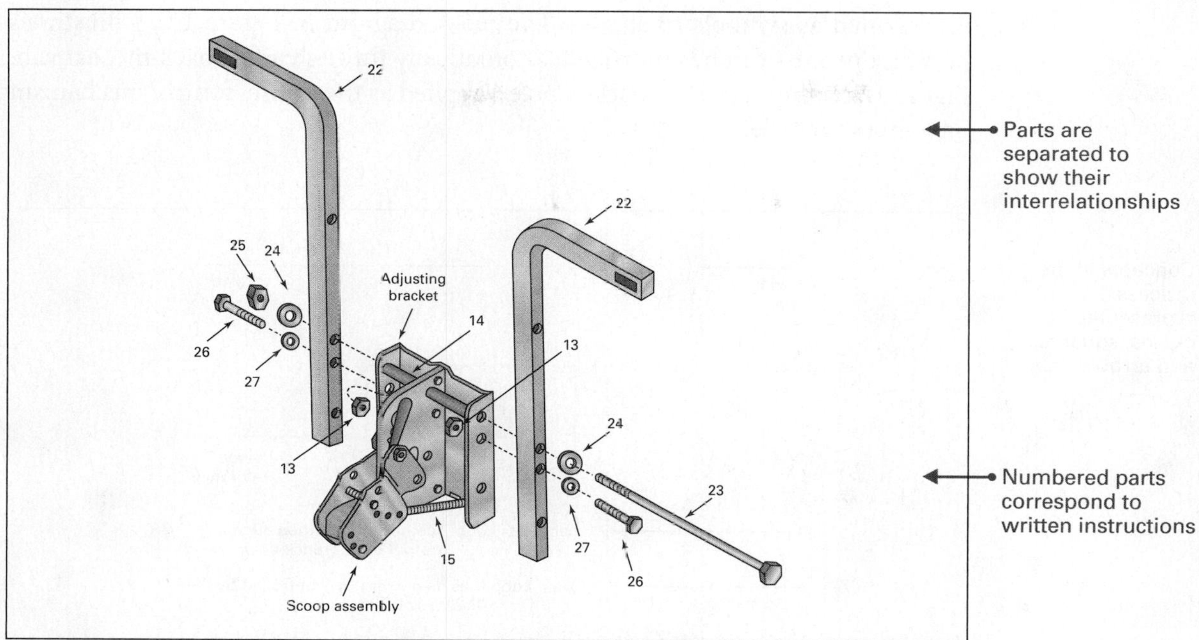

Parts are separated to show their interrelationships

Numbered parts correspond to written instructions

FIGURE 12.22 An Exploded Diagram of a Brace for an Adjustable Basketball Hoop Shows how the parts are assembled.

Source: Courtesy of Spalding.

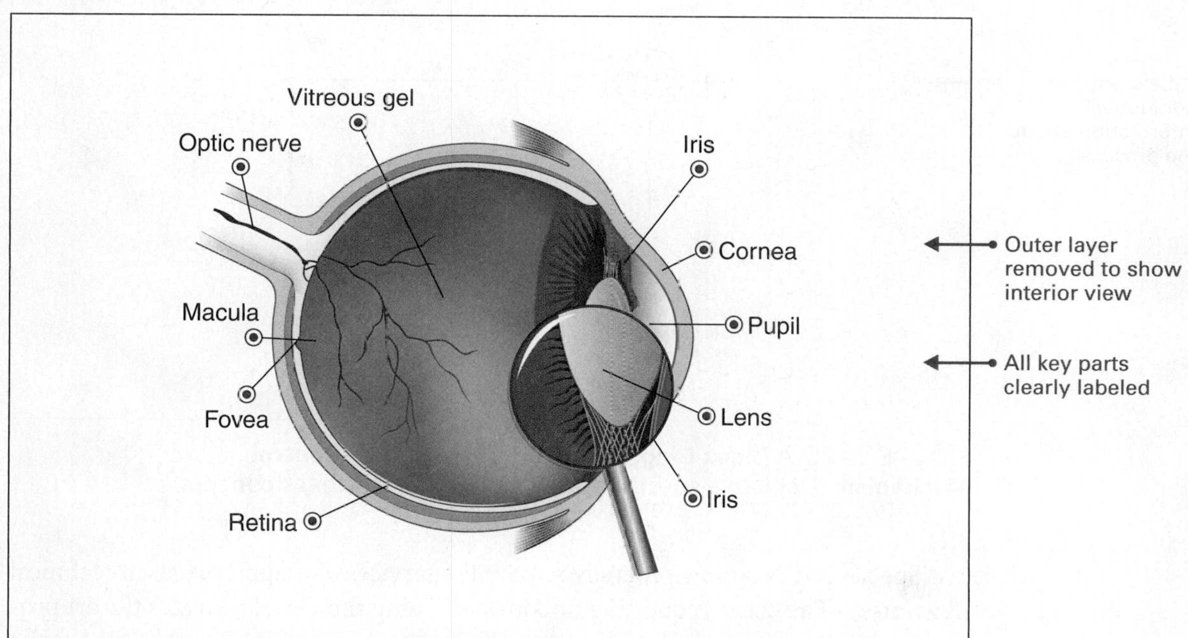

Outer layer removed to show interior view

All key parts clearly labeled

FIGURE 12.23 Cutaway Diagram of an Eye Shows what is inside.

Source: Courtesy of National Eye Institute, National Institutes of Health (NEI/NIH).

represented as symbols or shapes. The block diagram in Figure 12.24 illustrates how any process can be controlled automatically through a feedback mechanism. Figure 12.25 shows the feedback concept applied as the cruise-control mechanism on a motor vehicle.

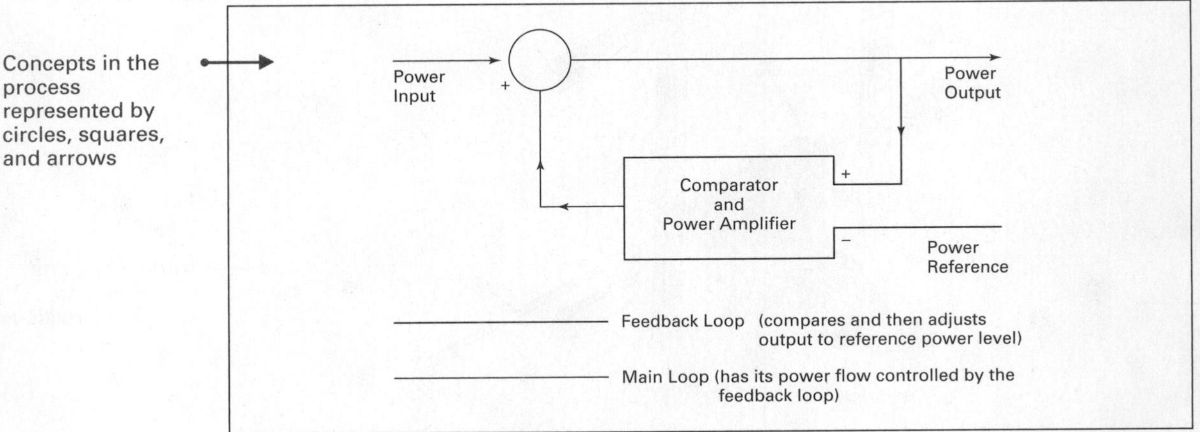

FIGURE 12.24 A Block Diagram Illustrating the Concept of Feedback

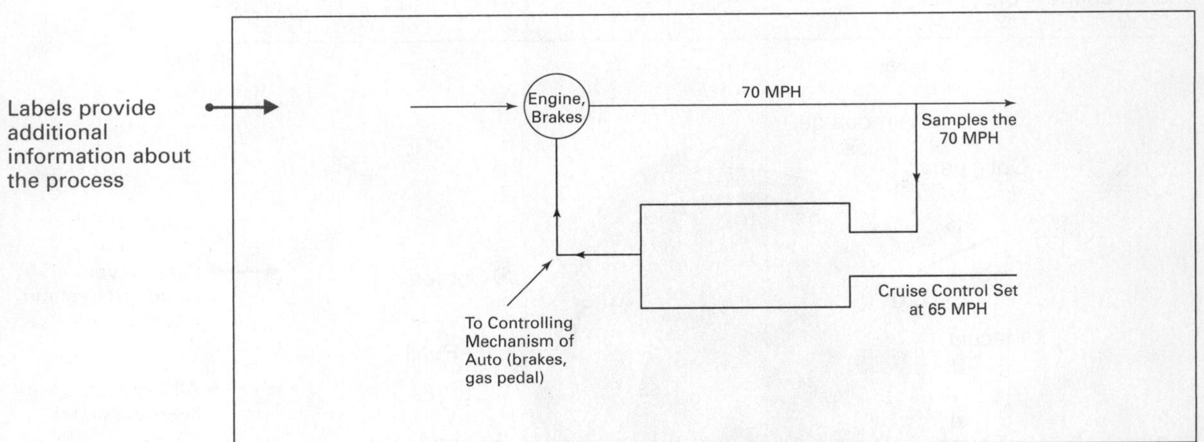

FIGURE 12.25 A Block Diagram Illustrating a Cruise-Control Mechanism Depicts a specific application of the feedback concept.

Specialized diagrams generally require the services of graphic artists or technical illustrators. The client requesting or commissioning the visual provides the art professional with an *art brief* (often prepared by writers and editors) that spells out the visual's purpose and specifications. The art brief is usually reinforced by a *thumbnail sketch,* a small, simple sketch of the visual being requested. For example, part of the brief addressed to the medical illustrator for Figure 12.23 might read as follows:

An art brief for Figure 12.23

- **Purpose:** to illustrate for laypersons major parts of internal anatomy of the eye
- **View:** full cutaway, sagittal
- **Range:** entire eyeball at roughly 500 percent scale
- **Depth:** medial cross-section
- **Structures omitted:** retinal blood vessels, sclera, ciliary and lateral rectus muscles, and other accessory structures
- **Structures included:** gross anatomy of eyeball—delineated by color, shape, shading, and texture, each connected with peripheral labels by roughly 1.5-point leader lines
- **Structures highlighted:** iris, cornea, pupil, lens, vitreous gel, retina, fovea, macula, and posterior junction with the optic nerve

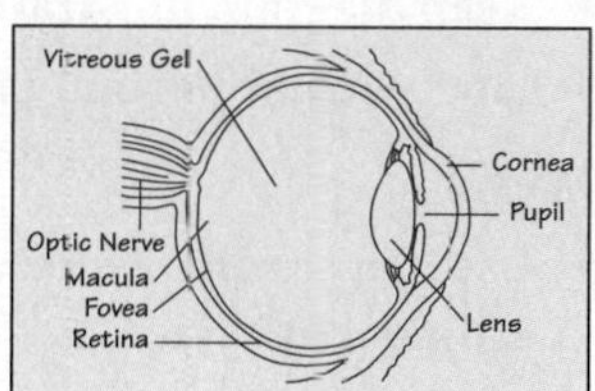

A thumbnail sketch of Figure 12.23

Maps

Besides being visually engaging, maps are especially useful for showing comparisons and for helping readers *visualize* position, location, and relationships among various data. Figure 12.26 synthesizes statistical information in a format that is accessible and understandable. Color enhances the comparisons.

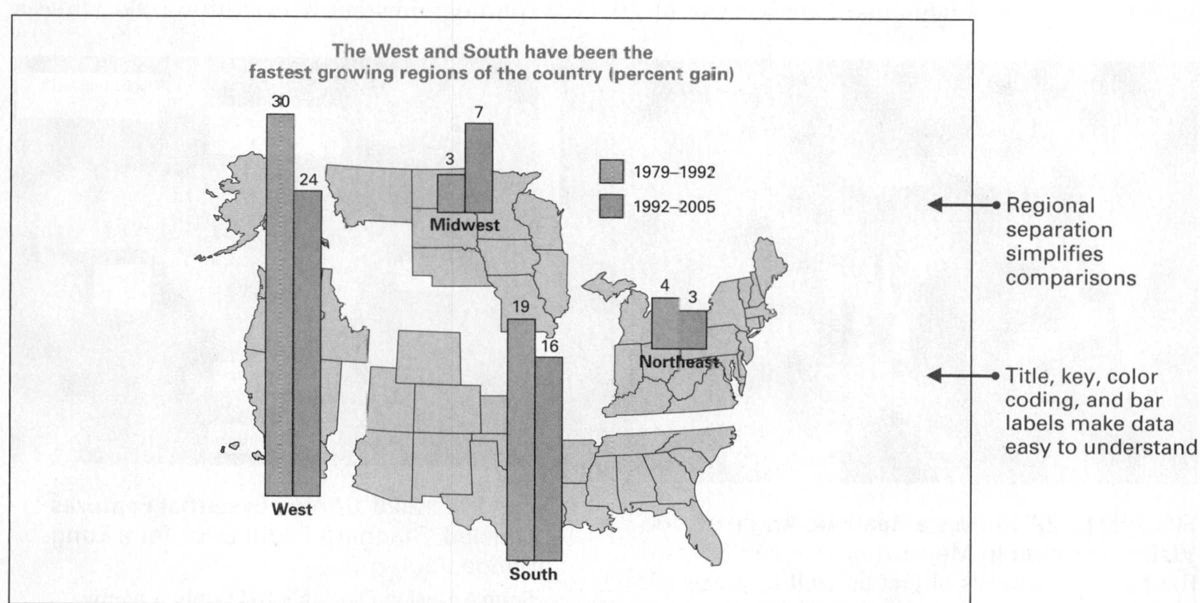

Regional separation simplifies comparisons

Title, key, color coding, and bar labels make data easy to understand

FIGURE 12.26 **A Map Rich in Statistical Significance** Shows the geographic distribution of data.

Source: U.S. Bureau of the Census.

GUIDELINES for Creating Graphic Illustrations

Drawings and Diagrams

- **Provide clear explanations.** Explain how diagram parts fit together or operate.
- **Use lines and arrows to indicate direction and motion.** For diagrams that show action, directional markers help viewers understand the action.
- **Keep diagram illustrations simple.** Only show viewers what they need to see.
- **Label each important part.**

Maps

- **Use maps from credible sources, such as the U.S. Census Bureau or other government agencies.**
- **Keep colors to a minimum, so that the maps are easy to read on a computer or in print.**

PHOTOGRAPHS

Photographs are especially useful for showing exactly how something looks (Figure 12.27) or how something is done (Figure 12.28). Unlike a diagram, which highlights certain parts of an item, photographs show everything. So while a

FIGURE 12.27 **Shows a Realistic Angle of Vision** Titration in Measuring Electron-Spin Resonance. (Shows object as well as person for sense of scale. Also shows angle that simulates operator's angle of vision. Photo has been cropped to remove needless detail.)
Source: RGB Ventures LLC dba SuperStock/Alamy.

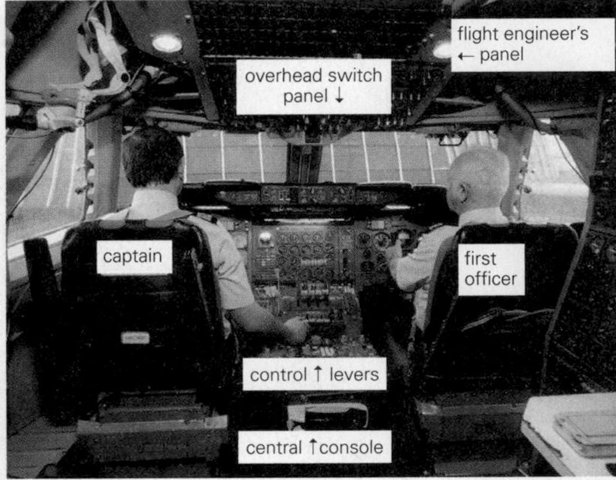

FIGURE 12.28 **Shows Essential Features Labeled** Standard Flight Deck for a Long-Range Jet.
Source: Design Pics Inc.—RM Content/Alamy.

photograph can be extremely useful, it also can provide too much detail or fail to emphasize the parts on which you want people to focus. For the most effective photographs, use a professional photographer who knows all about angles, lighting, lenses, and special film or digital editing options.

FIGURE 12.29 **Shows a Complex Mechanism** Free Tunable Laser.
Source: YuryZap/Shutterstock.

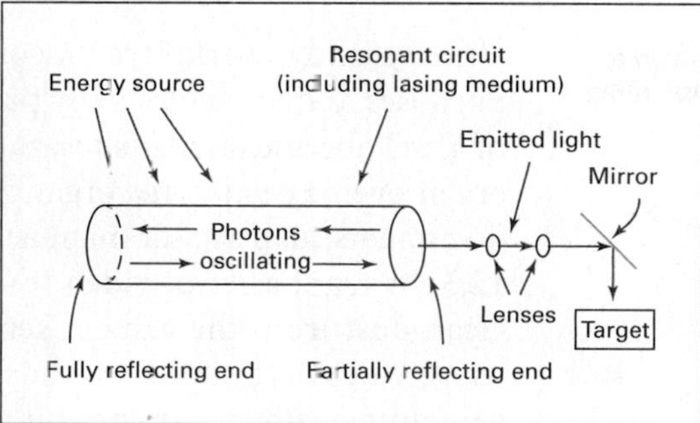

FIGURE 12.30 **A Simplified Diagram of Figure 12.29** Major Parts of the Laser.

GUIDELINES for Using Photographs

- **Simulate the readers' angle of vision.** Consider how they would view the item or perform the procedure (Figure 12.27).
- **Trim (crop) the photograph to eliminate needless detail** (Figure 12.27).
- **Provide a sense of scale for an object unfamiliar to readers.** Include a person, a ruler, or a familiar object (such as a hand) in the photo (Figure 12.27).
- **Label all the parts readers need to identify** (Figure 12.28).
- **Supplement the photograph with diagrams.** This way, you can emphasize selected features. (Figures 12.29 and 12.30).
- **If your document will be published, attend to the legal aspects.** Obtain a signed release from any person in the photograph and written permission from the copyright holder. Cite the photographer and/or the copyright holder.
- **Explain what readers should look for in the photo.** Do this in your discussion or use a caption.

Commercial vendors such as PhotoDisc, Inc. <www.photodisc.com> offer royalty-free stock photographs. (See page 278 for more Web sources.) For a fee, you can download photographs, edit or alter them as needed by using a program such as *Adobe Photoshop,* and then insert these images in your own documents.

NOTE *Make sure you understand what is legally and ethically permissible before including altered images.*

VIDEOS

Videos show a full-motion view

Until recently, workplace videos were typically used only for training and safety purposes and were filmed by professional videographers. Today, with the advent of YouTube and similar sites, as well as the ease of filming with a small video camera or even a cell phone, organizations are using videos to supplement traditional documents such as user manuals. For instance, the video frame captured in Figure 12.31 is from a set of video instructions for a product called Dust-Aid (used to clean dust from the camera sensor of a digital SLR camera). The principles for using videos are similar to those for photographs, except that videos are altered via editing rather than cropping. For more advice, see the annotations to Figure 12.31, the guidelines on page 277, and Chapter 20, pages 478–80.

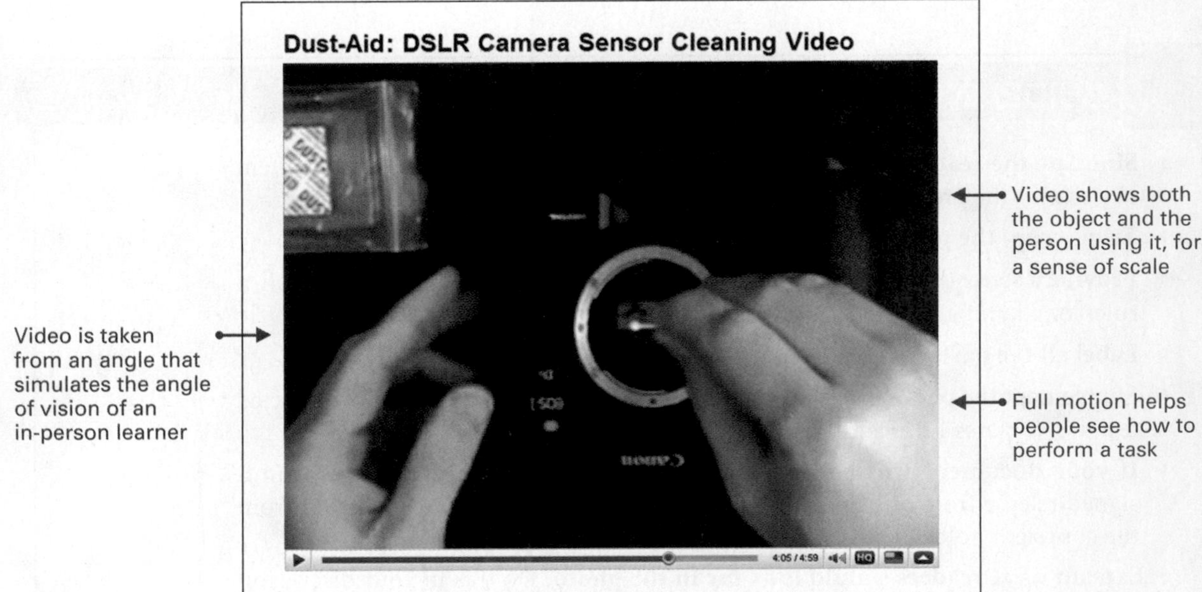

Dust-Aid: DSLR Camera Sensor Cleaning Video
Video shows both the object and the person using it, for a sense of scale
Video is taken from an angle that simulates the angle of vision of an in-person learner
Full motion helps people see how to perform a task
4:05 / 4:59
HQ

FIGURE 12.31 A Video Frame
Source: Reprinted with permission of Andrea Wordhouse.

GUIDELINES for Using Video

- **Provide a sense of scale.** Try to show both the object and a person using it (or a ruler or a hand).
- **In showing a procedure, simulate the angle of vision of the person actually performing each step.** In other words allow the viewer to "look over the person's shoulder."
- **Show only what the viewer needs to see.** For example, in a video of a long procedure, focus only on the part of the procedure that is most relevant.
- **Edit out needless detail.** If you have editing software, shorten the video to include only the essentials.
- **Avoid excess office or background noise when recording sound.**

SOFTWARE AND DOWNLOADABLE IMAGES

Many of the tasks formerly performed by graphic designers and technical illustrators now fall to people with little or no training. Whatever your career, you could be expected to produce high-quality graphics for conferences, presentations, and in-house publications. This text offers only a brief introduction to these matters. Your best bet is to take a graphic design class.

Using the Software

The more you know about different graphics software packages, the more choices you will have when it comes to creating effective visuals.

A sampling of resources for electronic visual design

- **Graphics software,** such as *Adobe Illustrator* or *CorelDraw,* allows you to sketch, edit, and refine your diagrams and drawings.
- **Presentation software,** such as *Microsoft PowerPoint* or *Apple Keynote,* lets you create slides, computer presentations, and overhead transparency sheets. Using a program such as *Adobe Macromedia Director,* you can create multimedia presentations that include sound and video.
- **Spreadsheet software,** such as *Microsoft Excel* or *Apple Numbers,* makes it easy to create charts and graphs.
- **Word-processing programs,** such as *Microsoft Word* or *Google Drive,* include simple image editors ("draw" feature) and other tools for working with visuals. More sophisticated page layout programs, such as *Adobe InDesign,* also provide ways to work with visual design.

Using Symbols and Icons

Symbols and icons can convey information visually to a wide range of audiences. Because such visuals do not rely on text, they are often more easily understood by international audiences, children, or people who may have difficulty reading. Symbols and icons are used in airports and other public places as well as in documentation, manuals, or training material. Some of these images are developed and approved by the International Organization for Standardization (ISO). The ISO makes sure the images have universal appeal and conform to a single standard, whether used in a printed document or on an elevator wall.

How symbols and icons differ

The words *symbol* and *icon* are often used interchangeably. Technically, icons tend to resemble the item they represent: An icon of a file folder on your computer, for example, looks like a real file folder. Symbols can be more abstract. Symbols still get the meaning across but may not resemble, precisely, what they represent. Figure 12.32 shows some familiar icons and symbols.

Simple drawings reduce chances for confusion

The first three images are icons (representative); the last two are symbols (abstract)

FIGURE 12.32 **Internationally Recognized Icons and Symbols**

Limitations of clip art

Ready-to-use icons and symbols can be found in clip-art collections, from which you can import and customize images by using a drawing program. Because of its generally unpolished appearance, consider using clip art only for in-house documents or for situations in which your schedule or budget preclude obtaining original artwork.

NOTE *Be sure the image you choose is "intuitively recognizable" to multicultural readers ("Using Icons" 3).*

Using Web Sites for Graphics Support

Following is a sampling of useful Web sites and gateways for finding visuals.

- **Clip art:** <www.clipart.com>
- **Photographs and video:** <www.gettyimages.com>
- **Maps:** <www.nationalgeographic.com/maps>
- **International symbols:** <www.iso.org>

NOTE *Be cautious about downloading and using visuals from the Web. Originators of any work, including Web-based visuals, own the work and the copyright. Even "free" clip art may be protected by copyright. Pay attention to the copyright and licensing* *information on the site where you obtain the visual. Check out the Creative Commons site for visuals and audio that are licensed for re-use at <www.creativecommons.org>. For more on copyright, see page 286.*

USING COLOR

Color often makes a presentation more interesting, focusing viewers' attention and helping them identify various elements. In Figure 12.18, for example, color helps viewers sort out the key schedule elements of a Gantt chart for a major project: activities, time lines, durations, and meetings. Color can help clarify a concept or dramatize how something works. In Figure 12.33, a strong solid color against a duller background enables readers to visualize how the tubular daylight device fits and functions.

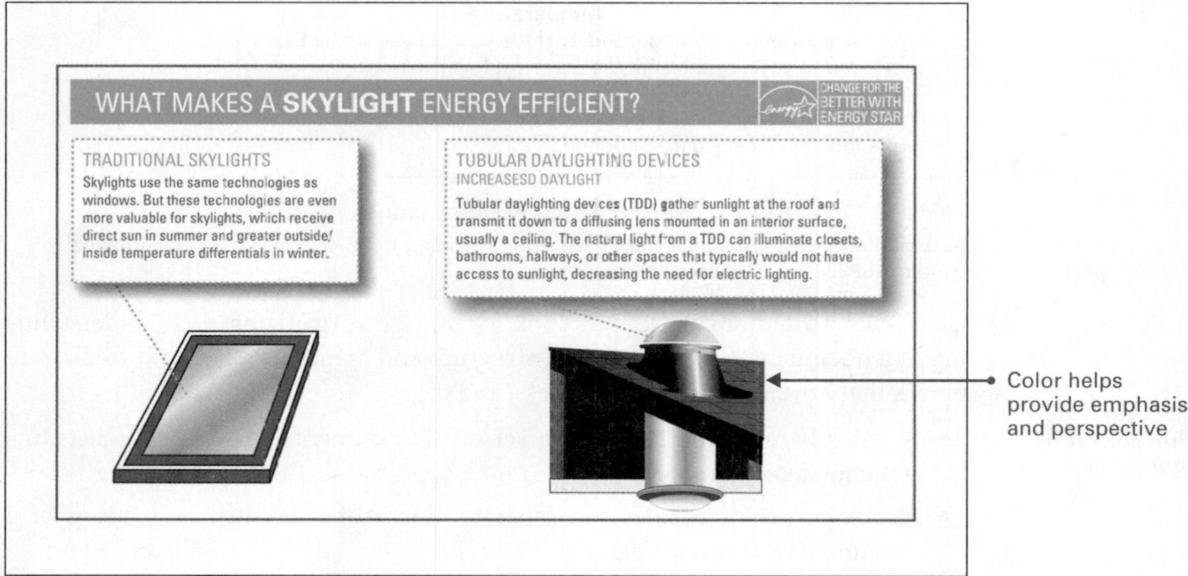

FIGURE 12.33 Color Used as a Visualizing Tool
Source: Courtesy of EnergyStar.

Color can help clarify complex relationships. In Figure 12.34, a world map using distinctive colors allows comparisons at a glance.

Color also can help guide readers through the material. Used effectively on a printed page, color helps organize the reader's understanding, provides orientation, and emphasizes important material. On a Web page, color can mirror the site's main theme or "personality," orient the reader, and provide cues for navigating the site. See Chapter 25 for more on color and Web page design.

Following are just a few possible uses of color in page design (White, *Color* 39–44; Keyes 647–49). For more on designing pages, see Chapter 13.

Color and shading help readers make instant comparisons

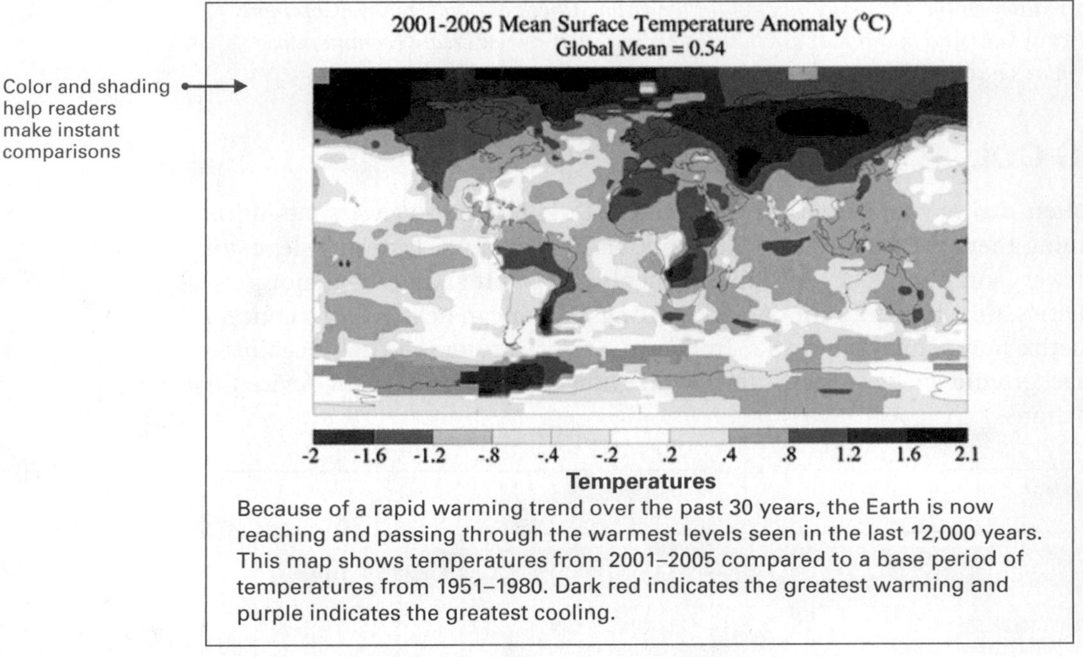

FIGURE 12.34 Colors Used to Show Relationships

Source: National Aeronautics and Space Administration (NASA) <www.nasa.gov/images/content/158226main_mean_surface_temp_lg.jpg>.

Use Color to Organize Readers look for ways of organizing their understanding of a document. Color can reveal structure and break material up into discrete blocks that are easier to locate, process, and digest.

How color reveals organization

- A color background screen can set off like elements such as checklists, instructions, or examples.
- Horizontal colored rules can separate blocks of text, such as sections of a document or areas of a page.
- Vertical rules can set off examples, quotations, captions, and so on.

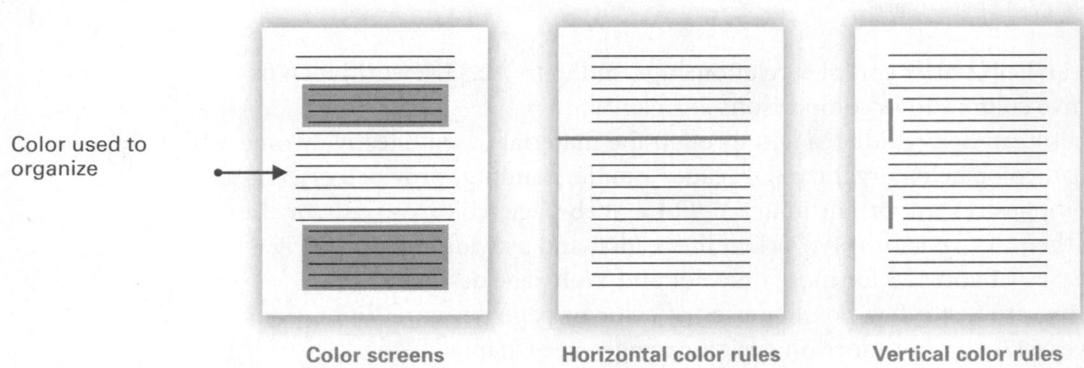

Use Color to Orient Readers look for signposts that help them find their place or locate what they need.

How color provides orientation

- Color can help headings stand out from the text and differentiate major headings from minor ones.
- Color tabs and boxes can serve as location markers.
- Color sidebars (for marginal comments), callouts (for labels), and leader lines (dotted lines for connecting a label to its referent) can guide the eyes.

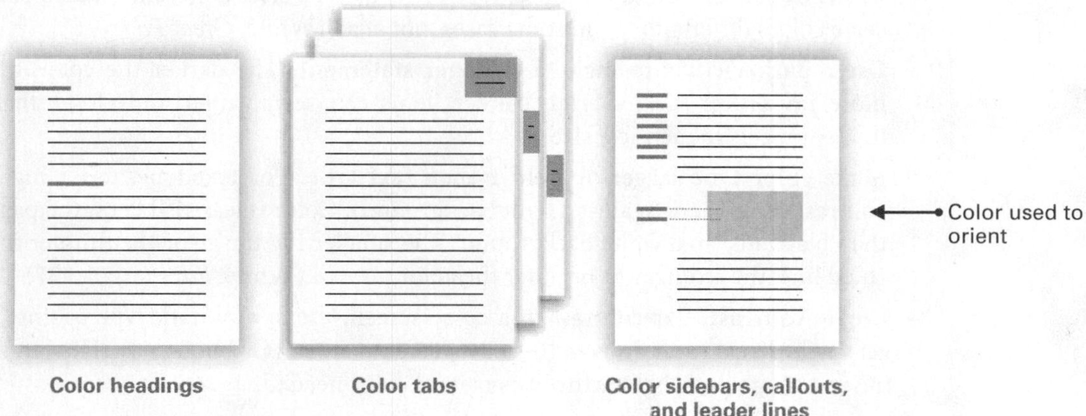

Color headings Color tabs Color sidebars, callouts, and leader lines

Use Color to Emphasize Readers look for places to focus their attention in the document.

How color emphasizes

- Color type can highlight key words or ideas.
- Color can call attention to cross-references or to links on a Web page.
- A color, ruled box can frame a warning, caution, note, hint, or any other item that needs to stick in people's minds.

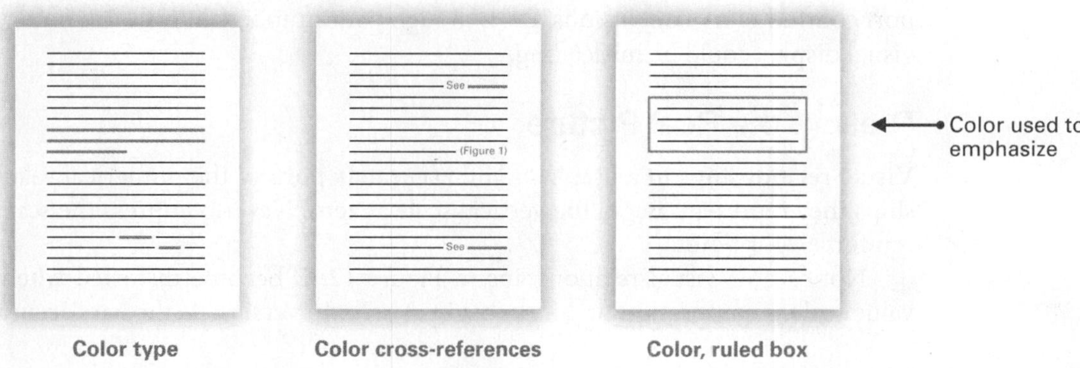

Color type Color cross-references Color, ruled box

GUIDELINES for Incorporating Color

- **Use color sparingly.** Color gains impact when used selectively. It loses impact when overused (*Aldus Guide* 39). Use no more than three or four distinct colors—including black and white (White, *Great Pages* 76).
- **Apply color consistently to like elements throughout your document.** (Wickens 117).
- **Make color redundant.** Be sure all elements are first differentiated in black and white: by shape, location, texture, type style, or type size. Different readers perceive colors differently or, in some cases, not at all (White, *Great Pages* 76).
- **Use a darker color to make a stronger statement.** The darker the color, the more important the material. Darker items can seem larger and closer than lighter objects of identical size.
- **Make color type larger or bolder than text type.** For text type, use a high-contrast color (dark against a light background). Color is less visible on the page than black ink on a white background. The smaller the image or the thinner the ruled line, the stronger or brighter the color needed (White, *Editing* 229, 237).
- **Create contrast.** For contrast in a color screen, use a very dark type against a very light background, say a 10 to 20 percent screen (Gribbons 70). The larger the screen area, the lighter the background color needed.

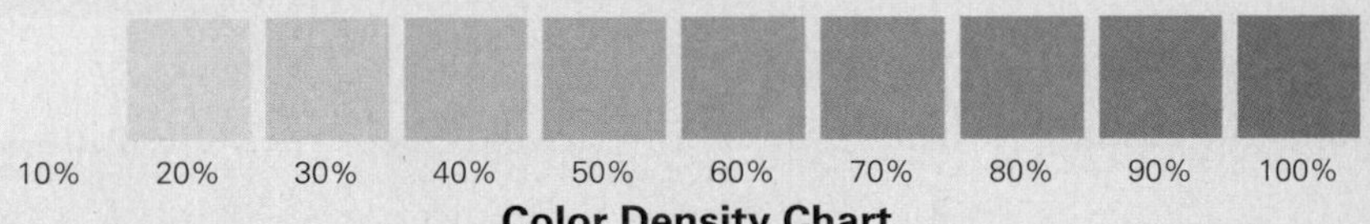

Color Density Chart

ETHICAL CONSIDERATIONS

Although you may be perfectly justified in presenting data in its best light, you are ethically responsible for avoiding misrepresentation. Any one set of data can support contradictory conclusions. Even though your numbers may be accurate, your visual display could be misleading.

Present the Real Picture

Visual relationships in a graph should accurately portray the numerical relationships they represent. Begin the vertical scale at zero. Never compress the scales to reinforce your point.

Notice how visual relationships in Figure 12.35 become distorted when the value scale is compressed or fails to begin at zero. In version A, the bars accurately

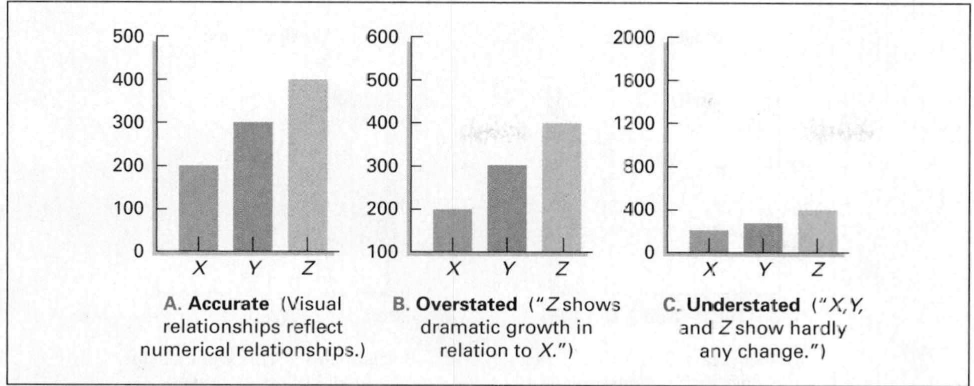

FIGURE 12.35 **An Accurate Bar Graph and Two Distorted Versions** Absence of a zero baseline in B shrinks the vertical axis and exaggerates differences among the data. In C, the excessive value range of the vertical axis dwarfs differences among the data.

depict the numerical relationships measured from the value scale. In version B, item *Z* (400) is depicted as three times *X* (200). In version C, the scale is overly compressed, causing the shortened bars to understate the quantitative differences.

Deliberate distortions are unethical because they imply conclusions that are contradicted by the actual data.

Present the Complete Picture

An accurate visual should include all essential data, without getting bogged down in needless detail. Figure 12.36 shows how distortion occurs when data that would provide a complete picture are selectively omitted. Version A accurately depicts the numerical relationships measured from the value scale. In version B, too few points are plotted. Always decide carefully what to include and what to leave out.

Don't Mistake Distortion for Emphasis

When you want to emphasize a point (a sales increase, a safety record, etc.), be sure your data support the conclusion implied by your visual. For instance, don't use inordinately large visuals to emphasize good news or small ones to downplay bad news. When using clip art, pictograms, or drawn images to dramatize a comparison, be sure the relative size of the images or icons reflects the quantities being compared.

A visual accurately depicting a 100 percent increase in phone sales at your company might look like version A in Figure 12.37. Version B overstates the good news by depicting the larger image four times the size, instead of twice the size, of the smaller image. Although the larger image is twice the height, it is also twice the *width,* so the total area conveys the visual impression that sales have *quadrupled.*

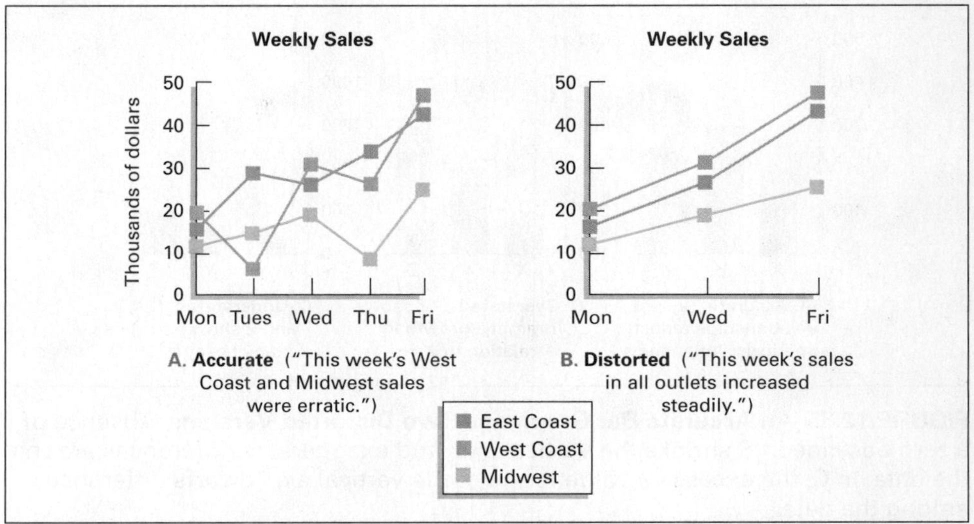

FIGURE 12.36 An Accurate Line Graph and a Distorted Version Selective omission of data points in B causes the lines to flatten, implying a steady increase rather than an erratic pattern of sales, as more accurately shown in A.

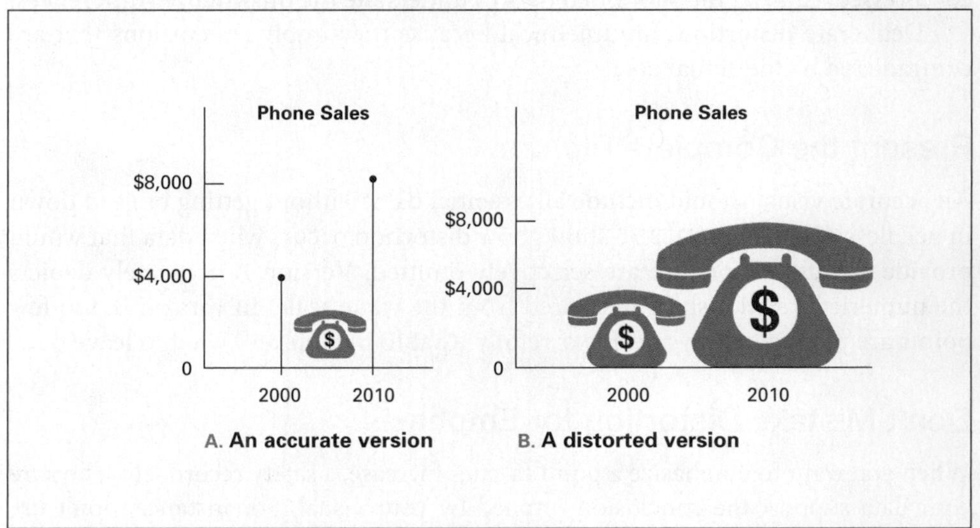

FIGURE 12.37 An Accurate Pictogram and a Distorted Version In B, the relative sizes of the images are not equivalent to the quantities they represent.

Visuals have their own rhetorical and persuasive force, which you can use to advantage—for positive or negative purposes, for the reader's benefit or detriment (Van Pelt 2). Avoiding visual distortion is ultimately a matter of ethics.

For additional guidance, use the planning sheet in Figure 12.38, and the checklist on page 288.

Focusing on Your Purpose

- What is this visual's purpose (to instruct, persuade, create interest)? ________________
- What forms of information (numbers, shapes, words, pictures, symbols) will this visual depict? ________________
- What kind of relationship(s) will the visual depict (comparison, cause-effect, connected parts, sequence of steps)? ________________
- What judgment, conclusion, or interpretation is being emphasized (that profits have increased, that toxic levels are rising, that *X* is better than *Y*)? ________________
- Is a visual needed at all? ________________

Focusing on Your Audience

- Is this audience accustomed to interpreting visuals? ________________
- Is the audience interested in specific numbers or an overall view? ________________
- Should the audience focus on one exact value, compare two or more values, or synthesize a range of approximate values? ________________
- Which type of visual will be most accurate, representative, accessible, and compatible with the type of judgment, action, or understanding expected from the audience? ________________
- In place of one complicated visual, would two or more straightforward ones be preferable? ________________
- Are there any specific cultural considerations? ________________

Focusing on Your Presentation

- What enhancements, if any, will increase audience interest (colors, patterns, legends, labels, varied typefaces, shadowing, enlargement or reduction of some features)? ________________
- Which medium—or combination of media—will be most effective for presenting this visual (slides, transparencies, handouts, large-screen monitor, flip chart, report text)? ________________
- For greatest utility and effect, where in the presentation does this visual belong? ________________

FIGURE 12.38 **A Planning Sheet for Preparing Visuals**

GUIDELINES for Obtaining and Citing Visual Material

Copyright

The Internet is a rich source for all kinds of visuals. It's tempting to simply cut and paste a visual from a Web page directly into your document. Most material on the Internet is subject to copyright laws, however. To avoid copyright problems when working with visuals, follow these guidelines:

- **Look for visuals that are copyright-free.** Many Web sites, such as <www.shutterstock.com>, offer images that don't require copyright permission.
- **Use public domain sources.** Some government sites, such as the U.S. Census Bureau, are a good source of charts, graphs, and tables that don't require copyright permission.
- **Follow fair use guidelines (see pages 148–50),** which allow for limited use of copyrighted material without permission (for example, for a class project that will not have widespread distribution).

Citing visuals created by someone else

- **Cite the source of the visual.** Even if you are following copyright guidelines, you should still properly cite the source of the visuals you use. *Failing to cite the source of a visual could constitute plagiarism.*
- **If the visual is available on the Internet, provide the Web address or other information so your reader can locate it.**

Attributing the source of your original visual

- **Cite the source of the data you used to create your visual.** Even if you create a visual yourself, the data for that visual may come from another source. For example, in Figure 12.9, the graph was created by a writer using Excel, but she used data downloaded from the U.S. Bureau of Labor Statistics.
- **If the data is available on the Internet, provide the Web address or other information so your reader can check the original source.**

CULTURAL CONSIDERATIONS

Meaning is in the eye of the beholder

Visual communication can serve as a universal language—as long as the graphic or image is not misinterpreted. For example, not all cultures read left to right, so a chart designed to be read left to right that is read in the opposite direction could be misunderstood. Color is also a cultural consideration: For instance, U.S. audiences associate red with danger and green with safety. But in Ireland, green or orange carry strong political connotations. In Muslim cultures, green is a holy color (Cotton 169). Icons and symbols as well can have offensive connotations. Hand gestures are especially problematic: some Arab cultures consider the left hand unclean; a pointing index finger—on either hand—signifies rudeness in Venezuela or Sri Lanka (Bosley 5–6).

GUIDELINES for Fitting Visuals with Text

- **Place the visual where it will best serve your readers.** If it is central to your discussion, place the visual as close as possible to the material it clarifies. (Achieving proximity often requires that you ignore the traditional "top or bottom" design rule for placing visuals on a page.) If the visual is peripheral to your discussion or of interest to only a few readers, place it in an appendix. Tell readers when to consult the visual and where to find it.
- **Never refer to a visual that readers cannot easily locate.** In a long document, don't be afraid to repeat a visual if you discuss it a second time.
- **Never crowd a visual into a cramped space.** Frame the visual with plenty of white space, and position it on the page for balance. To achieve proportion with the surrounding text, consider the size of each visual and the amount of space it will occupy.
- **Number the visual and give it a clear title and labels.** Your title should tell readers what they are seeing. Label all the important material and cite the source of data or of graphics.
- **Match the visual to your audience.** Don't make it too elementary for specialists or too complex for nonspecialists.
- **Introduce and interpret the visual.** In your introduction, tell readers what to expect:

  | As Table 2 shows, operating costs have increased 7 percent annually since 1990. — Informative

  | See Table 2. — Uninformative

- Visuals alone make ambiguous statements (Girill, "Technical Communication and Art" 35); pictures need to be interpreted. Instead of leaving readers to struggle with a page of raw data, explain the relationships displayed. Follow the visual with a discussion of its important features:

  | This cost increase means that...

- Always tell readers what to look for and what it means.
- **Use prose captions to explain important points made by the visual.** Use a smaller type size so that captions don't compete with text type (*Aldus Guide* 35).
- **Eliminate "visual noise."** Excessive lines, bars, numbers, colors, or patterns will overwhelm readers. In place of one complicated visual, use two or more straightforward ones.
- **Be sure the visual can stand alone.** Even though it repeats or augments information already in the text, the visual should contain everything readers will need to interpret it correctly.

CHECKLIST: Visuals

(Numbers in parentheses refer to the first page of discussion.)

Content

- ☐ Does the visual serve a valid purpose (clarification, not mere ornamentation)? (248)
- ☐ Is the level of complexity appropriate for the audience? (250)
- ☐ Is the visual titled and numbered? (251)
- ☐ Are all patterns identified by label or legend? (251)
- ☐ Are all values or units of measurement specified (grams per ounce, millions of dollars)? (256)
- ☐ Do the visual relationships represent the numeric relationships accurately? (282)
- ☐ Are captions and explanatory notes provided as needed? (253)
- ☐ Are all data sources cited? (251)
- ☐ Has written permission been obtained for reproducing or adapting a visual from a copyrighted source? (286)
- ☐ Is the visual introduced, discussed, interpreted, integrated with the text, and referred to by number? (287)
- ☐ Can the visual itself (along with any captions and labels) stand alone in terms of meaning? (287)

Style

- ☐ Is this the best type of visual for my purpose and audience? (250)
- ☐ Are all decimal points in each column of a table aligned vertically? (256)
- ☐ Is the visual uncrowded, uncluttered, and free of "visual noise"? (287)
- ☐ Is color used tastefully and appropriately? (282)
- ☐ Is the visual ethically acceptable? (282)
- ☐ Does the visual respect readers' cultural values? (286)

Placement

- ☐ Is the visual easy to locate? (287)
- ☐ Do all design elements (title, line thickness, legends, notes, borders, white space) achieve balance? (282)
- ☐ Is the visual positioned on the page to achieve balance? (287)
- ☐ Is the visual set off by adequate white space or borders? (287)
- ☐ Does the left side of a broadside table face the bottom of the page? (256)
- ☐ Is the visual placed near the text it is helping to describe? (251)

Projects

GENERAL

1. The following statistics are based on data from three colleges in a large western city. They compare the number of applicants to each college over six years.
   - In 2008 *X* college received 2,341 applications for admission, *Y* college received 3,116, and *Z* college 1,807.
   - In 2009 *X* college received 2,410 applications for admission, *Y* college received 3,224, and *Z* college 1,784.
   - In 2010 *X* college received 2,689 applications for admission, *Y* college received 2,976, and *Z* college 1,929.
   - In 2011 *X* college received 2,714 applications for admission, *Y* college received 2,840, and *Z* college 1,992.
   - In 2012 *X* college received 2,872 applications for admission, *Y* college received 2,615, and *Z* college 2,112.
   - In 2013 *X* college received 2,868 applications for admission, *Y* college received 2,421, and *Z* college 2,267.

   Display these data in a line graph, a bar graph, and a table. Which version seems most effective for someone who (a) wants exact figures, (b) wonders how overall enrollments are changing, or (c) wants to compare enrollments at each college in a certain year? Include a caption interpreting each version.
2. Devise a flowchart for a process in your field or area of interest. Include a title and a brief discussion.
3. Devise an organization chart showing the lines of responsibility and authority in an organization where you work.
4. Devise a pie chart to depict your yearly expenses. Title and discuss the chart.
5. Obtain enrollment figures at your college for the past five years by gender, age, race, or any other pertinent category. Construct a stacked-bar graph to illustrate one of these relationships over the five years.
6. In textbooks or professional journal articles, locate each of these visuals: a table, a multiple-bar graph, a multiline graph, a diagram, and a photograph. Evaluate each according to the revision checklist, and discuss the most effective visual in class.
7. Choose the most appropriate visual for illustrating each of these relationships.
   a. A comparison of three top brands of skis, according to cost, weight, durability, and edge control.
   b. A breakdown of your monthly budget.
   c. The changing cost of an average cup of coffee, as opposed to that of an average cup of tea, over the past three years.
   d. The percentage of college graduates finding desirable jobs within three months after graduation, over the last ten years.
   e. The percentage of college graduates finding desirable jobs within three months after graduation, over the last ten years—by gender.
   f. An illustration of automobile damage for an insurance claim.
   g. A breakdown of the process of corn-based ethanol production.
   h. A comparison of five cereals on the basis of cost and nutritional value.
   i. A comparison of the average age of students enrolled at your college in summer, day, and evening programs, over the last five years.
   j. Comparative sales figures for three items made by your company.
8. Display each of these sets of information in the visual format most appropriate for the stipulated audience. Complete the planning sheet in Figure 12.38 for each visual. Explain why you selected the type of visual as most effective for that audience.

Include with each visual a caption that interprets and explains the data.

a. (For general readers.) Assume that the Department of Energy breaks down energy consumption in the United States (by source) into these percentages: In 1980, coal, 18.5; natural gas, 32.8; hydro and geothermal, 3.1; nuclear, 1.2; oil, 44.4. In 1990, coal, 20.3; natural gas, 26.9; hydro and geothermal, 3.8; nuclear, 4.0; oil, 45.0. In 2000, coal, 23.5; natural gas, 23.8; hydro and geothermal, 7.3; nuclear, 4.1; oil, 41.3. In 2010, coal, 20.3; natural gas, 25.2; hydro and geothermal, 9.6; nuclear, 6.3; oil, 38.6.

b. (For experienced investors in rental property.) As an aid in estimating annual heating and air-conditioning costs, here are annual maximum and minimum temperature averages from 1975 to 2010 for five Sunbelt cities (in Fahrenheit degrees): In Jacksonville, the average maximum was 78.4; the minimum was 57.6. In Miami, the maximum was 84.2; the minimum was 69.1. In Atlanta, the maximum was 72.0; the minimum was 52.3. In Dallas, the maximum was 75.8; the minimum was 55.1. In Houston, the maximum was 79.4; the minimum was 58.2. (From U.S. National Oceanic and Atmospheric Administration.)

c. (For the student senate.) Among the students who entered our school four years ago, here are the percentages of those who graduated, withdrew, or are still enrolled: In Nursing, 71 percent graduated; 27.9 percent withdrew; 1.1 percent are still enrolled. In Engineering, 62 percent graduated; 29.2 percent withdrew; 8.8 percent are still enrolled. In Business, 53.6 percent graduated; 43 percent withdrew; 3.4 percent are still enrolled. In Arts and Sciences, 27.5 percent graduated; 68 percent withdrew; 4.5 percent are still enrolled.

d. (For the student senate.) Here are the enrollment trends from 2001 to 2013 for two colleges in our university. In Engineering: 2001, 455 students enrolled; 2002, 610; 2003, 654; 2004, 758; 2005, 803; 2006, 827; 2007, 1046; 2008, 1200; 2009, 1115; 2010, 1075; 2011, 1116; 2012, 1145; 2013, 1177. In Business: 2001, 922; 2002, 1006; 2003, 1041; 2004, 1198; 2005, 1188; 2006, 1227; 2007, 1115; 2008, 1220; 2009, 1241; 2010, 1366; 2011, 1381; 2012, 1402; 2013, 1426.

9. Anywhere on campus or at work, locate a visual that needs revision for accuracy, clarity, appearance, or appropriateness. Look in computer manuals, lab manuals, newsletters, financial aid or admissions or placement brochures, student or faculty handbooks, newspapers, or textbooks. Using the planning sheet in Figure 12.38 and the checklist (page 288) as guides, revise the visual. Submit a copy of the original, along with a memo explaining your improvements. Be prepared to discuss your revision in class.

10. Locate a document (news, magazine, or journal article, brief instructions) that lacks adequate or appropriate visuals. Analyze the document and identify where visuals would be helpful. In a memo to the document's editor or author, provide an art brief and a thumbnail sketch (page 273) for each visual you recommend, specifying its exact placement in the document.

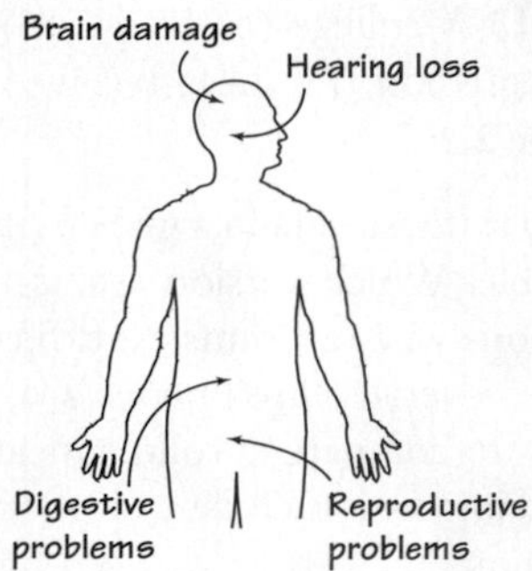

Source: U.S. Environmental Protection Agency. *Protect Your Family from Lead in Your Home*, 1995. 3.

Note: Be sure to provide enough detail for your audience to understand your suggestion clearly. For example, instead of merely recommending a "diagram of the toxic effects of lead on humans," stipulate a "diagram showing a frontal outline of the human body with the head turned sideways in profile view. Labels and arrows point to affected body areas to indicate brain damage, hearing problems, digestive problems, and reproductive problems."

11. Locate a Web page that uses color effectively to mirror the site's main theme or personality, to orient the reader, and to provide cues for easy navigation. Download the page and print it. Prepare a brief memo justifying your choice.
    Note: In a computer classroom, consider doing your presentation electronically.

TEAM

Assume that your instructor is planning to purchase five copies of a graphics software package for students to use in designing their documents. The instructor has not yet decided which general-purpose package would be most useful. Your group's task is to test one package and to make a recommendation.

In small groups, visit your school's computer lab and ask for a listing of available graphics packages. Select one package and learn how to use it. Design at least four representative visuals. In a memo or presentation to your instructor and classmates, describe the package briefly and tell what it can do. Would you recommend purchasing this package for general-purpose use by writing students? Explain. Submit your report, along with the sample graphics you have composed.

DIGITAL AND SOCIAL MEDIA

Compile a list of six Web sites that offer graphics support by way of advice, image banks, design ideas, artwork catalogs, and the like. Provide the address for each site, along with a description of the resources offered and their approximate cost. Report your findings in the format stipulated by your instructor. See page 278 for Web sites that will get you started.

GLOBAL

The International Organization for Standardization (ISO) is a group devoted to standardizing a range of material, including technical specifications and visual information. If you've ever been in an airport and seen the many international signs directing travelers to the restroom or informing them not to smoke, you have seen ISO signs. Go to the ISO Web site at <www.iso.org> to learn about ISO icons and symbols. Show some of the icons and symbols, and explain why these work for international audiences.

13 Designing Pages and Documents

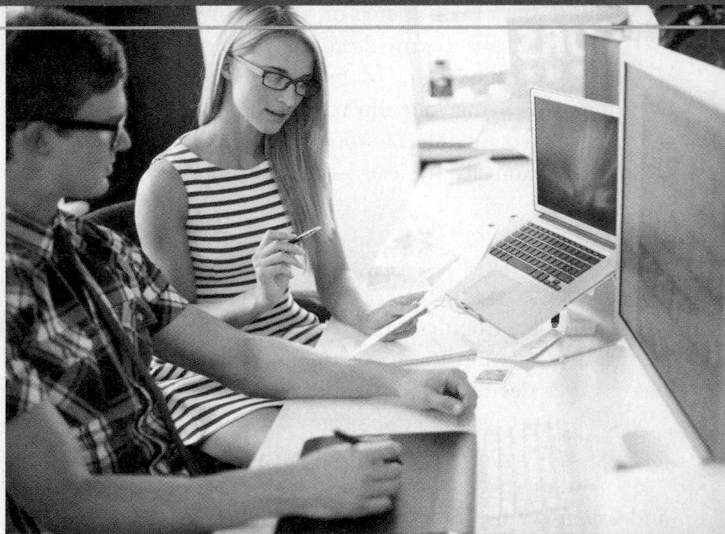

"Sometimes, even if a book I'm working on only needs a light revision, I end up designing the document, too. I have a coworker who designs documents professionally though, so if I need something fancy, he designs it and I follow the specs. If an email is long and complex, sometimes I try to impose some structure to it. If you are giving someone a written correspondence more than a page long, you probably should be worrying about the design of it. If you don't make things easy to follow, sometimes people panic and won't read what you've written."

—Lorraine Patsco, Director of Prepress and Multimedia Production

LEARNING OBJECTIVES FOR THIS CHAPTER

- Understand why document design is important
- Learn design skills that are needed in today's workplace
- Know how to use white space and margins
- Know how to choose typefaces and type sizes
- Know how to use color, shading, and other highlighting elements
- Know how to use headings, subheads, and running heads
- Understand that on-screen documents have special design requirements

Page design, the layout of words and graphics, determines the look of a document. Well-designed pages invite readers into the document, guide them through the material, and help them understand and remember the information.

In this electronic age the term "page" takes on broad meanings: On a computer screen or tablet, a page can scroll on endlessly. Also, *page* might mean a page of a report, but it can also mean one panel of a brochure or part of a reference card for installing printer software. The following discussion focuses mainly on traditional paper (printed) pages. See Designing Digital Documents later in this chapter for a discussion of pages in electronic documents.

PAGE DESIGN IN WORKPLACE DOCUMENTS

People read work-related documents only because they have to. If there are easier ways of getting the information, people will use them. In fact, busy readers often only skim a document, or they refer to certain sections during a meeting or presentation. Amid frequent distractions, readers want to be able to leave the document and then return and locate what they need easily.

Technical documents rarely get undivided attention

NOTE *Although many documents are available in both print and digital forms, the "paperless office" is largely a myth. People often prefer to read print copies of reports, proposals, and other longer documents. In some ways, information technology has produced more paper than ever.*

Readers are attracted by documents that appear inviting and accessible

In an age where visual information—on computer screens, televisions, and cell phones—surrounds us, a printed document competes for audience attention with these highly visual forms. Therefore, print documents need a clean, clear, attractive page design. Before actually reading a document, people usually scan it for a sense of what it's about and how it's organized. An audience's first impression tends to involve a purely visual, aesthetic judgment: "Does this look like something I want to read, or like too much work?" Instead of an unbroken sequence of paragraphs, readers look for charts, diagrams, lists, various type sizes and fonts, different levels of headings, and other aids to navigation. Having decided at a glance whether your document is visually appealing, logically organized, and easy to navigate, readers will draw conclusions about the value of your information, the quality of your work, and your overall credibility.

HOW PAGE DESIGN TRANSFORMS A DOCUMENT

To appreciate the impact of page design, consider Figures 13.1 and 13.2: Notice how the information in Figure 13.1 resists interpretation. Without design cues, we have no way of chunking that information into organized units of meaning. Figure 13.2 shows the same information after a design overhaul.

DESIGN SKILLS NEEDED IN TODAY'S WORKPLACE

As the number of page layout and design programs increases, you will likely be asked to prepare actual publications as part of your job—often without the help of clerical staff, print shops, and graphic artists. In such cases, you will need to master a variety of technologies and to observe specific guidelines.

Desktop Publishing

Desktop publishing helps you produce professional looking pages

Desktop publishing (DTP) systems such as *Adobe InDesign*, *Adobe Framemaker*, or *Quark* combine word processing, typesetting, and graphics. Using this software along with scanners and laser printers, one person, or a group working collaboratively, controls the entire production cycle: designing, illustrating, laying out, and printing the final document. Documents or parts of documents used repeatedly (*boilerplate*) can be retrieved when needed, or modified or inserted in some other document. With *groupware* (group authoring systems), writers from different locations can produce and distribute drafts online, incorporate reviewers' comments into their drafts, and publish documents collaboratively.

The Centers for Disease Control and Prevention (CDC) offer the following information on Chronic obstructive pulmonary disease, or COPD. COPD refers to a group of diseases that cause airflow blockage and breathing-related problems. It includes emphysema, chronic bronchitis, and in some cases asthma.

COPD is a leading cause of death, illness, and disability in the United States. In 2000, 11,900 deaths, 726,000 hospitalizations, and 1.5 million hospital emergency department visits were caused by COPD. An additional 8 million cases of hospital outpatient treatment or treatment by personal physicians were linked to COPD in 2000.

COPD has various causes. In the United States, tobacco use is a key factor in the development and progression of COPD, but asthma, exposure to air pollutants in the home and workplace, genetic factors, and respiratory infections also play a role. In the developing world, indoor air quality is thought to play a larger role in the development and progression of COPD than it does in the United States.

In the United States, an estimated 10 million adults had a diagnosis of COPD in 2000, but data from a national health survey suggest that as many as 24 million Americans are affected.

From 1980 to 2000, the COPD death rate for women grew much faster than the rate for men. For U.S. women, the rate rose from 20.1 deaths per 100,000 women to 56.7 deaths per 100,000 women over that 20-year span, while for men, the rate grew from 73.0 deaths per 100,000 men to 82.6 deaths per 100,000 men.

U.S. women also had more COPD hospitalizations (400,000) than men (322,000) and more emergency department visits (898,000) than men (551,000) in 2000. Additionally, 2000 marked the first year in which more women (59,936) than men (59,118) died from COPD.

However, the proportion of the U.S. population aged 25–54, both male and female, with mild or moderate COPD has declined over the past quarter century, suggesting that increases in hospitalizations and deaths might not continue.

The fact that women's COPD rates are rising so much faster than men's probably reflects the increase in smoking by women, relative to men, since the 1940s. In the United States, a history of currently or formerly smoking is the risk factor most often linked to COPD, and the increase in the number of women smoking in the past half-century is mirrored in the increase in COPD rates among women. The decreases in rates in both men and women aged 25–54 in the past quarter century reflect the decrease in overall smoking rates in the United States since the 1960s.

Document is untitled and provides no visual hierarchy: everything looks equal

Small margins make the document look crowded

Inadequate white space makes this version hard to read

Paragraphs look dense and intimidating

FIGURE 13.1 **Ineffective Page Design** This design provides no visual cues to indicate how the information is structured, what main ideas are being conveyed, or where readers should focus.

Masthead identifies the subject (COPD) and the information source (CDC)

COPD

Facts About Chronic Obstructive Pulmonary Disease

Title and headings provide a visual hierachy

What it is
Chronic obstructive pulmonary disease, or COPD, refers to a group of diseases that cause airflow blockage and breathing-related problems. It includes emphysema, chronic bronchitis, and in come cases asthma.

COPD is a leading cause of death, illness, and disability in the United States. In 2000, 119,000 deaths, 726,000 hospitalizations, and 1.5 million hospital emergency department visits were caused by COPD. An additional 8 million cases of hospital outpatient treatment or treatment by personal physicians were linked to COPD in 2000.

What causes it
In the United States, tobacco use is a key factor in the development and progression of COPD, but asthma, exposure to air pollutants in the home and workplace, genetic factors, and respiratory infections also play a role. In the developing world, indoor air quality is thought to play a larger role in the development and progression of COPD than it does in the United States.

Even from a distance, readers can see the document as a cohesive, single unit

Who has it
In the United States, an estimated 10 million adults had a diagnosis of COPD in 2000, but data from a national health survey suggest that as many as 24 million Americans are affected.

From 1980 to 2000, the COPD death rate for women grew much faster than the rate for men. For U.S. women, the rate rose from 20.1 deaths per 100,000 women to 56.7 deaths per 100,000 women over that 20-year span, while for men, the rate grew from 73.0 deaths per 100,000 men to 82.6 deaths per 100,000 men.

U.S. women also had more COPD hospitalizations (404,000) than men (322,000) and more emergency department visits (898,000) than men (551,000) in 2000. Additionally, 2000 marked the first year in which more women (59,936) than men (59,118) died from COPD.

However, the proportion of the U.S. population aged 25-54, both male and female, with mild or moderate COPD has declined over the past quarter century, suggesting that increases in hospitalizations and deaths might not continue.

Why women's COPD rates are rising so much faster than men's
These increases probably reflect the increase in smoking by women, relative to men, since the 1940s. In the United States, a history of currently or formerly smoking is the risk factor most often linked to COPD, and the increase in the number of women smoking over the past half-century is mirrored in the increase in COPD rates among women. The decreases in rates of mild and moderate COPD in both men and women aged 25-54 in the past quarter century reflect the decrease in overall smoking rates in the United States since the 1960s.

Page 1 of 2

Simple use of two colors helps readers focus on essential information

DEPARTMENT OF HEALTH AND HUMAN SERVICES
CENTERS FOR DISEASE CONTROL AND PREVENTION
SAFER · HEALTHIER · PEOPLE™

FIGURE 13.2 **Effective Page Design** Notice how this revision of Figure 13.1 uses a title, white space, headings, and color to help readers.

Source: Centers for Disease Control and Prevention <www.cdc.gov/nceh/airpollution/copd/pdfs/copdfaq.pdf>.

Electronic Publishing

Your work may involve electronic publishing, in which you use programs such as *Adobe RoboHelp* or *Adobe Dreamweaver* to create documents in digital format for the Web, the company intranet, or as online help screens. You also might produce Portable Document Files, PDF versions of a document, using software such as *Adobe Acrobat* or *Apple Preview*.

Electronic publishing works well for large, complex documents

For more on Web page design in particular, see Chapter 25.

Using Style Sheets and Style Guides

Style sheets are specifications that ensure consistency across a single document or among a set of documents. If you are working as part of a team, each writer needs to be using the same typefaces, fonts, headings, and other elements in identical fashion. Here are two examples of what you might find in a style sheet:

Style sheets provide design consistency

Possible style sheet entries

- The first time you use or define a specialized term, highlight it with *italics* or **boldface.**
- In headings, capitalize prepositions of five or more letters ("Between," "Versus").

The more complex the document, the more specific the style sheet should be. All writers and editors should have a copy. Consider keeping the style sheet on a shared document (Google Drive or other) for easy access and efficient updating.

In addition to style sheets for specific documents, some organizations produce style guides containing rules for proper use of trade names, appropriate punctuation, preferred formats for correspondence, and so on. Style guides help ensure a consistent look across a company's various documents and publications.

CREATING A DESIGN THAT WORKS FOR YOUR READERS

Approach your design decisions to achieve a consistent look, to highlight certain material, and to aid navigation. First, consider the overall look of your pages, and then consider the following three design categories: styling the words and letters, adding emphasis, and using headings for access and orientation.

> **NOTE** *All design considerations are influenced by the budget for a publication. For instance, adding a single color (say, to major heads) can double the printing cost.*

If your organization prescribes no specific guidelines, the general design principles that follow should serve in most situations.

Shaping the Page

In shaping a page, consider its look, feel, and overall layout. The following suggestions will help you shape appealing and usable pages.

Use the Right Paper. For routine documents (memos, letters, in-house reports) print in black, on low-gloss, white paper. Use rag-bond paper (20 pound or heavier) with a high fiber content (25 percent minimum).

For documents that will be published (manuals, marketing literature), consider the paper's grade and quality. Paper varies in weight, grain, and finish—from low-cost newsprint to specially coated paper with custom finishes. Choice of paper depends on the artwork to be included, the type of printing, and the intended aesthetic effect: For example, you might choose specially coated, heavyweight, glossy paper for an elegant effect in an annual report (Cotton 73).

Provide Page Numbers, Headers, and Footers. For a long document, count your title page as page i, without numbering it, and number all front matter pages, including the table of contents and abstract, with lowercase roman numerals (ii, iii, iv). Number the first text page and subsequent pages with arabic numerals (1, 2, 3). Along with page numbers, *headers* or *footers* (or *running heads* and *feet*) appear in the top or bottom page margins, respectively. These provide chapter or article titles, authors' names, dates, or other publication information. (For more on running heads and feet, see page 311.)

Use a Grid. Readers make sense of a page by looking for a consistent underlying structure, with the various elements located where they expect them. With a view of a page's Big Picture, you can plan the size and placement of your visuals and calculate the number of lines available for written text. Most important, you can rearrange text and visuals repeatedly to achieve a balanced and consistent design (White, *Editing* 58). Figure 13.3 shows a sampling of grid patterns. A two-column grid is commonly used in manuals. (See also the *Consider This* boxes in this text.) Brochures and newsletters typically employ a two- or three-column grid. Web pages often use a combined vertical/horizontal grid. Figure 13.2 uses a single-column grid, as do most memos, letters, and reports. (Grids are also used in storyboarding; see page 199.)

Use White Space to Create Areas of Emphasis. Sometimes, what is *not* on the page can make a big difference. Areas of text surrounded by white space draw the reader's eye to those areas.

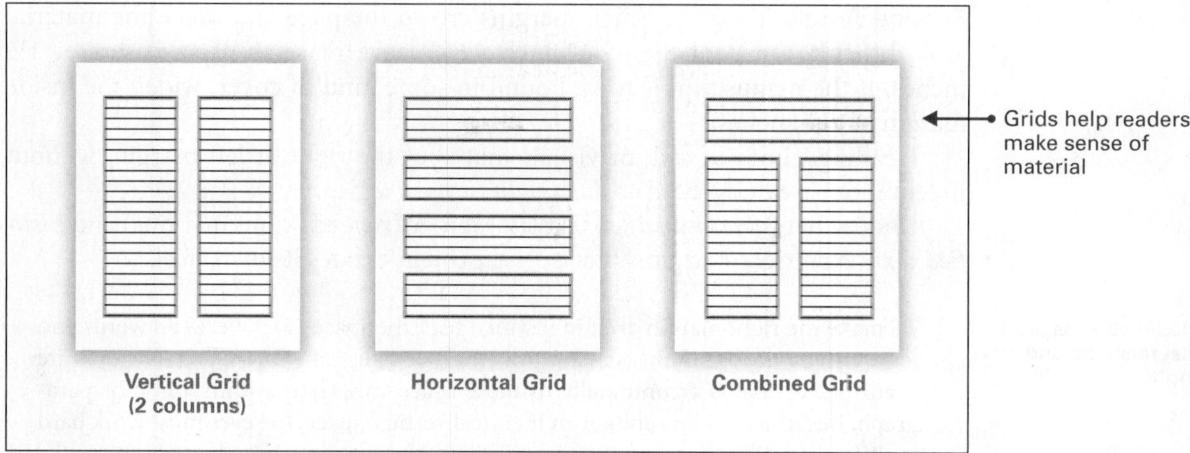
Vertical Grid
(2 columns)
Horizontal Grid
Combined Grid
Grids help readers make sense of material

FIGURE 13.3 Grid Patterns By subdividing a page into modules, grids provide a blueprint for your page design as well as a coherent visual theme for the document's audience.

Well-designed white space imparts a shape to the whole document, a shape that orients readers and lends a distinctive visual form to the printed matter by keeping related elements together, by isolating and emphasizing important elements, and by providing breathing room between blocks of information.

In the examples in Figure 13.4, notice how the white space pulls your eye toward the pages in different ways. Each example causes the reader to look at a different place on the page first. White space can keep a page from seeming too cluttered, and pages that look uncluttered, inviting, and easy to follow convey an immediate sense of reader-friendliness.

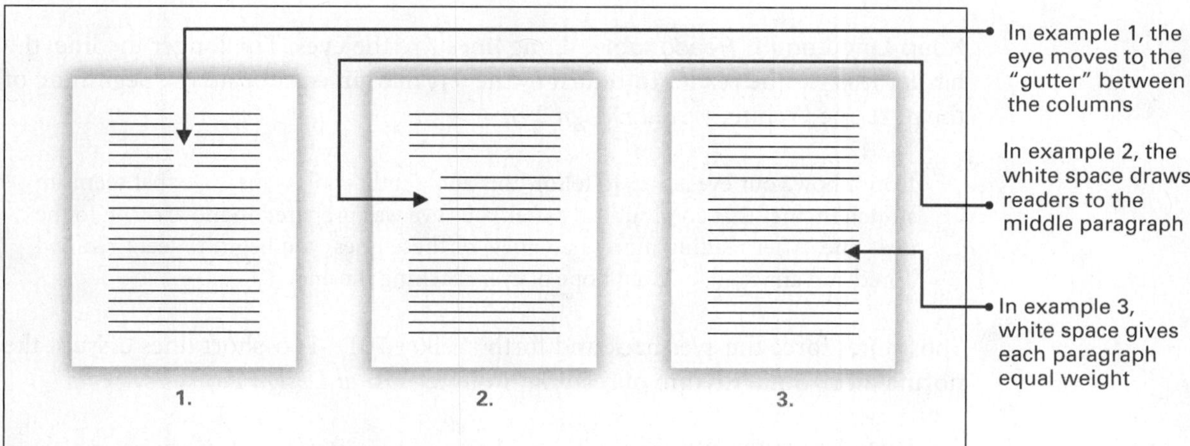
1.
2.
3.
In example 1, the eye moves to the "gutter" between the columns
In example 2, the white space draws readers to the middle paragraph
In example 3, white space gives each paragraph equal weight

FIGURE 13.4 White Space White space creates areas of emphasis.

Provide Ample Margins. Small margins crowd the page and make the material look difficult. On your 8½-by-11-inch page, leave margins of at least 1 or 1½ inches. If the manuscript is to be bound in some kind of cover, widen the inside margin to two inches.

Headings, lines of text, or visuals that abut the right or left margin, without indentation, are designated as *flush right* or *flush left*.

Choose between *unjustified* text (uneven or "ragged" right margins) and *justified* text (even right margins). Each arrangement creates its own "feel."

Justified lines are set flush left and right

> To make the right margin even in justified text, the spaces vary between words and letters on a line, sometimes creating channels or rivers of white space. The eyes are then forced to adjust continually to these space variations within a line or paragraph. Because each line ends at an identical vertical space, the eyes must work hard to differentiate one line from another (Felker 85). Moreover, in order to preserve the even margin, words at line's end are often hyphenated, and frequently hyphenated line endings can be distracting.

Unjustified lines are set flush left only

> Unjustified text, on the other hand, uses equal spacing between letters and words on a line, and an uneven right margin (as traditionally produced by a typewriter). For some readers, a ragged right margin makes reading easier. These differing line lengths can prompt the eye to move from one line to another (Pinelli et al. 77). In contrast to justified text, an unjustified page looks less formal, less distant, and less official.

Justified text is preferable for books, annual reports, and other formal materials. Unjustified text is preferable for more personal forms of communication such as letters, memos, and in-house reports.

Keep Line Length Reasonable. Long lines tire the eyes. The longer the line, the harder it is for the reader to return to the left margin and locate the beginning of the next line (White, *Visual Design* 25).

> Notice how your eye labors to follow this apparently endless message that seems to stretch in lines that continue long after your eye was prepared to move down to the next line. After reading more than a few of these lines, you begin to feel tired and bored and annoyed, without hope of ever reaching the end.

Short lines force the eyes back and forth (Felker 79). "Too-short lines disrupt the normal horizontal rhythm of reading" (White, *Visual Design* 25).

> Lines that are too
> short cause your eye
> to stumble from one

fragment to another
at a pace that too
soon becomes
annoying, if not
nauseating.

A reasonable line length is sixty to seventy characters (or nine to twelve words) per line for an 8½-by-11-inch single-column page. The number of characters will depend on print size. Longer lines call for larger type and wider spacing between lines (White, *Great Pages* 70).

Line length, of course, is affected by the number of columns (vertical blocks of print) on your page. Two-column pages often appear in newsletters and brochures, but research indicates that single-column pages work best for complex, specialized information (Hartley 148).

Keep Line Spacing Consistent. For any document likely to be read completely (letters, memos, instructions), single-space within paragraphs and double-space between paragraphs. Instead of indenting the first line of single-spaced paragraphs, separate them with one line of space. For longer documents likely to be read selectively (proposals, formal reports), increase line spacing within paragraphs by one-half space. Indent these paragraphs or separate them with one extra line of space.

> **NOTE** *Although academic papers generally call for double spacing, most workplace documents do not.*

Tailor Each Paragraph to Its Purpose. Readers often skim a long document to find what they want. Most paragraphs, therefore, begin with a topic sentence forecasting the content. As you shape each paragraph, follow these suggestions:

Shape each paragraph

- Use a long paragraph (no more than fifteen lines) for clustering material that is closely related (such as history and background, or any information best understood in one block).
- Use short paragraphs for making complex material more digestible, for giving step-by-step instructions, or for emphasizing vital information.
- Instead of indenting a series of short paragraphs, separate them by inserting an extra line of space.
- Avoid "orphans," leaving a paragraph's opening line at the bottom of a page, and "widows," leaving a paragraph's closing line at the top of the page.

Make Lists for Easy Reading. Whenever you find yourself writing a series of related items within a paragraph, consider using a list instead, especially if you are describing a series of tasks or trying to make certain items easy to locate. Types of items you might list: advice or examples, conclusions and recommendations, criteria for evaluation, errors to avoid, materials and equipment for a procedure, parts of a mechanism, or steps or events in a sequence. Notice how the items just mentioned, integrated into the previous sentence as an *embedded list*, become easier to grasp and remember when displayed below as a *vertical list*.

An embedded list is part of the running text

A vertical list draws readers' attention to the content of the list

Types of items you might display in a vertical list:

- advice or examples
- conclusions and recommendations
- criteria for evaluation
- errors to avoid
- materials and equipment for a procedure
- parts of a mechanism
- steps or events in a sequence

A list of brief items usually needs no punctuation at the end of each line. A list of full sentences or questions requires appropriate punctuation after each item. For more on punctuating embedded and vertical lists, see pages 702–03 or consult your organization's style guide.

Depending on the list's contents, set off each item with some kind of visual or verbal signal, as in Figure 13.5: If the items follow a strict sequence or chronology (say, parts of a mechanism or a set of steps), use arabic numbers (*1*, *2*, *3*) or the words *First*, *Second*, *Third*. If the items require no strict sequence (as in the sample vertical list above), use dashes, asterisks, or bullets. For a checklist, use open boxes.

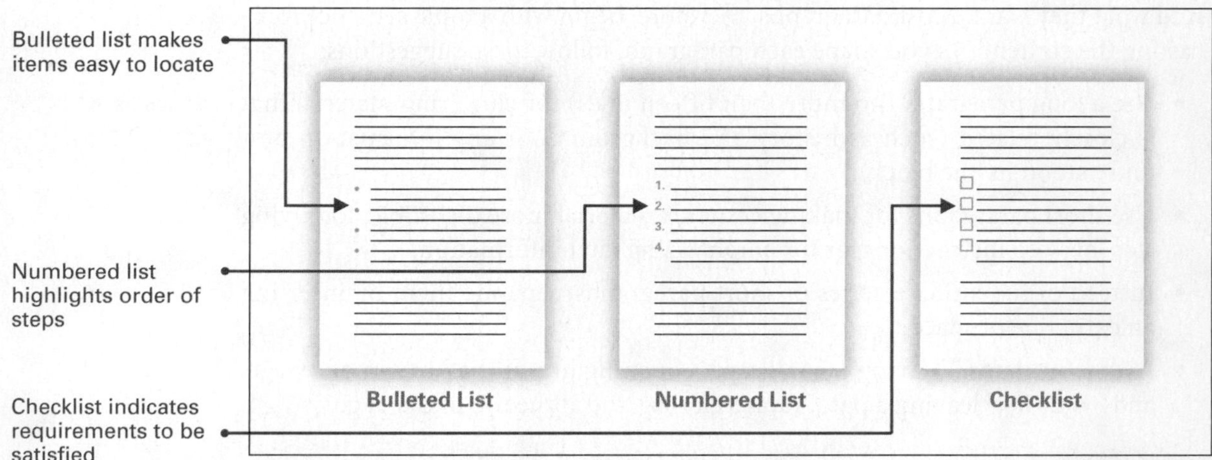
Bulleted list makes items easy to locate
Numbered list highlights order of steps
Checklist indicates requirements to be satisfied
Bulleted List
Numbered List
Checklist

FIGURE 13.5 Vertical Lists Lists help organize material for easy reading and comprehension.

Introduce your list with a forecasting phrase ("Topics to review for the exam:") or with a sentence ("To prepare for the exam, review the following topics:"). For more on introducing a list, see page 702.

Phrase all listed items in parallel grammatical form (page 684). When items suggest no strict sequence, try to impose some logical ranking (most to least important, alphabetical, or some such). Set off the list with extra white space above and below.

NOTE *A document with too many vertical lists appears busy, disconnected, and splintered (Felker 55). And long lists could be used by unethical writers to camouflage bad or embarrassing news.*

GUIDELINES for Shaping the Page

- **Picture the document's overall look and feel when you make design choices about pages.** If your company has other documents that resemble the one you are designing, use these to guide your choices.
- **Use the appropriate paper.** The feel of the page is conveyed by the kind of paper used. Visit a local print and copy shop to look at different samples.
- **Select an appropriate grid pattern.** Use a single-column grid for basic documents such as letters or reports; use a two-column grid for manuals, and either a two- or a three-column grid for brochures and newsletters.
- **Use white space to make pages easier to navigate.**
- **Use adequate margins.** On standard size paper (8½ × 11 inches), use 1-inch or 1.5-inch margins. For bound documents use a 2-inch margin on the bound side.
- **Keep line lengths easy on the eye.** Adequate margins help keep line length reasonable.

Styling the Words and Letters

After shaping the page, decide on the appropriate typefaces (fonts), type sizes, and capitalization.

Typography, the art of type styling, consists of choices among various typefaces. *Typeface*, or *font*, refers to all the letters and characters in one particular family such as Times, Helvetica, or New York. Each typeface has its own personality: Some convey seriousness; others convey humor; still others convey a technical or businesslike quality. Choice of typeface can influence reading speed by as much as 30 percent (Chauncey 36).

All typefaces divide into two broad categories: *serif* and *sans serif* (Figure 13.6). Serifs are the fine lines that extend horizontally from the main strokes of a letter:

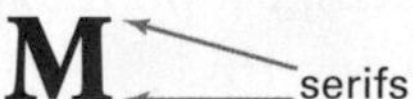

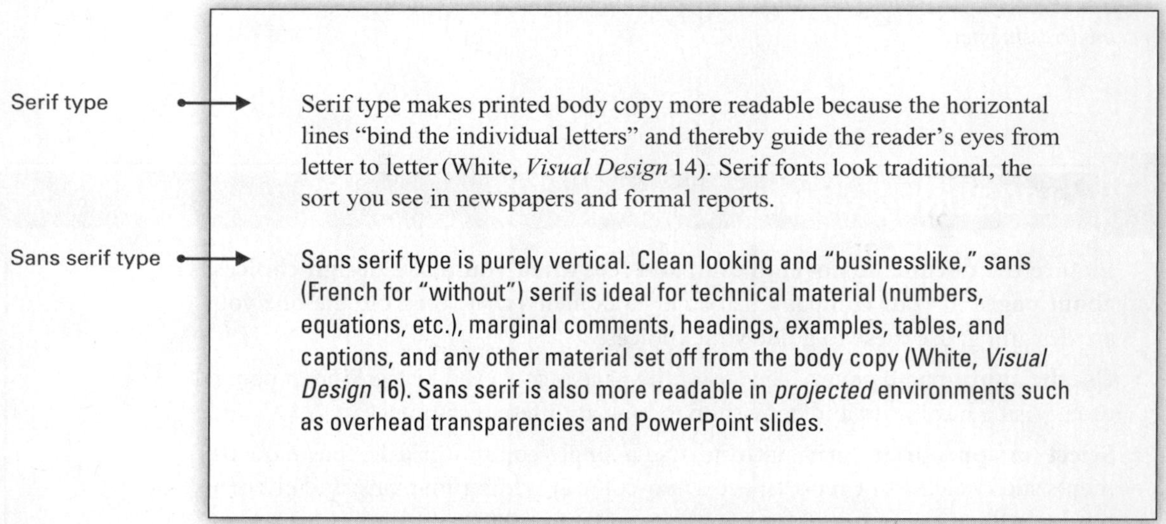

Serif type
Serif type makes printed body copy more readable because the horizontal lines "bind the individual letters" and thereby guide the reader's eyes from letter to letter (White, *Visual Design* 14). Serif fonts look traditional, the sort you see in newspapers and formal reports.
Sans serif type
Sans serif type is purely vertical. Clean looking and "businesslike," sans (French for "without") serif is ideal for technical material (numbers, equations, etc.), marginal comments, headings, examples, tables, and captions, and any other material set off from the body copy (White, *Visual Design* 16). Sans serif is also more readable in *projected* environments such as overhead transparencies and PowerPoint slides.

FIGURE 13.6 **Serif Versus Sans Serif Typefaces** Each version makes its own visual statement.

Readers from various cultures generally have their own font preferences. Learn all you can about the design conventions of the culture you are addressing.

Select an Appropriate Typeface. In selecting a typeface, consider the document's purpose. If the purpose is to help patients relax, choose a combination that conveys ease; fonts that imitate handwriting are often a good choice, but they can be hard to read if used in lengthy passages. If the purpose is to help engineers find technical data in a table or chart, use Helvetica or some other sans serif typeface—not only because numbers in sans serif type are easy to see but also because engineers will be more comfortable with fonts that look precise. Figure 13.7 offers a sampling of typeface choices.

For visual unity, use different sizes and versions (**bold,** *italic,* SMALL CAPS) of the same typeface throughout your document. For example, you might decide on

Times New Roman is a standard serif typeface.

Palatino is a slightly less formal serif alternative.

Helvetica is a standard sans serif typeface.

Arial seems a bit more readable than Helvetica.

Chicago makes a bold statement.

A font that imitates handwriting can be hard to read in long passages.

Ornate or whimsical fonts generally should be avoided.

FIGURE 13.7 **Sample Typefaces** Except for special emphasis, choose traditional typefaces (Times Roman, Helvetica). Decorative typefaces are hard to read and inappropriate for most workplace documents.

Times for an audience of financial planners, investors, and others who expect a traditional font. In this case, use Times 14 point bold for the headings, 12 point regular (roman) for the body copy, and 12 point italic, sparingly, for emphasis.

If the document contains illustrations, charts, or numbers, use Helvetica 10 point for these; use a smaller size for captions (brief explanation of a visual) or sidebars (marginal comments). You can also use one typeface (say, Helvetica) for headings and another (say, Times) for body copy. In any case, use no more than two different typeface families in a single document—and use them consistently.

Use Type Sizes That Are Easy to Read. To map out a page, designers measure the size of type and other page elements (such as visuals and line length) in picas and points (Figure 13.8).

The height of a typeface, the distance from the top of the *ascender* to the base of the *descender*, is measured in points.

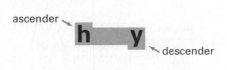

Select the appropriate point size

Standard type sizes for body copy run from 10 to 12 point, depending on the typeface. Use different sizes for other elements: headings, titles, captions, sidebars, or special emphasis. Whatever the element, use a consistent type size throughout your document. For overhead transparencies or computer projection in oral presentations, use 18 or 20 point type for body text and 20 or greater for headings.

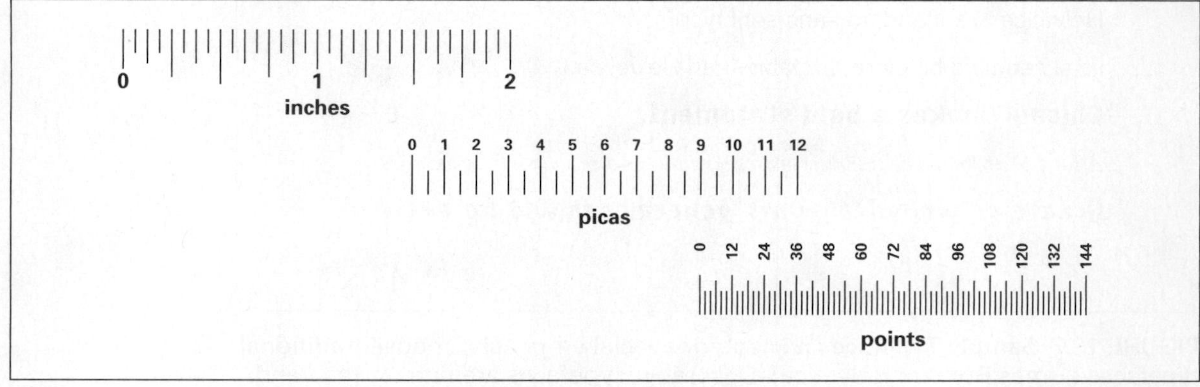

FIGURE 13.8 Sizing the Page Elements One pica equals roughly 1/6 of an inch and one point equals 1/12 of a pica (or 1/72 of an inch).

Use Full Caps Sparingly. Long passages in full capitals (uppercase letters) are hard to recognize and remember because uppercase letters lack ascenders and descenders, and so all words in uppercase have the same visual outline (Felker 87). The longer the passage, the harder readers work to grasp your emphasis.

Use full caps as section headings (INTRODUCTION) or to highlight a word or phrase (WARNING: NEVER TEASE THE ALLIGATOR). As with other highlighting options discussed below, use them sparingly.

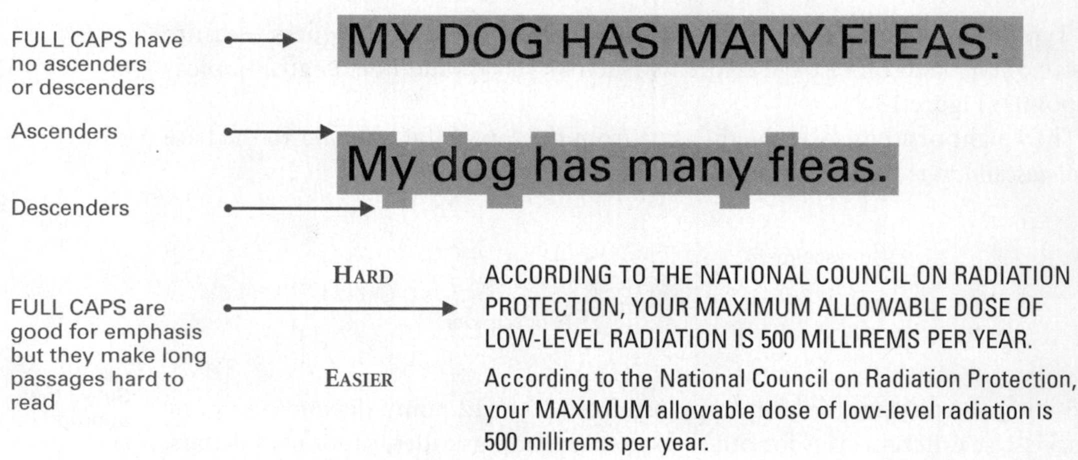

GUIDELINES for Styling the Words and Letters

- **Use a serif font (such as Times New Roman) for formal documents such as reports, legal communication, and letters.** Also use serif fonts for newspapers, magazines, and other documents where readers' eyes will need to move across long lines of text.
- **Use a sans serif font (such as Helvetica) for captions, most visuals (charts, graphs, and tables), and engineering specifications.**
- **Create visual unity by using the same typeface throughout.** Different sizes and versions (bold, italic) are fine within the same typeface.
- **Keep fonts at sizes that people can read.** Standard body copy should be between 10 and 12 points. Use different sizes for headings, titles, captions, and so on.

Adding Emphasis

Once you have selected the appropriate font, you can use different features, such as boldface or italics, to highlight important elements such as headings, special terms, key points, or warnings. The following guidelines offer some basic highlighting options.

GUIDELINES for Adding Emphasis

- You can indent (and use a smaller or a different type) to set off examples, explanations, or any material that should be differentiated from body copy.
- Using ruled horizontal lines, you can separate sections in a long document:

- Using ruled lines, broken lines, or ruled boxes, you can set off crucial information such as a warning or a caution.

Caution: Excessive highlights make a document look too busy.

(For more on background screens, ruled lines, and ruled boxes, see pages 280–81.)

When using typographic devices for highlighting, keep in mind that some options are better than others:

- **Boldface is good for emphasizing a single sentence or brief statement, and is seen by readers as "authoritative"** (*Aldus Guide* 42).

▶▶

GUIDELINES *continued*

- *More subtle than boldface, italics can highlight words, phrases, book titles, or anything else one might otherwise underline. But long passages of italic type can be hard to read.*
- Small type sizes (usually sans serif) work well for captions and credit lines and as labels for visuals or to set off other material from the body copy.
- ***Avoid large type sizes and dramatic typefaces—unless you really need to convey forcefulness.***
- Color is appropriate in some documents, but only when used sparingly. Pages 279–82 discuss how color can influence audience perception and interpretation of a message.

Whichever options you select, be consistent: Highlight all headings at one given level identically; set off all warnings and cautions identically. And never mix too many highlights.

Using Headings for Access and Orientation

Readers of a long document often look back or jump ahead to sections that interest them most. Headings announce how a document is organized, point readers to what they need, and divide the document into accessible blocks or "chunks." An informative heading can help a person decide whether a section is worth reading. Besides cutting down on reading and retrieval time, headings help readers remember information.

Lay Out Headings by Level. Like a good road map, your headings should clearly announce the large and small segments in your document. When you write your material, think of it in chunks and subchunks. In preparing any long document, you most likely have developed a formal outline (page 197). Use the logical divisions from your outline as a model for laying out the headings in your final draft.

Figure 13.9 shows how headings vary in their position and highlighting, depending on their rank. However, because of space considerations, Figure 13.9 does not show that each higher-level heading yields at least two lower-level headings.

Many variations of the heading format in Figure 13.9 are possible. For example, some heading formats use decimal notation. (For more on decimal notation, see page 197.)

Decide How to Phrase Your Headings. Depending on your purpose, you can phrase your headings in various ways (*Writing User-Friendly Documents* 17):

When to use which type of heading

HEADING TYPE	EXAMPLE	WHEN TO USE
Topic headings use a word or short phrase.	**Usable Page Design**	When you have lots of headings and want to keep them brief. Or to sound somewhat formal. Frequent drawback: too vague.
Statement headings use a sentence or explicit phrase.	**How to Create a Usable Page Design**	To assert something specific about the topic. Occasional drawback: wordy and cumbersome.
Question headings pose the questions in the same way readers are likely to ask them.	**How Do I Create a Usable Page Design?**	To invite readers in and to personalize the message, making people feel directly involved. Occasional drawbacks: too "chatty" for formal reports or proposals; overuse can be annoying.

To avoid verbal clutter, brief *topic headings* can be useful in documents that have numerous subheads (as in a textbook or complex report)—as long as readers understand the context for each brief heading. *Statement headings* work well for explaining how something happens or operates (say, "How the Fulbright Scholarship Program Works"). *Question headings* are most useful for explaining how to do something because they address the actual questions readers will have (say, "How Do I Apply for a Fulbright Scholarship?").

Phrase your headings to summarize the content as concisely as possible. But remember that a vague or overly general heading can be more misleading or confusing than no heading at all (Redish et al. 144). Compare, for example, a heading titled "Evaluation" versus "How the Fulbright Commission Evaluates a Scholarship Application"; the second version announces exactly what to expect.

Make Headings Visually Consistent and Grammatically Parallel. Feel free to vary the format shown in Figure 13.9—as long as you are consistent. When drafting your document, you can use the marks *h1*, *h2*, *h3*, and *h4* to indicate heading levels. All *h1* headings would then be set identically, as would each lower level of heading. For example, on a word-processed page, level one headings might use 14 point, bold upper case type, and be centered on the page; level two headings would then be 12 point, bold in upper and lower case and set flush left with the margin (or extended into the margin); level three headings would be 11 point bold, set flush left; level four would be 10 point bold, flush left, with the text run in.

SECTION HEADING

In a formal report, center each section heading on the page. Use full caps and a type size roughly 4 points larger than body copy (say, 16 point section heads for 12 point body copy), in boldface. Avoid overly large heads, and use no other highlights, except possibly a second color.

Major Topic Heading

Place major topic headings at the left margin (flush left), and begin each important word with an uppercase letter. Use a type size roughly 2 points larger than body copy, in boldface. Start the copy immediately below the heading, or leave one space below the heading.

Minor Topic Heading

Set minor topic headings flush left. Use boldface, italics (optional), and a slightly larger type size than in the body copy. Begin each important word with an uppercase letter. Start the copy immediately below the heading, or leave one space below the heading.

Subtopic Heading. Incorporate subtopic headings into the body copy they head. Place them flush left and set them off with a period. Use boldface and roughly the same type size as in the body copy.

FIGURE 13.9 **One Recommended Format for Headings** Note that each head is set one extra line space below any preceding text. Also, different type sizes reflect different levels of heads.

Along with being visually consistent, headings of the same level should also be grammatically parallel (see page 684). For example, if you phrase headings in the form of reader questions, make sure all are phrased in this way at that level. Or if you are providing instructions, begin each heading with the verb (shown in italics) that names the required action: "To avoid damaging your CDs: (1) *Clean* the CD drive heads. (2) *Store* CDs in appropriate containers—and so on.

GUIDELINES for Using Headings

- **Ordinarily, use no more than four levels of headings (section, major topic, minor topic, subtopic).** Excessive heads and subheads make a document seem cluttered or fragmented.
- **Divide logically.** Be sure that beneath each higher-level heading you have at least two headings at the next-lower level.
- **Insert one additional line of space above each heading.** For double-spaced text, triple-space before the heading and double-space after; for single-spaced text, double-space before the heading and single-space after.
- **Never begin the sentence right after the heading with "this," "it," or some other pronoun referring to the heading.** Make the sentence's meaning independent of the heading.
- **Never leave a heading floating as the final line of a page.** If at least two lines of text cannot fit below the heading, carry it over to the top of the next page.
- **Use running heads (headers) or feet (footers) in long documents.** Include a chapter or section heading across the top or bottom of each page (see Figure 13.10). In a document with single-sided pages, running heads or feet should always be placed consistently, typically flush right. In a document with double-sided pages, such as a book, the running heads or feet should appear flush left on left-hand pages and flush right on right-hand pages.

AUDIENCE CONSIDERATIONS IN PAGE DESIGN

In deciding on a format, work from a detailed audience and use profile. Know your audience and their intended use of your information. Create a design to meet their particular needs and expectations (Wight 11):

How readers' needs determine page design

- If people will use your document for reference only (as in a repair manual), make sure you have plenty of headings.
- If readers will follow a sequence of steps, show that sequence in a numbered list.

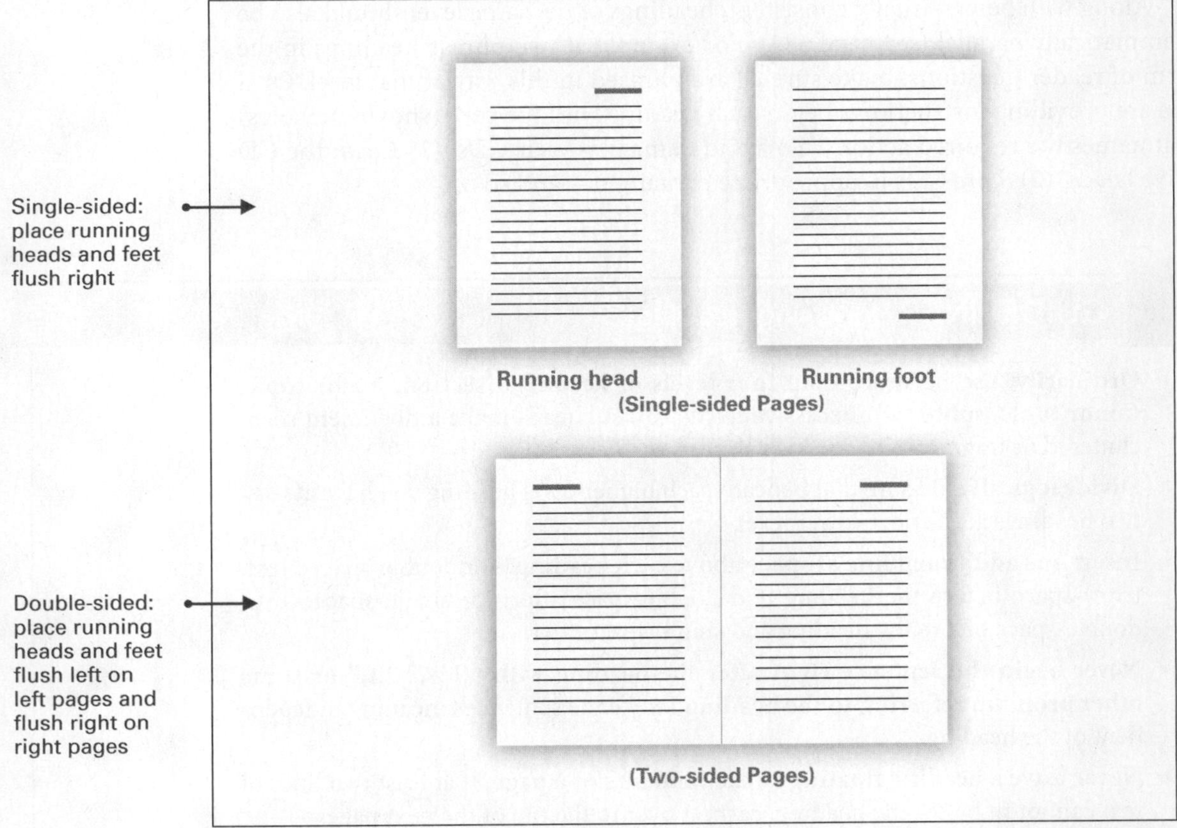
Single-sided: place running heads and feet flush right
Running head
Running foot
(Single-sided Pages)
Double-sided: place running heads and feet flush left on left pages and flush right on right pages
(Two-sided Pages)

FIGURE 13.10 Running Heads and Feet Running heads and feet help readers find material and stay oriented

- If readers need to evaluate something, give them a checklist of criteria (as in this book, at the end of most chapters).
- If readers need a warning, highlight the warning so that it cannot possibly be overlooked.
- If readers have asked for a one-page report or résumé, save space by using a 10 point type size.
- If readers will be encountering complex information or difficult steps, widen the margins, increase all white space, and shorten the paragraphs.

Regardless of the audience, never make the document look "too intellectually intimidating" (White, *Visual Design* 4).

Consider also your audience's cultural expectations. For instance, Arabic and Persian text is written from right to left instead of left to right (Leki 149). In other cultures, readers move up and down the page, instead of across. A particular culture might be offended by certain colors or by a typeface that seems too plain or too fancy (Weymouth 144). Ignoring a culture's design conventions can be interpreted as disrespect.

> **NOTE** *Even the most brilliant page design cannot redeem a document with worthless content, chaotic organization, or unreadable style. The value of any document ultimately depends on elements beneath the visual surface.*

DESIGNING DIGITAL DOCUMENTS

Print versus digital formats

Most of the techniques in this chapter are appropriate for both print and digital documents. In fact, many documents are designed for use in multiple formats. For instance, a manufacturer of lawn and gardening equipment might create a printed User Guide that accompanies its lawnmowers. But, because people often lose or misplace the User Guide, the company might also post the Guide to its Web site, in PDF format. Similarly, a company that makes medical devices (such as heart pacemakers) might supply a small print manual with each device, but might also provide a CD so that medical staff can download the manual onto their computers for future reference.

Whether you are designing for print or digital documents, follow the earlier guidelines in this chapter. For digital documents, pay special attention to the additional features discussed below.

Web Pages

Each "page" of a Web document typically stands alone as a discrete module (like a single page in a print document). But instead of the traditional introduction-body-conclusion sequence of pages, Web content is displayed in screen-sized chunks, with material often linked to other pages. Links can serve the same function as headings (discussed earlier) by providing visual cues and by guiding readers to new information.

The shape of Web pages

Because they are on a computer screen, Web pages need to be designed to accommodate small screen sizes, reduced resolution, and reader resistance to scrolling. Also, the shape of a typical computer screen is more "landscape" than "portrait" —wider than it is high. So, pages must provide for plenty of marginal width, and lines of text can't be too long.

Tools for creating Web pages

Word-processing software (such as *Microsoft Word* or *Apple Pages*) offers features that let you save documents as Web pages. This approach works well for simple Web pages. But most Web designers use more sophisticated tools, such as *Adobe Dreamweaver*, to create Web pages. Even with these tools, Web designers need to tinker with the margins, headings, fonts, and page makeup in order to achieve an accessible design.

NOTE *Because Web page design is complicated, you may want to take a class on this topic. Many organizations have Webmasters or Web designers on staff who could work with you on designing your Web page. See Chapter 25 for more on Web page design.*

Online Help

Like Web design, designing online help screens is a specialty. Many organizations, especially those that produce software, hire technical communicators who know how to produce online help screens. As with all page design, paper or electronic, producing online help screens requires consistency. For more on this topic see pages 477–78.

Adobe Acrobat™ and PDF Files

Unlike normal Web pages, which may display differently on different computers or browsers, PDF (Portable Document Format) documents retain their formatting and appear exactly as they were designed, both on the screen and when printed out. Also, unlike normal Web pages, PDF files typically cannot be altered or manipulated by other readers, thus protecting the integrity of your document. Created with *Adobe Acrobat* software, PDF files can be placed on the Web. Readers link to these just as they would to any Web site, using *Adobe Acrobat Reader* software, which usually can be downloaded free. PDF files also can be sent as email attachments (see page 342). PDF technology enables companies to make their reader documentation and product manuals available to anyone with a Web connection without having to reproduce and distribute the actual manuals in hard-copy form. For more information about PDF, go to <www.adobe.com/products/acrobat>.

CDs and Other Media

You can't predict the types of media that will be used to deliver your documents. You may design an instruction manual or a customer information brochure with the intent of printing it, but the document may eventually be delivered and read on the Web, on a hand-held device or a CD. For most media types, you can use *Adobe Acrobat's* PDF format to ensure that documents will look the same on the CD as they do in print. If designing for an iPod or smart phone, work within the current specifications and software required for these devices. In short, the best you can do is identify as early as possible the media in which your document might be delivered, and work with your organization's design team to ensure that your intended audience will be able to access the information.

CHECKLIST: Page Design

(Numbers in parentheses refer to the first page of discussion.)

Shape of the Page

- ☐ Is the paper of the right quality? (298)
- ☐ Are page numbers, headers, and footers used consistently? (298)
- ☐ Does the grid structure provide a consistent visual theme? (298)
- ☐ Does the white space create areas of emphasis? (298)
- ☐ Are the margins ample? (300)
- ☐ Is line length reasonable? (300)
- ☐ Is the right margin unjustified? (300)
- ☐ Is line spacing appropriate and consistent? (301)
- ☐ Is each paragraph tailored to suit its purpose? (301)
- ☐ Are paragraphs free of "orphan" lines or "widows"? (301)
- ☐ Is a series of parallel items within a paragraph formatted as a list (numbered or bulleted, as appropriate)? (301)

Style of Words and Letters

- ☐ In general, are versions of a single typeface used throughout the document? (303)
- ☐ If different typefaces *are* used, are they used consistently? (304)
- ☐ Are typefaces and type sizes chosen for readability? (305)
- ☐ Do full caps highlight only single words or short phrases? (306)

Emphasis, Access, and Orientation

- ☐ Is the highlighting consistent and tasteful? (307)
- ☐ Do headings clearly announce the large and small segments in the document? (308)
- ☐ Are headings formatted to reflect their specific level in the document? (308)
- ☐ Is the phrasing of headings consistent with the document's purpose? (308)
- ☐ Are headings visually consistent and grammatically parallel? (309)

Audience Considerations

- ☐ Does this design meet the audience's needs and expectations? (311)
- ☐ Does this design respect the cultural conventions of the audience? (312)

Projects

GENERAL

1. Find an example of effective page design. Photocopy a selection (two or three pages), and attach a memo explaining to your instructor and classmates why this design is effective. Be specific in your evaluation. Now do the same for an example of ineffective page design, making specific suggestions for improvement. Bring your examples and explanations to class, and be prepared to discuss them.

   As an alternative assignment, imagine that you are a technical communication consultant, and address each memo to the manager of the organization that produced each document.

2. The following are headings from a set of instructions for listening. Rewrite the headings to make them parallel.
   - You Must Focus on the Message
   - Paying Attention to Nonverbal Communication
   - Your Biases Should Be Suppressed
   - Listen for Main Ideas
   - Distractions Should Be Avoided
   - Provide Verbal and Nonverbal Feedback
   - Making Use of Silent Periods
   - Keeping an Open Mind Is Important

3. Using the checklist on page design, redesign an earlier assignment or a document you've prepared on the job. Submit to your instructor the revision and the original, along with a memo explaining your improvements. Discuss your design in class.

4. On campus or at work, locate a document with a design that needs revision. Candidates include career counseling handbooks, financial aid handbooks, student or faculty handbooks, software or computer manuals, medical information, newsletters, or registration procedures. Redesign the whole document or a two- to five-page selection from it. Submit to your instructor a copy of the original, along with a memo explaining your improvements. Be prepared to discuss your revision in class.

TEAM

Working in small groups, redesign a document you select or your instructor provides. Prepare a detailed explanation of your group's revision. Appoint a group member to present your revision to the class.

DIGITAL AND SOCIAL MEDIA

Many of today's technical documents are designed so they can be displayed on the computer and also printed and used in hard copy. The best choice for this approach is to create the document in PDF format (page 314). Locate a copy of your resume, a memo, or another document you wrote for work or class using a word-processing program. The careful attention you gave to page layout could change when someone else reads the document on a different computer or with a different version of the program. To retain your intended formatting, convert the document to PDF. Hint: in Microsoft Word, try File, Save As, then under Format select "PDF." In Apple Pages, use the Export function. Or, search on the Internet for other ways to create PDF documents.

GLOBAL

Find a document that presents the same information in several languages (assembly instructions for various products are often written in two or three languages, for example). Evaluate the design decisions made in these documents. For example, are the different languages presented side by side or in different sections? Write a memo to your instructor evaluating the document and making recommendations for improvement.

PART 4

Specific Documents and Applications

14 Memos

Considering Audience and Purpose

Memo Parts and Format

Memo Tone

Common Types of Memos

Guidelines for Memos

Checklist: Memos

Projects

"In my company memos circulate constantly. Everyone is busy, and you must be very clear about why they need to read your communication and, if appropriate, act on it. You are constantly competing to get the 'mindshare' of your readers. Memos—whether in hard copy, as PDF attachments, or even as the body of an email message—are less likely to be overlooked or deleted than regular email. In our company, memos are considered official communication and are written with great care. Maybe the difference between everyday email and a memo is in the deliberate steps of writing and revising a memo for content, format, and tone, and even printing it out and reading it over before distribution, instead of firing off a quick email that the writer, or the company, may end up regretting."

—Mary Hoffmann, Marketing Communication Manager for a major computer company

LEARNING OBJECTIVES FOR THIS CHAPTER

- Appreciate the vital role of memos in the workplace
- Picture a typical memo's audience and purpose
- Know the parts and format of a standard memo
- Understand the importance of proper tone in all memos
- Write various common types of memos
- Understand when to use hard copy, email, or PDF attachments

Definition of memos

The most traditional form of everyday workplace correspondence is the memo, or memorandum. The word *memorandum* is derived from the same Latin roots as the words *memorize*, *remember*, and *remind*. Accordingly, memos give directives, provide instructions, relay information, and make requests.

Typically distributed to employees within an organization and not to people outside the company, memos are easy to post in a workstation or office, and they provide a paper trail.

Memos have ethical and legal implications

Organizations rely on memos to trace decisions and responsibilities, track progress, and recheck data. Therefore, any memo you write can have far-reaching ethical and legal implications. Be sure your memo includes the date and your initials or signature. Also make sure that your information is specific, unambiguous, and accurate. Do as much research as needed to ensure that you have all your facts straight.

CONSIDERING AUDIENCE AND PURPOSE

Audience considerations

To determine your approach to any particular memo, identify the various audience members who will receive it. Some companies use standard memo distribution lists: a list for managers, a list for software developers, and so on.

Purpose considerations

The purpose of your memo should also be clear: Is it to inform your audience? To persuade people to support a new plan? To motivate them to take action? To announce bad news?

Memos versus email

Despite its explosive growth, email has not entirely taken the place of paper memos. (Memos are often turned into PDF files and attached to emails, or emails themselves can function as memos.) Although email leaves a digital trail, it is considered less formal than a memo. Also, an email message may be ignored when received in crowded in-boxes and may be inadvertently forwarded to the wrong parties. Organizations have different preferences about when hard-copy memos should be used in place of emails or PDF attachments. (For more on email, see Chapter 15.)

MEMO PARTS AND FORMAT

Standard parts of a memo

A standard memo has the word "Memo" or "Memorandum" centered at the top of the page and includes a heading (flush to the left margin) identifying the recipient(s), sender (and sender's initials), date, and subject. At the bottom of the memo, include a distribution notation if copies are to be sent to anyone not listed in the "To" line (usually managers who simply need to know that the memo was sent). Because memos are often read rapidly by busy recipients, they must follow this consistent, predictable format. Figures 14.1 and 14.2 show these standard elements.

The body copy (main text portion) of a memo should focus on one topic. Content should be complete yet compact, providing all the information readers need but not going into unnecessary detail. Organize the body of your memo by starting with a short introduction, and then a paragraph or two to address the main issue. Conclude by suggesting a course of action or asking your readers to follow up. Figure 14.3 shows a typical memo with all parts labeled.

MEMO TONE

As a form of "in-house" correspondence, memos circulate among colleagues, subordinates, and superiors to address questions like these:

What memo recipients want to know

- What are we doing right, and how can we do it better?
- What are we doing wrong, and how can we improve?
- Who's doing what, and when, and where?

Memo topics often involve evaluations or recommendations about policies, procedures, and, ultimately, the *people with whom we work*.

Because people are sensitive to criticism (even when it is merely implied) and often resistant to change, an ill-conceived or aggressive tone can spell disaster for the memo's author. So, be especially careful about your tone. Consider, for instance, this evaluation of one company's training program for new employees:

A hostile tone

> No one tells new employees what it's *really* like to work here—how to survive politically: For example, never tell anyone what you *really* think; never observe how few women are in management positions, or how disorganized things seem to be. New employees shouldn't have to learn these things the hard way. We need to demand clearer behavioral objectives.

Instead of sounding angry and demanding, the following version comes across as thoughtful and respectful:

A more reasonable tone

> New employees would benefit from a concrete guide to the personal and professional traits expected in our company. Training sessions could focus on appropriate attitudes, manners, and behavior in business settings.

NAME OF ORGANIZATION

MEMORANDUM   Center this label on the page or set it flush left (as shown)

To: Name and title of recipient
From: Your name and title (and initials or signature), for verification
Date: (also serves as a chronological record for future reference)
Subject: Elements of a Usable Memo (or, replace Subject with Re for *in reference to*)

Subject Line
Be sure that the subject line clearly announces your purpose: (Recommendations for Software Security Upgrades) instead of (Software Security Upgrades). Capitalize the first letter of all major words. (Some organizations also use boldface for the subject line. Follow the guidelines for your workplace.)

Memo Text
Unless you have reason for being indirect (see page 359), state your main point in the opening paragraph. Provide a context the recipient can recognize. (*As you requested in our January meeting, I am forwarding the results of our software security audit.*) For recipients unfamiliar with the topic, begin with a brief background paragraph.

Headings
When the memo covers multiple subtopics, include headings (as shown here). Headings (see page 308) help you organize and they help readers locate information quickly.

Graphic Highlights
To improve readability you might organize facts and figures in a table (see page 251) or in bulleted or numbered lists (see page 301).

Paragraph and Line Spacing
Do not indent a paragraph's first line. Single-space within paragraphs and double-space between.

Subsequent Page Header
Be as brief as possible. If you must exceed one page, include a running head on each subsequent page, naming the recipient and date (*J. Baxter, 6/12/11, page 2*).

Distribution and Enclosure Notations
These items are illustrated under "Workplace Letters" (see page 354), and used in the same way with memos, as needed.

FIGURE 14.1 **Standard Parts of a Memo** These elements can differ across organizations and professions, but most paper memos look like this. Because memos are often read rapidly by a busy recipient, the various pieces of important information have to be in predictable locations.

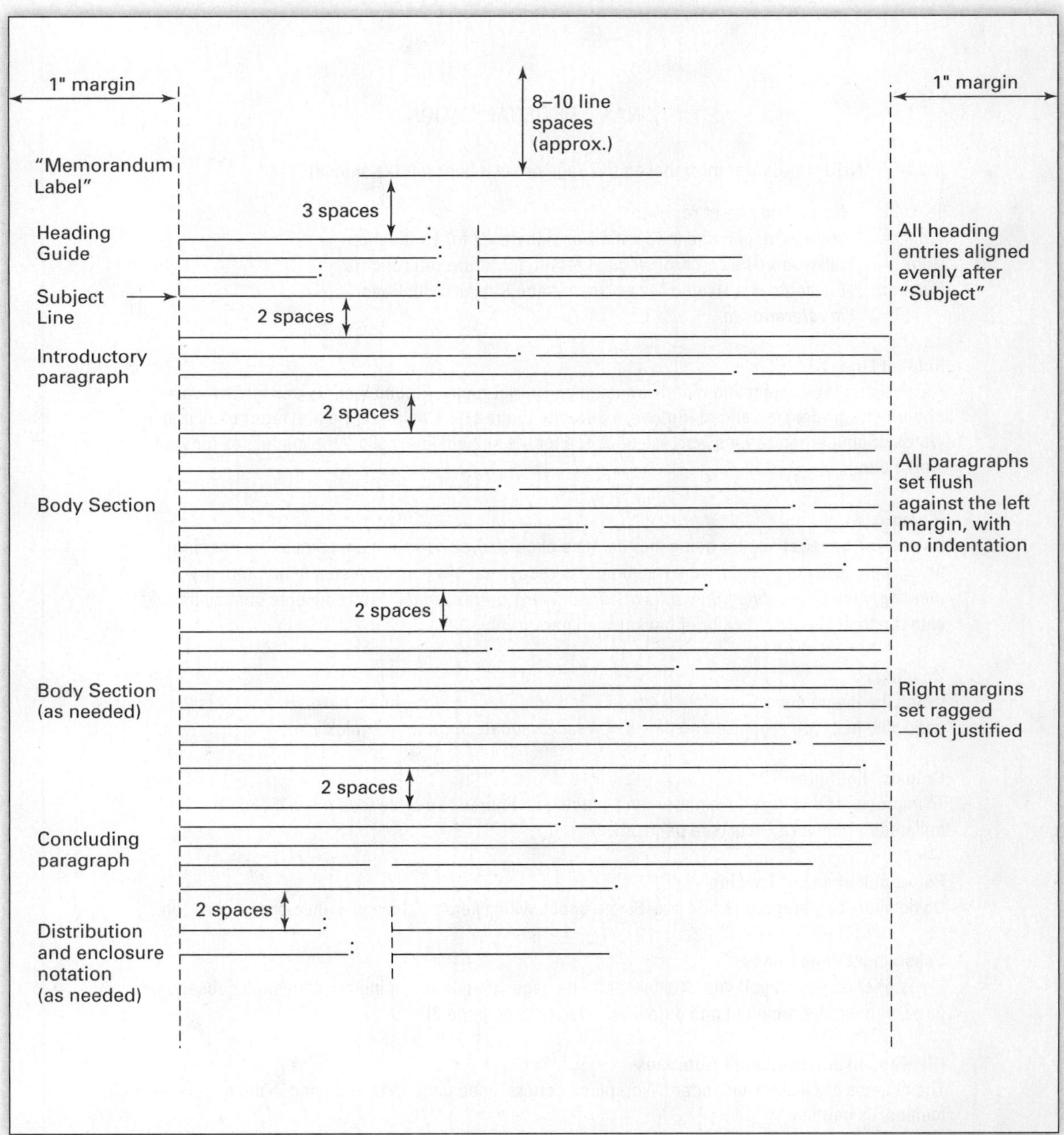

FIGURE 14.2 **Standard Memo Format** Any internal headings would be set two line spaces below the preceding paragraph and one line space above the following paragraph.

MEMORANDUM

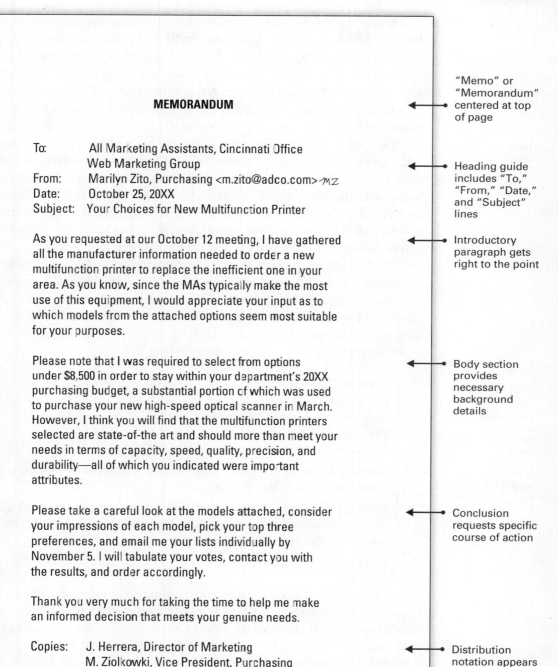

To: All Marketing Assistants, Cincinnati Office
Web Marketing Group
From: Marilyn Zito, Purchasing <m.zito@adco.com> MZ
Date: October 25, 20XX
Subject: Your Choices for New Multifunction Printer

As you requested at our October 12 meeting, I have gathered all the manufacturer information needed to order a new multifunction printer to replace the inefficient one in your area. As you know, since the MAs typically make the most use of this equipment, I would appreciate your input as to which models from the attached options seem most suitable for your purposes.

Please note that I was required to select from options under $8,500 in order to stay within your department's 20XX purchasing budget, a substantial portion of which was used to purchase your new high-speed optical scanner in March. However, I think you will find that the multifunction printers selected are state-of-the art and should more than meet your needs in terms of capacity, speed, quality, precision, and durability—all of which you indicated were important attributes.

Please take a careful look at the models attached, consider your impressions of each model, pick your top three preferences, and email me your lists individually by November 5. I will tabulate your votes, contact you with the results, and order accordingly.

Thank you very much for taking the time to help me make an informed decision that meets your genuine needs.

Copies: J. Herrera, Director of Marketing
M. Ziolkowski, Vice President, Purchasing

"Memo" or "Memorandum" centered at top of page

Heading guide includes "To," "From," "Date," and "Subject" lines

Introductory paragraph gets right to the point

Body section provides necessary background details

Conclusion requests specific course of action

Distribution notation appears at the bottom

FIGURE 14.3 **A Typical Memo** Note that the writer has initialed her memo (in the "From" line). Also she has provided a copy to each appropriate recipient—no one appreciates being left "out of the loop."

Achieving the right tone in your memos involves using some common sense. Put yourself in the shoes of your recipients and write accordingly. Be polite and avoid sounding bossy, condescending, and aggressive, or deferential and passive. Don't criticize, judge, or blame any individual or department. Don't resort to griping, complaining, and other negative commentary. Try to emphasize the positive. Finally, approach difficult situations reasonably. Instead of taking an extreme stance, or suggesting ideas that will never work, be practical and realistic.

Being direct or indirect

The tone of a memo also comes across in the sequence in which you deliver the information. Depending on the sensitivity of your memo's subject matter, you may want to take a direct or an indirect approach. A direct approach (as in Figure 14.3), begins with the "bottom line" in the first sentence (as well as in the subject line) and then presents the details or analysis to support your case. An indirect approach lays out the details of the case over several sentences (and leaves the subject line vague) before delivering the bottom line later in the paragraph.

Readers generally prefer the direct approach because they want to know the bottom line without being told in advance how to feel about it. Assume, for example, that a company Payroll Manager has to announce to employees that their paychecks will be delayed by two days: This manager should take a direct approach, announcing the troubling news in both the subject line and the opening sentence and then explaining the causes of the problem:

Direct approach: Subject line announces main point

Opening paragraph starts with bottom line

> MEMO
>
> To: All employees
> From: Meredith Rocteau, Payroll Manager MR
> Date: May 19, 20XX
> Subject: Delay in Paychecks
>
> I regret to inform you that those employees paid by direct deposit will experience a two-day delay in receiving their paychecks.
>
> This delay is due to a virus that infiltrated the primary computer server for our payroll system. Although we hired virus consultants to identify the virus and clean out the server, the process took nearly 48 hours.
>
> We apologize for the inconvenience.

However, when you need to convey exceedingly bad news or make an unpopular request or recommendation (as in announcing a strict new policy or employee layoffs), you might consider an indirect approach; this way you can present your case and encourage readers to understand your position before announcing the unpopular bottom line. The danger of the indirect approach, though, is that you may come across as evasive.

Indirect approach: Subject line is not specific about the main point

> MEMO
>
> To: All employees
> From: J. Travis Southfield, Director of Human Resources JTS

Date: September 19, 20XX
Subject: Difficult Economic Times

Each employee of the AutoWorld family is a valued member, and each of you has played an important role in our company's expansion over the past 10 years.

Yet as you all know, times are difficult right now for the automobile industry. Sales are down; financing is hard to obtain; and consumers are holding back on major purchases.

Offers an explanation before delivering the bottom line

In order to keep the company solvent, we must consider all options. Therefore, I have been informed by our company president, John Creaswell, that we must downsize. We will begin with options for retirement packages, but please be prepared for the possibility that layoffs may follow.

The bottom line

We will have more information for you at an all-hands meeting tomorrow.

(For more on direct versus indirect organizing patterns, see page 359.)

Delivering memos in the right medium to the right people

Finally, a memo's tone comes across in the way you handle its distribution. Use the appropriate delivery medium. If your topic is very short, not overly formal, and needs to reach everyone quickly, consider sending the memo as an email. But if your topic is more formal and more detailed, send out a traditional paper memo or brief email with PDF attachment. Also, be careful about who receives copies. Don't copy everyone at work when the content is only appropriate for a few, and don't leave vital people off your distribution list.

COMMON TYPES OF MEMOS

Memo format can also be used for distributing short, informal reports, discussed in Chapter 21. However, for the purposes of this introductory chapter, consider the following common and more basic types of memos.

Transmittal Memo

A transmittal memo accompanies a package of materials, such as a long report, a manuscript, or a proposal. Its purpose is to signal that the information is being sent from one place to another (providing a paper trail), to introduce the material, and to describe what is enclosed. A transmittal memo may be as simple as a sentence or a paragraph with a bulleted list describing the contents of the package, as in Figure 14.4.

Summary or Follow-up Memo

A summary or follow-up memo provides a written record of a meeting or conversation, or just a recap of a topic discussed that was not resolved at the time. In addition to providing evidence that the meeting or conversation took place, summary and follow-up memos also insure that each recipient has the same

MEMORANDUM

To: D. Spring, Director of Human Resources
From: M. Noll, Head, Biology Division, M.N.
Date: January 16, 20XX
Subject: Hiring of New Laboratory Manager

Introduction conveys the main point →

As you know, each unit manager has been asked to prepare a hiring plan for the coming year. Attached to this memo please find a brief report justifying the biology division's need for a new laboratory manager.

The attached report includes

Bullet list highlights major items →

- an overview of needs
- a job description
- a budget

Please let me know if you require any additional information. I look forward to hearing from you.

Enclosure notation names the document being transmitted →

Enclosure: Justification report

FIGURE 14.4 **A Transmittal Memo** A memo like this would be placed atop a longer document.

understanding of what was decided. Figure 14.5 shows a memo that performs both a summary and follow-up function.

Routine Miscellaneous Memo

Routine miscellaneous memos cover a virtually infinite variety of topics. Such a memo, for example, may contain some type of announcement or update, for example, announcing the closure of a parking ramp over the holidays for repair, or an upcoming awards ceremony on Friday. Other such memos may request information or action, reply to an inquiry, or describe a procedure. To save time and expense, these

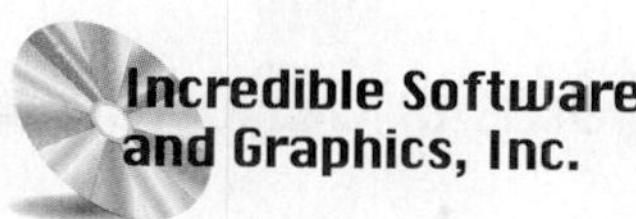

MEMO

To: Elaine Lamer and Mitchell Dramson, Software Development Team
From: Christopher Felts, Manager C.F.
Date: June 19, 20XX
Subject: Follow-Up to Today's Meeting

Thank you for meeting today to discuss next steps to complete the updated version of our animation software package. ← Refers to the earlier meeting

As you noted, the original release date of October 1 is probably too optimistic given the latest hiring freeze. Yet, as I mentioned, we can't afford to go beyond a date of October 15 if we hope to make our fourth quarter sales goals. So, let's agree on October 15 as the new due date. ← Summarizes what was discussed

Please communicate this information to the other members of your team. ← Requests specific action

cc: E. Hearly, Division Chief

FIGURE 14.5 A Summary or Follow-Up Memo This type of memo provides a written record.

memos are increasingly sent via email. But if the memo has a more formal purpose, a traditional paper version may be preferable, as in Figure 14.6, which reiterates an important company benefit and encourages employee participation.

Morris and Sutton, LLC

MEMORANDUM

To: All employees
From: Jorge Gonsalves, Human Resources J.G.
Date: January 12, 20XX
Subject: 401K Matching Policy

Describes the benefit plan →

As the new year begins, we in Human Resources would like to remind you about the company's generous 401K matching policy. We will match your 401K contributions 100% when you roll up to 10% of your salary into your 401K.

Encourages participation →

Many companies will match only up to 5% of an employee's salary, and, usually not at a 100% rate, so please take advantage of this program by enrolling now. Enrollment is only open until March 1st and will not be open again until next January.

Describes the procedure →

Please drop by the Human Resources office on the 6th floor to get a handout that provides more detailed information or to speak with an HR representative in person.

Thanks.

cc: Alison Sheffield, Manager, Human Resources

FIGURE 14.6 **A Routine Miscellaneous Memo** This type of memo can cover a wide variety of topics.

GUIDELINES for Memos

- **Do not overuse or misuse memos.** Use email or the telephone when you need to ask a quick question or resolve a simple issue. For a sensitive topic, prefer a face-to-face conversation whenever possible.
- **Use memos for in-house purposes only.** When sending a message to a client, use email if the message is informal and a letter if the message is more formal.
- **Focus on one topic.** If you need to address more than one topic, consider a format other than a memo (for instance, a report).
- **Be brief but sufficiently informative.** Recipients expect memos that are short and to the point but not at the expense of clarity.
- **Be sure the tone of your memo is polite and respectful.** Don't make enemies by "sounding off."
- **Avoid sounding too formal or too informal for the topic or audience.** A memo to the person in the next cubicle to ask for help on a project, for example, would be more informal than a memo to a company executive.
- **Use the appropriate organizational sequence (direct or indirect).** Prefer the direct approach when you need people to get the point quickly, and the indirect approach when you have something difficult to say that needs to be softened.
- **Follow the standard format illustrated throughout this chapter.** Refer to Figures 14.1 and 14.2 for spacing, margins, alignment, and other elements. Keep in mind that some organizations may have their own formatting requirements for various documents.
- **Use white space, headings, and bullets, as needed.** These features provide visible structure to your memo, as well as "chunking" all elements into easily digestible parts.
- **Use tables, charts, and other visuals to display quantitative information and to achieve emphasis, as needed.** See, for example, Figure 14.7.
- **Check spelling, grammar, and style.** Run the spelling and grammar checkers, but also proofread or ask a colleague to proofread the memo.
- **Be sure to initial your memo.** Initials beside your typed name certify that you are the author.
- **Determine whether to use paper or email to send your memo.** Paper memos take longer to reach the reader but may convey a more serious purpose, whereas digital distribution (such as email or email with a PDF attachment) is quicker but may be overlooked by the reader.
- **Distribute to the right people.** Do not "spam" people with your memo. Whether you are sending the memo on paper or as an email attachment, be sure it reaches only those who need the information. At the same time, don't leave out anyone who needs to read your message.

MEMO

To: Steve Bates, Director of Sales
From: Marcia Rogers, Sales Manager M.R.
Date: Feb. 1, 20XX
Subject: Yearly Sales Volumes in Regions 3, 5, 6

Steve, as I indicated at the meeting last week, Southwest sales continue to lag behind those in the Midwest and the Northwest. I still have no answer for the fourth quarter downturn. No doubt, the region's economic problems have caused everyone headaches, but we should be able to develop some new marketing strategies.

The Southwest region is diversifying quickly, and all economic indicators show slow but steady growth. A medical instrumentation industry such as ours should mirror that growth. But as the following chart illustrates, sales in the region have been erratic. We lost over $150,000 in the last quarter alone.

Visual provides emphasis

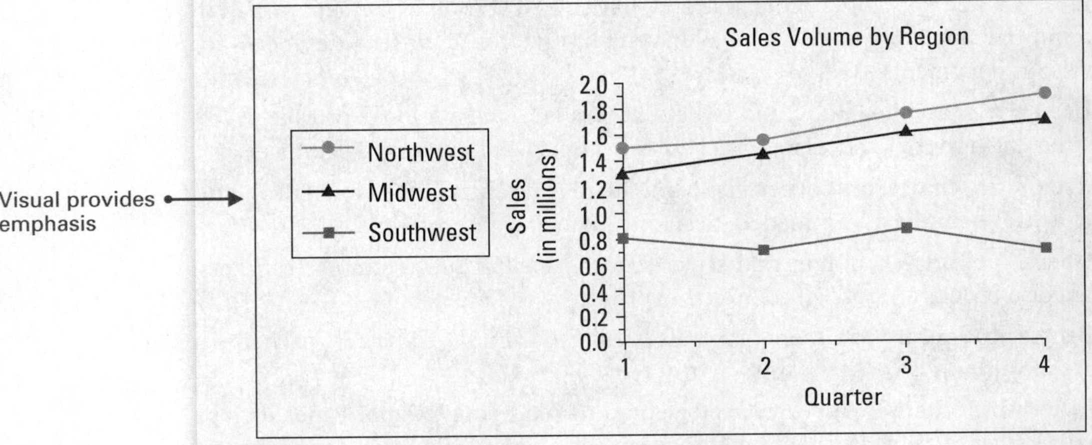

FIGURE 14.7 A Memo That Includes a Visual to Underscore a Point The line graph underscores and justifies the writer's concern about the company's unacceptable performance.

CHECKLIST: Memos

(Numbers in parentheses refer to the first page of discussion.)

Content

- ☐ Is the information based on careful research? (125)
- ☐ Is the message brief and to the point? (319)
- ☐ Are tables, charts, and other graphics used as needed? (329)
- ☐ Are recipients given enough information to make an *informed* decision? (319)
- ☐ Are the conclusions and recommendations clear? (320)

Organization

- ☐ Is the important information in an area of emphasis? (320)
- ☐ Is the direct or indirect pattern used appropriately to present the memo's bottom line? (359)
- ☐ Is the material "chunked" into easily digestible parts? (205)

Style

- ☐ Is the writing clear, concise, fluent, and exact? (211)
- ☐ Is the tone appropriate? (320)
- ☐ Has the memo been carefully proofread? (118)

Format

- ☐ Does the memo have a complete heading? (320)
- ☐ Does the subject line announce the memo's content and purpose? (321)
- ☐ Are paragraphs single-spaced within and double-spaced between? (321)
- ☐ Do headings announce subtopics, as needed? (321)
- ☐ If more than one reader is receiving a copy, does the memo include a distribution notation (cc:) to identify other recipients? (321)

Ethical, Legal, and Interpersonal Considerations

- ☐ Is the information specific, accurate, and unambiguous? (320)
- ☐ Does the medium (paper, email, PDF attachment, in person) fit the situation? (325)
- ☐ Is the message inoffensive to all parties? (324)
- ☐ Are all appropriate parties receiving a copy? (325)

Projects

GENERAL

1. Think of an idea you would like to see implemented in your job (e.g., a way to increase productivity, improve service, increase business, or improve working conditions). Write a routine miscellaneous memo requesting action and persuading your audience that your idea is worthwhile.
2. Write a memo as the sales director of a company to both in-house sales department employees and the sales representatives. Announce and outline a new dress code policy and diplomatically explain why the policy is more strict for the sales reps. Remember to keep an informal but professional tone, to format the memo properly, and to keep the memo brief but complete.

TEAM

Divide into teams and assume you own a company (create a name for it). Revise the following message so that it gets the intended results. Pay close attention to *tone*. Use a memo format. Make sure the subject line clearly forecasts your topic. Appoint one team member to present the revised memo in class.

> Too many employees are parking in front of the store rather than behind it. As a result of this infraction, customers have been complaining that they cannot find parking spaces. If employees don't start parking where they're supposed to, we'll lose customers. Lost customers means lost jobs. Since I've worked hard to build this company, I don't want to lose it because employees are too lazy to walk from the back lot. Let's keep our customers by keeping them happy.

DIGITAL AND SOCIAL MEDIA

Does the shape and layout of a memo influence how it is written? Conduct this small experiment. In teams of 3–4 people, consider a dangerous or inconvenient area or situation on campus (endless cafeteria lines, a poorly lit intersection, slippery stairs, a poorly timed traffic light). Select one of these situations (one that everyone is familiar with), and write a short memo to a decision maker (e.g., campus chief of police or head of food service). Each person should write his or her memo using one of the memo templates from *Microsoft Word*, Apple Pages, or other program (templates are predesigned formats that can be used to create memos and other documents). Compare the differences among the memos. Next, discuss whether for this audience the memo would be more effective if circulated in hard copy, sent as an email, or sent via email as a PDF attachment. (See the Digital and Social Media project in Chapter 13 (page 316) for hints on how to create a PDF.)

GLOBAL

Is the standard memo format discussed in this chapter a U.S. standard or an international standard? What sorts of memos are typically written in other countries? Interview someone who works in an international business, and write a short memo to your instructor explaining what you learned about memo writing in other countries.

15 Email and Text Messaging

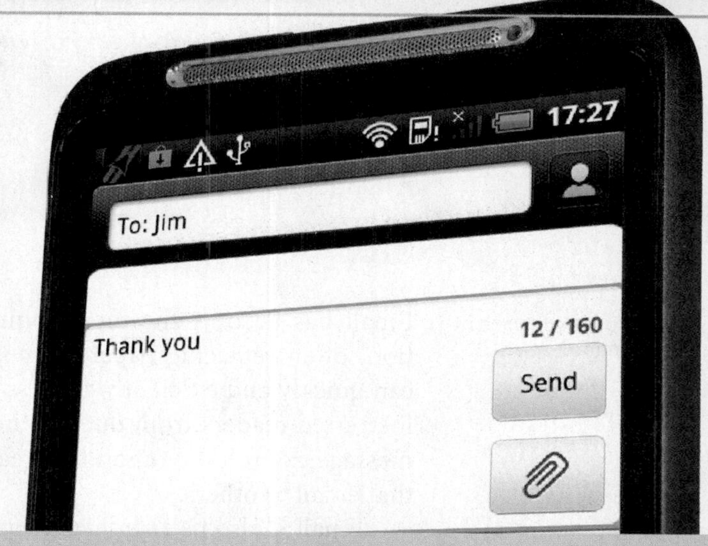

"I work for a bank, and our environment is regulated by U.S. government organizations, like the Securities and Exchange Commission, as well as laws like the Sarbanes-Oxley Act. We are regulated by international agencies and rules as well. Even though I write and read dozens of emails every day, I am aware that email is a form of written communication and that every email I write has potential legal implications. When I hire an intern or new employees, I always remind them to write email that is professional and factual and to avoid wisecracks and rude remarks. Also, at our company, we don't use email to send confidential information, and we don't use our work email for anything that is not work related."

— Aneta Dorrigan,
Financial Executive

LEARNING OBJECTIVES FOR THIS CHAPTER

- Identify the components of a workplace email message
- Organize an email message
- Write an email using a professional style and tone
- Recognize copyright and privacy issues affecting email use
- Write an email appropriate for a global audience
- Consider other media that may be more appropriate
- Understand the uses of text messaging in workplace settings

Workplace uses of email

Email has become the most common form of written workplace communication, often replacing paper memos and letters. Unlike paper documents, email can quickly and efficiently address an individual, a group within an organization, interested readers from outside the organization, or a mix of people. One email message can reach thousands of readers in seconds, and these readers can forward that email to others.

Email is also useful when people are in different time zones or have different working schedules: You can send an email at 2:00 A.M. if you are a night owl, and your early-bird colleague can read it in the morning. Email also provides an electronic paper trail for legal reasons or a record of ongoing conversation. Writers can include attachments, such as scans of print documents, to emails, thus eliminating the need for fax machines. Email messages are best used for routine, simple messages, such as quickly letting a coworker know the status of a project or asking your boss a simple question.

EMAIL PARTS AND FORMAT

Email parts

A standard email begins with a heading section containing “To,” “From,” “Date,” and “Subject” lines. Optional features include distribution notation, enclosure (or “attachment”) notation, sender’s contact information, and complimentary closing.

Email organization

Like any workplace document, an effective email message should have a brief introduction that gets right to the point, a clear body section with transitions between each paragraph, and a brief conclusion that often requests action (such as “please let me know your thoughts”). Also, emails often include headings, bullets, and other graphic highlights as a way to break up passages of text.

Figure 15.1 illustrates a standard workplace email.

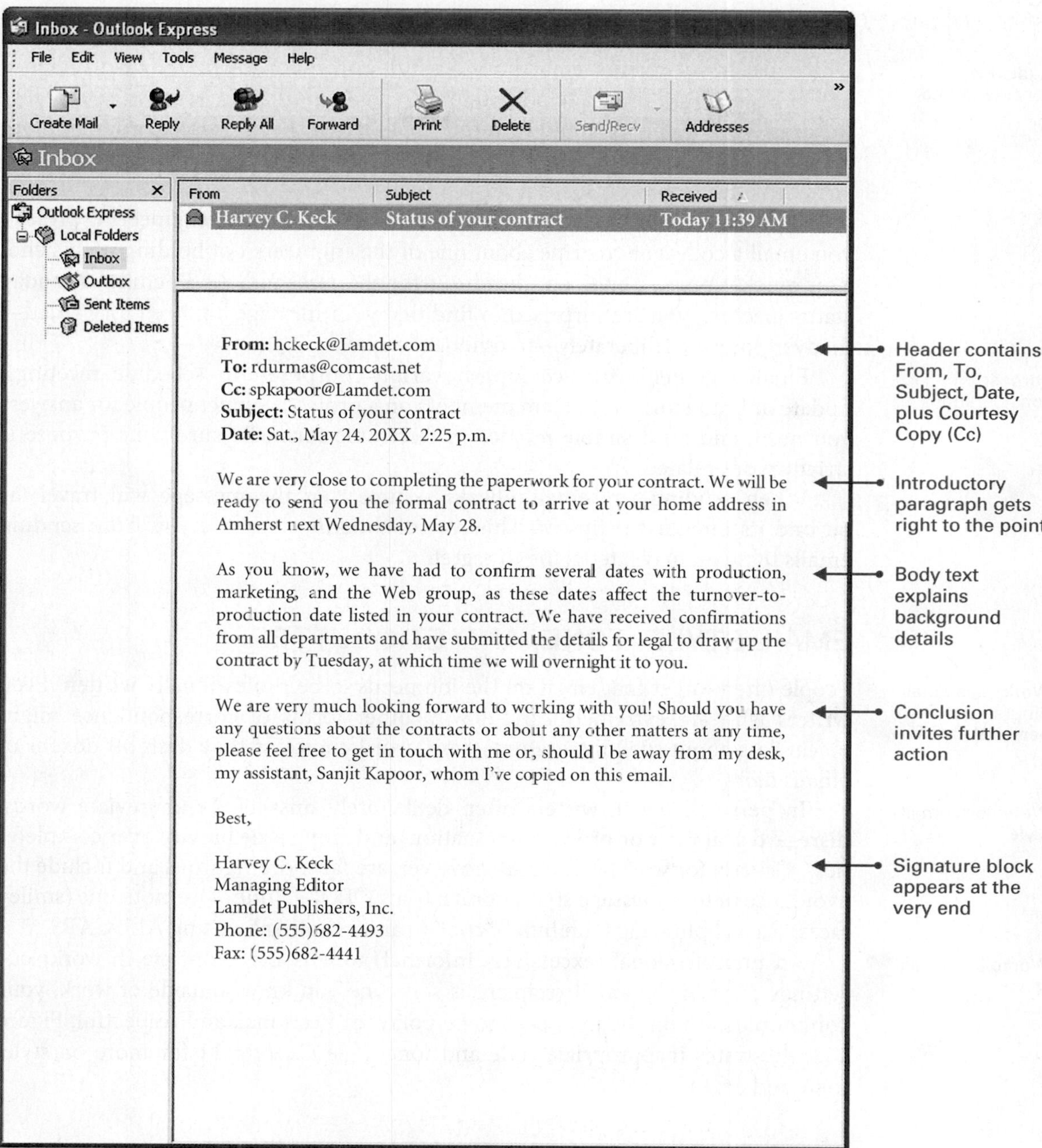

FIGURE 15.1 A Workplace Email This email includes all the required components and is organized in an introduction/body/conclusion structure.

Source: Outlook Express frame used with permission from Microsoft.

CONSIDERING AUDIENCE AND PURPOSE

Audience considerations

Unlike paper documents, email provides little control over who the final audience will be. You might intend to address only a small group, but because of easy forwarding, your audience could turn out much larger. People also tend to be more casual and off-the-cuff on email, sometimes more than in person; therefore, audience considerations become crucial.

Suppose, for example, that after a long week on a difficult engineering project, you email a colleague to gripe about one of the engineers not holding up his end. You quickly press "Send" and head out for the weekend. At a "chilly" Monday status meeting, you are surprised to find that your message has been forwarded—inadvertently or deliberately—to other colleagues.

Purpose considerations

Email can help you accomplish various purposes: to schedule meetings, update or brainstorm with team members on a project, contact people for answers you need, and send simple memos in electronic form. Be sure your purpose is strictly work related.

When sending any email, always assume that the message will travel far beyond its intended recipient. This way of thinking will save you from sending emails that you may later come to regret.

EMAIL STYLE, TONE, AND ETIQUETTE

Workplace email differs from personal email

People often forget that email on the job needs to be professionally written. Even writers who are extremely careful with other forms of correspondence might be careless about spelling, grammar, and word choice as they dash off dozens of emails daily.

Workplace email style

In personal email, writers often deliberately misspell or abbreviate words, disregard grammar or proper punctuation, and emphasize brevity over completeness. Criteria for workplace email, however, are far more rigorous and include the avoidance of text-message style abbreviations ("LOL," "imho"), emoticons (smiley faces), casual phrasing ("uh huh," "cool") , and shouting by using ALL CAPS.

Workplace email tone

An unprofessional (excessively informal) tone is inappropriate in workplace settings. Even if the email recipient is someone you know outside of work, your communication on the job needs to be polite, professional, and respectful. Figure 15.2 illustrates inappropriate style and tone. (See Chapter 11 for more on style, tone, and email.)

Interpersonal Issues and Email

Don't use email to avoid essential face-to-face contact

As described in Chapter 5 (pages 98, 99), email omits important social cues such as facial expressions, tone of voice, eye contact, and immediate feedback. An awkward situation, therefore, makes it tempting to send an email rather than use the

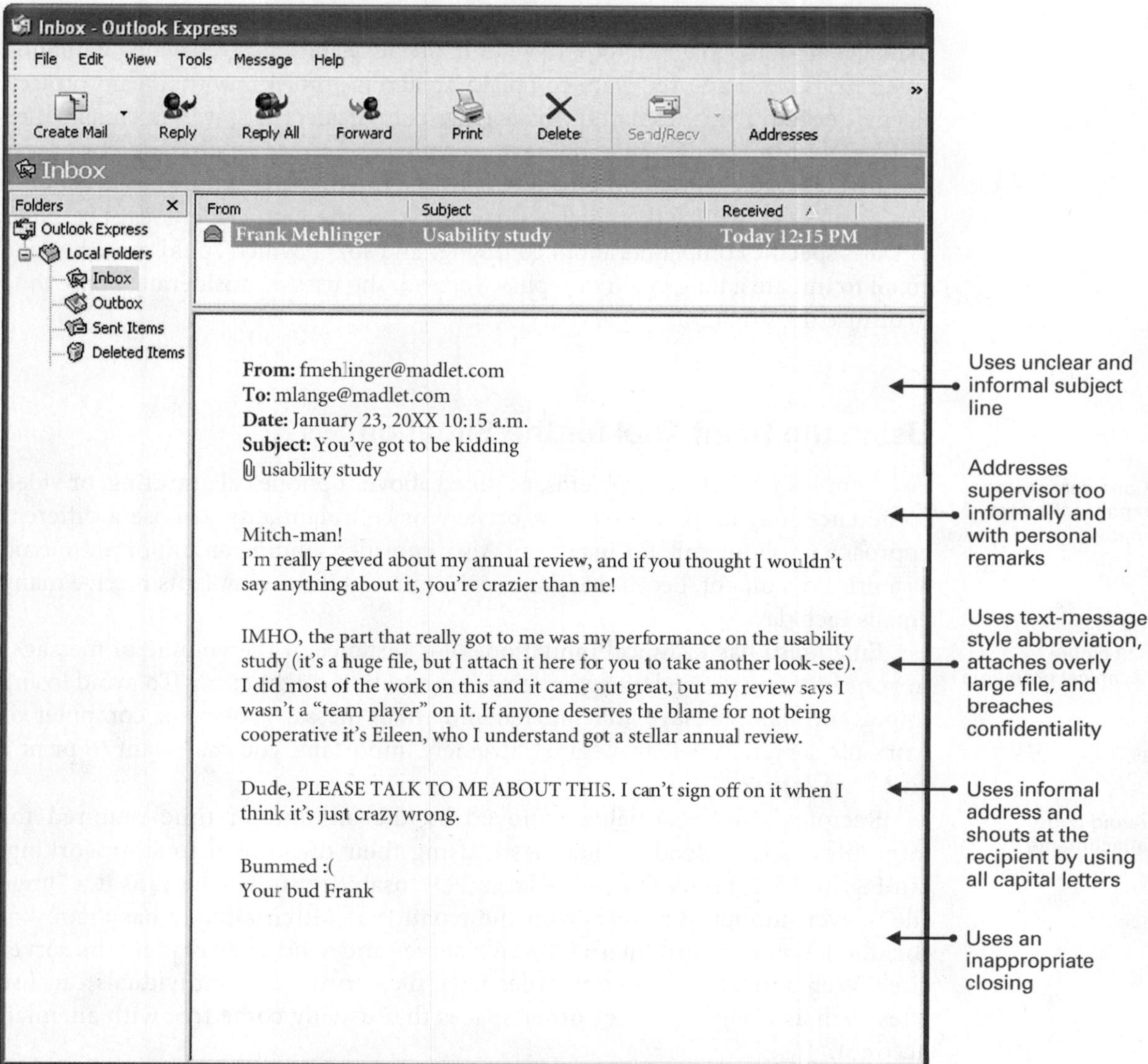

Inbox - Outlook Express
File Edit View Tools Message Help
Create Mail
Reply
Reply All
Forward
Print
Delete
Send/Recv
Addresses
Inbox
Folders
Outlook Express
Local Folders
Inbox
Outbox
Sent Items
Deleted Items
From
Subject
Received
Frank Mehlinger
Usability study
Today 12:15 PM
From: fmehlinger@madlet.com
To: mlange@madlet.com
Date: January 23, 20XX 10:15 a.m.
Subject: You've got to be kidding
usability study
Mitch-man!
I'm really peeved about my annual review, and if you thought I wouldn't say anything about it, you're crazier than me!
IMHO, the part that really got to me was my performance on the usability study (it's a huge file, but I attach it here for you to take another look-see). I did most of the work on this and it came out great, but my review says I wasn't a "team player" on it. If anyone deserves the blame for not being cooperative it's Eileen, who I understand got a stellar annual review.
Dude, PLEASE TALK TO ME ABOUT THIS. I can't sign off on it when I think it's just crazy wrong.
Bummed :(
Your bud Frank
Uses unclear and informal subject line
Addresses supervisor too informally and with personal remarks
Uses text-message style abbreviation, attaches overly large file, and breaches confidentiality
Uses informal address and shouts at the recipient by using all capital letters
Uses an inappropriate closing

FIGURE 15.2 A Workplace Email Lacking Professional Style and Tone
The style and tone of this email are inappropriate for the workplace.
Source: Outlook Express frame used with permission from Microsoft.

phone or meet personally. In Figure 15.2, Frank is upset about his annual performance review. Rather than wait, organize his thoughts, and request a meeting with his supervisor Mitch, Frank hurriedly writes an inappropriate email. Yet, like many volatile situations, this one would be easier to resolve face-to-face. If distance is an issue, a video conference or phone call is still a more personal approach.

Try to keep it simple

Don't use email for complex discussions. For example, in Figure 15.3, Rachel, a manager at a large manufacturer of vitamin products, has received a long, rambling email from her employee Dan, complaining about problems with a team project. Rachel realizes that these problems are too complicated to solve via email—they involve not just Dan but an entire team. The issues need to be discussed by everyone involved. Rachel therefore responds with a brief email asking Dan to set up a conference call. Notice that Rachel does not "take the bait"—she doesn't respond to Dan's specific complaints about colleagues and so on, which could cause her one email to initiate a long chain of replies. Instead, she uses a considerate, polite tone to diffuse the situation.

Using the Right Tool for the Situation

Consider whether email is the best medium

For complex projects or problems, as noted above, a phone call, meeting, or video conference may be preferable. For privacy or confidentiality, choose a different approach (a phone call, for instance). Also, consider sending an important memo as a print document, because email may be ignored if the recipients receive many emails each day.

Anticipate technical problems

Email also has technical limitations. For instance, if the volume of messages in your in-box gets too large, your email application might crash. To avoid losing important material, save attachments and email messages on your computer or work file server. When an item is extremely important, you may want to print a copy.

Avoid huge attachments

Recipients are justifiably annoyed by the amount of time required for large files to download, sometimes causing their own email to stop working. (In Figure 15.2, Frank attaches a large PDF usability study—he calls it a "huge file"—even though it's clear from the email that Mitch already has a copy of this file.) You can store these files on a server and send your readers the server site's Web address. Most companies have file servers, and individuals can use sites such as *Google Drive* or other spaces that usually come free with an email account.

USING VISUALS WITH EMAIL

Use conservative fonts, colors, and background

Stick with basic fonts such as Times Roman or Helvetica. Or choose "send as plain text" or the default font (usually Courier). Fancy fonts are inappropriate for workplace communication because they connote a frivolous tone (see Figure 15.4).

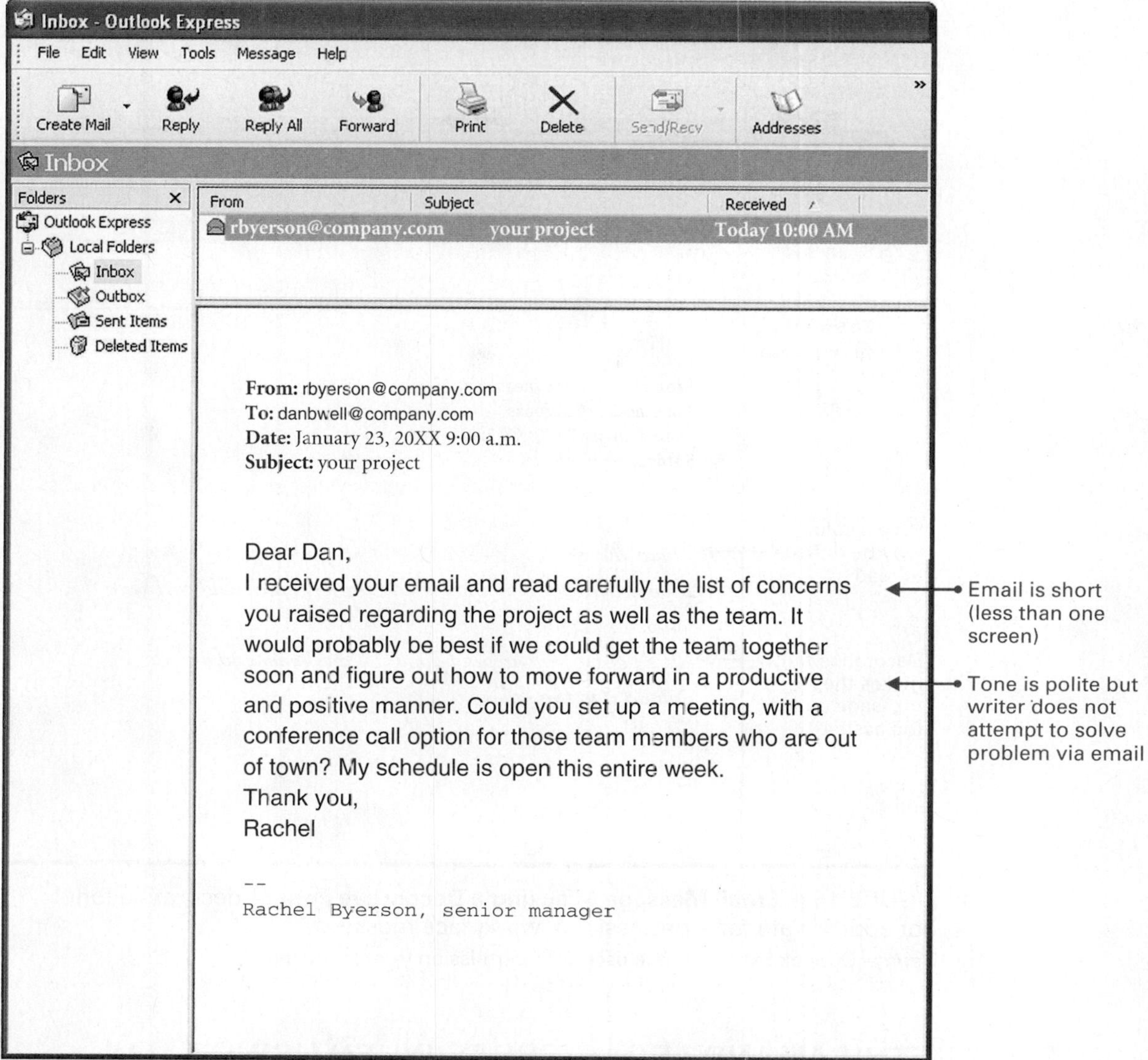

FIGURE 15.3 **A Response to a Long, Complicated Email** The writer attempts to diffuse a tense situation.
Source: Outlook Express frame used with permission from Microsoft.

If you include photographs, charts, graphs, and other visuals, do not paste these items directly into the email type. Instead, if the file is small (under 1 megabyte), add it as an attachment. If the file is larger, save it on a server and send recipients the Web address.

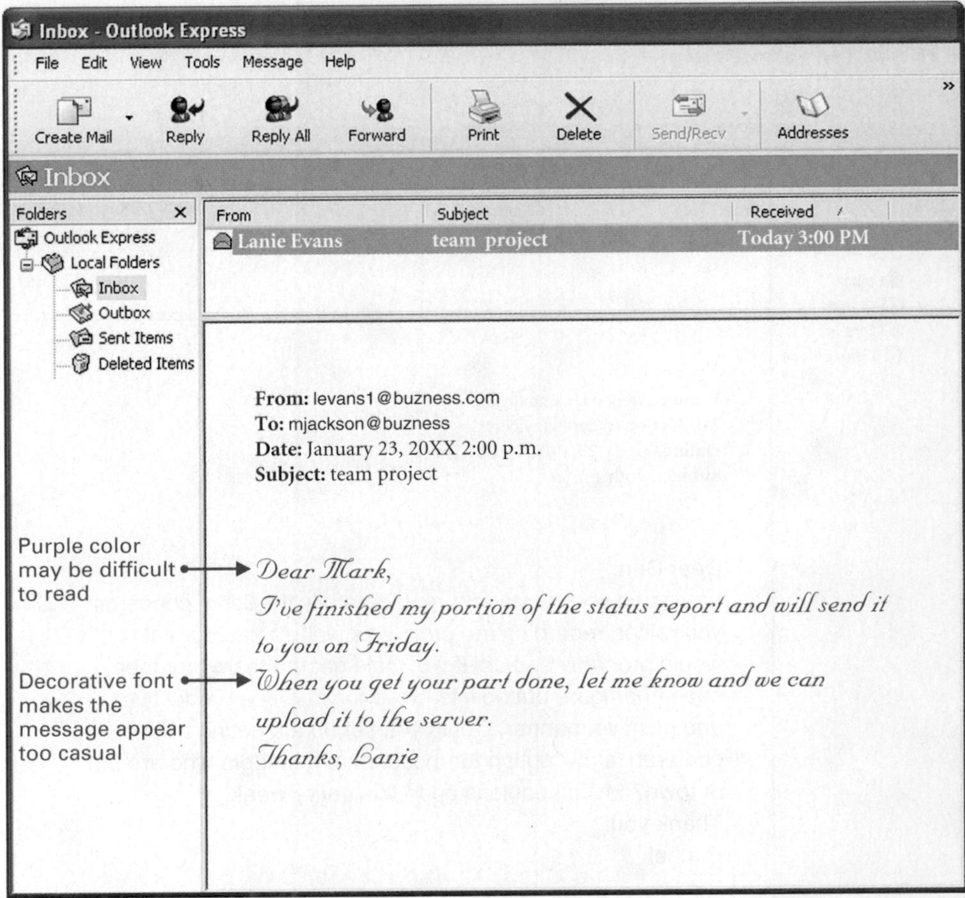

FIGURE 15.4 **Email Message Misusing a Decorative Font** A decorative font is not appropriate for a professional workplace message.
Source: Outlook Express frame used with permission from Microsoft.

ETHICAL AND LEGAL ISSUES WHEN USING EMAIL

When sent in a workplace setting, email is often archived and saved for years. Any workplace communication, including email, is subject to important ethical and legal considerations.

Copyright Issues

Email is subject to copyright

Any email message you receive is copyrighted by the person who wrote it or the organization that employs this person. Technically, under current law, forwarding this message to anyone for any purpose is a violation of the owner's copyright. Copyright also applies to the act of reproducing an email message as part of any type of publication. Yet forwarding is a common practice and typically is not a problem, if you use common sense. If unsure, seek permission from the person who wrote the original email.

Privacy Issues

Gossip, personal messages, risqué jokes, or complaints about the boss or a colleague—all might reach unintended recipients. While phone companies and other private carriers are governed by laws protecting privacy, no such legal protection yet exists for Internet communication (Peyser and Rhodes 82). The Electronic Privacy Act of 1986 offers limited protection against unauthorized reading of another person's email, but employers are exempt (Extejt 63).

Employers are legally entitled to monitor employee email

> In some instances it may be proper for an employer to monitor E-mail, if it has evidence of safety violations, illegal activity, racial discrimination, or sexual improprieties, for instance. Companies may also need access to business information, whether it is kept in an employee's drawer, file cabinet, or computer E-mail. (Bjerklie 15)

Email privacy can be compromised in other ways as well:

Email offers no privacy

- Everyone on a group mailing list—intended recipient or not—automatically receives a copy.
- Even when "deleted" from the system, messages can live on, saved in a backup file.
- Forwarding email without the author's consent violates that person's privacy.
- Anyone with access to your network and password can read your document, alter it, use parts of it out of context, pretend to be its author, forward it, plagiarize your ideas, or even author a document or conduct illegal activity in your name. (One partial safeguard is encryption software, which scrambles the message, and only people who possess the code can unscramble it. Another strategy is to circulate any sensitive document as a PDF attachment. PDF format makes it more difficult for someone to alter the document.)

The message in Figure 15.2 has legal implications in terms of the writer's job performance and future employment, and violates colleague confidentiality.

GLOBAL CONSIDERATIONS WHEN USING EMAIL

Email travels quickly. Just one click on the "Send" command, and your message can be routed to countless recipients. If these readers press "Forward," the message may travel to even more people. In any setting, but especially in companies that have international offices and clients, email can be read by people across the globe.

Email can quickly travel across countries

Chapter 5 (page 99) illustrates an email message that is inappropriate for a global audience. Figure 15.5 (page 344) shows a more appropriate message. The Guidelines box (page 342) lists items to consider as you email a global audience.

GUIDELINES for Writing and Using Email

Audience and Purpose

- **Consider your audience.** If you are writing to a customer, client, stranger, or someone in authority, use a more formal tone than for a coworker or immediate supervisor. Also, use a formal salutation and closing (see page 351).
- **Consider your purpose.** If the situation is complicated or requires discussion and back-and-forth exchange, don't use email. Consider setting up a meeting, conference call, or video conference.
- **Check and answer your email daily.** If you're really busy, at least acknowledge receipt and respond later.
- **Check your distribution list before each mailing.** Deliver your message to all intended recipients (but not to unintended ones).
- **Spell each recipient's name correctly.** There is no bigger turn-off for readers than seeing that their name is spelled incorrectly.

Formatting

- **For very brief email, stick with just one paragraph.** When more detail is required, follow the introduction/body/conclusion format shown in Figure 15.1.
- **Don't indent paragraphs.** Instead, double-space between paragraphs.
- **End with a signature block.** Include your contact information, and if you have the technology, your electronic signature.
- **Don't send huge or specially formatted attachments without first checking with the recipient.** Files over 1 megabyte can cause big problems for someone with a slow email connection. Also, use a standard format, such as PDF.

Style, Tone, and Interpersonal Issues

- **Write a clear subject line.** Instead of "Test Data" or "Data Request," be specific: "Request for Beta Test Data for Project 18." This line helps recipients decide whether to read the message immediately, and to file and locate the message later.
- **Keep it short.** Readers are impatient and don't want to scroll through long screens of information. Use an attachment (of under 1 megabyte in size) or direct readers to a Web document for more information.
- **Be polite and professional.** Formal language is appropriate for most workplace email. Avoid angry, personal attacks on other people (this behavior is often called "flaming" and has no place in business communication).
- **Use emoticons and abbreviations sparingly.** Use smiley faces and other emoticons strictly in informal messages to people you know well. Avoid these symbols when writing to international readers. The same goes for common email abbreviations such as BTW or HAND ("by the way"; "have a nice day").

- **Don't write in ALL CAPS.** This usage signals that you are SCREAMING.
- **Proofread and run the spell check before pressing "Send."** Misspellings not only affect your credibility and image but they also can confuse your readers.
- **Don't use email to avoid a situation in which personal contact is needed.** Although it may be uncomfortable, meeting with someone face-to-face is often the best way to resolve a complex problem or situation.

Visuals and Technology

- **Use formatting sparingly.** Headings, bullets, and font changes such as italics and bold may not display well on a recipient's email screen. Save the use of fonts for an attachment (word processing or PDF).
- **If you do use fonts, use those that are appropriate for the audience and purpose.** A decorative font is not a good choice for a workplace memo. Stick with Times Roman or Helvetica.
- **Don't use email as one giant filing cabinet.** Keep your in-box under 50 messages by creating folders for storing messages. Save important attachments and email messages on your computer or file server.

Global Issues

- **Avoid humor, slang, and idioms.** These items may be offensive in different cultures; also, this kind of language does not translate easily.
- **Write simple, short sentences that are easy to translate.**
- **Convey respect for your recipient.** A respectful tone and style is appreciated in any culture.
- **Don't be too direct or blunt.** Some cultures find directness offensive.
- **Be an active listener.** Don't respond immediately; read email carefully to get a sense of the cultural norms of the writer and the other readers.

Ethical and Legal Issues

- **Consider copyright issues.** Although it's common to forward email, if the situation is sensitive, request permission from the original writer.
- **Assume that your email is permanent and readable by anyone at any time.** "Forensic software" can find and revive deleted files.
- **Avoid wisecracks and rude remarks (flaming).** Any email judged harassing or discriminatory can have dire legal consequences.
- **Don't use email to send confidential information.** Avoid complaining, evaluating, or criticizing, and handle anything that should be kept private (say, an employee reprimand) in some other way.
- **Don't use your employer's email network for anything not work related.**
- **Before you forward a message, obtain permission from the sender.**

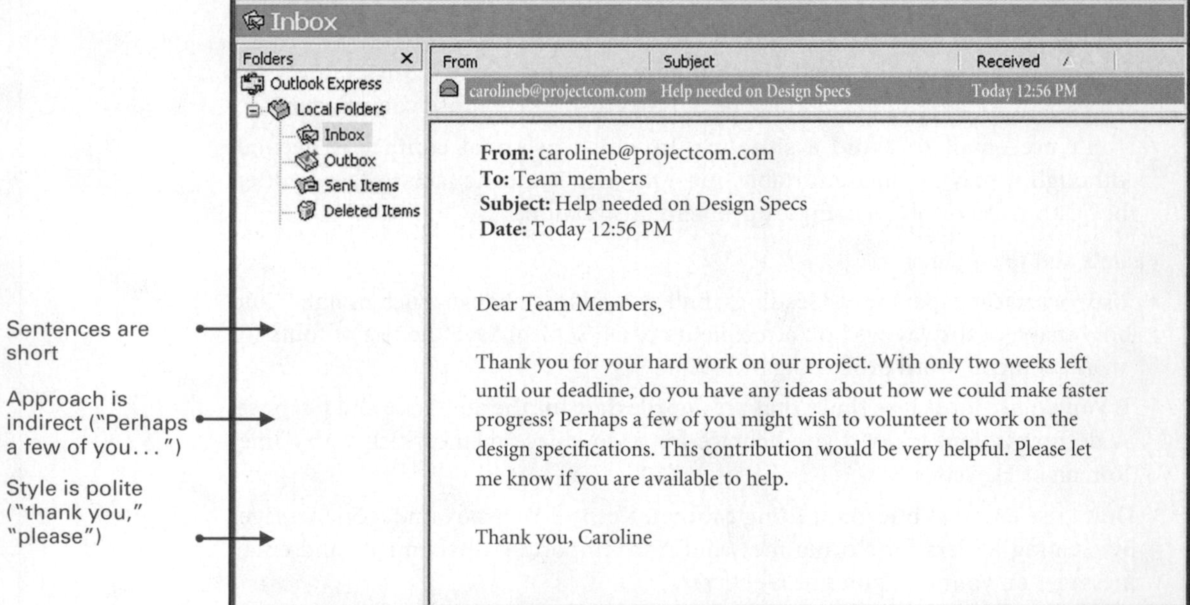

FIGURE 15.5 Email Message Written to a Global Audience
Source: Microsoft Corporation.

GUIDELINES for Choosing Email Versus Paper, Telephone, or Fax

Email is excellent for reaching a lot of people quickly with a relatively brief, informal message. And it is preferable to fax transmission when you wish to preserve the professional look of any well-formatted attachments. But there are often good reasons to transmit your message in traditional fashion, on paper—or to speak with the recipient directly.

- **Don't use email when a more personal medium is preferable.** Sometimes an issue is best resolved by a phone call, or even voice mail.
- **Don't use email for a complex message.** In contrast to a rapid-fire email message, preparing a paper document is more deliberate, giving you a chance to choose words carefully and to revise. Also, a well-crafted letter or memo is likely to be read more attentively. For in-house recipients, attach a file of your paper document to an introductory email.
- **Don't use email for most formal correspondence.** Don't use email to apply for or to resign from a job, request a raise, or respond to a formal letter unless recipients specifically request this method. Don't use it to send a thank-you or a follow-up after a job interview. (See Chapters 16 and 17 for more on formal letters and for job hunting.)

TEXT MESSAGING

A faster medium than email, text messages (texts) allow you to communicate with individuals or groups via cell phone. While texting has always been popular for personal communication, it is becoming increasingly more and more common for workplace communication as well. Texting can be an efficient way to get a quick answer to a simple question (I'm in the lobby. Where are you?), because people tend to read and respond faster to texts than to email messages. Texts are also are less intrusive than phone calls. Since most people send and receive texts on personal cell phones, few rules govern the use of texting in the workplace. For more on the nuances of sending and receiving texts at work, see the following Guidelines for Text Messaging.

Advantages of workplace text messaging

Consider your audience before deciding to text your colleagues for workplace conversation. Not everyone's cell phone package has a text messaging plan, and some plans charge extra per message. Even people who do use texting may prefer email instead, which requires timely, but not instant responses. Also, keep in mind that not everyone is familiar with the abbreviations and other shorthand used in most texts. As one expert notes.

Audience considerations

> "Office communication just isn't what it used to be. For folks over 40, the following instant message may look like nothing more than gobbledygook: '#s look gd . . . lnch @ 1/ back l8r.' But for younger employees, it's just simple shorthand for: 'The numbers look good. I'm leaving for lunch at 1 p.m., and I'll be back later.' " (Van Riper)

Although useful for rapid exchanges, texting is a poor choice for communication that requires careful planning, composing, and editing. Texting is also a bad choice if you need to keep a record of a conversation—texts are not stored for very long (days, or maybe weeks, depending on how much you text) or with as much care as workplace email messages. Use email if you need to attach longer documents or if a communication trail is needed for reference and legal reasons. Keep in mind that if the phone is provided by your employer, all content (both personal and business) can be monitored and reviewed (Privacy Rights Clearinghouse).

Purpose considerations

GUIDELINES for Text Messaging

- **Consider your audience and purpose.** Use text messaging with willing recipients only; ask if your recipient will incur charges before you text.
- **Keep text messages brief and to the point.** If making a statement, keep it simple ("Turned in paperwork today"). Ask questions that require simple answers ("Did you turn in the report?" "What time is the meeting?")
- **Avoid too many abbreviations.** Feel free to use common abbreviations (c u soon), as long as they are understood by all participants. But avoid obscure ones (audy—are you done yet?) that not everyone will recognize.

GUIDELINES *continued*

- **Know when to end the conversation.** Sometimes, text messages go on and on. When you've exhausted the topic, say goodbye.
- **Be professional in tone, style, and etiquette.** Avoid flaming and sexist or biased language, which could become the cause for a "textual harassment" grievance (Michael Best & Friedrich). When composing workplace texts, avoid the informal style you might use with friends.
- **Avoid discussing confidential topics.** Cell phones are easily lost or misplaced, so save confidential discussions for secure channels (secure workplace email, face-to-face meetings).

CHECKLIST: Email and Text Messages

(Numbers in parenthesis refer to the first page of discussion.)

Email

- ☐ Is the message short and to the point, with a clear subject line? (334)
- ☐ For a longer email, do I use introduction/body/conclusion format? (335)
- ☐ Is email the best medium in this situation, versus a call or visit? (338)
- ☐ If a situation is complicated, have I used email to acknowledge the issue, but suggested other avenues for solving the problem? (338)
- ☐ Is the tone professional and courteous, avoiding insults and accusations? (336)
- ☐ Have I avoided emoticons, ALL CAPS, and abbreviations? (336)
- ☐ Have I been careful not to send overly large attachments? (338)
- ☐ Have I avoided using excessive fonts, colors, and backgrounds? (338)
- ☐ Have I maintained confidentiality and privacy? (341)
- ☐ Will my email be easy to understand and inoffensive to global readers? (341)
- ☐ Have I proofread, spell checked, and verified my distribution list? (343)

Text Messages

- ☐ Have I determined whether texting is the best medium in this situation? (345)
- ☐ Have I checked with colleagues in advance to be sure it's OK to text? (345)
- ☐ Have I kept the message very short and on topic? (345)
- ☐ If asking a question, did I ask one where the answer will be brief? (345)
- ☐ Did I conclude the discussion when appropriate? (346)
- ☐ Have I been professional in the tone and style of my texts? (346)

Projects

GENERAL

1. Choose a topic and an audience, and write an email expressing your position on a debatable issue that affects your school, dorm, or community. Provide convincing support for your position.
2. Individually or in small groups, decide whether each of the following documents would be appropriate for transmission via a company email network. Be prepared to explain your decisions.

   Sarah Burnes's memo about benzene levels (page 13)
   The "Rational Connection" memo (page 42)
   The "better" memo to the maintenance director (page 45)
   Rosemary Garrido's letter to a potential customer (page 56)
   The medical report written for expert readers (page 21)
   A memo reporting illegal or unethical activity in your company
   A personal note to a colleague
   A request for a raise or promotion
   Minutes of a meeting
   Announcement of a no-smoking policy
   An evaluation or performance review of an employee
   A reprimand to an employee
   A notice of a meeting
   Criticism of an employee or employer
   A request for volunteers
   A suggestion for change or improvement in company policy or practice
   A gripe
   A note of praise or thanks
   A message you have received and have decided to forward to other recipients

TEAM

Work with a team to write a collaborative version of the "position" email (see General Project 1). Your team could plan this collaborative email by first conversing via IM about how it should be written.

DIGITAL AND SOCIAL MEDIA

Imagine a situation in which you you are waiting for a friend to arrive at the airport. Compose a text message to your friend asking if she has arrived yet and where the two of you should meet. Now imagine the same situation, but instead of a friend, you are waiting for a co-worker you've never met (someone from a different office location who is coming to your site for the week). Compose a text message to that person. In groups of 2–3 students, review each others' work and discuss the differences in tone, style, and other qualities between the two messages.

GLOBAL

You've been appointed by your manager to be team leader for an important new project. The team involves people from the following countries: China, Germany, India, Italy, and the United States. Your first assignment is to come up with a communication plan. You decide that given the time differences, the team should use email as its primary means of communication. But you know that when people write using email, there can be misunderstandings due to tone, style, and levels of directness. These issues might be amplified by the differences in cultures between team members. Use material in this chapter, Chapter 4, and on the Internet to research these issues. Write an email to the team outlining guidelines for communication for this project. Remember that the email you send needs to reflect the guidelines you are proposing.

16 Workplace Letters

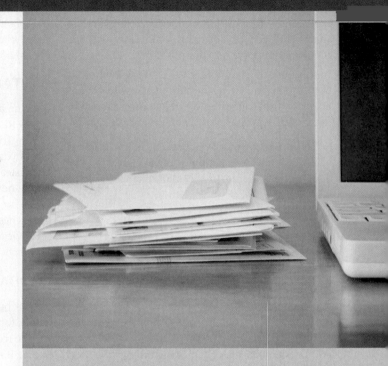

"One thing I've learned during my first year on the job is that workplace letters are a special breed of communication: They require a lot more attention than your typical memo, email, voicemail, and so on. A letter takes time to write, revise, print, and proofread, and during that time I've sometimes decided to make a few changes or countless changes—and at times have decided not to send the letter at all until a more experienced colleague has had a chance to review it. I think any effective letter is the product of many deliberate decisions on the writer's part."

—Foster Jankovich,
Claims Adjuster for an insurance company

LEARNING OBJECTIVES FOR THIS CHAPTER

- Know when to correspond by letter instead of memo or email
- Identify the standard and optional parts of a workplace letter
- Follow a conventional letter format
- Appreciate the importance of proper tone in any letter
- Understand that letters can have global and ethical implications
- Know how to convey bad or unwelcome news
- Write inquiry letters, claim letters, sales letters, and adjustment letters

Writers often have good reason to correspond in a more formal and personal medium than a memo or email message. A well-crafted letter is appropriate in situations like these:

When to send a letter instead of a memo or email

- To personalize your correspondence, conveying the sense that this message is prepared exclusively for your recipient
- To convey a dignified, professional impression
- To represent your company or organization
- To present a reasoned, carefully constructed case
- To respond to clients, customers, or anyone outside your organization
- To provide an official notice or record (as in a letter announcing legal action or confirming a verbal agreement)

A letter often has a *persuasive* purpose (see Chapter 3); therefore, proper tone is essential for connecting with the recipient. Because your signature certifies your approval—and your responsibility—for the message (which may serve as a legal document, as in Figure 16.1), precision is crucial.

This chapter covers four common letter types: inquiry letters, claim letters, sales letters, and adjustment letters. (Job application letters and letters of transmittal are discussed in Chapters 17 and 22, respectively.)

CONSIDERING AUDIENCE AND PURPOSE

Your overall approach to a workplace letter is determined by the letter's audience and purpose.

Audience considerations

Begin by focusing on your audience: Who will be the recipient of this letter? (When possible, write to a named person, not the title of a position.) What is your relationship to this person? Is this a potential employer, a client, an associate, a stranger? Exactly what information and level of formality does this person expect? How might this person react to the contents of your letter? Answering these questions in advance will help you craft a letter that connects with its recipient.

Purpose considerations

Next, focus on your purpose: What do you want the recipient to do after reading your letter—offer a job, provide advice, grant a favor, accept bad news? Do you have multiple purposes in mind as in, say, obtaining a refund for a faulty product while also preserving your business relationship with that supplier? Answering these questions in advance will help you craft a letter that achieves the outcome you seek.

LETTER PARTS, FORMATS, AND DESIGN ELEMENTS

Most workplace letters have the same basic components. This conventional and predictable arrangement enables recipients to locate what they need immediately, as in Figure 16.1.

Standard Parts

Many organizations have their own formats for letters. Depending on where you work, some of these parts may appear at different locations on the page. But in general a letter contains the elements listed here.

Heading and Date. If your stationery has a company letterhead, simply include the date a few lines below the letterhead, flush against the right or left margin. When you use your personal address, omit your name because that will appear below your signature at the letter's end.

Street address	154 Sea Lane
City, state, zip	Harwich, MA 02163
Month, day, year	July 15, 20XX

Use the Postal Service's two-letter state abbreviations (e.g., MA for Massachusetts, WY for Wyoming) in your heading, in the inside address, and on the envelope.

Inside Address. Two to six line spaces below the heading, flush against the left margin, is the inside address (the address of the recipient).

Name/position	Dr. Ann Mello, Dean of Students
Organization	Western University
Street address	30 Mogul Hill Road
City, state, zip	Stowe, VT 51350

Whenever possible, address a specifically named recipient, and include the person's title. Using "Mr." or "Ms." before the name is optional. (See page 237 for avoiding sexist usage in titles and salutations.)

> **NOTE** *Depending on the letter's length, adjust the vertical placement of your return address and inside address to achieve a balanced page.*

Salutation. The salutation, two line spaces below the inside address, begins with *Dear* and ends with a colon (*Dear Ms. Smith:*). If you don't know the recipient's name, use the position title (*Dear Manager*) or, preferably, an attention line (page 353). Only address the recipient by first name if that is the way you would address that individual in person.

Typical salutations

- Dear Ms. Smith:
- Dear Managing Editor:
- Dear Professor Trudeau:

No satisfactory guidelines exist for addressing several people within an organization. *Gentlemen* or *Dear Sirs* implies bias. *Ladies and Gentlemen* sounds too much like the beginning of a speech. *Dear Sir or Madam* is old-fashioned. *To Whom It May Concern* is vague and impersonal. Your best bet is to eliminate the salutation by using an attention line.

The shape of workplace letters

Text. Begin your letter text two line spaces below the salutation or subject line. Workplace letters typically include (1) a brief introductory paragraph (five or fewer lines) that identifies your purpose and connects with the recipient's interest, (2) one or more discussion paragraphs that present details of your message, and (3) a concluding paragraph that sums up and encourages action.

Keep the paragraphs short, usually fewer than eight lines. If a paragraph goes beyond eight lines, or if the paragraph contains detailed supporting facts or examples, as in Figure 16.1, consider using a vertical list.

Complimentary Closing. The closing, two line spaces (returns) below the last line of text, should parallel the level of formality used in the salutation and should reflect your relationship to the recipient (polite but not overly intimate). *Yours truly* and *Sincerely* are the most common. Others, in order of decreasing formality, include

Complimentary closings

- Respectfully,
- Cordially,
- Best wishes,
- Regards,
- Best,

Align the closing with the letter's heading.

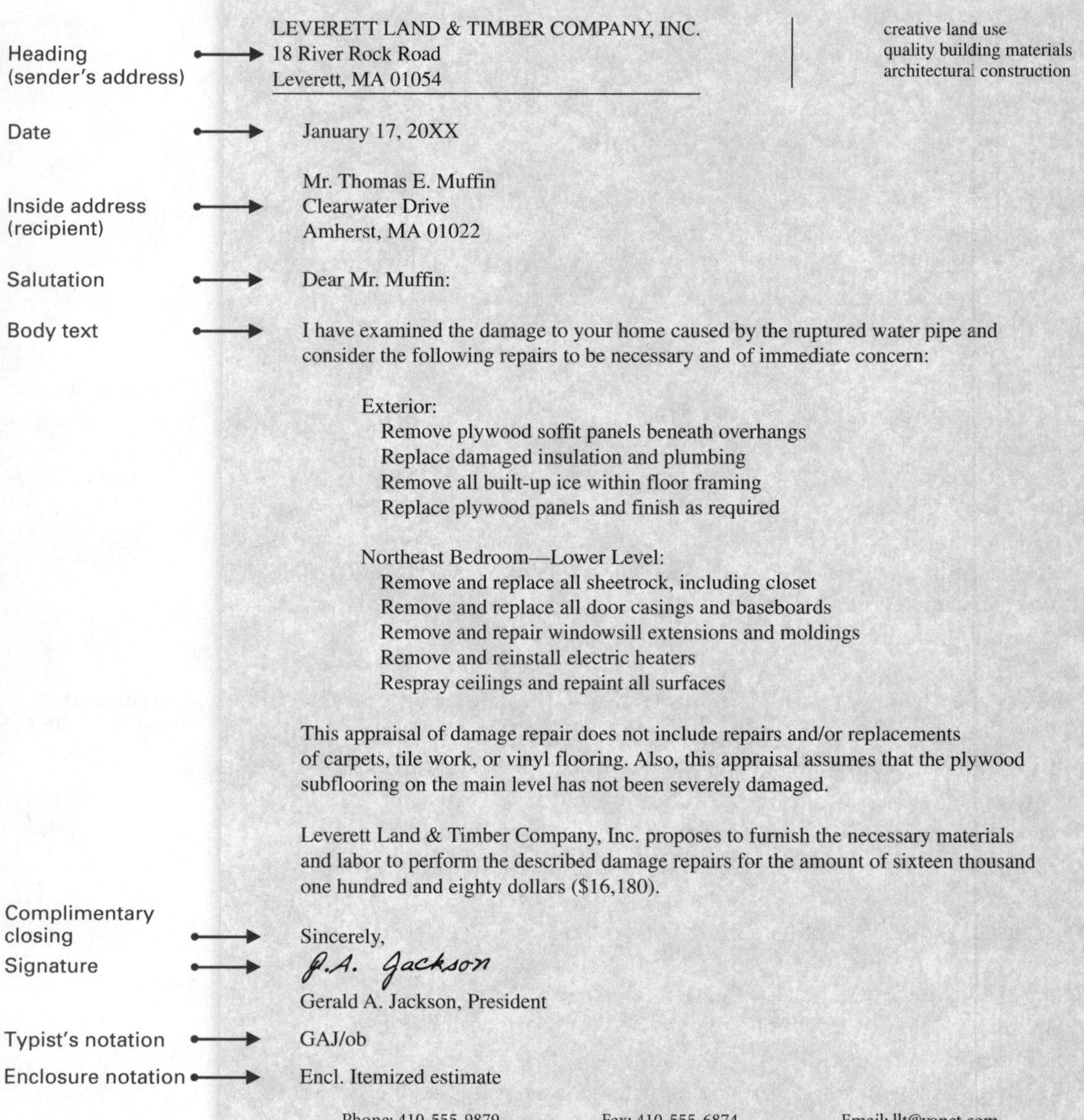

Heading (sender's address)
LEVERETT LAND & TIMBER COMPANY, INC.
18 River Rock Road
Leverett, MA 01054
creative land use
quality building materials
architectural construction
Date
January 17, 20XX
Inside address (recipient)
Mr. Thomas E. Muffin
Clearwater Drive
Amherst, MA 01022
Salutation
Dear Mr. Muffin:
Body text
I have examined the damage to your home caused by the ruptured water pipe and consider the following repairs to be necessary and of immediate concern:
Exterior:
Remove plywood soffit panels beneath overhangs
Replace damaged insulation and plumbing
Remove all built-up ice within floor framing
Replace plywood panels and finish as required
Northeast Bedroom—Lower Level:
Remove and replace all sheetrock, including closet
Remove and replace all door casings and baseboards
Remove and repair windowsill extensions and moldings
Remove and reinstall electric heaters
Respray ceilings and repaint all surfaces
This appraisal of damage repair does not include repairs and/or replacements of carpets, tile work, or vinyl flooring. Also, this appraisal assumes that the plywood subflooring on the main level has not been severely damaged.
Leverett Land & Timber Company, Inc. proposes to furnish the necessary materials and labor to perform the described damage repairs for the amount of sixteen thousand one hundred and eighty dollars ($16,180).
Complimentary closing
Sincerely,
Signature
G.A. Jackson
Gerald A. Jackson, President
Typist's notation
GAJ/ob
Enclosure notation
Encl. Itemized estimate
Phone: 410-555-9879
Fax: 410-555-6874
Email: llt@yonet.com

FIGURE 16.1 Standard Parts of a Workplace Letter This writer is careful to stipulate not only the exact repairs and costs, but also those items excluded from his estimate. In the event of legal proceedings, a formal letter signifies a contractual obligation on the sender's part.

Signature. Type your name and title on the fourth and fifth lines below and aligned with the closing. Sign in the space between the complimentary closing and typed name.

> Sincerely yours,
>
> *Martha S. Jones*
>
> Martha S. Jones
> Personnel Manager

The signature block

If you are representing your company or a group that bears legal responsibility for the correspondence, type the company's name in full caps two line spaces below your complimentary closing; place your typed name and title four line spaces below the company name and sign in the triple space between.

> Yours truly,
>
> HASBROUCK LABORATORIES
>
> *Lester Fong*
>
> L. H. Fong
> Research Associate

Signature block representing the company

Optional Parts

Some letters have one or more of the following specialized parts. (Examples appear in the sample letters in this chapter.)

Attention Line. Use an attention line when you write to an organization and do not know your recipient's name but are directing the letter to a specific department or position.

> Glaxol Industries, Inc.
> 232 Rogaline Circle
> Missoula, MT 61347
>
> ATTENTION: Director of Research and Development

An attention line can replace your salutation

Drop two line spaces below the inside address and place the attention line either flush with the left margin or centered on the page.

Subject Line. Typically, subject lines are used with memos, but if the recipient is not expecting your letter, a subject line is a good way of catching a busy reader's attention.

A subject line can attract attention

SUBJECT: *Placement of the Subject Line*

Place the subject line below the inside address or attention line with one line space before and after. You can italicize or capitalize the subject to make it prominent.

Typist's Notation. If someone else types your letter for you (common in the days of typewriters but rare today), your initials (in CAPS), a slash, and your typist's initials (in lower case) appear below the typed signature, flush with the left margin.

Typist's notation

JJ/pl

Enclosure Notation. If you enclose other documents in the same envelope, indicate this one line space below the typist's notation (or writer's name and position), flush against the left margin. State the number of enclosures.

Enclosure noted

Enclosure
Enclosures 2
Encl. 3

If the enclosures are important documents such as legal certificates, checks, or specifications, name them in the notation.

Enclosure named

Enclosures: 2 certified checks, 1 set of KBX plans

Copy (or distribution) Notation. If you distribute copies of your letter to other recipients, indicate this by inserting the notation "Copy" or "cc," followed by a colon, one line below the previous line (such as an enclosure line). The "cc" notation once stood for "carbon copy," but no one uses carbon paper any more, so now it is said to stand for "courtesy copy."

Copy notations

cc: office file
Melvin Blount

copy: S. Furlow
B. Smith

Most copies are distributed on an *FYI* (*For Your Information*) basis, but writers sometimes use the copy notation to maintain a paper trail or to signal the primary recipient that this information is being shared with others (e.g., superiors, legal authorities).

Multiple notations would appear in this order: typist, enclosures, and then copy.

Postscript. A postscript (typed or handwritten) draws attention to a point you wish to emphasize or adds a personal note. Do not use a postscript if you forget to mention a point in the body of the letter. Rewrite the body section instead.

> P. S. Because of its terminal position in your letter, a postscript can draw attention to a point that needs reemphasizing.

A postscript

Place the postscript two line spaces below any other notation, and flush against the left margin. Because readers often regard postscripts as sales gimmicks, use them sparingly in professional correspondence.

Formats and Design Features

The following elements help make workplace letters look inviting, accessible, and professional.

Letter Format. Although several formats are acceptable, and your company may have its own, the most popular format for workplace letters is *block* (Figure 16.2).

Digital Templates. Most word-processing software allows you to select from templates, or predesigned letter formats. These templates provide fields for you to insert your name, your company name, and your message. Some templates provide background artwork or other decorative features. As tempting as it may be to simply choose a template, make sure the one you use is appropriate for your audience and purpose. Unless the situation specifically calls for a decorative format, strive for a tasteful, conservative look. When in doubt, ignore the templates and work from a blank document.

Quality Stationery. Use high-quality, 20-pound bond, $8\frac{1}{2}'' \times 11''$ stationery with a minimum fiber content of 25 percent.

Uniform Margins and Spacing. When using stationery without a letterhead, frame your letter with $1\frac{1}{2}$-inch top margins, 1-inch side margins, and bottom margins of 1 to $1\frac{1}{2}$ inches. Use single spacing within paragraphs and double-spacing between. Vary these guidelines based on the amount of space required by the letter's text, but strive for a balanced look.

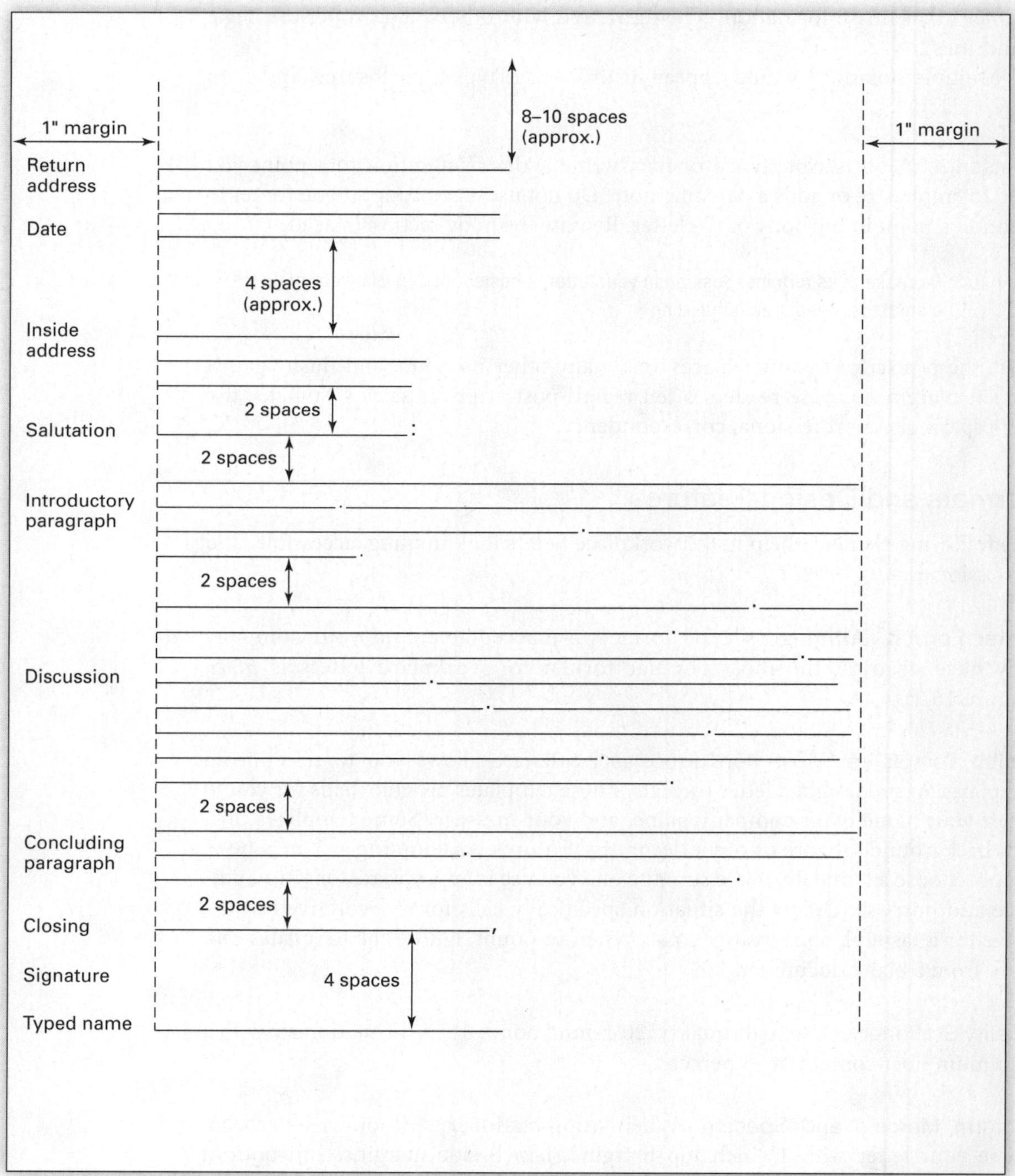

FIGURE 16.2 **Block Format** In the block format, every line begins at the left margin. This format is popular because it looks businesslike and saves keying time by eliminating the need to tab and center.

Headers for Subsequent Pages. Head each additional page with a notation identifying the recipient, date, and page number.

I Adrianna Fonseca, June 25, 20XX, p. 2

Subsequent-page header

Align your header with the right-hand margin. See page 57 for an example.

NOTE *Never use an additional page solely for the closing section. Instead, reformat the letter so that the closing appears on the first page, or so that at least two lines of text appear above the closing on the subsequent page.*

The Envelope. Your envelope (usually a #10 envelope) should be of the same quality as your stationery. Place the recipient's name and address at a fairly central point on the envelope. Place your own name and address in the upper-left corner. Single-space these elements. Most word-processing programs have envelope printing options that automatically place these elements. (See your printer's operating manual for instructions.)

LETTER TONE

The importance of a letter's tone

When you speak with someone face-to-face, you unconsciously modify your statements and facial expressions as you read and listen to the listener's signals: a smile, a frown, a raised eyebrow, a nod, a short vocal expression of agreement or disagreement. In a phone conversation, the person's voice can signal approval, dismay, anger, or confusion. Those cues allow you to modify your comments and vocal tone.

When writing a letter, however, you can easily forget that a flesh-and-blood person will be reacting to what you say—or seem to say. You will receive no visual or auditory clues to alter what you write before you send the letter. As a result, the tone of a letter is especially important to get right.

To achieve an appropriate tone, consider the factors discussed below that affect the relationship between sender and recipient. As you read through this section, refer to Figure 16.4 (page 365), which maintains an appropriate tone in conveying bad news.

Establish and Maintain a "You" Perspective

Prioritize the reader's needs, wants, and feelings

A letter displaying a "you" perspective puts the reader's interest and feelings first. To convey a "you" perspective, put yourself in the place of the person who will read your correspondence, and ask yourself how this recipient will react to what you have written. Even a single word or sentence, carelessly chosen or phrased, can offend. Consider the following sentence in a letter to a customer:

Offensive

> Our record keeping is very efficient and we have looked into it, so this is obviously your error.

This self-centered tone might be appropriate after numerous investigations into the customer's complaint and failed attempts to communicate your company's perspective to the customer, but in your initial correspondence it would be offensive. Here is a more considerate version. Instead of expressing only the writer's point of view, this second version conveys respect for the reader's viewpoint.

Considerate and respectful

> Although my paperwork shows that you were charged correctly, I will investigate this matter immediately by checking my files against our computer records.

Do not sign and mail the letter until you are certain that the needs and feelings of your reader consistently get top billing, even when you simultaneously must assert your own perspective.

Be Polite and Tactful

If you must express criticism, do so in a way that conveys good will and trust in the recipient. Avoid the following type of expression:

Tactless

> I am shocked that your company lacks the standards to design and manufacture an alarm clock that actually works.

Although a company representative would be required to write a polite and thoughtful response to the above complaint, he or she might be inclined to look closely at the clock's warranty and offer only the most basic reimbursement.

In contrast, a polite and thoughtful letter might yield a full refund or a brand new replacement:

Polite

> Although your clock worked reliably for several months, one of the internal mechanisms recently malfunctioned. I would appreciate your contacting me about an exchange or refund.

Use Plain English

Avoid *letterese*, the stuffy, puffed-up phrases some writers use to make their communications sound important. Even though a letter is more formal than a memo or an email, plain English still can get your point across. For example, consider the following closing section to an inquiry letter asking for help:

Letterese

> Humbly thanking you in anticipation of your kind assistance, I remain
>
> Faithfully yours,

The reader of this letter might feel spoken down to, and decide not to respond. However, in this next revised version, the reader would likely perceive the writer as a straight-talking equal and be more inclined to follow up:

Clear and direct

> I would greatly appreciate any help you could offer.
>
> Best wishes,

Here are a few stuffy phrasings, with clearer, more direct translations:

Letterese	**Clear and direct**
As per your request	As you requested
Contingent upon receipt of	As soon as we receive
Due to the fact that	Because

Be natural. Write as you would speak in a classroom or office: professionally and respectfully but clearly and directly.

NOTE *In the legal profession (and others), phrases such as those shown above are known as "terms of art" and connote a specific meaning. In these cases, you may not be able to avoid such elaborate phrases.*

Decide on a Direct or Indirect Organizing Pattern

The reaction you anticipate should determine the organizational plan of your letter: either *direct* or *indirect*. (Figure 16.3 illustrates the choices.)

Questions for organizing your message

- Will the recipient feel pleased, angry, or neutral?
- Will the message cause resistance, resentment, or disappointment?

When to be direct

The direct pattern puts the main point in the first paragraph, followed by the explanation. Be direct when you expect the recipient to react with approval or when you want to convey immediately the point of your letter (e.g., in good news, inquiry, or application letters—or other routine correspondence).

When to be indirect

If you expect the reader to resist or to need persuading, or if this person is from a different culture, consider an indirect plan. Give the explanation *before* the main point (as in requesting a pay raise or refusing a request).

Research indicates that "readers will always look for the bottom line" (*Writing User-Friendly Documents* 14). Therefore, a direct pattern, even for certain types of

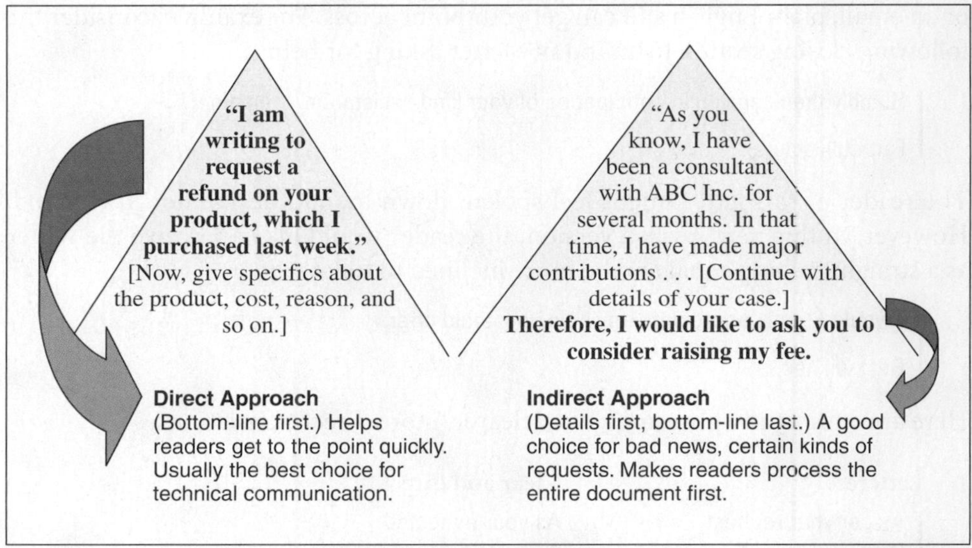

FIGURE 16.3 **Deciding on Your Writing Approach** Use a direct approach most of the time. But when you need to convey difficult or negative information, use an indirect approach. Be as brief as possible.

bad news, may be preferable—as in complaining about a faulty product. For more on conveying bad news, see the section later in this chapter.

> **NOTE** *Whenever you consider using an indirect pattern, think carefully about its ethical implications. Never try to deceive the recipient—and never create an impression that you have something to hide.*

For more on direct versus indirect organizing patterns, see page 324.

GLOBAL AND ETHICAL CONSIDERATIONS

Know your audience

In today's international marketplace, you can expect to communicate with people from numerous different countries and cultures. Many such people are non-native speakers of English and/or have a cultural background other than Anglo American. In such cases, relationship building is essential—and often more important than the topic being discussed.

How relationships can be damaged

Learn all you can about the letter recipient's culture and preferences before corresponding. Be aware that trouble can arise as early as the salutation: International audiences often consider an inappropriate salutation highly offensive. In France or England, for example, a person's title should be used in the salutation, as in "Monsieur le Professeur Larousse" or "Lord High Commissioner Jones" (Sabath 164). In England, "Dear Madam" and "Dear Sir" continue to be acceptable for people not known well by the writer (Scott 55). Know the conventions preferred by your particular readers.

After a bad opening, the letter's contents can spell more trouble, especially when a North American writer "gets right down to business," without focusing first on the relationship. For example, international audiences often expect a personalized introduction that compliments the recipient, inquires about the family, and dwells on other personal details before discussing the topic at hand. Also, North American readers value correspondence that is sufficiently clear and direct to ensure one interpretation only. In contrast, readers from other cultures often prefer ambiguity in their correspondence, thereby allowing the recipient to infer his/her own meaning: In short, countless people across the globe are insulted by a message that seems to be telling them what to think.

Discussing any controversial topic with international readers can be especially hazardous. Consider, for example, the page 358 response to a customer's inquiry about a possible billing error: That example (repeated below) shows respect for the recipient's viewpoint.

> Although my paperwork shows that you were charged correctly, I will investigate this matter immediately by checking my files against our computer records.

An acceptable version for an Anglo-American audience

However, while the previous version may be perfectly acceptable for a conventional North American audience, someone from a different culture might prefer a version like this one:

> Thank you for bringing your question about the possible billing error to my attention. I personally will investigate this matter immediately and do everything possible to answer your question to your full satisfaction.

A preferable version for an international audience

Take special care in expressing disagreement. For example, instead of writing "I'm not so sure that's the best approach," prefer "Are there any other approaches?" or "Do you think that is the best approach?" Or, instead of writing "I disagree" or "We need to discuss this," prefer "That viewpoint is interesting" or "I had not thought of that."

Finally, the letter's closing can create additional problems. For example, informal complimentary closings such as "Cheers" or "Best" often are considered offensive; instead, prefer a formal closing, such as "Respectfully," which seems to be a universally acceptable choice. Avoid excessive informality throughout your letter.

How good intentions can go wrong

Even the best intentions can violate ethical standards. For example, while trying to be polite and respectful, the writer might end up being evasive and misleading instead, thereby inadvertently deceiving the reader. In short, almost any type of international correspondence poses this dilemma: how to be clear and straightforward without appearing rude and insensitive. Do not allow your concern for diplomacy to overshadow the need for recipients to receive the information—as well as the understanding—they require in order to make sound decisions. Regardless of cultural differences, an ethical message ensures that the reader understands and interprets the information just as clearly and accurately as the writer does.

You can learn more about intercultural communication by reading credible Web pages and books. Also, workplace colleagues and faculty members may be good sources of advice. Never send off any global correspondence until you have done diligent homework. (For more on this topic, see Chapters 3 and 5.)

GUIDELINES for Letters in General

- **Determine whether the situation calls for a letter, memo, or email.** Use a letter to communicate formally with a client or customer (someone not in your organization).
- **Use proper letter format and include all the required parts.** Unless your organization has its own guidelines, use block format and the parts discussed earlier.
- **Place the reader's needs first.** Always write from the "you" perspective, putting yourself in your reader's place.
- **Decide on the direct or indirect approach.** Generally speaking, take the direct approach for good news and the indirect approach for bad news.
- **Maintain a courteous, professional tone.** A professional tone creates goodwill and is more effective in the long run.
- **Avoid letterese.** Use plain English, no matter how formal or important the letter. Stuffy language only comes across as phony.
- **Keep international readers in mind.** Don't assume that every letter you write is directed at a recipient whose first language is English or whose cultural values match your own.

CONVEYING BAD OR UNWELCOME NEWS

Bad news is a fact of life in the workplace

During your career you may have to say no to customers, employees, and job applicants. You may have to make difficult requests, such as asking employees to accept higher medical insurance premiums or seeking an interview with a beleaguered official. You may have to notify consumers or shareholders about accidents or product recalls. You may need to apologize for errors—the list of possibilities goes on. In conveying bad news, you face a *persuasive* challenge (see Chapter 3): You must convince people to accept your message. As the bearer of unwelcome news and requests, you will need to offer reasonable explanations, incentives, or justifications—and your tone will need to be diplomatic, as in Figure 16.4.

Decide if a direct or indirect approach is best

In each instance, you will have to decide whether to build your case first or get right to the main point. This will depend on the situation: If you are requesting a refund for a faulty printer, for example, you will probably want a direct approach, because the customer service person, who could easily receive hundreds of letters each day, will get to your point quickly. But if you are announcing a 15 percent increase in your client service fees, you might want readers to process your justification first.

The following general guidelines apply to many situations you will face; they also complement the guidelines for each specific type of letter covered in this chapter.

GUIDELINES for Conveying Bad News*

- **Don't procrastinate.** As much as people may dislike the news, they will feel doubly offended after being kept in the dark.
- **Never just blurt it out.** Set a considerate tone by prefacing your bad news with considerate terms such as *I regret*, *We're sorry*, or *Unfortunately*. Instead of flatly proclaiming *Your application has been denied*, give recipients information they can use: *Unfortunately, we are unable to offer you admission to this year's Program. This letter will explain why we made this decision and how you can reapply.* Provide a context that leads into your explanation.
- **Give a clear and honest explanation.** Don't make things worse by fogging or dodging the issue. (See the Guidelines for Persuasion, pages 53–55.)
- **When you need to apologize, do so immediately.** Place your apology right up front. Don't say *An error was made in calculating your construction bill.* Do say *We are sorry we made a mistake in calculating your construction bill.* Don't attempt to camouflage the error. Don't offer excuses or try to shift the blame.
- **Use the passive voice to avoid accusations but not to dodge responsibility.** Instead of *You used the wrong bolts*, say *The wrong bolts were used.*
- **Do not use "you" to blame the reader.** Instead of *You did not send a deposit,* say *We have not received your deposit.*

*Guidelines adapted from Dumont and Lannon 206–21; Timmerman and Harrison 382–87; U.S. Bureau of Land Management.

GUIDELINES *continued*

- **Keep the tone friendly and personal.** Avoid patronizing or impersonal jargon such as *company policy* or *circumstances beyond our control.*
- **Consider the format.** Take plenty of time to write and revise the letter, even by hand, if a personal note is warranted. For exceedingly bad news—say, denial of a promotion—consider sending the letter and following up with a meeting. Never use form letters for important matters, and don't use a formal letter for a relatively minor issue; for example, to notify employees that a company softball game has been cancelled, an email would be sufficient.
- **Consider the medium.** Don't be like one major electronics retailer who used an email list to notify hundreds of workers that they were laid off, effective immediately.

COMMON TYPES OF LETTERS

Among the many types of business letters you may write on the job, the common types are inquiry letters, claim letters, sales letters, and adjustment letters.

Inquiry Letters

Solicited and unsolicited inquiry letters

Inquiry letters ask questions and request a reply. They may be solicited (in response to an advertisement or announcement) or unsolicited (spontaneously written to request some type of information you need). For example, a computer repair technician might write a solicited inquiry to a computer manufacturer that offers free troubleshooting guides for repair specialists. If there has been no such advertised offer, the technician might write an unsolicited inquiry to the same company to ask if any troubleshooting information is available.

In a solicited inquiry, be brief and to the point, and be sure to reference the advertisement or announcement that prompted you to write. In an unsolicited inquiry, you are asking a busy person to spend the time to read your letter, consider your request, collect the information, and write a response. Therefore, keep your request reasonable and state the purpose clearly and concisely. Apologize for any imposition and express your appreciation. Avoid long, involved inquiries that are unlikely to be answered.

Figure 16.5 illustrates an unsolicited letter requesting information. Research consultant Alan Greene is preparing a report on the feasibility of harnessing solar energy for home heating in Alaska. After learning that a nonprofit research group has been experimenting with solar applications, Alan decides to write for details. Notice how he tries to make the respondent's task as easy as possible.

LEVERETT LAND & TIMBER COMPANY, INC.
18 River Rock Road
Leverett, MA 01054

creative land use
quality building materials
architectural construction

January 17, 20XX

Mr. Thomas E. Shaler
19 Clearwater Drive
Amherst, MA 01022

Dear Mr. Shaler:

Thank you for bringing the matter of the ruptured water pipe to my attention. I was pleased to hear from you again these months after our firm completed construction of your living room addition, though I was of course sorry to hear about the water damage not only to the new construction but to the living room as a whole.

← Establishes "you" perspective immediately

Naturally, I understand your desire to receive compensation for your home's damage, especially taking into account how recently the extension was completed. In reviewing the blueprints for the extension, however, I find that the pipes were state-of-the-art and were fully insulated. In fact, it is the practice of Leverett Land & Timber not only to use the best materials available but also to exceed piping insulation requirements by as much as 50 percent. For this reason, we cannot fulfill your request to replace the piping at no cost and repair the water-damaged areas.

← Takes an indirect approach by easing into the bad news, and saving it until the end of second paragraph

Undoubtedly, your insurance will cover the damage. I suspect that the rupture was caused by insufficient heating of the living room area during this unusually cold winter, but homeowner's insurance will cover damages resulting from cold-ruptured pipes 95 percent of the time.

← Speaks clearly and honestly—without blaming the reader

Our policy is to make repairs at a 20 percent discount in situations like this. Though the pipe rupture was not our fault, we feel personally close to every project we do and to every client we serve. Please get in touch if you would like to discuss this matter further. I would also be happy to speak with your insurance company if you wish.

← Remains polite and tactful, despite refusing the request

← Maintains the "you" perspective throughout

Sincerely,

G.A. Jackson

Gerald A. Jackson

FIGURE 16.4 **Bad News Letter** Note the "reader-friendly" tone throughout.

Solar Solutions, Inc.
234 Western Road
Fargo, ND 27116
March 10, 20XX

Rachel Cowans
Director of Energy Systems
The Earth Research Institute
Persham, ME 04619

Dear Ms. Cowans:

States the purpose →

As a Research Consultant at Solar Solutions, I am preparing a report (April 15 deadline) on the feasibility of solar energy for home heating in Arctic regions.

Makes a reasonable and courteous request →

In my research, I encountered references to your group's pioneering work in solar systems. Would you please allow me to benefit from your experience? Your answers to the following questions would be a great help.

1. At this stage of development, do you consider active or passive heating more practical? (Please explain briefly.)

Presents a list of specific questions →

2. Do you expect to surpass the 60 percent limit of heating needs supplied by the active system? If so, at what level of efficiency and how soon?

3. What is the cost of materials for building your active system, per cubic foot of living space?

Leaves space for response to each question →

4. What metal do you use in collectors, to obtain the highest thermal conductivity at the lowest maintenance costs?

Provides complete contact information →

Please record your answers in the spaces provided and return in the enclosed envelope. If an alternative medium is suitable, here is my contact information: phone: 555-986-6578; fax: 555-986-5432; email: agreene@solarsolutions.com

Offers to share findings →

I would be glad to send you a copy of my final document. Thank you for your help.

Sincerely,

Alan Greene

Alan Greene
Research Consultant

FIGURE 16.5 **An Unsolicited Inquiry Letter** This type of letter must be reader-friendly to increase the chance of getting a reply.

If your questions are too numerous or complex to be answered in print, you might alternately request an interview (assuming the respondent is nearby), as in Figure 16.6.

82 Mountain Street
New Bedford, MA 02720
March 8, 20XX

The Honorable Roger R. Grimes
Massachusetts House of Representatives
Boston, MA 02202

Dear Representative Grimes:

As a University of Massachusetts technical writing student, I am preparing a report evaluating the EPA's progress in removing PCB contaminants from New Bedford Harbor.

In my research, I encounter your name repeatedly. Your dedicated work has raised public awareness, and I am hoping to benefit from your knowledge. ← Gets right to the point of the letter

I was surprised to learn that, although this contamination is considered the most extensive anywhere, the EPA has not moved beyond conducting studies. My own study questions the need for such extensive data gathering. Your opinion, as I can ascertain from the news media, is that the EPA is definitely moving too slowly. ← Describes related research

The EPA refutes that argument by asserting they simply do not yet have the information necessary to begin a clean-up operation. ← Summarizes the ongoing controversy

As a New Bedford resident, I am very interested in your opinions on this issue. Could you possibly find time to grant me an interview? With your permission, I will phone your office in a few days to ask about arranging an appointment. ← Politely requests an interview

I would deeply appreciate your assistance and will gladly send you a copy of my completed report. ← Offers to share findings

Very truly yours,

Karen P. Granger

Karen P. Granger

FIGURE 16.6 Request for an Informative Interview Be as straightforward and polite as possible in order to get the reader interested in interviewing you.

GUIDELINES for Inquiry Letters

- **Don't wait until the last minute.** Provide ample time for a response.
- **Whenever possible, write to a specific person.** If you need the name, call the organization and ask to whom you should address your inquiry.
- **Do your homework to ask the right questions.** A vague request such as "Please send me your data on . . ." is likely to be ignored. Don't ask questions for which the answers are readily available elsewhere.
- **Explain who you are and how the information will be used.** If you appear to be from a competing company, your request will likely be ignored. But even in other situations, you will need to explain how you plan to use the requested data.
- **Write specific questions that are easy to understand and answer.** If you have multiple questions, put them in a numbered list to increase your chances of getting all the information you want. Consider leaving space for responses below each question.
- **Provide contact information.** If you can be reached via phone, email, and fax, provide all your numbers/addresses.
- **Include a stamped, self-addressed envelope.** This courteous gesture will increase the likelihood of a response.
- **Say thank you and offer to follow up.** Offer to send a copy of the document in which you plan to use the information, if appropriate.

Claim Letters

Routine and arguable claim letters

In the workplace, things do not always run smoothly. Sometimes people make mistakes, systems break down, or companies make promises that can't be kept. Claim (or complaint) letters request adjustments for defective goods or poor services, or they complain about unfair treatment or something similar. Such letters fall into two categories: *routine claims* and *arguable claims*. Each calls for a different approach. Routine claims typically take a direct approach because the customer's claim is not debatable. Arguable claims present more of a persuasive challenge because they convey unwelcome news and are open to interpretation; arguable claims, therefore, typically take an indirect approach.

Figure 16.7 shows a routine claim letter. Writer Jeffrey Ryder does not ask whether the firm will honor his claim; he assumes that it will, and asks directly how to return his defective skis for repair. Notice that, in place of a salutation, an attention line directs the claim to the appropriate department, while a subject line (and its reemphasis in the first sentence) makes clear the nature of the claim.

Ryder's Ski Shop
Box 2641-A
Pocatello, ID 83201
April 13, 20XX

Star Ski Manufacturing Company
P.O. Box 3049
St. Paul, MN 55165

Attention: Consumer Affairs Department
Subject: Delaminated Skis

This winter, four of the pairs of Tornado skis I purchased for rental at my ski shop began to delaminate. I want to take advantage of your lifetime guarantee to have them relaminated. ← States problem and action desired

I purchased the skis via your St. Paul Sales Representative in November 1989. Although I no longer have the sales slip, the registration numbers are P9906, P9961, P9965, and P9978. ← Provides details

I'm aware that you no longer make metal skis, but as I recall, your lifetime guarantee on the skis I bought was a major selling point. Only your company and one other were backing their skis so strongly. ← Explains basis for claim

Please let me know how to go about returning my delaminated skis for repair. ← Courteously states desired action

Yours truly,

Jeffrey Ryder

Jeffrey Ryder

FIGURE 16.7 A Routine Claim Letter This type of claim letter is not debatable, but still maintains a courteous tone.

Figure 16.8 shows an arguable claim letter. Because the reply may not necessarily be in her favor, writer Sandra Alvarez uses a tactful and reasonable tone and an indirect approach to present her argument. Although she is courteous, she is also somewhat forceful, to reflect her insistence on an acceptable adjustment. For example, the attention line creates an immediate businesslike tone.

Office Systems, Inc.
657 High Street
Tulsa, OK 74120

Fax (302) 655-5551 Phone (302) 655-5550 Email osys@sys.com

January 23, 20XX

Consumer Affairs Department
Hightone Office Supplies
93 Cattle Drive
Houston, TX 77028

ATTENTION: Ms. Dionne Dubree

Establishes early agreement → Your company has an established reputation as a reliable wholesaler of office supplies. For eight years we have counted on that reliability, but a recent episode has left us annoyed and disappointed.

On January 29, we ordered 5 cartons of 700 MB "hp" CDs (#A74-866) and 13 cartons of Epson MX 70/80 black cartridges (#A19-556).

Presents facts to support claim → On February 5, the order arrived. But instead of the 700 MB "hp" CDs ordered, we received 650 MB Everlast CDs. And the Epson cartridges were blue, not the black we had ordered. We returned the order the same day.

Offers more support → Also on the 5th, we called John Fitzsimmons at your company to explain our problem. He promised delivery of a corrected order by the 12th. Finally, on the 22nd, we did receive an order —the original incorrect one—with a note claiming that the packages had been water damaged while in our possession.

Includes all relevant information → Our warehouse manager insists the packages were in perfect condition when he released them to the shipper. Because we had the packages only five hours and had no

Sticks to the facts → rain on the 5th, we are certain the damage did not occur here.

Responsibility for damages therefore rests with either the shipper or your warehouse staff. What bothers us is our outstanding bill from Hightone ($2,049.50) for the faulty

Requests a specific adjustment → shipment. We insist that the bill be canceled and that we receive a corrected statement. Until this misunderstanding, our transactions with your company were excellent. We hope they can be again.

Stipulates a reasonable response time → We would appreciate having this matter resolved before the end of this month.

Yours truly,

Sandra Alvarez

Sandra Alvarez
Manager, Accounting

FIGURE 16.8 **An Arguable Claim Letter** This claim is debatable—be sure to state your claim thoroughly and professionally.

GUIDELINES for Claim Letters

Routine claim letters

- **Use a direct approach.** Describe the request or problem; explain the problem; close courteously, restating the action you request.
- **Be polite and reasonable.** Your goal is not to sound off but to achieve results: a refund, a replacement, or an apology. Press your claim objectively yet firmly by explaining it clearly and by stipulating the reasonable action that will satisfy you. Do not insult the reader or revile the company.
- **Provide enough detail to clarify the basis for your claim.** Explain the specific defect. Identify the faulty item precisely, giving serial and model numbers, and date and place of purchase.
- **Conclude by expressing goodwill and confidence in the company's integrity.** Do not make threats or create animosity.

Arguable claim letters

- **Use an indirect approach.** People are more likely to respond favorably *after* reading your explanation. Begin with a neutral statement both parties can agree to—but that also serves as the basis for your request.
- **Once you've established agreement, explain and support your claim.** Include enough information for a fair evaluation: date and place of purchase, order number, dates of previous letters or calls, and background.
- **Conclude by requesting a specific action.** Be polite but assertive in phrasing your request.

Sales Letters

Purpose and tone of sales letters

Sales letters are written to persuade a current or potential customer to buy a company's product or try its services. Because people are bombarded by sales messages—in magazines, on billboards, on television, on the Internet—your letter must be genuinely persuasive and must get to the point quickly. Engage the reader immediately with an attention-grabbing statement or an intriguing question. Describe the product or service you offer, and explain its appeal. Conclude by requesting immediate action.

In the letter in Figure 16.9, restaurant owner Jimmy Lekkas opens with an attention-grabbing question that is hard to ignore and has universal appeal: good food, for free, right in the neighborhood. He then makes his case by explaining the history of his restaurant (which provides immediate credibility) and offering vivid descriptions of the food. He closes by asking readers to take action by a specific date.

Jimmy's Greek Kitchen
24-52 28th Street
Astoria, NY 11102
Phone: (555) 274-5672
Fax: (555) 274-5671
Email: Jimmysgreek@comcast.net
Web site: http://www.jimmysgreekkitchen.com

July 16, 20XX

Adriana Nikolaidis
26-22 30th Street #5
Astoria, NY 11102

Dear Ms. Nikolaidis:

Opens with an attention-grabbing question →

Are you in the mood to sample the best Greek food in the neighborhood absolutely free of charge? We at the newly opened Jimmy's Greek Kitchen would like to say "Thank you for having us in your neighborhood" by inviting you to sample a variety of our authentic Greek specialties.

Describes the long history and appeal of the restaurant →

If you've heard of or visited the famous Jimmy's in Chicago, you know that our fare has been pleasing Chicago diners for over 40 years. At last, we have opened a companion restaurant in Astoria, and are proud to offer the same appetizers, entrees, and desserts, prepared to perfection. In fact, I trained our Astoria chef myself.

Maintains appeal by describing the menu →

Ranging from charbroiled meats and grilled seafoods to vegetarian specialties and Greek favorites like pastitsio and moussaka, Jimmy's is truly the best in town.

Ends by asking the reader to take action →

Please have a look at the enclosed menu to see our full range of tasty foods. Please take advantage of this special offer while it lasts. Until August 31, just bring this letter to Jimmy's and dinner is on the house. Choose any appetizer, entree, side order, beverage, and dessert on the menu—all free of charge. We hope that you will not only enjoy the dining experience but will tell others and come back to see us often.

Thank you,

Jimmy Lekkas

Jimmy Lekkas

FIGURE 16.9 A Sales Letter Sales letters must grab immediate attention, maintain interest, and evoke reader action.

GUIDELINES for Sales Letters

- **Begin with a question or other attention-grabbing statement.** Induce the recipient to take notice.
- **Get to the point.** People resist reading long opening passages, especially if the message is unsolicited.
- **Spell out the benefits for the recipients.** Answer this implied question from the reader: "What do I stand to gain from this?"
- **Persuade with facts and with appeals to the senses.** Facts (such as the history of your company) appeal to logic. Graphic descriptions (such as the colors of your new cars or the types of food you offer) appeal to a different part of the brain—the emotions. Use both.
- **Tell the truth.** Despite your desire to sell something, it is unethical to lie, distort, exaggerate, or underestimate to make the sale.
- **Close by asking readers to take action.** Either ask for some reasonable action (such as "go to our Web site"), or offer an incentive (such as a free sample) to encourage follow-up.

Adjustment Letters

Adjustment letters are written in response to a claim letter from a customer. Even though most people never make formal complaints or follow up on warranties or product guarantees, companies generally will make a requested adjustment that seems reasonable.

Positive adjustment letters

Rather than quibbling over questionable claims, companies usually honor the request and show how much they appreciate the customer, as in Figure 16.10. In that example, writer Jane Duval apologizes graciously for a mistake. She omits an explanation because the error is obvious: Someone sent the wrong software. Once the reader has the information and apology, Duval shifts attention to a positive feature: the gift certificate. Note the "you" perspective, the friendly tone, and the incentive for further business.

Negative adjustment letters

Of course, if a claim is unreasonable or unjustified, the recipient usually will refuse the request. In refusing to grant a refund for a 10-speed bicycle, Company representative Anna Jenkins needs to maintain a delicate balance (Figure 16.11). On the one hand, she must explain why she cannot grant the customer's request; on the other hand, she must be diplomatic in how she asserts that the customer is mistaken. Although Mrs. Gower may not be pleased by the explanation, it is thorough, reasonable, and courteous.

421 Fairview Road
Tulsa, OK 74321

May 2, 20XX

Mr. James Morris
P.O. Box 176
Little Rock, AR 54701

Dear Mr. Morris:

Apologizes immediately →

Your software should arrive by May 15. Sorry for the mixup. We don't make a practice of sending Apple software to PC owners, but we do slip up once in a while.

Offers compensation →

In appreciation for your patience and understanding, I've enclosed a $50 gift certificate. You can give it to a friend or apply it toward your next order. If you order by phone, just give the certificate number, and the operator will credit your account.

Looks toward the future →

Keep your certificate handy because you will be getting our new catalog soon. It features 15 new business and utility programs that you might find useful.

Sincerely,

Jane Duval

Jane Duval
Sales Manager

Encl. Gift Certificate

FIGURE 16.10 **A Positive Adjustment Letter** Positive responses to claims ensure customer loyalty.

People Power, Inc.

101 Salem Street, Springfield, Illinois 32456

March 8, 20XX

Mrs. Alma Gower
32 Wood Street
Lewiston, IL 32432

Dear Mrs. Gower:

When we advertise the Windspirit as the toughest, most durable ten-speed, we stress it's a racing or cruising bike built to withstand the long, grueling miles of intense competition. The bike is built of the strongest, yet lightest alloys available, and each part is calibrated to within 1/1000 of an inch. That's why we guarantee the Windspirit against defects resulting from the strain of competitive racing.

← Introduction starts off with the facts

The Windspirit, though, is not built to withstand the impact of ramp jumps such as those attempted by your son. The rims and front fork would have to be made from a much thicker gauge alloy, thereby increasing weight and decreasing speed. Since we build racing bikes, such a compromise is unacceptable.

← Writer doesn't accuse; she explains in a friendly tone

To ensure that buyers are familiar with the Windspirit's limits, in the owner's manual we stress that the bike should be carried over curbings and similar drops because even an eight-inch drop could damage the front rim. Damage from such drops is not considered normal wear and so is not covered by our guarantee.

← Refusal is professional, direct, and reasonable

Since your son appears to be more interested in a bike capable of withstanding the impact of high jumps, you could recoup a large part of the Windspirit's price by advertising it in your local newspaper. Many novice racers would welcome the chance to buy one at a reduced price. Or, if you prefer having it repaired, you could take it to Jamie's Bike Shop, the dealer closest to you.

← Closing is helpful

Yours truly,

Anna Jenkins

Anna Jenkins
Manager, Customer Services

FIGURE 16.11 A Negative Adjustment Letter Negative responses to claims say "no" diplomatically but emphatically.

GUIDELINES for Adjustment Letters

Granting Adjustments

- **Begin with the good news.** A sincere apology helps rebuild customers' confidence.
- **Explain what went wrong and how the problem will be corrected.** Without an honest explanation, you leave the impression that such problems are common or beyond your control.
- **Never blame employees as scapegoats.** To blame someone in the firm reflects poorly on the firm itself.
- **Do not promise that the problem never will recur.** Mishaps are inevitable.
- **End on a positive note.** Focus on the solution, not the problem.

Refusing Adjustments

- **Use an indirect organizational plan.** Explain diplomatically and clearly why you are refusing the request. Your goal is to convince the reader that your refusal results from a thorough analysis of the situation.
- **Be sure the refusal is unambiguous.** Don't create unrealistic expectations by using evasive language.
- **Avoid a patronizing or accusing tone.** Use the passive voice so as not to accuse the claimant, but do not hide behind the passive voice (see page 215).
- **Close courteously and positively.** Offer an alternative or compromise, when it is feasible to do so.

CHECKLIST: Letters

(Numbers in parentheses refer to the first page of discussion.)

Content

- ☐ Does the situation call for a formal letter rather than a memo or email? (349)
- ☐ Is the letter addressed to the correct and specifically named person? (351)
- ☐ Have you determined the position or title of your recipient? (351)
- ☐ Does the letter contain all the standard parts? (350)
- ☐ Does the letter have all needed specialized parts? (353)
- ☐ Is the letter's main point clearly stated? (351)
- ☐ Is all the necessary information included? (351)

Arrangement

- ☐ Does the introduction engage the reader and preview the body section? (351)
- ☐ Is the direct or indirect approach used appropriately? (359)
- ☐ Does the conclusion encourage the reader to act? (351)
- ☐ Is the format block? (355)

Style

- ☐ Does the letter convey a "you" perspective throughout? (357)
- ☐ Is the letter in plain English (free of letterese)? (358)
- ☐ Is the tone professional, polite, and appropriately formal? (357)
- ☐ Is the letter designed for a tasteful, conservative look? (355)
- ☐ Is the style clear, concise, fluent, exact, and likable? (211)
- ☐ Have you proofread with extreme care? (118)

Projects

GENERAL

1. Bring to class a copy of a business letter addressed to you or a friend. Compare letters. Choose the most and least effective.
2. Write and mail an unsolicited letter of inquiry about the topic you are investigating for an analytical report or research assignment. In your letter you might request brochures, pamphlets, or other informative literature, or you might ask specific questions. Submit a copy of your letter, and the response, to your instructor.
3. **a.** As a student in a state college, you learn that your governor and legislature have cut next year's operating budget for all state colleges by 20 percent. This cut will cause the firing of young and popular faculty members; drastically reduce admissions, financial aid, and new programs; and wreck college morale. Write a claim letter to your governor or representative, expressing your strong disapproval and justifying a major adjustment in the proposed budget.

   b. Write a claim letter to a politician about some issue affecting your school or community.

   c. Write a claim letter to an appropriate school official to recommend action on a campus problem.
4. Write a claim letter about a problem you've had with goods or services. State your case clearly and objectively, and request a specific adjustment.
5. *For Class Discussion:* Under what circumstances might it be acceptable to contact a potential inquiry respondent by email? When should you just leave the person alone?
6. The following sentences need to be overhauled before being included in a letter. Identify the weakness in each statement, and revise as needed. For example, you would revise the accusatory *You were not very clear* to *We did not understand your message.*

   a. I need all the information you have about methane-powered engines.

   b. You morons have sent me the wrong software!

c. It is imperative that you let me know of your decision by January 15.

d. I have become cognizant of your experiments and wish to ask your advice about the following procedure.

e. You will find the following instructions easy enough for an ape to follow.

f. As per your request I am sending the country map.

g. I am in hopes that you will call soon.

h. We beg to differ with your interpretation of this leasing clause.

TEAM

Working in groups, respond to the following scenario. Appoint one group member to present the letter in class.

> As director of Consumer Affairs, you've received an adjustment request from Brian Maxwell. Two years ago, he bought a pair of top-of-the-line Gannon speakers. Both speakers, he claims, are badly distorting bass sounds, and he states that his local dealer refuses to honor the three-year warranty. After checking, you find that the dealer refused because someone had obviously tampered with the speakers. Two lead wires had been respliced; one of the booster magnets was missing; and the top insulation also was missing from one of the speaker cabinets. Your warranty specifically states that if speakers are removed from the cabinet or subjected to tampering in any way, the warranty is void. You must refuse the adjustment; however, because Maxwell bought the speakers from a factory-authorized dealer, he is entitled to a 30 percent discount on repairs. Write the refusal, offering this alternative. His address: 691 Concord Street, Biloxi, MS 71690.

DIGITAL AND SOCIAL MEDIA

Word-processing programs such as *Microsoft Word* offer series of templates for writing letters. (Templates are preformatted layouts that can be used to create résumés, memos, letters, and other documents.) Templates can help you get started with the writing. Templates can also be a problem, however, because instead of thinking for yourself about the audience, purpose, and appropriate organizational pattern and language usage, you may end up letting the template do the thinking. Look at the various templates available in your word-processing program and on the Internet, and make a list of ways in which the template may or may not work for your purposes.

GLOBAL

Interview a person whose work takes him or her to one or more countries outside the United States. Ask that person to describe the way letters are used for international communication, and whether any special issues involving grammar, forms of address, direct or indirect organizational patterns, or other features make letter writing different when addressing international audiences.

17 Résumés and Other Job-Search Materials

"My company's recruiting and hiring team reviews dozens of entry-level job applications weekly. One main quality we look for in any candidate—regardless of technical qualifications—is that person's attention to detail. The first indication of this, of course, appears in the résumé and application letter. Whether these materials are submitted on paper or online, we expect them to be nothing less than professional in their content and presentation. Being a newly minted graduate is no excuse for a hastily contrived application."

—Carol Jiminez, Personnel Manager, large civil engineering firm

LEARNING OBJECTIVES FOR THIS CHAPTER

- Identify your personal assets as a job applicant
- Search for a job systematically
- Create an effective print résumé
- Adapt your print résumé for scanning, emailing, or posting online
- Write an effective application letter
- Prepare a dossier, portfolio, or webfolio
- Succeed in a job interview

In today's job market, many applicants compete for few openings. Whether you are applying for your first professional job or changing careers, you need to market your skills effectively. At each stage of the application process, you must stand out among the competition.

ASSESSING YOUR SKILLS AND APTITUDES

Identify your assets

Begin your job search by assessing those qualities and skills you can offer a potential employer:

- Do I communicate well, and am I also a good listener?
- Do I work well in groups and with people from different backgrounds?
- Do I have experience or aptitude for a leadership role?
- Can I solve problems and get things done?
- Can I perform well under pressure?
- Can I work independently, with minimal supervision?
- Do I have any special skills (public speaking, working with people, computer or other technical skills, aptitude with words, analytical skills, second or third languages, artistic/musical talent, mathematical aptitude)?
- Do I have any hobbies that could improve my job prospects?
- Would I prefer to work at a large company or a small one, or at a for-profit or a nonprofit organization?
- Do I like to travel, or would I prefer working in a single location?

Besides helping you focus your job search, your answers to these questions will come in handy when you write your résumé and prepare for job interviews.

RESEARCHING THE JOB MARKET

Search within a reasonable range, focusing on those fields that interest you most and fit you best.

Plan Your Strategy

Don't just dive in; work step by step

Begin your research well in advance of the time you need to have a job lined up. The question "Where do I start?" can be daunting: "Do I go to a career counselor first?" "Should I talk with friends and family members?" "Do I go straight to the Help Wanted section—in print or online?" "Which Web sites are the best?" Seemingly endless sources of information are available to job seekers. Proceed in a step-by-step, logical way—rather than going straight to the Internet and trying to navigate random Web sites.

Focus Your Search

Consult industry-specific resources

Before you apply for specific jobs, learn about the industry: Consult relevant books, magazines, journals, and Web sites. Join a professional group related to your industry and either attend meetings or interact online through sponsored chat groups. Identify the key companies and research those companies. Try to arrange an informational interview with a company in your field. Even busy professionals are often willing to speak with interested job seekers who are not applying for a specific job. These people can offer general advice about the industry as a whole as well as specific information about their own company.

Explore Online Resources

Look for specific job postings

Use nationwide job portals (such as *Monster.com, Careerbuilder.com*, and *SnagAJob.com*) to find jobs across the country or specific to your location; consult the online Help Wanted sections of your local newspapers' Web sites; locate industry-specific jobs on professional organization Web sites; or find jobs advertised only on the human resources Web sites of particular companies.

Learn to Network

The shortest route to a good job may be the *human connection*. Consider the following suggestions for exploring and establishing helpful contacts—in person as well as online.

Talk with helpful people

Networking in Person. Once you've narrowed choices of occupations, go to your campus job placement office to meet with a career counselor and to interview with recruiters who visit campus. Speak with faculty and others in the field. Network with acquaintances and family friends who may have other contacts.

Seek related experience

When it comes to landing a job, experience can count more than grades. Find a summer job or internship in your field or do related volunteer work. (Google for sites that list internship and volunteer opportunities.) Consider registering with agencies that provide temporary staffing. Even the most humble and temporary job offers the chance to make contacts and discover opportunities.

Explore social networking

Networking Online. In today's world of many applicants and fewer jobs, up-to-the-minute information sharing is essential. Social networking sites can help you stay connected, discover job openings, and advertise yourself. The most popular professional networking site is LinkedIn. On this and similar sites (such as Ryze or Spoke), you can keep your profile—including recent work experience, résumé, and references—up-to-date. The site can help connect you with former colleagues and classmates; these people are often your best bet for hearing about the most recent openings. Don't be shy about contacting people you don't know first-hand but to whom you are connected through a former coworker or classmate. Keep in mind that these are professional sites; make sure that anything you post is something you would want an employer to see.

How employers use online social networks

Many of us tend to think of social media such as Facebook and Twitter as sites for personal use, but the workplace is rapidly embracing such media for business purposes. Many companies maintain a Facebook page, and employers routinely check out the Facebook entries of potential employees. Twitter is another tool for employment-related communication. For example, companies such as Zappos (a popular online shoe store) are using Twitter to promote the company and recruit new employees. Other companies use Twitter to post job positions and to attract potential new hires (Doyle 2010). This advertisement for a resort management position with Liberty International (Figure 17.1) could be posted on a number of sites (Facebook, Twitter, LinkedIn) to increase coverage.

FIGURE 17.1 Electronic Job Posting Available on Twitter and LinkedIn
Employers know they can reach thousands of people this way.

NOTE *Always be discriminating about what you post on your Facebook and MySpace pages and other publicly available social networks.*

Using Twitter for job searching

When using Twitter, you can attract employer interest by creating a catchy user name (say "joanlandscapearchitect") and a brief profile that announces the skills you offer. Once you have set up an account (at Twitter.com), search by name for the companies that interest you. Sign up for instant updates via message feeds from those companies (as well as from alumni and friends who work in your field). Follow work-related conversations and contribute via your own tweets to establish your active presence. Provide a link to your own Web site or résumé. Visit related sites that match recruiters and candidates (say, TweetMyJobs.com) or sites that offer relevant job postings (say, TwitterJobSearch.com).

For more on workplace uses of social networks, see Chapter 26.

NOTE *Although online job listings and résumé postings have provided new tools for job seekers, today's job searches require the same basic approach and communication skills that people have relied on for decades.*

RÉSUMÉS

Essentially an applicant's personal advertisement for employment, a résumé gives an employer an instant overview. In fact, employers initially spend only 15 to 45 seconds looking at a résumé; during this scan, they are looking for a persuasive answer to the essential question: "What can you do for us?"

What employers expect in a résumé

Employers are impressed by a résumé that looks good, reads easily, appears honest, and provides only the relevant information an employer needs in order to determine whether the applicant should be interviewed. Résumés that are mechanically flawed, cluttered, sketchy, hard to follow, or seemingly dishonest simply get discarded.

Parts of a Résumé

What to include—and not include—in a résumé

Résumés contain these standard parts: contact information, career objectives, education, work experience, personal data and interests, and references. A résumé is not the place for such items as your desired salary and benefits or your requirements for time off. Also omit your photograph as well as information that employers are not allowed to legally request (such as race, age, or marital status).

As you read through this section, refer to Figure 17.2 (page 386), which includes all the required parts of a résumé.

Contact Information. Tell prospective employers how to reach you. If you are between addresses, provide both addresses and check each contact point regularly.

Be sure that your email address and phone number are accurate. If you use an answering machine or voice mail, record an outgoing message that sounds friendly and professional. If you have your own Web site (professional, not personal), include the Web address. Remember that employers may access your Facebook or MySpace pages, so be sure to keep those pages professional in tone and content.

Career Objectives. Spell out the kind of job you want. Avoid vague statements such as "A position in which I can apply my education and experience." Be specific: "An intensive-care nursing position in a teaching hospital, with the eventual goal of supervising and instructing." Tailor your career objective statement as you apply for different jobs, in order to match yourself with each position. State your immediate and long-range goals, including any plans to continue your education. If the company has branches, include *Willing to relocate.*

One hiring officer for a major computer firm offers this advice: "A statement should show that you know the type of work the company does and the type of position it needs to fill" (Beamon, qtd. in Crosby, *Résumés* 3).

NOTE *Below career objectives, you might insert a summary of qualifications. This section is vital in a computer-scannable résumé (Figure 17.4), but even in a conventional résumé, a "Qualifications" section can highlight your strengths. Make the summary specific and concrete: replace "proven leadership" with "team and project management," "special-event planning," or "instructor-led training"; replace "persuasive communicator" with "fundraising," "publicity campaigns," "environmental/ public-interest advocacy," or "door-to-door canvassing." In short, allow the reader to* ***visualize*** *your activities.*

Education. Begin with your most recent schooling and work backward. Include the name of the school, degree completed, year completed, and your major and minor. Omit high school, unless the high school's prestige or your achievements there warrant its inclusion. List courses that have directly prepared you for the job you seek. If your class rank or grade point average is favorable, list it. Include specialized training during military service. If you finance your education by working, say so, indicating the percentage of your contribution.

Work Experience. If your experience relates to the job, list it before your education. List your most recent job and then earlier jobs. Include employers' names and dates of employment. Indicate whether a job was full-time, part-time (hours weekly), or seasonal. Describe your exact duties for each job, indicating promotions. If it is to your advantage, state why you left each job. Include military experience and relevant volunteer work. If you lack paid experience, emphasize your education, including internships and special projects.

Personal Data and Interests. List any awards, skills, activities, and interests that are *relevant* to the given position, such as memberships in professional organizations, demonstrations of leadership, languages, special skills, and hobbies that may be of interest to the employer.

References. List three to five people who have agreed to provide strong assessments of your qualifications and who can speak on your behalf. Never list as references people who haven't first given you express permission. Your references should not be family members or non-work-related friends; instead, list former employers, professors, and community figures who know you well. If saving space is important, simply state at the end of your résumé, "References available upon request," to help keep the résumé to one page. But if the résumé already takes up more than one page, you probably should include your references. If you don't list references, prepare a separate reference sheet that you can provide on request. Include each person's job title, company address, and contact information.

> **NOTE** *Under some circumstances you may—if you wish—waive the right to examine your references. Some applicants, especially those applying to professional schools, as in medicine and law, waive this right in concession to a general feeling that a letter writer who is assured of confidentiality is more likely to provide a balanced, objective, and reliable assessment of a candidate. Before you decide, seek the advice of your major adviser or a career counselor.*

Portfolios. To illustrate your skills and experience in areas such as marketing, engineering, or other fields that generate actual documents or visual designs, assemble a portfolio showing samples of your work. If you do have a portfolio, indicate this on your résumé, followed by "Available on request," as in Figure 17.4. (See the Guidelines for preparing a portfolio, on page 400.)

Résumés from a Template

Programs such as *Microsoft Word* provide electronic templates that can be filled in with an individual's own personal data. Such programs organize the information keyed into the template, and the organization can be easily changed as needed.

While templates can help you organize your résumé, you still need to be aware of which organizational pattern is most appropriate.

Organizing Your Résumé

Organize your résumé to convey the strongest impression of your qualifications, skills, and experience. A résumé like the one in Figure 17.2 is known as a *reverse chronological résumé*, listing the most recent school and job first. If you have limited experience or education, gaps in your work history (e.g., due to illness, raising children), or if you have frequently switched career paths, create a *functional résumé* (Figure 17.3) to highlight skills relevant to a particular job.

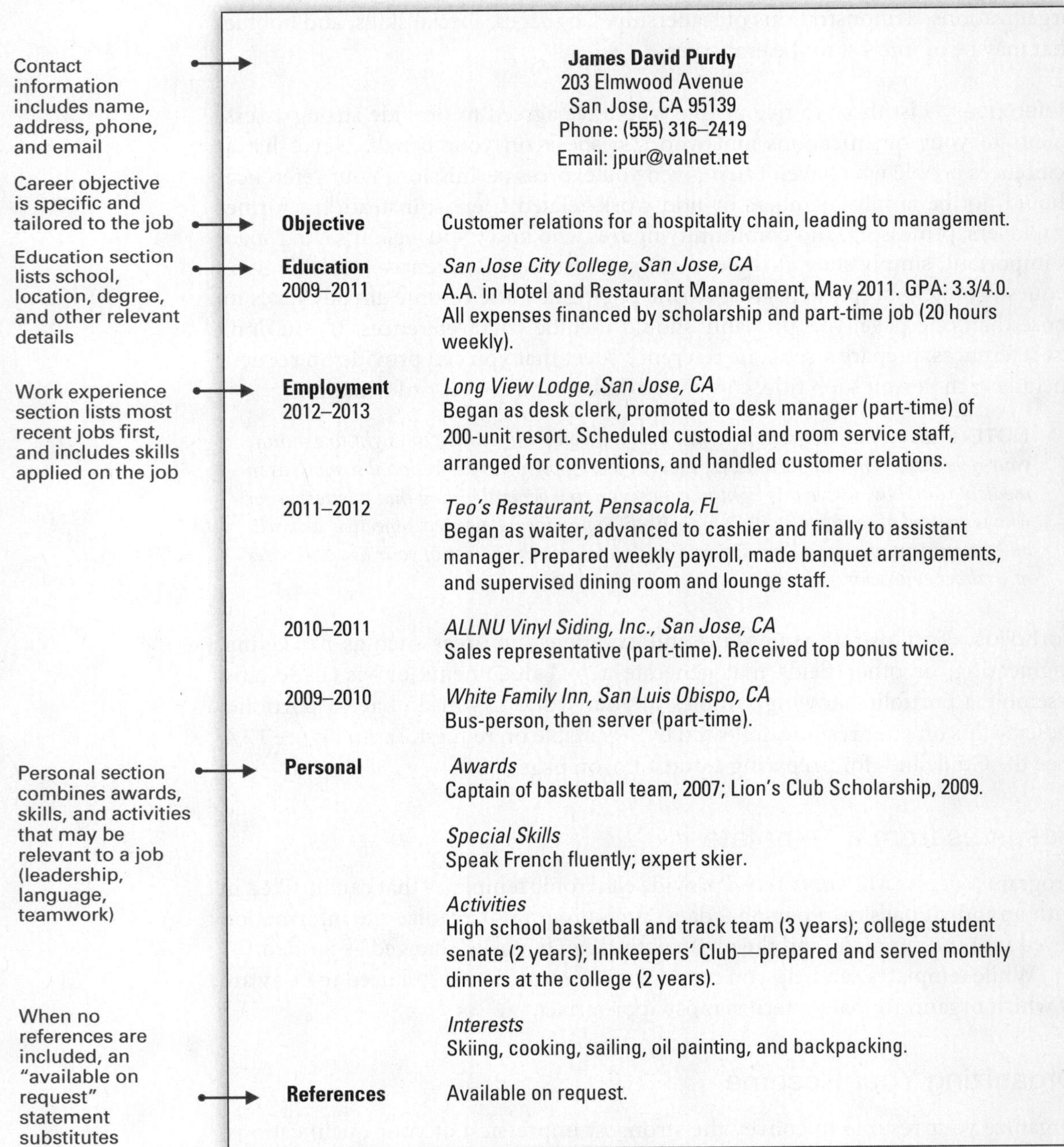

Contact information includes name, address, phone, and email
Career objective is specific and tailored to the job
Education section lists school, location, degree, and other relevant details
Work experience section lists most recent jobs first, and includes skills applied on the job
Personal section combines awards, skills, and activities that may be relevant to a job (leadership, language, teamwork)
When no references are included, an "available on request" statement substitutes
James David Purdy
203 Elmwood Avenue
San Jose, CA 95139
Phone: (555) 316–2419
Email: jpur@valnet.net
Objective
Customer relations for a hospitality chain, leading to management.
Education
2009–2011
San Jose City College, San Jose, CA
A.A. in Hotel and Restaurant Management, May 2011. GPA: 3.3/4.0.
All expenses financed by scholarship and part-time job (20 hours weekly).
Employment
2012–2013
Long View Lodge, San Jose, CA
Began as desk clerk, promoted to desk manager (part-time) of 200-unit resort. Scheduled custodial and room service staff, arranged for conventions, and handled customer relations.
2011–2012
Teo's Restaurant, Pensacola, FL
Began as waiter, advanced to cashier and finally to assistant manager. Prepared weekly payroll, made banquet arrangements, and supervised dining room and lounge staff.
2010–2011
ALLNU Vinyl Siding, Inc., San Jose, CA
Sales representative (part-time). Received top bonus twice.
2009–2010
White Family Inn, San Luis Obispo, CA
Bus-person, then server (part-time).
Personal
Awards
Captain of basketball team, 2007; Lion's Club Scholarship, 2009.
Special Skills
Speak French fluently; expert skier.
Activities
High school basketball and track team (3 years); college student senate (2 years); Innkeepers' Club—prepared and served monthly dinners at the college (2 years).
Interests
Skiing, cooking, sailing, oil painting, and backpacking.
References
Available on request.

FIGURE 17.2 A Reverse Chronological Résumé Use this format to show a clear pattern of job experience.

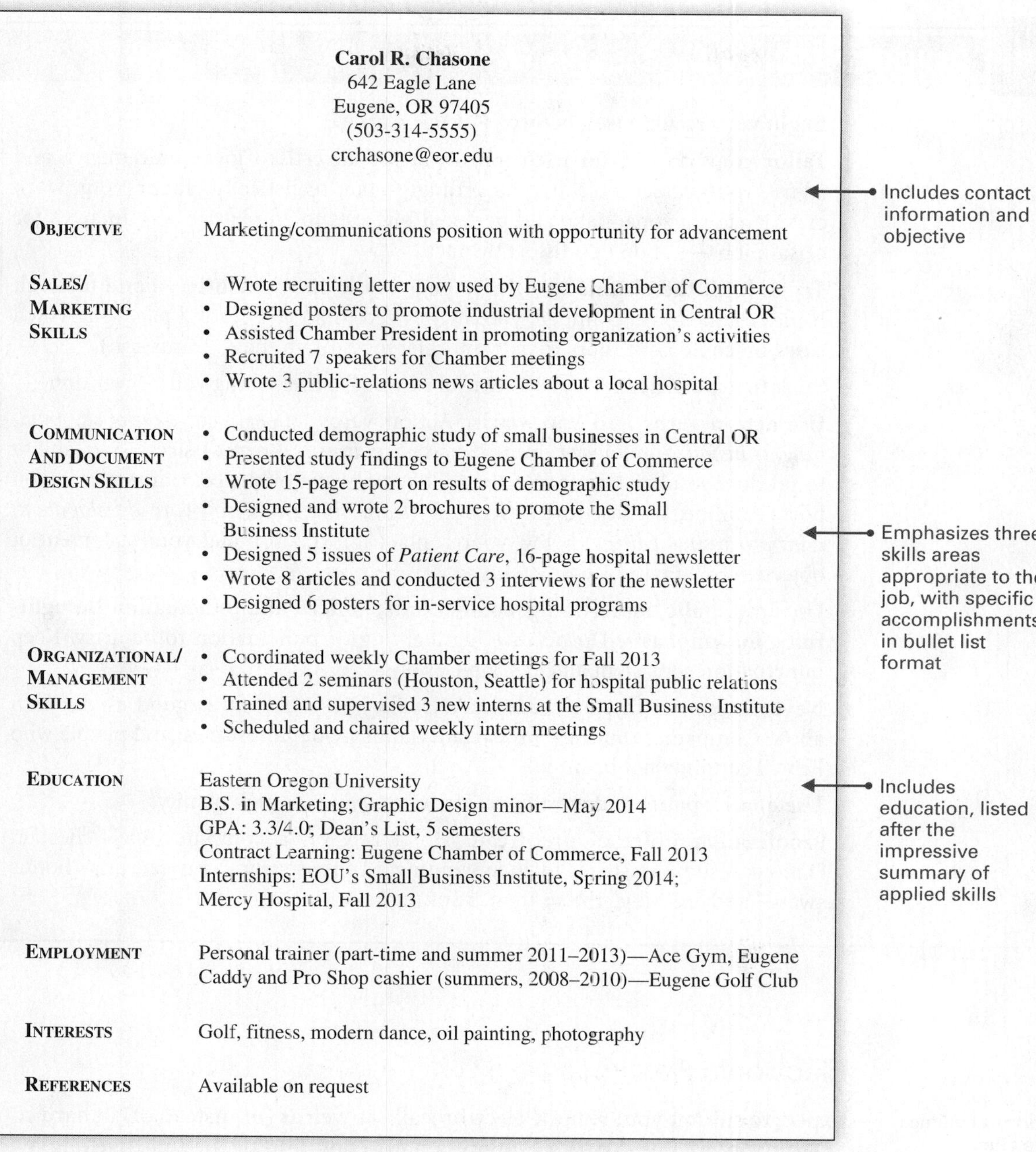

Carol R. Chasone
642 Eagle Lane
Eugene, OR 97405
(503-314-5555)
crchasone@eor.edu

OBJECTIVE Marketing/communications position with opportunity for advancement

SALES/ MARKETING SKILLS
- Wrote recruiting letter now used by Eugene Chamber of Commerce
- Designed posters to promote industrial development in Central OR
- Assisted Chamber President in promoting organization's activities
- Recruited 7 speakers for Chamber meetings
- Wrote 3 public-relations news articles about a local hospital

COMMUNICATION AND DOCUMENT DESIGN SKILLS
- Conducted demographic study of small businesses in Central OR
- Presented study findings to Eugene Chamber of Commerce
- Wrote 15-page report on results of demographic study
- Designed and wrote 2 brochures to promote the Small Business Institute
- Designed 5 issues of *Patient Care*, 16-page hospital newsletter
- Wrote 8 articles and conducted 3 interviews for the newsletter
- Designed 6 posters for in-service hospital programs

ORGANIZATIONAL/ MANAGEMENT SKILLS
- Coordinated weekly Chamber meetings for Fall 2013
- Attended 2 seminars (Houston, Seattle) for hospital public relations
- Trained and supervised 3 new interns at the Small Business Institute
- Scheduled and chaired weekly intern meetings

EDUCATION
Eastern Oregon University
B.S. in Marketing; Graphic Design minor—May 2014
GPA: 3.3/4.0; Dean's List, 5 semesters
Contract Learning: Eugene Chamber of Commerce, Fall 2013
Internships: EOU's Small Business Institute, Spring 2014;
Mercy Hospital, Fall 2013

EMPLOYMENT
Personal trainer (part-time and summer 2011–2013)—Ace Gym, Eugene
Caddy and Pro Shop cashier (summers, 2008–2010)—Eugene Golf Club

INTERESTS Golf, fitness, modern dance, oil painting, photography

REFERENCES Available on request

Includes contact information and objective
Emphasizes three skills areas appropriate to the job, with specific accomplishments in bullet list format
Includes education, listed after the impressive summary of applied skills

FIGURE 17.3 A Functional Résumé Use this format to focus on skills and potential instead of employment chronology. (Note that certain items in the above skills categories overlap.)

GUIDELINES for Hard-Copy Résumés

- **Begin your résumé well before your job search.**
- **Tailor your résumé for each job.** Read the advertised job requirements, and adjust your career objective accordingly—but realistically. Tailor your work experience, personal data, and personal interests to emphasize certain areas for certain jobs—but do not distort the facts.
- **Try to limit the résumé to a single page but keep it uncluttered and tasteful.** If the résumé looks cramped, you might need to go to a second page—in which case you could have room to list your references (with their permission).
- **Stick to experience relevant to the job.** Don't list everything you've ever done.
- **Use action verbs and key words.** Action verbs (*supervised, developed, built, taught, installed, managed, trained, solved, planned, directed*) stress your ability to produce results. If your résumé is likely to be scanned electronically or if you post it online, list keywords as nouns (*leadership skills, software development, data processing, editing*) below your contact information and your statement of objective (see Figure 17.4).
- **Use bold, italic, underlining, colors, fonts, bullets, and punctuation thoughtfully, for emphasis.** Do not use highlighting or punctuation to be artsy. Keep punctuation consistent and as simple as possible.
- **Never invent or distort credentials.** Make yourself look as good as the *facts* allow. Companies routinely investigate claims made in résumés, and people who lie will certainly not be hired.
- **Use quality paper and envelopes.** Use white paper of high quality.
- **Proofread, proofread, proofread.** Don't rely on a computer spell checker. Famous résumé mistakes include winning a "bogus award" instead of a "bonus award" and "ruining" rather than "running" a business.

Electronic Résumés

Today's résumés are often submitted electronically

Expect to submit your résumé electronically as well as (or instead of) in hard copy. Even if you are only asked to submit a hard-copy résumé, prospective employers may want to scan the hard copy into their computer systems, which requires special formatting. Many employers ask that résumés be submitted as email attachments, and you may want to post your résumé online, either on your own Web site or on a job search database (such as Monster.com). As you read through this section, refer to the sample résumé in Figure 17.4.

KAREN P. GRANGER
P.O. Box 6772
New Bedford, MA 02720
Phone: (555) 864-9318
Email: kgrang@swis.net

OBJECTIVE
A summer internship in software documentation.

QUALIFICATIONS
Software and hardware documentation. Editing. Desktop publishing. Usability testing. Web collaboration. Networking technology. Instructor-led training. DEC 20 mainframe and VAX 11/780 systems. Framemaker, RoboHelp, Web Works ePublisher, JavaScript, and Adobe Flash.

EDUCATION
University of Massachusetts Dartmouth (UMD): B.A. expected January 2014. English and Communications major. Computer Science minor. GPA 3.54. Class rank top 7 percent.

EXPERIENCE
Conway Communications, Inc., Marlboro, MA: Intern technical writer. LAN technology. Writing, designing, and testing hardware upgrade manuals. Designing and publishing of installation and maintenance manual. Specifying art and illustrations. Designing a fully linked home page and online help for the company intranet. Summers 2011 and 2012.

Writing and Reading Center, UMD: Tutor. Individual and group instruction. Training new tutors. Newsletter editing. Scriptwriting and acting in a training video. Designing home page. Fall 2010–present.

THE TORCH, UMD weekly newspaper: Managing editor. Conducting staff meetings. Generating story ideas. Writing editorials and articles. Supervising page layout, paste-up, and copyediting. Fall 2010–present.

ACHIEVEMENTS AND AWARDS
Writing samples published in TECHNICAL COMMUNICATION, 13th ed. (Longman, 2014).

Massachusetts State Honors Scholarship, 2010–2013.

Dean's list each semester.

ACTIVITIES
Student member, Society for Technical Communication and American Society for Training and Development.

Student representative, College Curriculum Committee. UMD Literary Society.

REFERENCES AND WRITING PORTFOLIO
Available on request.

For online confidentiality, uses a P.O. box, rather than a street address

Uses nouns instead of verb forms for keywords most likely to generate "hits" during scanning

Uses a simple font and format

All text is flush to the left margin

FIGURE 17.4 A Résumé That Can Be Scanned, Emailed, or Posted Online
Notice the standard print and the absence of fancy highlighting. For scannable résumé, use all caps (rather than bold or italics) for headings and publications titles.

Emailed résumés

Emailed and Scannable Résumés. Typically, résumés are submitted to employment sites (see below) or sent as email attachments. When submitting as an email attachment, format the résumé using a word-processing program that is compatible on both Macs and PCs. Or, if your word-processing software allows, save the résumé as a PDF document, to ensure that the formatting and page breaks will look identical on any computer.

Scannable résumés

Some organizations still request résumés be submitted on paper. In these cases, companies will often scan the paper résumé so it can be saved electronically. Electronic storage of hard-copy résumés enables employers to screen applicants, to compile a database of applicants (for later openings), and to evaluate all applicants fairly. An optical scanner feeds in the printed page, stores it as a file, and searches the file for keywords associated with the job opening. Résumés containing the most keywords ("hits") make the final cut.

To design a résumé that can be scanned or sent as an email attachment use the following Guidelines.

GUIDELINES for Emailed and Scannable Résumés

- **Use keywords.** Use words that are likely to get "hits" in keyword searches of a scannable résumé. You may want to create a "qualifications" section at the top of your résumé. Include keywords for general skills (conflict management, report and proposal writing), specialized skills (graphic design, XTML), credentials (B.S. in electrical engineering, Phi Beta Kappa), and job titles (manager, technician, intern). Use nouns for keywords whenever possible.
- **Consider making your scannable résumé slightly longer than your standard, hard-copy version.** The longer the résumé being scanned, the more hits possible.
- **Use a simple font.** Stick with those fonts that are the easiest to scan, such as Courier, Times, and Helvetica (Ariel).
- **Use simple formatting.** Avoid boldface, shading, italics, underlining, tabs, and centering. Place all text flush to the left margin. For emphasis, use ALL CAPS instead of boldface, italics, shading, or underlining.
- **Save your résumé in "text only" or "rich text" format.** This will ensure that all fancy fonts and formats are removed and will allow for smooth scanning and emailing.
- **Proofread your résumé.** Make sure the résumé is free of errors and that it emphasizes your most important skills and qualifications.
- **Do not staple or fold pages of a scannable résumé.**

Online Résumés. You may also want to place your résumé online, either on your own Web site (which might include a *webfolio*, see page 398) or on an employment Web site. For an employment Web site, follow the site's posting guidelines. For your own site or social networking page (such as LinkedIn or Facebook), use the following Guidelines.

GUIDELINES for Online Résumés

- **Add hyperlinks, if desired, for a searchable résumé.** If you post your résumé on your own Web site, consider adding hyperlinks so that readers can link to specific documents elsewhere on your page, such as scanned samples from your portfolio (see Figure 17.5).
- **Be sure your searchable résumé can download quickly.** Complex graphics and multimedia download slowly. Also verify that all links are functioning.
- **Include the searchable résumé's Web address on your hard-copy or scannable résumé.**
- **Prepare alternative delivery options.** In case an employer refuses to track down your résumé on a Web page, be prepared to email an attached copy.
- **Avoid personal information.** Do not expose yourself or your references to identity theft by posting photographs, home addresses (use a P.O. box or simply your city and email address), or birth dates. Also avoid frivolous personal information. Post only on sites that offer privacy options, such as Zoominfo, LinkedIn, or Ziggs.com; at these sites you can check, update, and correct your profile anytime.

APPLICATION LETTERS

An *application letter*, also known as a *cover letter*, complements your résumé. The letter's main purpose is to explain how your credentials fit the particular job and to convey a sufficiently informed, professional, and likable persona for the prospective employer to decide that you should be interviewed. Another purpose of the letter is to highlight specific qualifications or skills; for example, you might have listed "C++ programming" on your résumé, but for one particular job application you may wish to call attention to this item in your cover letter:

> My résumé notes that I am experienced with C++ programming. I also tutor C++ programming students in our school's learning center.

Solicited and unsolicited application letters

Sometimes you will apply for positions advertised in print or by word of mouth (*solicited applications*). At other times you will write prospecting letters to

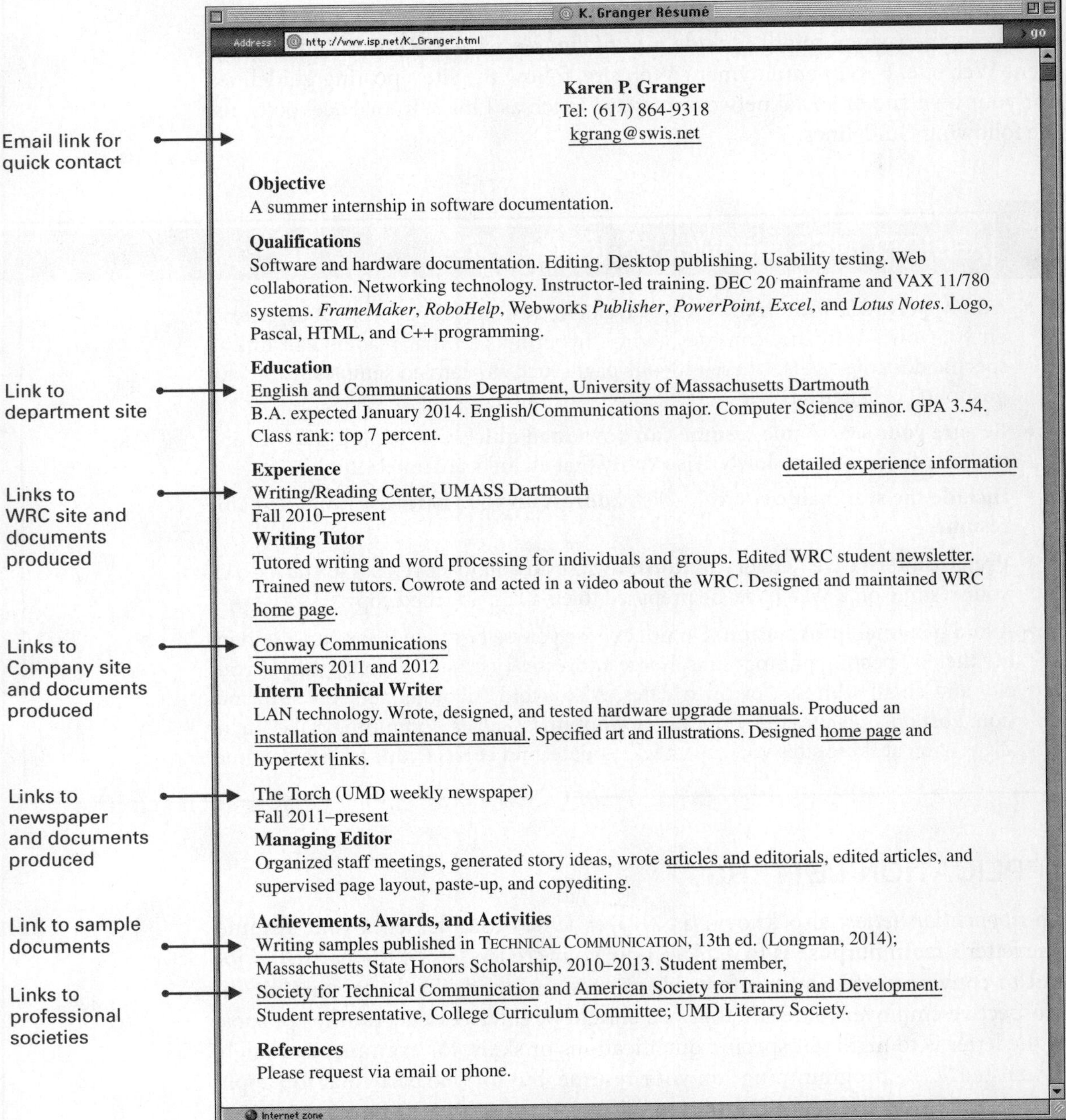

K. Granger Résumé
Address: http://www.isp.net/K_Granger.html
go
Karen P. Granger
Tel: (617) 864-9318
kgrang@swis.net
Email link for quick contact
Objective
A summer internship in software documentation.
Qualifications
Software and hardware documentation. Editing. Desktop publishing. Usability testing. Web collaboration. Networking technology. Instructor-led training. DEC 20 mainframe and VAX 11/780 systems. FrameMaker, RoboHelp, Webworks Publisher, PowerPoint, Excel, and Lotus Notes. Logo, Pascal, HTML, and C++ programming.
Education
Link to department site
English and Communications Department, University of Massachusetts Dartmouth
B.A. expected January 2014. English/Communications major. Computer Science minor. GPA 3.54. Class rank: top 7 percent.
Experience
detailed experience information
Links to WRC site and documents produced
Writing/Reading Center, UMASS Dartmouth
Fall 2010–present
Writing Tutor
Tutored writing and word processing for individuals and groups. Edited WRC student newsletter. Trained new tutors. Cowrote and acted in a video about the WRC. Designed and maintained WRC home page.
Links to Company site and documents produced
Conway Communications
Summers 2011 and 2012
Intern Technical Writer
LAN technology. Wrote, designed, and tested hardware upgrade manuals. Produced an installation and maintenance manual. Specified art and illustrations. Designed home page and hypertext links.
Links to newspaper and documents produced
The Torch (UMD weekly newspaper)
Fall 2011–present
Managing Editor
Organized staff meetings, generated story ideas, wrote articles and editorials, edited articles, and supervised page layout, paste-up, and copyediting.
Achievements, Awards, and Activities
Link to sample documents
Writing samples published in TECHNICAL COMMUNICATION, 13th ed. (Longman, 2014); Massachusetts State Honors Scholarship, 2010–2013. Student member,
Links to professional societies
Society for Technical Communication and American Society for Training and Development.
Student representative, College Curriculum Committee; UMD Literary Society.
References
Please request via email or phone.
Internet zone

FIGURE 17.5 A Searchable Résumé Links connect to various types of information, including several links to Karen's writing portfolio. For security reasons, personal contact information is limited to the applicant's phone number and email address.
Source: Microsoft Corporation.

organizations that have not advertised an opening but that might need someone like you (*unsolicited applications*). In either case, tailor your letter to the situation.

Solicited Application Letters

An application letter—whether solicited or unsolicited—consists of an introduction, body, and conclusion as in Figure 17.6. Imagine you are James Purdy (Figure 17.2). On one popular online job site, you read the advertisement in Figure 17.1 (page 382) and decide to apply. Now you plan and compose your letter.

Use the introduction to get right to the point

In your brief introduction (five lines or fewer), do these things: Name the job and where you have seen it advertised; identify yourself and your background; and, if possible, establish a connection by naming a mutual acquaintance who encouraged you to apply—but only if that person has given you permission.

Use the body section to demonstrate your qualifications

In the body, spell out your case. Without merely repeating your résumé, relate your qualifications specifically to this job. Also, be specific. Instead of referring to "much experience" or "increased sales," stipulate "three years of experience" or "a 35 percent increase in sales between June and October 2011." Support all claims with evidence. Instead of saying, "I have leadership skills," say, "I served as student senate president during my senior year and was captain of the lacrosse team."

Use the conclusion to restate interest

In the conclusion, restate your interest and emphasize your willingness to retrain or relocate if necessary. If the job is nearby, request an interview; otherwise, request a phone call or an email, suggesting a time you can be reached.

Unsolicited Application Letters

Do not limit your job search to advertised openings. In fact, fewer than 20 percent of all job openings are advertised. Unsolicited application letters are a good way to uncover possibilities. They do have drawbacks, however: You may waste time writing to organizations that have no openings, and you cannot tailor your letter to advertised requirements. But there are also advantages: Even employers with no openings often welcome and file impressive unsolicited applications or pass them on to another employer who has an opening.

Use the introduction to spark reader interest

Because an unsolicited letter arrives unexpectedly, you need to get the reader's immediate attention. Don't begin, "I am writing to inquire about the possibility of obtaining a position with your company." Instead, open forcefully by establishing a connection with a mutual acquaintance, or by making a strong statement or asking a persuasive question as in the following example:

A forceful opening

> Does your hotel chain have a place for a junior manager with a degree in hospitality management, a proven commitment to quality service, and customer relations experience that extends far beyond textbooks? If so, please consider my application for a position.

203 Elmwood Avenue
San Jose, CA 10462
April 22, 20XX

Sara Costanza
Personnel Director
Liberty International, Inc.
Lansdowne, PA 24153

Dear Ms. Costanza:

Writer identifies self and purpose →

Please consider my application for a junior management position at your Lake Geneva resort, as advertised on April 19 on Monster.com. I will graduate from San Jose City College on May 30 with an Associate of Arts degree in hotel and restaurant management. Dr. H. V. Garlid, my nutrition professor, described his experience as a consultant for Liberty International and encouraged me to apply.

Establishes a connection →

Relates specific qualifications from his résumé to the job opening →

As you can see from my enclosed résumé, for two years I worked as a part-time desk clerk, and I was promoted to manager, at a 200-unit resort. This experience, combined with earlier customer relations work in a variety of situations, has given me a clear and practical understanding of customers' needs and expectations.

Applies relevant personal interests to the job →

As an amateur chef, I'm well aware of the effort, attention, and patience required to prepare fine food. Moreover, my skiing and sailing background might be assets to your resort's recreation program.

Expresses confidence and enthusiasm throughout →

I have worked hard to hone my hospitality management skills. My experience, education, and personality have prepared me to work well with others and to respond creatively to challenges, crises, and added responsibilities.

Makes follow-up easy for the reader →

If my background meets your needs, please phone any weekday after 4:00 p.m. at (555) 316-2419 or email at jpur@valnet.net.

Sincerely,

James D. Purdy

James D. Purdy

Encl. Résumé

FIGURE 17.6 A Solicited Application Letter

March 1, 20XX
642 Eagle Lane
Eugene, OR 97405

Martha LaFrance, Personnel Director
Zithro Marketing Associates
132 Main Street
Portland, OR 42290

Dear Ms. LaFrance:

SUBJECT: Inquiry about a Marketing/Communications Position with Your Firm ← Subject line announces purpose of letter

Marketing Research, Marketing Management, Principles of Marketing, Business and Technical Communication, Visual Design, Photography, Typography: I believe such courses, along with two internships and relevant employment, have given me the theoretical background and practical experience employers would seek. ← Highlights special skills and opens forcefully

My experience includes writing and analyzing surveys, researching market trends, speaking before groups, and creating promotional materials. Could your firm use the services of an entry-level employee with this type of experience? ← Focuses on experience

Through internships with Mercy Hospital and the Small Business Institute, I have done public relations work, assisted in publishing the newsletter, written ads and public relations stories for local newspapers, interviewed key personnel, prepared layout and copy, and edited text. While working for the Chamber of Commerce, I wrote promotional letters, designed brochures and posters, organized events, and collaborated in promoting the organization's goals. Jobs as personal trainer and as salesperson not only have covered 75 percent of my college expenses but also have taught me a great deal about motivating and getting along with people. ← Relates background to employer's needs

My references will confirm that I am conscientious, disciplined, energetic, and reliable—someone willing to take on new projects and prepared to adapt quickly. ← Focuses on relevant personal traits

If you have an opening and you feel that I could make worthwhile contributions to your firm, I would welcome an interview at your convenience. ← Encourages follow-up

Sincerely,

Carol R. Chasone

Carol R. Chasone
Encl: Résumé

FIGURE 17.7 An Unsolicited Application Letter

Address your letter to the person most likely in charge of hiring. Consult company Web sites for names of company officers. Then call the company to verify the person's name and title. Also, consider using a "Subject" line to attract a busy reader's attention and to announce the purpose of your letter, as in Figure 17.7.

NOTE *Write to a specific person—not to a generic recipient such as "Director of Human Resources" or "Personnel Office." If you don't know who does the hiring, phone the company and ask for that person's name and title, and be sure you get the spelling right.*

GUIDELINES for Application Letters

- **Develop an excellent prototype letter.** Presenting a clear and concise picture of who you are, what you have to offer, and what makes you special is arguably the hardest—but most essential—part of the application process. Revise this prototype, or model, until it represents you in the best possible light. Keep it to a single page, if possible.
- **Customize each letter for the specific job opening.** Although you can base letters to different employers on the same basic prototype—with appropriate changes—prepare each letter afresh. Don't look for shortcuts.
- **Use caution when adapting sample letters.** Plenty of free, online sample letters provide ideas for approaching your own situation. But never borrow them whole. Most employers are able to spot a "canned" letter immediately.
- **Create a dynamic tone with active voice and action verbs.** Instead of "Management responsibilities were steadily given to me," say "I steadily assumed management responsibilities." Be confident without seeming arrogant. (For more on Tone, see pages 232–33.)
- **Never be vague.** Help readers visualize: Instead of saying, "I am familiar with the 1022 interactive database system and RUNOFF, the text-processing system," say "As a lab grader, I kept grading records on the 1022 database management system and composed lab procedures on the RUNOFF text-processing system."
- **Never exaggerate.** Liars get busted.
- **Convey some enthusiasm.** An enthusiastic attitude can sometimes be as important as your background (as in Figure 17.7).
- **Avoid flattery.** Don't say "I am greatly impressed by your remarkable company."
- **Be concise.** Review pages 216–22. Limit your letters to one page, unless your discussion truly warrants the additional space.

- **Avoid being overly informal or overly stiff.** Avoid informal terms that sound unprofessional ("Your company sounds like a cool place to work") as well as stuffy language ("Hitherto, I request the honor of your acquaintance").
- **Never settle for a first draft—or even a second or third.** The application letter is your one chance to introduce yourself to a prospective employer. Make it perfect by trimming excess wording, double-checking the tone, and ensuring that you have connected your qualifications directly to the job. After you are satisfied with the content, proofread repeatedly to spot any factual errors or typos.
- **Never send a photocopied letter.**

CONSIDER THIS: How Applicants Are Screened for Personal Qualities

As many as 25 percent of résumés contain falsified credentials, such as a nonexistent degree or a contrived affiliation with a prestigious school (Parrish 1+). A security director for one major employer estimates that 15 to 20 percent of job applicants have something personal to hide: a conviction for drunk driving or some other felony, trouble with the IRS, bad credit, or the like (Robinson 285).

With yearly costs of employee dishonesty or bad judgment amounting to billions of dollars, companies use preemployment screening for integrity, emotional stability, and a host of other personal qualities (Hollwitz and Pawlowski 203, 209).

Screening often begins with a background check of education, employment history, and references. One corporation checks up to ten references (from peers, superiors, and subordinates) per candidate (Justin Martin, "So" 78). In addition, roughly 95 percent of corporations check on the applicant's character, trustworthiness, and reputation: they may examine driving, credit, and criminal records, and interview neighbors and coworkers (Robinson 285).

The law affords some protection by requiring employers to notify the applicant before checking on character, reputation, and credit history and to provide a copy of any report that leads to a negative hiring decision (Robinson 285). Once an applicant is hired, however, the picture changes: more than 50 percent of companies provide personal information to credit agencies, banks, and landlords without informing employees, and 40 percent don't inform employees about what kinds of records are being kept on them (Karaim 72).

Beyond screening for background, employers use aptitude and personality tests to pinpoint desirable qualities. A sampling of test questions (Garner 86; Kane 56; Justin Martin, "So" 77, 78):

- *Ability to perform under pressure:* "Do you get nervous and confused at busy intersections?"
- *Emotional stability and even temper:* "Do you honk your horn often while driving?"
- *Sense of humor:* "Tell us a joke."

CONSIDER THIS *(continued)*

- *Ability to cope with people in stressful situations:* "Do you like to argue and debate?" "Are you good at taking control in a crisis?"
- *Persuasive skills:* "Write a brief memo to a client, explaining why X [stipulated on the test] can't be done on time."
- *Presentation skills:* "Prepare and give a five-minute speech on some aspect of the industry as it relates to this company."

These tests may be given online, before an applicant is considered for an interview.

Above all, most employers look for candidates who are *likable*. One employer checks with each person an applicant speaks with during the company visit—including the receptionist. Another employer has candidates join in a company softball game (Justin Martin, "So" 77).

DOSSIERS, PORTFOLIOS, AND WEBFOLIOS

An employer impressed by your résumé and application letter will have further questions about your credentials and your past work. These questions will be answered, respectively, by your dossier and your portfolio (or Webfolio).

Dossiers

What a dossier contains

Your dossier contains your credentials: college transcript, recommendation letters, and other items (such as a scholarship award or commendation letter) that offer evidence of your achievements. Prospective employers who decide to follow up on your application will request your dossier. By collecting recommendations in one folder, you spare your references from writing the same letter repeatedly.

Your college placement office will keep the dossier (or placement folder) on file and send copies to employers. Always keep your own copy as well, including any nonconfidential recommendation letters. Then, if an employer requests your dossier, you can photocopy and mail it, advising your recipient that the official placement copy is on the way, as dossiers are not always mailed immediately from a busy placement office.

Portfolios and Webfolios

What a portfolio contains

Your portfolio (or Webfolio, Figure 17.8) contains an introduction or mission statement explaining what you've included in your portfolio and why. Among the included items are your résumé, uploaded or scanned examples of your work, and anything else pertinent to your job search (such as copies of documents from your dossier). An organized, professional-looking portfolio or Webfolio shows that you can apply your skills and helps you stand out as a candidate. It also gives you concrete material to discuss during job interviews.

As you create your portfolio or Webfolio, seek advice and feedback from professors in your major and from other people in the field. If you have a portfolio, indicate this on your résumé, followed by "Available on request." If you have a Webfolio, provide the Web address on your résumé, but also bring printed copies of its contents to your interview. Keep copies of these items on hand to leave with the interviewer if requested.

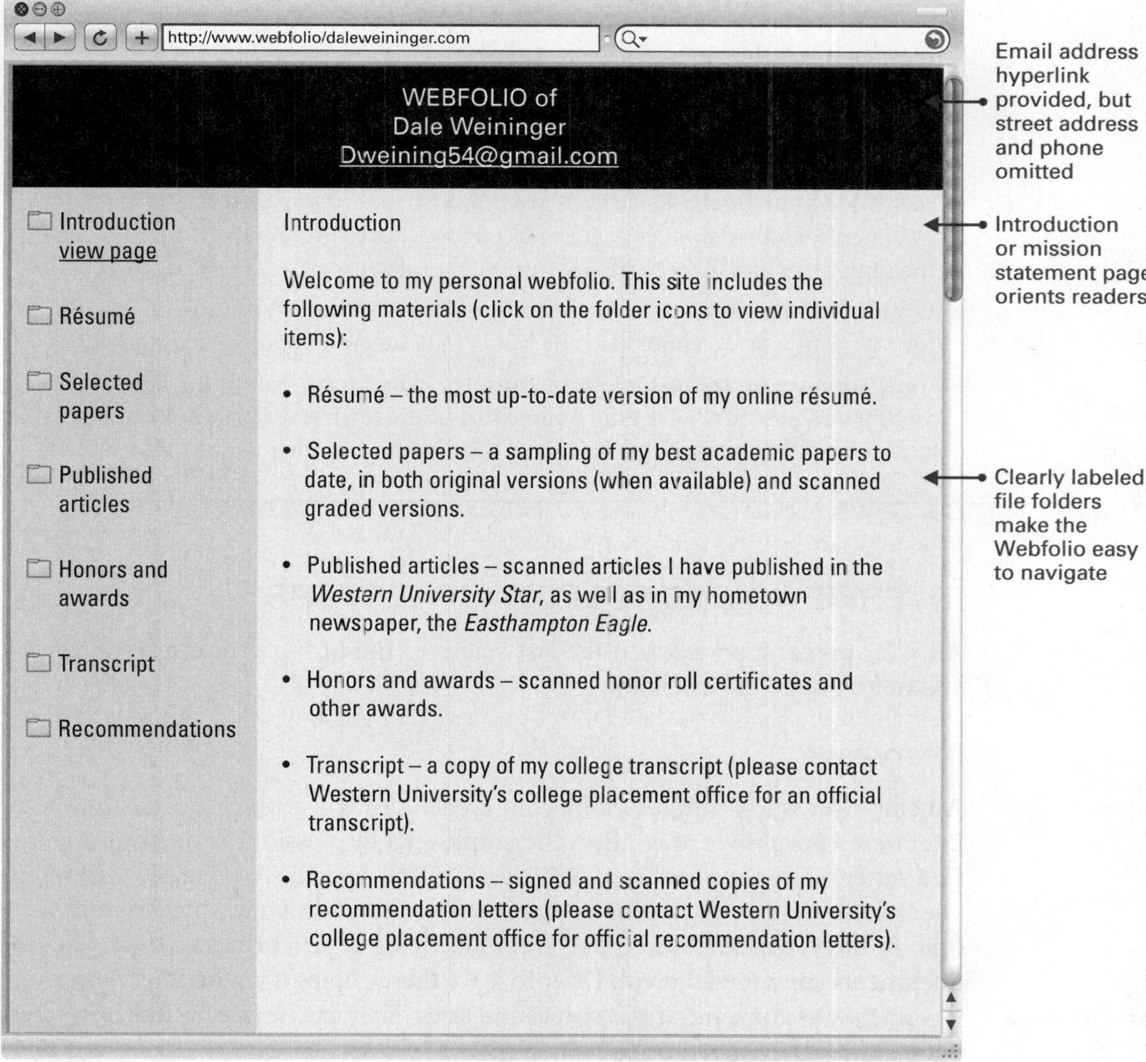

FIGURE 17.8 A Webfolio Be sure that your Webfolio is up to date. Check routinely to ensure that all links are functioning.
Source: Microsoft Corporation.

GUIDELINES for Dossiers, Portfolios, and Webfolios

- **Always provide an introduction or mission statement.** Place this page at the beginning, to introduce and explain the contents.
- **Collect relevant materials.** Gather documents or graphics you've prepared in school or on the job, presentations you've given, and projects or experiments you've worked on. Possible items: campus newspaper articles, reports on course projects, papers that earned an "A," examples of persuasive argument, documents from an internship, or visuals you've designed for an oral presentation.
- **Include copies of dossier materials.** Although they won't be official unless they go directly from your campus placement office to your prospective employer, post copies of your college transcript and recommendations on your Webfolio.
- **Assemble your items.** Place your résumé first (after your introduction/mission statement), and use divider pages or electronic files to group related items. Follow the same structure for a Webfolio. Aim for a professional look.
- **Omit irrelevant items.** Personal photographs and other items more appropriate for a MySpace or Facebook page do not belong in a portfolio or Webfolio.
- **Omit your street address or phone number from your Webfolio.** To maintain privacy and security, post only your email address. If you post your references, include only their names and the text of their letters, not their contact information.

INTERVIEWS AND FOLLOW-UP LETTERS

All your preparation leads to the last stages of the hiring process: the interview and follow-up to the interview.

Interviews

Purpose of interviews

An employer who is impressed by your credentials will arrange an interview. The interview's purpose is to confirm the employer's impressions from your application letter, résumé, references, and dossier. You will likely be asked to present your portfolio (if you have one) at the interview. In addition to your original portfolio or the Web address for your Webfolio, bring copies/printouts of all relevant documents contained therein. Offer to leave these copies with the interviewer.

Types of interview situations

Interviews come in various shapes and sizes. They can be face-to-face or via telephone or video conference. You might meet with a single interviewer, a hiring committee, or several committees in succession. You might be interviewed alone or as part of a group of candidates. Interviews can last an hour or less, a full day, or several days. The interview can range from a pleasant chat to a grueling interrogation. Some interviewers may antagonize you deliberately to observe your reaction.

How to prepare

Careful preparation is the key to a productive interview. If you haven't already done so, learn all you can about the company from trade journals, business magazines (such as *Forbes, Fortune*, and *Business Week*), the company's Web site, and other online resources. Request company literature, including the most recent annual report. Speak with people who know about the company, or (well in advance) arrange an informational interview with someone at the company. Once you've done all this, ask yourself, "Does this job seem like a good fit?"

NOTE *Taking the wrong job can be far worse than taking no job at all—especially for a recent graduate trying to build credentials.*

In addition to knowing about the company, be prepared in other ways. Dress and present yourself appropriately. Be psychologically prepared and confident (but not arrogant). Follow the rules of business etiquette. Unprepared interviewees make mistakes such as the following:

How people fail job interviews

- They know little about the company or what role they would play as an employee in this particular division or department.
- They have inflated ideas about their own worth.
- They have little idea of how their education prepares them for work.
- They dress inappropriately.
- They exhibit little or no self-confidence.
- They have only vague ideas of how they could benefit the employer.
- They inquire only about salary and benefits.
- They speak negatively of former employers or coworkers.

Practice answering interview questions

One important way to prepare for an interview is to practice answering typical questions. Think about how you would answer the following:

Questions to expect

- Why does this job appeal to you?
- What do you know about our company? About this division or unit?
- What do you know about our core values (for example, informal management structure, commitment to diversity, or to the environment)?
- What do you know about the expectations and demands of this job?
- What are the major issues affecting this industry?
- How would you describe yourself as an employee?
- What do you see as your biggest weakness? Biggest strength?
- Can you describe an instance in which you came up with a new and better way of doing something?
- What are your short-term and long-term career goals?

Prepare your own questions

Be sure to prepare your own list of well-researched questions about the job and the organization. You will be invited to ask questions, and what you ask can be as revealing as any answers you give.

Be truthful

Finally, tell the truth during the interview—doing so is both ethical and smart. Companies routinely verify an applicant's claims about education, prior employment, positions held, salary, and personal background. Perhaps you have some past infraction (such as a bad credit rating or a brush with the law), or some pressing personal commitment (such as caring for an elderly parent or a disabled child). Experts suggest that it's better to air these issues up front—before an employer learns from other sources. The employer will appreciate your honesty, and you will know exactly where you stand before accepting the job (Fisher, "Truth" 292).

Follow-Up Letters

There are two types of follow-up letters: thank you letters, and, if you are offered the job, acceptance or refusal letters.

Thank You Letters. Within a day or so after the interview, send a thank you letter (not an email or other electronic correspondence, which will seem lazy) to the person who interviewed you. If you were interviewed by multiple people, send each one an individual thank you letter. Not only is this courteous, but it also reinforces a positive impression. Keep your letter brief, but try to personalize your connection with the reader (Crosby, "Employment" 20).

Open by thanking the interviewer and reemphasizing your interest in the position. Then refer to some details from the interview or some aspect of your visit that would help the recipient reconnect with the interview experience. If you forgot to mention something important during the interview, include it here—briefly. Finally, close with genuine enthusiasm, and provide your contact information again to make it easy for the interviewer to respond. Following is the text of a thank you letter from James Purdy, the entry-level candidate in hotel-restaurant management, whose résumé and cover letter appeared earlier:

Refresh the employer's memory

> Thank you for your hospitality during my Tuesday visit to Lake Geneva resort. I am very interested in the restaurant-management position and was intrigued by our discussion about developing an eclectic regional cuisine.
>
> Everything about my tour was enjoyable, but I was especially impressed by the friendliness and professionalism of the resort staff. People seem to love working here, and it's not hard to see why.
>
> I'm convinced I would be a productive employee at Lake Geneva and would welcome the chance to prove my abilities. If you need additional information, please call me at (555) 316-2419.

Acceptance or Refusal Letters. You may receive a job offer by phone, letter, or email. If by phone, request a written offer and respond with a formal letter of acceptance. This letter may serve as part of your contract; spell out the terms you are accepting. Here is James Purdy's letter of acceptance:

> I am delighted to accept your offer of a position as assistant recreation supervisor at Liberty International's Lake Geneva Resort, with a starting salary of $44,500.
>
> As you requested, I will phone Elmer Druid in your Personnel Office for instructions on reporting date, physical exam, and employee orientation.
>
> I look forward to a long and satisfying career with Liberty International.

Accept an offer with enthusiasm

You may also have to refuse a job offer. Even if you refuse by phone, write a prompt and cordial letter of refusal, explaining your reasons, and allowing for future possibilities. A courteous refusal and explanation can let the employer know why you have chosen a competing employer or why you have decided against taking the job for other reasons. Purdy handled one job refusal this way:

> Although I thoroughly enjoyed my visit to your company's headquarters, I have to decline your offer of a position as assistant desk manager of your London hotel.
>
> I've decided to accept a position with Liberty International because the company has offered me the chance to participate in its manager-trainee program. Also, Liberty will provide tuition for courses in completing my B.A. degree in hospitality management.
>
> If any future openings should materialize at your Aspen resort, however, I would appreciate your considering me again as a candidate.
>
> Thank you for your confidence in me.

Decline an offer diplomatically

GUIDELINES for Interviews and Follow-Up Letters

- **Confirm the interview's exact time and location.** Arrive early, but no more than 10 minutes.

  NOTE *If you are offered a choice of interview times, choose mid-morning over late afternoon: According to an Accountemps survey of 1,400 managers, 69 percent prefer mid-morning for doing their hiring, whereas only 5 percent prefer late afternoon (Fisher, "My Company" 184).*

- **Don't show up empty-handed.** Bring a briefcase, pen, and notepad. Have your own questions written out. Bring extra copies of your résumé (unfolded) and a portfolio (if appropriate).

  NOTE *If you decide to take notes on a tablet or other electronic device, be sure the battery is fully charged. Do not take notes on a laptop; the screen could compromise your ability to make eye contact.*

GUIDELINES *continued*

- **Make a positive first impression.** Come dressed as if you already work for the company. Learn the name of your interviewer beforehand, so you can greet this person by name—but never by first name unless invited. Extend a firm handshake, smile, and look the interviewer in the eye. Wait to be asked to take a chair. Maintain eye contact much of the time, but don't stare. Do not fiddle with your face, hair, or other body parts.
- **Don't worry about having all the answers.** When you don't know the answer to a question, say so, and relax. Interviewers typically do most of the talking.
- **Avoid abrupt yes or no answers—as well as life stories.** Elaborate on your answers, but also keep them short and to the point.
- **Don't answer questions by merely repeating the material on your résumé.** Instead, explain how specific skills and types of experience could be assets to this particular employer. For concrete evidence refer to items in your portfolio whenever possible.
- **Remember to smile often and to be friendly and attentive throughout.** Qualifications are not the only reason a person gets hired. People often hire the candidate they *like* best.
- **Never criticize a previous employer.** Above all, interviewers like people who have positive attitudes.
- **Prepare to ask intelligent questions.** When questions are invited, focus on the nature of the job: travel involved, specific responsibilities, typical job assignments, opportunities for further training, types of clients, and so on. Avoid questions that could easily have been answered by your own prior research.
- **Take a hint.** When your interviewer hints that the meeting is ending, restate your interest, ask when a hiring decision is likely to be made, thank the interviewer, and leave.
- **Show some class.** If you are invited to lunch, don't order the most expensive dish on the menu; don't order an alcoholic beverage; don't smoke; don't salt your food before tasting it; don't eat too quickly; don't put your elbows on the table; don't speak with your mouth full; and don't order a huge dessert. And try to order last.
- **Expect a possible telephone interview.** Some employers interview initially by phone, usually calling to arrange a time beforehand. Ask for the interviewer's name (spelled) and contact information. Organize all your backup materials so you have them within easy reach. As the interview ends, encourage further contact by restating your interest in the position and your desire to visit and meet people in person.
- **Follow up as soon as possible.** Send a thank you note to each person with whom you interviewed. Be sure to get the spelling right for each person's name.

CHECKLIST: Résumés

(Numbers in parentheses refer to the first page of discussion.)

Content

- ☐ Is all my contact information accurate? (383)
- ☐ Does my statement of objective show a clear sense of purpose? (384)
- ☐ If I am willing to relocate, have I so indicated? (384)
- ☐ Did I include a summary of skills or qualifications, as needed? (384)
- ☐ Is my educational background clear and complete? (384)
- ☐ Did I accurately but briefly describe previous jobs? (384)
- ☐ Are personal data and interests included, as appropriate? (384)
- ☐ Did I list references or offer to provide them? (385)
- ☐ Did I offer to provide a portfolio, as appropriate? (385)
- ☐ Am I being scrupulously honest? (388)

Arrangement

- ☐ Did I place my strongest qualifications in positions of emphasis? (385)
- ☐ Are education versus experience presented in the most appropriate sequence to highlight my strengths? (384)
- ☐ Does my résumé's organization (reverse chronological or functional) put my best characteristics forward? (385)
- ☐ In my scannable résumé, did I use keywords and effective formatting? (390)
- ☐ If the résumé has hyperlinks, are they all functioning? (392)

Overall

- ☐ Did I limit the résumé to a single page, if possible? (388)
- ☐ Is the résumé uncluttered and tasteful? (388)
- ☐ Did I use quality (white) paper? (388)
- ☐ Did I use phrases instead of complete sentences? (388)
- ☐ Did I use action verbs and keywords? (388)
- ☐ Are highlighting and punctuation consistent and simple? (388)
- ☐ Have I proofread exhaustively? (388)

CHECKLIST: Application Letters

(Numbers in parentheses refer to the first page of discussion.)

Content

- ☐ Is my letter addressed to a specifically named person? (396)
- ☐ If my letter was solicited, did I indicate how I heard about the job? (393)
- ☐ If my letter was unsolicited, does it have a forceful opening? (393)
- ☐ Did I make my case without merely repeating my résumé? (393)
- ☐ Did I support all claims with evidence? (393)
- ☐ Did I avoid flattery? (396)
- ☐ Am I being scrupulously honest? (396)

Arrangement

- ☐ Does my introduction get directly to the point? (393)
- ☐ Does the body section expand on qualifications sketched in my résumé? (393)
- ☐ Does the conclusion restate my interest and request specific action? (393)

Overall

- ☐ Did I limit the letter to a single page, whenever possible? (396)
- ☐ Is my letter free of "canned" expressions? (396)
- ☐ Is my tone appropriate? (397)
- ☐ Did I convey enthusiasm and self-confidence without seeming arrogant? (396)
- ☐ Have I prepared a fresh letter for each job? (396)
- ☐ Have I proofread exhaustively? (397)

CHECKLIST: Supporting Materials

- ☐ Is my dossier complete, with letters of recommendation and other evidence of achievements? (398)
- ☐ Is my portfolio or Webfolio (if applicable) up-to-date? (398)
- ☐ If the portfolio has hyperlinks, are they all functioning? (399)
- ☐ Have I prepared for interviews? (400)
- ☐ Have I sent the appropriate follow-up correspondence? (402)

Projects

GENERAL

1. Prepare a hard-copy résumé. If you already have a résumé, revise it to follow this chapter's guidelines.
2. Write an application letter for a part-time or summer job in response to a specific ad and tailor your résumé for the job. Choose an organization related to your career goals. Identify the exact hours and calendar period during which you are free to work. Submit a copy of the ad along with your materials.
3. Make your résumé scannable and ready for sending via email or posting online. Be sure to use an easily scannable font; remove headers, boldface, underlining, bullets, tabs, and other formatting; and proofread it after you've converted the résumé to "text only" or "rich text" format.
4. A friend has asked you for help with the following application letter. Rewrite it as needed.

> Dear Ms. Brown,
>
> Please consider my application for the position of assistant in the Engineering Department. I am a second-year student majoring in electrical engineering technology. I am presently an apprentice with your company and would like to continue my employment in the Engineering Department.
>
> I have six years' experience in electronics, including two years of engineering studies. I am confident my background will enable me to assist the engineers, and I would appreciate the chance to improve my skills through their knowledge and experience.
>
> I would appreciate the opportunity to discuss the possibilities and benefits of a position in the Engineering Department at Concord Electric. Please phone me any weekday after 3:00 p.m. at (555) 568-9867. I hope to hear from you soon.
>
> Sincerely,

5. Write an unsolicited application letter to the human resources director of a company that interests you. Go to the company's Web site to research the various positions for which you may be qualified. Select one, and name that position in your letter. Also learn the name of the human resources director and address your letter to that person.

TEAM

In groups, prepare a listing of five Web sites that job seekers should visit for advice about cover letters and résumés, including online postings. Include a one-paragraph summary of material on each site. Compare findings of your group with those of others in your class. In addition to sites mentioned in this chapter, here are other sources (expand your search beyond these sites): <www.jobstar.org/tools/resume>, <www.eresumes.com>

DIGITAL AND SOCIAL MEDIA

Look at one or more of the following: <linkedin.com>, <careerbuilders.com>, and <monster.com>. Learn about how you would go about preparing a résumé to upload to one of these sites. If the site provides sample résumés, look at a few and compare these to the strategies provided in this chapter. Create a draft résumé for one of these sites and review it with your instructor.

GLOBAL

Assume that you and other students in your major would like to work in a particular country after graduation. Select a country and do some research on the economy, culture, and employment issues. Write a short memo that tells prospective students what they need to know about finding employment abroad.

18 Technical Definitions

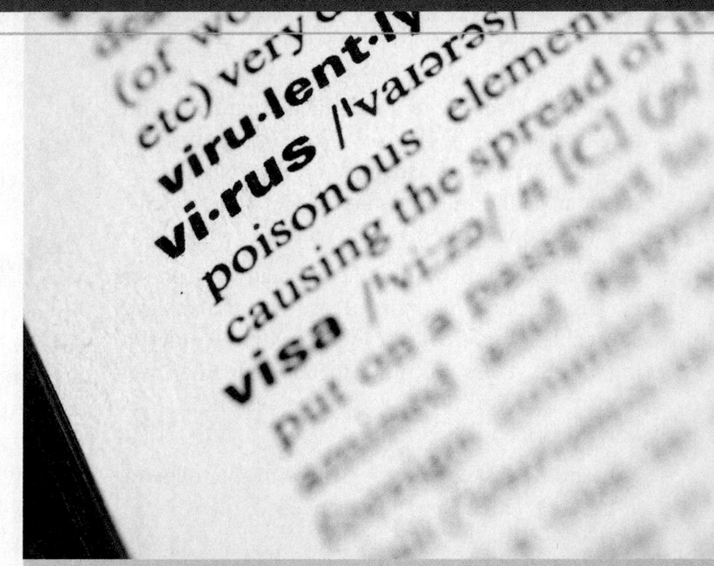

"As a nurse practitioner, much of my working day is spent defining specialized terms for patients and their families: medical conditions, treatments and surgical procedures, medications and side effects, and so on. Most of today's patients—especially those facing complex health decisions—expect to be well-informed about the medical issues that affect their lives. Clear, understandable definitions are an important first step in providing the information people need."

—Dana Ballinger,
Nurse Practitioner in a primary-care clinic

LEARNING OBJECTIVES FOR THIS CHAPTER

- Appreciate the role of definition in technical communication
- Know how audience and purpose indicate the need for definition
- Consider the role of definitions within and beyond the workplace
- Differentiate among levels of detail in a definition
- Select the right level of detail as your situation requires
- Write an expanded definition
- Place definitions effectively in your document

Definitions explain terms or concepts that are specialized and may be unfamiliar to people who lack expertise in a particular field. In many cases, a term may have more than one meaning or different meanings in different fields. Consider a word such as *atmosphere*: To an astronomer, it would refer to the envelope of gases that surrounds a planet ("the Earth's atmosphere"); to a politician or office manager, it would typically mean the mood of the country or the workplace ("an atmosphere of high hopes"); to a physicist it would stand for a unit of pressure ("a standard atmosphere is 101,325 pascal"); and to a novelist it would be associated with the mood of a novel ("a gothic atmosphere").

Why definitions must be precise

Precision is particularly important in specialized fields, in which field-specific terminology is common and undefined terms may prevent the overall document from making sense. Engineers talk about *elasticity* or *ductility*; bankers discuss *amortization* or *fiduciary relationships*. These terms must be defined if people both inside and outside of those fields are to understand the document as a whole. Imagine if a doctor continually used the words *myocardial infarction* in a patient brochure without ever defining the term. The fact that a myocardial infarction is the medical name for one form of *heart attack* would be lost on patients who need to have a clear understanding of the brochure.

CONSIDERING AUDIENCE AND PURPOSE

Audience considerations

Definitions answer one of two questions: "What, exactly, is it?" or "What, exactly, does it entail?" The first question spells out what makes an item, concept, or process unique. For example, an engineering student needs to understand the distinction between *elasticity* and *ductility*. People in any audience have to grasp precisely what "makes a thing what it is and distinguishes that thing from all other things" (Corbett 38). The second question spells out for your audience how they are affected by the item defined. For example, a person buying a new computer needs to understand exactly what "manufacturer's guarantee" or "expandable memory" means in the context of that purchase.

Purpose considerations

Consider the purpose of defining particular terms in your document by answering the question "Why does my audience need to understand this term?" The level of technicality you use must match the audience's background and experience. For a group of mechanical engineering students, your definition of a *solenoid*, for example, can use highly technical language:

A highly technical version

> A solenoid is an inductance coil that serves as a tractive electromagnet.

For general audiences, your definition will require language they can understand:

A nontechnical version

> A solenoid is a metal coil that converts electrical energy to magnetic energy capable of performing mechanical functions.

Unless you are certain that your audience already knows the exact meaning, always define a term the first time you use it.

LEGAL, ETHICAL, SOCIETAL, AND GLOBAL IMPLICATIONS

Definitions have legal implications

Precise definition is essential, because you (or the organization, if you write a document on its behalf) are legally responsible for that document. For example, contracts are detailed (and legally binding) definitions of the specific terms of an agreement. If you lease an apartment or a car, the printed contract will define both the *lessee's* and *lessor's* specific responsibilities. Likewise, an employment contract or employee handbook will spell out responsibilities for both employer and employee. In preparing an employee handbook for your company, you would need to define such terms as *acceptable job performance, confidentiality, sexual harassment*, and *equal opportunity*.

Definitions have ethical implications

Definitions have ethical implications, too. For example, the term *acceptable risk* had an ethical impact on January 28, 1986, when the space shuttle *Challenger* exploded 73 seconds after launch, killing all seven crew members. (Two rubber O-ring seals in a booster rocket had failed, allowing hot exhaust gases to escape and igniting the adjacent fuel tank.) Hours earlier—despite vehement objections from the engineers—management had decided that going ahead with the launch was a risk worth taking. In this case, management's definition of *acceptable risk* was based not on the engineering facts but rather on bureaucratic pressure to launch on schedule. Agreeing on meaning in such cases rarely is easy, but you are ethically bound to convey an accurate interpretation of the facts as you understand them.

Clear and accurate definitions help the public understand and evaluate complex technical and social issues. For example, as a first step in understanding the debate over the term *genetic engineering*, we need at least the following basic definition:

Definitions have societal implications

> Genetic engineering refers to [an experimental] technique through which genes can be isolated in a laboratory, manipulated, and then inserted stably into another organism. Gene insertion can be accomplished mechanically, chemically, or by using biological vectors such as viruses. (Office of Technology Assessment 20)

A general but informative definition

Of course, to follow the debate, we would need increasingly detailed information (about specific procedures, risks, benefits, and so on). But the above definition gets us started on a healthy debate by enabling us to visualize the basic concept and to mutually agree on the basic meaning of the term.

Ongoing threats to our planet's environment, the prospect of nuclear proliferation, and the perils of terrorism top a list of complex issues that make definitions vital to global communication. For example, on the environmental front, world audiences need a realistic understanding of concepts such as *greenhouse effect* or *ozone depletion*. On the nuclear proliferation front, the survival of our species could well depend on the clear definition of terms such as *nuclear non-proliferation treaty* or *non-aggression pact* by the nations who are parties to such agreements. On the terrorism front, the public wants to understand such terms as *biological terrorism* or *weapons of mass destruction.*

Definitions have global implications

In short, definition is more than an exercise in busy work. Figure 18.1 illustrates the informative power of an effective definition.

TYPES OF DEFINITION

Definitions fall into three distinct categories: *parenthetical, sentence,* and *expanded.* Decide how much detail your audience actually requires in order to grasp your exact meaning.

Three categories of definitions

Parenthetical Definitions

Often, you can clarify the meaning of a word by using a more familiar synonym or a clarifying phrase in parentheses, as in these examples:

When to use parenthetical definitions

> The *leaching field* (sievelike drainage area) requires crushed stone.
>
> The trees on the site are mostly *deciduous* (shedding foliage at season's end).

Parenthetical definitions

On a Web page or online help system, these types of short definitions can be linked to the main word or phrase. Readers who click on *leaching field* would be taken to a window containing a brief definition.

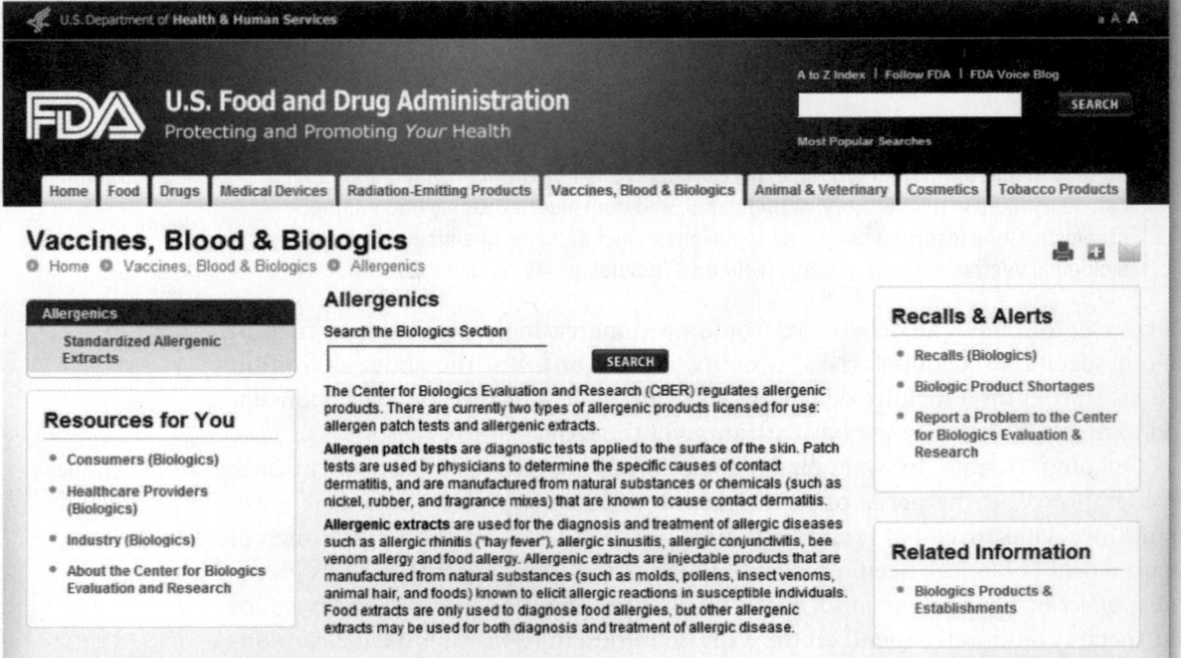

FIGURE 18.1 An Effective Definition In this example, *allergenics* is defined as consisting of two different types of products (patch tests and extracts). Each individual definition is then carefully written using short sentences; technical phrases such as "allergic rhinitis" are defined in simpler language ("hay fever") for non-expert readers. Because these definitions are available on a Web site, readers can search for more information, locate other definitions, and research any of the concepts within the definition.
Source: U.S. Food and Drug Administration.

Sentence Definitions

When to use sentence definitions

When a term requires more elaboration than a parenthetical definition can offer, use a sentence definition. Begin by stating the term. Then indicate the broader class to which this item belongs, followed by the features that distinguish it from other items in that general class. Here are examples:

Sentence definitions (termclass-features)

Term	Class	Distinguishing Features
A carburetor	a mixing device…	in gasoline engines that blends air and fuel into a vapor for combustion within the cylinders.

Diabetes	a metabolic disease...	caused by a disorder of the pituitary gland or pancreas and characterized by excessive urination, persistent thirst, and inability to metabolize sugar.
Stress	an applied force...	that strains or deforms a body.

The previous elements may be combined into one or more complete sentences:

> Diabetes is a metabolic disease caused by a disorder of the pituitary gland or pancreas. This disease is characterized by excessive urination, persistent thirst,and inability to metabolize sugar.

A complete sentence definition

Sentence definitions are especially useful if you plan to use a term often and need to establish a working definition that you will not have to repeat throughout the document:

> Throughout this report, the term *disadvantaged student* will refer to all students who lack adequate funds to pay for on-campus housing, food services, and medical care, but who are able to pay for their coursework and books through scholarships and part-time work.

A working definition

Expanded Definitions

When to use expanded definitions

Brief definitions are fine when your audience requires only a general understanding of a term. For example, the parenthetical definition of *leaching field* on page 411 might be adequate in a progress report to a client whose house you're building. But a document that requires more detail, such as a public health report on groundwater contamination from leaching fields, would call for an expanded definition.

Likewise, the nontechnical definition of "solenoid" on page 410 is adequate for a layperson who simply needs to know what a solenoid is. An instruction manual for mechanics, however, would define solenoid in much greater detail (as on page 419); mechanics need to know how a solenoid works and how to use and repair it.

Depending on audience and purpose, an expanded definition may be a short paragraph or may extend to several pages. For example, if a device, such as a digital dosimeter (used for measuring radiation exposure), is being introduced to an audience who needs to understand how this instrument works, your definition would require at least several paragraphs, if not pages.

METHODS FOR EXPANDING DEFINITIONS

An expanded definition can be created in any number of ways as described below. The method or methods you decide to use will depend on the questions you expect the audience will want answered, as illustrated in Figure 18.2.

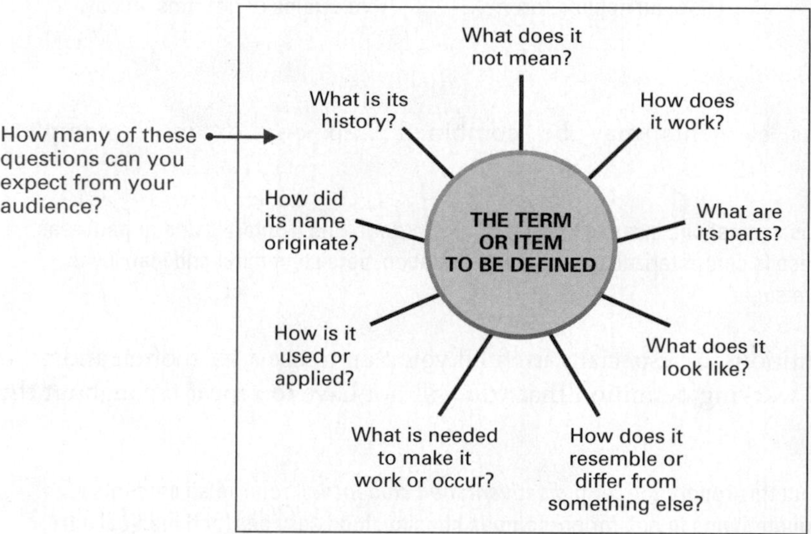

FIGURE 18.2 Questions for Expanding a Definition

As you read through the following sections, refer to the following sentence definition of the word *laser*, and consider how each expansion method provides detail in a different way:

Sentence definition

A laser is an electronic device that emits a highly concentrated beam of light.

Etymology

Sometimes, a word's origin (its development and changing meanings), also known as the word's etymology, can help clarify its meaning. For example, *biometrics* (the statistical analysis of biological data) is a word derived from the Greek *bio*, meaning "life," and *metron*, meaning "measure." You can use a dictionary to learn the origins of most words. Not all words develop from Greek, Latin, or other roots, however. For example, some terms are acronyms, derived from the first letters or parts of several words. Such is the case with the word *laser* (derived from *light amplification by stimulated emission of radiation*); therefore, to expand the sentence definition of *laser,* you might phrase your definition as follows:

"How did its name originate?"

The word *laser* is an acronym for *light amplification by stimulated emission of radiation*, and is the name for an electronic device that emits a highly concentrated beam of light.

History

In some cases, explaining the history of a term, concept, or procedure can be useful in expanding a definition. Specialized dictionaries and encyclopedias are good background sources. You might expand the definition of a laser by describing how the laser was invented:

> The early researchers in fiber optic communications were hampered by two principal difficulties—the lack of a sufficiently intense source of light and the absence of a medium which could transmit this light free from interference and with a minimum signal loss. Lasers emit a narrow beam of intense light, so their invention in 1960 solved the first problem. The development of a means to convey this signal was longer in coming, but scientists succeeded in developing the first communications-grade optical fiber of almost pure silica glass in 1970. (Stanton 28)

"What is its history?"

Negation

Some definitions can be clarified by an explanation of what the term *does not* mean. For example, the following definition of a laser eliminates any misconceptions an audience might already have about lasers:

> A laser is an electronic device that emits a highly concentrated beam of light. It is used for many beneficial purposes (including corrective eye and other surgeries), and not—as science fiction might tell you—as a transport medium to other dimensions.

"What does it not mean?"

Operating Principle

Anyone who wants to use a product correctly will need to know how it operates:

> Basically, a laser [uses electrical energy to produce] coherent light: light in which all the waves are in phase with each other, making the light hotter and more intense. (Gartaganis 23)

"How does it work?"

Analysis of Parts

To create a complete picture, be sure to list all the parts. If necessary, define individual parts as well, as in the following passage:

> A laser is an electronic device that emits a highly concentrated beam of light. To get a better idea of how a laser works, consider its three main parts:
>
> 1. [Lasers require] a source of energy, [such as] electric currents or even other lasers.
> 2. A resonant circuit... contains the lasing medium and has one fully reflecting end and one partially reflecting end. The medium—which can be a solid, liquid, or gas—absorbs the energy and releases it as a stream of photons [electromagnetic particles that emit light]. The photons... vibrate between the fully and partially reflecting ends of the resonant circuit, constantly accumulating energy—that is,

"What are its parts?"

they are amplified. After attaining a prescribed level of energy, the photons can pass through the partially reflecting surface as a beam of coherent light and encounter the optical elements.

3. Optical elements—lenses, prisms, and mirrors—modify size, shape, and other characteristics of the laser beam and direct it to its target. (Gartaganis 23)

Visuals

Make sure any visual you use is well labeled. Always introduce and explain your visual and place it near your discussion. If the visual is borrowed, credit the source. The following visual accompanies the previous analysis of parts:

"What does it look like?"

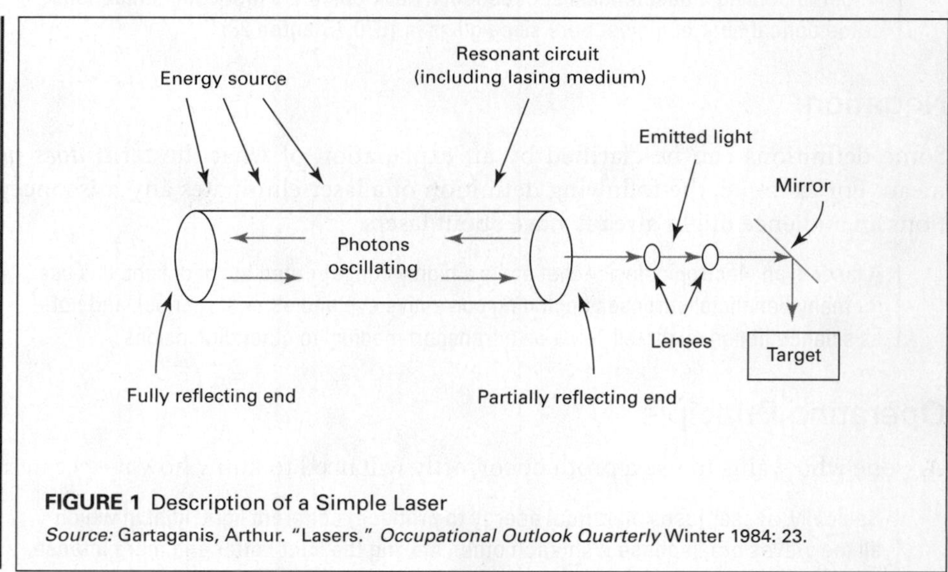

FIGURE 1 Description of a Simple Laser
Source: Gartaganis, Arthur. "Lasers." *Occupational Outlook Quarterly* Winter 1984: 23.

Comparison and Contrast

By comparing (showing similarities) or contrasting (showing differences) between new information and information your audience already understands, you help build a bridge between what people already know and what they don't. The following passage uses both comparison and contrast to expand upon a more basic definition of a laser:

"How does it resemble or differ from something else?"

Fiber optics technology results from the superior capacity of light waves to carry a communications signal. Sounds waves, radio waves, and light waves can all carry signals; their capacity increases with their frequency. Voice frequencies carried by telephone operate at 1000 cycles per second, or hertz. Television signals transmit at about 50 million hertz. Light waves, however, operate at frequencies in the hundreds of trillions of hertz. (Stanton 28)

Required Conditions

Some items or processes need special materials and handling, or they may have other requirements or restrictions. An expanded definition should include this important information:

> In order to emit a highly concentrated beam of light, the laser must absorb energy through the reflecting end of a resonant circuit, amplify the photons produced between the reflecting and partially reflecting end of the resonant circuit, and release the photons as a beam of light via a set of lenses, prisms, and mirrors.

"What is needed to make it work or occur?"

Examples

Examples are a powerful communication tool—as long as they are tailored to your audience's level of understanding. The following example shows how laser light is used in medical treatment:

> Lasers are increasingly used to treat health problems. Thousands of eye operations involving cataracts and detached retinas are performed every year by ophthalmologists.... Dermatologists treat skin problems.... Gynecologists treat problems of the reproductive system, and neurosurgeons even perform brain surgery—all using lasers transmitted through optical fibers. (Gartaganis 24–25)

"How is it used or applied?"

Depending on the complexity of what you need to define, you may need to combine multiple expansion methods, as in Figures 18.3 and 18.4. Whichever expansion strategies you use, be sure to document your information sources, as shown in "A Quick Guide to Documentation" (page 644).

Use as many expansion methods as needed

NOTE *An increasingly familiar (and user-friendly) format for expanded definition, especially for readers on the Web, is a listing of Frequently Asked Questions (FAQ), which organizes chunks of information as responses to questions people are likely to ask. This question-and-answer format creates a conversational style and conveys to readers the sense that their particular concerns are being addressed. Consider using a FAQ list whenever you want to increase reader interest and decrease resistance.*

SITUATIONS REQUIRING EXPANDED DEFINITIONS

The following two definitions (Figures 18.3 and 18.4) employ expansion methods suitable for their respective audiences' needs (and labeled in the margin). Like a good essay, both definitions are unified and coherent. Each paragraph is developed around one main idea and logically connected to other paragraphs. Transitions emphasize the connection between ideas. Visuals are incorporated. Each definition displays a level of technicality that is appropriate for the intended audience.

An Expanded Definition for Semitechnical Readers

The Situation. Ron Vasile, a lab assistant in his college's Electronics Engineering Technology program, has been asked to contribute to a reference manual for the program's incoming students. His first assignment is to prepare a section defining basic solenoid technology (Figure 18.3). As a way of getting started on this assignment, Ron creates the following audience and use profile.

Audience and Use Profile. The intended readers (future service technicians) are beginning student mechanics. Before they can repair a solenoid, they will need to know where the term *solenoid* comes from, what a solenoid looks like, how it works, how its parts operate, and how it is used. Diagrams will reinforce the explanations and enable readers to visualize this mechanism's parts and operating principle.

This definition is designed as an *introduction,* and so it offers only a general view of the mechanism. Because the readers are not engineering students, they do *not* need electromagnetic or mechanical theory (e.g., equations or graphs illustrating voltage magnitudes, joules, lines of force).

An Expanded Definition for Nontechnical Readers

The Situation. Amy Rogers has recently joined the public relations division of a government organization whose task is to explore the possible uses and applications of nanotechnology. She and other members of her division are helping to prepare a Web site that explains this complex topic to the general public. One of Amy's assignments is to prepare a definition of nanotechnology to be posted on the site. The definition shown in Figure 18.4 is written for hi-tech investors and other readers interested in new and promising technologies.

Audience and Use Profile. To understand *nanotechnology* and its implications, readers need an overview of what it is and how it developed, as well as its potential uses, present applications, health risks, and impact on the workforce. Question-type headings pose the questions in the same way readers are likely to ask them. Parenthetical definitions of *nanometer* and *micrometer* provide an essential sense of scale.

This audience would have little interest in the physics or physical chemistry involved, such as *carbon nanotubes* (engineered nanoparticles), *nanolasers* (advanced applications), or *computational nanotechnology* (theoretical aspects). They simply need the broadest possible picture, including a diagram that compares the size of nanoparticles with the size of more familiar items.

Each of these sample documents is developed from an audience and use profile based on the worksheet on page 31.

1

SOLENOID

A solenoid is an electrically energized coil that forms an electromagnet capable of performing mechanical functions. The term "solenoid" is derived from the word "sole," which in reference to electrical equipment means "a part of," or "contained inside, or with, other electrical equipment." The Greek word *solenoides* means "channel," or "shaped like a pipe."

A simple plunger-type solenoid consists of a coil of wire attached to an electrical source and an iron rod, or plunger, that passes in and out of the coil along the axis of the spiral. A return spring holds the rod outside the coil when the current is deenergized, as shown in Figure 1.

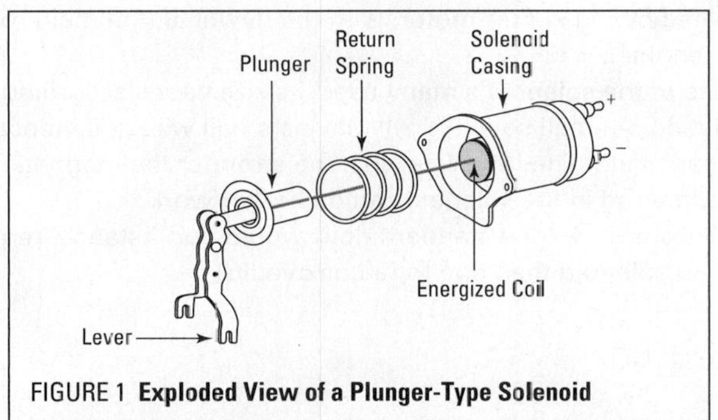

FIGURE 1 **Exploded View of a Plunger-Type Solenoid**

When the coil receives electric current, it becomes a magnet and thus draws the iron rod inside, along the length of its cylindrical center. With a lever attached to its end, the rod can transform electrical energy into mechanical force. The amount of mechanical force produced is the product of the number of turns in the coil, the strength of the current, and the magnetic conductivity of the rod.

The plunger-type solenoid in Figure 1 is commonly used in the starter-motor of an automobile engine. This type is 4.5 inches long and 2 inches in diameter, with a steel casing attached to the casing of the starter-motor. A linkage (pivoting lever) is attached at one end to the iron rod of the solenoid, and at the other end to the drive gear of the starter, as shown in Figure 2.

FIGURE 18.3 **An Expanded Definition for Semitechnical Readers**

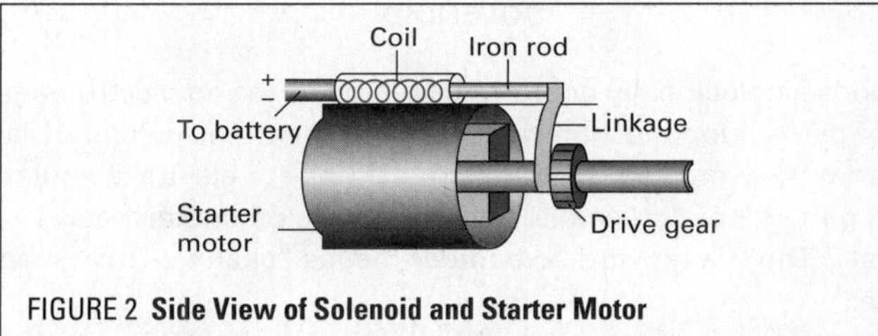

FIGURE 2 **Side View of Solenoid and Starter Motor**

When the ignition key is turned, current from the battery is supplied to the solenoid coil, and the iron rod is drawn inside the coil, thereby shifting the attached linkage. The linkage, in turn, engages the drive gear, activated by the starter-motor, with the flywheel (the main rotating gear of the engine).

Comparison of sizes and applications →

Because of the solenoid's many uses, its size varies according to the work it must do. A small solenoid will have a small wire coil, hence a weak magnetic field. The larger the coil, the stronger the magnetic field; in this case, the rod in the solenoid can do harder work.

An electronic lock for a standard door would, for instance, require a much smaller solenoid than one for a bank vault.

FIGURE 18.3 (*Continued*)

1

NANOTECHNOLOGY

What Is Nanotechnology?

Nanotechnology refers to the understanding and control of matter at dimensions of roughly 1 to 100 nanometers to produce new structures, materials, and devices. (A nanometer, µm, equals one-billionth of a meter; a sheet of paper is about 100,000 nanometers thick.) For further perspective, the diameter of DNA, our genetic material, is in the 2.5 nanometer range, while red blood cells are roughly 2.5 micrometers (a micrometer, mm, equals one-millionth of a meter), as shown in Figure 1.

Sentence definition

Parenthetical definitions

Comparison

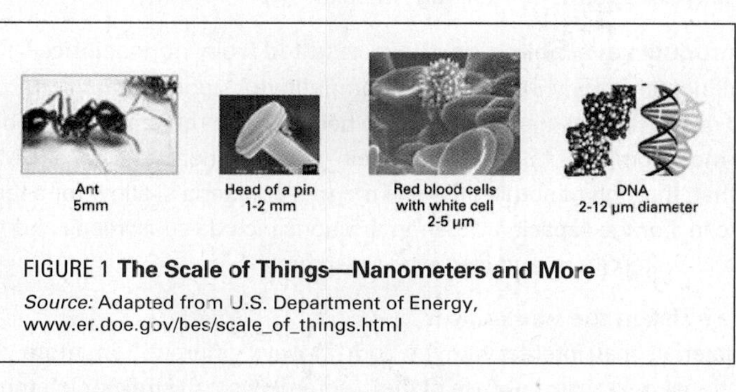

FIGURE 1 **The Scale of Things—Nanometers and More**

Source: Adapted from U.S. Department of Energy, www.er.doe.gov/bes/scale_of_things.html

A diagram comparing dimensions of nanoparticles with those of more familiar items

At the nanoscale level, the physical, chemical, and biological properties of materials differ from the properties of individual atoms and molecules or bulk matter. Nanotechnology research is directed toward understanding and creating improved materials, devices, and systems that exploit these new properties.

Contrast and operating principle

How did it develop?

Nanoscale science was enabled by advances in microscopy, most notably the electron, scanning-tunnel, and atomic-force microscopes, among others.

History

How is it used?

The use of nanoparticles is being researched and applied in many areas of technology and medicine, such as the following:

Examples

FIGURE 18.4 **An Expanded Definition for Nontechnical Readers** This type of question-and-answer format is often available on the Internet as a frequently asked questions, or FAQ, document.

Source: Adapted from Documents at the National Nanotechnology Initiative <www.nano.gov>.

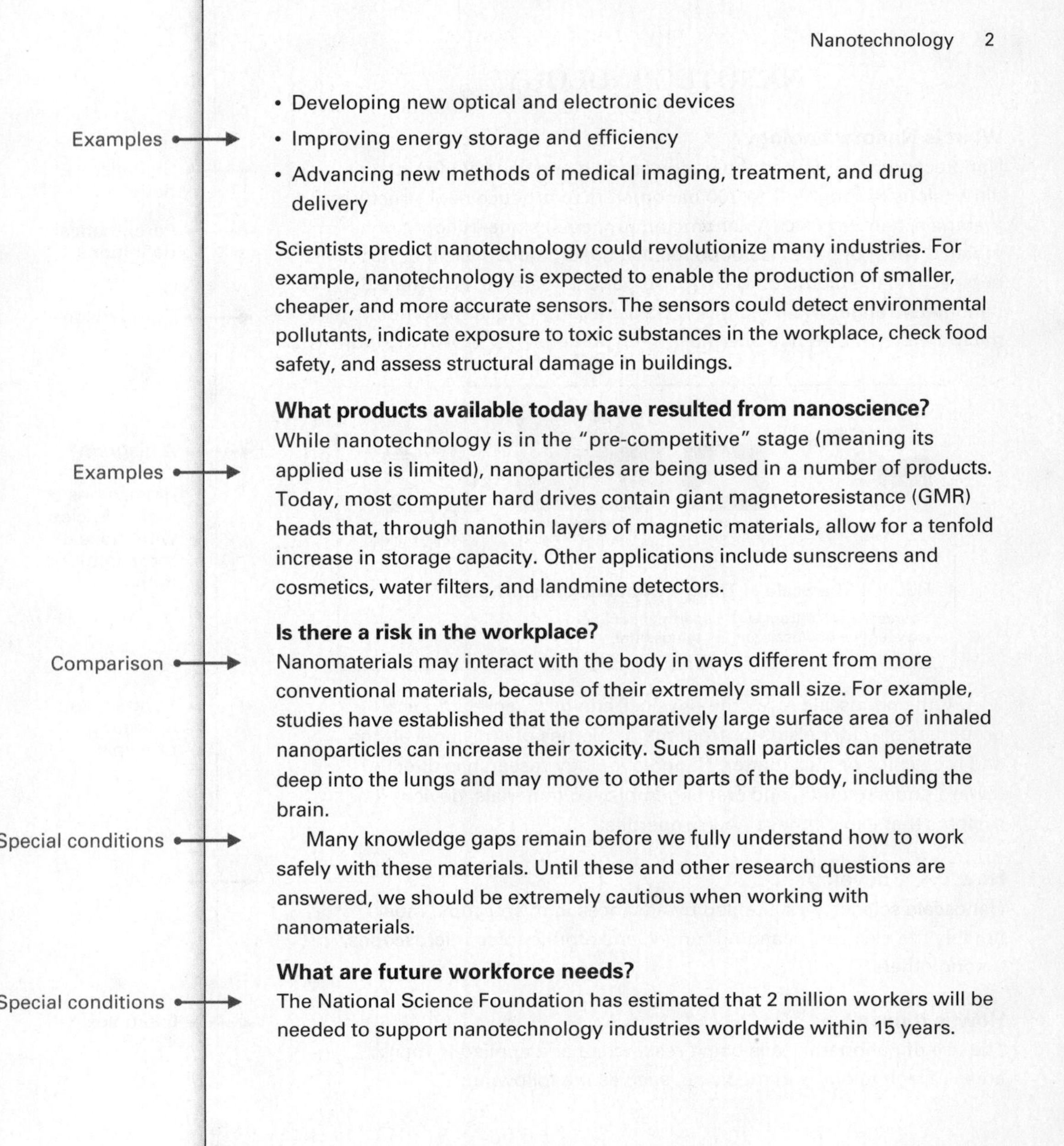

- Developing new optical and electronic devices
- Improving energy storage and efficiency
- Advancing new methods of medical imaging, treatment, and drug delivery

Scientists predict nanotechnology could revolutionize many industries. For example, nanotechnology is expected to enable the production of smaller, cheaper, and more accurate sensors. The sensors could detect environmental pollutants, indicate exposure to toxic substances in the workplace, check food safety, and assess structural damage in buildings.

What products available today have resulted from nanoscience?
While nanotechnology is in the "pre-competitive" stage (meaning its applied use is limited), nanoparticles are being used in a number of products. Today, most computer hard drives contain giant magnetoresistance (GMR) heads that, through nanothin layers of magnetic materials, allow for a tenfold increase in storage capacity. Other applications include sunscreens and cosmetics, water filters, and landmine detectors.

Is there a risk in the workplace?
Nanomaterials may interact with the body in ways different from more conventional materials, because of their extremely small size. For example, studies have established that the comparatively large surface area of inhaled nanoparticles can increase their toxicity. Such small particles can penetrate deep into the lungs and may move to other parts of the body, including the brain.

Many knowledge gaps remain before we fully understand how to work safely with these materials. Until these and other research questions are answered, we should be extremely cautious when working with nanomaterials.

What are future workforce needs?
The National Science Foundation has estimated that 2 million workers will be needed to support nanotechnology industries worldwide within 15 years.

FIGURE 18.4 (*Continued*)

PLACING DEFINITIONS IN A DOCUMENT

Placing printed definitions

Each time readers encounter an unfamiliar term or concept, that item should be defined. In a printed text, you can place brief definitions in parentheses or in the document's margin, aligned with the terms being defined. Sentence definitions should be part of the running text or, if they are numerous, listed in a glossary. Place an expanded definition either near the beginning of a long document or in an appendix (see page 535)—depending on whether the definition is essential to understanding the whole document or serves merely as a reference.

Using a glossary

A glossary alphabetically lists specialized terms and their definitions. It makes key definitions available to laypersons without interrupting technical readers. Use a glossary if your report contains numerous terms that may not be understood by all audience members. If fewer than five terms need defining, place them in the report introduction as working definitions, or use footnote definitions. If you use a glossary, announce its location: "(See the glossary at the end of this report)."

Figure 18.5 shows part of a glossary for a comparative analysis of two natural childbirth techniques, written by a nurse for expectant mothers.

GLOSSARY

Analgesic: a medication given to relieve pain during the first stage of labor.

Cervix: the neck-shaped anatomical structure that forms the mouth of the uterus.

Dilation: cervical expansion occurring during the first stage of labor.

First stage of labor: the stage in which the cervix dilates and the baby remains in the uterus.

Induction: the stimulating of labor by puncturing the membranes around the baby or by giving an oxytoxic drug (uterine contractant), or by doing both.

FIGURE 18.5 **A Partial Glossary**

How to prepare a glossary

Follow these suggestions for preparing a glossary:

- Define all terms unfamiliar to an intelligent layperson. When in doubt, over-defining is safer than underdefining.
- Define all terms by giving their class and distinguishing features (page 412), unless some terms need expanded definitions.
- List all terms in alphabetical order.
- On first use, place an asterisk in the text by each item defined in the glossary.
- List your glossary and its first page number in the table of contents.

On a Web site, you would use a link for each definition and/or provide a link to a separate glossary page. Web pages and hyperlinks are a good way to make definitions easily accessible, because readers can click on the item, read about it, and return to their original place on the page. See Figure 18.6 for a brochure that could also be set up as a web page, with links to specific definitions.

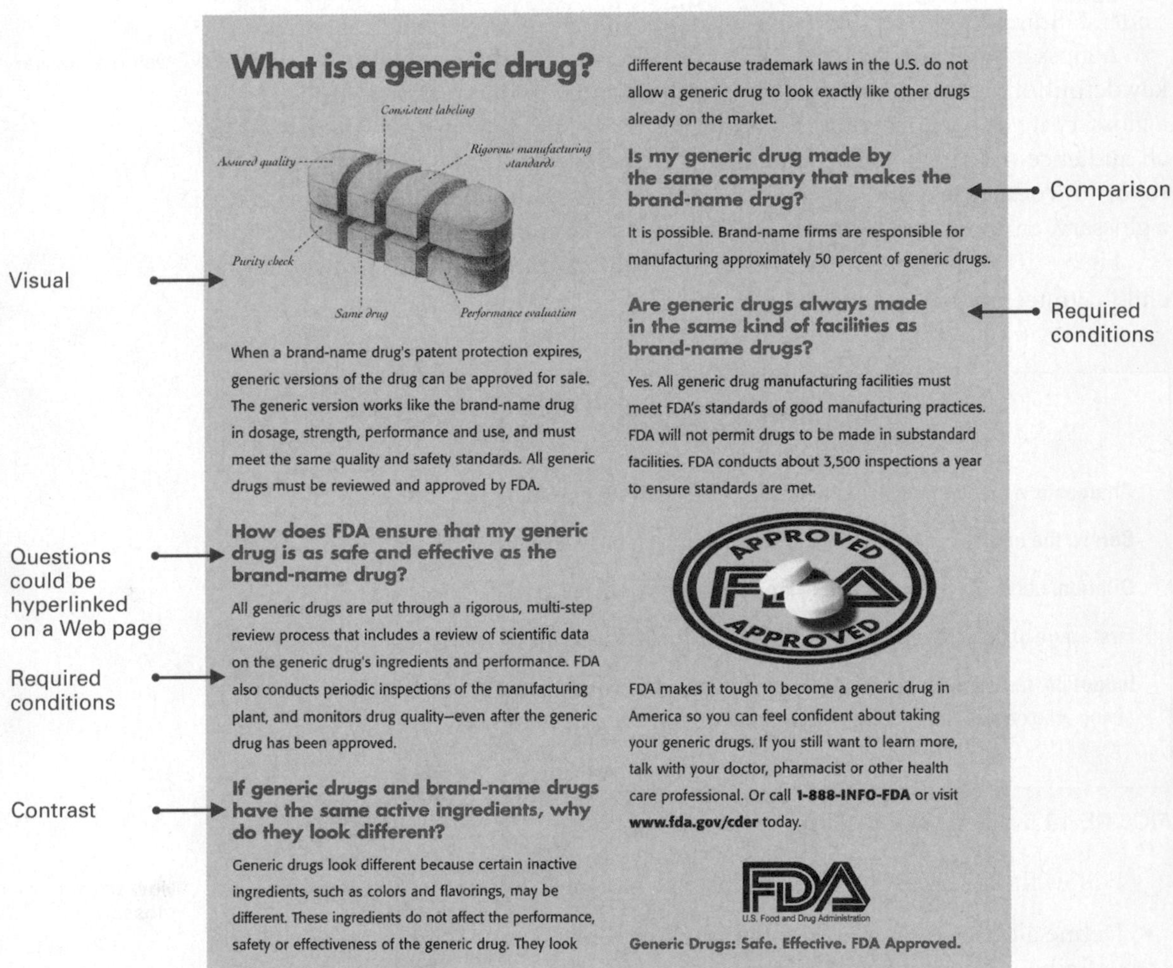

FIGURE 18.6 A Definition for Laypersons, Designed as a Two-Column Brochure

Source: U.S. Department of Health and Human Services. Food and Drug Administration.

GUIDELINES for Definitions

- **Decide on the level of detail you need.** Definitions vary greatly in length and detail, from a few words in parentheses to a multipage document. How much does this audience need in order to follow your explanation or grasp your point?
- **Classify the item precisely.** The narrower your class, the clearer your meaning. *Stress* is classified as an applied force; to say that stress "is what..." or "takes place when..." fails to denote a specific classification. Diabetes is precisely classified as a *metabolic disease,* not as a *medical term.*
- **Differentiate the item accurately.** If the distinguishing features are too broad, they will apply to more than the particular item you are defining. A definition of *brief* as a "legal document used in court" fails to differentiate *brief* from all other legal documents (*wills, affidavits,* and the like).
- **Avoid circular definitions.** Do not repeat, as part of the distinguishing feature, the word you are defining. "Stress is an applied force that places stress on a body" is a circular definition.
- **Expand your definition selectively.** Begin with a sentence definition and select the best combination of development strategies for your audience and purpose.
- **Use visuals to clarify your meaning.** No matter how clearly you explain, as the saying goes, a picture can be worth a thousand words—even more so when used with readable, accurate writing.
- **Know "how much is enough."** Don't insult people's intelligence by giving needless details or spelling out the obvious.
- **Consider the legal implications of your definition.** What does an "unsatisfactory job performance" mean in an evaluation of a company employee: that the employee should be fired, required to attend a training program, or given one or more chances to improve ("Performance Appraisal" 3–4)? Failure to spell out your meaning invites a lawsuit.
- **Consider the ethical implications of your definition.** Be sure your definition of a fuzzy or ambiguous term such as "safe levels of exposure," or "conservative investment," or "acceptable risk" is based on a fair and accurate interpretation of the facts. Consider, for example, a recent U.S. cigarette company's claim that cigarette smoking in the Czech Republic promoted "fiscal benefits," defined, in this case, by the fact that smokers die young, thus eliminating pension and health care costs for the elderly!
- **Place your definition in an appropriate location.** Allow readers to access the definition and then return to the main text with as little disruption as possible.
- **Cite your sources as needed.** See Appendix A.

CHECKLIST Definitions

(Numbers in parentheses refer to the first page of discussion.)

Content

- ☐ Is the type of definition (parenthetical, sentence, expanded) suited to its audience and purpose? (411)
- ☐ Does the definition adequately classify the item? (425)
- ☐ Does the definition adequately differentiate the item? (425)
- ☐ Will the level of technicality connect with the audience? (410)
- ☐ Have circular definitions been avoided? (425)
- ☐ Is the expanded definition developed adequately for its audience? (425)
- ☐ Is the expanded definition free of needless details for its audience? (425)
- ☐ Are visuals used adequately and appropriately? (416)
- ☐ Are all information sources properly documented? (425)
- ☐ Is the definition ethically and legally acceptable? (425)

Arrangement

- ☐ Is the expanded definition unified and coherent (like an essay)? (417)
- ☐ Are transitions between ideas adequate? (417)
- ☐ Is the definition appropriately located in the document? (423)

Style and Page Design

- ☐ Is the definition in plain English? (410)
- ☐ Are sentences clear, concise, and fluent? (210)
- ☐ Is word choice precise? (225)
- ☐ Is the definition grammatical? (680)
- ☐ Is the page design inviting and accessible? (293)

Projects

GENERAL

Choose a situation and an audience, and prepare an expanded definition designed for this audience's level of technical understanding. Use at least four expansion strategies, including at least one visual. In preparing your expanded definition, consult no fewer than four outside references. Cite and document each source as shown in "A Quick Guide to Documentation" (page 644).

TEAM

Divide into groups by majors or interests. Appoint one person as group manager. Decide on an item, concept, or process that would require an expanded definition for laypersons. Some examples follow:

From computer science: an algorithm, binary coding, or systems analysis
From nursing: a pacemaker, coronary bypass surgery, or natural childbirth

Complete an Audience and Use Profile (page 31). Once your group has decided on the appropriate expansion strategies, the group manager will assign each member to work on one or two specific strategies as part of the definition. As a group, edit and incorporate the collected material into an expanded definition, revising as often as needed. The group manager will assign one member to present the definition in class.

Your instructor may stipulate a brochure format for your definition, as in Figure 18.6. (For more on this format, refer to "brochures" in this book's Index.)

DIGITAL AND SOCIAL MEDIA

Convert your expanded definition from the General Project into a Web page. Include links to your information sources using a question and answer format, as in Figure 18.6.

GLOBAL

Any definition you write may be read by someone for whom English is not a first language. Locate an expanded definition on Wikipedia that may be difficult for a non-American or non–native English speaker to understand for some reason (use of idioms, use of abbreviations, use of American metaphors such as sports metaphors not used in other countries). Explain how the definition could be reworded so that most readers would understand it.

19 Technical Descriptions, Specifications, and Marketing Materials

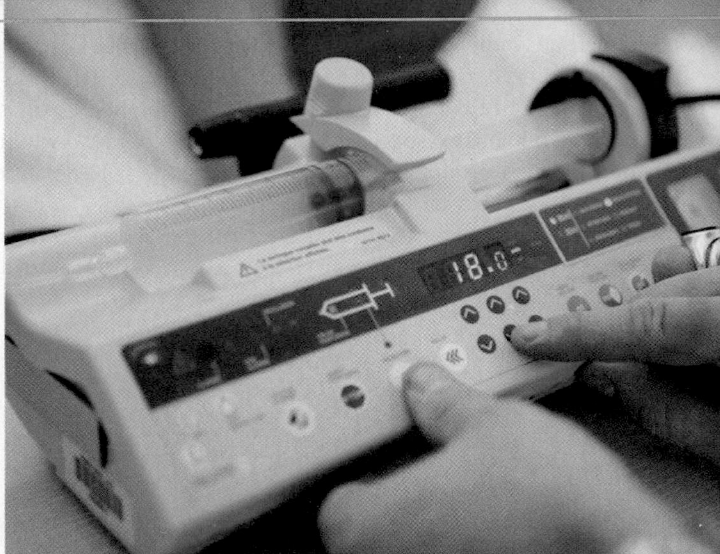

"My company manufactures devices for the medical industry. I find that much of my writing involves descriptions, specifications, and even marketing materials. My audiences range from highly technical ones (say, industrial designers or nurses) to legal (say, government regulators), to nontechnical (say, patients and their families). In all cases, I have to be sure that my materials serve the exact information needs and purposes of the intended audience."

—Zach Bowen,
Biomedical Engineer

LEARNING OBJECTIVES FOR THIS CHAPTER

- Understand the role of audience and purpose in technical description
- Differentiate between product and process descriptions
- Appreciate the requirement for objectivity in such descriptions
- Recognize the main components of a technical description
- Write a product and/or process description
- Write a set of specifications
- Write a technical marketing document

Description (creating a picture with words and images) is part of all writing. But a technical description conveys information about a product or mechanism to someone who will use it, operate it, assemble it, or manufacture it, or to someone who needs to know more about it. Any item can be visualized from countless different perspectives. Therefore, the way you describe something—your perspective—depends on your purpose and the audience's needs.

CONSIDERING AUDIENCE AND PURPOSE

Audience considerations

Descriptions and definitions often go hand in hand and provide the foundation for many types of technical explanation. Definitions answer the questions "What is it?" or "What does it entail?" To help readers to *visualize*, descriptions answer additional questions that include "What does it look like?" "What are its parts?" "What does it do?" "How does it work?" or "How does it happen?"

Purpose considerations

Consider exactly what you want readers to know and why they need to know it. Before writing your description, you may want to jot down an audience and purpose statement such as: "The purpose of this description is to help plumbing apprentices understand the parts of the Heatwave home water heater and how those parts work together to produce hot water."

TYPES OF TECHNICAL DESCRIPTIONS

Product versus process descriptions

Technical descriptions divide into two basic types: *product* descriptions and *process* descriptions. Anyone learning to use a particular device (say, a stethoscope) relies on product description. Anyone wanting to understand the steps or stages in a complex event (say, how lightning is produced) relies on process description.

For example, the product description in Figure 19.1, part of an owner's manual, gives do-it-yourself homeowners a clear image of the overall device and its parts. The accompanying process description in Figure 19.2 shows the device in action.

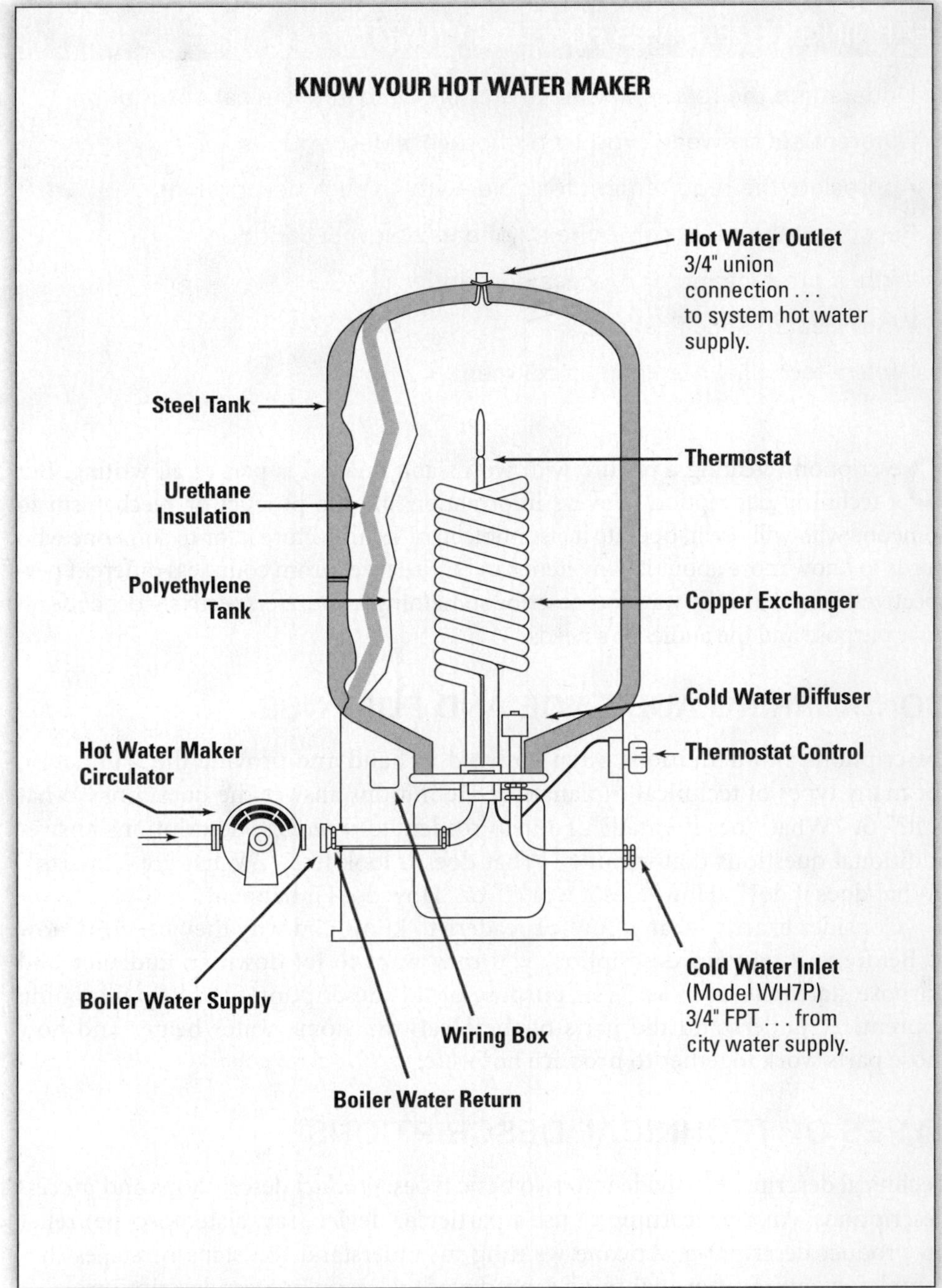

FIGURE 19.1 **A Product Description** This description allows readers to visualize the basic parts and the relationships among the parts.

Source: Courtesy of AMTROL Inc.

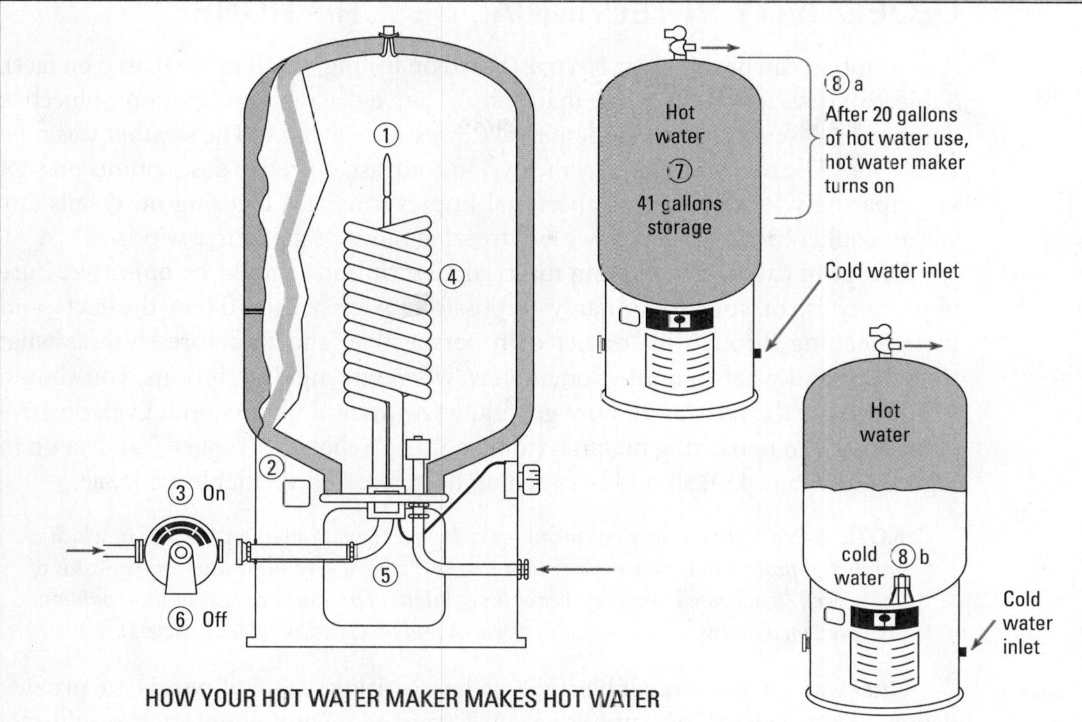

HOW YOUR HOT WATER MAKER MAKES HOT WATER

1. The thermostat calls for energy to make hot water in your Hot Water Maker.
2. The built-in relay signals your boiler/burner to generate energy by heating boiler water.
3. The Hot Water Maker circulator comes on and circulates hot boiler water through the inside of the Hot Water Maker heat exchanger.
4. Heat energy is transferred, or "exchanged" from the boiler water inside the exchanger to the water surrounding it in the Hot Water Maker.
5. The boiler water, after the maximum of heat energy is taken out of it, is returned to the boiler so it can be reheated.
6. When enough heat has been exchanged to raise the temperature in your Hot Water Maker to the desired temperature, the thermostat will de-energize the relay and turn off the Hot Water Maker circulator and your boiler/burner. This will take approximately 23 minutes—when you first start up the Hot Water Maker. During use, reheating will be approximately 9–12 minutes.
7. You now have 41 gallons of hot water in storage . . . ready for use in washing machines, showers, sinks, etc. This 41 gallons of hot water will stay hot up to 10 hours, if you don't use it, without causing your boiler/burner to come on. (Unless, of course, you need it for heating your home in the winter.)
8. When you do use hot water, you will be able to use approximately 20 gallons, before the Hot Water Maker turns on. Then you will still have 21 gallons of hot water left for use, as your Hot Water Maker "recoups" 20 gallons of cold water. This means, during normal use (3 1/2 GPM Flow), you will never run out of hot water.

You can expect substantial energy savings with your Hot Water Maker, as its ability to store hot water and efficiently transfer energy to make more hot water will keep your boiler off for longer periods of time.

FIGURE 19.2 **A Process Description** This description allows readers to visualize the sequence of events in producing the hot water.
Source: Courtesy of AMTROL Inc.

OBJECTIVITY IN TECHNICAL DESCRIPTIONS

Subjective versus objective descriptions

A description can be mainly *subjective* (based on feeling) or *objective* (based on fact). Subjective descriptions do more than simply convey factual information; subjective descriptions use sensory and judgmental expressions such as "The weather was miserable" or "The room was terribly messy." In contrast, objective descriptions present an impartial view, filtering out personal impressions and focusing on details any viewer could observe ("All day, we had freezing rain and gale-force winds").

Why descriptions should be objective

Descriptions have ethical implications

Except in cases of marketing material, descriptions should be objective. Pure objectivity is, of course, humanly impossible. Each writer filters the facts and their meaning through his or her own perspective, and therefore chooses what to include and what to omit. Nonetheless, when writing descriptions, you should communicate the facts as they are generally known and understood. Even positive claims made in marketing material (for example, "reliable," "rugged," and so on in Figure 19.9, page 450) should be based on objective and verifiable evidence.

> **NOTE** *Being objective does not mean forsaking personal evaluation in cases in which a product or process may be unsafe or unsound. An ethical communicator, in the words of one expert, "is obligated to express her or his opinions of products, as long as these opinions are based on objective and responsible research and observation" (MacKenzie 3).*

How to remain objective

One way to maintain objectivity when writing descriptions is to provide details that are visual, not emotional. Ask yourself what any observer would recognize, or what a camera would record. For example, instead of saying, "His office has a depressing atmosphere" (not everyone would agree), say "His office has broken windows looking out on a brick wall, missing floorboards, broken chairs, and a ceiling with chunks of plaster missing."

A second way to maintain objectivity is to use precise and informative language. For instance, specify location and position, exact measurements, weights, and dimensions, instead of using inexact and subjective words like *large, long*, and *near*.

> **NOTE** *Never confuse precise language with overly complicated technical terms or needless jargon. For example, don't say "phlebotomy specimen" instead of "blood," "thermal attenuation" instead of "insulation," or "proactive neutralization" instead of "damage control." General readers prefer nontechnical language—as long as the simpler words do the job.*

ELEMENTS OF A USABLE DESCRIPTION

Clear and Limiting Title

Give an immediate forecast

An effective title promises exactly what the document will deliver—no more and no less. For example, the title "A Description of a Velo Ten-Speed Racing Bicycle" promises a comprehensive description. If you intend to describe the braking mechanism only, be sure your title indicates this focus: "A Description of the Velo's Center-Pull Caliper Braking Mechanism."

Appropriate Level of Detail and Technicality

Give enough detail to convey a clear picture, but do not burden readers needlessly. Identify your audience and its reasons for using your description. Focus carefully on your purpose.

The descriptions of the hot water maker in Figures 19.1 and 19.2 focus on *what this model looks like, what it's made of,* and *how it works.* Its intended audience of do-it-yourselfers will know already what a hot water maker is and what it does. That audience will need no background. (A description of *how this product was put together* appears with the installation and maintenance instructions later in the owner's manual.)

Give readers exactly and only what they need

In contrast, *specifications* (page 443) for manufacturing the hot water maker would describe each part in exacting detail (e.g., the steel tank's required thickness and pressure rating as well as required percentages of iron, carbon, and other constituents in the steel alloy).

Visuals

Use drawings, diagrams, or photographs generously—with captions and labels that help readers interpret what they are seeing. Notice how the diagram in Figure 19.3 provides a simple but dynamic picture of a process in action. Economy in a visual often equals clarity. Avoid verbal and visual clutter.

Let the visual repeat, restate, or reinforce the prose

Sources for descriptive graphics include drawing or architectural drafting programs, clip art, electronic scans, and downloads from the Internet. (See page 278 for a sampling of Web sites and discussion of legal issues regarding the use of online graphics.)

Clearest Descriptive Sequence

Any item or process usually has its own logic of organization, based on (1) the way it appears as a static object, (2) the way its parts operate in order, or (3) the way its parts are assembled. As a writer you can describe these relationships, respectively, in spatial, functional, or chronological sequence.

Organize for the reader's understanding

Spatial Sequence. Part of all physical descriptions, a spatial sequence answers these questions: *What does it do? What does it look like? What parts and materials is it made of?* Use this sequence when you want readers to visualize a static item or a mechanism at rest (an office interior, the Statue of Liberty, a plot of land, a chainsaw, or a computer keyboard). Can readers best visualize this item from front to rear, left to right, top to bottom? (What logical path do the parts create?) A retractable pen, for example, would logically be viewed from outside to inside. The specifications in Figure 19.6 (page 445) proceed from the ground upward.

A spatial sequence parallels the reader's angle of vision in viewing the item

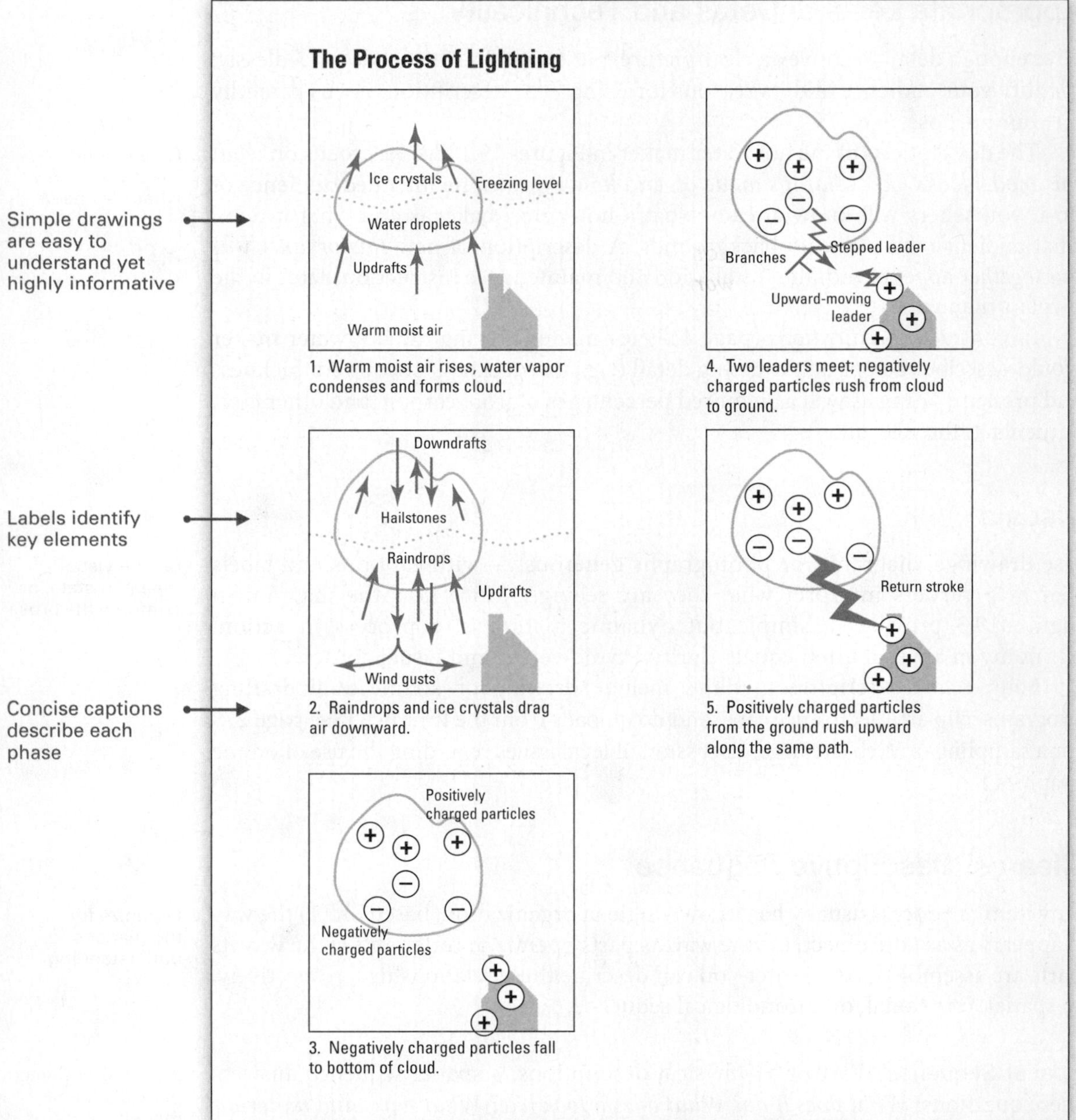

The Process of Lightning
Ice crystals
Freezing level
Water droplets
Updrafts
Warm moist air
1. Warm moist air rises, water vapor condenses and forms cloud.
Branches
Stepped leader
Upward-moving leader
4. Two leaders meet; negatively charged particles rush from cloud to ground.
Downdrafts
Hailstones
Raindrops
Updrafts
Wind gusts
2. Raindrops and ice crystals drag air downward.
Return stroke
5. Positively charged particles from the ground rush upward along the same path.
Positively charged particles
Negatively charged particles
3. Negatively charged particles fall to bottom of cloud.
Simple drawings are easy to understand yet highly informative
Labels identify key elements
Concise captions describe each phase

FIGURE 19.3 A Process Description That Minimizes Distracting Detail In an experiment, students who were given this visual alone were better able to understand the process of lightning than students who were given 550 words of text along with the visual.

Source: From Richard E. Mayer, et al. "When Less Is More: Meaningful Learning From Visual and Verbal Summaries of Science Textbook Lessons," *Journal of Educational Psychology,* Vol. 88, No. 1, pp. 64-73. Copyright © 1996 by the American Psychological Association. Reprinted by permission of the American Psychological Association and Richard E. Mayer.

Functional Sequence. The functional sequence answers this question: *How does it work?* It is best used in describing a mechanism in action, such as a 35-millimeter camera, a nuclear warhead, a smoke detector, or a car's cruise-control system. The logic of the item is reflected by the order in which its parts function. Like the hot water maker in Figure 19.2, a mechanism usually has only one functional sequence.

A functional sequence parallels the order in which parts operate

Chronological Sequence. A chronological sequence answers these questions: *How is it assembled? How does it work? How does it happen?* Use the chronological sequence for an item that is best visualized in terms of its order of assembly (such as a piece of furniture, a tent, or a prehung window or door unit). Architects might find a spatial sequence best for describing a proposed beach house to clients; however, they would use a chronological sequence (of blueprints) for specifying for the builder the prescribed dimensions, materials, and construction methods at each stage of the process.

A chronological sequence parallels the order in which parts are assembled or stages occur

NOTE *Combine these sequences as needed. For example, in describing an automobile jack (for a car owner's manual) you would employ a spatial sequence to help readers recognize this item, a functional sequence to show them how it works, and a chronological sequence to help them assemble and use the jack correctly.*

AN OUTLINE FOR PRODUCT DESCRIPTION

Description of a complex mechanism almost invariably calls for an outline. This model is adaptable to any description.

I. Introduction: General Description[1]
- A. Definition, Function, and Background of the Item
- B. Purpose (and Audience—for classroom only)
- C. Overall Description (with general visuals, if applicable)
- D. Principle of Operation (if applicable)
- E. Preview of Major Parts

II. Description and Function of Parts
- A. Part One in Your Descriptive Sequence
  1. Definition
  2. Shape, dimensions, material (with specific visuals)
  3. Subparts (if applicable)
  4. Function
  5. Relation to adjoining parts

[1]In most descriptions, the subdivisions in the introduction can be combined and need not appear as individual headings in the document.

6. Mode of attachment (if applicable)

B. Part Two in Your Descriptive Sequence (and so on)

III. Conclusion and Operating Description

A. Summary (used only in a long, complex description)

B. Interrelation of Parts

C. One Complete Operating Cycle

You might modify, delete, or combine certain components of this outline to suit your subject, purpose, and audience.

A SITUATION REQUIRING PRODUCT DESCRIPTION

The following description of a solar collector, aimed toward a general audience, adapts the previous outline model.

A Mechanism Description for a Nontechnical Audience

The Situation. Roxanne Payton is a mechanical engineer specializing in green energy technologies. Roxanne prepared this description (Figure 19.4) as part of an informational booklet on solar energy systems distributed by her company, Eco-Solutions.

Audience and Use Profile. The audience here will be homeowners or potential homeowners interested in incorporating solar flat-plate collectors as a heating source. Although many of these people probably lack technical expertise, they presumably have some general knowledge about active solar heating systems. Therefore, this description will focus on the collectors rather than on the entire system, while omitting specific technical data (for example, the heat conducting and corrosive properties of copper versus aluminum in the absorber plates). The team of engineers who designed the collector would include such data in research-and-development reports for the manufacturer. Informed laypersons, however, need only the information that will help them visualize and understand how a basic collector operates.

Diagrams will be especially effective descriptive tools because they simplify the view by removing distracting features; labels will help readers interpret what they are seeing.

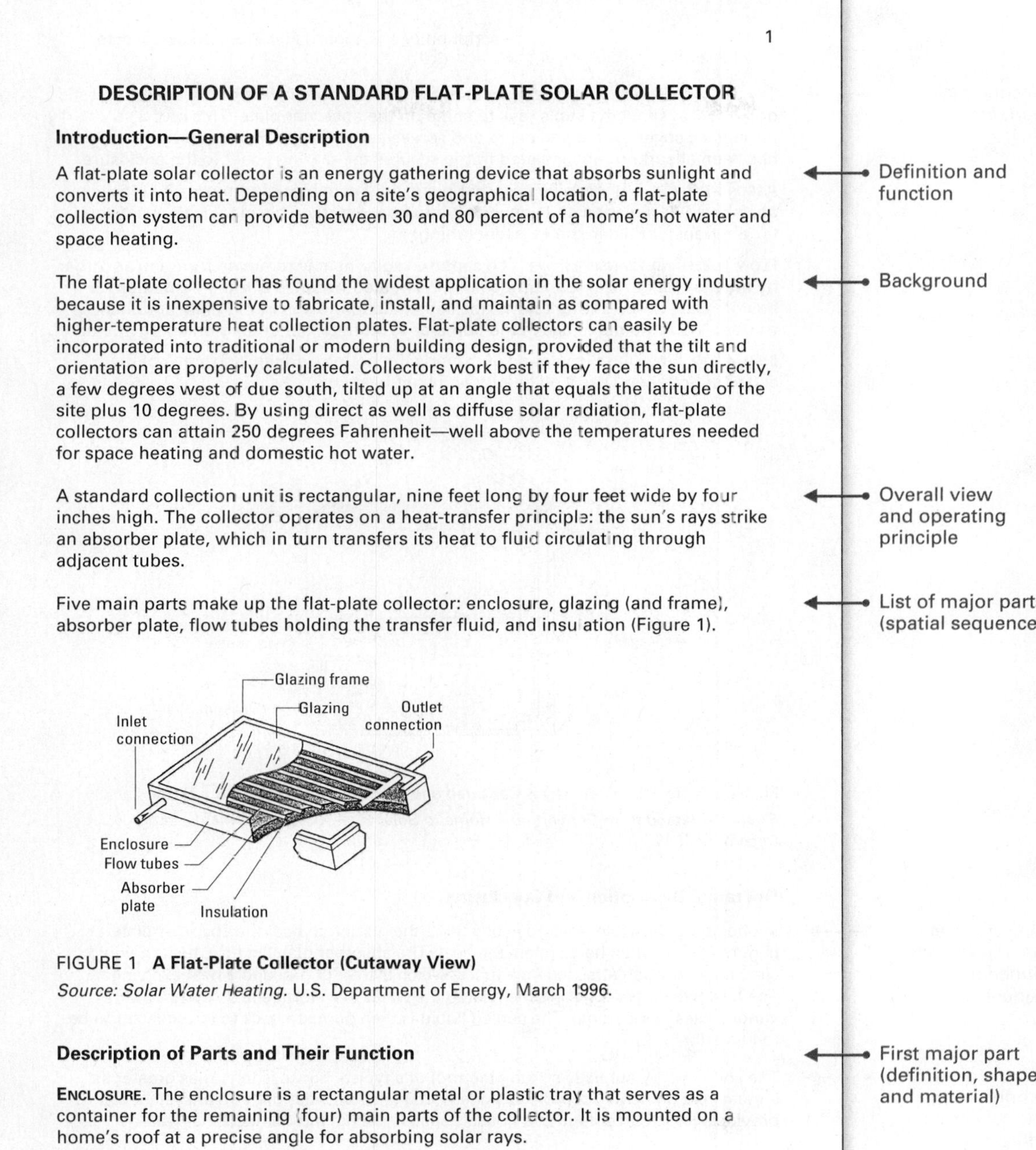

1

DESCRIPTION OF A STANDARD FLAT-PLATE SOLAR COLLECTOR

Introduction—General Description

A flat-plate solar collector is an energy gathering device that absorbs sunlight and converts it into heat. Depending on a site's geographical location, a flat-plate collection system can provide between 30 and 80 percent of a home's hot water and space heating.

← Definition and function

The flat-plate collector has found the widest application in the solar energy industry because it is inexpensive to fabricate, install, and maintain as compared with higher-temperature heat collection plates. Flat-plate collectors can easily be incorporated into traditional or modern building design, provided that the tilt and orientation are properly calculated. Collectors work best if they face the sun directly, a few degrees west of due south, tilted up at an angle that equals the latitude of the site plus 10 degrees. By using direct as well as diffuse solar radiation, flat-plate collectors can attain 250 degrees Fahrenheit—well above the temperatures needed for space heating and domestic hot water.

← Background

A standard collection unit is rectangular, nine feet long by four feet wide by four inches high. The collector operates on a heat-transfer principle: the sun's rays strike an absorber plate, which in turn transfers its heat to fluid circulating through adjacent tubes.

← Overall view and operating principle

Five main parts make up the flat-plate collector: enclosure, glazing (and frame), absorber plate, flow tubes holding the transfer fluid, and insulation (Figure 1).

← List of major parts (spatial sequence)

FIGURE 1 **A Flat-Plate Collector (Cutaway View)**
Source: Solar Water Heating. U.S. Department of Energy, March 1996.

Description of Parts and Their Function

← First major part (definition, shape, and material)

Enclosure. The enclosure is a rectangular metal or plastic tray that serves as a container for the remaining (four) main parts of the collector. It is mounted on a home's roof at a precise angle for absorbing solar rays.

FIGURE 19.4 **A Mechanism Description for a Nontechnical Audience** Readers are given only as much detail as they need to understand and visualize the item.

Second major part, etc.

Glazing (and Frame). The glazing consists of one or more layers of transparent plastic or glass that allow the sun's rays to shine on the absorber plate. This part also provides a cover for the enclosure and serves as insulation by trapping the heat that has been absorbed. An insulated frame secures the glazing sheet to the enclosure.

Absorber Plate. The metallic absorber plate, coated in black for maximum efficiency, absorbs solar radiation and converts it into heat energy. This plate is the heat source for the transfer fluid in the adjacent tubing.

Flow Tubes and Transfer Fluid. The captured solar heat is removed from the absorber by means of a transfer medium; generally, treated water. The transfer medium is heated as it passes through flow tubes attached to the absorbing plate and then transported to points of use in the home or to storage, depending on energy demand.

Insulation. Fiberglass insulation surrounds the bottom, edges, and sides of the collector, to retain absorbed energy and limit heat loss.

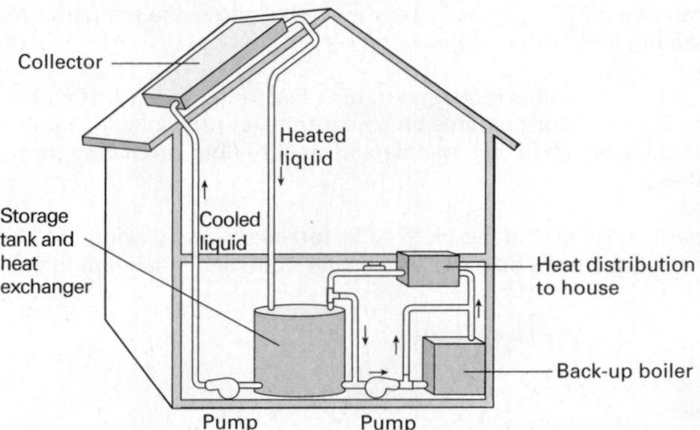

FIGURE 2 **How Solar Energy Is Captured and Distributed Throughout a Home**
Source: Adapted from *Converting a Home to Solar Heat.* U.S. Department of Energy, December 1995.

Operating Description and Conclusion

One complete operating cycle (functional sequence)

In one operating cycle, solar rays penetrate the glazing to heat the absorber plate (Figure 2). Insulation helps retain the heat. The absorber plate, in turn, heats a liquid circulating through attached flow tubes, which is then pumped to a heat exchanger. The heat exchanger transfers the heat to the water in a storage tank, pumped to various uses in the home. The cooled liquid is then pumped back to the collector to be re-heated.

A conclusion emphasizing the collector's efficiency

The solar energy annually striking the roof of a typical house is ten times greater its annual heat demand. Properly designed and installed, a flat-plate solar system can provide a large percentage of a house's space heating and domestic hot water.

FIGURE 19.4 (*Continued*)

AN OUTLINE FOR PROCESS DESCRIPTION

A description of how things work or happen divides the process into its parts or principles. Colleagues and clients need to know how stock and bond prices are governed, how your bank reviews a mortgage application, how an optical fiber conducts an impulse, and so on. A process description must be detailed enough to allow readers to follow the process step by step.

Much of your college writing explains how things happen. Your audience is your professor, who will evaluate what you have learned. Because this person knows *more* than you do about the subject, you often discuss only the main points, omitting the types of details that uninformed readers would require.

But your real challenge comes in describing a process for audiences who know *less* than you do, and who are neither willing nor able to fill in the blank spots; you then become the teacher, and the audience members become your students.

Introduce your description by telling what the process is, and why, when, and where it happens. In the body, tell how it happens, analyzing each stage in sequence. In the conclusion, summarize the stages, and describe one full cycle of the process.

Sections from the following general outline can be adapted to any process description:

I. Introduction
- A. Definition, Background, and Purpose of the Process
- B. Intended Audience (usually omitted for workplace audiences)
- C. Prior Knowledge Needed to Understand the Process
- D. Brief Description of the Process
- E. Principle of Operation
- F. Special Conditions Needed for the Process to Occur
- G. Definitions of Special Terms
- H. Preview of Stages

II. Stages in the Process
- A. First Major Stage
  1. Definition and purpose
  2. Special conditions needed for the specific stage
  3. Substages (if applicable)
     a.
     b.
- B. Second Stage (and so on)

III. Conclusion
- A. Summary of Major Stages
- B. One Complete Process Cycle

Adapt this outline to the process you are describing.

A SITUATION REQUIRING PROCESS DESCRIPTION

The following document is patterned after the sample outline.

A Process Description for a Nontechnical Audience

The Situation. Bill Kelly belongs to an environmental group studying the problem of acid rain in its Massachusetts community. (Massachusetts is among the states most affected by acid rain.) To gain community support, the environmentalists must educate citizens about the problem. Bill's group is publishing and mailing a series of brochures. The first brochure explains how acid rain is formed (Figure 19.5).

Audience and Use Profile. Some will already be interested in the problem; others will have no awareness (or interest). Therefore, explanation is given at the lowest level of technicality (no chemical formulas, equations). But the explanation needs to be vivid enough to appeal to less aware or less interested readers. Visuals create interest and illustrate the situation simply. To give an explanation thorough enough for broad understanding, the process is divided into three chronological steps: how acid rain develops, spreads, and destroys.

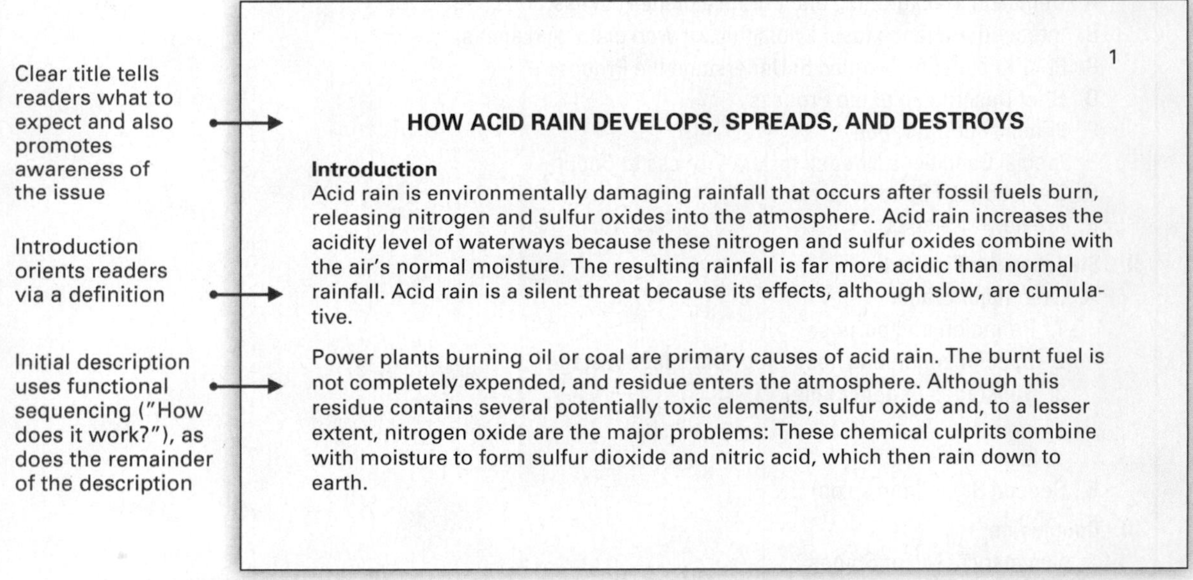

Clear title tells readers what to expect and also promotes awareness of the issue

Introduction orients readers via a definition

Initial description uses functional sequencing ("How does it work?"), as does the remainder of the description

1

HOW ACID RAIN DEVELOPS, SPREADS, AND DESTROYS

Introduction

Acid rain is environmentally damaging rainfall that occurs after fossil fuels burn, releasing nitrogen and sulfur oxides into the atmosphere. Acid rain increases the acidity level of waterways because these nitrogen and sulfur oxides combine with the air's normal moisture. The resulting rainfall is far more acidic than normal rainfall. Acid rain is a silent threat because its effects, although slow, are cumulative.

Power plants burning oil or coal are primary causes of acid rain. The burnt fuel is not completely expended, and residue enters the atmosphere. Although this residue contains several potentially toxic elements, sulfur oxide and, to a lesser extent, nitrogen oxide are the major problems: These chemical culprits combine with moisture to form sulfur dioxide and nitric acid, which then rain down to earth.

FIGURE 19.5 A Process Description for a Nontechnical Audience Readers can follow the process as it unfolds.

2

The Process

How Acid Rain Develops. Once fossil fuels have been burned, their usefulness ends. It is here that the acid rain problem begins (Figure 1).

Headers in "The Process" mirror the description's title

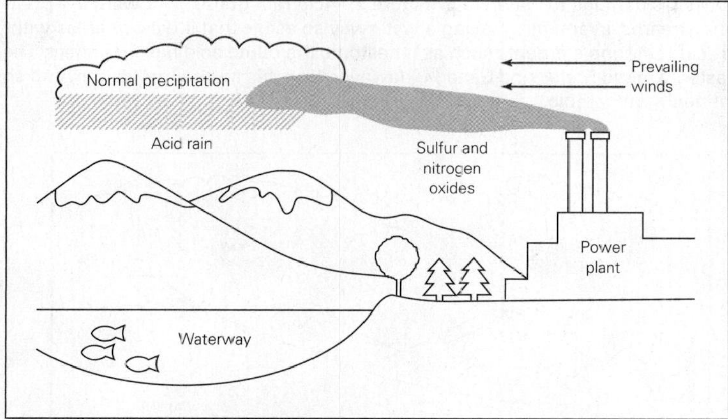

FIGURE 1 **How Acid Rain Develops and Spreads**

Clearly labeled visual enhances prose description of process

Acid level is measured by pH readings. The pH scale runs from 0 through 14—a pH of 7 is neutral. (Distilled water has a pH of 7.) Numbers above 7 indicate increasing alkalinity. (Household ammonia has a pH of 11.) Numbers below 7 indicate increasing acidity. Movement in either direction on the scale means multiplying by 10. Lemon juice, with a pH value of 2, is 10 times more acidic than apples, with a pH of 3, and 1,000 times more acidic than carrots, with a pH of 5.

Additional definition introduces a new concept ("pH")

Because of carbon dioxide (an acid substance) normally present in air, unaffected rainfall has a pH of 5.6. At this time, the pH of precipitation in the northeastern United States and Canada is between 4.5 and 4. In Massachusetts, rain and snowfall have an average pH reading of 4.1. A pH reading below 5 is considered abnormally acidic, and therefore a threat to aquatic populations.

How Acid Rain Spreads. Although we might expect areas containing power plants to be most severely affected, acid rain can in fact travel thousands of miles from its source. Stack gases escape and drift with the wind currents, traveling great distances before they return to earth as acid rain (Figure 1).

For roughly two to five days after emission, the gases follow the prevailing winds far from the point of origin. Estimates show that about 50 percent of the acid rain that affects Canada originates in the United States; conversely, 15 to 25 percent of U.S. acid rain originates in Canada.

The tendency of stack gases to drift makes acid rain a widespread menace. More than 200 lakes in the Adirondacks, hundreds of miles from any industrial center, cannot support life because their water has become so acidic.

FIGURE 19.5 (*Continued*)

3

How Acid Rain Destroys. Acid rain causes damage wherever it falls. It erodes various types of building rock such as limestone, marble, and mortar. Damage to buildings, houses, monuments, statues, and cars is widespread. Many priceless monuments have already been destroyed, and even trees of some varieties are dying.

More crucial is damage to waterways (Figure 2). Acid rain gradually lowers the pH in lakes and streams, eventually making a waterway so acidic that it dies. In areas with natural acid-buffering elements such as limestone, the dilute acid has less effect. The northeastern United States and Canada, however, lack this natural protection, and so are continually vulnerable.

Second labeled visual provides graphic illustration of the process

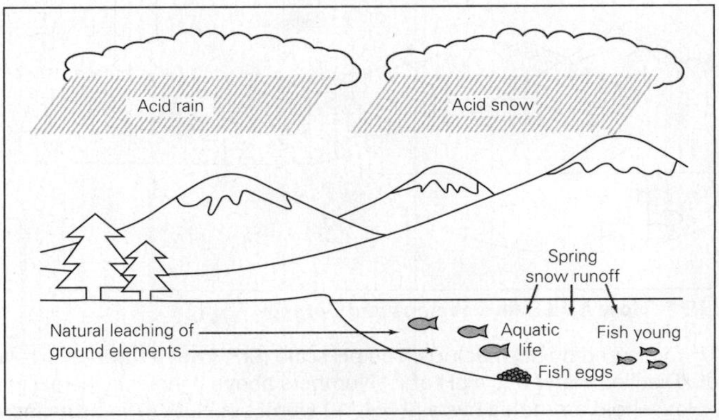

FIGURE 2 **How Acid Rain Infiltrates Waterways**

The pH level in an affected waterway drops so low that some species cease to reproduce. A pH of 5.1 to 5.4 means that entire fisheries are threatened: once a waterway reaches a pH of 4.5, fish reproduction ceases.

In the northeastern United States and Canada, the acidity problem is compounded by the runoff from acid snow. During winter, acid snow sits with little melting, so that by spring thaw, the acid released is greatly concentrated. Aluminum and other heavy metals normally present in soil are also released by acid rain and runoff. These concentrated toxins leach into waterways, affecting fish in all stages of development.

Conclusion summarizes the process and implicitly solicits audience support

Summary

Acid rain develops from nitrogen and sulfur oxides emitted by the burning of fossil fuels. In the atmosphere, these oxides combine with ozone and water to form precipitation with a low pH. This acid precipitation returns to earth miles from its source, damaging waterways that lack natural buffering agents. The northeastern United States and Canada are the most severely affected areas in North America.

FIGURE 19.5 (*Continued*)

GUIDELINES for Descriptions

- **Take a look at the product or process.** Study your subject. For a product description, get your hands on the item if you can; weigh it, measure it, take it apart. For a process description, observe the process yourself, if possible.
- **Analyze your audience.** Determine your primary and secondary audiences. Then ask yourself exactly what your audience needs to know: "What does it look like?" "What are its parts?" "What does it do?" "How does it work?" or "How does it happen?" Decide upon the appropriate level of technicality for your audience.
- **Analyze your purpose.** Ask yourself why your audience needs this description.
- **Maintain objectivity.** Think in terms of visual (not emotional) details and specific language when describing location, measurements, weights, and dimensions.
- **Be concise.** Provide only what your audience needs, without distracting details.
- **Include all necessary parts.** Include a clear and limiting title, an orienting introduction, the appropriate sequence of topics (spatial, functional, chronological—or a combination), and a conclusion that brings readers full circle.
- **Incorporate visuals.** Enhance your verbal description using visuals, particularly if the product or process is too complicated to describe only in words.

SPECIFICATIONS

Airplanes, bridges, smoke detectors, and countless other technologies are produced according to certain *specifications*. A particularly exacting type of description, specifications (or "specs") prescribe standards for performance, safety, and quality. For almost any product and process, specifications spell out the following:

Specifications describe products and processes

- methods for manufacturing, building, or installing a product
- materials and equipment to be used
- size, shape, and weight of the product
- specific testing, maintenance, and inspection procedures

Specifications are often used to ensure compliance with a particular safety code, engineering standard, or government or legal ruling.

Specifications have ethical and legal implications

Because specifications define an "acceptable" level of quality, any product "below specifications" may provide grounds for a lawsuit. When injury or death results (as in a bridge collapse or an airline accident), the contractor, subcontractor or supplier is criminally liable.

Types of Specifications

Federal and state regulatory agencies routinely issue specifications to ensure safety. For example, the Consumer Product Safety Commission specifies that power lawn mowers be equipped with a "kill switch" on the handle, a blade guard to prevent foot injuries, and a grass thrower that aims downward to prevent eye and facial injury. This same agency issues specifications for baby products, such as the fire retardancy of pajama fabric. Passenger airline specifications for aisle width, seat belt configurations, and emergency equipment are issued by the Federal Aviation Administration. State and local agencies issue specifications in the form of building codes, fire codes, and other standards for safety and reliability.

Government departments (Defense, Interior, and so on) issue specifications for all types of military hardware and other equipment. A set of NASA specifications for spacecraft parts can be hundreds of pages long, prescribing the standards for even the smallest nuts and bolts, down to screw-thread depth and width in millimeters.

The private sector issues specifications for countless products or projects, to help ensure that customers get exactly what they want. Figure 19.6 shows partial specifications drawn up by an architect for a medical clinic building. This section of the specs covers only the structure's "shell." Other sections detail the requirements for plumbing, wiring, and interior finish work.

Considering Audience and Purpose

Specifications like those in Figure 19.6 must be clear enough for *identical* interpretation by a broad audience with varied purposes (Glidden 258–59).

Specifications address a diverse audience

- **The customer,** who has the big picture of what is needed and who wants the best product at the best price
- **The designer** (architect, engineer, computer scientist, etc.), who must translate the customer's wishes into the actual specification
- **The contractor or manufacturer,** who won the job by making the lowest bid, and so must preserve profit by doing only what is prescribed
- **The supplier,** who must provide the exact materials and equipment
- **The workforce,** who will do the actual assembly, construction, or installation (managers, supervisors, subcontractors, and workers—some working on only one part of the product, such as plumbing or electrical)
- **The inspectors** (such as building, plumbing, or electrical inspectors), who evaluate how well the product conforms to the specifications

Each of these parties needs to understand and agree on exactly *what* is to be done and *how* it is to be done. In the event of a lawsuit over failure to meet specifications, the readership broadens to include judges, lawyers, and jury.

Ruger, Filstone, and Grant
Architects

MATERIAL SPECIFICATIONS FOR THE POWNAL CLINIC BUILDING

Foundation

footings: 8" x 16" concrete (load-bearing capacity: 3,000 lbs. per sq. in.)
frost walls: 8" x 4' @ 3,000 psi
slab: 4" @ 3,000 psi, reinforced with wire mesh over vapor barrier

Exterior Walls

frame: eastern pine #2 timber frame with exterior partitions set inside posts
exterior partitions: 2" x 4" kiln-dried spruce set at 16" on center
sheathing: 1/4" exterior-grade plywood
siding: #1 red cedar with a 1/2" x 6" bevel
trim: finished pine boards ranging from 1" x 4" to 1" x 10"
painting: 2 coats of Clear Wood Finish on siding; trim primed and finished with one coat of bone white, oil base paint

Roof System

framing: 2" x 12" kiln-dried spruce set at 24" on center
sheathing: 5/8" exterior-grade plywood
finish: 240 Celotex 20-year fiberglass shingles over #15 impregnated felt roofing paper
flashing: copper

Windows

Anderson casement and fixed-over-awning models, with white exterior cladding, insulating glass and screens, and wood interior frames

Landscape

driveway: gravel base, with 3" traprock surface
walks: timber defined, with traprock surface
cleared areas: to be rough graded and covered with wood chips
plantings: 10 assorted lawn plants along the road side of the building

FIGURE 19.6 **Specifications for a Building Project (Partial)** These specifications ensure that all parties agree on the specific materials to be used.

In addition to guiding a product's design and construction, specifications can facilitate the product's use and maintenance. For instance, specifications in a computer manual include the product's performance limits, or *ratings*: its power requirements; its processing and storage capacity; its operating environment requirements; the makeup of key parts; and so on. Product support literature for appliances, power tools, and other items routinely contains ratings to help customers select a good operating environment or replace worn or defective parts. The specifications in Figure 19.9, on page 450, list the main components and performance capacities of a complete power system.

GUIDELINES for Specifications

- **Analyze your audience.** Determine who will be reading the specs.
- **Know the minimum governmental and industry standards.** If your product is for specific customers, also consider the standards they expect you to meet.
- **Focus on consistency, quality, and safety.** Specifications fulfill all three purposes. Everyone who reads the document needs to be "on the same page" (consistency); the product you describe must satisfy quality requirements; and it must also meet safety requirements.
- **Use a standard format when applicable.** If your organization uses a standard format for specifications, follow that format.
- **Include a brief introduction or descriptive title.** Include some kind of overview, be it a one- or two-sentence introduction, a brief summary, or an abstract (see Chapter 9 for more on summaries and abstracts). For an audience completely familiar with the material, a clear and descriptive title will suffice.
- **List all parts and materials.** Group items into categories if needed.
- **Refer to other documents or specs, as needed.** Often one set of specifications will refer to another set, or to government or industry standards. If your specifications are online, link to other specifications you refer to.
- **Use a consistent terminology.** Use the same terms for the same parts or materials throughout your specifications. If you refer to an "ergonomic adapter" in one section, do not substitute "iMac mouse adapter" in a later section.
- **Include retrieval aids.** Especially in longer specifications, some readers may be interested in only one portion. For example, someone working on a subset of a larger project may only want to look up technical details for that part of the project. Use clear headings and a table of contents.
- **Keep it simple.** People look at specifications because they want quick access to items, parts, technical requirements, and so on. If you can, limit your specs to short lists, using longer prose passages only as necessary.
- **Check your use of technical terms.** Use terms that are standard for the field.

TECHNICAL MARKETING MATERIALS

Audience and purpose considerations

Technical marketing materials are designed to sell a product or service. Unlike proposals (Chapter 23), which also offer products or services, technical marketing materials tend to be less formal and more dynamic, colorful, and varied. A typical proposal is tailored to one client's specific needs and follows a fairly standard format while marketing literature seeks to present the product in its best light for a broad array of audiences and needs. Also, technical marketing documents describe science and technology products and are often aimed at knowledgeable readers. A team of scientists looking to purchase a new electron microscope, for example, want specific technical information. Even when directed toward a general audience (say, home computer users), technical marketing materials must deal with specialized concepts.

Engineers and people in other technical disciplines who have a creative flair are often hired as technical marketing specialists. (For an intimate look at technical marketing as a career, see Richard Larkin's report in Chapter 22.)

Some situations that call for technical marketing materials include the following:

Common uses of technical marketing materials

- *Cold calls*—sales representatives sending material to potential new customers
- *On-site visits*—sales representatives and technical experts visiting a customer to see if a new product or service might be of interest
- *Display booths*—booths at industry trade shows displaying engaging, interesting materials that people can take and read at their leisure
- *Web information*—Web pages acting as the primary place for information on a technical product or service

Common formats for marketing documents

Marketing documents range from simple "fact sheets" to brochures, booklets, or Web sites with colorful photographs and other visuals. Here are some common types:

- **Web pages.** Most companies use the Web to display their marketing materials. The advantage of a Web page (Figure 19.7) over a printed document is that you can update price, specifications, or other features of the product. Web pages also allow interactivity: Customers can provide feedback, request additional information, or place orders. Facebook and Twitter are also used for marketing, typically referring customers to a Web site for more details.
- **Brochures.** Brochures are used to introduce a product or service, provide pricing information, and explain how customers can contact the company. A typical brochure (Figure 19.8) is a standard-size page (8-1/2 × 11 inches) folded in thirds, but brochures can assume various shapes and sizes, depending on purpose, audience, and budget.

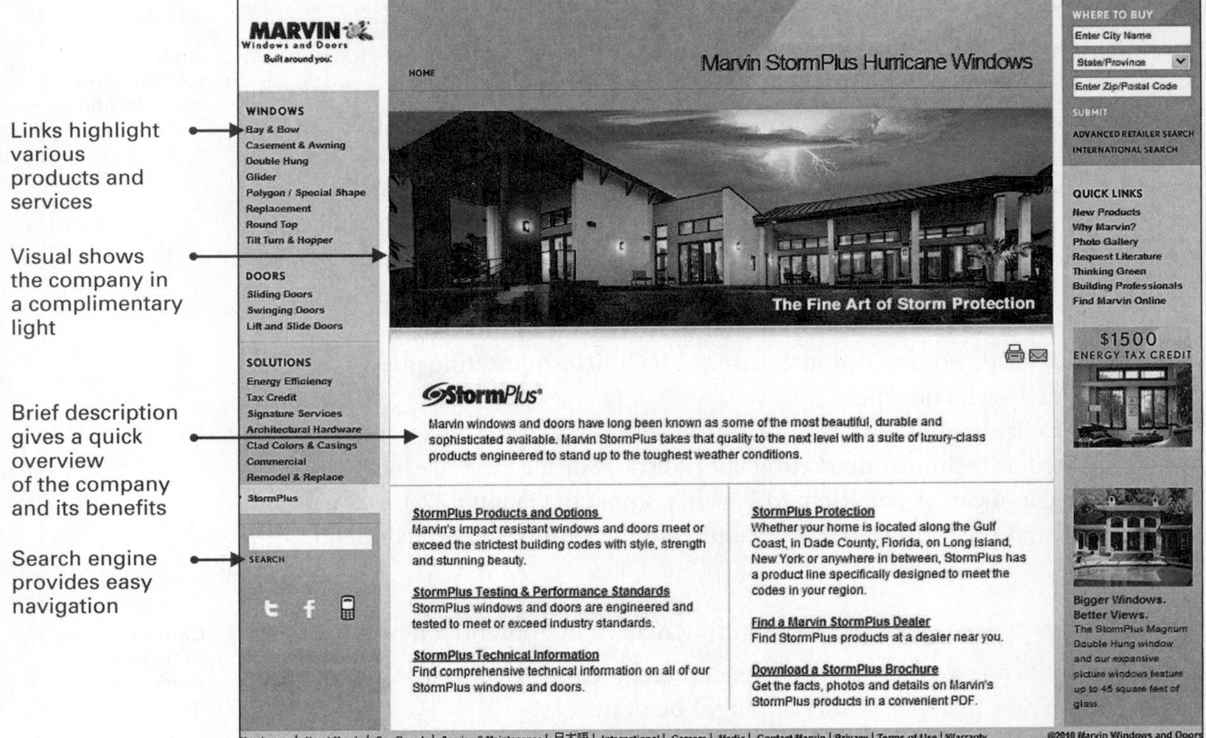

FIGURE 19.7 A Technical Marketing Web Page
Source: Courtesy of Marvin Windows and Doors.

- **Fact sheets.** Fact sheets offer basic data about the product or service, usually on a 8-1/2 × 11-inch page. Figure 19.9 shows a double-sided fact sheet. Although that document contains a great deal of technical information, it is designed to be inviting and navigable: Visuals are easy to interpret; paragraphs are concise and readable; headings forecast each section; and the most complex data is chunked into clearly labeled lists.
- **Letters.** Business letters are the most personal types of marketing documents. If a potential customer requests details about a product or service, you may send this information and include a brief cover letter. Thank the customer for his or her interest and point out specific features of your product or service that match this customer's needs. See, for example, how Rosemary Garrido's letter on page 56 creates a persuasive connection with a potential customer.
- **Large color documents.** Some technical marketing materials are far more elaborate than a typical brochure. Consider the glossy booklets for a new car: The high-quality photography, slick color printing, and glossy feel are designed to evoke the feeling of owning such a car. These booklets include technical specifications, such as engine horsepower and wheel base size.

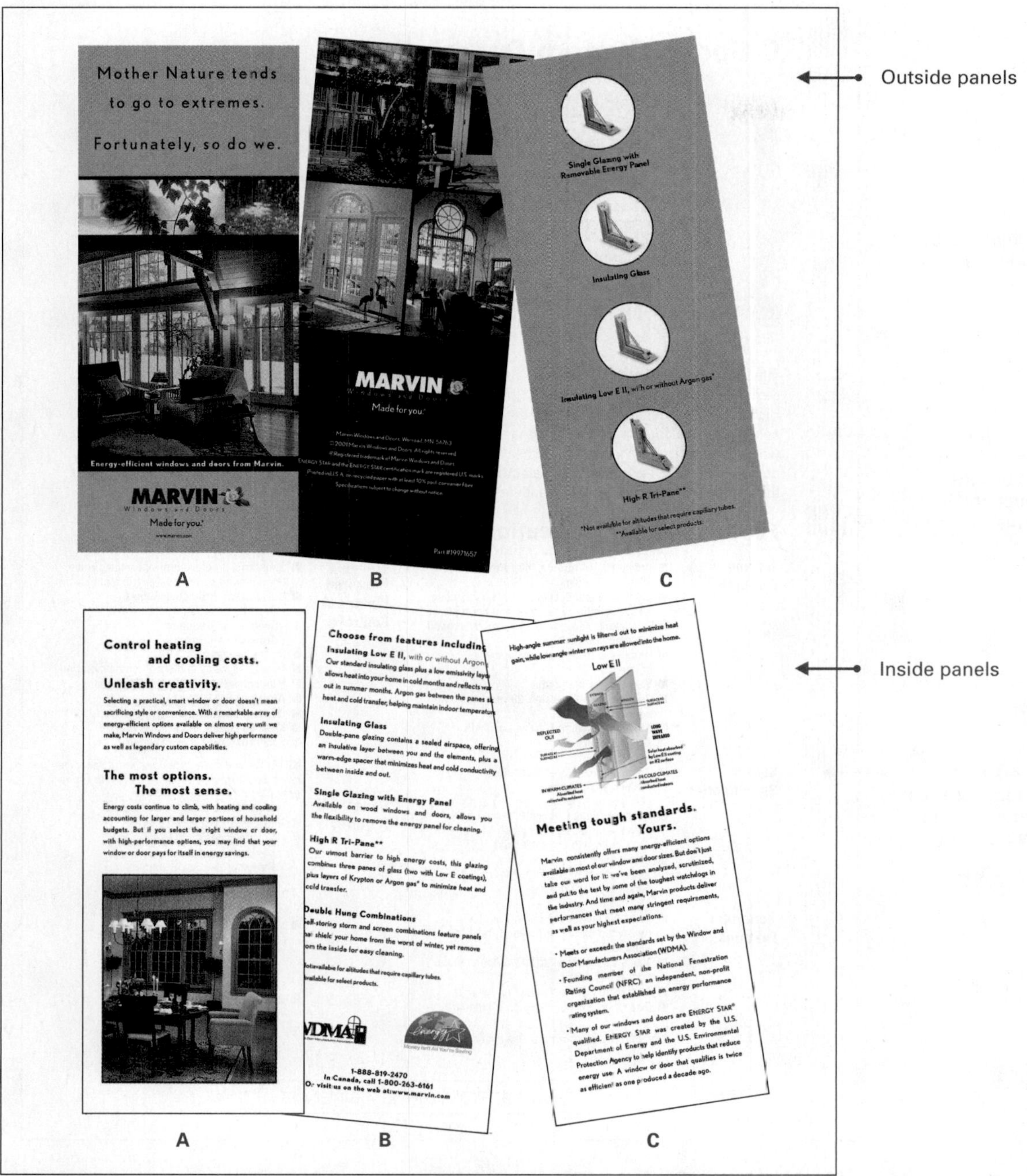

FIGURE 19.8 A Technical Marketing Brochure The upbeat message and engaging photo in outside Panel A situate the product in an aesthetic light. Inside Panel A stresses product benefits (energy savings, beauty, and versatility). Inside Panel B focuses on technical features and options, and offers contact information. Inside Panel C describes the standards Marvin products meet. Outside Panel C shows insulating options. Photos in outside Panel B echo the aesthetic focus of the opening panel.

Source: Courtesy of Marvin Windows and Doors.

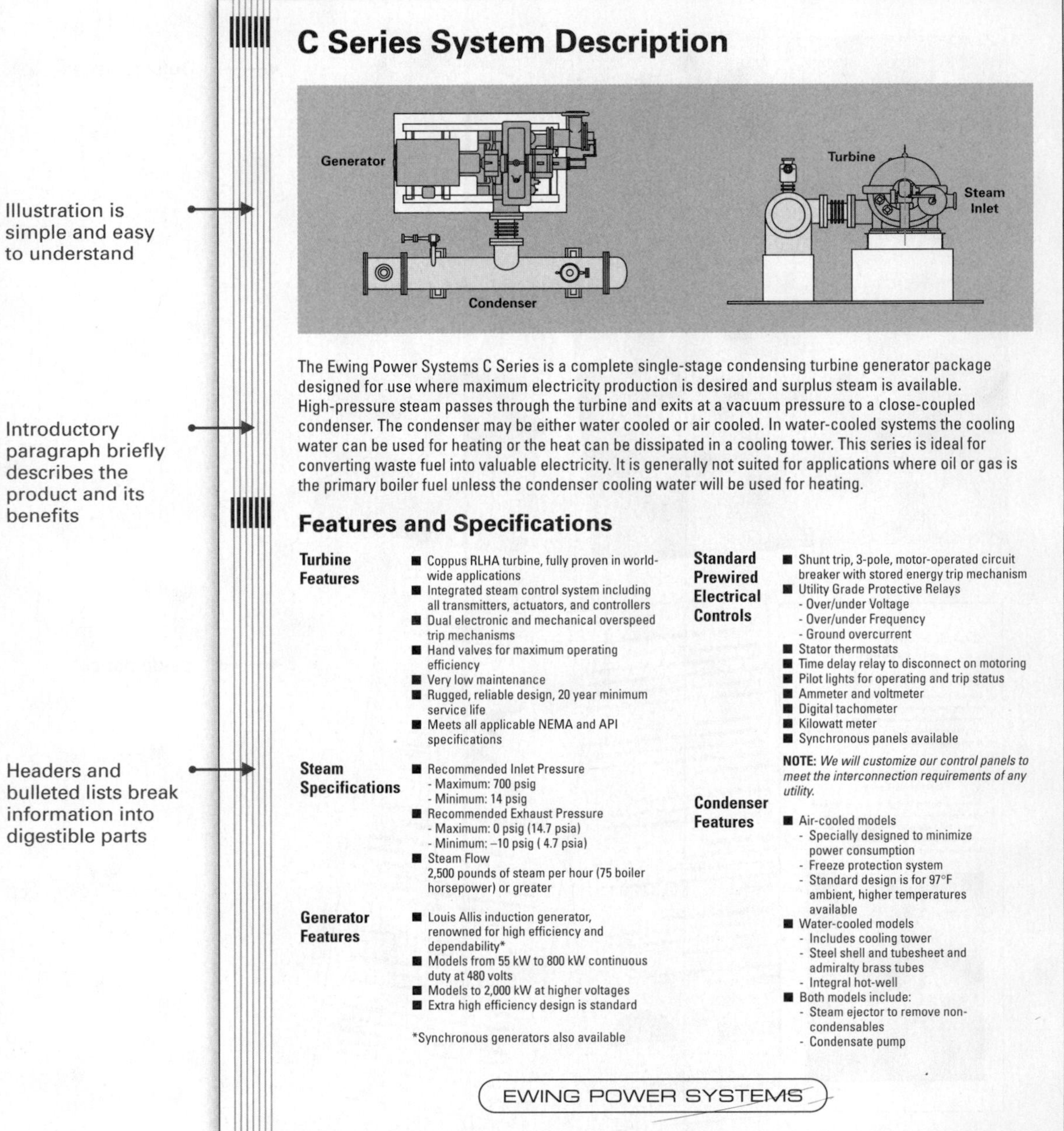

C Series System Description

Illustration is simple and easy to understand

The Ewing Power Systems C Series is a complete single-stage condensing turbine generator package designed for use where maximum electricity production is desired and surplus steam is available. High-pressure steam passes through the turbine and exits at a vacuum pressure to a close-coupled condenser. The condenser may be either water cooled or air cooled. In water-cooled systems the cooling water can be used for heating or the heat can be dissipated in a cooling tower. This series is ideal for converting waste fuel into valuable electricity. It is generally not suited for applications where oil or gas is the primary boiler fuel unless the condenser cooling water will be used for heating.

Introductory paragraph briefly describes the product and its benefits

Features and Specifications

Turbine Features

- Coppus RLHA turbine, fully proven in world-wide applications
- Integrated steam control system including all transmitters, actuators, and controllers
- Dual electronic and mechanical overspeed trip mechanisms
- Hand valves for maximum operating efficiency
- Very low maintenance
- Rugged, reliable design, 20 year minimum service life
- Meets all applicable NEMA and API specifications

Steam Specifications

- Recommended Inlet Pressure
  - Maximum: 700 psig
  - Minimum: 14 psig
- Recommended Exhaust Pressure
  - Maximum: 0 psig (14.7 psia)
  - Minimum: –10 psig (4.7 psia)
- Steam Flow
  2,500 pounds of steam per hour (75 boiler horsepower) or greater

Headers and bulleted lists break information into digestible parts

Generator Features

- Louis Allis induction generator, renowned for high efficiency and dependability*
- Models from 55 kW to 800 kW continuous duty at 480 volts
- Models to 2,000 kW at higher voltages
- Extra high efficiency design is standard

*Synchronous generators also available

Standard Prewired Electrical Controls

- Shunt trip, 3-pole, motor-operated circuit breaker with stored energy trip mechanism
- Utility Grade Protective Relays
  - Over/under Voltage
  - Over/under Frequency
  - Ground overcurrent
- Stator thermostats
- Time delay relay to disconnect on motoring
- Pilot lights for operating and trip status
- Ammeter and voltmeter
- Digital tachometer
- Kilowatt meter
- Synchronous panels available

NOTE: *We will customize our control panels to meet the interconnection requirements of any utility.*

Condenser Features

- Air-cooled models
  - Specially designed to minimize power consumption
  - Freeze protection system
  - Standard design is for 97°F ambient, higher temperatures available
- Water-cooled models
  - Includes cooling tower
  - Steel shell and tubesheet and admiralty brass tubes
  - Integral hot-well
- Both models include:
  - Steam ejector to remove non-condensables
  - Condensate pump

EWING POWER SYSTEMS

FIGURE 19.9 A Technical Marketing Fact Sheet After a product diagram and a brief introduction to the C Series Cogeneration System, the description focuses on the product's major components and specifications.

Source: Reprinted by the permission of Recycled Energy Development, LLC.

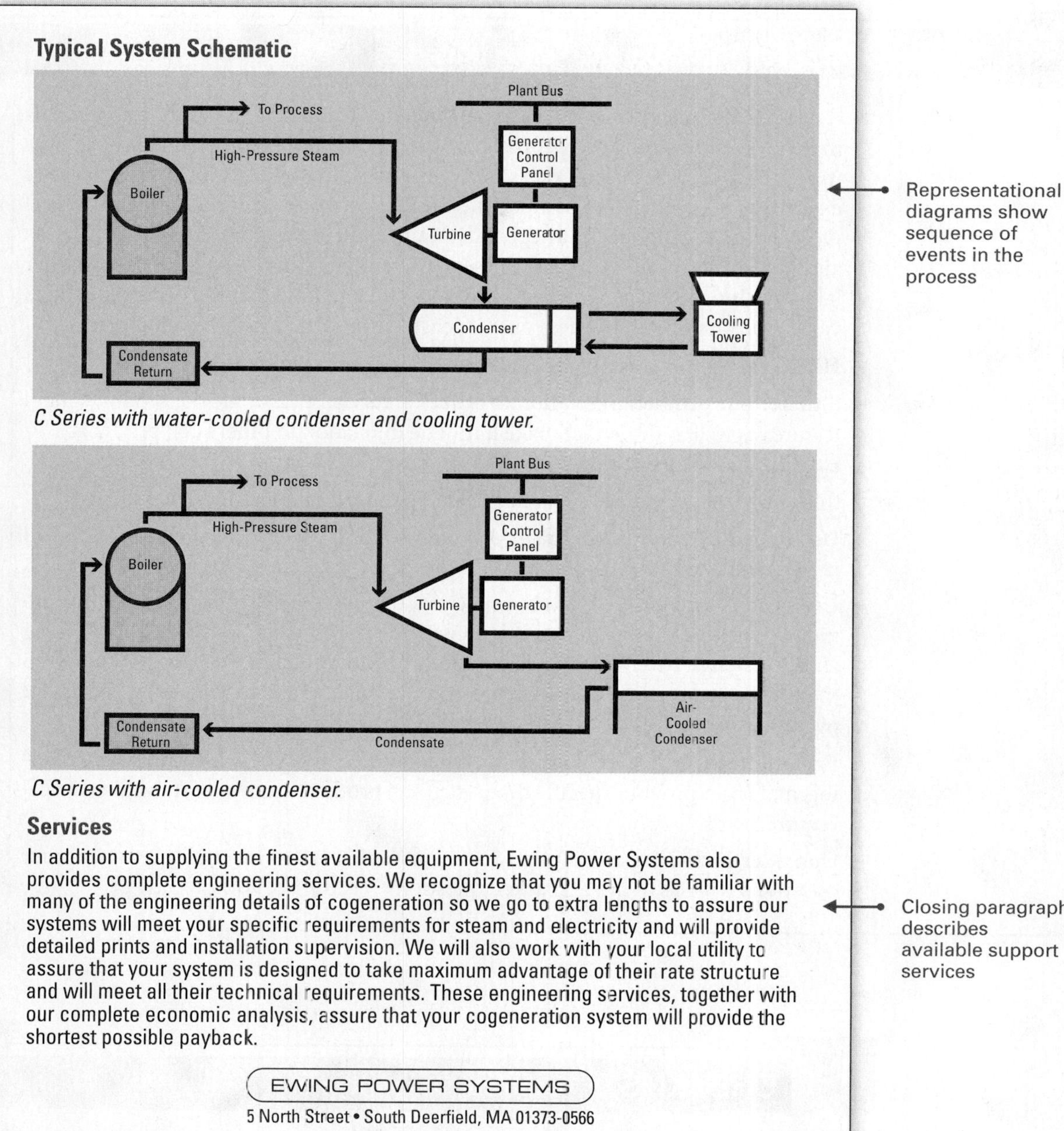

Typical System Schematic

C Series with water-cooled condenser and cooling tower.

C Series with air-cooled condenser.

Services

In addition to supplying the finest available equipment, Ewing Power Systems also provides complete engineering services. We recognize that you may not be familiar with many of the engineering details of cogeneration so we go to extra lengths to assure our systems will meet your specific requirements for steam and electricity and will provide detailed prints and installation supervision. We will also work with your local utility to assure that your system is designed to take maximum advantage of their rate structure and will meet all their technical requirements. These engineering services, together with our complete economic analysis, assure that your cogeneration system will provide the shortest possible payback.

EWING POWER SYSTEMS

5 North Street • South Deerfield, MA 01373-0566

Representational diagrams show sequence of events in the process

Closing paragraph describes available support services

FIGURE 19.9 (*Continued*)

GUIDELINES for Technical Marketing Materials

- **Research the background and experience of decision makers.** Your materials may be read by a range of people, but your main goal is to persuade those who make the final purchasing decisions. Gear the document toward their level of expertise and needs. For example, the turbine generator fact sheet in Figure 19.9 uses technical language ("integrated steam control system," and so on) for its audience of engineers, whereas the window brochure in Figure 19.8 uses simpler language for a more general audience. Also, if you know that the decision makers value a product's effectiveness over its cost, emphasize quality and not price.
- **Highlight the product's name.** Display the name prominently and often.
- **Situate your product in relation to others of its class.** Describe the product's main features as well as those that make it unique in relation to other such products.
- **Emphasize the special appeal of this product or service.** Briefly explain how this item fits the reader's exact needs, and support your claim with evidence.
- **Use upbeat, dynamic language.** Be careful not to overdo it, though. Technical people tend to dislike an obvious sales pitch.
- **Use visuals and color.** Visuals, especially diagrams and color photographs, are highly effective. Color images can convey the item's shape and feel while adding emotional and visual appeal (see Figure 19.8). If you create both print and Web materials, make sure to coordinate your color choices to convey a consistent overall look and feel for your company and product.
- **Provide technical specifications, as needed.** Many types of technical marketing materials provide specifications such as product size, weight, and electrical requirements.
- **Consider including a FAQ list.** Some marketing materials anticipate customer questions with a "frequently asked questions" (FAQ) section.

CHECKLIST: Technical Descriptions

(Numbers in parentheses refer to first page of discussion.)

Content

- ☐ Is the description objective? (432)
- ☐ Does the title promise exactly what the description delivers? (432)
- ☐ Are the item's overall features described, as well as each part? (435)

- ☐ Is each part defined before it is discussed? (435)
- ☐ Is the function of each part explained? (435)
- ☐ Do visuals appear whenever they can provide clarification? (433)
- ☐ Will readers be able to visualize the item? (429)
- ☐ Are any details missing, needless, or confusing for this audience? (433)
- ☐ Is the description ethically acceptable? (432)

Arrangement

- ☐ Does the description follow the clearest possible sequence? (433)
- ☐ Are relationships among the parts clearly explained? (435)

Style and Page Design

- ☐ Is the language informative and precise? (225)
- ☐ Is the level of technicality appropriate for the audience? (433)
- ☐ Is the description in plain English? (226)
- ☐ Is each sentence clear, concise, and fluent? (211)
- ☐ Is the description grammatical? (680)
- ☐ Is the page design inviting and accessible? (293)

CHECKLIST: for Specifications

Content

- ☐ Are the specifications appropriately detailed for the audience? (444)
- ☐ Do the specifications meet the requirements for consistency, quality, and safety? (446)
- ☐ Do the specifications adhere to prescribed standards? (443)

Arrangement

- ☐ Are other specifications or documents referred to, if needed? (446)
- ☐ Do the specifications follow a standard format, if applicable? (446)
- ☐ Is a brief introduction or descriptive title included? (446)
- ☐ Are the component parts or materials listed? (446)

Style and Page Design

- ☐ Is the terminology consistent? (446)
- ☐ Do short lists replace long prose passages wherever possible? (446)
- ☐ Are technical terms standard for the field? (446)
- ☐ Are the specifications easy to navigate, with clear headings and other retrieval aids? (446)

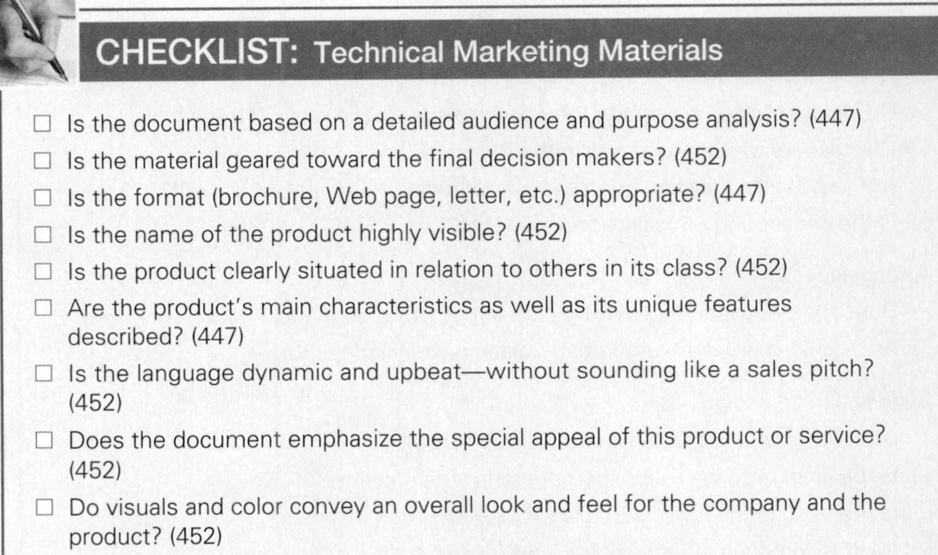

CHECKLIST: Technical Marketing Materials

- ☐ Is the document based on a detailed audience and purpose analysis? (447)
- ☐ Is the material geared toward the final decision makers? (452)
- ☐ Is the format (brochure, Web page, letter, etc.) appropriate? (447)
- ☐ Is the name of the product highly visible? (452)
- ☐ Is the product clearly situated in relation to others in its class? (452)
- ☐ Are the product's main characteristics as well as its unique features described? (447)
- ☐ Is the language dynamic and upbeat—without sounding like a sales pitch? (452)
- ☐ Does the document emphasize the special appeal of this product or service? (452)
- ☐ Do visuals and color convey an overall look and feel for the company and the product? (452)
- ☐ Are the product's technical specifications included, as needed? (452)
- ☐ Is a FAQ list included, as needed? (452)

Projects

GENERAL

1. Choose a product requiring a description. Identify the audience and purpose, and prepare a description for this audience's level of technical understanding. As you prepare your description, refer to the Guidelines on page 443.

2. Select a specialized process that you understand well and that has several distinct steps. Using the process description on page 440 as a model, explain this process to classmates who are unfamiliar with it.

3. The solar-collector description in this chapter is aimed toward a general audience. Evaluate its effectiveness for this audience. In one or two paragraphs, discuss your evaluation and suggest revisions.

4. How do specifications function in your workplace or home? Find one example of specifications used in your home or workplace and analyze it in terms of its usability. Are the specifications written for consistency, quality, and safety? How? What could the writers have done to improve the usability of this document?

TEAM

1. Divide into groups. Assume your group works in the product development division of a diversified manufacturing company. Your division has just thought of an idea for an inexpensive consumer item with a potentially vast market (choose a simple mechanism, such as nail clippers or a stapler). Your group's assignment is to prepare three descriptions of this invention:

a. one for company executives who will decide whether to produce and market the item

b. one for the engineers, machinists, and so on, who will design and manufacture the item

c. one for the customers who might purchase and use the item

Before writing for each audience, complete an Audience and Purpose Profile sheet (page 31). Appoint a group manager, who will assign tasks to members (visuals, typing, etc.). When the descriptions are prepared, the group manager will appoint one member to present the documents and explain their differences in class.

2. Select a specialized process you understand well or that you can learn about quickly by searching the Web (e.g., how gum disease develops, how an earthquake occurs, how steel is made, how a computer compiles and executes a program). Write a brief description of the process, incorporating at least one visual. Exchange your description with a classmate. Study your classmate's description for 15 minutes and then write the description in your own words. Now, evaluate your classmate's version of your original description. Does it show that your description was understood? If not, why not? Discuss your conclusions in a memo to your instructor, submitted with all samples. Be sure to document your information sources.

3. Assume your group is an architectural firm designing buildings at your college. Develop a set of specifications for duplicating the interior of the classroom in which this course is held. Focus only on materials, dimensions, and equipment (whiteboard, desk, etc.), and use visuals as appropriate. Your audience includes the firm that will construct the classroom, teachers, and school administrators. Use the same format as in Figure 19.6, or design a better one. Appoint one member to present the completed specifications in class. Compare versions from each group for accuracy and clarity.

DIGITAL AND SOCIAL MEDIA

Use the Internet to search for a description of a product or process that is related to your field of study. Look for places where the description might be confusing for general readers, and rewrite the description for their understanding.

GLOBAL

Descriptions, especially those for nonspecialized or nontechnical audiences, are often written by comparing the item being described to an item that is already familiar to readers. For instance, the human heart is often described as a pump and compared to a pump people already know about (the pump for a swimming pool or a car's water pump). While descriptions based on these types of comparisons can be useful, they can also be problematic if your readers are from different countries and cultures. For instance, if you describe the human heart in relation to the pump for a swimming pool, people from parts of the United States or certain countries that don't have pools will not understand the comparison. Working with 2–3 other students, pick an item for which you'd like to write a description that will be distributed both within the United States and to at least one other country. Discuss whether or not to use a comparison and how you will decide which comparison(s) to use.

20 Instructions and Procedures

"Clear, accurate instructions and procedures are essential to the work we do in aerospace engineering. We need to ensure that the mechanics, ground control personnel, and pilots have the information they need to perform tasks and conduct safety and operations checks. These instructional documents can't have too much detail or be too wordy, and they need a clear list of steps. Hazard and warning material needs to show up easily, usually through the use of a visual. At our company, teams of engineers and technical writers work together to design, write, and evaluate all of our instructions, which we then print on quick-reference cards and make available on CDs."

—Farid Akina, Aerospace Engineer, at an international aerospace design firm

LEARNING OBJECTIVES FOR THIS CHAPTER

- Know how instructions and procedures are used in the workplace
- Recognize the various formats for hard-copy instructions
- Understand how instructions have serious legal implications
- Compare the benefits of print, digital, online, and video instructions
- Understand how procedures differ from instructions
- Write a set of instructions and a set of procedures
- Evaluate the usability of instructional documents

Instructions spell out the steps required for completing a task or a series of tasks (say, installing printer software on your computer or operating an electron microscope). The audience for a set of instructions might be someone who doesn't know how to perform the task or someone who wants to perform it more effectively. In either case, effective instructions enable people to complete a job safely and efficiently.

Procedures, a special type of instructions, serve also as official guidelines. Procedures ensure that all members of a group (such as employees at the same company) follow the same steps to perform a particular task. For example, many companies have procedures in place that must be followed for evacuating a building or responding to emergencies.

The role of instructions on the job

Almost anyone with a responsible job writes and reads instructions. For example, you might instruct new employees on how to activate their voice mail system or advise a customer about shipping radioactive waste. An employee going on vacation typically writes instructions for the person filling in. People who buy a computer or cell phone usually look at the print or online instruction manual to get started.

CONSIDERING AUDIENCE AND PURPOSE

Audience considerations

Before preparing instructions, find out how much your audience already knows about the task(s) involved. For example, technicians who have done this procedure often (say, fixing a jammed photocopier), will need only basic guidelines rather than detailed explanations. But a more general audience (say, consumers trying to set up and use a digital scanner), will need step-by-step guidance. A mixed audience (some experienced people and some novices) may require a layered approach: for instance, some initial basic information with a longer section later that has more details.

Purpose considerations

The general purpose of instructions is to help people perform a task. The task may be simple (inserting a new toner cartridge in a printer) or complex (using an electron microscope). Whatever the task, people will have some basic questions:

What people expect to learn from a set of instructions

- Why am I doing this?
- How do I do it?
- What materials and equipment will I need?
- Where do I begin?
- What do I do next?
- What could go wrong?

Because they focus squarely on the person who will "read" and then "do," instructions must meet the highest standards of excellence.

FORMATS FOR INSTRUCTIONAL DOCUMENTS

Instructional documents take various formats, in hard copy or electronic versions (usually as PDF documents on a company Web site). Here are some of the most commonly used:

Common formats for instructional documents

- **Manuals** (Figure 20.1) contain instructions for all sorts of tasks. A manual also may contain descriptions and specifications for the product, warnings, maintenance and troubleshooting advice, and any other information the reader is likely to need. For complex products (such as an ozone-mapping spectrometer) or procedures (such as cleaning a hazardous-waste site), the manual can be a sizable book. Most manuals (of any size) are available in both print and PDF format.
- **Brief reference cards** (Figure 20.2) typically fit on a single page or less. The instructions usually focus on the basic steps for people who want only enough information to start on a task and to keep moving through it.
- **Instructional brochures** (Figure 20.3) can be displayed, handed out, mailed, or otherwise distributed to a broad audience. They are especially useful for advocating procedures that increase health and safety.
- **Hyperlinked instructions** (Figure 20.4) enable people to explore various levels and layers of information and to choose the layers that match their needs.
- **Online instructions** (Figure 20.9) provide the contents of a hard-copy manual as a link on a Web site. Whereas people with less experience tend to prefer paper documentation, online help is especially popular among people with more experience.

Regardless of its format, any set of instructions must meet the strict legal and usability requirements discussed on the following pages.

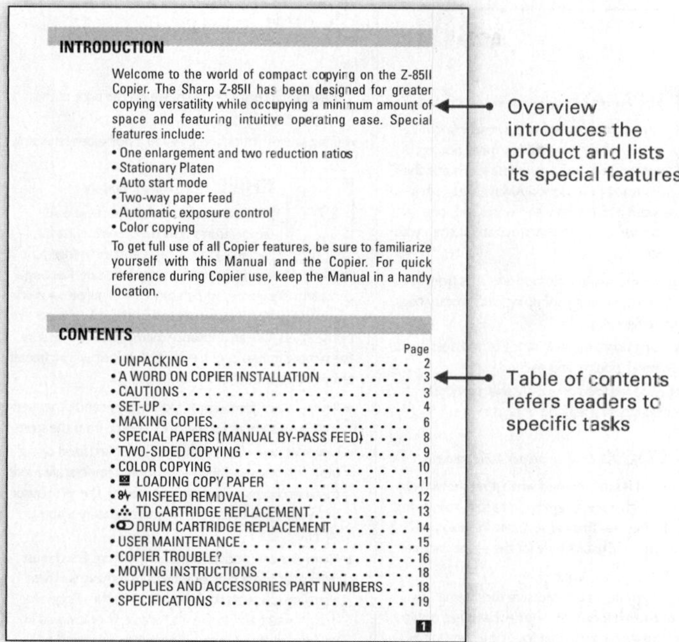

INTRODUCTION

Welcome to the world of compact copying on the Z-85II Copier. The Sharp Z-85II has been designed for greater copying versatility while occupying a minimum amount of space and featuring intuitive operating ease. Special features include:

- One enlargement and two reduction ratios
- Stationary Platen
- Auto start mode
- Two-way paper feed
- Automatic exposure control
- Color copying

To get full use of all Copier features, be sure to familiarize yourself with this Manual and the Copier. For quick reference during Copier use, keep the Manual in a handy location.

CONTENTS

	Page
• UNPACKING	2
• A WORD ON COPIER INSTALLATION	3
• CAUTIONS	3
• SET-UP	4
• MAKING COPIES	6
• SPECIAL PAPERS (MANUAL BY-PASS FEED)	8
• TWO-SIDED COPYING	9
• COLOR COPYING	10
• LOADING COPY PAPER	11
• MISFEED REMOVAL	12
• TD CARTRIDGE REPLACEMENT	13
• DRUM CARTRIDGE REPLACEMENT	14
• USER MAINTENANCE	15
• COPIER TROUBLE?	16
• MOVING INSTRUCTIONS	18
• SUPPLIES AND ACCESSORIES PART NUMBERS	18
• SPECIFICATIONS	19

1

Overview introduces the product and lists its special features
Table of contents refers readers to specific tasks

FIGURE 20.1 Table of Contents from the *Sharp Compact Copier Z-8511 Operation Manual*

Source: Courtesy of Sharp Electronics Corporation.

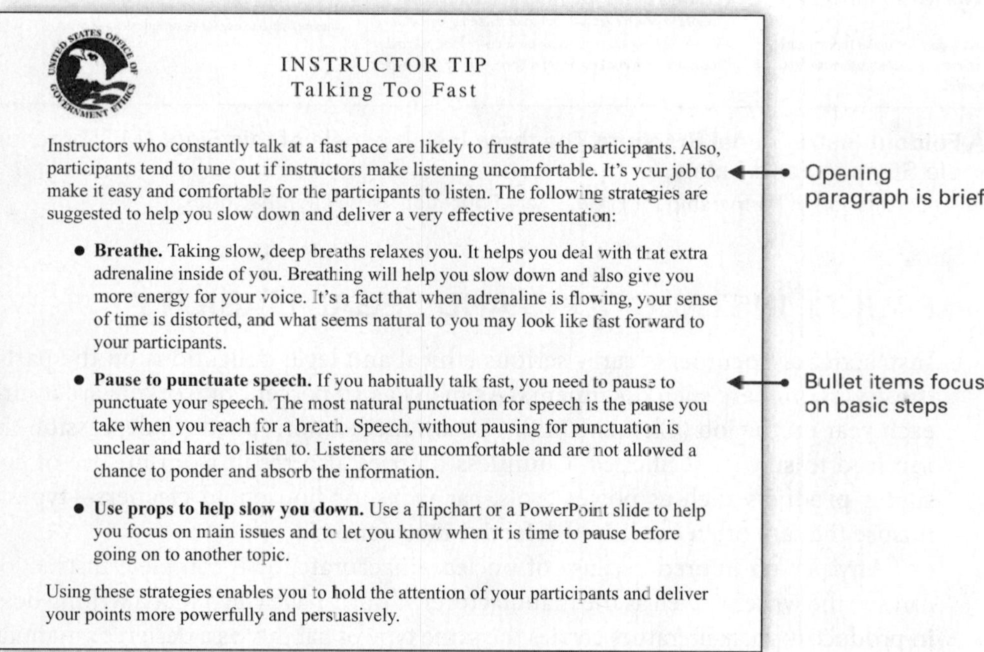

INSTRUCTOR TIP

Talking Too Fast

Instructors who constantly talk at a fast pace are likely to frustrate the participants. Also, participants tend to tune out if instructors make listening uncomfortable. It's your job to make it easy and comfortable for the participants to listen. The following strategies are suggested to help you slow down and deliver a very effective presentation:

- **Breathe.** Taking slow, deep breaths relaxes you. It helps you deal with that extra adrenaline inside of you. Breathing will help you slow down and also give you more energy for your voice. It's a fact that when adrenaline is flowing, your sense of time is distorted, and what seems natural to you may look like fast forward to your participants.
- **Pause to punctuate speech.** If you habitually talk fast, you need to pause to punctuate your speech. The most natural punctuation for speech is the pause you take when you reach for a breath. Speech, without pausing for punctuation is unclear and hard to listen to. Listeners are uncomfortable and are not allowed a chance to ponder and absorb the information.
- **Use props to help slow you down.** Use a flipchart or a PowerPoint slide to help you focus on main issues and to let you know when it is time to pause before going on to another topic.

Using these strategies enables you to hold the attention of your participants and deliver your points more powerfully and persuasively.

UNITED STATES OFFICE OF GOVERNMENT ETHICS
Opening paragraph is brief
Bullet items focus on basic steps

FIGURE 20.2 A Brief Reference Card

Source: Reprinted by permission of United States Office of Government Ethics <www.usoge.gov>.

BAC (foodborne bacteria) could make you and those you care about sick. In fact, even though you can't see BAC—or smell him, or feel him—he and millions more like him may have already invaded the food you eat. But you have the power to *Fight BAC!®*.

Foodborne illness can strike anyone. Some people are at a higher risk for developing foodborne illness, including pregnant women, young children, older adults and people with weakened immune systems. For these people the following four simple steps are critically important:

CLEAN: *Wash hands and surfaces often*

Bacteria can be spread throughout the kitchen and get onto hands, cutting boards, utensils, counter tops and food. To *Fight BAC!®*, always:

- Wash your hands with warm water and soap for at least 20 seconds before and after handling food and after using the bathroom, changing diapers and handling pets.
- Wash your cutting boards, dishes, utensils and counter tops with hot soapy water after preparing each food item and before you go on to the next food.
- Consider using paper towels to clean up kitchen surfaces. If you use cloth towels wash them often in the hot cycle of your washing machine.
- Rinse fresh fruits and vegetables under running tap water, including those with skins and rinds that are not eaten.
- Rub firm-skin fruits and vegetables under running tap water or scrub with a clean vegetable brush while rinsing with running tap water.

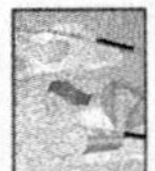

SEPARATE: *Don't cross-contaminate*

Cross-contamination is how bacteria can be spread. When handling raw meat, poultry, seafood and eggs, keep these foods and their juices away from ready-to-eat foods. Always start with a clean scene— wash hands with warm water and soap. Wash cutting boards, dishes, countertops and utensils with hot soapy water.

- Separate raw meat, poultry, seafood and eggs from other foods in your grocery shopping cart, grocery bags and in your refrigerator.
- Use one cutting board for fresh produce and a separate one for raw meat, poultry and seafood.
- Never place cooked food on a plate that previously held raw meat, poultry, seafood or eggs.

COOK: *Cook to proper temperatures*

Food is safely cooked when it reaches a high enough internal temperature to kill the harmful bacteria that cause illness. Refer to the chart on the back of this brochure for the proper internal temperatures.

- Use a food thermometer to measure the internal temperature of cooked foods. Make sure that meat, poultry, egg dishes, casseroles and other foods are cooked to the internal temperature shown in the chart on the back of this brochure.
- Cook ground meat or ground poultry until it reaches a safe internal temperature. Color is not a reliable indicator of doneness.
- Cook eggs until the yolk and white are firm. Only use recipes in which eggs are cooked or heated thoroughly.
- When cooking in a microwave oven, cover food, stir and rotate for even cooking. Food is done when it reaches the internal temperature shown on the back of this brochure.
- Bring sauces, soups and gravy to a boil when reheating.

CHILL: *Refrigerate promptly*

Refrigerate foods quickly because cold temperatures slow the growth of harmful bacteria. Do not over-stuff the refrigerator. Cold air must circulate to help keep food safe. Keeping a constant refrigerator temperature of 40°F or below is one of the most effective ways to reduce the risk of foodborne illness. Use an appliance thermometer to be sure the temperature is consistently 40°F or below. The freezer temperature should be 0°F or below.

- Refrigerate or freeze meat, poultry, eggs and other perishables as soon as you get them home from the store.
- Never let raw meat, poultry, eggs, cooked food or cut fresh fruits or vegetables sit at room temperature more than two hours before putting them in the refrigerator or freezer (one hour when the temperature is above 90°F).
- Never defrost food at room temperature. Food must be kept at a safe temperature during thawing. There are three safe ways to defrost food: in the refrigerator, in cold water, and in the microwave. Food thawed in cold water or in the microwave should be cooked immediately.
- Always marinate food in the refrigerator.
- Divide large amounts of leftovers into shallow containers for quicker cooling in the refrigerator.
- Use or discard refrigerated food on a regular basis. Check USDA cold storage information at ***www.fightbac.org*** for optimum storage times.

FIGURE 20.3 A Foldout Instructional Brochure The three inside panels of this *Fight BAC!* brochure offer "Four Simple Steps to Food Safety."
Source: Reprinted by permission of Partnership for Food Safety Education <www.fightbac.org>.

FAULTY INSTRUCTIONS AND LEGAL LIABILITY

Ethical implications of instructions

Instructional documents carry serious ethical and legal obligations on the part of those who prepare such documents. As many as 10 percent of workers are injured each year on the job (Clement 149). Certain medications produce depression that can lead to suicide (Caher 5). Countless injuries also result from misuse of consumer products such as power tools, car jacks, or household cleaners—types of misuse that are often caused by defective instructions.

Legal implications of instructions

Any person injured because of unclear, inaccurate, or incomplete instructions can sue the writer as well as the manufacturer. Courts have ruled that a writing defect in product support literature carries the same type of liability as a design or manufacturing defect in the product itself (Girill, "Technical Communication and Law" 37).

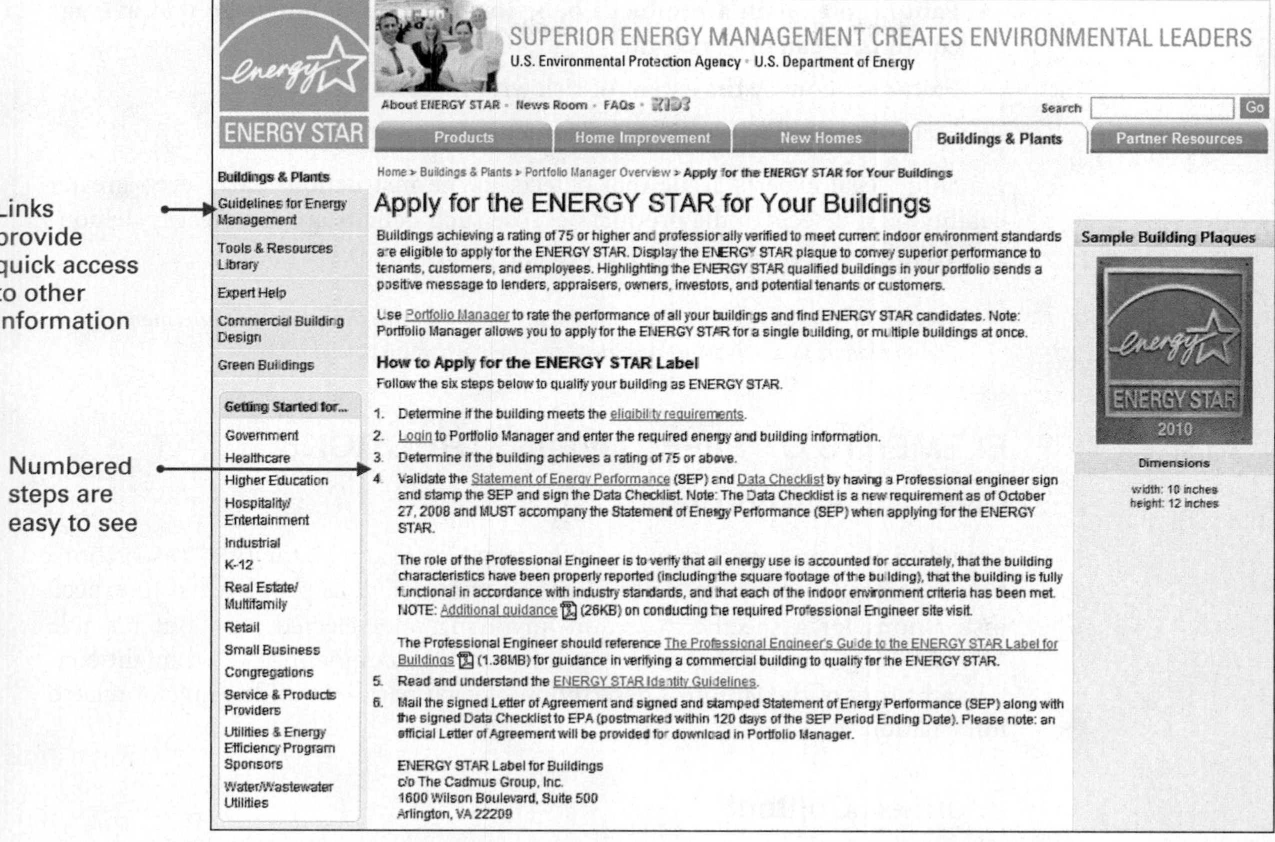

FIGURE 20.4 Hyperlinked Instructions Note the links to specific steps.
Source: U.S. Department of Energy.

Those who prepare instructions are potentially liable for damage or injury resulting from information omissions such as the following (Caher 5–7; Manning 13; Nordenberg 7):

Examples of faulty instructions that create legal liability

- **Failure to instruct and caution readers in the proper use of a product:** for example, a medication's proper dosage or possible interaction with other drugs or possible side effects.
- **Failure to warn against hazards from proper use of a product:** for example, the risk of repetitive stress injury resulting from extended use of a keyboard.
- **Failure to warn against the possible misuses of a product:** for example, the danger of child suffocation posed by plastic bags or the danger of toxic fumes from spray-on oven cleaners.

- **Failure to explain a product's benefits and risks in language that average consumers can understand.**
- **Failure to convey the extent of risk with forceful language.**
- **Failure to display warnings prominently.**

Some legal experts argue that defects in the instructions carry even greater liability than defects in the product because such deficits are more easily demonstrated to a nontechnical jury (Bedford and Stearns 128).

NOTE *Among all technical documents, instructions have the strictest requirements for giving readers precisely what they need precisely when they need it.*

ELEMENTS OF EFFECTIVE INSTRUCTIONS

Clear and Limiting Title

Provide a clear and exact preview of the task. For example, the title "Instructions for Cleaning the Drive Head of a Laptop Computer" tells people what to expect: instructions for a specific procedure involving one selected part. But the title "The Laptop Computer" gives no such forecast; a document so titled might contain a history of the laptop, a description of each part, or a wide range of related information.

Informed Content

Know the procedure

Make sure that you know exactly what you are talking about. Ignorance, inexperience, or misinformation on your part makes you no less liable for faulty or inaccurate instructions:

Ignorance provides no legal excuse

> If the author of [a car repair] manual had no experience with cars, yet provided faulty instructions on the repair of the car's brakes, the home mechanic who was injured when the brakes failed may recover [damages] from the author. (Walter and Marsteller 165)

Unless you have performed the task often, do not try to write instructions for other people confronting this task.

Visuals

Instructions often include a persuasive dimension: to promote interest, commitment, or action. In addition to showing what to do, visuals attract the reader's attention and help keep words to a minimum.

Types of visuals especially suited to instructions include icons, representational and schematic diagrams, flowcharts, photographs, and prose tables.

Visuals to accompany instructions can be created using a variety of software packages. Other sources for instructional graphics include clip art, scanning, and downloading from the Internet. (Page 278 describes useful Web sites and discusses legal issues in the use of computer graphics.)

To use visuals effectively, consider these suggestions:

How to use instructional visuals

- Illustrate any step that might be hard for readers to visualize. The less specialized your readers, the more visuals they are likely to need.
- Parallel the reader's angle of vision in performing the activity or operating the equipment. Name the angle (side view, top view) if you think people will have trouble figuring it out for themselves.
- Avoid illustrating any action simple enough for readers to visualize on their own, such as "PRESS RETURN" for anyone familiar with a keyboard.

Visuals can be used without words, too, especially for international audiences. Often called *wordless instructions*, these diagrams use clear, simple line drawings, arrows, and call-outs to let people see how to do something. Figure 20.5 shows a wordless instruction for setting up a printer.

Arrows indicate motions or action
Line drawing is simple
Call-outs show important items in detail

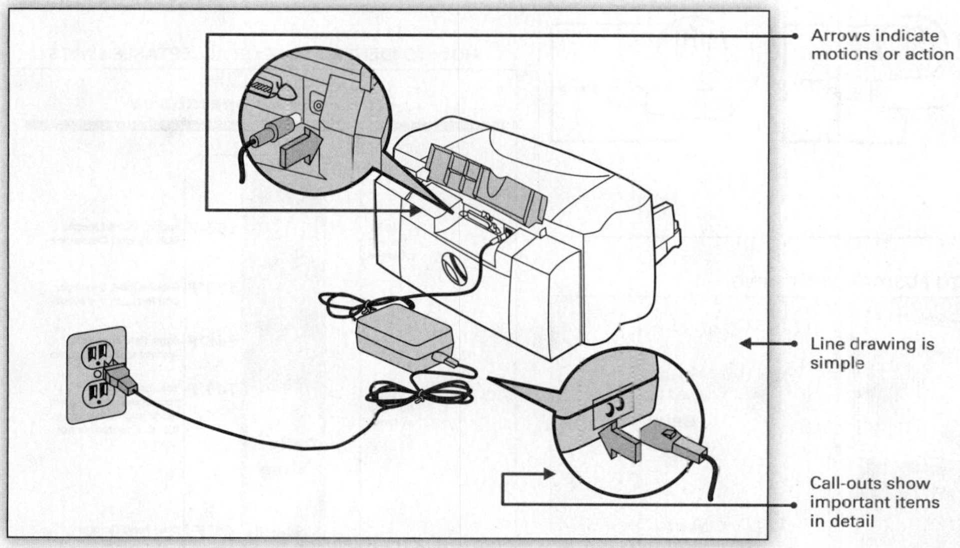

FIGURE 20.5 Wordless Instructions Instructions with only images, and no words, are suitable for most readers, including international audiences.
Source: Copyright Hewlett-Packard Development Company, L.P. Reproduced with Permission.

Figure 20.6 presents an array of visuals and their specific instructional functions. Each of these visuals is easily constructed and some could be further enhanced, depending on your production budget and graphics capability.

HOW TO LOCATE SOMETHING

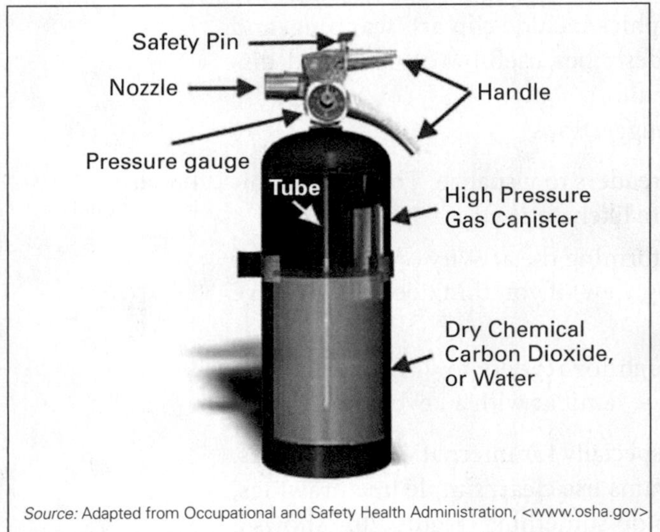

Source: Adapted from Occupational and Safety Health Administration, <www.osha.gov>

HOW TO OPERATE SOMETHING

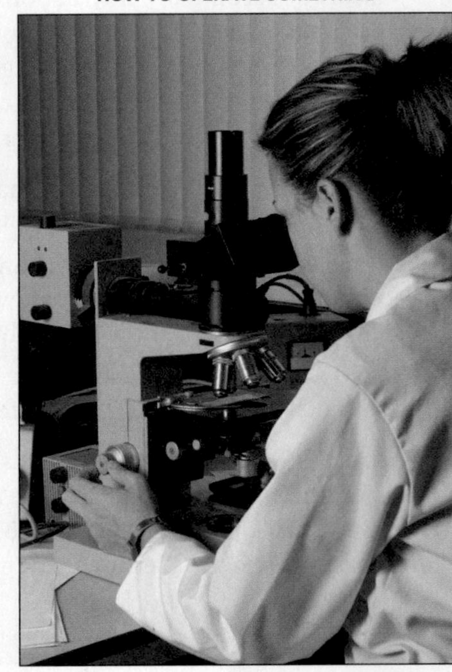

HOW TO REPAIR SOMETHING

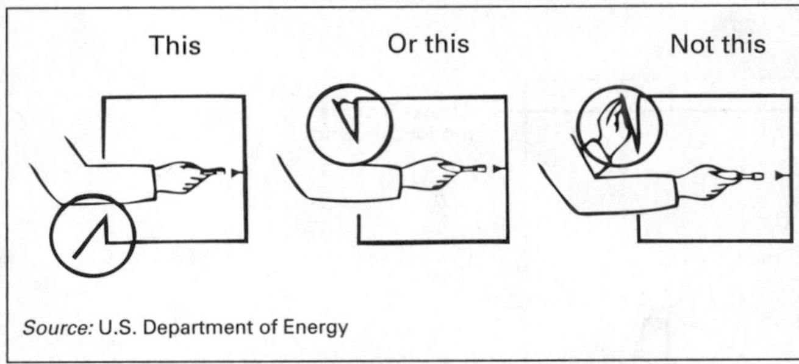

Source: U.S. Department of Energy

HOW TO IDENTIFY SAFE OR ACCEPTABLE LIMITS

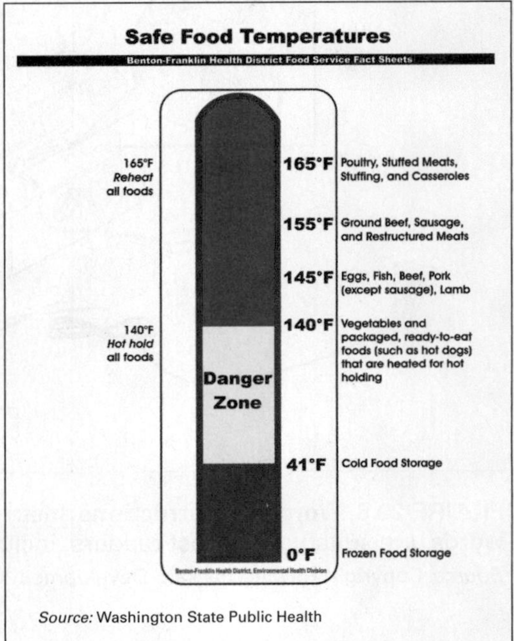

Source: Washington State Public Health

HOW TO POSITION SOMETHING

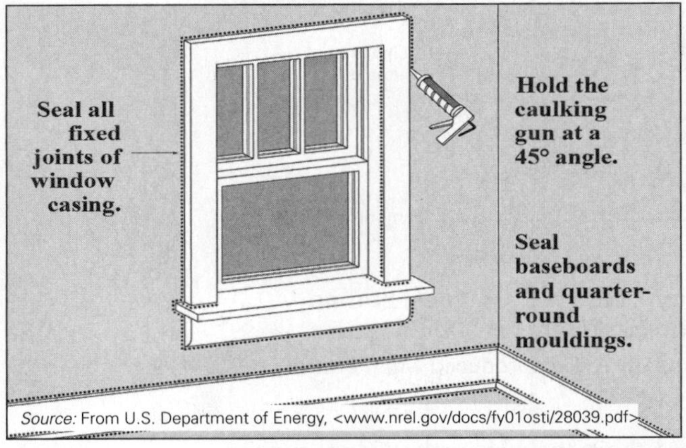

Source: From U.S. Department of Energy, <www.nrel.gov/docs/fy01osti/28039.pdf>

FIGURE 20.6 Common Types of Instructional Visuals and Their Functions

Appropriate Level of Detail and Technicality

Unless you know your readers have the relevant background and skills, write for a general audience, and do three things:

1. Give readers enough background to understand why they need to follow these instructions.
2. Give enough detail to show *what* to do.
3. Give enough examples so each step can be visualized clearly.

Provide exactly and only what readers need

These three procedures are explained and illustrated on the following pages.

1. Provide Background. Begin by explaining the purpose of the task.

You might easily lose information stored on a flash drive if

- the drive is damaged by repeated use, moisture, or extreme temperature;
- the drive is erased by a power surge, a computer malfunction, or a user error; or
- the stored information is scrambled by a nearby magnet (telephone, computer terminal, or the like).

Always use another back-up device, such as a Firewire hard drive, for important material.

Tell readers why they are doing this

Also, state your assumptions about your reader's level of technical understanding.

To follow these instructions, you should be able to identify these parts of your iMac: computer, monitor, keyboard (wireless or USB), mouse, and an external USB or FireWire hard drive (for backup).

Spell out what readers should already know

Define any specialized terms that appear in your instructions.

Initialize: Before you can store or retrieve information on a new CD, you must initialize the disk. Initializing creates a format that computers and CD players can understand—a directory of specific memory spaces on the disk where you can store information and retrieve it as needed.

Tell readers what each key term means

When the reader understands *what* and *why,* you are ready to explain *how* he or she can complete the task.

2. Provide Adequate Detail. Include enough detail for people to understand and perform the task successfully. Omit general information that readers probably know, but do not overestimate the audience's background, as in the following example.

Make instructions complete but not excessive

Inadequate detail for laypersons

First Aid for Electrical Shock

1. Check vital signs.
2. Establish an airway.
3. Administer CPR as needed.
4. Treat for shock.

Not only are the above details inadequate, but terms such as "vital signs" and "CPR" are too technical for laypersons. Such instructions posted for workers in a high-voltage area would be useless. Illustrations and explanations are needed, as in the instructions in Figure 20.7 for item 3 above, administering CPR.

Don't assume that people know more than they really do, especially when you can perform the task almost automatically. (Think about when a relative or friend taught you to drive a car—or perhaps you tried to teach someone else.) Always assume that your readers know less than you. A colleague will know at least a little less; a layperson will know a good deal less—maybe nothing—about this procedure.

Exactly how much information is enough? The following guidelines can help you find an answer:

GUIDELINES for Providing Appropriate Detail

- **Provide *all* the necessary information.** The instructions must be able to stand alone.
- **Don't provide unnecessary information.** Give only what readers need. Don't tell them how to build a computer when they only need to know how to copy a file.
- **Instead of focusing on the *product,* focus on the *task*.** "How does it work?" "How do I use it?" or "How do I do it?" (Grice, "Focus" 132).
- **Omit steps that are obvious.** "Seat yourself at the computer," for example.
- **Divide the task into simple steps and substeps.** Allow people to focus on one step at a time.
- **Adjust the *information rate*.** This is "the amount of information presented in a given page" (Meyer 17), adjusted to the reader's background and the difficulty of the task. For complex or sensitive steps, slow the information rate. Don't make people do too much too fast.
- **Reinforce the prose with visuals.** Don't be afraid to repeat information if it saves readers from going back to look something up.
- **Keep it simple.** When writing instructions for consumer products, assume "a barely literate reader" (Clement 151).
- **Recognize the persuasive dimension of the instructions.** Readers may need persuading that this procedure is necessary or beneficial, or that they can complete this procedure with relative ease and competence.

THE ABC'S OF CARDIOPULMONARY RESUSCITATION (CPR)

Cardiopulmonary resuscitation (CPR) is an emergency medical procedure for restoring breathing and heartbeat to persons who have suffered an electrical shock, heart attack, or other instance of cardiac arrest. CPR keeps oxygenated blood flowing to the brain until medical professionals arrive. Following are three simple "ABC" steps for CPR.

Adequate introductory detail for laypersons

Step 1: A for Airway: Make sure the airway is not constricted.

Clearly numbered steps

- First, call 911 immediately or have someone else call.
- Check if the victim is breathing. If not, carefully roll the victim onto his or her back in one movement.
- Gently push back the forehead with one hand and lift the chin with your other hand to unblock tongue from airway.
- Listen for breathing and watch for chest movement. Move quickly to Step 2 if the victim is still not breathing.

Step 2: B for Breathing: Administer rescue breathing to keep the blood oxygenated.

- Continue to hold down the forehead and lift the neck to keep the airway open.
- Pinch the nose with the thumb and forefinger of the hand holding back the forehead.
- Take a deep breath and seal your lips around the victim's mouth.
- Blow one breath steadily into the mouth for one second; then administer a second breath.
- Do not wait to see if the victim resumes independent breathing. Move quickly to Step 3.

Troubleshooting notes for laypersons

Step 3: C for Circulation: Perform chest compressions to keep the blood circulating.

- Kneel at the side of the victim's head and shoulders. Do not spend time checking for a pulse.
- Place the heel of one hand over the notch at the center of the victim's chest.
- Place the palm of your other hand over the first hand and, using your body weight, press down firmly and quickly, compressing the chest about two inches.
- Allow the chest to return to its original position before the next compression.
- Administer chest compressions at about two compressions per second for 20 seconds.
- Return to Step 2, first ensuring that the airway is open.
- Cycle between Steps 2 and 3 thereafter until help arrives.

Troubleshooting notes for laypersons

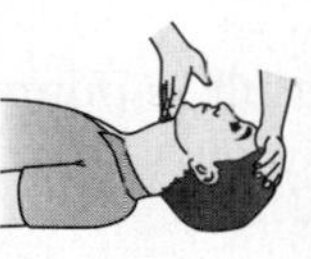
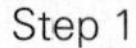

Step 1

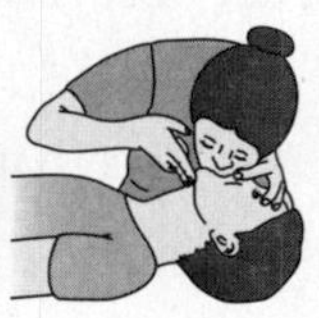

Step 2

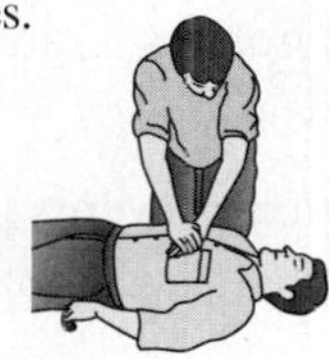
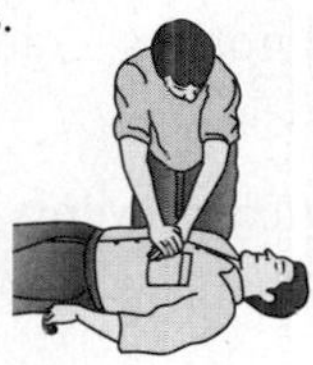

Step 3

Visuals reinforce each step

FIGURE 20.7 Adequate Detail for Laypersons

Give plenty of examples

3. Offer Examples. Instructions require specific examples (how to load a program, how to order a part) to help people follow the steps correctly:

> To load your program, type this command:
>
> Load "Style Editor"
>
> Then press RETURN.

Like visuals, examples *show* readers what to do. Examples, in fact, often appear as visuals.

Include Troubleshooting Advice. Anticipate things that commonly go wrong when this task is performed—the paper jams in the printer, the tray of the DVD drive won't open, or some other malfunction. Explain the probable cause(s) and offer solutions.

Explain what to do when things go wrong

> NOTE: IF *X* doesn't work, first check *Y* and then do *Z*.

Logically Ordered Steps

Instructions are almost always arranged in chronological order, with warnings and precautions inserted for specific steps.

Show how the steps are connected

> You can't splice two wires to make an electrical connection until you have removed the insulation. To remove the insulation, you will need. . . .

Notes and Hazard Notices

Alert readers to special considerations

Following are the only items that normally should interrupt the steps in a set of instructions (Van Pelt 3):

- A *note* clarifies a point, emphasizes vital information, or describes options or alternatives.

> NOTE: If you don't name a newly initialized hard drive, the computer automatically names it "Untitled."

While a note is designed to enhance performance and prevent error, the following hazard notices—ranked in order of severity—are designed to prevent damage, injury, or death.

- A *caution* prevents possible mistakes that could result in injury or equipment damage:

The least forceful notice

> CAUTION: A momentary electrical surge or power failure may erase or damage the contents of an internal hard drive. To avoid losing your work, save your files to a backup disk on a regular basis.

- A *warning* alerts readers to potential hazards to life or limb:

> WARNING: To prevent electrical shock, always disconnect your printer from its power source before cleaning internal parts.

A moderately forceful notice

- A *danger* notice identifies an immediate hazard to life or limb:

> DANGER: The red canister contains DEADLY radioactive material. **Do not break the safety seal** under any circumstances.

The most forceful notice

Inadequate notices of warning, caution, or danger are a common cause of lawsuits (page 461). Each hazard notice is legally required to (1) describe the specific hazard, (2) spell out the consequences of ignoring the hazard, and (3) offer instruction for avoiding the hazard (Manning 15).

Content requirements for hazard notices

Even the most emphatic verbal notice might be overlooked by an impatient or inattentive reader. Direct attention with symbols, or icons, as a visual signal (Bedford and Stearns 128):

Use hazard symbols

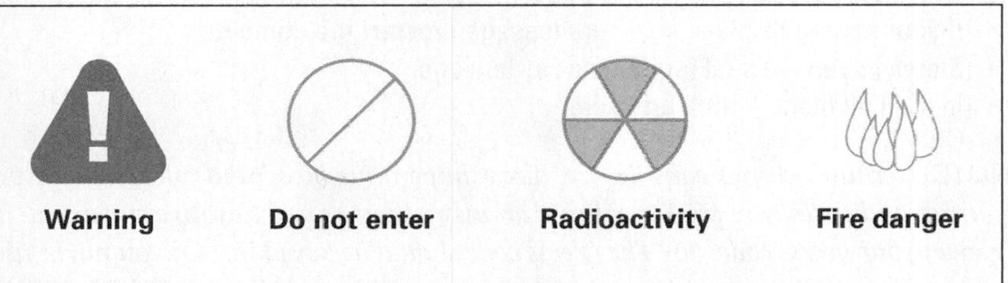

Keep the hazard notices prominent: Preview the hazards in your introduction and place each notice, *clearly highlighted* (by a ruled box, a distinct typeface, larger typesize, or color), immediately before the respective step.

NOTE *Use hazard notices only when needed; overuse will dull their effect, and readers may overlook their importance.*

Readability

Instructions must be understood on the first reading because people want to take *immediate* action.

Write instructions that are easy to read quickly

Like descriptions (page 428), instructions name parts, use location and position words, and state exact measurements, weights, and dimensions. Instructions additionally require your strict attention to phrasing, sentence structure, and paragraph structure.

Use Direct Address, Active Voice, and Imperative Mood. Write instructions in the second person, as direct address, in order to emphasize the role of the reader.

In general, begin all steps and substeps with action verbs, using the *active voice* and *imperative mood* ("Insert the disk" instead of "The disk should be inserted" or "You should insert the disk").

Indirect or confusing

- The user keys in his or her access code.
- You should key in your access code.
- It is important to key in the access code.
- The access code is keyed in.

In this next version, the opening verb announces the specific action required.

Clear and direct

Key in your access code.

In certain cases, you may want to provide a clarifying word or phrase that precedes the verb (*Read Me* 130):

Information that might precede the verb

- [To log on,] **key in** your access code.
- [If your screen displays an error message,] **restart** the computer.
- [Slowly] **scan** the seal for gamma ray leakage.
- [In the Edit menu,] **click** on Paste.

NOTE *Certain cultures consider the direct imperative bossy and offensive. For cross-cultural audiences, you might rephrase an instruction as a declarative statement: from "Key in your access code" to "The access code should be keyed in." Or you might use an indirect imperative such as "Be sure to key in your access code" (Coe, "Writing" 18).*

Use Short and Logically Shaped Sentences. Use shorter sentences than usual, but never "telegraph" your message by omitting articles (*a, an, the*). Use one sentence for each step, so that people can perform one step at a time.

If a single step covers two related actions, describe these actions in their required sequence:

Confusing

Before switching on the computer, insert the DVD in the drive.

Logical

Insert the DVD in the drive; then switch on the computer.

Simplify explanations by using a familiar-to-unfamiliar sequence:

Hard

You must initialize a blank CD before you can store information on it.

Easier

Before you can store information on a blank CD, you must initialize the CD.

Use Parallel Phrasing. Parallelism is important in all writing but especially so in instructions, because repeating grammatical forms emphasizes the step-by-step organization. Parallelism also increases readability and lends continuity to the instructions.

> To connect to the file server, follow these steps:
> 1. Switch the terminal to "on."
> 2. The CONTROL key and C key are pressed simultaneously.
> 3. Typing LOGON, and pressing the ESCAPE key.
> 4. Type your user number, and then press the ESCAPE key.

Not parallel

All steps should be in identical grammatical form:

> To connect to the file server, follow these steps:
> 1. Switch the terminal to "on."
> 2. Press the CONTROL key and C key simultaneously.
> 3. Type LOGON, and then press the ESCAPE key.
> 4. Type your user number, and then press the ESCAPE key.

Parallel

Phrase Instructions Affirmatively. Research shows that people respond more quickly and efficiently to instructions phrased affirmatively rather than negatively (Spyridakis and Wenger 205).

> Verify that your camera lens is not contaminated with dust.

Negative

> Examine your camera lens for dust.

Affirmative

Use Transitions to Mark Time and Sequence. Transitional expressions (see page 701) provide a bridge between related ideas. Some transitions ("first," "next," "meanwhile," "finally," "ten minutes later," "the next day," "immediately afterward") mark time and sequence. They help readers understand the step-by-step process, as in the next example.

> **PREPARING THE GROUND FOR A TENT**
>
> Begin by clearing and smoothing the area that will be under the tent. This step will prevent damage to the tent floor and eliminate the discomfort of sleeping on uneven ground. **First,** remove all large stones, branches, or other debris within a level area roughly 10 × 10 feet. Use your camping shovel to remove half-buried rocks that cannot easily be moved by hand. **Next,** fill in any large holes with soil or leaves. **Finally,** make several light surface passes with the shovel or a large, leafy branch to smooth the area.

Transitions enhance continuity

Effective Design

Instructions rarely get undivided attention. The reader, in fact, is doing two things more or less at once: interpreting the instructions and performing the task. An effective instructional design conveys the sense that the task is within a qualified person's range of abilities. The more accessible and inviting the design, the more likely your readers will follow the instructions.

GUIDELINES for Designing Instructions

- **Use informative headings.** Tell readers what to expect; emphasize what is most important; provide cues for navigation. A heading such as "How to Initialize Your Compact Disk" is more informative than "Compact Disk Initializing."
- **Arrange all steps in a numbered list.** Unless the procedure consists of simple steps (as in "Preparing the Ground for a Tent," above), list and number each step. Numbered steps not only announce the sequence of steps, but also help readers remember where they left off. (For more on using lists, see page 301.)
- **Separate each step visually.** Single-space within steps and double-space between.
- **Double-space to signal a new paragraph, instead of indenting.**
- **Make warning, caution, and danger notices highly visible.** Use ruled boxes or highlighting, and plenty of white space.
- **Make visual and verbal information redundant.** Let the visual repeat, restate, or reinforce the prose.
- **Keep the visual and the step close together.** If room allows, place the visual right beside the step; if not, right after the step. Set off the visual with plenty of white space.
- **Consider a multicolumn design.** If steps are brief and straightforward and require back-and-forth reference from prose to visuals, consider multiple columns.
- **Keep it simple.** Readers can be overwhelmed by a page with excessive or inconsistent designs.
- **For lengthy instructions, consider a layered approach.** In a complex manual, for instance, you might add a "Quick-Use Guide" for getting started, with cross-references to pages containing more detailed and technical information.

For additional design considerations, see Chapter 13.

NOTE *Online instructions have their own design requirements, discussed on page 477. Also, despite the increasing popularity of online documentation, many people continue to find printed manuals more convenient and easier to navigate (Foster 10).*

AN OUTLINE FOR INSTRUCTIONS

You can adapt the following outline to any instructions. Here are the possible components to include:

I. Introduction
- A. Definition, Benefits, and Purpose of the Procedure
- B. Intended Audience (often omitted for workplace audiences)
- C. Prior Knowledge and Skills Needed by the Audience
- D. Brief Overall Description of the Procedure
- E. Principle of Operation
- F. Materials, Equipment (in order of use), and Special Conditions
- G. Working Definitions (always in the introduction)
- H. Warnings, Cautions, Dangers (previewed here and spelled out at steps)
- I. List of Major Steps

II. Required Steps
- A. First Major Step
  - 1. Definition and purpose
  - 2. Materials, equipment, and special conditions for this step
  - 3. Substeps (if applicable)
    - a. First substep
    - b. Second substep (and so on)
- B. Second Major Step (and so on)

III. Conclusion
- A. Review of Major Steps (for a complex procedure only)
- B. Interrelation of Steps
- C. Troubleshooting or Follow-up Advice (as needed)

This outline is only tentative; you might modify, delete, or combine some components, depending on your subject, purpose, and audience.

Introduction

The introduction should help readers to begin "doing" as soon as they are able to proceed safely, effectively, and confidently (van der Meij and Carroll 245–46). Most people are interested primarily in "how to use it or fix it," and will require only a general understanding of "how it works." You don't want to bury your readers in a long introduction, nor do you want to set them loose on the procedure without adequate preparation. Know your audience—what they need and don't need.

Body: Required Steps

In the body section (labeled Required Steps), give each step and substep in order. Insert warnings, cautions, and notes as needed. Begin each step with its definition or purpose or both. Readers who understand the reasons for a step will do a better job. A numbered list is an excellent way to segment the steps. Or, begin each sentence in a complex stage on a new line.

Conclusion

The conclusion of a set of instructions has several possible functions:

- Summarize the major steps in a long and complex procedure, to help people review their performance.
- Describe the results of the procedure.
- Offer follow-up advice about what could be done next or refer the reader to further sources of documentation.
- Give advice about troubleshooting if anything goes wrong.

You might do all these things—or none of them. If your procedural section has provided all that is needed, omit the conclusion altogether.

A SITUATION REQUIRING INSTRUCTIONS

Figure 20.8 shows a complete set of instructions written for a nontechnical audience. These instructions follow the basic outline by offering an overview, a list of equipment needed, and simple numbered instructions. The design, which uses informative headings, numbered steps, and simple visual diagrams, is easy to use.

A Complete Set of Instructions for a Nontechnical Audience

The Situation. The owner of your town's local hardware store tells you that he often is asked the same questions by customers who want to make simple home repairs. One common question is about how to replace a worn faucet washer. He decides to hire a technical writing student (you) to help him write and design a simple, yet effective, set of instructions.

Audience and Use Profile. These customers come from a wide range of backgrounds, but most of them are not engineers or plumbers. They are just regular homeowners who are confident in their ability to work with basic tools and comfortable trying a new task. They don't want a lot of detail about the history of faucets or the various types of faucets. They just want to know how to fix the problem. These people are busy—they have lots of chores to do on the weekend, and they want instructions that are easy to follow and use.

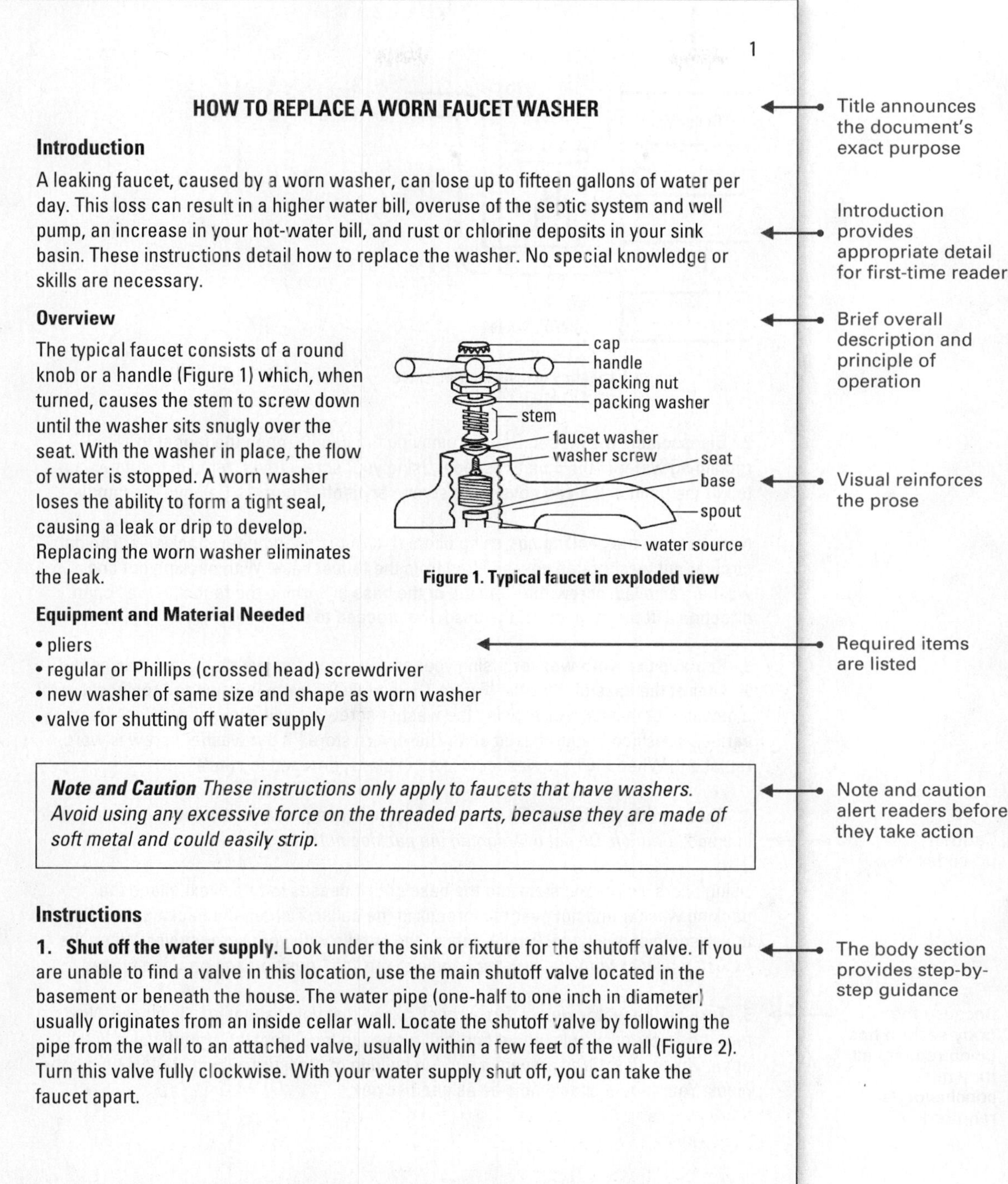

1

HOW TO REPLACE A WORN FAUCET WASHER

Introduction

A leaking faucet, caused by a worn washer, can lose up to fifteen gallons of water per day. This loss can result in a higher water bill, overuse of the septic system and well pump, an increase in your hot-water bill, and rust or chlorine deposits in your sink basin. These instructions detail how to replace the washer. No special knowledge or skills are necessary.

Overview

The typical faucet consists of a round knob or a handle (Figure 1) which, when turned, causes the stem to screw down until the washer sits snugly over the seat. With the washer in place, the flow of water is stopped. A worn washer loses the ability to form a tight seal, causing a leak or drip to develop. Replacing the worn washer eliminates the leak.

cap
handle
packing nut
packing washer
stem
faucet washer
washer screw
seat
base
spout
water source

Figure 1. Typical faucet in exploded view

Equipment and Material Needed

- pliers
- regular or Phillips (crossed head) screwdriver
- new washer of same size and shape as worn washer
- valve for shutting off water supply

Note and Caution *These instructions only apply to faucets that have washers. Avoid using any excessive force on the threaded parts, because they are made of soft metal and could easily strip.*

Instructions

1. **Shut off the water supply.** Look under the sink or fixture for the shutoff valve. If you are unable to find a valve in this location, use the main shutoff valve located in the basement or beneath the house. The water pipe (one-half to one inch in diameter) usually originates from an inside cellar wall. Locate the shutoff valve by following the pipe from the wall to an attached valve, usually within a few feet of the wall (Figure 2). Turn this valve fully clockwise. With your water supply shut off, you can take the faucet apart.

Title announces the document's exact purpose
Introduction provides appropriate detail for first-time readers
Brief overall description and principle of operation
Visual reinforces the prose
Required items are listed
Note and caution alert readers before they take action
The body section provides step-by-step guidance

FIGURE 20.8 **A Complete Set of Instructions**

2

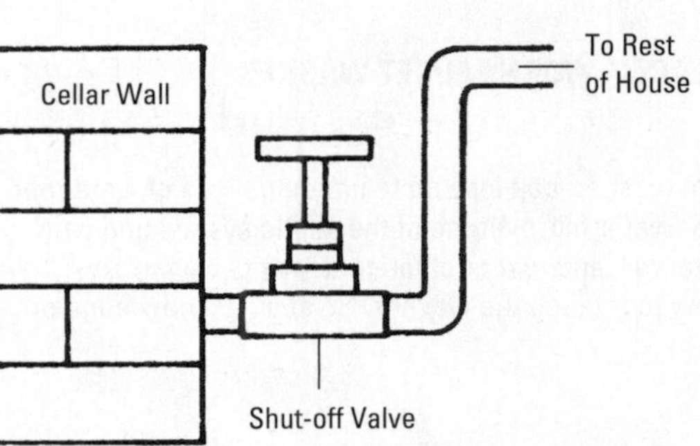

Figure 2. Location of main shut-off valve

2. **Disassemble the faucet.** Before removing the handle, open the faucet to allow remaining water in the pipe to escape. Using your screwdriver, remove the screw on top of the handle. If a cap covers the screw, pry it off (Figure 1). Remove the handle.

Next, remove the packing nut, using pliers to turn the nut counter-clockwise. The flat circular nut washer can now be lifted from the faucet base. With packing nut and washer removed, screw the stem out of the base by turning the faucet in the "open" direction. Lift the stem out of the base and proceed to step 3.

3. **Replace the worn washer.** Using your screwdriver, remove the screw holding the washer at the base of the stem (Figure 1). Remove the worn washer and replace it with a new one of the same size, using the washer screw to hold it in place. (Washers of various sizes can be purchased at any hardware store.) If the washer screw is worn, replace it. When the new washer is fixed in place, proceed to step 4.

Caution precedes step

4. **Reassemble the faucet.** To reassemble your faucet, reverse the sequence described in step 2. *Caution: Do not overtighten the packing nut!*

Using pliers, screw the stem into the base until it ceases to turn. Next, place the packing washer and nut over the threads in the collar. Tighten the packing nut using the strength of one hand. Finally, secure the handle with your screwdriver. When the faucet is fully assembled, turn the handle to the "off" position and proceed to step 5.

Because the body section has given readers all they need, no conclusion is required

5. **Turn on the water supply.** First, check to see that your faucet is fully closed. Next, turn the water on slowly (about one-half turn each time) until the shutoff valve is fully open. These slow turns prevent a sudden buildup of pressure, which could damage the pipes. Your faucet should now be as good as new.

FIGURE 20.8 *(Continued)*

DIGITAL AND ONLINE INSTRUCTIONS

The rising cost of printing and updating instructions, particularly instructions that can be accessed easily online, has shifted much instructional material to digital formats. A common method of placing instructional material online is to use Portable Document Format, or PDF. These files retain their original formatting, so they look identical in print or on the screen. Figure 20.8, the instructions for replacing a worn faucet washer, would be easy to convert to a PDF file (using *Adobe Acrobat, Apple Pages*, or similar software). These instructions could then be posted on the hardware store's Web site.

PDF documents allow instructions to be accessed online

For some products, printed manuals have been replaced with CD versions. For example, when you buy new computer software, such as *Microsoft Word* or *Adobe Illustrator*, the program may come with a brief, printed, installation guide. These small guides are often titled "Getting Started" and look like small brochures. But the full-scale user manual will be available on the accompanying CD that you can download to your computer.

Some instructions come on a CD

Most software also provides the "help" information within the program itself. Online instructions (Figure 20.9) can be updated through the computer's "automatic update" feature, and they are designed to provide the following information:

Some instructions are built into the program

Examples of online documentation

- error messages and troubleshooting advice
- reference guides to additional information or instructions
- tutorial lessons that include interactive exercises with immediate feedback
- help and review options to accommodate different learning styles
- link to software manufacturer's Web site

Instead of leafing through a printed manual or searching a digital version, people find what they need by typing a simple command, clicking a mouse button, using a help menu, or following an electronic prompt.

Special software such as *RoboHelp* or *Doc-to-Help* can convert print material into online help files that appear as dialog boxes that ask the person to input a response or click on an option, or as pop-up or balloon help that appears when the person clicks on an icon or points to an item on the screen for more information. (Explore, for example, the online help resources on your own computer.)

Like Web pages (Chapter 25), online information should be written in well-organized chunks (page 205). It should never be paper documentation merely converted into an electronic file because some tasks that people perform with the paper document may not be possible with the online version without substantial modifications. In short, creating effective online documentation requires much training and practice.

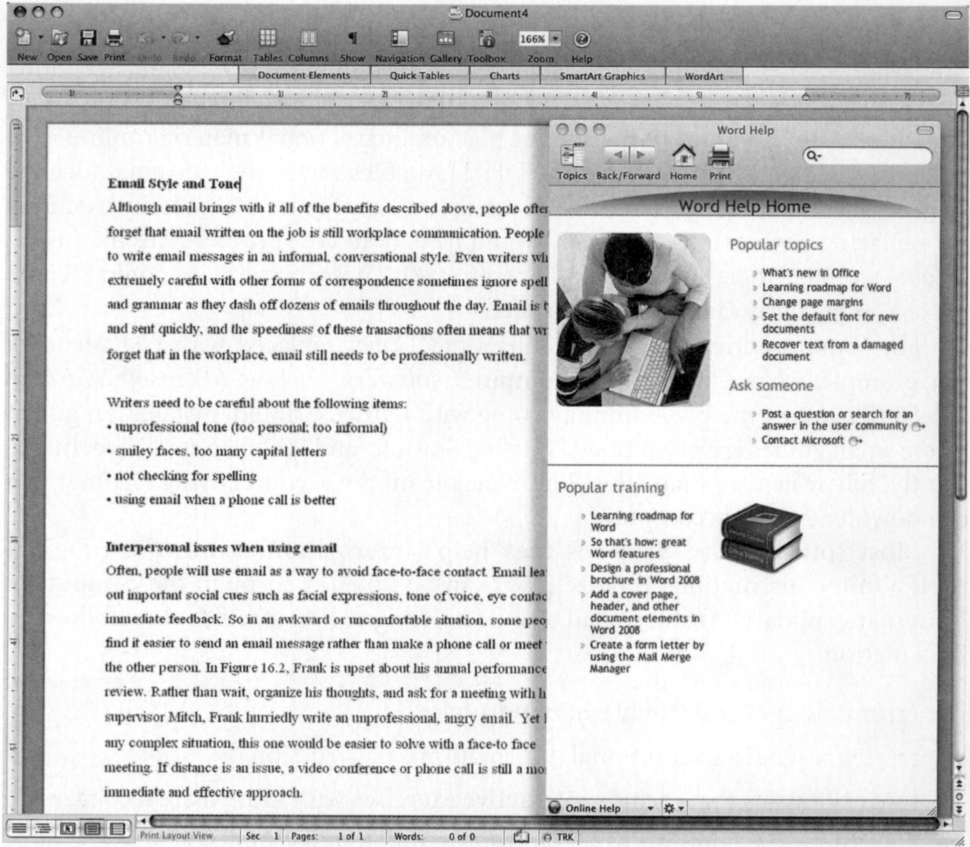

FIGURE 20.9 An Online Help Screen This electronic index offers instant access to any of the topics in the entire online manual.
Source: Microsoft Corporation.

VIDEO INSTRUCTIONS

Along with providing CDs and online instructions, many organizations are creating instructions in video format and posting them on a video-sharing site (such as YouTube) or on the company Web site. By combining sound, movement, color, speech, narration, and text, video instructions can show the full range of actions required to assemble the product or perform the task. *Showing* is a powerful teaching technique. People like to *see* how something is done and often will ask a friend or neighbor for advice about a given task before even reading the instruction manual.

Scripting Online Videos

Start by creating an outline

For a video, the outline takes the form of a script but serves the same function—to plan and sketch what you intend to create. The script outlines the narration, images, motion, and other features that will comprise the complete video. For an instructional video, begin by writing a printed set of instructions. Then adapt the print instructions to a video format: decide on background and foreground details, determine camera placement, decide where and when to include music or text, and write out the full narrative to be delivered.

Script the video (and then edit) to provide separate segments that orient the viewer, give a list of parts, supply step-by-step instructions, and offer a conclusion (such as a shot of the assembled product in action and a closing remark). Remove any unnecessary background or foreground clutter. Position the camera to keep the object or procedure at the center of the frame, at a distance that allows viewers to see clearly. Keep music to a minimum, usually only at the beginning and end. If text is included, make it easy-to-read on the screen—concise, clear, and to the point. Finally, accompany each step with narration, spoken clearly and slowly, with transitions between each step, and concise information.

Figure 20.10 features selected stills from an instructional video on how to properly apply insecticides, known as ant baits, to control fire ants. This video combines text, sound, images and narration. The script for these four slides would resemble the example shown on page 480.

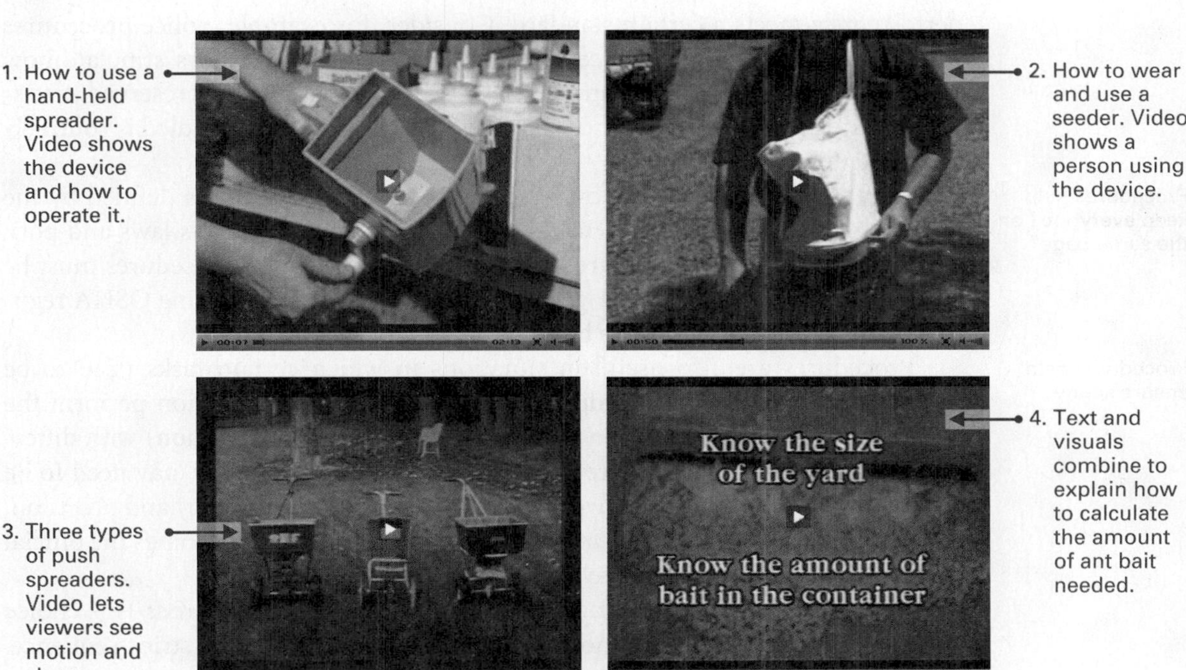

1. How to use a hand-held spreader. Video shows the device and how to operate it.
2. How to wear and use a seeder. Video shows a person using the device.
3. Three types of push spreaders. Video lets viewers see motion and shape.
Know the size of the yard
Know the amount of bait in the container
4. Text and visuals combine to explain how to calculate the amount of ant bait needed.

FIGURE 20.10 Stills from a Set of Video Instructions

Source: Used with permission of the Alabama Cooperative Extension System (Alabama A&M University and Auburn University). All rights to the original material are reserved by the Alabama Cooperative Extension System.

Sample script for Figure 20.10

- **Video still 1:** After opening music and slide, begin with video footage demonstrating how to use the hand seed spreader. Narration: "The most effective way to apply bait is to broadcast it."
- **Video still 2:** Close shot of a person wearing a seeder. Follow the person as he walks across the yard, toward camera.
- **Video still 3:** Still shot of three types of push spreaders. Narration: "Bait can be applied with the same spreader you use for fertilizer."
- **Video still 4:** Combine text and visual shot of how to calculate the amount of ant bait.

PROCEDURES

How instructions and procedures differ

Instructions show an uninitiated person how to perform a task. *Procedures,* on the other hand, provide rules and guidance for people who usually know how to perform the task but who are required to follow accepted practice. To ensure that everyone does something in exactly the same way, procedures typically are aimed at groups of people who need to coordinate their activities so that everyone's performance meets a certain standard. Consider, for example, police procedures for properly gathering evidence from a crime scene: Strict rules stipulate how evidence should be collected and labeled and how it should be preserved, transported, and stored. Evidence shown to have been improperly handled is routinely discredited in a courtroom.

Procedures help keep everyone "on the same page"

Organizations need to follow strict safety procedures, say, as defined by the U.S. Occupational Safety and Health Administration (OSHA). As laws and policies change, such procedures are often updated. The written procedures must be posted for employees to read. Figure 20.11 shows one page outlining OSHA regulations for evacuating high-rise buildings.

Procedures help ensure safety

Procedures are also useful in situations in which certain tasks need to be standardized. For example, if different people in your organization perform the same task at different times (say, monitoring groundwater pollution) with different equipment, or under different circumstances, this procedure may need to be standardized to ensure that all work is done with the same accuracy and precision. A document known as a *Standard Operating Procedure (SOP)* becomes the official guideline for that task, as shown in Figure 20.12.

The steps in a procedure may or may not need to be numbered. This choice will depend on whether or not steps must be performed in strict sequence. Compare for example, Figure 20.11 versus Figure 20.12.

Heading identifies this as a government (OSHA) procedure

Questions that readers might have

Bullets break out each step visually

OSHA FACT Sheet

Evacuating High-Rise Buildings

The National Fire Protection Association defines "high-rise building" as a building greater than 75 feet (25 m) in height where the building height is measured from the lowest level of fire department vehicle access to the floor of the highest occupiable story. Appropriate exits, alarms, emergency lighting, communication systems, and sprinkler systems are critical for employee safety. When designing and maintaining exits, it is essential to ensure that routes leading to the exits, as well as the areas beyond the exits, are accessible and free from materials or items that would impede individuals from easily and effectively evacuating. State and local building code officials can help employers ensure that the design and safety systems are adequate.

When there is an emergency, getting workers out of high-rise buildings poses special challenges. Preparing in advance to safely evacuate the building is critical to the safety of employees who work there.

What actions should employers take to help ensure safe evacuations of high-rise buildings?

- Don't lock fire exits or block doorways, halls, or stairways.
- Test regularly all back-up systems and safety systems, such as emergency lighting and communication systems, and repair them as needed.
- Develop a workplace evacuation plan, post it prominently on each floor, and review it periodically to ensure its effectiveness.
- Identify and train floor wardens, including back-up personnel, who will be responsible for sounding alarms and helping to evacuate employees.
- Conduct emergency evacuation drills periodically.
- Establish designated meeting locations outside the building for workers to gather following an evacuation. The locations should be a safe distance from the building and in an area where people can assemble safely without interfering with emergency response teams.
- Identify personnel with special needs or disabilities who may need help evacuating and assign one or more people, including back-up personnel, to help them.
- Ensure that during off-hour periods, systems are in place to notify, evacuate, and account for off-hour building occupants.
- Post emergency numbers near telephones.

What should workers know before an emergency occurs?

- Be familiar with the worksite's emergency evacuation plan;
- Know the pathway to at least two alternative exits from every room/area at the workplace;
- Recognize the sound/signaling method of the fire/evacuation alarms;
- Know who to contact in an emergency and how to contact them;
- Know how many desks or cubicles are between your workstation and two of the nearest exits so you can escape in the dark if necessary;
- Know where the fire/evacuation alarms are located and how to use them; and
- Report damaged or malfunctioning safety systems and back-up systems

What should employers do when an emergency occurs?

- Sound appropriate alarms and instruct employees to leave building.
- Notify police, firefighters, or other appropriate emergency personnel.
- Take a head count of employees at designated meeting locations, and notify emergency personnel of any missing workers.

What should employees do when an emergency occurs?

- Leave the area quickly but in an orderly manner, following the worksite's emergency evacuation plan. Go directly to the nearest fire-free and smoke-free stairwell recognizing that in some circumstances the only available exit route may contain limited amounts of smoke or fire.

FIGURE 20.11 Safety Procedures This page defines general safety and evacuation procedures to be followed by employers and employees. Each building in turn is required to have its own specific procedures, based on such variables as location, design, and state law.

Source: U.S. Occupational Safety and Health Administration, 2007 <www.osha.gov>.

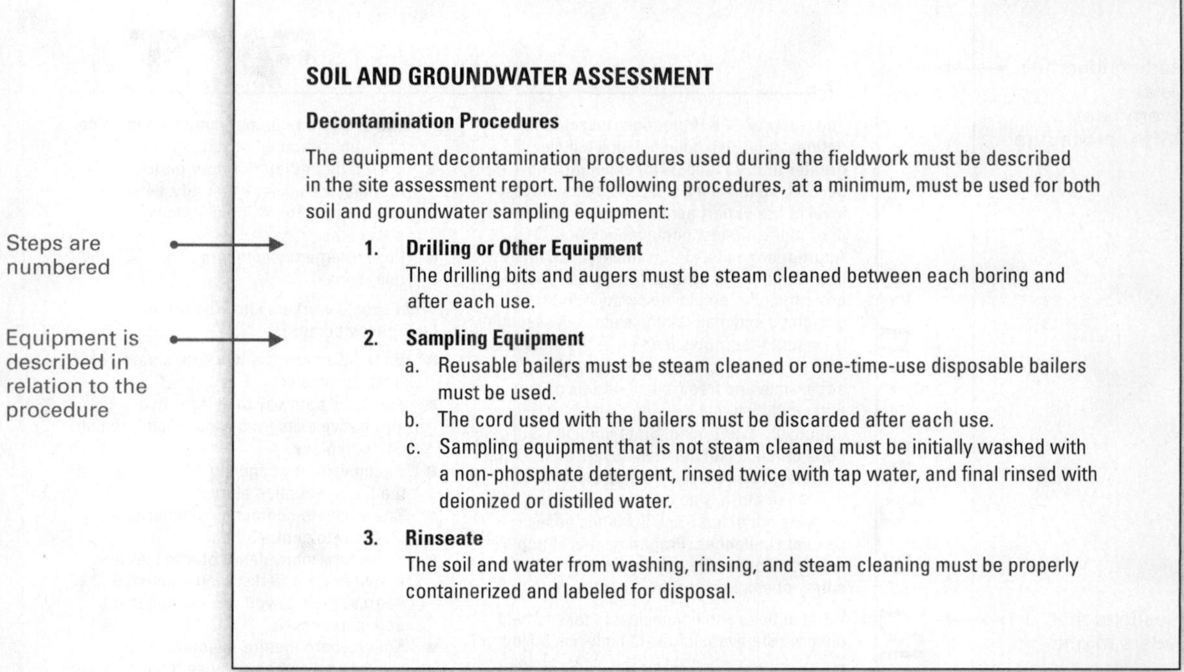
Steps are numbered

Equipment is described in relation to the procedure

SOIL AND GROUNDWATER ASSESSMENT

Decontamination Procedures

The equipment decontamination procedures used during the fieldwork must be described in the site assessment report. The following procedures, at a minimum, must be used for both soil and groundwater sampling equipment:

1. **Drilling or Other Equipment**
   The drilling bits and augers must be steam cleaned between each boring and after each use.
2. **Sampling Equipment**
   a. Reusable bailers must be steam cleaned or one-time-use disposable bailers must be used.
   b. The cord used with the bailers must be discarded after each use.
   c. Sampling equipment that is not steam cleaned must be initially washed with a non-phosphate detergent, rinsed twice with tap water, and final rinsed with deionized or distilled water.
3. **Rinseate**
   The soil and water from washing, rinsing, and steam cleaning must be properly containerized and labeled for disposal.

FIGURE 20.12 **A Standard Operating Procedure** Part of a manual for dealing with leaking underground fuel tanks, this SOP is aimed at technicians already familiar with techniques such as "steam cleaning" and "containerizing." However, to prevent contamination of testing equipment, each technician must follow strict steps.
Source: Courtesy of *Ventura County LUFT Guidance Manual*. Ventura, CA. April 2001.

EVALUATING THE USABILITY OF INSTRUCTIONS AND PROCEDURES

As discussed in Chapter 2, a usable document enables readers to easily locate the information they need, understand this information immediately, and use it safely and effectively (Coe, *Human Factors* 193; Spencer 74). When you write and design any type of workplace or technical document, the end goal is for people to be able to *use* the document successfully. Although usability is an important feature of all documents, it is critical with instructions and procedures because of safety and liability concerns (see Faulty Instructions and Legal Liability, pages 460–62).

Once you have created a first draft, you can conduct some basic usability evaluations to see how people use your document and to determine whether you need to revise the instructional material. Obtaining this feedback in the early stages enables you to correct errors or problems before the instructions are finalized.

Usability and the Goals of Your Readers

You can evaluate usability by observing how people read, respond to, and work with your document. Begin by identifying the performance objectives—the precise tasks or goals readers must accomplish successfully, or the precise knowledge they must acquire (Carliner, "Physical" 564; Zibell 13). For example, the tasks involved in Figure 20.8 (instructions for replacing a worn faucet washer) are evident by the numbered steps. Readers must successfully complete each of these main steps as well as the tasks within each step. For instance, Step 2, "Disassemble the faucet," contains sub-steps (open the faucet; remove the screw; remove the handle; remove the packing nut). Your document is considered usable if readers are able to successfully complete these tasks, from start to finish.

Usability testing on documents that involve regulation (medical devices, for example, which are regulated by the Food and Drug Administration) or in other high-stakes settings is usually conducted by experts with training and experience in this area. Yet all instructional and procedural documents can benefit from basic usability testing. Conducting such testing and revising your document before publication can save your organization time, money, and potential legal challenges.

Approaches for Evaluating a Document's Usability

Using the Audience and Use Profile in Chapter 2 (page 31), expand on the "Intended use of document" and "Information needs" items. What are the precise tasks readers need to accomplish using this document? How much time will readers typically have: a few minutes, or several hours? What other factors are key to your understanding of what will make your instructions or procedures usable?

Once you have answered these questions, check your document using the overall Usability Checklist in Chapter 2 (page 32), along with the specific checklist for the given document (as on page 485). Revise if necessary. Then, you can use two approaches to test the document's usability. Be sure to run your tests on people who represent the typical audience for the situation. For instance, if your audience for Figure 20.8 is homeowners who have experience using basic tools and doing simple home repairs, do not test your documents with people who have never used a pair of pliers.

Revise your document based on what you learn from the usability evaluations.

Think-Aloud Evaluation. In this approach, you will need 3 to 5 people but should test them one at a time. Each person is provided with your instructions and a way he or she can actually test the document. For instance, if your instructions explain how to connect a digital camera to a computer, provide a camera, cable, and laptop. Ask subjects to "think out loud" (talk about what they are doing) as they try to follow your instructions. Note those places where people are successful and where

Basic Usability Survey

1. Briefly describe why this document is used.
2. Evaluate the *content:*
   - Identify any irrelevant information.
   - Indicate any gaps in the information.
   - Identify any information that seems inaccurate.
   - List other problems with the content.
3. Evaluate the *organization:*
   - Identify anything that is out of order or hard to locate or follow.
   - List other problems with the organization.
4. Evaluate the *style:*
   - Identify anything you misunderstood on first reading.
   - Identify anything you couldn't understand at all.
   - Identify expressions that seem wordy, inexact, or too complex.
   - List other problems with the style.
5. Evaluate the *design:*
   - Indicate any headings that are missing, confusing, or excessive.
   - Indicate any material that should be designed as a list.
   - Give examples of material that might be clarified by a visual.
   - Give examples of misleading or overly complex visuals.
   - List other problems with design.
6. Identify anything that seems misleading or that could create legal problems or cross-cultural misunderstanding.
7. Please suggest other ways of making this document easier to use.

FIGURE 20.13 **A Basic Usability Survey** Versions of these questions can serve as a basis for testing your document.

(*Source:* Based on Carliner, "Demonstrating Effectiveness" 258.)

they get stuck. Don't coach them, but do remind them to describe their thinking (sometimes when people are concentrating, they will stop talking, and you need to ask them "what are you thinking now?"). After the test is concluded, follow up with questions about places where your document seemed unclear or where people seemed to have particular problems. Take good notes and at the end of your tests, compare findings to look for common themes.

Focus Groups. In this approach, 8 to 10 people are provided with the instructions and are asked to complete the task. Based on a targeted list of questions about the document's content, organization, style, and design (Basic Usability Survey, Figure 20.13), focus group members are asked to complete the survey and then describe (out loud) what information they think is missing or excessive, what they like or dislike, and what they find easy or hard to understand. They may also suggest revisions for graphics, format, word choice, or level of technicality.

CHECKLIST: Instructions and Procedures

(Numbers in parentheses refer to first page of discussion.)

Content

- ☐ Does the title promise exactly what the instructions deliver? (462)
- ☐ Is the background adequate for the intended audience? (465)
- ☐ Do explanations enable readers to understand what to do? (465)
- ☐ Do examples enable readers to see how to do it correctly? (465)
- ☐ Are the definition and purpose of each step given as needed? (470)
- ☐ Are all obvious steps and needless information omitted? (466)
- ☐ Do notes, cautions, or warnings appear before or with the step? (468)
- ☐ Is the information rate appropriate for the reader's abilities and the difficulty of this procedure? (466)
- ☐ Are visuals adequate for clarifying the steps? (462)
- ☐ Do visuals repeat prose information whenever necessary? (472)
- ☐ Is everything accurate and based on your thorough knowledge? (462)

Organization

- ☐ Is the introduction adequate without being excessive? (473)
- ☐ Do the instructions follow the exact sequence of steps? (474)
- ☐ Is each step numbered, if appropriate? (472)

▶▶

CHECKLIST: (*continued*)

- ☐ Is all the information for a particular step close together? (472)
- ☐ For lengthy instructions, is a layered approach, with a brief reference card, more appropriate? (472)
- ☐ Is the conclusion necessary and, if necessary, adequate? (474)

Style

- ☐ Does the familiar material appear *first* in each sentence? (470)
- ☐ Do steps generally have short sentences? (470)
- ☐ Does each step begin with an action verb? (470)
- ☐ Are all steps in the active voice and imperative mood? (470)
- ☐ Do all steps have parallel and affirmative phrasing? (471)
- ☐ Are transitions adequate for marking time and sequence? (471)

Page Design

- ☐ Does each heading clearly tell readers what to expect? (472)
- ☐ Are steps single-spaced within, and double-spaced between? (472)
- ☐ Is the overall design simple and accessible? (472)
- ☐ Are notes, cautions, or warnings set off or highlighted? (472)
- ☐ Are visuals beside or near the step, and set off by white space? (472)

Projects

GENERAL

1. Improve readability by revising the style and design of these instructions.

> **What to Do Before Jacking Up Your Car**
>
> Whenever the misfortune of a flat tire occurs, some basic procedures should be followed before the car is jacked up. If possible, your car should be positioned on as firm and level a surface as is available. The engine has to be turned off; the parking brake should be set; and the automatic transmission shift lever must be placed in "park" or the manual transmission lever in "reverse." The wheel diagonally opposite the one to be removed should have a piece of wood placed beneath it to prevent the wheel from rolling. The spare wheel, jack, and lug wrench should be removed from the luggage compartment.

2. Select part of a technical manual in your field or instructions for a general audience and make a copy of the material. Using the checklist on pages 485–86, evaluate the sample's usability. In a memo to your instructor, discuss the strong and weak points of the instructions. Or explain your evaluation in class.

3. Assume that colleagues or classmates will be serving six months as volunteers in agriculture, education, or a similar capacity in a developing country. Do the research and create a set of procedures that will prepare individuals for avoiding diseases and dealing with medical issues in that specific country. Topics might include safe food and water, insect protection, vaccinations, medical emergencies, and the like. Be sure to provide background on the specific health risks travelers will face. Design your instructions as a two-sided brief reference card, as a chapter to be included in a longer manual, or in some other format suggested by your instructor.

Hint: Begin your research for this project by checking out the National Centers for Disease Control's Web site at <www.cdc.gov/travel/.

4. Choose a topic from your major, or an area of interest. Using the general outline in this chapter as a model, prepare instructions for a task that requires at least three major steps. Address a general audience, and begin by completing an audience and use profile. Include (a) all necessary visuals, or, (b) an "art brief" (pages 272–73) and a rough diagram for each visual, or (c) a "reference visual" (a copy of a visual published elsewhere) with instructions for adapting your visual from that one. (If you borrow visuals from other sources, provide full documentation.)

5. Select any one of the instructional visuals in Figure 20.5 and write a prose version of those instructions—without using visual illustrations or special page design. Bring your version to class and be prepared to discuss the conclusions you've derived from this exercise.

6. Find a set of instructions or some other technical document that is easy-to-use. Assume that you are Associate Director of Communications for the company that produced this document and you are doing a final review before the document is released. With the Checklist for Instructions and Procedures as a guide, identify those features that make the document usable and prepare a memo to your boss that justifies your decision to release the document.

Following the identical scenario, find a document that is hard to use, and identify the features that need improving. Prepare a memo to your boss that spells out the needed improvements. Submit both memos and the examples to your instructor.

TEAM

1. Draw a map of the route from your classroom to your dorm, apartment, or home—whichever is closest. Be sure to include identifying landmarks. When your map is completed, write instructions for a classmate who will try to duplicate your map from the information given in your written instructions. Be sure your classmate does not see your map! Exchange your instructions and try to duplicate your classmate's map. Compare your results with the original map. Discuss your conclusions about the usability of these instructions.

2. Divide into small groups and visit your computer center, library, or any place on campus or at work where you can find operating manuals for computers, lab or office equipment, or the like. (Or look through the documentation for your own computer hardware or software.) Locate fairly brief instructions that could use revision for improved content, organization, style, or format. Choose instructions for a procedure you are able to perform. Make a copy of the instructions, test them for usability, and revise as needed. Submit all materials to your instructor, along with a memo explaining the improvements. Or be prepared to discuss your revision in class.

3. Test the usability of a document prepared for this course. As a basis for your test, adapt the Audience and Use Profile Sheet on page 31, the general Checklist for Usability (page 32), whichever specific checklist applies to this particular document (as on pages 485–86, for example), and the Basic Usability Survey on page 484.

Revise the document based on your findings. Obtain your data through focus group discussions and/or think-aloud evaluation.

Appoint a group member to explain the usability testing procedure and the results to the class.

DIGITAL AND SOCIAL MEDIA

Do the research and prepare a set of instructions that will show general readers how to become more environmentally informed consumers and how to find, identify, evaluate, and compare environmentally friendly consumer goods such as appliances, building materials, and household products. Design your instructions as a foldout brochure (page 460) or a one-page (double-sided) handout, or in a format requested by your instructor. *Hint:* Begin your research by checking out the following Web sites:

- *The Environment at MIT* at <web.mit.edu/environment/reduce/env_living.html/>
- The U.S. Environmental Protection Agency's *Energy Star* site at <www.energystar.gov>
- *Buyer's Guide for the Ethical consumer* site at <www.ethicalconsumer.org/FreeBuyersGuides.aspx>

GLOBAL

In many cultures, the use of imperative mood is considered impolite or too direct. For instance, instructions that state "Place the disk into the disk drive" may sound bossy and inconsiderate. Find a set of instructions that use imperative mood (for example, Figure 20.8 in this chapter) and rewrite these for a cross-cultural audience where the imperative mood would be offensive. For instance, you might use an indirect imperative ("Be sure to insert the disk into the drive").

21 Informal Reports

"In a large corporation like this one, short, informal reports keep vital day-to-day information moving along: Employees or groups report to managers or to one another; managers report to company department heads; department heads report to company officers, who, in turn report to the CEO. These reports address any conceivable topic—based on the need or crisis at the time. Depending on the urgency and importance of the issue, a given report might be issued as an email, a PDF attachment, or a paper document. All such documents serve as a permanent record and are filed for later reference and retrieval, as needed."

—Elaine Hering,
Division Chief for a major auto-parts supplier

LEARNING OBJECTIVES FOR THIS CHAPTER

- Understand the role and purposes of informal reports
- Differentiate between informal and formal reports
- Differentiate between informational and analytical reports
- Write informational reports
- Write analytical reports

Informal versus formal reports

When you think of reports, you probably picture long, formal documents that contain many pages of research, information, charts and graphs, footnotes, and other details. Yet in the workplace, for every long, formal report that is written, there are countless specific shorter reports created. These *informal reports* help people make decisions on matters as diverse as the most comfortable office chairs to buy or the best recruit to hire for management training. Unlike long formal reports (discussed in Chapter 22), most informal reports require no extended planning, are prepared quickly, contain little or no background information, and have no *front* or *end matter* supplements (title page, table of contents, glossary, works cited, index).

Format of informal reports

Although various formats can be used, informal reports most often take the form of a memorandum. Memo reports are usually distributed via email (as PDF attachments) and sometimes in hard copy. See Chapter 14 for more on memos.

INFORMATIONAL VERSUS ANALYTICAL REPORTS

Informational versus analytical reports

In the professional world, decision makers rely on two types of informal reports: some reports focus primarily on information ("what we're doing now," "what we did last month," "what our customer survey found," "what went on at the department meeting"). Other reports also include analysis ("what this information means for us," "what courses of action should be considered," "what we recommend, and why").

Types of informational reports

Informational reports answer basic questions such as how much progress has been made on a project (progress reports), what activity transpired during a given period (activity reports), what activity took place during a business trip (trip reports), or what discussions occurred in a meeting (meeting minutes). These reports help keep an organization running from day to day by providing short, timely updates.

Types of analytical reports

Analytical reports offer information as well as interpretations and conclusions based on the information. Analysis is the heart of technical communication. Analysis involves evaluating information, interpreting it accurately, drawing valid conclusions, and making persuasive recommendations. Although gathering and reporting information are essential workplace skills, analysis is ultimately what professionals do to earn their pay. Analytical reports evaluate whether a project or situation is feasible (feasibility reports), make recommendations on how to proceed (recommendation reports), constructively critique the work of others (peer review reports), or justify the writer's position on an issue (justification reports).

PROGRESS REPORTS

Audience and purpose considerations

Organizations depend on *progress reports* (also called status reports) to monitor progress and problems on various projects. Progress reports may be written either for internal personnel or outside clients. In the case of internal audiences, managers use progress reports to evaluate projects, monitor employees, decide how to allocate funds, and keep track of delays or expense overages that could dramatically affect outcomes and project costs. In the case of external audiences, progress reports explain to clients how time and money are being spent and how difficulties have been overcome. The reports can therefore be used to assure the client that the project will be completed on schedule and within the budget.

Many contracts stipulate the dates and stages when progress will be reported. Failing to report on time may invoke contractual penalties. Some organizations require regular progress reports (daily, weekly, monthly), whereas others only use progress reports as needed, such as when a project milestone has been reached.

Figure 21.1 shows a progress report from a training manager to a company vice president. Because the audience is internal, the writer has chosen memo format. A report like this to an external client might be written in letter format and on company letterhead as a legal record. Notice also how the report provides only those details essential to the reader.

GUIDELINES for Progress Reports

- **Choose an appropriate format.** Routine, regular reports may be delivered in email format, whereas more infrequent reports might be better delivered via a signed memo (or a letter, when the report is for an external client).
- **Provide a clear subject line.** All progress reports should clearly identify their purpose in the subject line of a memo, email, or letter.
- **Present information efficiently.** Because readers of progress reports are managers or clients who want the bottom line information as quickly as possible, chunk the information into logically headed sections and use bulleted or numbered lists. Leave out information readers will already know, but do not omit anything that they might need to know.
- **Use a timeline structure to answer the anticipated questions.** First identify what has been accomplished since the last report. Then discuss any important details such as outcomes of meetings, problems encountered and solutions implemented, deadlines met or missed, and resources/materials needed. Conclude with steps to be completed in time for the next report, with specific dates, if available.

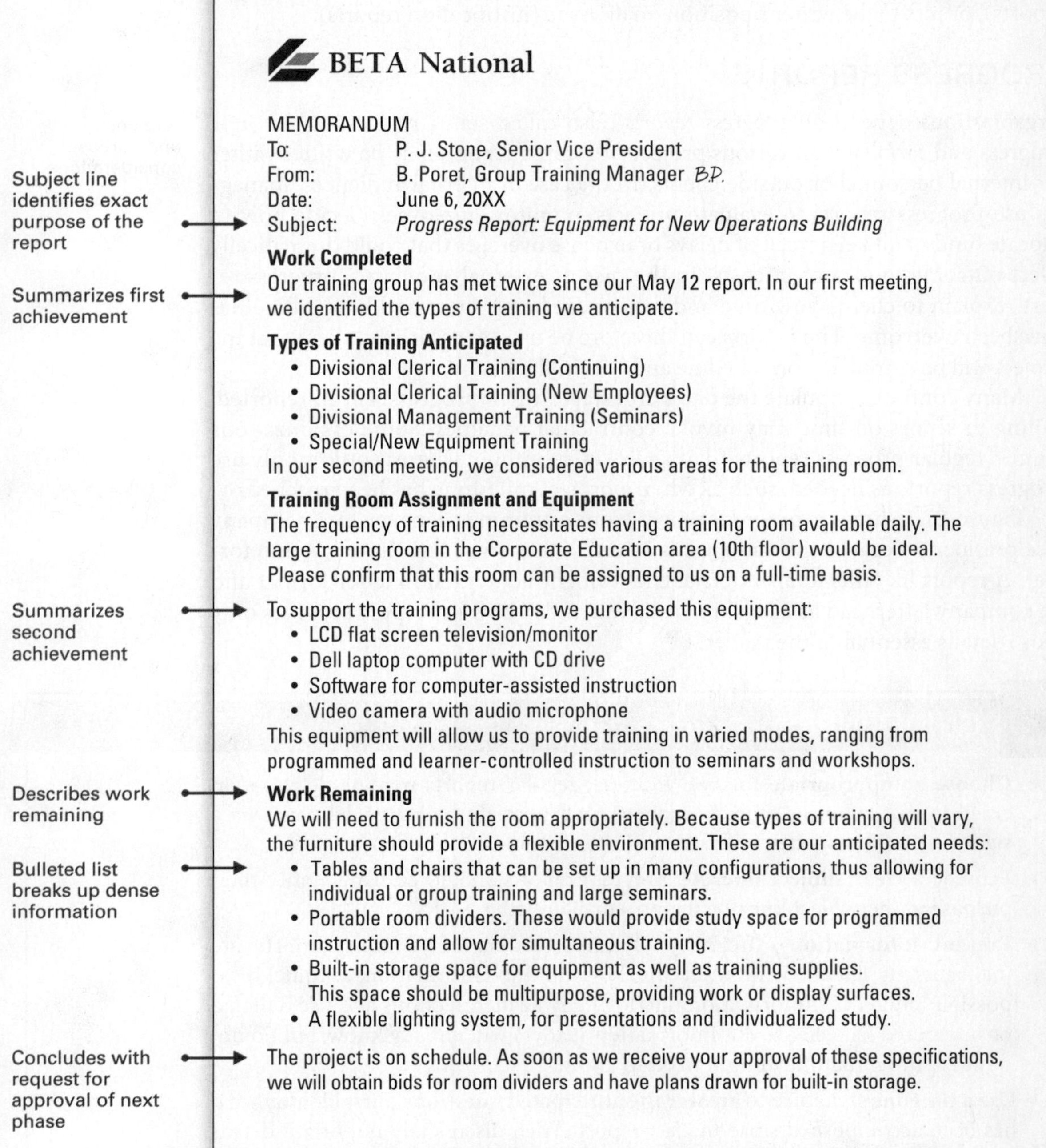

Subject line identifies exact purpose of the report

Summarizes first achievement

Summarizes second achievement

Describes work remaining

Bulleted list breaks up dense information

Concludes with request for approval of next phase

BETA National

MEMORANDUM

To: P. J. Stone, Senior Vice President
From: B. Poret, Group Training Manager *B.P.*
Date: June 6, 20XX
Subject: *Progress Report: Equipment for New Operations Building*

Work Completed

Our training group has met twice since our May 12 report. In our first meeting, we identified the types of training we anticipate.

Types of Training Anticipated

- Divisional Clerical Training (Continuing)
- Divisional Clerical Training (New Employees)
- Divisional Management Training (Seminars)
- Special/New Equipment Training

In our second meeting, we considered various areas for the training room.

Training Room Assignment and Equipment

The frequency of training necessitates having a training room available daily. The large training room in the Corporate Education area (10th floor) would be ideal. Please confirm that this room can be assigned to us on a full-time basis.

To support the training programs, we purchased this equipment:

- LCD flat screen television/monitor
- Dell laptop computer with CD drive
- Software for computer-assisted instruction
- Video camera with audio microphone

This equipment will allow us to provide training in varied modes, ranging from programmed and learner-controlled instruction to seminars and workshops.

Work Remaining

We will need to furnish the room appropriately. Because types of training will vary, the furniture should provide a flexible environment. These are our anticipated needs:

- Tables and chairs that can be set up in many configurations, thus allowing for individual or group training and large seminars.
- Portable room dividers. These would provide study space for programmed instruction and allow for simultaneous training.
- Built-in storage space for equipment as well as training supplies. This space should be multipurpose, providing work or display surfaces.
- A flexible lighting system, for presentations and individualized study.

The project is on schedule. As soon as we receive your approval of these specifications, we will obtain bids for room dividers and have plans drawn for built-in storage.

FIGURE 21.1 A Progress Report

As you work on a longer report or term project, your instructor may require a progress report. In Figure 21.2, Karen Granger documents progress made on her term project: an evaluation of the Environmental Protection Agency's effectiveness in cleaning a heavily contaminated harbor at a major New England fishery.

Progress Report

To: Dr. John Lannon
From: Karen P. Granger *KG*
Date: April 17, 20XX
Subject: Evaluation of the EPA's ***Remedial Action Master Plan***

Project Overview
As my term project, I have been evaluating the issues of politics, scheduling, and safety surrounding the EPA's published plan to remove Polychlorinated biphenyl (PCB) contaminants from New Bedford Harbor.

Work Completed

February 23: Began general research on the harbor contamination.

March 8: Decided to analyze the *Remedial Action Master Plan* (*RAMP*) in order to determine whether residents are being "studied to death" by the EPA.

March 9–19: Drew a map of the harbor to show areas of contamination. Obtained the *RAMP* from Pat Shay of the EPA.

Interviewed State Representative Grimes briefly by phone; Scheduled an in-depth interview with Grimes and environmentalist Sharon Dean. Interviewed Patricia Chase, President, New England Sierra Club, by phone.

March 24: Obtained *Public Comments on the New Bedford RAMP*, a collection of reactions to the plan.

April 13: Interviewed Grimes and Dean; searched Grimes's files for information. Also searched the files of Raymond Soares, New Bedford Coordinator, EPA.

Summarizes achievements to date

Work in Progress
Contacting by phone and email a cross section of respondents who have commented on the *RAMP*.

FIGURE 21.2 Progress Report on a Term Project

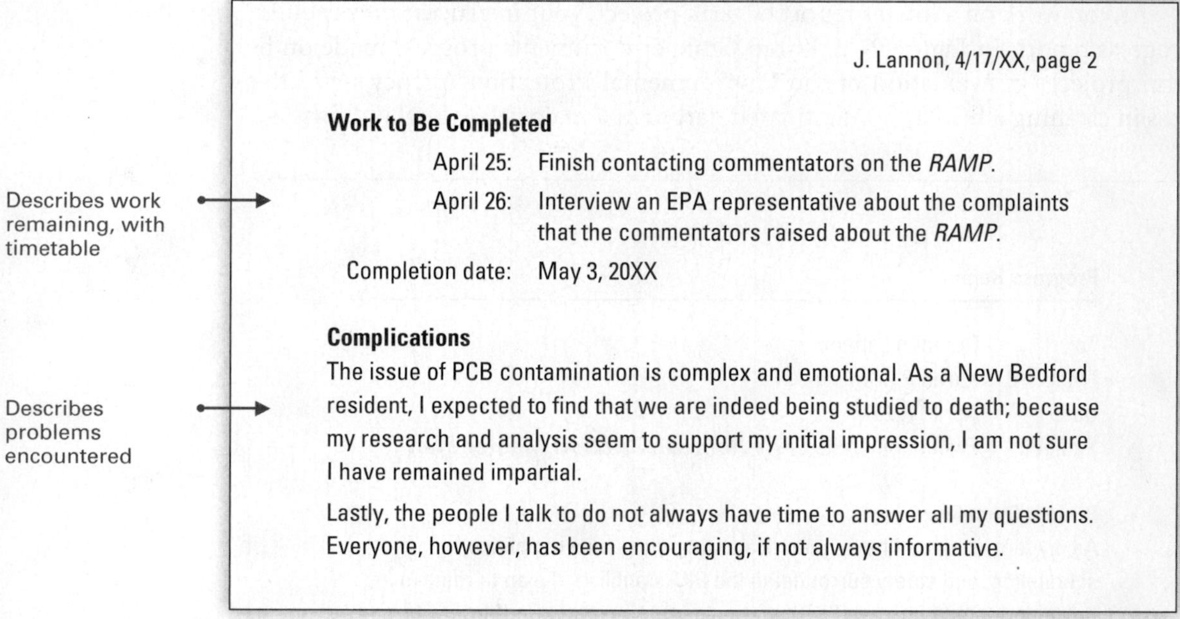

J. Lannon, 4/17/XX, page 2

Work to Be Completed

April 25: Finish contacting commentators on the *RAMP*.

April 26: Interview an EPA representative about the complaints that the commentators raised about the *RAMP*.

Completion date: May 3, 20XX

Complications

The issue of PCB contamination is complex and emotional. As a New Bedford resident, I expected to find that we are indeed being studied to death; because my research and analysis seem to support my initial impression, I am not sure I have remained impartial.

Lastly, the people I talk to do not always have time to answer all my questions. Everyone, however, has been encouraging, if not always informative.

Describes work remaining, with timetable
Describes problems encountered

FIGURE 21.2 *(Continued)*

PERIODIC ACTIVITY REPORTS

Audience and purpose considerations

Periodic activity reports resemble progress reports in that they summarize activities over a specified period. But unlike progress reports, which summarize specific accomplishments on a particular project, periodic activity reports summarize general activities during a particular period. Periodic activity reports are almost always internal, written by employees to update their supervisors on their activities as a whole, in order to help managers monitor workload. In many companies, these reports, usually written weekly or monthly, are called "status reports."

Fran DeWitt's report (Figure 21.3) answers her boss's primary question: *What did you accomplish last month?* Her response has to be detailed and informative.

NOTE *Both progress reports and periodic activity reports inform management and clients about what employees are doing and how well they are doing it. Therefore, accuracy, clarity, and appropriate detail are essential, as is the ethical dimension. Make sure that recipients have all the vital facts, and that they understand these facts as clearly as you do.*

GUIDELINES for Periodic Activity Reports

- **Choose an appropriate format.** Periodic activity reports are usually written as emails or memos to a supervisor. However, some organizations require a predesigned form.
- **Provide a clear subject line.** Identify the exact purpose and time frame of the report in a subject line, such as "Monthly activity report for August."

- **Present information efficiently.** Report readers just want the bottom line. Omit minor details but include all the essentials. Use headings to chunk information, and bulleted and numbered lists to break up dense prose for easier reading.
- **Make sure your report answers the expected questions.** Describe your key accomplishments during the period (such as progress on an ongoing project). Then describe other relevant activity since the last report, (such as completion of one-time projects, attendance at meetings, problems encountered, or changes).

TRIP REPORTS

Trip reports focus on business-related travel during a given period. Employers who pay travel expenses need to know that the company is getting its money's worth. Employers also need to know what employees learn through their travels.

Audience and purpose considerations

Figure 21.4 (page 497) shows a trip report from an employee who has traveled to a branch office to inspect the site and interview the office staff about absenteeism and hiring problems at that branch.

GUIDELINES for Trip Reports

- **Take accurate notes.** If you must interview people, either record the conversation—with their permission—or take careful notes. Transcribe interviews immediately, while your memory is fresh. If you investigate a location or site, take careful notes.
- **Begin with a clear subject line and purpose statement.** The subject line identifies the exact trip, including date(s), while the purpose statement prevents any possible confusion about your reasons for the trip.
- **Record the names of people and places.** Specify whom you spoke with (spelling names correctly and getting job titles right) and places visited.
- **Account for times and locations.** If you visit more than one location, be clear about what occurred at each site.
- **Use a format that is easy to navigate.** Provide clear headings to chunk information and use bulleted/numbered lists.
- **Describe findings completely and objectively.** Include all vital information and omit irrelevant material. Do not insert personal impressions—stick to the facts.
- **Offer to follow up.** Because trip reports may evoke further questions from a supervisor, indicate that you are available to help provide clarification. Unless you have been specifically asked, do not make recommendations.

Subject line announces the topic

Gives overview of recent activities, and their purpose

Gives details

Explains the benefits of these activities

■ Mammon Trust

MEMORANDUM

Date: 6/18/XX

To: N. Morgan, Assistant Vice President

From: F. C. DeWitt *FCD*

Subject: **Recent Meetings for Computer-Assisted Instruction**

Overview

For the past month, I've been working on a cooperative project with the Banking Administration Institute, Computron Corporation, and several banks. My purpose has been to develop training programs, specific to banking, appropriate for computer-assisted instruction (CAI). We focus on three areas: Proof/Encoding Training for entry-level personnel, Productivity Skills for Management, and Banking Principles for Supervisors.

Meetings Hosted

I hosted two meetings for this task force. On June 6, we discussed Proof/ Encoding Training, and on June 7, Productivity Training. The objective for the Proof/Encoding meeting was to compare ideas, information, and available training packages. We are now designing a course.

The objective for the Productivity meeting was to explore methods for increasing Banking Operations skills. Discussion included instances in which computer-assisted instruction is appropriate. Computron also described software applications used to teach productivity. Other banks outlined their experiences with similar applications.

Meeting Attended

On June 10, I attended a meeting in Washington, D.C. to design a course in basic banking principles for high-level clerical/supervisory-level employees. We also discussed the feasibility of adapting this course to CAI. This type of training, not currently available through Corporate Education, would meet a definite supervisor/management need in the division.

Benefits

My involvement in these meetings has two benefits. First, structured discussions with trainers in the banking industry provide an exchange of ideas, methods, and experiences. This involvement expedites development of our training programs because it saves me time on research. Second, with a working knowledge of these systems and applications, I am able to assist my group in designing programs specific to our needs.

FIGURE 21.3 Periodic Activity Report

To: Monica Herrera, Director of Human Resources, Boston office
From: Bill Moskowicz, Human Resources Specialist *B.M.*
Date: March 30, 20XX
Subject: **March 20 Visit to the Eastfield Office**

Subject line identifies trip and its date

Purpose

On March 20th, I visited the Eastfield office to explore these two issues:

- Higher than average rate of employee absenteeism at that office
- Difficulties hiring qualified employees to work and live in or near the Eastfield Fort Channel area

Begins with a purpose statement

To pinpoint the causes of these problems, I decided to interview three individuals face-to-face, in hopes of getting more candid and detailed responses than I would via phone or email, particularly regarding the sensitive absenteeism problem.

Schedule

Provides an accounting of how time was spent

I spoke with the following people individually: Susan Sheehan, Director of HR (9:00 a.m.–10:00 a.m.); Sammy Lee, Marketing Manager for the gourmet desserts division (10:00 a.m.–11 :00 a.m.); and Megan Fields, an Administrative Assistant in the distribution division (11:00 a.m.–12:00 p.m.). Then we all had lunch and continued the discussion between noon and 2:00 p.m., at which time I transcribed my recordings and headed back to Boston.

Interviews

Includes discussion of what was learned

The interviews were illuminating. Essentially all three pointed out how the absenteeism and hiring problems are not entirely separate issues; in fact, they are closely linked. While once a thriving, safe, and low-crime city (including the branch's Fort Channel area), Eastfield has now fallen upon difficult economic times, particularly in the last year. All three employees identified the following problems:

- Increased gang activity and vagrancy in the Fort Channel area
- Lack of safe public transportation to and from the office or a secure, on-site parking facility

Uses bulleted list (and headings) to break up text and identify key points

FIGURE 21.4 A Trip Report

M. Herrera, 3/30/XX, page 2

- An increasing decline in amenities, especially lunch venues or safe public areas nearby
- Decreased security resulting from a busy police force and high security guard turnover

While Susan and Sammy can both afford to occasionally take cabs and leave the Fort Channel area for lunch, Megan pointed out her limitations due to salary and an insufficient reimbursement program.

The Fort Channel area's problems have all had a direct impact on employee hiring in recent months. Both Susan and Sammy reported losing promising potential employees following interviews. According to Susan, while United Foods manufactures and distributes gourmet products, attracting those who wish to work in an upscale environment, potential employees are often frightened away, preferring employment at either the Boston office or with competitors located elsewhere in the state. At the same time, very few have opted to relocate from the Boston to Eastfield offices to help account for imbalances.

Conclusion

Offers to follow up →

While the goal of this trip was not for me to make recommendations, I have some specific ideas. I would be glad to speak with you further to answer any questions and to share those ideas with you.

FIGURE 21.4 *(Continued)*

MEETING MINUTES

Audience and purpose considerations

Many team or project meetings require someone to record the proceedings. *Meeting minutes* are the records of such meetings. Copies of minutes usually are distributed (often via email) to all members and interested parties to track the proceedings and to remind members about their responsibilities. Usually one person is appointed to record the minutes. Often, the person assigned will type minutes on a laptop and email them out as soon as the meeting is completed.

GUIDELINES for Meeting Minutes

- **Take good notes during the meeting.** Don't rely on your memory, even if you write up the minutes immediately after the meeting. Write down who said what, especially if an important point was raised.
- **Complete the minutes immediately after the meeting.** Even if you take good notes, you may forget the context of a particular point if you wait too long.
- **Include a clear title and the meeting date.** Indicate the meeting's exact purpose ("sales conference planning meeting"), and include the date to prevent confusion with similar meetings.
- **List all attendees.** If the meeting was chaired or moderated, indicate by whom.
- **Describe all agenda items.** Make sure all topics discussed are recorded. Your own memory (and that of other meeting attendees) of meeting topics is usually fleeting.
- **Record all decisions or conclusions.** If everyone agreed on a point, or if a vote was taken, include those outcomes.
- **Make the minutes easy to navigate.** Use headings, lists, and other helpful design features.
- **Make the minutes precise and clear.** Describe each topic fully yet concisely. Don't omit important nuances, but stick to the facts.
- **Keep personal commentary, humor, and "sidebar" comments out of meeting minutes.** Comments ("As usual, Ms. Jones disagreed with the committee") or judgmental expressions ("good," "poor," "irrelevant") are not appropriate.
- **Proofread.** Check the spelling of attendees' names.
- **Try to anticipate any unintended consequences.** Consider how you have described any politically sensitive or confidential issues before sending out minutes. Remember, email can travel widely.

Figure 21.5 shows minutes from a personnel managers' meeting.

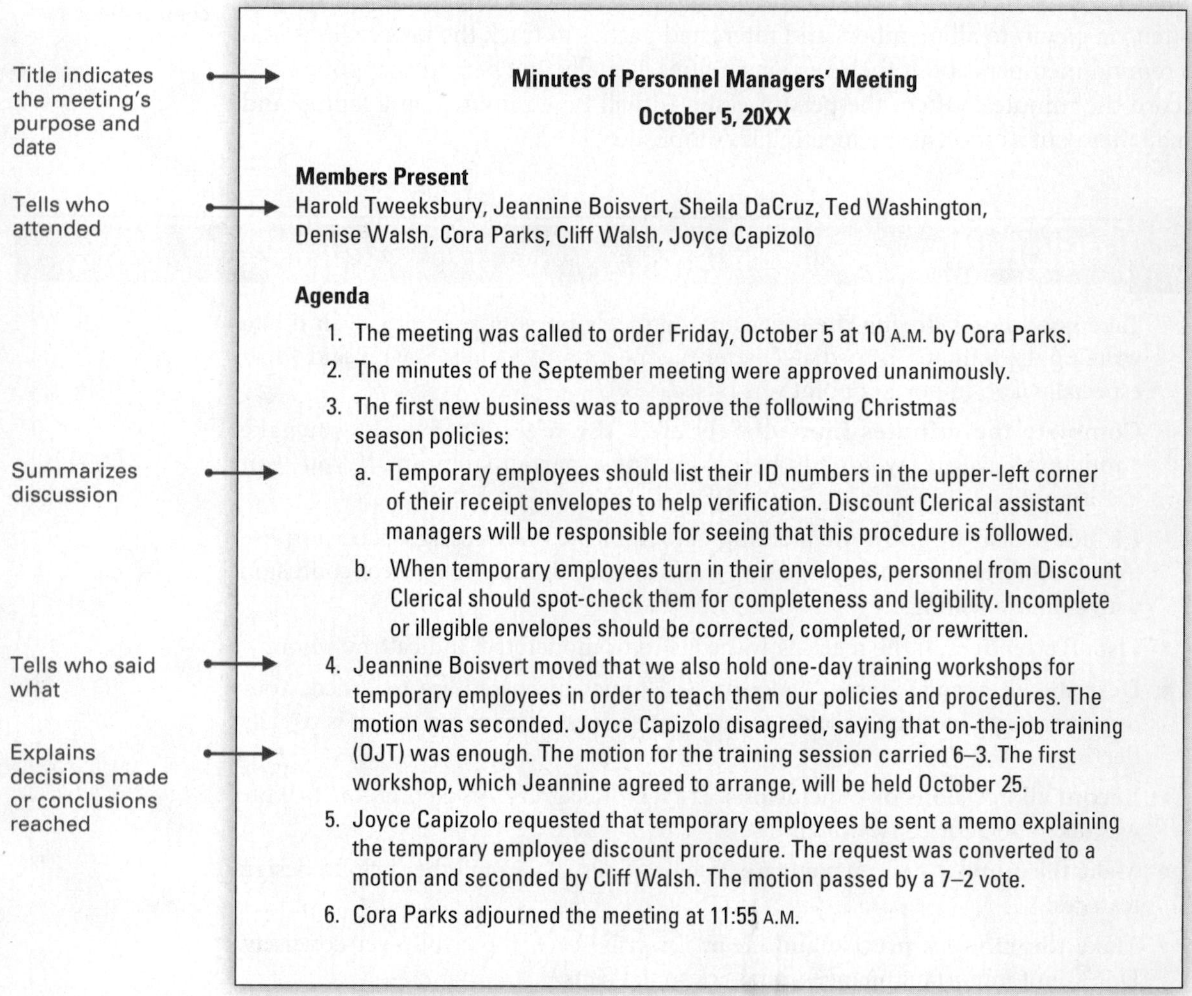
Title indicates the meeting's purpose and date
Tells who attended
Summarizes discussion
Tells who said what
Explains decisions made or conclusions reached

Minutes of Personnel Managers' Meeting
October 5, 20XX

Members Present
Harold Tweeksbury, Jeannine Boisvert, Sheila DaCruz, Ted Washington, Denise Walsh, Cora Parks, Cliff Walsh, Joyce Capizolo

Agenda

1. The meeting was called to order Friday, October 5 at 10 A.M. by Cora Parks.
2. The minutes of the September meeting were approved unanimously.
3. The first new business was to approve the following Christmas season policies:
   a. Temporary employees should list their ID numbers in the upper-left corner of their receipt envelopes to help verification. Discount Clerical assistant managers will be responsible for seeing that this procedure is followed.
   b. When temporary employees turn in their envelopes, personnel from Discount Clerical should spot-check them for completeness and legibility. Incomplete or illegible envelopes should be corrected, completed, or rewritten.
4. Jeannine Boisvert moved that we also hold one-day training workshops for temporary employees in order to teach them our policies and procedures. The motion was seconded. Joyce Capizolo disagreed, saying that on-the-job training (OJT) was enough. The motion for the training session carried 6–3. The first workshop, which Jeannine agreed to arrange, will be held October 25.
5. Joyce Capizolo requested that temporary employees be sent a memo explaining the temporary employee discount procedure. The request was converted to a motion and seconded by Cliff Walsh. The motion passed by a 7–2 vote.
6. Cora Parks adjourned the meeting at 11:55 A.M.

FIGURE 21.5 Meeting Minutes

FEASIBILITY REPORTS

Audience and purpose considerations

Feasibility reports help decision makers assess whether an idea, plan, or course of action is realistic and practical. An idea that seems to make perfect sense from one perspective may not be feasible for one reason or another, perhaps, say, because of timing. For example, a manufacturing company may want to switch to a more automated process, which would reduce costs over the long term. But in the short term, the resulting layoffs would have a negative impact on morale.

A feasibility report provides answers to questions such as these:

Typical questions about feasibility

- What is the problem or situation, and how should we deal with it?
- Is this course of action likely to succeed?
- Do the benefits outweigh the drawbacks or risks?
- What are the pros and cons, and the alternatives?
- Should anything be done at all? Should we wait? Is the timing right?

The answers are based on the writer's careful research and analysis.

Managers and other decision makers are the primary audience for feasibility reports. These busy people expect the recommendation or answer at or near the beginning of the document, followed by supporting evidence and reasoning. A feasibility report generally uses the "bottom line first" organizing pattern: here is the situation; here is our recommendation; and here is why this approach is feasible at this time.

Figure 21.6 shows a report in which a securities analyst for a state pension fund reports to the fund's manager on the feasibility of investing in a rapidly growing computer maker.

GUIDELINES for Feasibility Reports

- **Make the subject line clear.** Always use the word "feasibility" (or a synonym) in the title ("Subject: Feasibility of . . .").
- **Provide background if needed.** Your readers may not always need background information, but if they do, make it brief.
- **Offer the recommendation early.** State the "bottom line" explicitly at the beginning of the report, or just after the background information.
- **Follow up with details, data, and criteria.** Include supporting data, such as costs, equipment needed, and results expected. Include only the directly relevant details that will persuade readers to support your recommendation.
- **Explain why your recommendation is the most feasible among all the choices.** Your readers may prefer other options. Persuade them that your suggested course of action is the best.
- **End with a call to action.**

MEMORANDUM

To: Mary K. White, Fund Manager

From: Martha Mooney MM

Date: April 1, 20XX

Clear subject line leaves no doubt as to purpose of report →

Subject: **The Feasibility of Investing in WBM Computers, Inc.**

Gives brief background →

Our Treasury bonds, composing 3.5 percent of the Fund's investment portfolio, mature on April 15. Current inflationary pressures make fixed-income investments less attractive than equities. As you requested, I have researched and compared investment alternatives based on these criteria: market share, earnings, and dividends.

Recommendation

Makes a direct recommendation →

Given its established market share, solid earnings, and generous dividends, WBM Computers, Inc. is a sound and promising company. I recommend that we invest our maturing bond proceeds in WBM's Class A stock.

Market Share

Explains the criteria supporting the recommendation →

Though only ten years old, WBM competes strongly with established computer makers. Its market share has grown steadily for the past five years. This past year, services and sales ranked 367th in the industrial U.S., with orders increasing from $750 million to $1.25 billion. Net income places WBM 237th nationally, and 13th on return to investors.

Earnings

WBM's net profit on sales is 9 percent, a roughly steady figure for the past three years. Whereas 2000 earnings were only $.09 per share, this year's are $1.36 per share. Included in these ten-year earnings is a two-for-one stock split issued November 2, 2004. Barring a global sales downturn WBM's outlook for continued strong earnings is promising.

Dividends

Investors are offered two types of common stock. The assigned par value of both classes is $.50 per share. Class A stock pays an additional $.25 per share dividend but restricts voting privileges to one vote for every ten shares held by the investor. Class B stock does not pay the extra dividend but carries full voting rights. The additional dividend from Class A shares would enhance income flow into our portfolio.

Encourages reader action →

WBM shares now trade at 14 times earnings and current share price of $56.00, a bargain in my estimation. An immediate investment would add strength and diversity to our portfolio.

FIGURE 21.6 **A Feasibility Report**

RECOMMENDATION REPORTS

Audience and purpose considerations

Whereas a feasibility report sets out to prove that a particular course of action is the right one, a *recommendation report* shortens or even skips the feasibility analysis (since it has already occurred or been discussed) and gets right to the recommendation. Recommendation reports, like feasibility reports, may include supporting data, but they also state an affirmative position ("Here's what we should do and why") rather than examining whether the approach will work ("Should we do it?"). Like feasibility reports, recommendation reports are for the eyes of decision makers, and these documents take a direct stance.

Figure 21.7 shows a recommendation report from a health and safety officer at an airline company to a vice president, regarding workstation comfort of reservation and booking agents. After receiving numerous employee complaints about chronic discomfort, this writer's boss has asked him to study the problems and recommend improvements in the work environment.

NOTE *Before making any recommendation, be sure you've gathered the right information. For the report in Figure 21.7, the writer did enough research to rule out one cause of the problem (computer screens as the cause of employee headaches) before settling on the actual cause (excessive glare on display screens from background lighting).*

GUIDELINES for Recommendation Reports

- **Provide a clear subject line.** Make sure the subject line announces the purpose of the report.
- **Keep the background brief.** But do discuss how feasibility has already been determined.
- **Summarize the problem or situation prior to making recommendations.** Outline the issue that the recommended actions will resolve. Then discuss the recommendations in as much detail as necessary.
- **Use an authoritative tone.** Take a strong stance and write with confidence, knowing that the recommendation already is considered feasible.
- **Use informative headings.** Instead of using the vague heading "Problem," be specific ("Causes of Agents' Discomfort"). Remember that you are writing to a "bottom line" audience.
- **End with a list of benefits for taking action.** Rather than appealing for action, assume it will be taken. Reemphasize the benefits.

• TRANS GLOBE AIRLINES •

MEMORANDUM

To: R. Ames, Vice President, Personnel

From: B. Doakes, Health and Safety *B.D.*

Date: August 15, 20XX

Subject line states exact purpose of report →

Subject: **Recommendations for Reducing Agents' Discomfort**

Provides immediate orientation by giving brief background and main point →

In our July 20 staff meeting, we discussed physical discomfort among reservation and booking agents, who spend eight hours daily at workstations. They complain of headaches, eyestrain, blurred or double vision, backaches, and stiff joints. This report outlines the apparent causes and recommends ways of reducing discomfort.

Causes of Agents' Discomfort

For the time being, computer display screens can be ruled out as a cause of headaches and eye problems for the following reasons:

Statement of problem or situation precedes recommendations →

1. Our new display screens have excellent contrast and no flicker.
2. Research about effects of low-level radiation from computer screens is inconclusive.

The headaches and eye problems seem to be caused by excessive glare on display screens from background lighting.

Other discomforts, such as backaches and stiffness, apparently result from the agents' sitting in one position for up to two hours between breaks.

Recommended Changes

Makes general recommendations →

We can eliminate much discomfort by improving background lighting, workstation conditions, and work routines and habits.

Background Lighting. To reduce the glare on display screens, these are recommended changes in background lighting:

Expands on each recommendation →

1. Decrease all overhead lighting by installing lower-wattage bulbs.
2. Keep all curtains and adjustable blinds on the south and west windows at least half-drawn, to block direct sunlight.
3. Install shades to direct the overhead lighting straight downward, so that it is not reflected on the screens.

Workstation Conditions. These are recommended changes in the workstations:

1. Reposition all screens so light sources are neither at front nor back.
2. Wash the surface of each screen weekly.
3. Adjust each screen so the top is slightly below the operator's eye level.
4. Adjust all keyboards so they are 27 inches from the floor.
5. Replace all fixed chairs with pneumatic, multi-task chairs.

FIGURE 21.7 **A Recommendation Report**

R. Ames, 8/15/XX, page 2

Work Routines and Habits. These are recommended changes in agents' work routines and habits:

1. Allow frequent rest periods (10 minutes hourly instead of 30 minutes twice daily).
2. Provide yearly eye exams for agents, as part of our routine healthcare program.
3. Train agents to adjust screen contrast and brightness whenever the background lighting changes.
4. Offer workshops on improving posture.

These changes will give us time to consider more complex options such as installing hoods and antiglare filters on display screens, replacing fluorescent lighting with incandescent, covering surfaces with nonglare paint, or other disruptive procedures.

Discusses benefits of the following recommendations

cc: J. Bush, Medical Director
M. White, Manager of Physical Plant

FIGURE 21.7 *(Continued)*

JUSTIFICATION REPORTS

Audience and purpose considerations

Many recommendation reports respond to reader requests for a solution to a problem (as in Figure 21.7); others originate with the writer, who has recognized a problem and has devised a solution. This latter type is often called a *justification report*; such reports justify the writer's position by answering this key question for recipients: *Why should we follow your recommendation?*

Unsolicited recommendations—no matter how sound the reasoning behind them—present a complex persuasive challenge and they *always* carry the possibility of inviting a hostile or defensive response from a surprised or offended recipient. ("Who asked for your two cents worth?") Never come across as presumptuous. Give readers notice beforehand; feel them out on the issue.

GUIDELINES for Justification Reports

- **State the problem and your recommended solution.** Unless you expect total resistance to your idea, get to the point quickly and make your case (as **in Figure 21.8**) by using some version of the direct organizational plan described on page 359.
- Highlight the benefits of your plan before presenting the ***costs***. An expensive "bottom line" is often an audience deterrent.
- **If needed, explain how your plan can be implemented.**
- **Conclude by encouraging the reader to act.**

Global Biosolutions, Inc.

MEMORANDUM

To: D. Spring, President

From: M. Marks, Chief, Biology Division MM

Date: April 18, 20XX

Subject: **The Need to Hire Additional Personnel**

Introduction and Recommendation

Opens with the problem →

With 56 active employees, GBI has been unable to keep up with scheduled contracts. As a result, we have a contract backlog of roughly $700,000. This backlog is caused by understaffing in the biology and chemistry divisions.

Recommends a solution →

To increase production and ease the workload, I recommend that we hire three general laboratory assistants.

Expands on the recommendation →

The lab assistants would be responsible for cleaning glassware and general equipment; feeding and monitoring fish stocks; preparing yeast, algae, and shrimp cultures; preparing stock solutions; and assisting scientists in various procedures.

Benefits and Costs

Shows how benefits would offset costs →

Three full-time lab assistants would have a positive effect on overall productivity:

- Dirty glassware would no longer pile up.
- Because other employees would no longer need to work more than forty hours weekly, morale would improve.
- Research scientists would be freed from general maintenance work.
- With our backlog eliminated, clients would no longer be impatient.

Costs: Initial yearly salaries (at $12.00/hour) for three lab assistants would come to $74,880; medical insurance would add roughly $30,000. Accounting assures me that this expenditure would be more than offset by anticipated revenue growth.

Conclusion

Encourages acceptance of the recommendation →

Increased productivity at GBI is essential to maintaining good client relations. These additional personnel would allow us to continue a reputation of prompt and efficient service, thus ensuring our steady growth and development.

Could we meet to discuss this request in detail? I will contact you Monday.

FIGURE 21.8 **A Justification Report** The tone here is confident yet diplomatic—appropriate for an unsolicited recommendation to an executive. For more on connecting with a reluctant audience, see Chapter 3.

PEER REVIEW REPORTS

Peer review reports provide a way for people (peers) to give each other constructive criticism and feedback. Because such reports are shared by colleagues wishing to preserve good workplace relationships, they must be written very tactfully.

Audience and purpose considerations

Figure 21.9 can serve as a model for reviewing the work of other students in the classroom. (For move on peer review, see pages 95–96.)

GUIDELINES for Peer Review Reports

- **Start with the positives.** Briefly enumerate the good points of the reviewed document as a way of leading into and balancing against the criticisms.
- **Organize by topic area.** Provide separate sections for suggestions about the reviewed document's writing style, design, use of visuals, and other elements.
- **Always provide constructive criticism.** Remember that you are reviewing the work of a colleague or colleagues. Review their work tactfully, as you would want yours reviewed. However, don't ignore problem areas.
- **Support your critique with examples and advice.** Point to particular examples in the reviewed document as you discuss various elements. Suggest alternatives, if possible. Point to helpful resources, if applicable.
- **Close positively.** End with a friendly, encouraging tone. If the reviewed document is particularly problematic, state as much—but diplomatically.

CHECKLIST: Informal Reports

Review the Guidelines boxes for your specific report type.

- ☐ Have I determined the right report type (status report, recommendation report, etc.) for this situation?
- ☐ For a progress or status report, have I determined how much detail to include?
- ☐ When taking minutes for a meeting, have I included all the key decisions and discussion items and omitted unnecessary detail?
- ☐ If I have decided to write a recommendation or justification report, has the feasibility of the project or idea already been determined, or is a feasibility study and report more appropriate at this time?
- ☐ Depending on the audience, have I used a memo, email, or letter format?
- ☐ Is the subject line clear?
- ☐ Is the tone professional and polite but direct?
- ☐ Have I done enough research so that my position is credible?

TO: Catie Noll, Advertising Associate
FROM: David Summer, Advertising Supervisor *D.S.*
DATE: May 1, 20XX
SUBJECT: **Review of Your Feasibility Report for the Garvey Account**

Begins with a friendly tone and says something positive before suggesting changes →

I have reviewed the first draft of your report for the Garvey account. Thank you for your good work! You have done a great job organizing the material and getting started. I would like to offer the following suggestions:

Suggested changes are clear and organized by area →

Voice: You use passive voice in a number of places where active voice would be more appropriate. For instance, at the bottom of page 7, you might want to change "A mistake was made" to "We made a mistake." I would recommend that you review the entire draft for this usage.

Reviewer provides rationale behind suggestions →

Organization: As a reader, I did not know what you were recommending in this report until I reached the very end. I would suggest that you move your recommendation up to the beginning of the report, then follow it with the supporting data. Our supervisors will want to know the bottom line right away.

Reviewer provides specific advice to help the writer improve the document →

Research: I noticed that most of your research was based on commercial Web sites. You should probably look at more reliable peer-reviewed sources, such as well-respected business newspapers, journal articles, and online publications of professional organizations.

Visuals/font: Great use of images, especially the maps on page 9. You might want to increase the font size of the base text.

Uses a polite closing →

I hope my recommendations are helpful as you complete this project. Your report is well on the way, offering solid reasons that should persuade the managers to try winning the Garvey account from our competitors. Please let me know if you have any questions.

FIGURE 21.9 A Peer Review Report

Projects

GENERAL

1. For this or another class, write a progress report to your instructor, describing the progress you've made on a project (your final project, for instance). Use the guidelines suggested in this chapter. Or, write a peer review report of a classmate's draft of an upcoming assignment.
2. For a current or past job or internship, write a periodic activity report in which you report on the past week's activities (actual or typical). Follow the guidelines in this chapter.
3. Take notes at the next group event or meeting that you attend. Write up minutes for the meeting, thinking about how much detail to include and what kinds of information will be useful to the other members of the team.

TEAM

With 2–3 other classmates, identify a dangerous or inconvenient area or situation on campus or in your community (endless cafeteria lines, an unsafe walkway, slippery stairs, a bad campus intersection). Observe the problem for several hours during a peak use period. Write a recommendation report to a specifically identified decision maker (the head of campus security, for example) describing the problem, listing your observations, and making a recommendation.

DIGITAL AND SOCIAL MEDIA

Many Web-based recommendation reports are not in the brief memo or email format described in this chapter. Examine some Web-based recommendation reports and describe the differences in length, format, look, and feel for these Web-based reports. For instance, the page at www.cdc.gov/mmwr/preview/mmwrhtml/rr5704a1.htm is a report about the prevention of certain diseases in pregnant women and infants. Why did the Centers for Disease Control choose a Web-based format and not a shorter memo report? Write a memo to your instructor answering this question.

GLOBAL

Assume that you are a team leader of a company based in the United States but with offices worldwide. You have been assigned a new manager who is a citizen of another country. This week you need to write a report recommending that all the staff on your team receive bonuses. You know the tone you would take if your manager were from the United States, but you are uncertain about what tone or level of politeness is appropriate for this new manager. Pick a country and do some research on the Internet about tone, style, and politeness in different cultures, remembering that not everyone in a country or culture is exactly alike. Write a short memo to your instructor explaining what you have learned and how you would shape your recommendation report in this situation.

22 Formal Analytical Reports

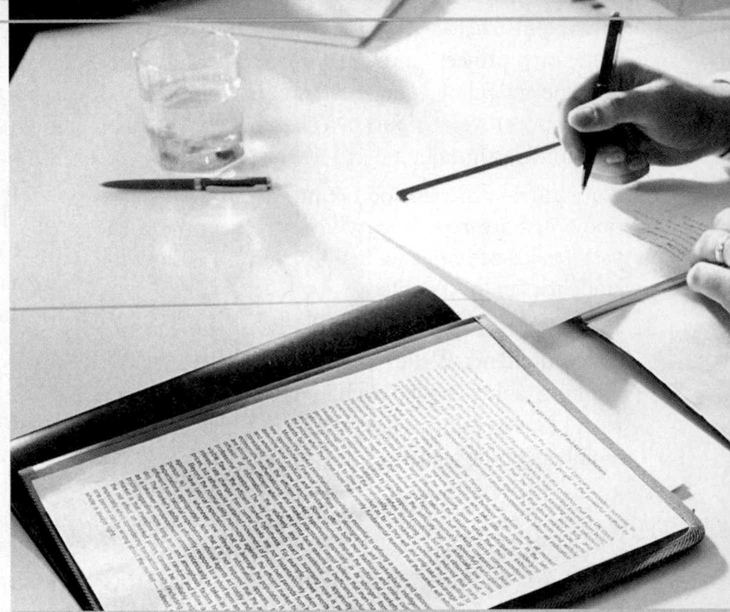

"Our clients make investment decisions based on feasibility and strategy for marketing new products. Our job is to research consumer interest in these potential products (say, a new brand of low-calorie chocolate). In designing surveys, I have to translate the client's information needs into precise questions. I have to be certain that the respondents are answering exactly the question I had in mind, and not inventing their own version of the question. Then I have to analyze these data and translate them into accurate interpretations and recommendations for our clients."

—James North, Senior Project Manager, market research firm

LEARNING OBJECTIVES FOR THIS CHAPTER

- Appreciate the role of formal analytical reports in the workplace
- Understand the role of audience and purpose for such reports
- Identify three major types of analyses: casual, comparative, and feasibility
- Know the criteria for sound analytical reasoning
- Identify the parts that typically accompany a long report (front matter and end matter)
- Write a formal analytical report

The formal analytical report, like the shorter versions discussed in Chapter 21, usually leads to recommendations. The formal report replaces the memo when the topic requires lengthy discussion. Formal reports generally include a title page, table of contents, a system of headings, a list of references or works cited, and other front-matter and end-matter supplements discussed on pages 533–36.

An essential component of workplace problem solving, analytical reports are designed to answer these questions:

What readers of an analytical report want to know

- Based on the information gathered about this issue, what do we know?
- What conclusions can we draw?
- What should we do or not do?

Assume, for example, that you receive this assignment from your supervisor:

A typical analytical problem

> Recommend the best method for removing the heavy-metal contamination from our company dump site.

First, you will have to learn all you can about the problem. Then you will compare the advantages and disadvantages of various options based on the criteria you are using to assess feasibility: say, cost-effectiveness, time required versus time available for completion, potential risk to the public and the environment. For example, the cheapest option might also pose the greatest environmental risk and could result in heavy fines or criminal charges. But the safest option might simply be too expensive for this struggling company to afford. Or perhaps the Environmental Protection Agency has imposed a legal deadline for the cleanup. In making your recommendation, you will need to weigh all the criteria (cost, safety, time) very carefully, or you could land in jail.

Recommendations have legal and ethical implications

The above situation calls for critical thinking (Chapter 9) and research (Chapters 7–9). Besides interviewing legal and environmental experts, you might search the literature and the Web. From these sources you can discover whether anyone has been able to solve a problem like yours, or learn about the newest technologies for toxic waste cleanup. Then you will have to decide how much, if any, of what others have done applies to your situation. (For more on analytical reasoning, see pages 515–21.)

CONSIDERING AUDIENCE AND PURPOSE

Using analysis on the job

On the job, you may be assigned to evaluate a new assembly technique on the production line, or to locate and purchase the best equipment at the best price. You might have to identify the cause behind a monthly drop in sales, the reasons for low employee morale, the causes of an accident, or the reasons for equipment failure. You might need to assess the feasibility of a proposal for a company's expansion or merger or investment. You will present your findings in a formal report.

Audience considerations

Because of their major impact on the decision-making process, formal reports are almost always written for an audience of decision makers such as government officials or corporate managers. You need to know whom you are writing for and whether the report will be read primarily by an individual, a team, or a series of individuals with differing roles in the company.

Purpose considerations

To determine the purpose of the report, consider what question or questions it will ultimately answer. Also, consider why this particular topic is timely and useful to the intended audience. Use the Audience and Use Profile Sheet on page 31 to begin mapping out your audience and purpose for the report.

TYPICAL ANALYTICAL PROBLEMS

Far more than an encyclopedia presentation of information, the analytical report traces your inquiry, your evidence, and your reasoning to show exactly how you arrived at your conclusions and recommendations.

Workplace problem solving calls for skills in three broad categories: *causal analysis, comparative analysis,* and *feasibility analysis.* Each approach relies on its own type of reasoning.

Causal Analysis: "Why Does *X* Happen?"

Designed to reveal a problem at its source, the causal analysis answers questions such as this: *Why do so many apparently healthy people have sudden heart attacks?*

CASE The Reasoning Process in Causal Analysis

Medical researchers at the world-renowned Hanford Health Institute recently found that 20 to 30 percent of deaths from sudden heart attacks occur in people who have none of the established risk factors (weight gain, smoking, diabetes, lack of exercise, high blood pressure, or family history). *Identify the problem*

To better identify people at risk, researchers are now tracking down new and powerful risk factors such as bacteria, viruses, genes, stress, anger, and depression. *Examine possible causes*

Once researchers identify these factors and their mechanisms, they can recommend preventive steps such as careful monitoring, lifestyle and diet changes, drug treatment, or psychotherapy (H. Lewis 39–43). *Recommend solutions*

A different version of causal analysis employs reasoning from effect to cause, to answer questions such as this: *What are the health effects of exposure to electromagnetic radiation?* For more on causal reasoning, see pages 161–67.

NOTE *Keep in mind that faulty causal reasoning is extremely common, especially when we ignore other possible causes or we confuse correlation with causation (page 165).*

Comparative Analysis: "Is *X* OR *Y* Better for Our Needs?"

Designed to rate competing items on the basis of specific criteria, the comparative analysis answers questions such as this: *Which type of security (firewall/encryption) program should we install on our company's computer system?*

CASE The Reasoning Process in Comparative Analysis

XYZ Corporation needs to identify exactly what information (personnel files, financial records) or functions (in-house communication, file transfer) it wants to protect from whom. Does it need both virus and tamper protection? Does it wish to restrict network access or encrypt email and computer files so they become unreadable to unauthorized persons? Does it wish to restrict access to or from the Web? In addition to the level of protection, how important are ease of maintenance and user friendliness? *Identify the criteria*

After identifying their specific criteria, XYZ decision makers need to rank them in order of importance (for example, 1. tamper protection, 2. user-friendliness, 3. secure financial records, and so on). *Rank the criteria*

On the basis of these ranked criteria, XYZ will assess relative strengths and weaknesses of competing security programs and recommend the best one (Schafer 93–94). *Compare items according to the criteria, and ecommend the best one*

For more on comparative analysis, see page 416.

Feasibility Analysis: "Is This a Good Idea?"

Designed to assess the practicality of an idea or a plan, the feasibility analysis answers questions such as this: *Should healthy young adults be encouraged to receive genetic testing to measure their susceptibility to various diseases?*

CASE The Reasoning Process in Feasibility Analysis

As a step toward "[translating] genetic research into health care," a National Institutes of Health (NIH) study is investigating the feasibility of offering genetic testing to healthy young adults at little or no cost. The testing focuses on diseases such as melanoma, diabetes, heart disease, and lung cancer. This study will measure not only the target audience's interest but also how those people tested "will interpret and use the results in making their own health care decisions in the future."

Arguments in favor of testing include the following:

Consider the trength of supporting reasons

- Young people with a higher risk for a particular disorder might consider preventive treatments.
- Early diagnosis and treatment could be "personalized," tailored to an individual's genetic profile.
- Low-risk test results might "inspire healthy people to stay healthy" by taking precautions such as limiting sun exposure or changing their dietary, exercise, and smoking habits.

Arguments against testing include the following:

Consider the trength of opposing reasons

- The benefits of early diagnosis and treatment for a small population might not justify the expense of testing the population at large.
- False positive results are always traumatic, and false negative results could be disastrous.
- Any positive result could subject a currently healthy young person to biased treatment from employers or disqualification for health and life insurance (National Institutes of Health; Notkins 74, 79).

Weigh the pros and cons, and recommend a course of action

After assessing the benefits and drawbacks of testing in this situation, NIH decision makers can make the appropriate recommendations.

For more on feasibility analysis, see pages 500–01.

Combining Types of Analysis

Analytical categories overlap considerably. Any one study may in fact require answers to two or more of the previous questions. The sample report on pages 538–49 is both a feasibility analysis and a comparative analysis. It is designed to answer these questions: *Is technical marketing the right career for me? If so, which is my best option for entering the field?*

ELEMENTS OF AN EFFECTIVE ANALYSIS

The formal analytical report incorporates many elements from documents in earlier chapters, along with the suggestions that follow.

Clearly Identified Problem or Purpose

To solve any problem or achieve any goal, you must first identify the issues precisely. Always begin by defining the main questions and thinking through any subordinate questions they may imply. Only then can you determine what to look for, where to look, and how much information you will need.

Define your purpose

Your employer, for example, might pose this question: Will a low-impact aerobics program significantly reduce stress among my employees? The aerobics question obviously requires answers to three other questions: What are the therapeutic claims for aerobics? Are they valid? Will aerobics work in this situation? With the main questions identified, you can formulate an audience and purpose statement:

> My goal is to examine and evaluate claims about the therapeutic benefits of low-impact aerobic exercise and to recommend a course of action to my employer.

Audience and purpose statement

Words such as *examine* and *evaluate* (or *compare, identify, determine, measure, describe,* and so on) help readers understand the specific analytical activity that forms the subject of the report. (For more on asking the right questions, see pages 126–27.)

Adequate But Not Excessive Data

A superficial analysis is basically worthless. Worthwhile analysis, in contrast, examines an issue in depth. In reporting on your analysis, however, you filter that material for the audience's understanding, deciding what to include and what to leave out. "Do decision makers in this situation need a closer look or am I presenting excessive detail when only general information is needed?" Is it possible to have too much information? In some cases, yes—as behavioral expert Dietrich Dorner explains:

Decide how much is enough

> The more we know, the more clearly we realize what we don't know. This probably explains why... organizations tend to [separate] their information-gathering and decision-making branches. A business executive has an office manager; presidents have... advisers; military commanders have chiefs of staff. The point of this separation may well be to provide decision makers with only the bare outlines of all the available information so they will not be hobbled by excessive detail when they are obliged to render decisions. Anyone who is fully informed will see much more than the bare outlines and will therefore find it extremely difficult to reach a clear decision. (99)

Excessive information hampers decision making

Confusing the issue with excessive information is no better than recommending hasty action on the basis of inadequate information (Dorner 104).

When you might consult an abstract or summary instead of the complete work

As you research the issue you may want to filter material for your own understanding as well. Your decision about whether to rely on the abstract or summary or to read the complete text of a specialized article or report depends on the question you're trying to answer and the level of technical detail your readers expect. If you are an expert in the field, writing for other experts, you probably want to read the entire document in order to assess the methods and reasoning behind a given study. But if you are less than expert, a summary or abstract of this study's findings might suffice. The fact sheet in Figure 22.1, for example, summarizes a detailed feasibility study for a general reading audience. Readers seeking more details, including nonclassified elements of the complete report, could visit the Transportation Security Administration's Web site at <www.tsa.gov>.

NOTE *If you have relied merely on the abstract or summary instead of the full article, be sure to indicate this ("Abstract," "Press Release" or the like) when you cite the source in your report (as shown on pages 655, 673).*

Accurate and Balanced Data

Give readers all they need to make an informed judgment

Avoid stacking the evidence to support a preconceived point of view. Assume, for example, that you are asked to recommend the best chainsaw brand for a logging company. Reviewing test reports, you come across this information:

> Of all six brands tested, the Bomarc chainsaw proved easiest to operate. However, this brand also offers the fewest safety features.

In citing these equivocal findings, you need to present both of them accurately, and not simply the first—even though the Bomarc brand may be your favorite. Then argue for the feature (ease of use or safety) you think should receive priority. (Refer to pages 126, 156 for more on exploring and presenting balanced and reasonable evidence.)

Fully Interpreted Data

Explain the significance of your data

Interpretation shows the audience "what is important and what is unimportant, what belongs together and what does not" (Dorner 44). For example, you might interpret the above chainsaw data in this way:

Explain the meaning of your evidence

> Our logging crews often work suspended by harness, high above the ground. Also, much work is in remote areas. Safety features therefore should be our first requirement in a chainsaw. Despite its ease of operation, the Bomarc saw does not meet our safety needs.

FACT SHEET: Train and Rail Inspection Pilot, Phase I

U.S. DEPARTMENT OF HOMELAND SECURITY
Transportation Security Administration
FOR IMMEDIATE RELEASE – June 7, 20XX
TSA Press Office: (571) 227-2829

Objective:
Implement a pilot program to determine the feasibility of screening passengers, luggage and carry-on bags for explosives in the rail environment.

TRIP I Background:

- Homeland Security Secretary announced TRIP on March 22, 20XX, to test new technologies and screening concepts.
- The program is conducted in partnership with the Department of Transportation, Amtrak, Maryland Rail Commuter, and Washington D.C.'s Metro.
- The New Carrollton, Md. station was selected because it serves multiple types of rail operations and is located close to Washington, D.C.

TRIP I Facts:

- Screening for Phase I of TRIP began on May 4 and was completed on May 26 20XX.
- A total of 8,835 passengers and 9,875 pieces of baggage were screened during the test.
- The average time to wait in line and move through the screening process was less than 2 minutes.
- Customer Feedback cards reflect a 93 percent satisfaction rate with both the screening process and the professional demeanor of TSA personnel.

Lessons Learned:

- Results indicate efficient checkpoints throughout with minimal customer inconvenience.
- Passengers were overwhelmingly receptive to the screening process.
- Providing a customer service representative on-site during all screening operations helped Amtrak ensure passengers received outstanding customer service.
- Skilled TSA screeners from the agency's National Screening Force were able to quickly transition to screening in the rail environment.
- Most importantly, Phase I showed that currently available technology could be utilized to screen for explosives in the rail environment.

FIGURE 22.1 **A Summary Description of a Feasibility Study** Notice that the criteria for assessing feasibility include passenger wait times, passenger receptiveness to screening, and—most important—effectiveness of screening equipment in this environment.
Source: Transportation Security Administration.

By saying "therefore" you engage in analysis—not just information sharing. Don't merely list your findings, explain what they mean.

Subordination of Personal Bias

Evaluate and interpret evidence impartially

To arrive at the *truth* of the matter (page 157), you need to see clearly. Don't let your biases fog up the real picture. Each stage of analysis requires decisions about what to record, what to exclude, and where to go next. You must evaluate your data (Is this reliable and important?), interpret your evidence (What does it mean?), and make recommendations (What action is needed?). An ethically sound analysis presents a balanced and reasonable assessment of the evidence. Do not force viewpoints that are not supported by dependable evidence. (Refer to page 158.)

Appropriate Visuals

Use visuals generously

Graphs are especially useful in an analysis of trends (rising or falling sales, radiation levels). Tables, charts, photographs, and diagrams work well in comparative analyses. Be sure to accompany each visual with a fully interpreted "story."

NOTE *As the simplicity of Figure 22.2 and its brief caption illustrate, a powerful visual does not need to be complex and fancy, nor its accompanying story long and involved. Sometimes, less can be more.*

Valid Conclusions and Recommendations

Be clear about what the audience should think and do

Along with the informative abstract (page 184), conclusions and recommendations are the sections of a long report that receive the most audience attention. The goal of analysis is to reach a valid conclusion—an overall judgment about what all the material means (that *X* is better than *Y*, that *B* failed because of *C*, that *A* is a good plan of action). The following example shows the conclusion of a report on the feasibility of installing an active solar heating system in a large building.

Offer a final judgment

1. Active solar space heating for our new research building is technically feasible because the site orientation will allow for a sloping roof facing due south, with plenty of unshaded space.
2. It is legally feasible because we are able to obtain an access easement on the adjoining property, to ensure that no buildings or trees will be permitted to shade the solar collectors once they are installed.
3. It is economically feasible because our sunny, cold climate means high fuel savings and faster payback (fifteen years maximum) with solar heating. The long-term fuel savings justify our short-term installation costs (already minimal because the solar system can be incorporated during the building's construction—without renovations).

Conclusions are valid when they are logically derived from accurate interpretations.

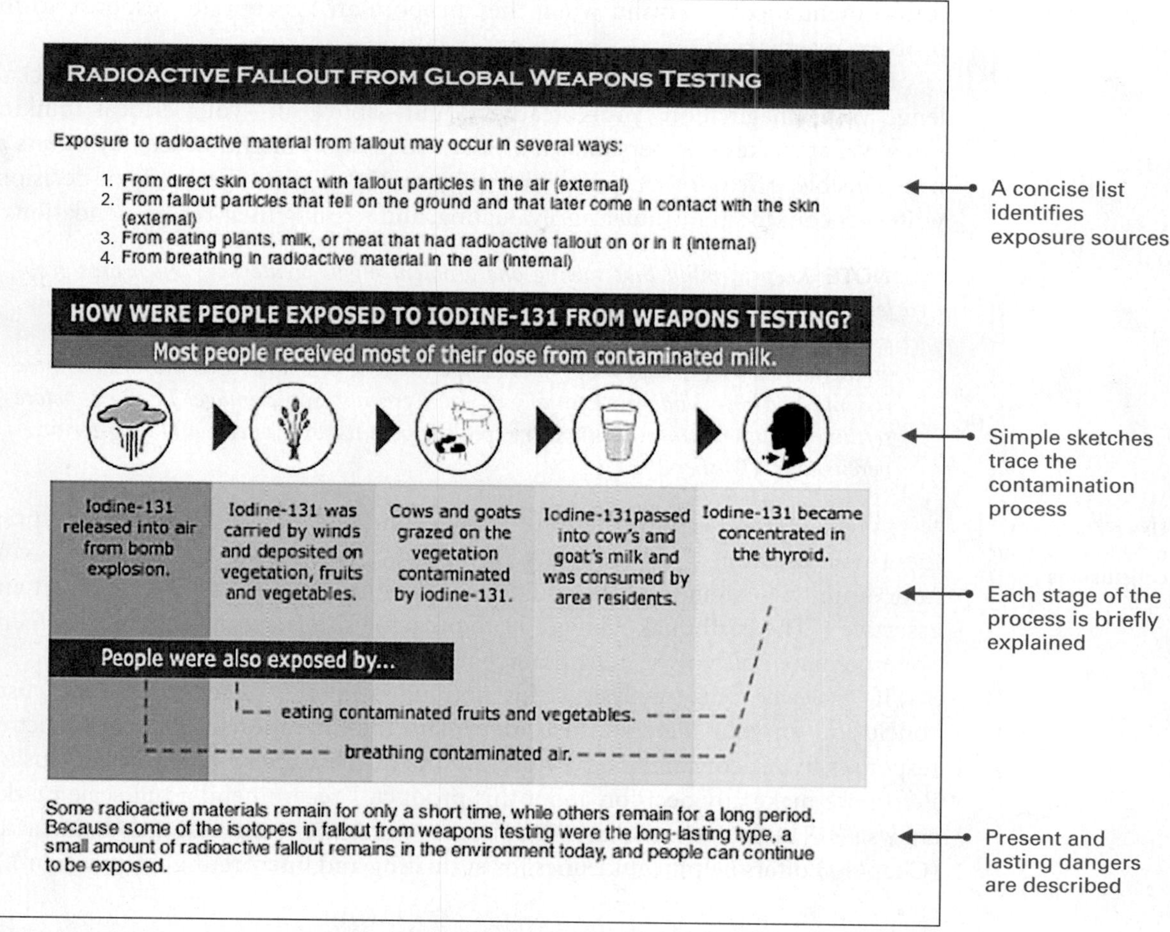

RADIOACTIVE FALLOUT FROM GLOBAL WEAPONS TESTING
Exposure to radioactive material from fallout may occur in several ways:
1. From direct skin contact with fallout particles in the air (external)
2. From fallout particles that fell on the ground and that later come in contact with the skin (external)
3. From eating plants, milk, or meat that had radioactive fallout on or in it (internal)
4. From breathing in radioactive material in the air (internal)
HOW WERE PEOPLE EXPOSED TO IODINE-131 FROM WEAPONS TESTING?
Most people received most of their dose from contaminated milk.
Iodine-131 released into air from bomb explosion.
Iodine-131 was carried by winds and deposited on vegetation, fruits and vegetables.
Cows and goats grazed on the vegetation contaminated by iodine-131.
Iodine-131passed into cow's and goat's milk and was consumed by area residents.
Iodine-131 became concentrated in the thyroid.
People were also exposed by...
eating contaminated fruits and vegetables.
breathing contaminated air.
Some radioactive materials remain for only a short time, while others remain for a long period. Because some of the isotopes in fallout from weapons testing were the long-lasting type, a small amount of radioactive fallout remains in the environment today, and people can continue to be exposed.
A concise list identifies exposure sources
Simple sketches trace the contamination process
Each stage of the process is briefly explained
Present and lasting dangers are described

FIGURE 22.2 A Simple but Highly Informative Visual
Source: Radiation Studies, Centers for Disease Control (CDC) <www.cdc.gov/nceh/radiation/fallout/RF-GWT_exposure.htm>.

Having explained *what it all means,* you then recommend *what should be done.* Taking all possible alternatives into account, your recommendations urge the most feasible option (to invest in *A* instead of *B,* to replace *C* immediately, to follow plan *A,* or the like). Here are the recommendations based on the previous conclusions:

1. I recommend that we install an active solar heating system in our new research building.
2. We should arrange an immediate meeting with our architect, building contractor, and solar heating contractor. In this way, we can make all necessary design changes before construction begins in two weeks.
3. We should instruct our legal department to obtain the appropriate permits and easements immediately.

Tell what should be done

Recommendations are valid when they propose an appropriate response to the problem or question.

Because they culminate your research and analysis, recommendations challenge your imagination, your creativity, and—above all—your critical thinking skills. What strikes one person as a brilliant suggestion might be seen by others as irresponsible, offensive, or dangerous. (Figure 22.3 depicts the kinds of decisions writers encounter in formulating, evaluating, and refining their recommendations.)

> **NOTE** *Keep in mind that solving one problem might create new and worse problems—or unintended consequences. For example, to prevent crop damage by rodents, an agriculture specialist might recommend trapping and poisoning. While rodent eradication may increase crop yield temporarily, it also increases the insects these rodents feed on—leading eventually to even greater crop damage. In short, before settling on any recommendation, try to anticipate its "side effects and long-term repercussions" (Dorner 15).*

Use a confident tone to state your conclusions

When you do achieve definite conclusions and recommendations, express them with assurance and authority. Unless you have reason to be unsure, avoid noncommittal statements ("It would seem that" or "It looks as if"). Be direct and assertive ("The earthquake danger at the reactor site is acute," or "I recommend an immediate investment"). Announce where you stand.

If, however, your analysis yields nothing definite, do not force a simplistic conclusion on your material. Instead, explain the limitations ("The contradictory responses to our consumer survey prevent me from reaching a definite conclusion. Before we make any decision about this product, I recommend a full-scale market analysis"). The wrong recommendation is far worse than no recommendation at all. (Chapter 8 offers helpful guidelines for evaluating and interpreting information.)

Self-Assessment

Assess your analysis continuously

The more we are involved in a project, the larger our stake is in its outcome—making self-criticism less likely just when it is needed most! For example, it is hard to admit that we might need to backtrack, or even start over, in instances like these (Dorner 46):

Things that might go wrong with your analysis

- During research you find that your goal isn't clear enough to indicate exactly what information you need.
- As you review your findings, you discover that the information you have is not the information you need.
- After making a recommendation, you discover that what seemed like the right course of action turns out to be the wrong one.

If you meet such obstacles, acknowledge them immediately, and revise your approach as needed.

Consider All the Details

- What exactly should be done—if anything at all?
- How exactly should it be done?
- When should it begin and be completed?
- Who will do it, and how willing are they?
- What equipment, material, or resources are needed?
- Are any special conditions required?
- What will this cost, and where will the money come from?
- What consequences are possible?
- Whom do I have to persuade?
- How should I order my list (priority, urgency, etc.)?

Locate the Weak Spots

- Is anything unclear or hard to follow?
- Is this course of action unrealistic?
- Is it risky or dangerous?
- Is it too complicated or confusing?
- Is anything about it illegal or unethical?
- Will it cost too much?
- Will it take too long?
- Could anything go wrong?
- Who might object or be offended?
- What objections might be raised?

Make Improvements

- Can I rephrase anything?
- Can I change anything?
- Should I consider alternatives?
- Should I reorder my list?
- Can I overcome objections?
- Should I get advice or feedback before I submit this?

FIGURE 22.3 How to Think Critically About Your Recommendations
Source: Ruggiero, Vincent R., *The Art of Thinking: A Guide to Critical and Creative Thought*, 8th Ed., (c) 2007, pp.188–189. Adapted and Electronically reproduced by permission of Pearson Education, Inc., Upper Saddle River, New Jersey.

AN OUTLINE AND MODEL FOR ANALYTICAL REPORTS

Whether you outline earlier or later, the finished report depends on a good outline. This model outline can be adapted to most analytical reports.

I. Introduction

A. Definition, Description, and Background

B. Purpose of the Report, and Intended Audience

C. Method of Inquiry

D. Limitations of the Study

E. Working Definitions (here or in a glossary)

F. Scope of the Inquiry (topics listed in logical order)

G. Conclusion(s) of the Inquiry (briefly stated)

II. Collected Data

A. First Topic for Investigation

1. Definition
2. Findings
3. Interpretation of findings

B. Second Topic for Investigation

1. First subtopic
   a. Definition
   b. Findings
   c. Interpretation of findings
2. Second subtopic (and so on)

III. Conclusion

A. Summary of Findings

B. Overall Interpretation of Findings (as needed)

C. Recommendations (as needed and feasible)

(This outline is only tentative. Modify the components as necessary.)

Two sample reports in this chapter follow the model outline. The first one, "Children Exposed to Electromagnetic Radiation: A Risk Assessment" (minus the front matter and end matter that ordinarily accompany a long report), begins on page 523. The second report, "Feasibility Analysis of a Career in Technical Marketing," appears in Figure 22.4.

Each report responds to slightly different questions. The first tackles these questions: *What are the effects of* X *and what should we do about them?* The second tackles two questions: *Is* X *feasible, and which version of* X *is better for my purposes?* At least one of these reports should serve as a model for your own analysis.

Introduction

The introduction engages and orients the audience, and provides background as briefly as possible for the situation. Often, writers are tempted to write long introductions because they have a lot of background knowledge. But readers generally don't need long history lessons on the subject.

Identify your topic's origin and significance, define or describe the problem or issue, and explain the report's purpose. (Generally, stipulate your audience only in the version your instructor will read and only if you don't attach an audience and use profile.) Briefly identify your research methods (interviews, literature searches, and so on) and explain any limitations or omissions (person unavailable for interview, research still in progress, and so on). List working definitions, but if you have more than two or three, use a glossary. List the topics you have researched. Finally, briefly preview your conclusion; don't make readers wade through the entire report to find out what you recommend or advise.

NOTE *Not all reports require every component. Give readers only what they need and expect.*

As you read the following introduction, think about the elements designed to engage and orient the audience (i.e., local citizens), and evaluate their effectiveness. (Review page 126 for the situation that gave rise to this report.)

CHILDREN EXPOSED TO ELECTROMAGNETIC RADIATION: A RISK ASSESSMENT

LAURIE A. SIMONEAU

INTRODUCTION

Wherever electricity flows—through the largest transmission line or the smallest appliance—it emits varying intensities of charged waves: an *electromagnetic field* (EMF). Some medical studies have linked human exposure to EMFs with definite physiologic changes and possible illness including cancer, miscarriage, and depression.

Definition and background of the problem

Experts disagree over the health risk, if any, from EMFs. Some question whether EMF risk is greater from high-voltage transmission lines, the smaller distribution lines strung on utility poles, or household appliances. Conclusive research may take years; meanwhile, concerned citizens worry about avoiding potential risks.

In Bocaville, four sets of transmission lines—two at 115 Kilovolts (kV) and two at 500 kV —cross residential neighborhoods and public property. The Adams elementary school is less than 100 feet from this power line corridor. EMF risks—whatever they may be—are thought to increase with proximity.

Description of the problem

Purpose and methods of this inquiry

Based on examination of recent research and interviews with local authorities, this report assesses whether potential health risks from EMFs seem significant enough for Bocaville to (a) increase public awareness, (b) divert the transmission lines that run adjacent to the elementary school, and (c) implement widespread precautions in the transmission and distribution of electrical power throughout Bocaville.

Scope of this inquiry

This report covers five major topics: what we know about various EMF sources, what research indicates about physiologic and health effects, how experts differ in evaluating the research, what the power industry and the public have to say, and what actions are being taken locally and nationwide to avoid risk.

Conclusions of the inquiry (briefly stated)

The report concludes by acknowledging the ongoing conflict among EMF research findings and by recommending immediate and inexpensive precautionary steps for our community.

Body

The body section (or data section) describes and explains your findings. Present a clear and detailed picture of the evidence, interpretations, and reasoning on which you will base your conclusion. Divide topics into subtopics, and use informative headings as aids to navigation.

> **NOTE** *Remember your ethical responsibility for presenting a fair and balanced treatment of the material, instead of "loading" the report with only those findings that support your viewpoint. Also, keep in mind the body section can have many variations, depending on the audience, topic, purpose, and situation.*

As you read the following section, evaluate how effectively it informs readers, keeps them on track, reveals a clear line of reasoning, and presents an impartial analysis.

DATA SECTION

First major topic

Sources of EMF Exposure

Definition

Electromagnetic intensity is measured in *milligauss* (mG), a unit of electrical measurement. The higher the mG reading, the stronger the field. Studies suggest that consistent exposure above 1–2 mG may increase cancer risk significantly, but no scientific evidence concludes that exposure even below 2.5 mG is safe.

Findings

Table 1 gives the EMF intensities from electric power lines at varying distances during average and peak usage.

Interpretation

As Table 1 indicates, EMF intensity drops substantially as distance from the power lines increases.

Although the EMF controversy has focused on 2 million miles of power lines crisscrossing the country, potentially harmful waves are also emitted by household wiring, appliances, computer terminals—and even from the earth's natural magnetic field. The background magnetic field (at a safe distance from any electrical appliance) in

Table 1 EMF Emissions from Power Lines (in milligauss)

Types of Transmission Lines	Maximum on Right-of-Way	Distance from lines			
		50'	100'	200'	300'
115 Kilovolts (kV)					
Average usage	30	7	2	0.4	0.2
Peak usage	63	14	4	0.9	0.4
230 Kilovolts (kV)					
Average usage	58	20	7	1.8	0.8
Peak usage	118	40	15	3.6	1.6
500 Kilovolts (kV)					
Average usage	87	29	13	3.2	1.4
Peak usage	183	62	27	6.7	3.0

Source: United States Environmental Protection Agency. *EMF in Your Environment.* Washington: GPO, 1992. Data from Bonneville Power Administration.

the average American home varies from 0.5 to 4.0 mG (United States Environmental 10). Table 2 compares intensities of various sources.

EMF intensity from certain appliances tends to be higher than from transmission lines because of the amount of current involved.

Interpretation

Table 2 EMF Emissions from Selected Sources (in milligauss)

Source	*Range*[a,b]
Earth's magnetic field	0.1–2.5
Blowdryer	60–1400
Four in. from TV screen	40–100
Four ft from TV screen	0.7–9
Fluorescent lights	10–12
Electric razor	1200–1600
Electric blanket	2–25
Computer terminal (12 inches away)	3–15
Toaster	10–60

[a]Data from Miltane, John. Interview 5 Apr. 2013; National Institute of Environmental Health. *EMF Electric and Magnetic Fields Associated with the Use of Electric Power.* Washington: GPO, 2002: 32-35.

[b]Readings are made with a gaussmeter, and vary with technique, proximity of gaussmeter to source, its direction of aim, and other random factors.

Voltage measures the speed and pressure of electricity in wires, but *current* measures the volume of electricity passing through wires. Current (measured in *amperage*) is what produces electromagnetic fields. The current flowing through a transmission line typically ranges from 200 to 400 amps. Most homes have a 200-amp

Definitions

Finding

service. This means that if every electrical item in the house were turned on at the same time, the house could run about 200 amps—almost as high as the transmission line. Consumers then have the ability to put 200 amps of current-flow into their homes, while transmission lines carrying 200 to 400 amps are at least 50 feet away (Miltane).

Proximity and duration of exposure, however, are other risk factors. People are exposed to EMFs from home appliances at close proximity, but appliances run only periodically: exposure is therefore sporadic, and intensity diminishes sharply within a few feet (Figure 1).

As Figure 1 indicates, EMF intensity drops dramatically over very short distances from the typical appliance.

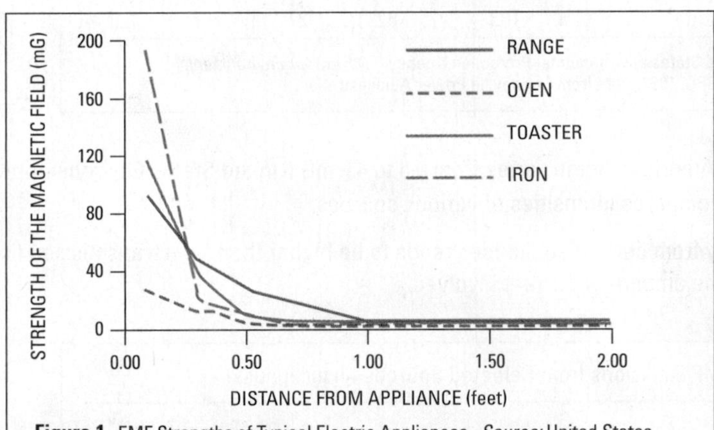

Figure 1 EMF Strengths of Typical Electric Appliances *Source:* United States Environmental Protection Agency. *EMF In Your Environment.* Washington: GPO, 1992.

Finding

Power line exposure, on the other hand, is at a greater distance (usually 50 feet or more), but it is constant. Moreover, its intensity can remain strong well beyond 100 feet (Miltane).

Interpretation

Research has yet to determine which type of exposure might be more harmful: briefly, to higher intensities or constantly, to lower intensities. In any case, proximity seems most significant because EMF intensity drops rapidly with distance.

Second major topic

Physiologic Effects and Health Risks from EMF Exposure

Research on EMF exposure falls into two categories: epidemiologic studies and laboratory studies. The findings are sometimes controversial and inconclusive, but also disturbing.

First subtopic
Definition

Epidemiologic Studies. Epidemiologic studies look for statistical correlations between EMF exposure and human illness or disorders. Of 77 such studies in recent decades, over 70 percent suggest that EMF exposure increases the incidence of the following conditions (Pinsky 155–215):

General findings

- cancer, especially leukemia and brain tumors
- miscarriage
- stress and depression
- learning disabilities
- heart attacks

Following, for example, are summaries of several noted epidemiologic studies implicating EMFs in occurrences of cancer.

Detailed findings

A Landmark Study of the EMF/Cancer Connection. A 1979 Denver study by Wertheimer and Leeper was the first to implicate EMFs as a cause of cancer. Researchers compared hundreds of homes in which children had developed cancer with similar homes in which children were cancer free. Victims were two to three times as likely to live in "high-current homes" (within 130 feet of a transmission line or 50 feet of a distribution line).

Critiques of findings

This study has been criticized because (1) it was not "blind" (researchers knew which homes cancer victims were living in), and (2) researchers never took gaussmeter readings to verify their designation of "high-current" homes (Pinsky 160–62; Taubes 96).

Detailed findings

Follow-up Studies. Several major studies of the EMF/cancer connection have confirmed Wertheimer's findings:

- In 1988, Savitz studied hundreds of Denver houses and found that children with cancer were 1.7 times as likely to live in high-current homes. Unlike his predecessors, Savitz did not know whether a cancer victim lived in the home being measured, and he took gaussmeter readings to verify that houses could be designated "high-current" (Pinsky 162–63).
- In 1990, London and Peters found that Los Angeles children had 2.5 times more risk of leukemia if they lived near power lines (Brodeur 115).
- In 1992, a massive Swedish study found that children in houses with average intensities greater than 1 mG had twice the normal leukemia risk; at greater than 2 mG, the risk nearly tripled; at greater than 3 mG, it nearly quadrupled (Brodeur 115).
- In 2002, British researchers evaluated findings from 34 studies of power line EMF effects (a *meta-analysis*). This study found "a degree of consistency in the evidence suggesting adverse health effects of living near high voltage power lines" (Henshaw et al. 1).

Workplace Studies. More than 80 percent of 51 studies from 1981 to 1994—most notably a 1992 Swedish study—concluded that electricians, electrical engineers, and power line workers constantly exposed to an average of 1.5 to 4.0 mG had a significantly elevated cancer risk (Brodeur 115; Pinsky 177–209).

Two additional workplace studies seem to support or even amplify the above findings.

- A 1995 University of North Carolina study of 138,905 electric utility workers concluded that occupational EMF exposure roughly doubles brain cancer risk. This study, however, found no increased leukemia risk (Cavanaugh 8; Moore 16).
- A Canadian study of electrical-power employees published in 2000 indicates that those who had worked in strong electric fields for more than 20 years had "an eight- to tenfold increase in the risk of leukemia," along with a significantly elevated risk of lymphoma ("Strong Electric Fields" 1–2).

Interpretation

Although none of the above studies can be said to "prove" a direct cause-effect relationship, their strikingly similar results suggest a conceivable link between prolonged EMF exposure and illness.

Second subtopic

Laboratory Studies. Laboratory studies assess cellular, metabolic, and behavioral effects of EMFs on humans and animals. EMFs directly cause the following physiologic changes (Brodeur 88; Pinsky 24–29; Raloff, "EMFs'" 30):

General findings

- reduced heart rate
- altered brain waves
- impaired immune system
- interference with the synthesis of genetic material
- disrupted regulation of cell growth
- interaction with the biochemistry of cancer cells
- altered hormonal activity
- disrupted sleep patterns

These changes are documented in the following summaries of several significant laboratory studies.

Detailed findings

EMF Effects on Cell Chemistry. Other studies have demonstrated previously unrecognized effects on cell growth and division. Most notably, a 2000 study by Michigan State University found that EMFs equal to the intensity that occurs "within a few feet" of outdoor power lines caused cells with cancer-related genetic mutations to multiply rapidly (Sivitz 196).

EMF Effects on Hormones. Studies have found that EMF exposure (say, from an electric blanket) inhibits production of melatonin, a hormone that fights cancer and depression, stimulates the immune system, and regulates bodily rhythms. A 1997 study at the Lawrence National Laboratory found that EMF exposure can suppress both melatonin and the hormone-like, anticancer drug Tamoxifen (Raloff, "EMFs' " 30). In 1996, physiologist Charles Graham found that EMFs elevate female estrogen levels and depress male testosterone levels—hormone alterations associated with risk of breast or testicular cancer, respectively (Raloff, "EMFs' " 30).

Although laboratory studies seem more conclusive than the epidemiologic studies, what these findings *mean* is debatable.

Interpretation

Debate over Quality, Cost, and Status of EMF Research

Third major topic

Experts differ over the meaning of EMF research findings largely because of the following limitations attributed to various studies.

Limitations of Various EMF Studies. Epidemiologic studies are criticized for overstating evidence. For example, some critics claim that so-called EMF-cancer links are produced by "data dredging" (making countless comparisons between cancers and EMF sources until random correlations appear) (Taubes 99). Other critics argue that news media distort the issue by publicizing positive findings while often ignoring negative or ambiguous findings (N. Goodman). Some studies are also accused of mistaking *coincidence* for *correlation,* without exploring "confounding factors" (e.g., exposure to toxins or to other adverse conditions—including the earth's natural magnetic field) (Moore 16).

First subtopic

Critiques of population studies

Supporters of EMF research respond that the sheer volume of epidemiologic evidence seems overwhelming (Kirkpatrick 81, 83). Moreover, the Swedish studies cited earlier seem to invalidate the above criticisms (Brodeur 115).

Response to critiques

Laboratory studies are criticized—even by scientists who conduct them—because effects on an isolated culture of cells or on experimental animals do not always equal effects on the total human organism (Jauchem 190–94).

Critiques of lab studies

Until recently critics argued that no scientist had offered a reasonable hypothesis to explain the possible health effects of EMFs (Palfreman 26). However, a 2004 University of Washington study showed that a weak electromagnetic field can break DNA strands and lead to brain cell death in rats, presumably because of cell-damaging agents known as free radicals (Lai and Singh).

Response to critiques

Costs of EMF Research. Critics claim that research and publicity about EMFs are becoming a profit venture, spawning "a new growth industry among researchers, as well as marketers of EMF monitors" ("Electrophobia" I). Environmental expert Keith Florig identifies adverse economic effects of the EMF debate that include decreased property values, frivolous lawsuits, expensive but needless "low field" consumer appliances, and costly modifications to schools and public buildings (Monmonier 190).

Cost objections

Present Status of EMF Research. In July 1998, an editor at the *New England Journal of Medicine* called for the ending of EMF/cancer research. He cited studies from the National Cancer Institute and other respected sources that showed "little evidence" of any causal connection. In a parallel development, federal and industry funding for EMF research has been reduced drastically (Stix 33). But, in August 1998, experts from the Energy Department and the National Institute of Environmental Health Sciences (NIEHS) proposed that EMFs should be officially designated a "possible human carcinogen" (Gross 30).

Conflicting scientific opinions

However, one year later, in a report based on its seven-year review of EMF research, NIEHS concluded that "the scientific evidence suggesting that... EMF exposures pose any health risk is weak." But the report also conceded that such exposure "cannot be recognized at this time as entirely safe" (National Inst., *Health* 1–2). In 2005, the National Cancer Institute fueled the controversy, concluding that the EMF–cancer connection is supported by only "limited evidence" and "inconsistent associations" (1). In a 2009 update, NIEHS announced "that the overall pattern of results suggests a weak association between exposure to EMFs and increased risk of childhood leukemia" (National Inst., *Electric* 1). Recently, noted epidemiologist Daniel Wartenberg has testified in support of the "Precautionary Principle," arguing that policy decisions should be based on "the possibility of risk." Specifically, Wartenberg advocates "prudently lowering exposures of greatest concern [i.e., of children] in case the possible risk is shown eventually to be true" (6).

Interpretation

In short, after more than twenty-five years of study, the EMF/illness debate continues, even among respected experts. While most scientists agree that EMFs exert measurable effects on the human body, they disagree about whether a real hazard exists. Given the drastic cuts in research funding, definite answers are unlikely to appear any time soon.

Fourth major topic

Views from the Power Industry and the Public

While the experts continue their debate, other viewpoints are worth considering as well.

First subtopic

The Power Industry's Views. The Electrical Power Research Institute (EPRI), the research arm of the nation's electric utilities, claims that recent EMF studies have provided valuable but inconclusive data that warrant further study (Moore 17). What does our local power company think about the alleged EMF risk? Marianne Halloran-Barney, Energy Service Advisor for County Electric, expressed this view in an email correspondence:

Findings

> There are definitely some links, but we don't know, really, what the effects are or what to do about them.... There are so many variables in EMF research that it's a question of whether the studies were even done correctly.... Maybe in a few years there will be really definite answers.

Echoing Halloran-Barney's views, John Miltane, Chief Engineer for County Electric, added this political insight:

> The public needs and demands electricity, but in regard to the negative effects of generation and transmission, the pervasive attitude seems to be "not in my back yard!" Utilities in general are scared to death of the EMF issue, but at County Electric we're trying to do the best job we can while providing reliable electricity to 24,000 customers.

Miltane stresses that County Electric takes the EMF issue very seriously: Whenever possible, new distribution lines are run underground and configured to diminish EMF intensity.

Public Perception. Industry views seem to parallel the national perspective among the broader population: Informed people are genuinely concerned, but remain unsure about what level of anxiety is warranted or what exactly should be done. A survey by the Edison Electric Institute did reveal that EMFs are considered a serious health threat by 33 percent of the American public (Stix 33).

Second subtopic

Risk-Avoidance Measures Being Taken

Fifth major topic

Although conclusive answers may require decades of research, concerned citizens are already taking action against potential EMF hazards.

Risk Avoidance Nationwide. Following are examples of steps taken by various communities to protect schoolchildren from EMF exposure:

First subtopic

Findings

- Hundreds of individuals and community groups have taken legal action to block proposed construction of new power lines. A single Washington law firm has defended roughly 140 utilities in cases related to EMFs (Dana and Turner 32).
- Houston schools "forced a utility company to remove a transmission line that ran within 300 feet of three schools. Cost: $8 million" (Kirkpatrick 85).
- California parents and teachers are pressuring reluctant school and public health officials to investigate cancer rates in the roughly 1,000 schools located within 300 feet of transmission lines, and to close at least one school (within 100 feet) in which cancer rates far exceed normal (Brodeur 118).

Although critics argue that the questionable risks fail to justify the costs of such measures, widespread concern about EMF exposure continues to grow.

Risk Avoidance Locally. Local awareness of the EMF issue seems low. The main public concern seems to be with property values. According to Halloran-Barney, County Electric receives one or two calls monthly from concerned customers, including people buying homes near power lines. The lack of public awareness adds another dimension to the EMF problem: People can't avoid a health threat that they don't know exists.

Second subtopic

Before risk avoidance can be considered on a broader community level, the public must first be informed about EMFs and the associated risks of exposure.

Interpretation

Conclusion

The conclusion is likely to interest readers most because it answers the questions that originally sparked the analysis.

NOTE *Many workplace reports are submitted with the conclusion preceding the introduction and body sections.*

In the conclusion, you summarize, interpret, and recommend. Although you have interpreted evidence at each stage of your analysis, your conclusion presents a broad interpretation and suggests a course of action, where appropriate. The summary and interpretations should lead logically to your recommendations.

Elements of a logical conclusion

- The summary accurately reflects the body of the report.
- The overall interpretation is consistent with the findings in the summary.
- The recommendations are consistent with the purpose of the report, the evidence presented, and the interpretations given.

NOTE *Don't introduce any new facts, ideas, or statistics in the conclusion.*

As you read the following conclusion, evaluate how effectively it provides a clear and consistent perspective on the whole document.

CONCLUSION

Review of major findings

Summary and Overall Interpretation of Findings

Electromagnetic fields exist wherever electricity flows; the stronger the current, the higher the EMF intensity. While no "safe" EMF level has been identified, long-term exposure to intensities greater than 2.5 milligauss is considered dangerous. Although home appliances can generate high EMFs during use, power lines can generate constant EMFs, typically at 2 to 3 milligauss in buildings within 150 feet. Our elementary school is less than 100 feet from a high-voltage power line corridor.

Notable epidemiologic studies implicate EMFs in increased rates of medical disorders such as cancer, miscarriage, stress, depression, and learning disabilities—all directly related to intensity and duration of exposure. Laboratory studies show that EMFs cause the kinds of cellular and metabolic changes that could produce these disorders.

An overall judgment about what the findings mean

Though still controversial and inconclusive, most of the various findings are strikingly similar and they underscore the need for more research and for risk avoidance, especially as far as children are concerned.

Concerned citizens nationwide have begun to prevail over resistant school and health officials and utility companies in reducing EMF risk to schoolchildren. And even though our local power company is taking reasonable risk-avoidance steps, our community can do more to learn about the issues and diminish potential risk.

Recommendations

In light of the conflicting evidence and interpretations, any type of government regulation any time soon seems unlikely. Also, considering the limitations of what we know, drastic and enormously expensive actions (such as burying all the town's power lines or increasing the height of utility towers) seem inadvisable. In fact, these might turn out to be the wrong actions.

Despite this climate of uncertainty, however, our community still can take some immediate and inexpensive steps to address possible EMF risk. Please consider the following recommendations:

Feasible and realistic course of action

- Relocate the school playground to the side of the school most distant from the power lines.
- Discourage children from playing near any power lines.
- Distribute a version of this report to all Bocaville residents.
- Ask our school board to hire a licensed contractor to take milligauss readings throughout the elementary school, to determine the extent of the problem, and to suggest reasonable corrective measures.
- Ask our Town Council to meet with County Electric Company representatives to explore options and costs for rerouting or burying the segment of the power lines near the school.
- Hold a town meeting to answer citizens' questions and to solicit opinions.
- Appoint a committee (consisting of at least one physician, one engineer, and other experts) to review emerging research as it relates to our school and town.

As we await conclusive answers, we need to learn all we can about the EMF issue, and to do all we can to diminish this potentially significant health issue.

A call to action

WORKS CITED

[*The Works Cited section for the preceding report appears in A Quick Guide to Documentation (Part 5, Pages 663–64). This author uses MLA documentation style.*]

FRONT MATTER AND END MATTER SUPPLEMENTS

Most formal reports or proposals consist of the front matter, the text of the report or proposal, and the end matter. (Some parts of the front and end matter may be optional.) Submit your completed document with these supplements, in this order:

Front matter precedes the report

- letter of transmittal
- title page
- table of contents
- list of tables and figures
- abstract
- **text of the report** (introduction, body, conclusion)

End matter follows the report

- glossary (as needed)
- appendices (as needed)
- Works Cited page (or alphabetical or numbered list of references)

For discussion of the above supplements, see below. For examples in a formal report or proposal, see Figures 22.4 and 23.4.

Front Matter

Preceding the text of the report is the front matter: letter of transmittal, title page, table of contents, list of tables and figures (if appropriate), and abstract or executive summary.

Letter of Transmittal

Many formal reports or proposals include a letter of transmittal, addressed to a specific reader or readers, which precedes the document. This letter might acknowledge people that helped with the document, refer readers to sections of special interest, discuss any limitations of the study or any problems in gathering data, offer personal (or off-the-record) observations, or urge readers to take immediate action. See page 538 for a sample letter of transmittal.

Title Page. The title page provides the document title, the names of all authors and their affiliations (and/or the name of the organization that commissioned the report), and the date the report was submitted. The title announces the report's purpose and subject by using descriptive words such as *analysis, comparison, feasibility,* or *recommendation*. Be sure the title fully describes your report, but avoid an overly long and involved title. Make the title the most prominent item, highest on the page, followed by the name of the recipient(s), the author(s), and the date of submission. See page 539 for a sample title page.

Table of Contents. For any long document, the table of contents helps readers by listing the page number for each major section, including any front matter that falls after the table of contents. (Do not include the letter of transmittal, title page, or the table of contents itself, but do include the list of tables and figures, along with the abstract or executive summary.)

Indicate page numbers for front matter in lowercase Roman numerals (i, ii, iii). Note that the title page, though not numbered itself or listed on the table of contents, is counted as page i. Number the report text pages using Arabic numerals (1, 2, 3), starting with the first page of the report. Number end matter using Arabic numerals continuing from the end of the report's text.

Make sure headings and subheadings in the table of contents match exactly the headings and subheadings in the document. Indicate headings of different levels (a-level, b-level, c-level) using different type styles or indentations. Use *leader lines* (........) to connect headings with their page numbers. For a sample table of contents, see page 540.

List of Tables and Figures. On a separate page following the table of contents (or at the end of the table of contents, if it fits), list the tables and figures in the report. If the report contains only one or two tables and figures, you may skip this list. For a sample list, see page 540.

Abstract or Executive Summary. Instead of reading an entire formal report, readers interested only in the big picture may consult the abstract or executive summary that commonly precedes the report proper (see Chapter 9). The purpose of this summary is to explain the issue, describe how you researched it, and state your conclusions (and, in the case of an executive summary, indicate what action the conclusions suggest). Busy readers can then flip through the document to locate sections important to them.

Make the abstract or executive summary as brief as possible. Summarize the report without adding new information or leaving out crucial information. Write for a general audience and follow a sequence that moves from the reason the report was written to the report's major findings, to conclusions and recommendations. For a sample abstract, see page 541.

Text of the Report

The text of the report consists of the introduction, the body, and the conclusion, as discussed and illustrated on pages 542–49.

End Matter

Following the report text (as needed) is the end matter, which may include a glossary, appendices, and/or a list of references cited in your report. Readers can refer to any of these supplements or skip them altogether, according to their needs.

Glossary. Use a glossary if your report contains more than five technical terms that may not be understood by all intended readers. If five or fewer terms need defining, place them in the report's introduction as working definitions, or use footnote definitions. If you do include a separate glossary, announce its location when you introduce technical terms defined there ("see the glossary at the end of this report"). Page 423 shows a glossary.

Appendices. If you have large blocks of material or other documents that are relevant but will bog readers down, place these in an appendix. For example, if your report on the cost of electricity at your company refers to another report issued by the local utility company, you may wish to include this second report as an appendix. Other items that belong in an appendix include complex formulas, interview questions and responses, maps, photographs, questionnaires and tabulated responses, and texts of laws and regulations.

Do not stuff appendices with needless information or use them to bury bad or embarrassing news that belongs in the report itself. Title each appendix clearly: "Appendix A: Projected Costs." Mention the appendixes early in the introduction, and refer to them at appropriate points in the report: ("see Appendix A"). The sample proposal in Figure 23.4 includes an appendix on pages 587.

References or Works Cited List. If you have used outside sources in your report (and typically you should), you must provide a list of References (per APA style) or of Works Cited (per MLA style). For detailed advice on documenting sources using APA or MLA style, see A Quick Guide to Documentation. The report in Figure 22.4 uses APA style and includes a References list, which appears in A Quick Guide to Documentation (Part 5), page 677. The report shown on pages 523–33 uses MLA style and includes a Works Cited list, which is shown in Part 5, pages 663–64.

A SITUATION REQUIRING AN ANALYTICAL REPORT

The formal report that follows, patterned after the model outline (page 522), combines a feasibility analysis with a comparative analysis.

A Formal Report

The Situation. Richard Larkin, author of the following report, has a work-study job fifteen hours weekly in his school's placement office. His boss, John Fitton (placement director), likes to keep up with trends in various fields. Larkin, an engineering major, has developed an interest in technical marketing and sales. Needing a report topic for his writing course, Larkin offers to analyze the feasibility of a technical marketing and sales career, both for his own decision making and for technical and science graduates in general. Fitton accepts Larkin's offer, looking forward to having the final report in his reference file for use by students choosing careers. Larkin wants his report to be useful in three ways: (1) to satisfy a course requirement, (2) to help him in choosing his own career, and (3) to help other students with their career choices.

With his topic approved, Larkin begins gathering his primary data, using interviews, letters of inquiry, telephone inquiries, and lecture notes. He supplements these primary sources with articles in recent publications. He will document his findings in APA (author-date) style.

As a guide for designing his final report (Figure 22.4), Larkin completes the following audience and use profile (based on the worksheet on page 31).

Audience and Use Profile. The primary audience consists of John Fitton, Placement Director, and the students who will refer to the report. The secondary audience is the writing instructor.

Because he is familiar with the marketing field, Fitton will need very little background to understand the report. Many student readers, however, will have questions like these:

- What, exactly, is technical marketing and sales?
- What are the requirements for this career?
- What are the pros and cons of this career?
- Could this be the right career for me?
- How do I enter the field?

Readers affected by this document are primarily students making career choices. Readers' attitudes likely will vary:

- Some readers should have a good deal of interest, especially those seeking a people-oriented career.
- Others might be only casually interested as they investigate a range of possible careers.
- Some readers might be skeptical about something written by a fellow student instead of by some expert. To connect with all these people, this report needs to persuade them that its conclusions are based on reliable information and careful reasoning.

All readers expect things spelled out, but concisely. Visuals will help compress and emphasize material throughout.

Essential information will include an expanded definition of technical marketing and sales, the skills and attitudes needed for success, the career's advantages and drawbacks, and a description of various paths for entering the career.

This report combines feasibility and comparative analysis, so the structure of the report must reveal a clear line of reasoning: in the feasibility section, reasons for and reasons against; in the comparison section, a block structure and a table that compares the four entry paths point by point. The report will close with recommendations based on solid conclusions.

For various readers who might not wish to read the entire report, an informative abstract will be included.

NOTE *This report's end matter (list of references) is shown and discussed on pages 676, 677.*

Letter of transmittal targets and thanks specific reader and provides additional context

165 Hammond Way
Hyannis, MA 02457
April 29, 20XX

John Fitton
Placement Director
University of Massachusetts
North Dartmouth, MA 02747

Dear Mr. Fitton:

Here is my report, Feasibility Analysis of a Career in Technical Marketing. In preparing this report, I've learned a great deal about the requirements and modes of access to this career, and I believe my information will help other students as well. Thank you for your guidance and encouragement throughout this process.

Although committed to their specialties, some technical and science graduates seem interested in careers in which they can apply their technical knowledge to customer and business problems. Technical marketing may be an attractive choice of career for those who know their field, who can relate to different personalities, and who communicate well.

Technical marketing is competitive and demanding, but highly rewarding. In fact, it is an excellent route to upper-management and executive positions. Specifically, marketing work enables one to develop a sound technical knowledge of a company's products, to understand how these products fit into the marketplace, and to perfect sales techniques and interpersonal skills. This is precisely the kind of background that paves the way to top-level jobs.

I've enjoyed my work on this project, and would be happy to answer any questions. Please phone at 690-555-1122 or email at larkin@com.net anytime.

Sincerely,

Richard B. Larkin

Richard B. Larkin, Jr.

FIGURE 22.4 A Formal Report

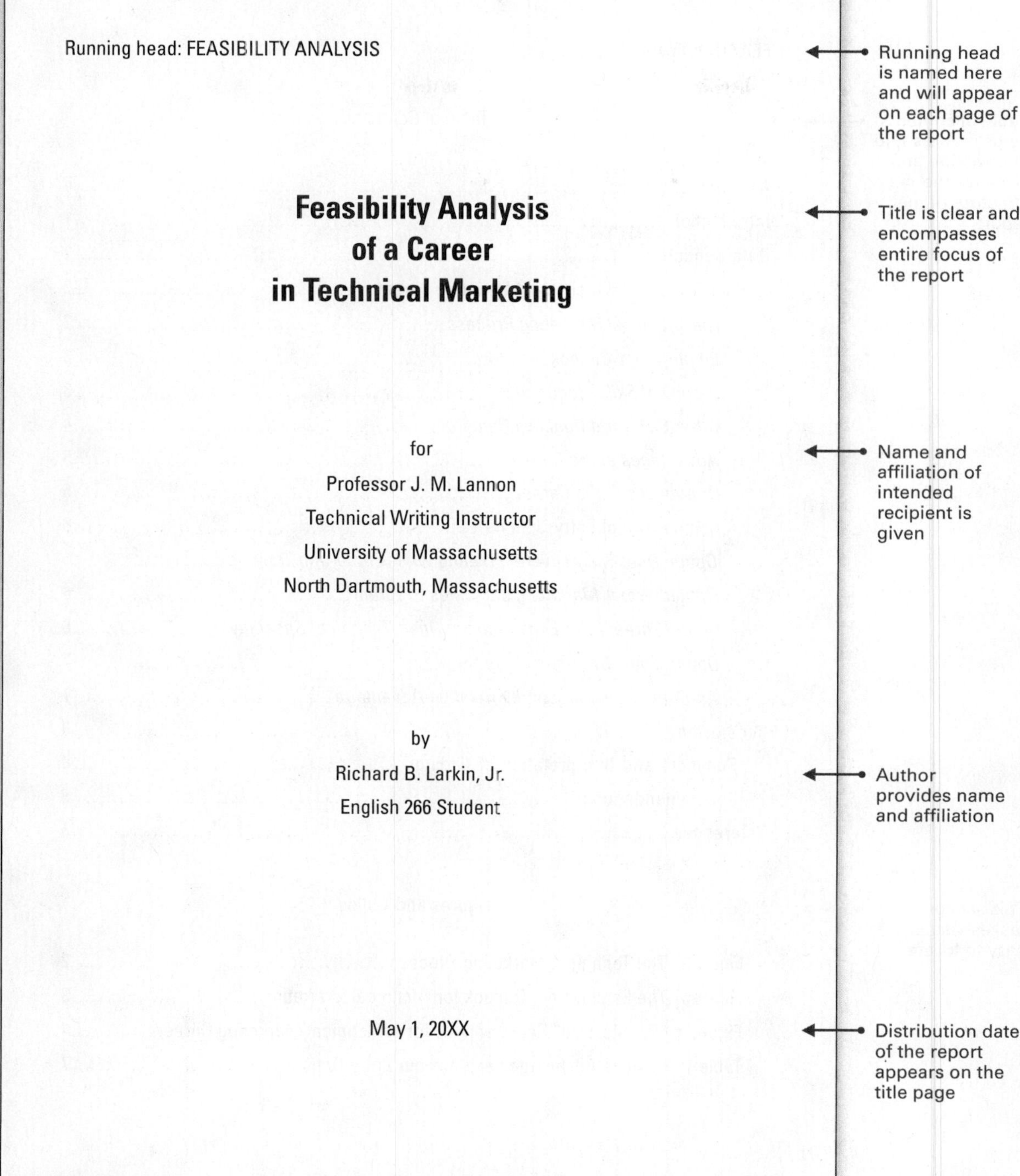
Running head: FEASIBILITY ANALYSIS

Feasibility Analysis of a Career in Technical Marketing

for

Professor J. M. Lannon
Technical Writing Instructor
University of Massachusetts
North Dartmouth, Massachusetts

by

Richard B. Larkin, Jr.
English 266 Student

May 1, 20XX

Running head is named here and will appear on each page of the report
Title is clear and encompasses entire focus of the report
Name and affiliation of intended recipient is given
Author provides name and affiliation
Distribution date of the report appears on the title page

FIGURE 22.4 (*Continued*)

Table of contents helps readers find information and visualize the structure of the report

FEASIBILITY ANALYSIS

Table of Contents

This section makes visuals easy to locate

Figures and Tables

FIGURE 22.4 (*Continued*)

FEASIBILITY ANALYSIS iii

Abstract

Abstract fully summarizes the content of the report

The feasibility of technical marketing as a career is based on a college graduate's interests, abilities, and expectations, as well as on possible entry options

Technical marketing is a feasible career for anyone who is motivated, who can communicate well, and who knows how to get along. Although this career offers job diversity and potential for excellent income, it entails almost constant travel, competition, and stress.

College graduates enter technical marketing through one of four options: entry-level positions that offer hands-on experience, formal training programs in large companies, prior experience in one's specialty, or graduate programs. The relative advantages and disadvantages of each option can be measured in resulting immediacy of income, rapidity of advancement, and long-term potential.

Anyone considering a technical marketing career should follow these recommendations:

- Speak with people who work in the field.
- Weigh the implications of each entry option carefully.
- Consider combining two or more options.
- Choose options for personal as well as professional benefits.

FIGURE 22.4 *(Continued)*

Introduction

Introduction identifies the problem

In today's global business climate, graduates in science and engineering face narrowing career opportunities because of "offshoring" of hi-tech jobs to low-wage countries. Government research indicates that more than two-thirds of the 40 occupations "most prone to offshoring" are in science and engineering (Bureau of Labor Statistics [BLS], 2006, p. 14). Experts Hira and Hira have suggested that the offshoring situation threatens the livelihood of some of the best-paid workers in America (2005, p. 12). University career counselor Troy Behrens offers the disturbing fact that the U.S. graduated 30,000 engineers in 2006, whereas India and China graduated 3 million (cited in Jacobs, 2007).

Proposes a possible solution

Given such bleak prospects, graduates might consider alternative careers. Technical marketing is one field that combines science and engineering expertise with "people skills"— those least likely to be offshored (BLS, 2006, p. 12). Engineers, for example, might seek jobs as *sales engineers*, specially trained professionals who market and sell highly technical products and services (BLS, 2009a, p. 1).

What specific type of work do technical marketers perform? *The Occupational Outlook Handbook* offers this job description:

Definition

> They [technical marketing specialists] possess extensive knowledge of [technologically and scientifically advanced] products, including…the components, functions, and scientific processes that make them work. They use their technical skills to explain the benefit of their products to potential customers and to demonstrate how their products are better than the products of their competitors. Often they modify and adjust products to meet customers' specific needs (BLS, 2009a, p.1).

(For a more detailed job description, refer to "The Technical Marketing Process," on page 2.)

Clear purpose statement leads into the body of the report

Undergraduates interested in technical marketing need answers to the following basic questions:

- *Is this the right career for me?*
- *If so, how do I enter the field?*

To help answer these questions, this report analyzes information gathered from professionals as well as from the literature. After defining *technical marketing,* the analysis examines employment outlook, required skills and personal qualities, career benefits and drawbacks, and entry options.

FIGURE 22.4 (*Continued*)

FEASIBILITY ANALYSIS 2

Data Section

Key Factors in a Technical Marketing Career
Anyone considering technical marketing needs to assess whether this career fits his or her interests, abilities, and aspirations.

Headings help keep readers oriented throughout

The technical marketing process. The classic process (identifying, reaching, and selling to customers) entails six key activities (Cornelius & Lewis, 1983, p. 44):

All information from outside sources is cited

1. *Market research:* assessing size and character of the target market.
2. *Product development and management:* producing the goods to fill a need.
3. *Cost determination and pricing:* measuring every expense in the product's production, distribution, advertising, and sales to determine its price.
4. *Advertising and promotion:* developing strategies for reaching customers.
5. *Product distribution:* coordinating all elements of a technical product or service, from conception through final delivery to the customer.
6. *Sales and technical support:* creating and maintaining customer accounts, and servicing and upgrading products.

Engaged in all these activities, the technical marketing professional gains detailed understanding of the industry, the product, and the customer's needs (Figure 1).

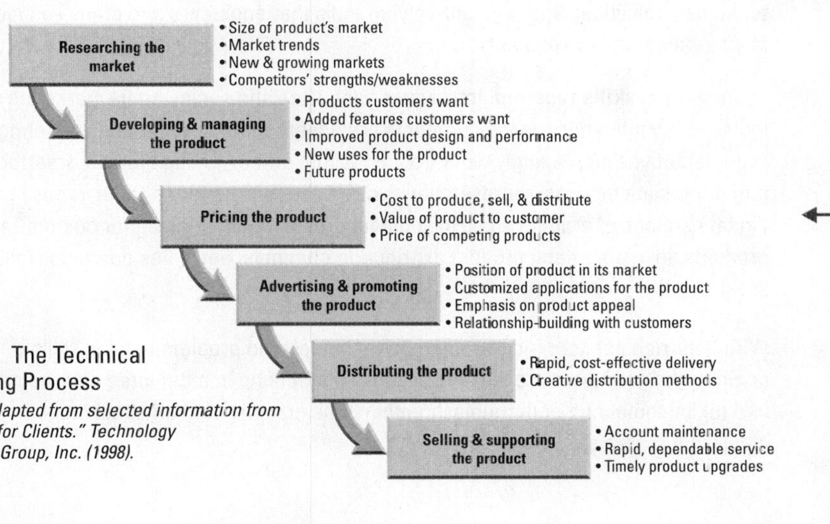

Visual reinforces the prose list above

Figure 1 The Technical Marketing Process
Source: Adapted from selected information from "Services for Clients." Technology Marketing Group, Inc. (1998).

FIGURE 22.4 (*Continued*)

Employment outlook. For graduates with the right combination of technical and personal qualifications, the outlook for technical marketing (and management) is excellent. Most engineering jobs will increase at less than average for jobs requiring a Bachelor's degree, while marketing and marketing management jobs will exceed the average rate (Figure 2).

Visual provides instant comparison

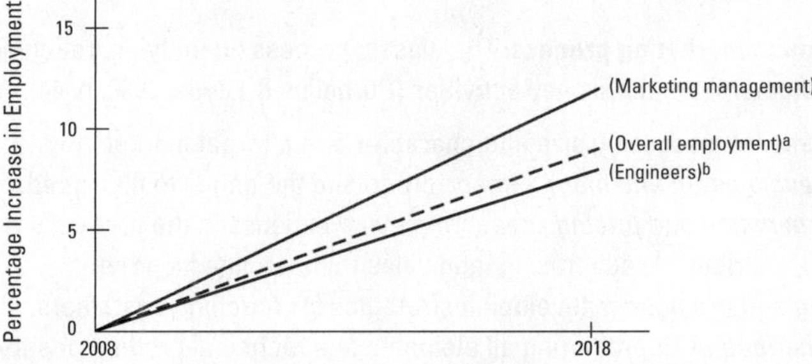

Figure 2 The Employment Outlook for Technical Marketing

[a]Jobs requiring a Bachelor's degree.

[b]Excluding outlying rates for specialties at the positive end of the spectrum (environmental engineers: +31%; biomedical: +72%; civil: +24%; petroleum: +18%).

Source: Data from U.S. Department of Labor. Bureau of Labor Statistics. (2009). http://www.bls.gov/oco/ocos027.htm

Although highly competitive, these marketing positions call for the very kinds of technical, analytical, and problem-solving skills that engineers can offer—especially in an automated environment.

Technical skills required. Interactive Web sites and social media marketing will increasingly influence the way products are advertised and sold. Also marketing representatives increasingly work from a "virtual office." Using laptops, smartphones, and other such devices, representatives out in the field have real-time access to digital catalogs of product lines, multimedia presentations, pricing for customized products, inventory data, product distribution channels, and sales contacts (Tolland, 2013).

With their rich background in computer, technical, and problem-solving skills, engineering graduates are ideally suited for (a) working in automated environments, and (b) implementing and troubleshooting these complex and often sensitive electronic systems.

FIGURE 22.4 (*Continued*)

FEASIBILITY ANALYSIS 4

Other skills and qualities required. *Business Week*'s Peter Coy offers this distinction between routine versus non routine work:

> The jobs that will pay well in the future will be ones that are hard to reduce to a recipe. These attractive jobs—from factory floor management to sales to teaching to the professions—require flexibility, creativity, and lifelong learning. They generally also require subtle and frequent interactions with other people, often face to face. (2004, p. 50)

For emphasis, select sources are quoted directly

Technical marketing is just such a job: it involves few "cookbook-type" tasks and requires "people skills." Besides a strong technical background, success in this field calls for a generous blend of those traits summarized in Figure 3.

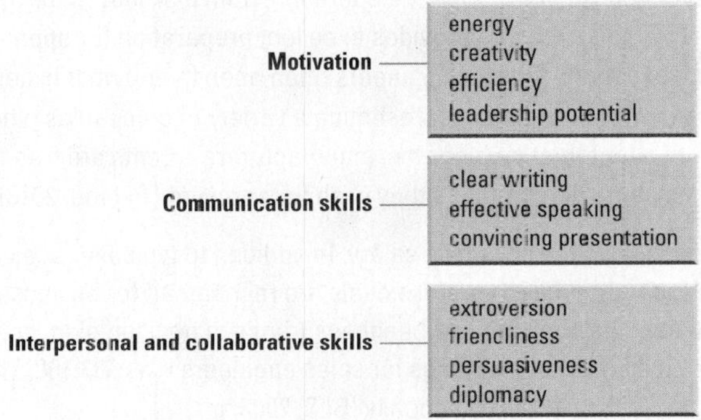

Figure 3 Required People Skills for a Technical Marketing Career

Motivation is essential in marketing. Professionals must be energetic and able to function with minimal supervision. Career counselor Phil Hawkins describes the ideal candidates as people who can plan and program their own tasks, can manage their time, and have no fear of hard work (personal interview, February 11, 2013). Leadership potential, as demonstrated by extracurricular activities, is an asset.

Report is based on primary as well as secondary research

Motivation alone, however, provides no guarantee of success. Marketing professionals are paid to communicate the value of their products and services, orally, online, on paper, and face to face. They routinely prepare such documents as sales proposals, product descriptions, and user manuals. Successful job candidates typically have taken courses in advertising, public speaking, technical communication, and—increasingly— foreign language (BLS, 2009a, pp. 2-3).

FIGURE 22.4 (*Continued*)

FEASIBILITY ANALYSIS 5

Skilled oral presentation is vital to any sales effort, as Phil Hawkins points out. Technical marketing professionals need to speak confidently and persuasively—to represent their products and services in the best light (personal interview, February 11, 2013). Sales presentations often involve public speaking at conventions and trade shows.

The ultimate requirement for success in marketing is interpersonal and collaborative skills: "tact, good judgement, and exceptional ability to establish and maintain relationships with supervisory and professional staff and client firms" (BLS, 2009b, p. 4).

Offers balanced coverage: advantages versus drawbacks (below)

Advantages of the career. As shown in Figure 1, technical marketing offers experience in every phase of a company's operation, from a product's design to its sales and service. Such broad exposure provides excellent preparation for upper-management positions. In fact, experienced sales engineers often open their own businesses as freelance "manufacturers' agents" representing a variety of companies who have no marketing staff. In effect their own bosses, manufacturers' agents are free to choose, from among many offers, the products they wish to represent (Tolland, 2013).

Another career benefit is the attractive salary. In addition to typically receiving a base pay plus commissions, marketing professionals are reimbursed for business expenses. Other employee benefits often include health insurance, a pension plan, and a company car. In 2008, the median annual earnings for sales engineers was $83,100. The highest 10 percent earned more than $136,000 annually (BLS, 2008, p.1).

The interpersonal and communication skills that marketing professionals develop are highly portable. This is vital in our rapidly shifting economy, in which job security is disappearing in the face of more and more temporary positions (Tolland, 2013).

Provides a realistic view

Drawbacks of the career. Technical marketing is by no means a career for every engineer or technology professional. Sales engineer Roger Cayer cautions that personnel might spend most of their time traveling to meet potential customers. Success requires hard work over long hours, evenings, and occasional weekends. Above all, the job entails constant pressure to meet sales quotas (phone interview, February 8, 2013). Anyone considering this career should be able to work and thrive in a competitive environment. The Bureau of Labor Statistics (2009a, p. 2) adds that the expanding global economy means that "international travel, to secure contracts with foreign customers, is becoming more common"—placing more pressure on an already hectic schedule.

FIGURE 22.4 (*Continued*)

FEASIBILITY ANALYSIS 6

A Comparison of Entry Options

Engineers and other technical graduates enter this field through one of four options. Some join small companies and learn their trade directly on the job. Others join companies that offer formal training programs. Some begin by getting experience in their technical specialty. Others earn a graduate degree beforehand. These options are compared below.

Each option in the comparison is previewed

Option 1: Entry-level marketing with on-the-job training. Smaller manufacturers offer marketing positions in which people learn on the job. Elaine Carto, president of ABCO Electronics, believes small companies offer a unique opportunity; entry-level salespersons learn about all facets of an organization, and often enjoy rapid advancement (personal interview, February 10, 2013). Career counselor Phil Hawkins says, "It's all a matter of whether you prefer to be a big fish in a small pond or a small fish in a big pond" (personal interview, February 11, 2013).

Entry-level marketing offers immediate income and a chance for early promotion. But one disadvantage might be the loss of any technical edge acquired in college.

Here and below, interpretations clarify the pros and cons of each entry option

Option 2: A marketing and sales training program. Formal training programs offer the most popular entry. Larger companies offer two formats: (a) a product-specific program, focused on a particular product or product line, or (b) a rotational program, in which trainees learn about an array of products and work in the various positions outlined in Figure 1. Programs last from weeks to months. Intel Corporation, for example, offers 30-month training programs titled "Sales and Marketing Rotation," to prepare new graduates for positions as technical sales engineer, marketing technical engineer, and technical applications engineer.

Like direct entry, this option offers the advantage of immediate income and early promotion. With no chance to practice in their specialty, however, trainees might eventually find their technical expertise compromised.

Option 3: Prior experience in one's technical specialty. Instead of directly entering marketing, some candidates first gain experience in their specialty. This option combines direct exposure to the workplace with the chance to sharpen technical skills in practical applications. In addition, some companies, such as Roger Cayer's, will offer marketing and sales positions to outstanding staff engineers as a step toward upper management (phone interview, February 8, 2013).

FIGURE 22.4 (*Continued*)

FEASIBILITY ANALYSIS 7

Although the prior-experience option delays entry into technical marketing, industry experts consider direct workplace and technical experience key assets for career growth in any field. Also, work experience becomes an asset for applicants to top MBA programs (Shelley, 1997, pp. 30–31).

Option 4: Graduate program. Instead of direct entry, some people choose to pursue an MS in their specialty or an MBA. According to engineering professor Mary McClane, MS degrees are usually unnecessary for technical marketing unless the particular products are highly complex (personal interview, April 2, 2013).

In general, jobseekers with an MBA have a competitive advantage. Also, new MBAs with a technical bachelor's degree and one to two years of experience command salaries from 10 to 30 percent higher than MBAs who lack work experience and a technical bachelor's degree. In fact, no more than 3 percent of candidates offer a "techno-MBA" specialty, making this unique group highly desirable to employers (Shelley, 1997, p. 30). A motivated student might combine graduate degrees. Dora Anson, president of Susimo Systems, sees the MS/MBA combination as ideal preparation for technical marketing (2013).

Interprets evidence impartially

One disadvantage of a full-time graduate program is lost salary, compounded by school expenses. These costs must be weighed against the prospect of promotion and monetary rewards later in one's career.

An overall comparison by relative advantage. Table 1 compares the four entry options on the basis of three criteria: immediate income, rate of advancement, and long-term potential.

Table summarizes the prior information, for instant comparisons

Table 1 Relative Advantages Among Four Technical-Marketing Entry Options

	Relative Advantages		
Option	Early, immediate income	Greatest advancement in marketing	Long-term potential
Entry level, no experience	yes	yes	no
Training program	yes	yes	no
Practical experience	yes	no	yes
Graduate program	no	no	yes

FIGURE 22.4 (*Continued*)

FEASIBILITY ANALYSIS 8

Conclusion

Summary of Findings

Technical marketing and sales requires solid technical background, motivation, communication skills, and interpersonal skills. This career offers job diversity and excellent income potential, balanced against relentless pressure to perform.

Graduates interested in this field confront four entry options: (1) direct entry with on-the-job training, (2) a formal training program, (3) prior technical experience, and (4) graduate programs. Each option has benefits and drawbacks based on immediacy of income, rate of advancement, and long-term potential.

Interpretation of Findings

For graduates with strong technical backgrounds and the right skills and motivation, technical marketing offers attractive prospects. Anyone contemplating this career, however, needs to enjoy customer contact and thrive in a competitive environment.

Those who decide that technical marketing is for them have various entry options:

- For hands-on experience, direct entry is the logical option.
- For intensive sales training, a formal program with a large company is best.
- For sharpening technical skills, prior work in one's specialty is invaluable.
- If immediate income is not vital, graduate school is an attractive option.

Recommendations

If your interests and abilities match the requirements, consider these suggestions:

1. For a firsthand view, seek the advice and opinions of people in the field. You might begin by contacting professional organizations such as the Manufacturers' Agents National Association at www.manaonline.org
2. Before settling on an entry option, consider its benefits and drawbacks and decide whether this option best coincides with your career goals.
3. When making any career decision, consider career counselor Phil Hawkins' advice: "Listen to your brain and your heart" (personal interview, February 11, 2013). Seek not only professional advancement but also personal satisfaction.

References

[The complete list of references is shown and discussed on pages 676, 677.]

Summary accurately and concisely reflects the report's body section

Overall interpretation explains what the findings mean

Recommendations are clear about what the audience should think and do

FIGURE 22.4 (*Continued*)

GUIDELINES for Reasoning through an Analytical Problem

Audiences approach an analytical report with this basic question:

Is this analysis based on sound reasoning?

Whether your report documents a causal, comparative, or feasibility analysis (or some combination) you need to trace your line of reasoning so that readers can follow it clearly. As you prepare your report, refer to the usability checklist on page 32 and observe the following guidelines:

For Causal Analysis

1. **Be sure the cause fits the effect.** Keep in mind that faulty causal reasoning is extremely common, especially when we ignore other possible causes or when we confuse mere coincidence with causation. For more on this topic, refer to pages 161–63.
2. **Make the links between effect and cause clear.** Identify the immediate cause (the one most closely related to the effect) as well as the distant cause(s) (the ones that often precede the immediate cause). For example, the immediate cause of a particular airplane crash might be a fuel-tank explosion, caused by a short circuit in frayed wiring, caused by faulty design or poor quality control by the airplane manufacturer. Discussing only the immediate cause often just scratches the surface of the problem.
3. **Clearly distinguish between possible, probable, and definite causes.** Unless the cause is obvious, limit your assertions by using *perhaps, probably, maybe, most likely, could, seems to, appears to,* or similar qualifiers that prevent you from making an insupportable claim. Keep in mind that "certainty" is elusive, especially in causal relationships.

For Comparative Analysis

1. **Rest the comparison on clear and definite criteria: costs, uses, benefits/drawbacks, appearance, results.** In evaluating the merits of competing items, identify your specific criteria (cost, ease of use, durability, and so on) and rank these criteria in order of importance.
2. **Give each item balanced treatment.** Discuss points of comparison for each item in identical order.
3. **Support and clarify the comparison or contrast through credible examples.** Use research, if necessary, for examples that readers can visualize.

4. **Follow either a block pattern or a point-by-point pattern.** In the block pattern, first one item is discussed fully, then the next. Choose a block pattern when the overall picture is more important than the individual points.

   In the point-by-point pattern, one point about both items is discussed, then the next point, and so on. Choose a point-by-point pattern when specific points might be hard to remember unless placed side by side.

Block pattern	**Point-by-point pattern**
Item A first point second point, etc.	first point of A/first point of B, etc.
Item B first point second point, etc.	second point of A/second point of B, etc.

5. **Order your points for greatest emphasis.** Try ordering your points from least to most important or dramatic or useful or reasonable. Placing the most striking point last emphasizes it best.
6. **In an evaluative comparison ("X is better than Y"),** offer your final judgment. Base your judgment squarely on the criteria presented.

For Feasibility Analysis

1. **Consider the strength of supporting reasons.** Choose the best reasons for supporting the action or decision being considered—based on your collected evidence.
2. **Consider the strength of opposing reasons.** Remember that people—including ourselves—usually see only what they want to see. Avoid the temptation to overlook or downplay opposing reasons, especially for an action or decision that you have been promoting. Consider alternate points of view; examine and evaluate all the evidence.
3. **Recommend a realistic course of action** After weighing all the pros and cons, make your recommendation—but be prepared to reconsider if you discover that what seemed like the right course of action turns out to be the wrong one.

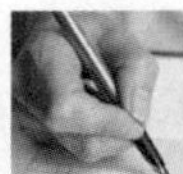

CHECKLIST: Analytical Reports

For evaluating your research methods and reasoning, refer also to the checklist on page 171. (Numbers in parentheses refer to the first page of discussion.)

Content

- ☐ Does the report address a clearly identified problem or purpose? (515)
- ☐ Is the report's length and detail appropriate for the subject? (515)
- ☐ Is there enough information for readers to make an informed decision? (515)
- ☐ Are all limitations of the analysis clearly acknowledged? (523)
- ☐ Is the information accurate, unbiased, and complete? (516)
- ☐ Are visuals used whenever possible to aid communication? (518)
- ☐ Are all data fully interpreted? (516)
- ☐ Are the conclusions logically derived from accurate interpretation? (518)
- ☐ Do the recommendations constitute an appropriate and reasonable response to the question or problem? (519)
- ☐ Is each source and contribution properly cited? (643)
- ☐ Are all needed front and end matter supplements included? (533)

Arrangement

- ☐ Is there a distinct introduction, body, and conclusion? (513)
- ☐ Does the introduction provide sufficient orientation to the issue or problem? (523)
- ☐ Does the body section present a clear picture of the evidence and reasoning? (524)
- ☐ Does the conclusion answer the question that originally sparked the analysis? (531)
- ☐ Are there clear transitions between related ideas? (701)

Style and Page Design

- ☐ Is the level of technicality appropriate for the primary audience? (20)
- ☐ Are headings informative and adequate? (308)
- ☐ Is the writing clear, concise, and fluent? (211)
- ☐ Is the language precise, and informative? (225)
- ☐ Is the report grammatical? (680)
- ☐ Is the page design inviting and accessible? (293)

Projects

GENERAL

Prepare an analytical report, using this procedure:

a. Choose a problem or question for analysis from your major or a subject of interest.

b. Restate the main question as a declarative sentence in your audience and purpose statement.

c. Identify an audience—other than your instructor—who will use your information for a specific purpose.

d. Hold a private brainstorming session to generate major topics and subtopics.

e. Use the topics to make a working outline based on the model outline in this chapter.

f. Make a tentative list of all sources (primary and secondary) that you will investigate. Verify that adequate sources are available.

g. In a proposal memo to your instructor (page 559), describe the topic and your plan for analysis. Attach a tentative bibliography.

h. Use your working outline as a guide to research.

i. Submit a progress report (page 491) to your instructor describing work completed, problems encountered, and work remaining.

j. Compose an audience and use profile. (Use the sample on page 29 as a model, along with the profile worksheet on page 31.)

k. Write the report for your stated audience. Work from a clear statement of audience and purpose, and be sure that your reasoning is shown clearly. Verify that your evidence, conclusions, and recommendations are consistent. Be especially careful that your recommendations observe the critical-thinking guidelines in Figure 22.3.

l. After writing your first draft, make any needed changes in the outline and revise your report according to the revision checklist. Include front matter and end matter.

m. Exchange reports with a classmate for further suggestions for revision.

n. Prepare an oral report of your findings for the class as a whole.

TEAM

1. Divide into small groups. Choose a topic for group analysis—preferably, a campus issue—and brainstorm. Draw up a working outline that could be used as an analytical report on this subject.

2. In the workplace, it is common for reports to be written in teams. Think of an idea for a report for this class that might be a team project. How would you divide the tasks and ensure that the work was being done fairly? What are the advantages and disadvantages of a team approach to a report? In groups of 2–3, discuss these issues. If your instructor indicates that your report is to be team-based, write a memo (as a team) to your instructor indicating the role of each team member and the timeline.

DIGITAL AND SOCIAL MEDIA

Many reports, particularly government reports, are turned into PDF documents and are available on the Web. When you have a draft of your report, turn it into a PDF file. See the Digital and Social Media project in Chapter 13 (page 316) for hints on how to create a PDF. Read a few pages of the PDF version, then read the same pages in hard copy. Do you find yourself reading more quickly with the on-screen (PDF) version? What are the pros and cons of PDF versus print? Write a short memo to your classmates explaining your observations.

GLOBAL

Use the Internet to look for reports written in English by government agencies of different countries. Look for similarities to the reports you are familiar with in the United States (or the one you are preparing for class), as well as differences in features such as organization, word choice, formatting, use of visuals, levels of politeness, and so on.

23 Proposals

Considering Audience and Purpose

The Proposal Process

Types of Proposals

Elements of a Persuasive Proposal

An Outline and Model for Proposals

Guidelines for Proposals

A Situation Requiring a Formal Proposal

Checklist: Proposals

Projects

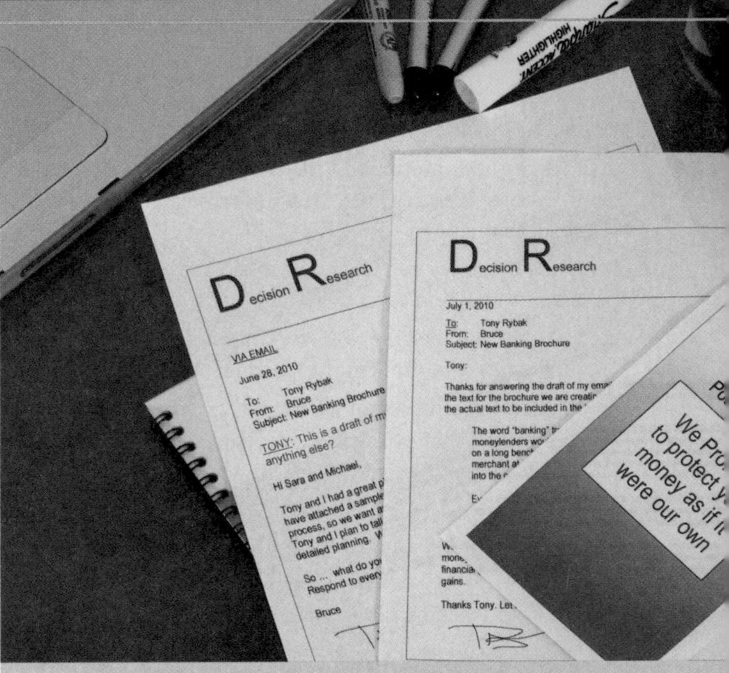

"My work is all about proposal writing—it's my full-time job. While some of our museum's financial support comes from private donors, most of it is generated from grants. I mainly write for panels or committees reviewing grant proposals to decide whether to fund them: for example, corporate officers making a decision on a corporate gift, trustees of private foundations deciding on a foundation gift, and so on. Any such proposal (prepared for, say, The National Endowment for the Arts) usually has to be submitted on a yearly basis in order for funding to continue. And each proposal must compete yearly with proposals from similar institutions. It's a continuous challenge!"

—Ellen Catabia,
Grant Writer for a major museum

LEARNING OBJECTIVES FOR THIS CHAPTER

- Understand the persuasive purpose of proposals
- Understand the expectations of people who read proposals
- Differentiate between solicited and unsolicited proposals
- Differentiate between formal and informal proposals
- Understand the different functions of planning, research, and sales proposals
- Write an informal proposal
- Write a formal proposal

Proposals attempt to *persuade* an audience to take some form of action: to authorize a project, accept a service or product, or support a specific plan for solving a problem or improving a situation.

You might write as a proposal a letter to your school board to suggest changes in the English curriculum; you might write a memo to your firm's vice president to request funding for a training program for new employees; or you might work on a team preparing an extensive document to bid on a Defense Department contract (competing with proposals from other firms). As a student or as an intern at a nonprofit agency, you might submit a *grant proposal*, requesting financial support for a research or community project.

You might work alone or collaboratively. Developing and writing the proposal might take hours or months. If your job depends on funding from outside sources, proposals might be the most important documents you produce.

CONSIDERING AUDIENCE AND PURPOSE

Audience considerations

In science, business, government, or education, proposals are written for decision makers: managers, executives, directors, clients, board members, or community leaders. Inside or outside your organization, these people review various proposals and then decide whether a specific plan is worthwhile, whether the project will materialize, or whether the service or product is useful.

Before accepting a particular proposal, reviewers look for persuasive answers to these basic questions:

What proposal reviewers want to know

- What exactly is the problem or need, and why is this such a big deal?
- Why should we spend time, money, and effort on this?
- What exactly is your plan, and how do we know it is feasible?

- Why should we accept the items that seem costly about your plan?
- What action are we supposed to take?

A proposal involves these basic persuasive tasks

Connect with your audience by addressing the previous questions early and systematically. Here are the persuasive tasks involved:

1. **Spell out the problem (and its causes) clearly and convincingly.** Supply enough detail for your audience to appreciate the problem's importance.
2. **Point out the benefits of solving the problem.** Explain specifically what your readers stand to gain.
3. **Offer a realistic, cost-effective solution.** Stick to claims or assertions you can support. (For more on feasibility, see pages 500, 514.)
4. **Address anticipated objections to your solution.** Consider carefully your audience's level of skepticism about this issue.
5. **Convince your audience to act.** Decide exactly what you want your readers to do and give reasons why they should be the ones to take action.

Pages 563–69 offer examples and strategies for completing each of these tasks. And the page 575 Guidelines supply more detail.

Purpose considerations

The singular purpose of your proposal is to convince your audience to accept your plan: "Yes. Let's move ahead on this."

How proposals and reports differ in purpose

While they may contain many of the same basic elements as a report, proposals have a primarily *persuasive* purpose. Of course, reports can also contain persuasive elements, as in recommending a specific course of action or justifying an equipment purchase. But reports typically serve a variety of *informative* purposes as well—such as keeping track of progress, explaining why something happened, or predicting an outcome.

A report often precedes a proposal. For example, a report on high levels of chemical pollution in a major waterway typically leads to various proposals for cleaning up that waterway. In short, once the report has *explored* a particular need, a proposal will be developed to *sell* the idea for meeting that need.

THE PROPOSAL PROCESS

Proposals in the commercial sector

The basic proposal process can be summarized like this: Someone offers a plan for something that needs to be done. This process has three stages:

Stages in the proposal process

1. Client *X* needs a service or product.
2. Firms *A*, *B*, and *C* propose a plan for meeting the need.
3. Client *X* awards the job to the firm offering the best proposal.

Following is a typical scenario.

CASE Submitting a Competitive Proposal

You manage a mining engineering firm in Tulsa, Oklahoma. You regularly read the *Commerce Business Daily*, an essential online reference tool for anyone whose firm seeks government contracts. This publication lists the government's latest needs for services (salvage, engineering, maintenance) and for supplies, equipment, and materials (guided missiles, engine parts, and so on). On Wednesday, February 19, you spot this announcement:

> **Development of Alternative Solutions to Acid Mine Water Contamination from Abandoned Lead and Zinc Mines** near Tar Creek, Neosho River, Ground Lake, and the Boone and Roubidoux aquifers in northeastern Oklahoma. This will include assessment of environmental effects of mine drainage followed by development and evaluation of alternate solutions to alleviate acid mine drainage in receiving streams. An optional portion of the contract to be bid on as an add-on and awarded at the discretion of the OWRB will be to prepare an Environmental Impact Assessment for each of three alternative solutions as selected by the OWRB. The project is expected to take six months to accomplish, with an anticipated completion date of September 30, 20XX. The projected effort for the required task is thirty person-months. The request for proposal is available at www.owrb.gov. Proposals are due March 1.
>
> Oklahoma Water Resources Board
> P.O. Box 53585
> 1000 Northeast 10th Street
> Oklahoma City, OK 73151
> (405) 555–2541

Your firm has the personnel, experience, and time to do the job, so you decide to compete for the contract. Because the March 1 deadline is fast approaching, you immediately download the request for proposal (RFP). The RFP will give you the guidelines for developing and submitting the proposal—guidelines for spelling out your plan to solve the problem (methods, timetables, costs).

You then get right to work with the two staff engineers you have appointed to your proposal team. Because the credentials of your staff could affect the client's acceptance of the proposal, you ask team members to update their résumés for inclusion in an appendix to the proposal.

In situations like the one above, the client will award the contract to the firm submitting the best proposal, based on the following criteria (and perhaps others):

Criteria by which reviewers evaluate proposals

- understanding of the client's needs, as described in the RFP
- clarity and feasibility of the plan being offered
- quality of the project's organization and management
- ability to complete the job by deadline
- ability to control costs

- firm's experience on similar projects
- qualifications of staff to be assigned to the project
- firm's performance record on similar projects

A client's specific evaluation criteria are often listed (in order of importance or on a point scale) in the RFP. Although these criteria may vary, every client expects a proposal that is *clear, informative*, and *realistic*.

Proposals in the nonprofit sector

In contrast to proposals prepared for commercial purposes, museums, community service groups, and other nonprofit organizations prepare *grant proposals* that request financial support for worthwhile causes. Government and charitable granting agencies such as the Department of Health and Human Services, the Pugh Charitable Trust, or the Department of Agriculture solicit proposals for funding in areas such as medical research, educational TV programming, and rural development. Submission and review of grant proposals follow the same basic process used for commercial proposals.

Submitting paperless proposals

In both the commercial and nonprofit sectors, the proposal process increasingly occurs online. The National Science Foundation's *Fastlane* Web site <www.fastlane.nsf.gov>, for example, allows grant applicants to submit proposals in electronic format. This enables applicants to include sophisticated graphics, to revise budget estimates, to update other aspects of the plan as needed, and to maintain real-time contact with the granting agency while the proposal is being reviewed.

TYPES OF PROPOSALS

Solicited and unsolicited proposals

Proposals may be either *solicited* or *unsolicited*. Solicited proposals are those that have been requested by a manager, client, or customer (see the case on page 557). Unsolicited proposals are those that have not been requested. If you are a new advertising agency in town, you may send out unsolicited proposals to local radio stations to suggest they use your agency for their advertising.

Because the audience for a solicited proposal has made a specific request, you will not need to spend time introducing yourself or providing background on the product or service. For an unsolicited proposal (sometimes termed a "cold call" in sales), you will need to catch readers' attention quickly and provide incentives for them to continue reading—perhaps by printing a price comparison of your fees on the first page, for example.

Informal and formal proposals

Proposals may also be *informal* or *formal*. Informal proposals can take the form of an email or memo (if distributed within an organization), or a letter (when sent outside of an organization). Formal proposals, meanwhile, take on the same format as formal reports (see Chapter 22), including front matter, the proposal text, and end matter, if applicable.

Both solicited and unsolicited proposals, whether informal or formal, fall into three categories: planning proposals, research proposals, and sales proposals.

Planning Proposals

The role of planning proposals

Planning proposals offer solutions to a problem or suggestions for improvement. A planning proposal might be a request for funding to expand the campus newspaper (as in the formal proposal in this chapter), an architectural plan for new facilities at a ski area, or a plan to develop energy alternatives to fossil fuels.

Figure 23.1 is the first page of a solicited, informal planning proposal. Architects from Brewster Architectural, Inc. have been meeting with personnel from Southeastern Massachusetts University to discuss installing an elevator in an older campus building. Because the project is complicated (need to maintain the building's historic elements but install an elevator fully compliant with the Americans with Disabilities Act), the architects need to persuade the client that their analysis and research are sound and their methods will succeed. Because this proposal is addressed to an external reader, it is cast as a letter. To save space, only the salutation and first page are shown here. (Some planning proposals for far less complex situations are purposely brief, such as the proposal from Leverett Land & Timber Company, shown in Figure 16.1, page 352.)

Notice that the word choice ("Chris," "we've," "thanks") creates a friendly, yet still professional tone—appropriate for this document since the architects and their clients have spent many hours together already. Notice also the "Limitations" section, where the architects are careful to remind their clients that any construction project may have unanticipated surprises.

This proposal does not need a lengthy introduction or problem statement: Southeastern Massachusetts University, having solicited the proposal, is aware of the problem.

Research Proposals

The role of research proposals

Research (or grant) proposals request approval (and often funding) for some type of study. For example, a university chemist might address a research proposal to the Environmental Protection Agency to request funds to identify toxic contaminants in local groundwater. Research proposals are solicited by many agencies, including the National Science Foundation and the National Institutes of Health. Each agency has its own requirements and guidelines for proposal format and content. Successful research proposals follow those guidelines and carefully articulate the goals of the project. In these cases, proposal readers will generally be other scientists; therefore, writers can use language that is appropriate for other experts.

Other research proposals might be submitted by students requesting funds or approval for, say, independent study, or a thesis project. A technical writing student usually submits an informal research proposal that will lead to the term project. For example, in the following research proposal (Figure 23.2), Tom Dewoody requests his instructor's authorization to do a feasibility study (Chapter 22) that will produce an analytical report for potential investors. Dewoody's proposal clearly answers the questions about *what, why, how, when,* and *where.* Because this proposal is addressed to an internal reader, it is cast as a memo.

States the document's purpose

Summarizes the background and problem

Outlines the client's needs

Proposes a solution

Sets realistic expectations

Dear Chris and team:

Thanks for meeting over the past few weeks to help us gather the necessary information so we can provide a plan for the elevator project in Bass Hall.

Background

To make the building fully accessible, Bass Hall needs an elevator. Last month, you contacted us requesting a proposal for this project. Although Bass Hall is not an officially designated historic building, it has distinct historic features that you wish to retain. In addition to historic preservation issues, timing of this project is very important for the building occupants.

Needs assessment

We've met with project managers, the University building committee, and the building's tenants (Department of Chemistry). Based on those meetings and a review of blueprints and other documents, we have identified the following needs as important:

- Maintain the historic east-facing facade of Bass Hall
- Locate the elevator shaft so it begins in the underground parking garage
- Avoid any physical changes to the Department of Chemistry's student lab
- Ensure the fewest disruptions during the academic semester
- Use code compliant elevator doors that preserve the historic look of other entrances
- Avoid disturbing the marble portico at the building entrance

Proposed Plan

Based on the needs identified above, and on the overall University master building plan, city and state codes and guidelines, and the timeline you have outlined, we propose to install a handicap-accessible elevator, starting at the underground parking garage level and terminating on the 4th floor, with the following conditions:

- Situate the elevator shaft in the middle of the building, thus allowing it to terminate in the underground parking garage
- Locate the elevator on the north side of the hallway. Although this location will require relocating one faculty office, using the north side avoids the student chemistry lab, marble portico, and other important building features
- Work with our historic preservation team to create custom entrance doors and hardware
- Begin demolition on June 1, so that the most disruptive work will be completed before the fall semester begins and the final project can be finished by December

Limitations

Older buildings bring unanticipated issues. For instance, although Bass Hall recently underwent asbestos abatement, should any additional asbestos be located during initial testing, we would need to reconsider the timing of this proposal to allow for removal.

Please see the next several pages for schematic drawings and other details.

FIGURE 23.1 A Planning Proposal. The complete proposal contains several schematic drawings (two pages additional) for the client to review.

To: Dr. John Lannon
From: T. Sorrells Dewoody
Date: March 16, 20XX
Subject: *Proposal for Determining the Feasibility of Marketing Dead Western White Pine*

Introduction
Over the past four decades, huge losses of western white pine have occurred in the northern Rockies, primarily attributable to white pine blister rust and the attack of the mountain pine beetle. Estimated annual mortality is 318 million board feet. Because of the low natural resistance of white pine to blister rust, this high mortality rate is expected to continue indefinitely.

Opens with background and causes of the problem

If white pine is not harvested while the tree is dying or soon after death, the wood begins to dry and check (warp and crack). The sapwood is discolored by blue stain, a fungus carried by the mountain pine beetle. If the white pine continues to stand after death, heart cracks develop. These factors work together to cause degradation of the lumber and consequent loss in value.

Statement of Problem
White pine mortality reduces the value of white pine stumpage because the commercial lumber market will not accept dead wood. The major implications of this problem are two: first, in the face of rising demand for wood, vast amounts of timber lie unused; second, dead trees are left to accumulate in the woods, where they are rapidly becoming a major fire hazard here in northern Idaho and elsewhere.

Describes problem

Proposed Solution
One possible solution to the problem of white pine mortality and waste is to search for markets other than the conventional lumber market. The last few years have seen a burst of popularity and growing demand for weathered barn boards and wormy pine for interior paneling. Some firms around the country are marketing defective wood as specialty products. (These firms call the wood from which their products come "distressed," a term I will use hereafter to refer to dead and defective white pine.) Distressed white pine quite possibly will find a place in such a market.

Describes one possible solution

Scope
To assess the feasibility of developing a market for distressed white pine, I plan to pursue six areas of inquiry:

Defines scope of the proposed study

FIGURE 23.2 A Research Proposal

1. What products presently are being produced from dead wood, and what are the approximate costs of production?
2. How large is the demand for distressed-wood products?
3. Can distressed white pine meet this demand as well as other species meet it?
4. Does the market contain room for distressed white pine?
5. What are the costs of retrieving and milling distressed white pine?
6. What prices for the products can the market bear?

Methods

Describes how study will be done →

My primary data sources will include consultations with Dr. James Hill, Professor of Wood Utilization, and Dr. Sven Bergman, Forest Economist—both members of the College of Forestry, Wildlife, and Range. I will also inspect decks of dead white pine at several locations and visit a processing mill to evaluate it as a possible base of operations. I will round out my primary research with a letter and telephone survey of processors and wholesalers of distressed material.

Mentions literature review →

Secondary sources will include publications on the uses of dead timber, and a review of a study by Dr. Hill on the uses of dead white pine.

My Qualifications

Cites a major reference and gives the writer's qualifications for this project →

I have been following Dr. Hill's study on dead white pine for two years. In June of this year I will receive my B.S. in forest management. I am familiar with wood milling processes and have firsthand experience at logging. My association with Drs. Hill and Bergman gives me the opportunity for an in-depth feasibility study.

Conclusion

Encourages reader acceptance →

Clearly, action is needed to reduce the vast accumulations of dead white pine in our forests—among the most productive forests in northern Idaho. By addressing the six areas of inquiry mentioned earlier, I can determine the feasibility of directing capital and labor to the production of distressed white pine products. With your approval I will begin research at once.

FIGURE 23.2 *(Continued)*

Sales Proposals

Sales proposals offer services or products and may be either solicited or unsolicited. If the proposal is solicited, several firms may be competing for the contract; in such cases, submitted proposals may be ranked by a committee.

The role of sales proposals

A successful sales proposal persuades customers that your product or service surpasses those of competitors. In the following solicited proposal (Figure 23.3), the writer explains why her machinery is best for the job, how the job can be done efficiently, what qualifications her company can offer, and what costs are involved. To protect herself, she points out possible causes of increased costs. Because this document is addressed to an external reader, it is cast as a letter.

NOTE *Never underestimate costs by failing to account for and acknowledge all variables—a sure way to lose money or clients.*

The proposal categories (planning, research, and sales) discussed in this section are not mutually exclusive. A research proposal, for example, may request funds for a study that will lead to a planning proposal. The Vista proposal partially shown here combines planning and sales features; if clients accept the preliminary plan, they will hire the firm to install the automated system.

NOTE *Proposals can be cast as letters if the situation calls for them to be brief. If the situation requires a longer proposal, you may need to include most or all of the components listed in the proposal outline (page 570) as well as supplements (discussed on page 569 in this chapter and listed on pages 533-36 in Chapter 22).*

ELEMENTS OF A PERSUASIVE PROPOSAL

Proposal reviewers expect a clear, informative, and realistic presentation. They will evaluate your proposal on the basis of the following quality indicators. (See also the criteria listed on pages 557–58.)

A Forecasting Title or Subject Line

Provide a clear forecast

Announce the proposal's purpose and content with an informative title such as "Recommended Wastewater Treatment System for the Mudpie Resorts and Spa" (for a formal proposal) or with a subject line (in an informal proposal). Instead of a vague title such as "Proposed Office Procedures for Vista Freight Company," be specific: "A Proposal for Automating Vista's Freight Billing System." An overworked reviewer facing a stack of proposals might very well decide that the proposal lacking a clear, focused title or subject line probably also will be unclear and unfocused in its content—and set it aside.

Modern Landscaping
23–44 18th Street
Sunnyside, NY 11104

October 4, 20XX

Martin Haver
35–66 114th Avenue
Jamaica, NY 11107

Subject: *Proposal to Dig a Trench and Move Boulders at Bliss Site*

Dear Mr. Haver:

Describes the subject and purpose →

I've inspected your property and would be happy to undertake the landscaping project necessary for the development of your farm.

Gives the writer's qualifications →

The backhoe I use cuts a span 3 feet wide and can dig as deep as 18 feet—more than an adequate depth for the mainline pipe you wish to lay. Because this backhoe is on tracks rather than tires and is hydraulically operated, it is particularly efficient in moving rocks. I have more than twelve years of experience with backhoe work and have completed many jobs similar to this one.

Explains how the job will be done →

Maintains a confident tone throughout →

After examining the huge boulders that block access to your property, I am convinced they can be moved only if I dig out underneath and exert upward pressure with the hydraulic ram while you push forward on the boulders with your D-9 Caterpillar. With this method, we can move enough rock to enable you to farm that now inaccessible tract. Because of its power, my larger backhoe will save you both time and money in the long run.

Gives a qualified cost estimate →

This job should take 12 to 15 hours, unless we encounter subsurface ledge formations. My fee is $200 per hour. The fact that I provide my own dynamiting crew at no extra charge should be an advantage to you because you have so much rock to be moved.

Encourages reader acceptance by emphasizing economy and efficiency →

Please phone or email me at your convenience for more information. I'm sure we can do the job economically and efficiently.

Sincerely yours,

Sharon Ingram

Sharon Ingram

Phone: (814) 555-1212 **Fax:** (814) 551-1222 **Email:** SCAPES@gmail.com

FIGURE 23.3 A Sales Proposal

Background Information

A background section can be brief or long. If the reader is familiar with the project, a quick reminder of the context is sufficient:

> **Background**
>
> Vista provides two services: (1) It locates freight carriers for its clients. The carriers, in turn, pay Vista a 6 percent commission for each referral. (2) Vista handles all shipping paperwork for its clients. For this auditing service, clients pay Vista a monthly retainer.

Brief background, for readers familiar with the context

In an unsolicited proposal, you may need to provide a longer introduction. If the topic warrants, the background section may take up several pages.

Statement of the Problem

The problem and its resolution form the backbone of any proposal. Show that you clearly understand your clients' problems and their expectations, and then offer an appropriate solution.

> **Statement of the Problem**
>
> Although Vista's business has increased steadily for the past three years, record keeping, accounting, and other paperwork are still done manually. These inefficient procedures have caused a number of problems, including late billings, lost commissions, and poor account maintenance. Updated office procedures seem crucial to competitiveness and continued growth.

Describes problem and its effects

Description of Solution

The proposal audience wants specific suggestions for meeting their specific needs. Their biggest question is: "What will this plan do for me?" In the following proposal for automating office procedures at Vista, Inc., Gerald Beaulieu begins with a clear assessment of needs and then moves quickly into a proposed plan of action.

> **Objective**
>
> This proposal offers a realistic and effective plan for streamlining Vista's office procedures. We first identify the burden imposed on your staff by the current system, and then we show how to reduce inefficiency, eliminate client complaints, and improve your cash flow by automating most office procedures.

Describes plan to solve the problem

A Clear Focus on Benefits

Do a detailed audience and use analysis to identify readers' major concerns and to anticipate likely questions and objections. Show that you understand what readers (or their organization) will gain by adopting your plan. The following list spells the exact tasks Vista employees will be able to accomplish once the proposed plan is implemented.

Relates benefits directly to client's needs

> Once your automated system is operational, you will be able to
>
> - identify cost-effective carriers
> - coordinate shipments (which will ensure substantial client discounts)
> - print commission bills
> - track shipments by weight, miles, fuel costs, and destination
> - send clients weekly audit reports on their shipments
> - bill clients on a 25-day cycle
> - produce weekly or monthly reports
>
> Additional benefits include eliminating repetitive tasks, improving cash flow, and increasing productivity.

(Each of these benefits will be described at length later in the "Plan" section.)

Honest and Supportable Claims

Promise only what you can deliver

Because they typically involve expenditures of large sums of money as well as contractual obligations, proposals require a solid ethical and legal foundation. Clients in these situations often have doubts or objections about time and financial costs and a host of other risks involved whenever any important project is undertaken. Your proposal needs to address these issues openly and honestly. For example, if you are proposing to install customized virus-protection software, be clear about what this software cannot accomplish under certain circumstances. False or exaggerated promises not only damage reputations, but also invite lawsuits. (For more on supporting your claims, see pages 48–51.)

Here is how the Vista proposal qualifies its promises:

Anticipates a major objection and offers a realistic approach

> As countless firms have learned, imposing automated procedures on employees can create severe morale problems—particularly among senior staff who feel coerced and often marginalized. To diminish employee resistance, we suggest that your entire staff be invited to comment on this proposal. To help avoid hardware and software problems once the system is operational, we have included recommendations and a budget for staff training. (Adequate training is essential to the automation process.)

If the best available solutions have limitations, say so. Notice how the above solutions are qualified ("diminish" and "help avoid" instead of "eliminate") so as not to promise more than the plan can achieve.

A proposal can be judged fraudulent if it misleads potential clients by

Major ethical and legal violations in a proposal

- making unsupported claims,
- ignoring anticipated technical problems, or
- knowingly underestimating costs or time requirements.

For a project involving complex tasks or phases, provide a realistic timetable (perhaps using a Gantt chart, pages 266, 267) to show when each major phase will begin and end. Also provide a realistic, accurate budget, with a detailed cost breakdown (for supplies and equipment, travel, research costs, outside contractors, or the like) to show clients exactly how the money is being spent. For a sample breakdown of costs, see the construction repair proposal (Figure 16.1, page 352).

NOTE *Be certain that you spend every dollar according to the allocations that have been stipulated. For example, if a grant award allocates a certain amount for "a research assistant," be sure to spend that exact amount for that exact purpose—unless you receive written permission from the granting agency to divert funds for other purposes. Keep strict accounting of all the money you spend. Proposal experts Friedland and Folt remind us that "Financial misconduct is never tolerated, regardless of intent" (161). Even an innocent mistake or accounting lapse on your part can lead to charges of fraud.*

Appropriate Detail

Vagueness in a proposal is fatal. Spell everything out. Instead of writing, "We will install state-of-the-art equipment," enumerate the products or services to be provided.

> To meet your requirements, we will install 12 iMac desktop computers each with 500 GB hard drives. The system will be networked for secure file transfer between office locations. The plan also includes network printers with four HP LaserJet CP2020 color printers and one HP Deskjet 6940 color printer.

Spells out what will be provided

To avoid misunderstandings that could produce legal complications, a proposal must elicit *one* interpretation only.

Place support material (maps, blueprints, specifications, calculations) in an appendix so as not to interrupt the discussion.

NOTE *While concrete and specific detail is vital, never overburden reviewers with needless material. A precise audience and use analysis (Chapter 2) can pinpoint specific information needs.*

Readability

A readable proposal is straightforward, easy to follow, and understandable. Avoid language that is overblown or too technical for your audience. Review Chapter 11 for style strategies.

A Tone That Connects with Readers

Your proposal should move people to action. Review Chapter 4 for persuasion guidelines. Keep your tone confident and encouraging, not bossy and critical. For more on tone, see pages 232–38.

Visuals

Emphasize key points in your proposal with relevant tables, flowcharts, and other visuals (Chapter 12), properly introduced and discussed.

Visual repeats, restates, or reinforces the prose

As the flowchart (Figure 1) illustrates, Vista's routing and billing system creates redundant work for your staff. The routing sheet alone is handled at least six times. Such extensive handling leads to errors, misplaced paperwork, and late billing.

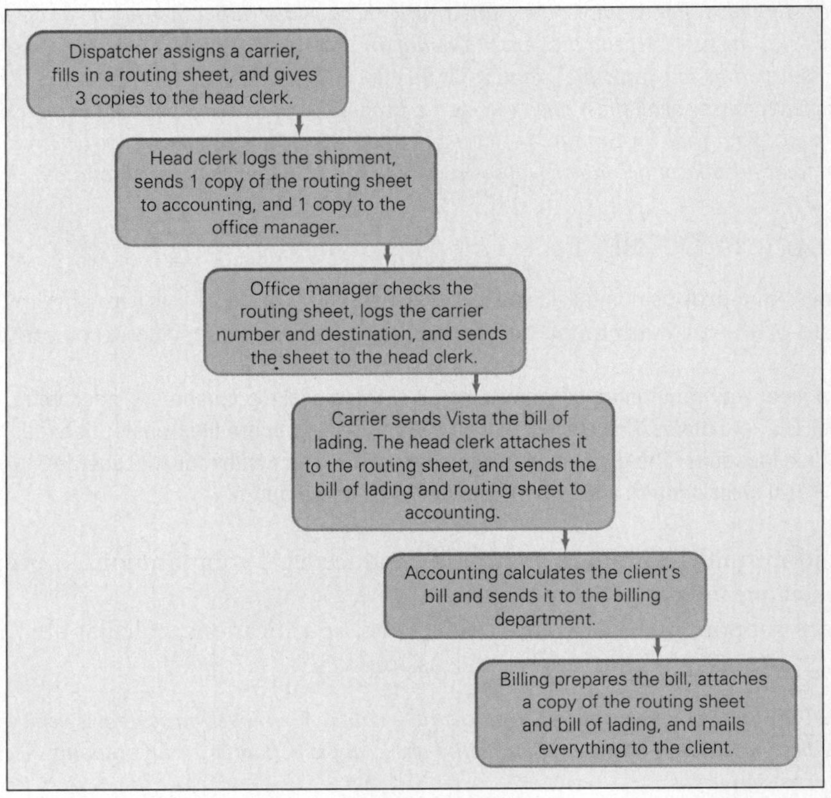

FIGURE 1 Flowchart of Vista's Manual Routing and Billing System

Accessible Page Design

Yours might be one of several proposals being reviewed. Help the audience to find what they need quickly. Review Chapter 13 for design strategies.

Supplements Tailored for a Diverse Audience

Analyze the specific needs and interests of each major reviewer

A single proposal often addresses a diverse audience: executives, managers, technical experts, attorneys, politicians, and so on. Various reviewers are interested in different parts of your proposal. Experts look for the technical details. Others might be interested in the recommendations, costs, timetable, or expected results, but they will need an explanation of technical details as well.

Give each major reviewer what he or she expects

If the primary audience is expert or informed, keep the proposal text itself technical. For uninformed secondary reviewers (if any), provide an informative abstract, a glossary, and appendices explaining specialized information. If the primary audience has no expertise and the secondary audience does, write the proposal itself for laypersons, and provide appendices with the technical details (formulas, specifications, calculations) that experts will use to evaluate your plan. See Chapter 22 for front-matter and end-matter supplements.

If you are unsure about which supplements to include in an internal proposal, ask the intended audience or study similar proposals. For a solicited proposal (to an outside agency), follow the agency's instructions exactly.

Proper Citation of Sources and Contributors

Proposals rarely emerge from thin air. Whenever appropriate, especially for topics that involve ongoing research, you need to credit key information sources and contributors. Proposal experts Friedland and Folt offer these suggestions (22, 135–36):

How to cite sources and contributors

- **Review the literature on this topic.** Limit your focus to the major background studies.
- **Don't cite sources of "common knowledge" about this topic.** Information available in multiple sources or readily known in your discipline usually qualifies as common knowledge. (For more, see page 649.)
- **Provide adequate support for your plan.** Cite all key sources that serve to confirm your plan's feasibility.
- **Provide up-to-date principal references.** Although references to earlier, ground-breaking studies are important, recent studies can be most essential.
- **Present a balanced, unbiased view.** Acknowledge sources that differ from or oppose your point of view; explain the key differences among the various viewpoints before making your case.
- **Give credit to all contributors.** Recognize everyone who has worked on or helped with this proposal: for example, coauthors, editors, data gatherers, and people who contributed ideas.

Proper citation is not only an ethical requirement, but also an indicator of your proposal's feasibility. See "A Quick Guide to Documentation" (page 643 for more on citation techniques.

AN OUTLINE AND MODEL FOR PROPOSALS

Depending on a proposal's complexity, each section contains some or all of the components listed in the following general outline:

I. Introduction
- A. Statement of Problem and Objective/Project Overview
- B. Background and Review of the Literature (as needed)
- C. Need
- D. Benefits
- E. Qualifications of Personnel
- F. Data Sources
- G. Limitations and Contingencies
- H. Scope

II. Plan
- A. Objectives and Methods
- B. Timetable
- C. Materials and Equipment
- D. Personnel
- E. Available Facilities
- F. Needed Facilities
- G. Cost and Budget
- H. Expected Results
- I. Feasibility

III. Conclusion
- A. Summary of Key Points
- B. Request for Action

IV. Works Cited

These components can be rearranged, combined, divided, or deleted as needed. Not every proposal will contain all components; however, each major section must persuasively address specific information needs as illustrated in the sample proposal that begins on page 571.

Introduction

From the beginning, your goal is *to sell your idea*—to demonstrate the need for the project, your qualifications for tackling the project, and your clear understanding of what needs to be done and how to proceed. Readers quickly lose interest in a wordy, evasive, or vague introduction.

Following is the introduction for a planning proposal titled "Proposal for Solving the Noise Problem in the University Library." Jill Sanders, a library work-study student, addresses her proposal to the chief librarian and the administrative staff. Because this proposal is unsolicited, it must first make the problem vivid through details that arouse concern and interest. This introduction is longer than it would be in a solicited proposal, whose audience would already agree on the severity of the problem.

NOTE *Title page, informative abstract, table of contents, and other front-matter and end-matter supplements that ordinarily accompany long proposals of this type are omitted here to save space. See Chapter 22 for discussion and examples of each type of supplement. Also see Figure 22.4 (page 538–49).*

INTRODUCTION

Statement of Problem

During the October 20XX Convocation at Margate University, students and faculty members complained about noise in the library. Soon afterward, areas were designated for "quiet study," but complaints about noise continue. To create a scholarly atmosphere, the library should take immediate action to decrease noise.

Concise descriptions of problem and objective immediately alert the readers

Objective

This proposal examines the noise problem from the viewpoint of students, faculty, and library staff. It then offers a plan to make areas of the library quiet enough for serious study and research.

Sources

My data come from a university-wide questionnaire; interviews with students, faculty, and library staff; inquiry letters to other college libraries; and my own observations for three years on the library staff.

This section comes early because it is referred to in the next section

Details of the Problem

This subsection examines the severity and causes of the noise.

Details help readers understand the problem

Severity. Since the 20XX Convocation, the library's fourth and fifth floors have been reserved for quiet study, but students hold group study sessions at the large tables and disturb others working alone. The constant use of computer terminals on both floors adds to the noise, especially when students converse. Moreover, people often chat as they enter or leave study areas.

On the second and third floors, designed for reference, staff help patrons locate materials, causing constant shuffling of people and books, as well as loud conversation. At the computer service desk on the third floor, conferences between students and instructors create more noise.

The most frequently voiced complaint from the faculty members interviewed was about the second floor, where people using the Reference and Government Documents services converse loudly. Students complain about the lack of a quiet spot to study, especially in the evening, when even the "quiet" floors are as noisy as the dorms.

Shows how campus feels about problem

Shows concern is widespread and pervasive

More than 80 percent of respondents (530 undergraduates, 30 faculty, 22 graduate students) to a university-wide questionnaire (Appendix A) insisted that excessive noise discourages them from using the library as often as they would prefer. Of the student respondents, 430 cited quiet study as their primary reason for wishing to use the library.

The library staff recognizes the problem but has insufficient personnel. Because all staff members have assigned tasks, they have no time to monitor noise in their sections.

Causes. Respondents complained specifically about these causes of noise (in descending order of frequency):

Identifies specific causes

1. Loud study groups that often lapse into social discussions.
2. General disrespect for the library, with some students' attitudes characterized as "rude," "inconsiderate," or "immature."
3. The constant clicking of typing at computer terminals on all five floors, and of laptops on the first three.
4. Vacuuming by the evening custodians.

All complaints converged on lack of enforcement by library staff. Because the day staff works on the first three floors, quiet-study rules are not enforced on the fourth and fifth floors. Work-study students on these floors have no authority to enforce rules not enforced by the regular staff. Small, black-and-white "Quiet Please" signs posted on all floors go unnoticed, and the evening security guard provides no deterrent.

Needs

This statement of need evolves logically and persuasively from earlier evidence

Excessive noise in the library is keeping patrons away. By addressing this problem immediately, we can help restore the library's credibility and utility as a campus resource. We must reduce noise on the lower floors and eliminate it from the quiet-study floors.

Scope

Previews the plan

The proposed plan includes a detailed assessment of methods, costs and materials, personnel requirements, feasibility, and expected results.

Body

The body (or plan section) of your proposal will receive the most audience attention. The main goal of this section is to prove your plan will work. Here you spell out your plan in enough detail for the audience to evaluate its soundness. If this section is vague, your proposal stands no chance of being accepted. Be sure that your plan is realistic and promises no more than you can deliver.

PROPOSED PLAN

This plan takes into account the needs and wishes of our campus community, as well as the available facilities in our library.

Phases of the Plan

Noise in the library can be reduced in three complementary phases: (1) improving publicity, (2) shutting down and modifying our facilities, and (3) enforcing the quiet rules.

Tells how plan will be implemented

Improving Publicity. First, the library must publicize the noise problem. This assertive move will demonstrate the staff's interest. Publicity could include articles by staff members in the campus newspaper, leaflets distributed on campus, and a freshman library orientation acknowledging the noise problem and asking for cooperation from new students. All forms of publicity should detail the steps being taken by the library to solve the problem.

Describes first phase

Shutting Down and Modifying Facilities. After notifying campus and local newspapers, you should close the library for one week. To minimize disruption, the shutdown should occur between the end of summer school and the beginning of the fall term.

Describes second phase

During this period, you can convert the fixed tables on the fourth and fifth floors to cubicles with temporary partitions (six cubicles per table). You could later convert the cubicles to shelves as the need increases.

Then you can take all unfixed tables from the upper floors to the first floor, and set up a space for group study. Plans are already under way for removing the computer terminals from the fourth and fifth floors.

Enforcing the Quiet Rules. Enforcement is the essential long-term element in this plan. No one of any age is likely to follow all the rules all the time—unless the rules are enforced.

Describes third phase

First, you can make new "Quiet" posters to replace the present, innocuous notices. A visual-design student can be hired to draw up large, colorful posters that attract attention. Either the design student or the university print shop can take charge of poster production.

Next, through publicity, library patrons can be encouraged to demand quiet from noisy people. To support such patron demands, the library staff can begin monitoring the fourth and fifth floors, asking study groups to move to the first floor, and revoking library privileges of those who refuse. Patrons on the second and third floors can be asked to speak in whispers. Staff members should set an example by regulating their own voices.

Estimates costs and materials needed

Costs and Materials

- The major cost would be for salaries of new staff members who would help monitor. Next year's library budget, however, will include an allocation for four new staff members.
- A design student has offered to make up four different posters for $200. The university printing office can reproduce as many posters as needed at no additional cost.
- Prefabricated cubicles for 26 tables sell for $150 apiece, for a total cost of $3,900.
- Rearrangement on various floors can be handled by the library's custodians.

The Student Fee Allocations Committee and the Student Senate routinely reserve funds for improving student facilities. A request to these organizations would presumably yield at least partial funding for the plan.

Describes personnel needed

Personnel

The success of this plan ultimately depends on the willingness of the library administration to implement it. You can run the program itself by committees made up of students, staff, and faculty. This is yet another area where publicity is essential to persuade people that the problem is severe and that you need their help. To recruit committee members from among students, you can offer Contract Learning credits.

The proposed committees include an Antinoise Committee overseeing the program, a Public Relations Committee, a Poster Committee, and an Enforcement Committee.

Assesses probability of success

Feasibility

On March 15, 20XX, I mailed survey letters to twenty-five New England colleges, inquiring about their methods for coping with noise in the library. Among the respondents, sixteen stated that publicity and the administration's attitude toward enforcement were main elements in their success.

Improved publicity and enforcement could work for us as well. And slight modifications in our facilities, to concentrate group study on the busiest floors, would automatically lighten the burden of enforcement.

Offers a realistic and persuasive forecast of benefits

Benefits

Publicity will improve communication between the library and the campus. An assertive approach will show that the library is aware of its patrons' needs and is willing to meet those needs. Offering the program for public inspection will draw the entire community into improvement efforts. Publicity, begun now, will pave the way for the formation of committees.

The library shutdown will have a dual effect: It will dramatize the problem to the community, and it will provide time for the physical changes. (An antinoise program begun with carpentry noise in the quiet areas would hardly be effective.) The shutdown will be both a symbolic and a concrete measure, leading to reopening of the library with a new philosophy and a new image.

Continued strict enforcement will be the backbone of the program. It will prove that staff members care enough about the atmosphere to jeopardize their friendly image in the eyes of some users, and that the library is not afraid to enforce its rules.

Conclusion

The conclusion reaffirms the need for the project and induces the audience to act. End on a strong note, with a conclusion that is assertive, confident, and encouraging—and keep it short.

CONCLUSION AND RECOMMENDATION

The noise in Margate University Library has become embarrassing and annoying to the whole campus. Forceful steps are needed to restore the academic atmosphere.

Aside from the intangible question of image, close inspection of the proposed plan will show that it will work if the recommended steps are taken and—most important—if daily enforcement of quiet rules becomes a part of library policy.

Reemphasizes need and feasibility and encourages action

In long, formal proposals, especially those beginning with a comprehensive abstract, the conclusion can be omitted.

GUIDELINES for Proposals

- **Understand the audience's needs.** Demonstrate a clear understanding of the audience's problem, and then offer an appropriate solution.
- **Perform research as needed.** For example, you might research the very latest technology for solving a problem; compare the costs, benefits, and drawbacks of various approaches; contact others in your field for their suggestions; or find out what competitors are up to.
- **Credit all information sources and contributors.** If anything in your proposal represents the work or input of others, document the sources.
- **Use an appropriate format.** For an informal proposal distributed internally, use email or memo format. For an informal proposal distributed externally, use letter format. For a formal proposal, include all the required front matter and end matter.
- **Provide a clear title or subject line and background information.** Tell readers what to expect, and orient them with the appropriate background information.
- **Spell out the problem (and its causes).** Answer the implied question, "Why is this such a big deal?"
- **Point out the benefits of solving the problem.** Answer the implied question, "Why should we spend time, money, and effort to do this?"
- **Offer a realistic solution.** Stick to claims or assertions you can support. Answer the implied question, "How do we know this will work?" If the solution involves accounting for costs, budgeting time, or proving your qualifications, include this information.

▶▶

GUIDELINES *continued*

- **Address anticipated objections to your plan.** Decision makers typically approach a proposal with skepticism, especially if the project will cost them money and time. Answer the implied question, "Why should we accept the items that seem costly with your plan?"
- **Include all necessary details, but don't overload.** Include as much supporting detail as you need to induce readers to say yes. Leave nothing to guesswork. At the same time, don't overload readers with irrelevant information.
- **Write clearly and concisely.** Use action verbs and plain English. Avoid terms that are too technical for your audience. If necessary for a mixed audience with differing technical levels, include a glossary.
- **Express confidence.** You are trying to sell yourself, your ideas, or your services to a skeptical audience. Offer the supporting facts ("For the third year in a row, our firm has been ranked as the number 1 architecture firm in the Midwest") and state your case directly ("We know you will be satisfied with the results").
- **Make honest and supportable claims.** If the solutions you offer have limitations, make sure you say so.
- **Induce readers to act.** Decide exactly what you want readers to do, and give reasons why they should be the ones to act. In your conclusion, answer the implied question, "What action am I supposed to take?"

A SITUATION REQUIRING A FORMAL PROPOSAL

The proposal that follows is essentially a grant proposal, since it requests funding for a nonprofit enterprise. Notice how it adapts elements from the sample outline (page 570). As in any funding proposal, a precise, realistic plan and an itemized budget provide the justification for the requested financial support.

A Formal Proposal

The Situation. Southeastern Massachusetts University's newspaper, the SMU *Torch*, is struggling to meet rising production costs. The paper's yearly budget is funded by the Student Fee Allocation Committee, which disburses money to various campus organizations. Drastic budget cuts have resulted in reduced funding for all state schools. As a result, the newspaper has received no funding increase for the last three years. Meanwhile, production costs keep rising.

Bill Trippe, the *Torch*'s business manager, has to justify a requested increase of 17.3 percent for the coming year's budget. Before drafting his proposal (Figure 23.4), Bill constructs an audience and use profile (based on the worksheet, page 58).

Audience and Use Profile. The primary audience includes all members of the Student Fee Allocation Committee. The secondary audience is the newspaper staff, who will implement the proposed plan—if it is approved by the committee.

The primary audience will use this document as perhaps the sole basis for deciding whether to grant the additional funds. Most of these readers have overseen the newspaper budget for years, and so they already know quite a bit about the newspaper's overall operation. But they still need an item-by-item explanation of the conditions created by problems with funding and ever-increasing costs. Probable questions Bill can anticipate:

- Why should the paper receive priority over other campus organizations?
- Just how crucial is the problem?
- Are present funds being used efficiently?
- Can any expenses be reduced?
- How would additional funds be spent?
- How much will this increase cost?
- Will the benefits justify the cost?

The primary audience often has expressed interest in this topic. But they are likely to object to any request for more money by arguing that everyone has to economize in these difficult times. Thus their attitude could be characterized as both receptive and hesitant. (Almost every campus organization is trying to make a case for additional funds.)

Bill knows most of the committee members pretty well, and he senses that they respect his management skills. But he still needs to spell out the problem and propose a realistic plan, showing that the newspaper staff is sincere in its intention to eliminate nonessential operating costs. At a time when everyone is expected to make do with less, this proposal needs to make an especially strong case for salary increases (to attract talented personnel).

The primary audience has solicited this proposal, and so it is likely to be carefully read—but also scrutinized and evaluated for its soundness. Especially in a budget request, this audience expects no shortcuts: Every expense will have to be itemized, and the Costs section should be the longest part of the proposal.

To further justify the budget request, the proposal needs to demonstrate just how well the newspaper manages its present funds. In the Feasibility section, Bill provides a detailed comparison of funding, expenditures, and the size of the *Torch* in relation to the size of the newspapers of the four other local colleges. These are the facts most likely to persuade readers that the plan is cost-effective.

To organize his document, Bill (1) identifies the problem, (2) establishes the need, (3) proposes a solution, (4) shows that the plan is cost-effective, and (5) concludes with a request for action.

This audience expects a confident and businesslike—but not stuffy—tone.

SMU *Torch*

Old Westport Road
North Dartmouth, Massachusetts 02747

May 1, 20XX

Charles Marcus, Chair
Student Fee Allocation Committee
Southeastern Massachusetts University
North Dartmouth, MA 02747

Dear Dean Marcus:

Letter of transmittal provides additional context and persuasion

No one needs to be reminded about the effects of increased costs on our campus community. We are all faced with having to make do with less.

Accordingly, we at the *Torch* have spent long hours devising a plan to cope with increased production costs—without compromising the newspaper's tradition of quality service. I think you and your colleagues will agree that our plan is realistic and feasible. Even the "bare-bones" operation that will result from our proposed spending cuts, however, will call for a $6,478.57 increase in next year's budget.

We have received no funding increase in three years. Our present need is absolute. Without additional funds, the *Torch* simply cannot continue to function as a professional newspaper. I therefore submit the following budget proposal for your consideration.

Respectfully,

William Trippe

William Trippe
Business Manager, SMU *Torch*

FIGURE 23.4 **A Formal Proposal**

A Funding Proposal
for
The SMU *Torch*
(20XX–XX)

Provides a clear title

Prepared for
The Student Fee Allocation Committee
Southeastern Massachusetts University
North Dartmouth, Massachusetts

by
William Trippe
Torch Business Manager

Writer, affiliation, and date always appear on the title page

May 1, 20XX

FIGURE 23.4 *(Continued)*

Table of contents orients readers and demonstrates proposal's structure

ii

TABLE OF CONTENTS

FIGURE 23.4 *(Continued)*

INFORMATIVE ABSTRACT

The SMU *Torch*, the student newspaper at Southeastern Massachusetts University, is crippled by inadequate funding, having received no budget increase in three years. Increased costs and inadequate funding are the major problems facing the *Torch*. Increases in costs of technology upgrades and in printing have called for cutbacks in production. Moreover, our low staff salaries are inadequate to attract and retain qualified personnel. A nominal pay increase would make salaries more competitive.

Our staff plans to cut costs by reducing page count and by hiring a new press for the *Torch*'s printing work. The only proposed cost increase (for staff salaries) is essential.

A detailed breakdown of projected costs establishes the need for a $6,478.57 budget increase to keep the paper a weekly publication with adequate page count to serve our campus.

Compared with similar newspapers at other colleges, the *Torch* makes much better use of its money. The comparison figures in the Appendix illustrate the cost-effectiveness of our proposal.

Abstract accurately encapsulates entire document

FIGURE 23.4 *(Continued)*

INTRODUCTION

Overview

Opens with an overview of the situation

Our campus newspaper faces the contradictory challenge of surviving ever-growing production costs while maintaining its reputation for quality. The following proposal addresses that crisis. This plan's ultimate success, however, depends on the Allocation Committee's willingness to approve a long-overdue increase in the *Torch*'s upcoming yearly budget.

Background

Provides relevant background

In ten years, the *Torch* has grown in size, scope, and quality. Roughly 6,000 copies (24 pages/issue) are printed weekly for each fourteen-week semester. Each week, the *Torch* prints national and local press releases, features, editorials, sports articles, announcements, notices, classified ads, a calendar column, and letters to the editor. A vital part of university life, our newspaper provides a forum for information, ideas, and opinions—all with the highest professionalism. This year we published a Web-based version as well.

Statement of Problem

Describes the problem concisely

With much of its staff about to graduate, the *Torch* faces next year with rising costs in every phase of production, and the need to replace outdated and worn equipment.

Our newspaper also suffers from a lack of student involvement: Despite gaining valuable experience and potential career credentials, few students can be expected to work without some kind of remuneration. Most staff members do receive nominal weekly salaries: from $20 for the distributor to $90 for the Editor-in-Chief. But salaries averaging barely $5 per hour cannot possibly compete with the minimum wage. Since more and more SMU students must work part-time, the *Torch* will have to make its salaries more competitive.

The newspaper's operating expenses can be divided into four categories: hardware and software upgrades, salaries, printing costs, and miscellaneous (office supplies, mail, and so on). The first three categories account for nearly 90 percent of the budget. Over the past year, costs in all categories have increased: from as little as 2 percent for miscellaneous expenses to as much as 19 percent for technology upgrades. Printing costs (roughly one-third of our total budget) rose 9 percent in the past year, and another price hike of 10 percent has just been announced.

FIGURE 23.4 *(Continued)*

Funding Proposal 2

Need

Despite growing production costs, the *Torch* has received no increase in its yearly budget allocation ($37,400) in three years. Inadequate funding is virtually crippling our newspaper.

Proposes a logical solution to the problem, based on evidence

Scope

The following plan includes

1. Methods for reducing production costs while maintaining the quality of our staff
2. Projected costs for technology upgrades, salaries, and services during the upcoming year
3. A demonstration of feasibility, showing our cost-effectiveness
4. A summary of attitudes shared by our personnel

Previews the plan before getting into details

PROPOSED PLAN

This plan is designed to trim operating costs without compromising quality.

Methods

We can overcome our budget and staffing crisis by taking these steps:

Itemizes realistic ways to save money and retain staff

Reducing Page Count. By condensing free notices for campus organizations, abolishing "personal" notices, and limiting press releases to one page, we can reduce page count per issue from 24 to 20, saving nearly 17 percent in production costs. (Items deleted from hard copy could be linked as add-ons in the *Torch*'s Web-based version.)

Reducing Hard-Copy Circulation. Reducing circulation from 6,000 to 5,000 copies barely will cover the number of full-time students, but will save 17 percent in printing costs. The steadily increasing hits on our Web site suggest that more and more readers are using the electronic medium. (We are designing a fall survey to help determine how many readers rely on the Web-based version.)

Hiring a New Press. We can save money by hiring Arrow Press for printing. Other presses (including our present printer) bid at least 25 percent higher than Arrow. With its state-of-the art production equipment, Arrow will import our "camera-ready" digital files to produce the hard-copy version. Moreover, no other company offers the rapid turnover time (from submission to finished product) that Arrow promises.

FIGURE 23.4 *(Continued)*

Upgrading Our Desktop Publishing Technology. To meet Arrow's specifications for submitting digital files, we must upgrade our equipment. Upgrade costs will be largely offset the first year by reduced printing costs. Also, this technology will increase efficiency and reduce labor costs, resulting in substantial payback on investment.

Increasing Staff Salaries. Although we seek talented students who expect little money and much experience, salaries for all positions must increase by an average of 25 percent. Otherwise, any of our staff could earn as much money elsewhere by working only a little more than half the time. In fact, many students could exceed the minimum wage by working for local newspapers. To illustrate: The *Standard Beacon* pays $60 to $90 per news article and $30 per photo; the *Torch* pays nothing for articles and $6 per photo.

A striking example of low salaries is the $4.75 per hour we pay our desktop publishing staff. Our present desktop publishing cost of $3,038 could be as much as $7,000 or even higher if we had this service done by an outside firm, as many colleges do. Without this nominal salary increase, we cannot possibly attract qualified personnel.

Costs

Our proposed budget is itemized in Table 1, but the main point is clear: If the *Torch* is to remain viable, increased funding is essential for meeting our projected costs.

Table 1 Projected Costs and Requested Funding for Next Year's *Torch* Budget

Provides detailed breakdown of costs—the central issue in the situation

PROJECTED COSTS	
Hardware/Software Upgrades	
Apple iMac w/ 4 GB RAM, 500 GB HD (3.06GHz processor)	$1,162.00
HP Pavilion 2709m 27" (second monitor)	355.00
Seagate 500 GB external hard drive (for backups)	128.99
Olympus Stylus 9000 digital camera	299.98
HP Scanjet 5000 sheet-feed scanner	799.00
Microsoft Office 2013 Professional Upgrade	499.00
Adobe Creative Suite 5 Master Collection	2,450.00
Subtotal	**$5,693.97**

FIGURE 23.4 *(Continued)*

Funding Proposal 4

Wages and Salaries	
Desktop-publishing staff (35 hr/wk at $6.00/hr x 28 wk)	$5,880.00
Editor-in-Chief	3,150.00
News Editor	1,890.00
Features Editor	1,890.00
Advertising Manager	2,350.00
Advertising Designer	1,575.00
Webmaster	2,520.00
Layout Editor	1,890.00
Art Director	1,260.00
Photo Editor	1,890.00
Business Manager	1,890.00
Distributor	560.00
Subtotal	**$26,745.00**

Miscellaneous Costs	
Graphics by SMU art students (3/wk @ $10 each)	$ 840.00
Mailing	1,100.00
Telephone	1,000.00
Campus print shop services	400.00
Copier fees	100.00
Subtotal	**$3,440.00**

Fixed Printing Costs (5,000 copies/wk x 28/wk)	**$24,799.60**
TOTAL YEARLY COSTS	**$60,678.57**
Expected Advertising Revenue ($600/wk x 28 wks)	**($16,800.00)**
Total Costs Minus Advertising Revenue	**$45,109.39**
TOTAL FUNDING REQUEST	**$43,878.57**

FIGURE 23.4 *(Continued)*

Funding Proposal 5

Assesses probability of success

Feasibility

Beyond exhibiting our need, we feel that the feasibility of this proposal can be measured through an objective evaluation of our cost-effectiveness: Compared with newspapers at similar schools, how well does the *Torch* use its funding?

In a survey of the four area college newspapers, we found that the *Torch*—by a sometimes huge margin—makes the best use of its money per page. Table 1A in the Appendix shows that, of the five newspapers, the *Torch* costs students the least, runs the most pages weekly, and spends the least money per page, *despite a circulation two to three times the size of the other papers.*

The *Torch* has the lowest yearly cost of all five newspapers, despite having the largest circulation. With the requested budget increase, the cost would rise by only $0.88, for a yearly cost of $9.00 to each student. Although Alden College's newspaper costs each student $8.58, it is published only every third week, averages 12 pages per issue, and costs more than $71.00 yearly per page to print—in contrast to our yearly printing cost of $55.65 per page. As the figures in the Appendix demonstrate, our cost management is responsible and effective.

Addresses important issue of personnel

Personnel

The *Torch* staff is determined to maintain the highest professionalism. Many are planning careers in journalism, writing, editing, advertising, photography, Web design, or public relations. In any *Torch* issue, the balanced, enlightened coverage is evidence of our judicious selection and treatment of articles and our shared concern for quality.

CONCLUSION

Reemphasizes need and encourages action

As a broad forum for ideas and opinions, the *Torch* continues to reflect a seriousness of purpose and a commitment to free and responsible expression. Its role in campus life is more vital than ever during these troubled times.

Every year, allocations to student organizations increase or decrease based on need. Last year, for example, eight allocations increased by an average of $4,332. The *Torch* has received no increase in three years.

Presumably, increases are prompted by special circumstances. For the *Torch*, these circumstances derive from increasing production costs and the need to update vital equipment. We respectfully urge the Committee to respond to the *Torch*'s legitimate needs by increasing next year's allocation to $43,878.57.

FIGURE 23.4 *(Continued)*

APPENDIX (Comparative Performance)

Table 1A Allocations and Performance of Five Local College Newspapers

	Stonehorse College	Alden College	Simms University	Fallow State	SMU
Enrollment	1,600	1,400	3,000	3,000	5,000
Fee paid (per year)	$65.00	$85.00	$35.00	$50.00	$65.00
Total fee budget	$104,000	$119,000	$105,000	$150,000	$325,000
Newspaper budget	$18,300	$8,580	$36,179	$52,910	$37,392 $45,109[a]
Yearly cost per student	$12.50	$8.58	$16.86	$24.66	$8.12 $9.00[a]
Publication rate	Weekly	Every third week	Weekly	Weekly	Weekly
Average no. of pages	8	12	18	12	24
Average total pages	224	120	504	336	672 560[a]
Yearly cost per page	$81.60	$71.50	$71.78	$157.47	$55.65 $67.12[a]

[a]These figures are next year's costs for the SMU *Torch*.

Source: Figures were quoted by newspaper business managers in April 20XX.

Appendix provides detailed breakdown of cost comparisons

FIGURE 23.4 *(Continued)*

CHECKLIST: Proposals

(Numbers in parentheses refer to the first page of discussion.)

Content

- ☐ Are all required proposal elements included? (563)
- ☐ Does the title or subject line provide a clear forecast? (563)
- ☐ Is the background section appropriate for this audience's needs? (565)
- ☐ Is the problem clearly identified? (565)
- ☐ Is the objective clearly identified? (565)
- ☐ Does the proposal demonstrate a clear understanding of the client's problems and expectations? (565)
- ☐ Is the proposed solution, service, or product stated clearly? (565)
- ☐ Are the claims honest and supportable? (566)
- ☐ Does the proposal maintain a clear focus on benefits? (565)
- ☐ Does it address anticipated objections? (556)
- ☐ Are the proposed solutions feasible and realistic? (566)
- ☐ Are all foreseeable limitations and contingencies identified? (566)
- ☐ Is every *relevant* detail spelled out? (567)
- ☐ Is the cost and budget section accurate and easy to understand? (567)
- ☐ Are visuals used effectively? (568)
- ☐ Is each source and contribution properly cited? (569)
- ☐ Is the proposal ethically acceptable? (566)

Arrangement

- ☐ Does the introduction spell out the problem and preview the plan? (570)
- ☐ Does the body section explain *how, where, when,* and *how much*? (572)
- ☐ Does the conclusion encourage acceptance of the proposal? (575)
- ☐ Is the informal proposal cast as a memo or letter, as appropriate? (575)
- ☐ Does the formal proposal have adequate front matter and end matter supplements to serve the needs of different readers? (569)

Style and Page Design

- ☐ Is the level of technicality appropriate for primary readers? (20)
- ☐ Does the tone encourage acceptance of the proposal? (568)
- ☐ Is the writing clear, concise, and fluent? (567)
- ☐ Is the language precise? (567)
- ☐ Is the proposal grammatical? (682)
- ☐ Is the page design inviting and accessible? (568)

Projects

GENERAL

1. After identifying your primary and secondary audience, write a short planning proposal for improving an unsatisfactory situation in the classroom, on the job, or in your dorm or apartment (e.g., poor lighting, drab atmosphere, health hazards, poor seating arrangements). Choose a problem or situation whose solution or resolution is more a matter of common sense and lucid observation than of intensive research. Be sure to (a) identify the problem clearly, give a brief background, and stimulate interest; (b) clearly state the methods proposed to solve the problem; and (c) conclude with a statement designed to gain audience support.
2. Write a research proposal to your instructor (or an interested third party) requesting approval for your final term project (a formal analytical report or formal proposal). Verify that adequate primary and secondary sources are available. Convince your audience of the soundness and usefulness of the project.
3. As an alternate term project to the formal analytical report (Chapter 22), develop a long proposal for solving a problem, improving a situation, or satisfying a need in your school, community, or job. Choose a subject sufficiently complex to justify a formal proposal, a topic requiring research (mostly primary). Identify an audience (other than your instructor) who will use your proposal for a specific purpose. Complete an audience and use profile.

TEAM

Working in groups of four, develop an unsolicited planning proposal for solving a problem, improving a situation, or satisfying a need in your school, community, or workplace. Begin by brainstorming as a group to come up with a list of possible issues or problems to address in your proposal. Narrow your list, and work as a group to focus on a specific issue or idea. Your proposal should address a clearly identified audience of decision makers and stakeholders in the given issue. Complete an audience and use profile.

DIGITAL AND SOCIAL MEDIA

As noted earlier, solicited proposals are usually written in response to a formal "request for proposal" (RFP). Most RFPs are available on the Web. For instance, the National Science Foundation's site at <www.nsf.gov/funding/> provides links for all sorts of research funding opportunities. There is a link for undergraduate students, for graduate students, for K–12 educators, and for many program areas such as engineering, geosciences, and so on. Go to this site and click on a link that interests you and locate the RFP. Write a memo to your instructor explaining why you are interested in this research and what focus your proposal would take. For instance, you might have a good idea for a proposal in response to the Research Experiences for Undergraduates (REU) RFP. What topic would you choose and how would you make your best case?

GLOBAL

Compare the sorts of proposals regularly done in the United States with those created in other countries. For example, is the format the same? Are there more proposals for certain purposes in the United States than in another country? You can learn about this topic by interviewing an expert in international business (someone you meet on the job, during an internship, or through your adviser). You can also search the Web for information on international technical communication. Describe your findings in a short memo that you will share with your classmates.

24 Oral Presentations and Webinars

"In any particular week, I give at least 2–3 presentations. Sometimes these are brief and informal, designed to provide my team an update on our project's status. Other times, the presentation needs to be quite detailed and formal—for instance, when I present to my manager and other division heads. Since it's never clear who will be attending in person and who will be connecting via video conference or Webinar, I always make sure that my visuals are easy to understand and not too cluttered. Regardless of the technology, my primary goal is to make sure that I'm providing just the right amount of information for my audience and focusing on content that they need to know about."

—Nick Hillman
Industrial engineer for a medical device company

LEARNING OBJECTIVES FOR THIS CHAPTER

- Analyze your audience and purpose
- Select the type of presentation you want to make
- Choose the appropriate technology
- Perform research, write an outline, prepare visuals
- Create audience-friendly slides using presentation software
- Deliver your presentation
- Understand how and when to use Webinars or slide sharing tools

Workplace professionals need to present ideas effectively in person. Oral presentations vary in style, complexity, and formality. They may include convention speeches, reports at national meetings, technical briefings for colleagues, and speeches to community groups. These talks may be designed to *inform* (e.g., to describe new government safety requirements); to *instruct* (e.g., to show volunteers how to safely clean up an oil spill); to *persuade* (e.g., to induce company officers to vote for a pay raise); or to achieve all three of the above. The higher your status, on the job or in the community, the more you can expect to give oral presentations.

ADVANTAGES AND DRAWBACKS OF ORAL PRESENTATIONS

Advantages

Unlike written documents, oral presentations are truly interactive. In face-to-face communication, you can use body language (vocal tone, eye contact, and gestures) to establish credibility and rapport with your audience. A likable personality can have a powerful effect on audience receptiveness. Also, oral presentations provide for give-and-take, which does not happen with traditional written documents. As you see how your audience reacts, you can adjust your presentation as you go, and audiences can get questions answered immediately.

Drawbacks

In a written report you generally have plenty of time to think about what you're saying and how you're saying it, and to revise until the message is just right. For an oral report, one attempt is basically all you get, and the pressure makes it easier to stumble. (People consistently rank fear of public speaking higher than fear of dying!) Also, an oral report is limited in the amount and complexity of information it can present. Readers of a written report can follow at their own pace and direction, going back and forth, perhaps skimming some sections and studying others. In an oral presentation, you establish the pace and the information flow, thereby creating the risk of "losing" or boring the listeners.

AVOIDING PRESENTATION PITFALLS

An oral presentation is only the tip of a pyramid built from many earlier labors. But such presentations often serve as the concrete measure of your overall job performance. In short, your audience's only basis for judgment may be the brief moments during which you stand before them.

The podium or lectern can be a lonely and intimidating place. In the words of two experts, "most persons in most presentational settings do not perform well" (Goodall and Waagen 14–15). Despite the fact that they can help make or break a person's career, oral presentations often turn out to be boring, confusing, unconvincing, or too long. Many are delivered ineptly, with the presenter losing her or his place, fumbling through notes, apologizing for forgetting something, or reading word-for-word the bullet points on the screen. Table 24.1 lists some of the things that go wrong. Avoid such difficulties through careful analysis, planning, and preparation.

Speaker • • •	Visuals * * *	Setting ▪ ▪ ▪
• makes no eye contact	* are nonexistent	▪ is too noisy
• seems like a robot	* are hard to see	▪ is too hot or cold
• hides behind the lectern	* are hard to interpret	▪ is too large or small
• speaks too softly/loudly	* are out of sequence	▪ is too bright for visuals
• sways, fidgets, paces	* are shown too rapidly	▪ is too dark for notes
• rambles or loses her/his place	* are shown too slowly	▪ has equipment missing
• never gets to the point	* have typos/errors	▪ has broken equipment
• fumbles with notes or visuals	* are word-filled	
• has too much material		

TABLE 24.1 Common Pitfalls in Oral Presentations

PLANNING YOUR PRESENTATION

Analyze Your Audience and Purpose

Analyzing audience and purpose is a slightly different proposition when speaking rather than writing. Therefore, use the Audience and Purpose Profile Sheet in Figure 24.1.

Audience considerations

Do all you can to find out exactly who will be attending your presentation. Determine their roles within the organization. Learn about their attitudes and experiences regarding your subject. For example, managers may focus on the bottom

AUDIENCE

Primary audience members:______________________________
(names, titles)

Secondary audience members:__________________________

____

Are most attendees of this presentation members of the same team or group?
Y N

Relationship with audience members:______________________
(client, employer, other)

Technical background of audience:________________________
(layperson, expert, other)

Cultural background of audience:_________________________

How many people will attend? 2–6 7–12 12–20 more than 20

PURPOSE

Primary purpose:__________________(to inform or instruct; to persuade; to propose an action; to sell something)

Secondary purpose(s):__________________________________

ROOM or LOCATION for presentation

Conference table:______________________________________

Theater style:____

TECHNOLOGY REQUIRED

PowerPoint or other presentation software

Overhead projector

Flip chart

Whiteboard or chalkboard

FIGURE 24.1 Audience and Purpose Profile Sheet for an Oral Presentation

line, while engineers may care more about the difficulties involved in the project you are proposing. Oral presentations are often delivered to a mixed group, so consider the attitudes of the group as a whole and speak to the needs of various factions. The group is also likely to consist of people from various cultural and linguistic backgrounds, so be sure to account for these differences.

Formulate on paper an audience and purpose statement. Who are your listeners? What do you want listeners to think, know, or do? (This statement can also serve as the introduction to your presentation.)

Assume, for example, that you represent an environmental engineering firm that has completed a study of groundwater quality in your area. The organization that sponsored your study has asked you to present an oral version of your written report, titled "Pollution Threats to Local Groundwater," at a town meeting.

After careful thought, you settle on this statement:

Audience and purpose statement

> **Audience and Purpose:** By informing Cape Cod residents about the dangers to the Cape's freshwater supply posed by rapid population growth, this report is intended to increase local interest in the problem.

Now you are prepared to focus on the listeners and the speaking situation by asking these questions:

Questions for analyzing your listeners and purpose

- Who are my listeners (strangers, peers, superiors, clients)?
- What is their attitude toward me or the topic (hostile, indifferent, needy, friendly)?
- Why are they here (they want to be here, are forced to be, are curious)?
- What kind of presentation do they expect (brief, informal; long, detailed; lecture)?
- What do these listeners already know (nothing, a little, a lot)?
- What do they need or want to know (overview, bottom line, nitty-gritty)?
- How large is their stake in this topic (about layoffs, new policies, pay raises)?
- Do I want to motivate, mollify, inform, instruct, or warn my listeners?
- What are their biggest concerns or objections about this topic?
- What do I want them to think, know, or do?

Analyze Your Speaking Situation

The more you can discover about the circumstances, the setting, and the constraints for your presentation, the more deliberately you will be able to prepare.

Ask yourself these questions:

Questions for analyzing your speaking situation

- How much time will I have to speak?
- Will other people be speaking before or after me?

- How formal or informal is the setting?
- How large is the audience?
- How large is the room?
- How bright and adjustable is the lighting?
- What equipment is available?
- How much time do I have to prepare?

Later parts of this chapter explain how to incorporate your answers to the above questions in your preparation.

Select a Type of Presentation

Your primary purpose determines the type of presentation required: informative presentation, training/instructional presentation, persuasive presentation, action plan presentation, or sales presentation.

Types of oral presentations

Informative Presentations. Informative presentations are often given at conferences, product update meetings, briefings, or class lectures. Your goal is to be as impartial as possible and to provide the best information you can If your primary purpose is informative, observe these criteria:

Informative presentations provide facts and explanations

- Keep the presentation title clear and factual.
- Stipulate at the outset that your purpose is simply to provide information.
- Be clear about the sources of information that you present or draw upon.

Training/Instructional Presentations. Training (or instructional) presentations can cover such topics as how to ensure on-the-job safety, how to use a specific software application, or how to exit a capsized kayak. Some technical communicators specialize in giving training presentations. If your primary purpose is instructional, observe these criteria:

Training/instructional presentations show how to perform a task

- Use a title that indicates the training purpose of the presentation.
- Provide an overview of the learning outcomes—what participants can expect to learn from the presentation.
- Create slides or a handout that participants can reference later, when they are trying to perform the task(s) on their own.

Persuasive Presentations. To influence people's thinking, give a persuasive presentation. For example, an engineer at a nuclear power plant may wish to persuade her peers that a standard procedure is unsafe and should be changed. In a

Persuasive presentations attempt to gain support or change an opinion

persuasive situation, you need to perform adequate research so that you are well informed on all sides of the issue. If your primary purpose is persuasive, observe these criteria:

- Be clear from the start that you are promoting a point of view.
- Use research and visual data (charts, graphs, etc.) to support your stance.
- Consider and address counterarguments in advance ("Some might say that this approach won't work, but here is why it will"), and be prepared to take questions that challenge your view.

Action plan presentations motivate people to take action

Action Plan Presentations. To get something done, give an action plan presentation. For example, if you wanted your company to address a design flaw in one of its products, you would give a presentation that outlined the problem, presented a specific solution, and then encouraged audience members to implement the solution. If your primary purpose is to move people to take action, observe these criteria:

- Be clear up front about your purpose ("My primary purpose today is to ask you to act on this matter").
- Present the research to back up the need for your plan.
- Show that you have considered other plans but that yours is the most effective.
- In closing, restate what you want your audience to do.

Sales presentations inform and persuade

Sales Presentations. Technical sales presentations need to be well researched. (At many high-tech companies, technical sales representatives are often scientists or engineers who understand the product's complexities and also are effective communicators.) If your primary purpose is to sell something, observe these criteria:

- Let the facts tell the story. Use examples to help explain why your product or service is the right one.
- Know your product or service—and those of your competitors—inside and out. Thorough knowledge of your own product or service and a well-researched competitive analysis will make your presentation that much more persuasive.
- Display sincere interest in the needs and concerns of your customers.
- Provide plenty of time for questions. You may think you have made an airtight case for your product or service, but you will need extra face-to-face time to field questions and convince skeptical audience members.

Select a Delivery Method

Your presentation's effectiveness will depend largely on *how* the presentation connects with listeners. Different types of delivery create different connections.

The Memorized Delivery. This type of delivery takes a long time to prepare, offers no chance for revision during the presentation, and spells disaster if you lose your place. Avoid a memorized delivery in most workplace settings.

The Impromptu Delivery. An impromptu (off-the-cuff) delivery can be a natural way of connecting with listeners—but only when you really know your material, feel comfortable with your audience, and are in an informal speaking situation (group brainstorming, or responding to a question: "Tell us about your team's progress on the automation project"). Avoid impromptu deliveries for complex information, no matter how well you know the material. If you have minimal warning beforehand, at least jot down a few notes about what you want to say.

The Scripted Delivery. For a complex technical presentation, a conference paper, or a formal speech, you may want to read your material verbatim from a prepared script. Scripted presentations work well if you have many details to present, are talkative, have a strict time limit (e.g., at a conference), or if this audience makes you nervous. Consider a scripted delivery when you want the content, organization, and style of your presentation to be as near perfect as possible.

Although a scripted delivery helps you control your material, it offers little chance for audience interaction and it can be boring.

If you *do* plan to read aloud, allow ample preparation time. Leave plenty of white space between lines and paragraphs. Rehearse until you are able to glance up from the script periodically without losing your place. Plan on roughly two minutes per double-spaced page.

The Extemporaneous Delivery. An extemporaneous delivery is carefully planned, practiced, and based on notes that keep you on track. In this natural way of addressing an audience, you glance at your material and speak in a conversational style. Extemporaneous delivery is based on key ideas in sentence or topic outline form, often projected as overhead transparencies or as slides generated from presentation software such as *Microsoft PowerPoint*.

The dangers in extemporaneous delivery are that you might lose track of your material, forget something important, say something unclearly, or exceed your time limit. Careful preparation is the key.

Table 24.2 summarizes the various uses and drawbacks of the most common types of delivery. In many instances, some combination of methods can be effective. For example, in an orientation for new employees, you might prefer the flexibility

Delivery Method	* Main Uses *	• Main Drawbacks •
IMPROMPTU (inventing as you speak)	* in-house meetings * small, intimate groups * simple topics	• offers no chance to prepare • speaker might ramble • speaker might lose track
SCRIPTED (reading verbatim from a written work)	* formal speeches * large, unfamiliar groups * strict time limit * cross-cultural audiences * highly nervous speaker	• takes a long time to prepare • speaker can't move around • limits human contact • can appear stiff and unnatural • might bore listeners • makes working with visuals difficult
EXTEMPORANEOUS (speaking from an outline of key points)	* face-to-face presentations * medium-sized, familiar groups * moderately complex topics * somewhat flexible time limit * visually based presentations	• speaker might lose track • speaker might leave something out • speaker might get tongue-tied • speaker might exceed time limit • speaker might fumble with notes, visuals, or equipment

TABLE 24.2 A Comparison of Oral Presentation Methods

of an extemporaneous format but also read a brief passage aloud from time to time (e.g., excerpts from the company's formal code of ethics). Most workplace presentations are extemporaneous.

PREPARING YOUR PRESENTATION

To stay in control and build confidence, plan the presentation systematically.

Research Your Topic

Be prepared to support each assertion, opinion, conclusion, and recommendation with evidence and reason. Check your facts for accuracy. Begin gathering material well ahead of time. Use summarizing techniques from Chapter 9. If your presentation is merely a spoken version of a written report, you can simply expand your outline for the written report into a sentence outline.

Aim for Simplicity and Conciseness

Boil the material down to a few main points. A typical attention span is about twenty minutes. Time yourself in practice sessions and trim as needed.

(If your situation requires a lengthy presentation, plan a short break, about halfway.)

Anticipate Audience Questions

Consider those parts of your presentation that listeners might question or challenge. You might need to clarify or justify information that is new, controversial, disappointing, or surprising.

Outline Your Presentation

If your presentation is based on a written report, you can use the outline from the report to help shape the presentation (see also Chapter 10 for more on outlining). For most presentations, follow the introduction-body-conclusion outline format.

Set the stage

Introduction. The introduction should accomplish three things:

1. Capture your audience's attention by telling a quick story, asking a question, or relating your topic to a current event or to something else the audience cares about.
2. Establish credibility by stating your credentials or explaining where you obtained your information.
3. Preview your presentation by listing the main points and the overall conclusion.

Use small chunks and transitions in the body

Body. Readers who get confused or want to know the scope of a print document can look back at the headings, table of contents, or previous pages. But oral presentations offer no such options. To make your presentation easy to follow, structure the material into small chunks. To signal that you are moving from one main point to another, use a transition statement such as, "Now that I've explained how to separate good information from bad, let me suggest how you can contribute to medical discussions on the Internet."

Tie everything together

Conclusion. Your conclusion should return full circle to your introduction. Remind your audience of the big picture, restate the main points you've just covered, and leave listeners with some final advice or tips for locating more information. You can also distribute handouts at this time.

The next page illustrates a complete presentation outline using the introduction, body, conclusion format. Notice how each sentence is a topic sentence for a paragraph that a well-prepared speaker can develop in detail.

Presentation outline

Pollution Threats to Local Groundwater

Arnold Borthwick

Introduction

I. Introduction to the Problem

A. Do you know what you are drinking when you turn on the tap and fill a glass?

B. The quality of our water is good, but not guaranteed to last forever.

C. Cape Cod's rapid population growth poses a serious threat to our freshwater supply.

D. Measurable pollution in some town water supplies has already occurred.

E. What are the major causes and consequences of this problem and what can we do about it?

Body, divided into sections

II. Description of the Aquifer

A. The groundwater is collected and held in an aquifer.

1. This porous rock formation creates a broad, continuous arch beneath the entire Cape.
2. The lighter freshwater flows on top of the heavier saltwater.

B. This type of natural storage facility, combined with rapid population growth, creates potential for disaster.

III. Hazards from Sewage and Landfills

A. With increasing population, sewage and solid waste from landfill dumps increasingly invade the aquifer.

B. The Cape's sandy soil promotes rapid seepage of wastes into the groundwater.

C. As wastes flow naturally toward the sea, they can invade the drawing radii of town wells.

IV. Hazards from Saltwater Intrusion

A. Increased population also causes overdraw on some town wells, resulting in saltwater intrusion.

B. Salt and calcium used in snow removal add to the problem by seeping into the aquifer from surface runoff.

V. Long-Term Environmental and Economic Consequences

A. The environmental effects of continuing pollution of our water table will be far-reaching.

1. Drinking water will have to be piped in more than 100 miles from Quabbin Reservoir.
2. The Cape's beautiful freshwater ponds will be unfit for swimming.
3. Aquatic and aviary marsh life will be threatened.
4. The Cape's sensitive ecology might well be damaged beyond repair.

B. Such environmental damage would, in turn, spell economic disaster for Cape Cod's major industry—tourism.

VI. Conclusion and Recommendations Conclusion

A. This problem is becoming more real than theoretical.

B. The conclusion is obvious: If the Cape is to survive ecologically and financially, we must take immediate action to preserve our *only* water supply.

C. These recommendations offer a starting point for action.

1. Restrict population density in all Cape towns by creating larger building lot requirements.
2. Keep strict watch on proposed high-density apartment and condominium projects.
3. Create a committee in each town to educate residents about water conservation.
4. Prohibit salt, calcium, and other additives in sand spread on snow-covered roads.
5. Explore alternatives to landfills for solid waste disposal.

D. Given its potential effects on our quality of life, such a crucial issue deserves the active involvement of every Cape resident.

If you are not using *PowerPoint* or another program that creates notes for you, transfer your presentation outline to notecards (one side only, each card numbered and perhaps color-coded), which you can hold in one hand and shuffle as needed. Or insert the outline pages in a looseleaf binder for easy flipping. Type or print clearly, leaving enough white space so you can locate material at a glance.

PLANNING AND CREATING YOUR VISUALS

Using visuals as part of your presentation is a great way to increase the audience's interest, focus, understanding, and retention of material. Nothing is more boring than a presentation filled with slide after slide containing only text. Yet you don't want to overuse visuals, either. Select those that will clarify and enhance your talk—without making you or your main points fade into the background. Focus on the following decisions.

Decide Which Visuals to Use and Where to Use Them

Should you use tables (numbers or text), graphics, charts, illustrations, or diagrams? How complex or simple should the visuals be for this audience? Chapter 12 can help you answer these questions. Then, decide *where* to use these visuals. Visuals are best used to emphasize a point, or any place where *showing* is more effective than just *telling*.

Also, decide how many visuals are appropriate. For international audiences, visuals may be better than text. But don't overuse them, either. Strike a balance: A good ratio would be one visual slide for every 2–3 text slides.

Create a Storyboard

A presentation storyboard is a double-column format in which your discussion is outlined in the left column and aligned with the specific supporting visuals in the right column (Figure 24.2).

Pollution Threats to Local Groundwater

I. Introduce the Problem	(slide: *forecast of presentation*)
A. Do you know what you are drinking when you turn on the tap and fill the glass?	(slide: *showing opening question and photo of glass of water*)
B. The quality of our water is good, but not guaranteed to last forever.	
C. Cape Cod's rapid population growth poses a serious threat to our freshwater supply.	(poster: *a line graph showing twenty-year population growth*)
D. Measurable pollution in some town water supplies has already occurred.	(poster: *two side-by-side tables showing twenty-year increases in nitrate and chloride concentrations in three town wells*)
E. What are the major causes and consequences of this problem and what can we do about it?	(slide: *a list that previews my five subtopics*)

FIGURE 24.2 **A Partial Storyboard** Each section of the presentation outline (page 600) will have its own storyboard.

Decide Which Visuals You Can Realistically Create

Fit each visual to the situation. The visuals you select will depend on the room, the equipment, and the production resources available.

Fit each visual to the situation

How large is the room and how is it arranged? Some visuals work well in small rooms, but not large ones, and vice versa. How well can the room be darkened? Which lights can be left on? Can the lighting be adjusted selectively? What size should visuals be, to be seen clearly by the whole room? (A smaller, intimate room is usually better than a room that is too big.)

What hardware is available (overhead projector, CD player, computer projector)? What graphics programs are available? Which program is best for your purpose and listeners? How far in advance does this equipment have to be requested?

Prepare Your Visuals

As you prepare visuals, focus on economy, clarity, and simplicity.

Be Selective. Use a visual only when it truly serves a purpose. Use restraint in choosing what to highlight with visuals. Try not to begin or end the presentation with a visual. At those times, listeners' attention should be focused on the presenter, not a visual.

Make Visuals Easy to Read and Understand. Think of each visual as an image that flashes before your listeners. They will not have the luxury of studying the visual at leisure. Listeners need to know at a glance what they are looking at and what it means. In addition to being able to *read* the visual, listeners need to *understand* it. See the guidelines that follow.

GUIDELINES for Readable and Understandable Visuals

- **Make visuals large enough to be read anywhere in the room.**
- **Don't cram too many words, ideas, designs, or type styles into a single visual.**
- **Distill the message into the fewest words and simplest images possible.**
- **Chunk material into small sections.**
- **Summarize with key words, phrases, or short sentences.**
- **Use 18–24 point type size and sans serif typeface.**
- **Display only one point per visual—unless previewing or reviewing parts of your presention.**
- **Give each visual a title that announces the topic.**
- **Use color, sparingly, to highlight key words, facts, trends, or the bottom line.**
- **Use the brightest color for what is most important.**
- **Label each part of a diagram or illustration.**
- **Proofread each visual carefully.**

When your material is extremely detailed or complex, prepare handouts for listeners so they can jot notes as you discuss specific material. For more on using and managing handouts effectively, refer to page 612.

Use the Appropriate Technology to Prepare Your Visuals The most common way to prepare visuals such as charts and graphs is to use. Spreadsheet programs (such as *Microsoft Excel* or *Apple Numbers*) can generate charts and graphs based on numeric data sets. Word-processing programs (such as *Microsoft Word* or *Apple Pages*) let you create prose tables and simple graphics easily. Many people use the "draw" tool in presentation programs (such as *Microsoft PowerPoint* or *Apple Keynote*) to create graphs, charts, and simple diagrams. More sophisticated programs such as *Adobe Illustrator* or *CorelDRAW* can be used for line drawings and diagrams. You might also be able to take a simple photograph using a basic digital camera, or find a copyright-free photograph on the Internet. For more on creating visuals, see Chapter 12.

CHOOSING THE RIGHT VISUAL MEDIUM

Consider all the options

In most workplace settings, presentation software (such as *PowerPoint*) has become the standard medium for oral presentations. Most of the time, presentation software is what you will use on the job. But other media are available, and you should choose the medium that best fits the situation. Which medium or combination is best for your topic, setting, and audience? How fancy do listeners expect the presentation to be? Which media are appropriate for this occasion?

Fit the medium to the situation

- For a weekly meeting with department colleagues, scribbling on a blank transparency, chalkboard, or dry-erase markerboard might suffice.
- For interacting with listeners, you might use a chalkboard to record audience responses to your questions.
- For immediate orientation, you might begin with a poster that lists key visuals/ideas/themes to which you will refer repeatedly.
- For helping listeners take notes, absorb data, or remember complex material, you might distribute a presentation outline as a preview or provide handouts.
- For a presentation to investors, clients, or upper management, you might require polished and professionally prepared visuals, including computer graphics, such as an electronic slide presentation using *PowerPoint* or simple software.

Figure 24.3 presents the various media that you can use for a presentation.

> **NOTE** *Keep in mind that the more technology you use in your presentation, the more prepared you must be.*

Whiteboard/Chalkboard

Uses

- simple, on-the-spot visuals
- recording audience responses
- informal settings
- small, well-lighted rooms

Tips

- copy long material in advance
- make it legible and visible to all
- use washable markers
- speak to the listeners—not to the board

Overhead Projection

Uses

- on-the-spot or prepared visuals
- formal or informal settings
- small- or medium-sized rooms
- rooms needing to remain lighted

Tips

- use cardboard mounting frames for your acetate transparencies
- write discussion notes on each frame
- check your sequence beforehand
- turn projector off when not using it
- face the audience—not the screen
- point directly on the transparency
- use erasable color markers to highlight items

Poster

Uses

- overviews, previews, emphasis
- recurring themes
- small, well-lighted rooms

Tips

- use 20" × 30" posterboard (or larger)
- use intense, washable colors
- keep each poster simple and uncrowded
- arrange/display posters in advance
- point to what you are discussing

Film and Video

Uses

- necessary display of moving images
- coordinated sound and visual images

Tips

- introduce segment to be shown; tell viewers what to expect
- show only relevant segments
- if the segment is complex, replay it where needed, using slow-motion replay
- practice beforehand

Flip Chart

Uses

- a sequence of visuals
- back-and-forth movement
- small, well-lighted rooms

Tips

- use an easel pad and easel
- use intense, washable colors
- check your sequence beforehand
- point to what you are discussing

Handouts

Uses

- present complex material
- help listeners follow along, take notes, and remember

Tips

- staple or bind the packet
- number the pages
- try saving for the end
- if you distribute up front, ask audience to read only when instructed

Computer Projection

Uses

- sophisticated charts, graphs, maps
- multimedia presentations
- formal settings
- small, dark rooms

Tips

- take lots of time to prepare/practice
- work from a storyboard
- check the whole system beforehand
- have a default plan in case something goes wrong

FIGURE 24.3 **Media Choices for Visual Presentations**

USING PRESENTATION SOFTWARE

Overview of presentation software

Microsoft PowerPoint (the most widely used) or other software, such as *Apple*'s *Keynote* or *Open Office*'s *Impress* allow you to create visual presentations simply and quickly. You can include images, sounds, movies, animations, and video links to Web sites. *Prezi*, a newer program, offers even more options.

In a world in which images are everywhere and electronic communication is the mode, *PowerPoint* and similar software is often regarded—rightly or wrongly—as "an indispensable corporate survival tool" (Nunberg 330).

Using presentation software, you can

Selected design and display features of presentation software

- Create slide designs in various colors, shading, and textures.
- Create drawings or graphs and import clip art, photos, or other images.
- Create animated text and images: say, bullets that flash one-at-a-time on the screen or bars and lines on a graph that are highlighted individually, to emphasize specific characteristics of the data.
- Create dynamic transitions between each slide, such as having one slide dissolve toward the right side of the screen as the following slide uncovers from the left.
- Amplify each slide with speaker notes that are invisible to the audience.
- Sort your slides into various sequences.
- Precisely time your entire presentation.
- Show your presentation on the computer screen or large-screen projector, online via the Web, as overhead transparencies, or as printed handouts.

Figure 24.4 shows parts of a sample presentation based in part on the outline on page 600.

Ethics and the Use of Presentation Software

The presentation software debate

Many people feel that presentation software's bullet-style points help structure the story or the argument and help the presenter organize and stay on course. But critics argue that the mere content outline provided by the slides can oversimplify complex issues and that an endless list of bullets or animations, colors, and sounds can distract from the deeper message. Also, people's learning styles differ, and presentation software (like PowerPoint) may be more suited for those who prefer a clear sequence versus those who learn best when the discussion is more open (Weimer).

In the end, technological tools are merely a supplement to your presentation. They are no substitute for the facts, ideas, examples, numbers, and interpretations that make up the clear and complete message audiences expect.

Title slide give overall forecast of presentation →

POLLUTION THREATS TO LOCAL GROUNDWATER

Arnold Borthwick
B.S. student in soil and water science

GROUNDWATER
What are you drinking when you fill your glass?

← Introductory slide offers an engaging question and visual

Overview lets the audience know what's coming →

OVERVIEW

- The problem
- Our local aquifer
- Hazards (sewage, landfill, saltwater)
- Consequences (environmental, economic)
- Conclusions and recommendations

HAZARDS--SEWAGE & SALTWATER INTRUSION

- Increasing population = more sewage invades aquifer
- Cape Cod's sandy soil promotes rapid seepage
- As waste flows towards sea, it can invade wells
- Increased population = overdrawn town wells
- Overdrawn town wells can cause saltwater intrusion
- Salt/calcium from snow removal can add to the problem

← This slide, which appears later in the presentation, corresponds with the third overview bullet

Visual effectively illustrates the problem →

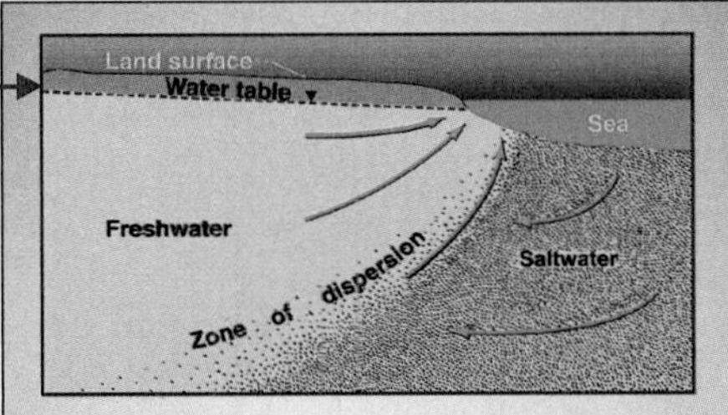

SALTWATER INTRUSION

Source: Barlow 2000A, Ground-Water Resources for the Future – Atlantic Coastal Zone, U.S. Geological Survey Fact Sheet 085-00, August 2000. Figure modified from Cooper, H. H., 1964, A hypothesis concerning the dynamic balance of fresh water and salt water in a coastal aquifer: U.S. Geological Survey Water-Supply Paper 1613-C, p. 1-12.

CONCLUSIONS & RECOMMENDATIONS

- Restrict population density (larger building lots)
- Keep strict watch on high-density apartments/condos
- Create a committee in each town to educate residents
- Prohibit salt, calcium, and other ice melt chemicals
- Explore alternatives for solid waste landfills

← Easy to read conclusion slide reinforces the main points

FIGURE 24.4 **Sample Presentation.** These six slides are from a longer presentation (13 slides total).

CASE *PowerPoint* and the Space Shuttle *Columbia* Disaster

On February 1, 2003, the space shuttle *Columbia* burned up upon reentering the Earth's atmosphere. The *Columbia* had suffered damage during launch when a piece of insulating foam had broken off the shuttle and damaged the wing.

While *Columbia* was in orbit, NASA personnel tried to assess the damage and to recommend a course of action. It was decided that the damage did not seem serious enough to pose a significant threat, and reentry proceeded on schedule. (Lower-level suggestions that the shuttle fly close to a satellite that could have photographed the damage, for a clearer assessment, were overlooked and ultimately ignored by the decision makers.)

The *Columbia* Accident Investigation Board concluded that a *PowerPoint* presentation to NASA officials had played a role in the disaster: Engineers presented their findings in a series of confusing and misleading slides that obscured errors in their own engineering analysis. Design expert Edward Tufte points out that one especially crucial slide was so crammed with data and bullet points and so lacking in analysis that it was impossible to decipher accurately (8–9).

The Board's findings:

> As information gets passed up an organization's hierarchy, from people who do analysis to mid-level managers to high-level leadership, key explanations and supporting information are filtered out. In this context, it is easy to understand how a senior manager might read this *PowerPoint* slide and not realize that it addresses a life-threatening situation.
>
> At many points during its investigation, the Board was surprised to receive similar presentation slides from NASA officials in place of technical reports. The Board views the endemic use of *PowerPoint* briefing slides instead of technical papers as an illustration of the problematic methods of technical communication at NASA. (*Columbia* Accident, *Report* 191)

GUIDELINES for Using Presentation Software

- **Don't let the software do the thinking.** Use your own research, sense of audience and purpose, and other original ideas to shape the presentation. Then use the software to help make the material accessible and interesting. The shape and content should come from you, not from the software.
- **Have a backup plan in case the technology fails.** Bring handouts to the presentation and be prepared to give the presentation without the software. Don't distribute handouts until you are ready to discuss them; otherwise, people will start reading the handouts instead of paying attention to you.
- **Start with an overview slide.** Orient your audience by showing an opening slide that indicates what you plan to cover and in what order.

- **Find a balance between text and visuals.** Excessive text is boring; excessive visuals can be confusing. Each visual should serve a purpose: to summarize information, to add emphasis, to set a tone, and so on. Avoid overcrowding the slides: Include no more than 7–9 lines per slide (including the heading) with no more than 6–9 words per bulleted item.
- **Avoid overcrowding the slide.** In general, include no more than one key point per slide. If you are the kind of person who likes to embellish and enjoys speaking to a crowd, use fewer slides.
- **Avoid merely reciting the slides.** Instead, discuss each slide, with specific examples and details that round out the idea—but try not to digress or ramble.
- **Don't let the medium obscure the message.** The audience should be focused on what you have to say, and not on the slide. Avoid colors and backgrounds that distract from the content. Avoid the whooshing and whiz-bang and other sounds unless absolutely necessary. Be conservative with any design and display feature.
- **Keep it simple but not simplistic.** Spice things up with a light dose of imported digital photos, charts, graphs, or diagrams, but avoid images that look so complex that they require detailed study.
- **Keep viewers oriented.** Don't show a slide until you are ready to discuss it. Present one topic per slide, bringing bullets (subtopics) on one at a time as you discuss them. Let your audience digest the slide data *while* you speak, and not before or after.
- **End with a "conclusions" or "questions" slide.** Give your audience a sense of having come full circle. On a "conclusions" slide, summarize the key points. A "questions" slide can simply provide a heading and a visual. Allow time at the end of your presentation for questions and/or comments.

DELIVERING YOUR PRESENTATION

You have planned and prepared carefully. Now consider the following simple steps to make your actual presentation enjoyable instead of terrifying.

Rehearse Your Delivery

Hold ample practice sessions to become comfortable with the organization and flow of your presentation. Try to rehearse at least once in front of friends, or use a full-length mirror and a recorder. Assess your delivery from listener comments or from your recorded voice (which will sound high to you). Use the evaluation checklist on page 618 as a guide.

If at all possible, rehearse using the actual equipment (computer projector and so on) in the actual setting, to ensure that you have all you need and that everything works. Rehearsing a computer-projected presentation is essential.

Check the Room and Setting Beforehand

Make sure you have enough space, electrical outlets, and tables for your equipment. If you will be addressing a large audience by microphone and plan to point to features on your visuals, be sure the microphone is movable. Pay careful attention to lighting, especially for chalkboards, flip charts, and posters. Don't forget a pointer if you need one.

Cultivate the Human Landscape

A successful presentation involves relationship building with the audience.

Get to Know Your Audience. Try to meet some audience members before your presentation. We all feel more comfortable with people we know.

Be Reasonable. Don't make your point at someone else's expense. If your topic is controversial (layoffs, policy changes, downsizing), decide how to speak candidly and persuasively with the least chance of offending anyone. For example, in your presentation about groundwater pollution (page 600), you don't want to attack the building developers, since the building trade is a major producer of jobs, second only to tourism, on Cape Cod. Avoid personal attacks.

Display Enthusiasm and Confidence. Nobody likes a speaker who seems half dead. Clean up verbal tics ("er," "ah," "uuh"). Overcome your shyness; research indicates that shy people are seen as less credible, trustworthy, likable, attractive, and knowledgeable. Don't be afraid to smile.

Don't Preach. Speak like a person talking—not someone giving a sermon or the Gettysburg Address. Use *we, you, your, our,* to establish commonality with the audience. Avoid jokes or wisecracks.

Keep Your Listeners Oriented

Help your listeners focus their attention and organize their understanding. Give them a map, some guidance, and highlights.

Open with a Clear and Engaging Introduction The introduction to a presentation is your chance to set the stage. For most presentations, you have three main tasks:

1. Show the listeners how your presentation has meaning for them. Show how your topic affects listeners personally by telling a quick story, asking a question, or referring to a current event or something else the audience cares about.
2. Establish your credibility by stating your credentials or explaining where you obtained your information.
3. Preview your presentation by listing the main points and the overall conclusion.

An introduction following this format might sound something like this:

> Do you know what you are drinking when you turn on the tap and fill a glass? The quality of Cape Cod's drinking water is seriously threatened by rapid population growth. My name is Arnold Borthwick, and I've been researching this topic for a term project. Today, I'd like to share my findings with you by discussing three main points: specific causes of the problem, the foreseeable consequences, and what we can do to avoid disaster.

An appeal to listeners' concerns

A presentation preview

Outline your main points by using an overview slide.

Give Concrete Examples. Good examples are informative and persuasive.

> Overdraw from town wells in Maloket and Tanford (two of our most rapidly growing towns) has resulted in measurable salt infusion at a yearly rate of 0.1 mg per liter.

A concrete example

Use examples that focus on listener concerns.

Provide Explicit Transitions. Alert listeners whenever you are switching gears:

> For my next point. . . .
>
> Turning now to my second point. . . .

Explicit transitions

Repeat key points or terms to keep them fresh in listeners' minds.

Review and Interpret. Last things are best remembered. Help listeners remember the main points:

> To summarize the dangers to our groundwater, . . .

A review of main points

Also, be clear about what this material means. Be emphatic about what listeners should be doing, thinking, or feeling:

An emphatic conclusion

> The conclusion is obvious: If the Cape is to survive, we must. . . .

Try to conclude with a forceful answer to this implied question from each listener: "What does all this mean to me personally?"

Plan for How You Will Use Any Non-Computer Visual Aids

If you plan to work with a whiteboard, chalkboard, flip chart, poster, or other aid, you need to prepare and organize. Presenting material effectively in these formats is a matter of good timing and careful management.

Prepare. If you plan to draw on a chalkboard or poster, do the drawings beforehand (in multicolors). Otherwise, listeners will be sitting idly while you draw away.

Prepare handouts if you want listeners to remember or study certain material. In most cases, distribute these *after* your talk. (You want the audience to be looking at and listening to you, instead of reading the handout.) Distribute handouts before or during the talk only if you want people to take notes—or if your equipment breaks down. When you do distribute handouts beforehand, ask listeners to await your instructions before they turn to a particular page.

Organize. Make sure you organize your media materials and the physical layout beforehand, to avoid fumbling during the presentation. Check your visual sequence against your storyboard.

Follow a Few Simple Guidelines. Make your visuals part of a seamless presentation. Avoid listener distraction, confusion, and frustration by observing the following suggestions.

GUIDELINES for Presenting Visuals

- **Try not to begin with a visual.**
- **Try not to display a visual until you are ready to discuss it.**
- **Tell viewers what they should be looking for in the visual.**
- **Point to what is important.**
- **Stand aside when discussing a visual, so everyone can see it.**
- **Don't turn your back on the audience.**
- **After discussing the visual, remove it promptly.**
- **Switch off equipment that is not in use.**
- **Try not to end with a visual.**

Manage Your Presentation Style

Think about how you are moving, how you are speaking, and where you are looking. These are all elements of your personal style.

Use Natural Movements and Reasonable Postures. Move and gesture as you normally would in conversation, and maintain reasonable postures. Avoid foot shuffling, pencil tapping, swaying, slumping, or fidgeting.

Adjust Volume, Pronunciation, and Rate. With a microphone, don't speak too loudly. Without one, don't speak too softly. Be sure you can be heard clearly without shattering eardrums. Ask your audience about the sound and speed of your delivery after a few sentences.

Nervousness causes speakers to gallop along and mispronounce words. Slow down and pronounce clearly. Usually, a rate that seems a bit slow to you will be just right for listeners.

Maintain Eye Contact. Look directly into listeners' eyes. With a small audience, eye contact is one of your best connectors. As you speak, establish eye contact with as many listeners as possible. With a large group, maintain eye contact with those in the first rows. Establish eye contact immediately—before you even begin to speak—by looking around.

Manage Your Speaking Situation

Do everything you can to keep things running smoothly.

Be Responsive to Listener Feedback. Assess listener feedback continually and make adjustments as needed. If you are laboring through a long list of facts or figures and people begin to doze or fidget, you might summarize. Likewise, if frowns, raised eyebrows, or questioning looks indicate confusion, skepticism, or indignation, you can backtrack with a specific example or explanation. By tuning in to your audience's reactions, you can keep listeners on your side.

Stick to Your Plan. Say what you came to say, then summarize and close—politely and on time. Don't punctuate your speech with digressions that pop into your head. Unless a specific anecdote was part of your original plan to clarify a point or increase interest, avoid excursions. We often tend to be more interested in what we have to say than our listeners are! Don't exceed your time limit.

Leave Listeners with Something to Remember. Before ending, take a moment to summarize the major points and reemphasize anything of special importance.

Are listeners supposed to remember something, have a different attitude, take a specific action? Let them know! As you conclude, thank your listeners.

Allow Time for Questions and Answers. At the very beginning, tell your listeners that a question-and-answer period will follow. Use the following suggestions for managing listener questions diplomatically and efficiently.

GUIDELINES for Managing Listener Questions

- **Announce a specific time limit for the question period.**
- **Listen carefully to each question.**
- **If you can't understand a question, ask that it be rephrased.**
- **Repeat every question, to ensure that everyone hears it.**
- **Be brief in your answers.**
- **If you need extra time for an answer, arrange for it after the presentation.**
- **If anyone attempts lengthy debate, offer to continue after the presentation.**
- **If you can't answer a question, say so and move on.**
- **End the session with a clear signal.** Say something such as, "We have time for one more question."

GUIDELINES for Delivering Oral Presentations

- **Be rehearsed and prepared.** The best way to calm your nerves is to remind yourself of the preparation and research you have done. Practice your delivery so that it is professional and appropriate but natural for you.
- **Memorize a brief introduction.** If you begin your presentation smoothly and confidently, you won't be as nervous going forward. Do not open by saying "I'm a little bit nervous today" or "I have a slight cold. Can everyone hear me in the back?" Just begin. A memorized introduction will help you avoid having to ad-lib (potentially badly) when you are most anxious.
- **Dress for success.** Wear clothes that suggest professionalism and confidence.
- **Stand tall and use eye contact.** Good posture and frequent eye contact convey a sense of poise, balance, and confidence. Practice in front of a mirror. If looking people directly in the eye makes you nervous, aim just above people's heads. Or find a friendly face or two and look at those people first. As you gain confidence, be sure to cast your gaze around the entire room or conference table.

- **Take charge.** If you get interrupted but don't want to take questions until the end, remember that you are in control. Be polite but firm: "Thank you for that good question. I'll save it and other questions until the end of my presentation."
- **Gesture naturally.** Don't force yourself to move around or be theatrical if this is not your style. But do not act like a robot, either. Unless you are speaking from a podium or lectern, move around just a bit. And when it's time to take questions, consider moving closer to the audience. In a conference room setting, if everyone else is seated, you should stand.

CONSIDER THIS Cross-Cultural Audiences May Have Specific Expectations

Imagine that you've been assigned to represent your company at an international conference or before international clients (e.g., of passenger aircraft or mainframe computers). As you plan and prepare your presentation, remain sensitive to various cultural expectations.

For example, some cultures might be offended by a presentation that gets right to the point without first observing formalities of politeness, well wishes, and the like.

Certain communication styles are welcomed in some cultures, but are considered offensive in others. In southern Europe and the Middle East, people expect direct and prolonged eye contact as a way of showing honesty and respect. In Southeast Asia, this may be taken as a sign of aggression or disrespect (Gesteland 24). A sampling of the questions to consider:

- *Should I smile a lot or look serious? (Hulbert, "Overcoming" 42)*
- *Should I rely on expressive gestures and facial expressions?*
- *How loudly or softly, rapidly or slowly should I speak?*
- *Should I come out from behind the podium and approach the audience or keep my distance?*
- *Should I get right to the point or take plenty of time to lead into and discuss the matter thoroughly?*
- *Should I focus only on the key facts or on all the details and various interpretations?*
- *Should I be assertive in offering interpretations and conclusions, or should I allow listeners to reach their own conclusions?*
- *Which types of visuals and which media might or might not work?*
- *Should I invite questions from this audience, or would this be offensive?*

To account for language differences, prepare a handout of your entire script for distribution after the presentation, along with a copy of your visuals. This way, your audience will be able to study your material at their leisure.

WEBINARS AND DISTANCE PRESENTATIONS

Web-based presentations help bridge distances

The best way to deliver an oral presentation is in person, in a face-to-face setting. Facial expressions, tone of voice, and the back and forth exchange of ideas are most effective when everyone is in the same room. But in some situations, especially when audience members are at different sites (often, in different countries), a face-to-face presentation may not be possible. In these situations, companies use distance delivery options to avoid the cost (and impracticality) of transporting everyone to the same location. Distance delivery of oral presentations ensures that everyone on the team can still attend and participate.

Webinars

Webinars (Web-based seminars) allow you to deliver a presentation via the Internet. Audience members connect to the Webinar site via their computer and an Internet connection. Some companies have internal Webinar software unique to that particular workplace. Most companies, however, find it more cost-effective to use the services of commercial sites, such as *WebEx, GoToMeeting*, or *Adobe Connect*.

Webinar sites provide a number of useful features. Consider how you might use some or all of the following features if you were to give your presentation via a Webinar.

Tools you can use with a webinar presentation

- ***PowerPoint* or other presentation slides** can be uploaded and displayed in real time. You can change slides, point to specific items, and use transitions to move from one slide to another, much as you would do in any real-time presentation.
- **Digital whiteboards** let you draw and make notes that everyone can see.
- **Real-time chat tools** allow your audience to ask questions and engage in discussions.
- **Video** can be used if you want people to actually see each other (versus just seeing each other's chat postings). Video can complicate the Webinar, however, because some participants may not have video cameras.

For a Webinar to work, everyone must be available at the same time. So if you are on the East Coast of the United States, for example, and some of your audience is in Europe, there could be an eight or nine hour difference. You may need to start the Webinar at 7 AM so that your international colleagues can attend in the early afternoon. Webinars with audiences in Asia require even more careful time calculations.

Slide Sharing and Other Tools

A Webinar may not be the right choice for all your audience members. There may be too many changes in time zones or it may be impossible to find a time when everyone can attend. In these cases, you can use *slide sharing* technologies to make your slides available to those who can't attend.

Among the available slide sharing tools, *Slideshare* (<www.slideshare.net>) lets you upload slides in a variety of formats—*Microsoft PowerPoint, Apple Keynote, Adobe* PDF—and make these available to your audience.

You may want to work on the presentation with input from others. *Google Drive* (<docs.google.com>) allow you to create a slide show collaboratively. You and anyone with your permission can revise and edit a presentation, using the Google presentation software tool. You can then open up the file for viewing by anyone (public access) or just by those who have permission.

GUIDELINES for Webinars and Distance Presentations

- **Prepare your slides well in advance.**
- **Test your slides on the Webinar site.** Ask one or two colleagues to sign in the day before the presentation for a trial run.
- **Decide which Webinar features to use.** Options include slides, real-time chat, and video.
- **Post your slides on the company's server (Intranet) or on a slide sharing site.** In this way, people unable to attend the Webinar will still be able to view your presentation.
- **If you decide to post your slides, consider adding audio (narration).** People can then listen to you speak as they view the slides. *PowerPoint* and other tools have an audio feature.
- **Use slide sharing sites to allow those who can't attend the Webinar to access your slides.**
- **When appropriate, use collaboration tools to work on a team presentation.** Don't use a site such as *Google Drive* for confidential work-related material. Instead, use whatever tools your company has authorized.

CHECKLIST: Oral Presentations

Presentation Evaluation for (name/topic) ____________

Content — ***Comments***

- ☐ Stated a clear purpose. ____________
- ☐ Created interest in the topic. ____________
- ☐ Showed command of the material. ____________
- ☐ Supported assertions with evidence. ____________
- ☐ Used adequate and appropriate visuals. ____________
- ☐ Used material suited to this audience's needs, knowledge, concerns, and interests. ____________
- ☐ Acknowledged opposing views. ____________
- ☐ Gave the right amount of information. ____________

Organization

- ☐ Began with a clear overview. ____________
- ☐ Presented a clear line of reasoning. ____________
- ☐ Moved from point to point effectively. ____________
- ☐ Stayed on course. ____________
- ☐ Used transitions effectively. ____________
- ☐ Avoided needless digressions. ____________
- ☐ Summarized before concluding. ____________
- ☐ Was clear about what the listeners should think or do. ____________

Style

- ☐ Dressed appropriately. ____________
- ☐ Seemed confident relaxed, and likable. ____________
- ☐ Seemed in control of the speaking situation. ____________
- ☐ Showed appropriate enthusiasm. ____________
- ☐ Pronounced, enunciated, and spoke well. ____________
- ☐ Used no slang whatsoever. ____________
- ☐ Used appropriate gestures, tone, volume, and delivery rate. ____________
- ☐ Had good posture and eye contact. ____________
- ☐ Interacted with the audience. ____________
- ☐ Kept the audience actively involved. ____________
- ☐ Answered questions concisely and convincingly. ____________

Overall professionalism: Superior ________ **Acceptable** ________ **Needs work** ________

Evaluator's signature: ____________________

Projects

GENERAL

1. In a memo to your instructor, identify and discuss the kinds of oral reporting duties you expect to encounter in your career.
2. Prepare an oral presentation for your class, based on your written long report. Develop a sentence outline and a storyboard that includes at least three visuals. If your instructor requests, create one or more of your presentation visuals using *PowerPoint* software.

   Practice your presentation with a tape recorder, video camera, or a friend. Use the checklist on page 648 to assess and refine your delivery.
3. Observe a lecture or speech, and evaluate it according to the Checklist. Write a memo to your instructor (without naming the speaker), identifying strong and weak areas and suggesting improvements.

TEAM

In today's work world, presentations are often prepared by, and sometimes delivered by, more than one person. In groups of 3–4 people, come up with a simple presentation topic that everyone can work on. (You might want to base this topic on a group writing activity from earlier in the semester.) Discuss how, as a team, you will approach the research, planning, and creation of the presentation. For example, will one person be responsible for the research? Will another person assemble the slides? Create a brief presentation for your instructor and classmates (using presentation software), describing the process you will take and the decisions your team made.

DIGITAL AND SOCIAL MEDIA

Using the prior Team Project, and in the same group of 3–4 people, investigate how you would create a presentation if each of you worked in a different location (too remote from each other to have a face-to-face meeting). If everyone has a Google account, try creating a shared Google presentation (click on Google drive, then Create, then Presentation). Or, use PowerPoint and share the file by email. In class, give a short presentation on the pros and cons of working on a presentation in this manner.

GLOBAL

Imagine that you've been assigned to represent your company at an international conference or before international clients. As you plan and prepare your presentation, what can you do to remain sensitive to various cultural expectations? For example, some cultures might be offended by a presentation that gets right to the point without first observing formalities of politeness, well wishes, and the like. Use the Internet to research issues about presentation etiquette for a particular culture (choose one). Then create a short presentation on this topic for the class.

25 Web Pages

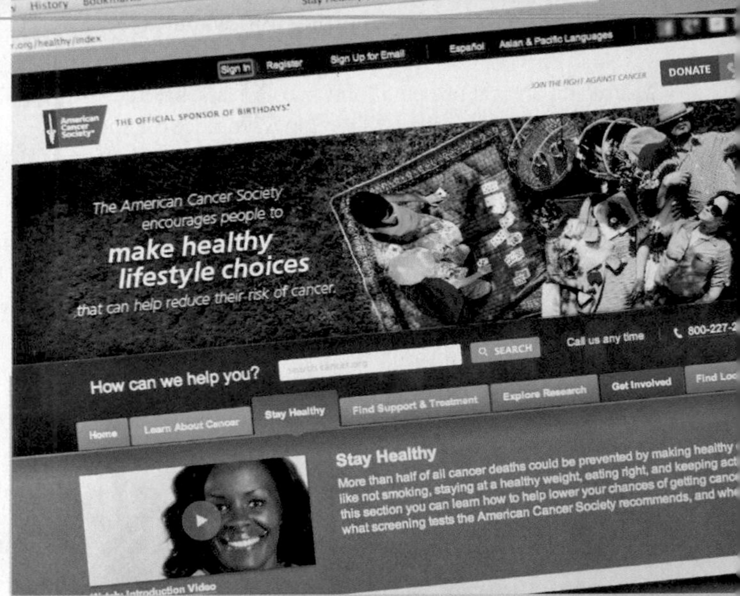

"My job involves working on the instructions and specifications for our technical racing bikes. We also have a pretty complex company Web site, and I work with a team of designers and programmers to make sure the Web content is easy to read, quick to access, and up to date. The writing skills I use for print documents are important on the Web, too. People who visit our site are impatient and want information that's quick and to the point."

—Lori Huberman,
Senior Technical Writer,
international racing cycle company

LEARNING OBJECTIVES FOR THIS CHAPTER

- Identify audience and purpose for Web pages
- Understand what readers expect from Web pages
- Write appropriate Web-based content
- Design a basic Web page
- Identify software used for creating Web pages
- Recognize the role of teams in Web design
- Create Web pages for intercultural audiences

Web pages save on printing costs and can be kept updated

Once a document is printed on paper, it remains fixed. If the document needs updating, a new (and costly) print run is required. After the new document is printed, it must be distributed, too. Web-based information, on the other hand, can be updated quickly and at minimal cost, and without the expense of shipping a new document. For example, if an organization discovers a mistake in some key information presented on its Web site, this information can be revised immediately and readers informed by a simple email message or notice on the site.

Web pages are interactive.

The Web also offers a level of interactivity that printed texts do not. Readers can search the information, forward material to others, ask questions, download files, and click on links that lead to other sources of information. Various types and levels of information, suitable for different audiences, are easy to access from the same page. Figure 25.1 shows a Web page from the U.S. Food and Drug Administration on bug bites and bee stings. Interactive features include a list of consumer updates (links) in the left margin, a list of questions (such as "When is medical attention needed?") that readers can click for more information, a search box, and a "Resources for You" section.

NOTE *Web site refers to an entire site: the main Web page and all the other pages that can be accessed via links on the main page. Web page refers to one single page, such as the page in Figure 25.1.*

CONSIDERING AUDIENCE AND PURPOSE

Audiences for Web pages

Because the Web can be accessed by countless readers, think carefully about your intended audience and purpose for a Web page. Who are the primary readers? Are they potential customers seeking product or support information? Are they people with questions about a medical condition? Because Web-based information is easy

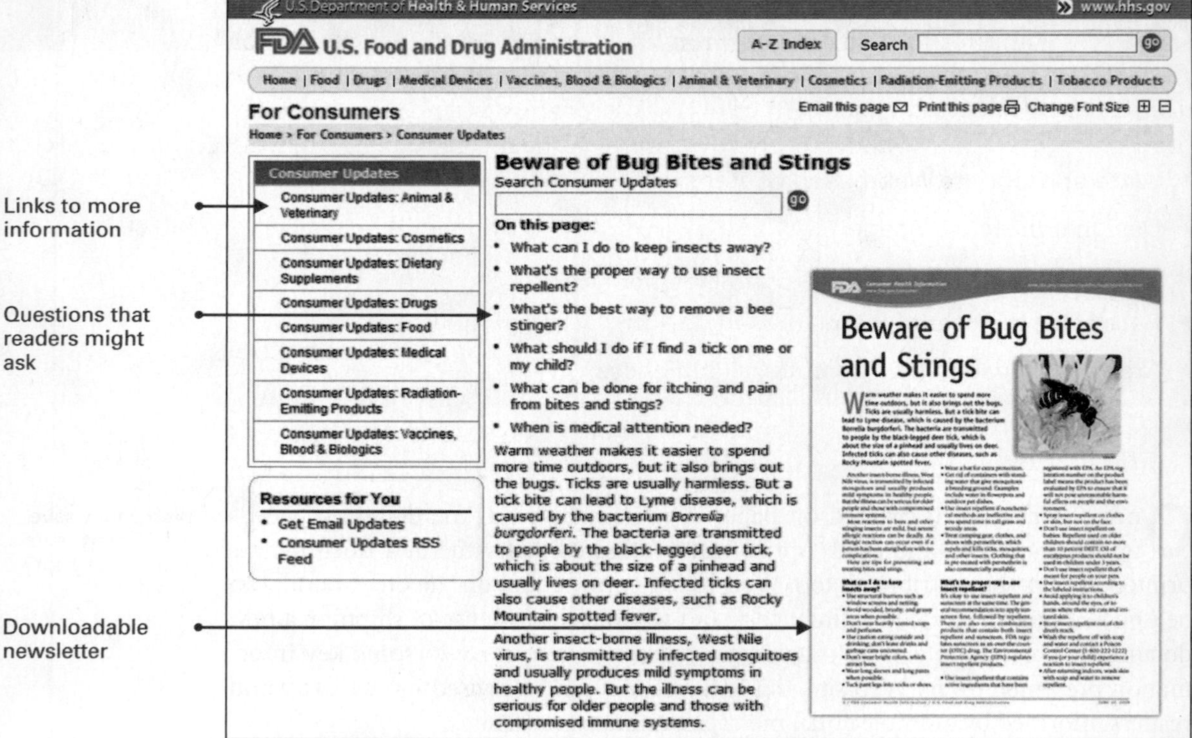

FIGURE 25.1 An Interactive Web Page This page includes a variety of links to other information and a downloadable newsletter.

Source: U.S. Food and Drug Administration From <http://www.fda.gov/ForConsumers/ConsumerUpdates/ucm048022.htm>.

to forward to others, consider the many potential secondary audiences for a Web page. For instance, Figure 25.1 is written and designed for general readers (people without medical training) who want to learn more about bug bites and bee stings. But even though that page is written for non-experts, a doctor or nurse might access other pages on the site, skipping over the section titled "For Consumers" and going straight for the main FDA Web page, which provides links for medical professionals.

Purposes for Web pages

Learn what you can about the purpose of the Web page. What do people want to do with the information? The writers of the content in Figure 25.1 avoid technical terms, use questions to address readers' main concerns, and provide links to other sites. Readers of Web pages expect to access exactly what they are looking for, and they will leave a page if they don't find what they want.

Web site development is a complex process that changes as the related technologies evolve. Most commercial and organizational Web sites are developed and maintained by a team trained in graphic design, information architecture, marketing, computer programming, technical writing, and other areas. In smaller organizations (a small non-profit, for example), the team may be smaller, but rarely does a single person create and maintain a professional Web site. Large or small, any Web site development process benefits greatly from having a technical communicator on the team. Technical communicators bring special attention to issues such as audience and purpose, clear writing style and tone, and use of visuals.

The role of technical communicators in Web site development

HOW PEOPLE READ WEB PAGES

In general, when people read a Web page, they want information quickly, and they typically share the following expectations.

What readers expect from Web pages

- **Accessibility.** Web pages should be easy to enter, navigate, and exit. Instead of reading word-for-word, readers tend to skim, looking for key material without having to scroll through pages of text. They look for chances to interact (for example, links to click on), and they want to download material quickly.
- **Worthwhile Content.** Web pages should contain all the information readers need and want. Content (such as product and price updates) should be accurate and up to date. Readers look for links to other high-quality sites as indicators of credibility. They look for a "search" tool and for contact information that is easy to find.
- **Sensible Arrangement.** Readers want to know where they are and where they are going. They expect a reasonable design and layout, with links easily navigated forward or backward. They look for navigation features to be labeled ("Company Information," "Ordering," "Job Openings," and so on).
- **Clean, Crisp Page Design.** Readers want a page design that is easy to navigate quickly, with plenty of white space and a balance of text, visuals, and color.
- **Good Use of Visuals and Special Effects.** Readers expect high-quality visuals (photographs, charts and graphs, company logos) used in a balanced manner (not too many on the page). Special effects, such as fonts that blink, can be annoying.

One person rarely tackles all the areas described above. There are two areas—writing the content and designing the pages—where technical communicators can make contributions as part of a Web design team.

WRITING FOR THE WEB

When writing content for Web pages, remember that readers will be busy. They will lack the patience to wade through long passages of prose. The following Guidelines offer suggestions for writing Web content for busy readers.

Web writing should be accessible

GUIDELINES for Writing Web Pages

- **Chunk the information.** Break long paragraphs into shorter passages that are easy to access and quick to read. Chunking is also used in paper documents (see Chapter 13), but is especially important for Web pages. Chunking can also be used to break information into sections that address different audiences.
- **Write with a readable style.** Write clear, concise, and fluent sentences. Use a friendly but professional tone. Avoid abbreviations and technical terms that some audience members might not understand.
- **Keep sentences short.** Long sentences not only bog down the reader, but may also display poorly on a Web page.
- **Keep paragraphs short.** Long paragraphs can make a Web page look prose-heavy. Make your online text at least 50 percent shorter than what you would write in a print document.
- **Catch reader attention in the first two paragraphs.** One expert suggests that "the first two paragraphs must state the most important information" (Nielsen).
- **Write in a factual, neutral tone.** Even on overtly political Web sites (such as a site for a political candidate), readers prefer writing that is fact-based and maintains a neutral tone.
- **Choose words that are meaningful.** Start headings, subheads, and bulleted items with "information-carrying words" (Nielsen) that have immediate meaning for readers. Instead of a word like "Introduction," you could use the phrase "Welcome to the Park," as in Figure 25.2.
- **Write with interactive features in mind.** Use hyperlinks to provide more information about a technical term or a concept; think about when to link to other Web pages (within and outside your site). When you do create outside links, consider the ethical and legal implications (pages 629–30).
- **Remember that most Web pages are globally accessible.** Avoid confusing readers for whom English is not a first language. Avoid violating cultural expectations. For more on writing for global audiences, see pages 628–29.

DESIGNING WEB PAGES

An effective Web page—one that people will want to read and explore—uses a clean, attractive, uncluttered design. The page strikes a good balance between text and visuals, offers inviting and complementary colors, and uses white space effectively.

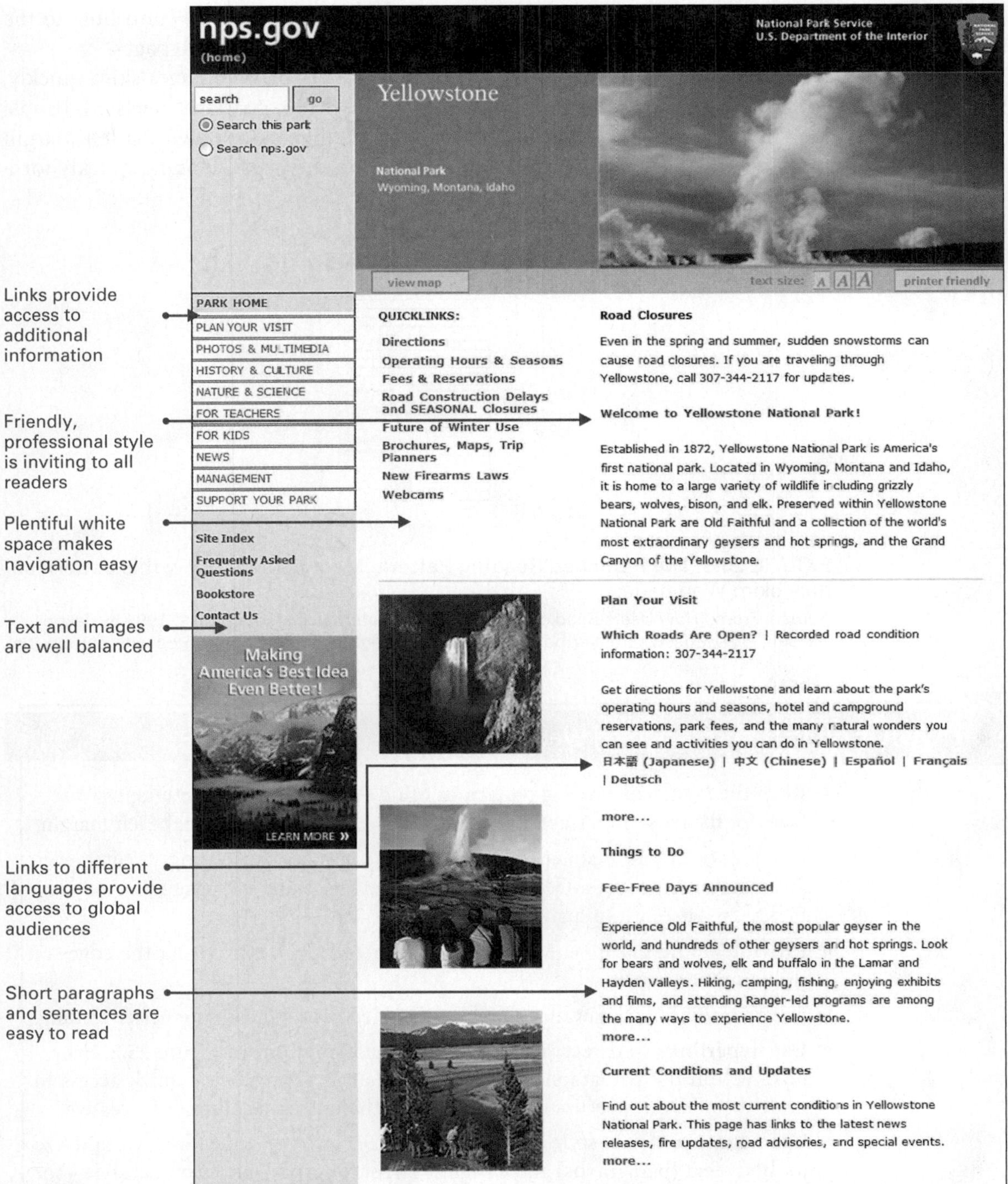

FIGURE 25.2 **A Well Written and Designed Web Page** This Web page features chunked information and a variety of design features to make it easy for readers to use.

Source: Yellowstone home page, National Park Service, <www.nps.gov/yell>.

Ample margins, consistent use of fonts, and clear headings all contribute to the design. The Guidelines box offers suggestions for designing Web pages.

Use an "F-shaped" layout pattern

Even more than with print documents, readers of Web pages skim quickly, employing what one expert calls the "F-shaped" reading pattern (Nielsen). People look across the page a few times (horizontally), then skim down the left margin (making an F shape, roughly, with their eyes on the page), looking quickly for a point of interest or a link to click on (see Figure 25.3).

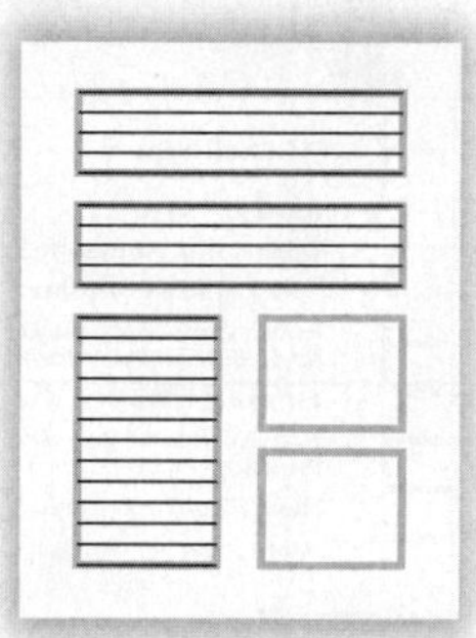

FIGURE 25.3 The F-Shaped Reading Pattern Most people follow this pattern as they skim Web pages.

Source: From "How Users Read on the Web" by Jakob Nielsen, copyright © 1997 by Jakob Nielsen, <www.useit.com/alertbox/9710a.html>. All rights reserved. Reprinted with permission.

GUIDELINES for Designing Web Pages

- **Keep the F-shaped reading pattern in mind.** Use the top two paragraphs or sections for the most important information. Place additional links in the left margin.
- **Use plenty of white space.** Cluttered Web pages are frustrating. White space gives the page an open feel and allows the eye to skim the page more quickly. Figure 25.2 uses white space effectively.
- **Provide ample margins.** Margins keep your text from blurring at the edges of the computer screen.
- **Use an unjustified right margin.** An unjustified margin makes for easier reading.
- **Use hyperlinks to direct readers to other information.** In Figure 25.2, hyperlinks within the paragraphs and down the left margin provide quick access to more detail. Don't overuse hyperlinks. More than ten in a column is excessive.
- **Use a consistent font style and size.** Figure 25.2 uses the same font style and size for body text (paragraphs) and a slightly larger font size—but identical style—for headings. Don't mix and match typefaces randomly.

- **Don't use underlining for emphasis.** On a Web page, underlining is only used to indicate a hyperlink.
- **Use ample headings.** People skimming a Web page look for headings as guides to the content areas they seek.
- **Use visuals (charts, graphs, photographs) effectively.** Excessive visuals confuse readers. Inadequate visuals cause readers to avoid the page. Figure 25.2 takes advantage of the F-shaped reading pattern to use visuals: a horizontal visual across the top, and small square visuals along the left vertical margin. Photographs are nicely balanced with text.
- **Use a balanced color palette.** Color can make a Web page attractive and easier to navigate. In Figure 25.2, all primary headings are green; secondary headings are tan. Colors of text and visuals need to reflect the theme of the Web page (e.g., the use of greens, tan, blues, and browns mirror the earth tone theme of a national park). For more on color, see Chapter 12.

TECHNIQUES AND TECHNOLOGIES FOR CREATING WEB SITES

Creating a Web site typically involves two major steps. First, you need to plan your overall approach to the site. To do this, you and the team would sketch out a plan for the site, using a storyboard or other approach. After this high-level planning comes the detail work involved in writing and designing each individual Web page on the site. Storyboarding, teamwork, and using the right tools and technologies are all essential to the process.

Planning Web Sites Using Storyboarding

Use storyboarding to get started

When planning a print document, you might create an outline (see Chapter 10 for more on outlining). But to plan a Web site, use a storyboard—a sketch of the site, as in Figure 25.4. This type of storyboard for a Web site is often called a site map. The site map gives you (and others on the design team) an overall view of what the site will contain. (For more on storyboarding, see Chapter 5.)

Teamwork When Creating Web Sites

Get the team started via meetings and brainstorming

As discussed earlier, workplace Web sites are typically developed by a team whose members need to connect their different areas of expertise. Meetings, especially during the early planning stages, allow everyone to have input. Chapter 5 offers advice for conducting meetings. Early in the process, use creative thinking,

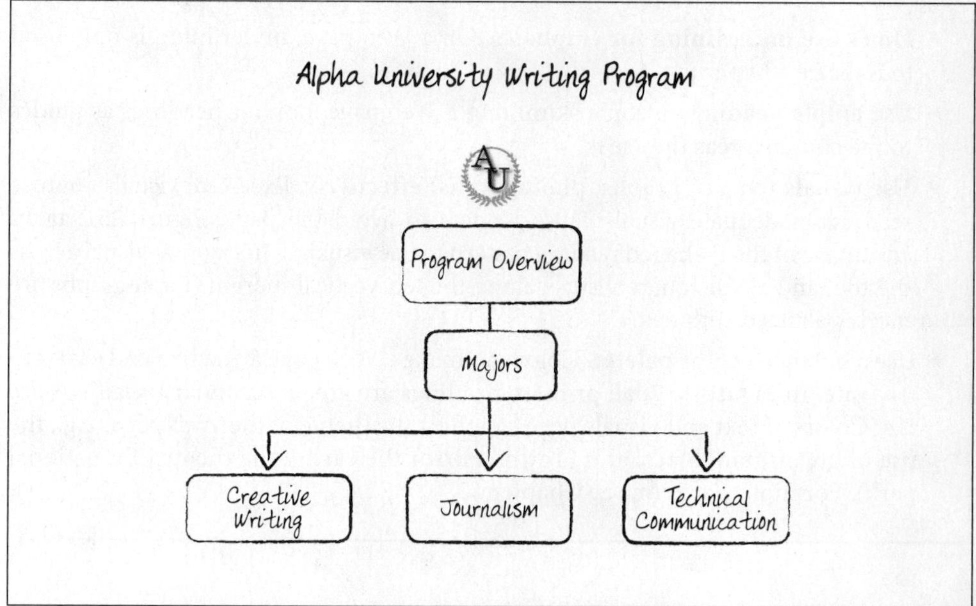

FIGURE 25.4 **A Storyboard Map for a Web Site for Alpha University's Writing Program** Each node represents a different Web page. The top node (Program Overview) represents the main Web page (home page).

especially brainstorming and storyboarding (page 93) to develop a unified vision for the site.

Creating Web Pages Using Word Processing and Other Software

Software for creating Web sites

Simple Web pages can be created with everyday software, such as word-processing programs. These programs typically allow you to export a *Word* (or similar) document to a Web page. For more complicated Web sites, programs such as *Adobe Dreamweaver* and *NVU* (an open source program) are the norm. Professional Web designers and programmers use these tools to create complex sites that include interactive features, animation, online shopping links, and more. To learn about Web design, look for a workshop or short course through your school, community education center, or local library.

GLOBAL ISSUES AND WEB PAGES

Most Web pages have global audiences

Readers of Web pages may come from a variety of countries and cultures. Keep these global audiences in mind as you write and design your site. Word choice, visuals, tone, and even color choices can have different meanings for different cultures.

NOTE *Some countries censor which parts of the Internet users can access, but even in these cases, many Web sites are still available.*

GUIDELINES for Addressing Global Audiences

- **Write in clear, simple English, in a way that makes translation easy.** Most Web pages originate in the United States and are written in English, but not every reader speaks English as a first language. Follow the suggestions on page 100, on writing for translation.
- **Avoid cultural references and humor.** These references are not only hard to translate but can also be offensive to some cultures. See Chapter 5, pages 99–100.
- **Offer different language options.** For a global audience, Web sites should include links to information in different languages. National parks have international visitors; readers of Figure 25.2 can click on links for Japanese, Chinese, Spanish, French, and German languages.
- **Use colors and visuals appropriately.** If your Web site is aimed at specific cultural groups, find out whether certain colors or images will be offensive. See Chapter 12, page 286, for more on cultural considerations when presenting visual information.

ETHICAL AND LEGAL CONSIDERATIONS

The power of a Web page to convey information instantaneously and worldwide increases the writer's or designer's need for sound ethical and legal judgment.

Ethical Considerations

How a Web page can be unethical

Consider the speed of the Internet, its global reach, and a Web page's ability to combine sound, color, images, text, and interactivity. These features create the potential for manipulation and distortion. Imagine a Web site for an herbal remedy that some people feel is helpful for anxiety. This remedy may not have FDA approval and may carry harmful side effects. But a site promoting this product could easily, and at little cost, be set up to look scientific and factual. Fancy logos from quasi-scientific organizations might convey a sense of professional credibility. Statistics, charts, and links to other sites might create the appearance of a valid medical site. As a communicator, you need to question the possible outcome for users and the overall risks to society of setting up such a site.

Legal Considerations

Legal considerations in preparing Web pages include copyright issues and privacy considerations.

Copyright issues

Verify the ownership of everything you include on a Web page. If you have located a bar chart elsewhere on the Web that you'd like to insert, it is technically very easy to cut and paste or download the bar chart to your page. But is this use legal? Even if the chart has no copyright symbol ©, in the United States all expressions fixed in a tangible medium are copyrighted. The © symbol is not absolutely necessary. Therefore, downloading and including the chart in your document could be a copyright infringement. When in doubt, use copyright-free visuals or obtain written permission, even if you are only linking from your Web page to another Web page. See Chapter 7 for more information about copyright.

Privacy considerations

Web pages raise privacy concerns as well, especially in regard to gathering the personal information of visitors to the site. Many organizations create privacy statements that can be accessed on their Web sites. Such statements let readers know how information will be used and what rights readers have. Privacy statements should be readily available on a site, and they should be written in language that anyone can understand. As a technical communicator, you may be asked to help write such a privacy statement.

CHECKLIST: Writing and Designing Web Pages

(Numbers in parentheses refer to the first page of discussion)

Audience and Purpose

- ☐ Is the page easy to enter, navigate, and exit? (623)
- ☐ Is the content useful and worthwhile? (623)
- ☐ Is the page at the right level of technicality for its primary audience? (621)

Writing

- ☐ Is the most important information contained in the early paragraphs? (624)
- ☐ Is the information chunked for easy access and quick reading? (624)
- ☐ Are sentences and paragraphs short and to the point? (624)
- ☐ Is the content written in a factual, neutral tone? (624)

Design

- ☐ Does the page follow an "F-shaped" reading pattern? (626)
- ☐ Are text and images well balanced? (623)
- ☐ Is there plenty of white space and margins to help guide the eye? (626)

- ☐ Are paragraphs visually compact and short? (624)
- ☐ Are hyperlinks used to direct readers to other information? (626)
- ☐ Is the page easy for the eye to scan? (623)
- ☐ Is key material highlighted by headings, color, and so on? (627)
- ☐ Are visuals used effectively? (623)
- ☐ Is the entire Web site sketched out using a storyboard? (627)

Teamwork

- ☐ Is there a meeting schedule for the project? (84)
- ☐ Has the team used brainstorming to get started? (92)
- ☐ Has the team determined what role (writer, designer, programmer, researcher) each person will play? (84)

Global Issues

- ☐ Is the writing clear enough for non-native speakers of English to understand and can it be easily translated? (629)
- ☐ Does the page avoid cultural references and humor? (629)
- ☐ If appropriate, does the page offer different language options? (629)
- ☐ Are colors and visuals used appropriately? (629)

Ethical and Legal Issues

- ☐ Are text and visuals truthful and not distorted or manipulative? (629)
- ☐ Has permission been granted to use items on the page where copyright is a concern? (630)
- ☐ If appropriate, does the page link to the organization's privacy policy? (630)

Projects

GENERAL

1. With a classmate, locate one or two Web sites you might use as research sources for a project. Using the guidelines in this chapter, assess these sites for quality of structure, style, use of visuals, and design. Write up your findings in an email message to your instructor. Include the Web address for each site you used.
2. Design a new Web page for your major. *Note*: Do not use any such existing page on your school or department Web site as a model.

TEAM

Divide into groups by major. As a team, compare the versions of the Web page you each designed individually for General Project 2, above. Now, create a team version of that same Web page.

DIGITAL AND SOCIAL MEDIA

Do some research to develop your own "top ten" list of effective Web design principles. Begin by reviewing this chapter and exploring the two Web sites listed below. Then find other resources on Web style and

Web design. Based on what you find, assemble your list. Using your list as a guide, find three sites that exemplify the principles of effective Web design and style. Prepare a short presentation on your exemplary sites, and explain why you selected them as examples of good design.

- <webstyleguide.com/wsg3/index.html>: *Web Style Guide*, by Lynch and Horton, widely regarded as a "bible" of Web design.
- <www.nngroup.com/articles/be-succinct-writing-for-the-web/>: *Writing for the Web*, by Jakob Nielsen, a leading Web usability expert.

GLOBAL

Find Web sites that are in different languages or based in different countries. Besides differences in language, note any other differences between non-U.S. Web sites and those that originate in the United States. Here are some features to look for:

- **Use of color.** Different cultures often associate unique meanings with certain colors. For example, red may be used in India to mean procreation or life, while in the United States it is often associated with danger or warnings (Hoft 267).
- **Issues of privacy.** U.S. sites often send out *cookies* (files sent to your computer that give Web site providers information about you), but other countries, such as Germany, allow no personal information to be used without an individual's permission. Note if any of the sites mention their privacy policy in this regard.

Keep track of what you find, and present your findings in class.

26 Social Media

"As director of social media for a local non-profit, my job is to use blogs, wikis, and social networks to raise awareness of environmental issues. These tools help us stay in touch with our regular supporters, and they help us reach out to new supporters, too. The interactivity is great—anyone can post a comment to the blog or update an entry on our wiki, although I do exercise some editorial control to ensure quality. Our social network page makes it easy for us to connect with people who share similar goals and interests. We keep our social network page professional and fact-based."

—Geoffrey Wersan,
Director of Social Media,
environmental advocacy group

LEARNING OBJECTIVES FOR THIS CHAPTER

- Understand audience and purpose for social media
- Understand how to write for social media
- Recognize different types of social media
- Understand uses of social media for workplace communication
- Consider the legal and ethical implications of these media
- Understand how these media are changing the ways we work and learn

Importance of social media

Social media are playing an increasingly important role in the workplace. In technical communication, social media can serve as a resource for staying in touch with colleagues, acquiring information from technical experts, learning more about customer preferences, sharing updated information with customers, and keeping professionals connected. On the job, you might use social media to research a report or proposal, to post a job announcement, or to learn more about the professional background of a job candidate. You might also be asked to help write, maintain, and update these sites.

Social media can help organizations disseminate cutting-edge technical and scientific research—and get feedback from people who may not be experts but who have first-hand experience. In one case, the Mayo Clinic used Twitter to announce a new research study about celiac disease (an autoimmune disease that prevents the digestion of wheat gluten). The Clinic was able to track how the Twitter messages spread and to send a prepublication copy of the article to select readers from the Twitter stream. Mayo gave these readers permission to blog about the study (adapted from Ruiz).

Jobs for "social media director" are on the rise. For example, organizations such as Ford Motor Company are hiring people who specialize in social media marketing; duties include keeping the company's social media sites (blog, Facebook page) up to date and reviewing and measuring online customer behavior (such as how often people click on a link or search parts of the site) (Monty). These jobs require strong writing skills along with an ability to understand the audience, purpose, and specific technology used for the site.

CONSIDERING AUDIENCE AND PURPOSE

Internal and external audience and purpose

In the workplace, social media can have two kinds of audiences: internal (people inside the organization) and external (people outside the organization). Internal audiences typically don't need a lot of explanation or background; they already understand the specialized language of the field and customs of the organization. These audiences want straightforward content that will help them complete a project. External audiences, on the other hand, may know little about the topic and need more detailed information, including definitions of technical terms, links to explanations, and illustrations.

Because social media has a wide reach across different time zones and countries, the audience can be vast. For external audiences, social media can reach millions of people quickly and easily. In October 2012, Facebook, the most popular social networking site, reported more than one billion participants. During large-scale events (elections, natural disasters, major news or business stories), Twitter feeds can have millions of followers.

Audience as Contributor

External audience members can be important contributors to social media sites. For instance, many companies encourage customers to provide feedback via a customer review site, such as Yelp or TripAdvisor. Increasingly, product instructions and user documentation (see Chapter 20) are posted online, with a blog or wiki available so readers can report or update the documentation if they notice problems or errors. When audience members become contributors, there are more chances to collect important information. But there is also a greater need for fact-checking.

As one technical communication expert noted:

> "The challenge for the professional communicator is to contribute at a higher level, welcoming community involvement and building on it. For the technical writer, that may mean doing less writing and more curating of content—for example, identifying and promoting the best wiki contributions, correcting errors, clarifying unclear language, adding illustrations, and improving organization" (Carr).

See "Ethical and Legal Considerations," page 641 in this chapter.

USING SOCIAL MEDIA FOR TECHNICAL COMMUNICATION

"Social media" covers a wide range of applications, including blogs, wikis, networking sites, customer review sites, and Twitter feeds. Each application requires a different approach to audience and purpose.

Variety of social media

Blogs

Blogs (short for Web logs) began as tools to keep track of email discussions. Rather than search through old email, people could view messages in reverse chronological order on a blog. Soon, blogs became popular for discussions on

Use of internal and external blogs

political topics, hobbies, and other mutual interests. Organizations saw the benefits of using blogs—both internally and externally—to share information and provide spaces for discussion. Companies such as Apple, Intel, and others use blogs to help employees share information. These internal blogs, accessible only to those within the company, are focused on audiences such as engineers, managers, technical writers, and others. Companies also create external blogs, designed for more general audiences outside the company.

Internal blogs enhance workflow and morale. In large organizations, blogs can provide an alternative to email for routine in-house communication. Anyone in the network can post a message or comment on other messages. In the blogging environment, meetings can be conducted without the time and location constraints of face-to-face meetings. Employee training can be delivered, and updates about company developments can be circulated. Blogs are especially useful for collaborating. For example, someone in a company's engineering department can create a forum to discuss various solutions to a technical problem. Colleagues can then weigh in with their suggestions.

External blogs facilitate customer feedback on products and services, enhance marketing and public relations, provide timely news and updates, and help personalize a large organization. Blogs give businesses a chance to show a personal, informal side, to respond amiably and quickly to customer concerns, and to allow customers to provide ideas and feedback. Tone, of course, is critical in an organization's blog; it needs to sound friendly, welcoming, and sincere. The blog should invite readers in.

Marriott International, for example, has created a "Marriott on the Move" blog (Figure 26.1) to provide customers with updates about travel and hotel specials. Customers can use the blog to make comments, too, providing the company with immediate feedback. Non-profits and government organizations, such as the Centers for Diseases Control (CDC) and the National Wildlife Federation also use blogs, aimed primarily at external audiences and designed to keep the public updated on timely topics.

Blogs are typically written and edited by one person or a small group of people. Many other people can comment, but only a few individuals serve as authors. In this way, the organization can maintain control over the accuracy and tone of the message.

Wikis

Uses of internal and external wikis

A wiki (from the Hawaiian phrase *wiki wiki*, meaning "quick") is a type of Web site used to collect and keep information updated. Most people are familiar with *Wikipedia*, the online encyclopedia that allows anyone to write and revise its content. Companies and other organizations also use wikis to update content in a wide variety of technical and scientific areas. As with blogs, organizations maintain both internal and external wikis, depending on the project and need.

FIGURE 26.1 An External Corporate Blog
Source: Reprinted with permission of Marriott International, Inc.

But unlike blogs, which typically have only a few people serving as authors, wikis encourage everyone to contribute to the site's content.

Internal wikis provide a one-stop site for employees seeking information about a project or topic. Employees can add to and update the content; the wiki keeps track of the date of entries and revisions. Members of an engineering team working on an airline hydraulic system, for example, might create a wiki to track the latest information about fluid pressure, landing gear, wings and flaps, and so forth. As the project develops, the wiki could be updated by the engineers and other team members. To ensure confidentiality, internal wikis can only be accessed by authorized users. Usually a login and password are required.

External wikis allow people to locate and update content that is specific to their area of expertise. Because external wikis are open to countless people with all sorts of knowledge, these sites can be excellent sources of information. But the lack of gatekeeping by a central editor (as in peer-reviewed journal articles or books) also creates the potential for inaccuracy. A well-managed external wiki, one that balances open access with some level of editorial control, can be a valuable resource.

Take a look at <plastics.inwiki.org/Main_Page>, a wiki designed for chemists and technicians who work with plastics. These specialists can access the information and also contribute, revise, and update entries.

GUIDELINES for Writing and Using Blogs and Wikis

- **Use standard software.** Readers expect blogs and wikis to have a certain look and feel. Tools such as *Blogger* (<www.blogger.com>) and *Wikispaces* (<www.wikispaces.com>) can be adapted to confidential workplace environments.
- **Keep Web writing guidelines in mind.** Like Web pages, blogs and wikis work best when information is written in chunks, using short sentences and a clear, readable style. See Chapter 25, "Guidelines for Writing Web Pages," page 624.
- **Write differently for internal versus external audiences.** Internal audiences do not require as much background. External audiences may require more explanation.
- **Think carefully before posting comments.** An internal blog is considered workplace communication; an external blog represents the organization. In both cases, keep your ideas factual and tone professional.
- **For an external blog, focus on the customer's priorities and needs.** A friendly, encouraging tone goes a long way in good customer relations.
- **Check blog and wiki entries for credibility.** Check the content to see when it was last updated (on a wiki, this information is usually under the "history" tab).
- **Before editing or adding to a wiki, get your facts and your tone straight.** If you spot some type of error, be diplomatic in your correction—and be sure you aren't creating some other type of error.

Social Networking Sites

Uses of Facebook and other social networking sites

Social networks connect people to each other and to sites of mutual interest. Facebook is the most popular social networking site. Originally developed for college students, Facebook is now used by friends, families, professional associates, political campaigns, non-profits, and businesses. Many organizations maintain a Facebook page to highlight or promote a particular product or service within the company. For example, a soft drink company might create a Facebook page to promote a new beverage. Government agencies use Facebook to share news events, provide updates and photos, and allow other Facebook users to comment and share information with friends. NASA's Mars Curiosity Rover has a Facebook page, which has been "liked" by almost half a million people.

Facebook's most popular use continues to be by individuals, who use the site to keep up with friends and family. Although you may think of your personal Facebook page as unrelated to your work life, keep in mind that employers regularly check Facebook and other social networking sites as part of the job interview process.

Job and Professional Networking Sites

Uses of LinkedIn and other professional networking sites

Whereas Facebook is used mainly for staying in touch with friends and family (and showcasing companies and products), LinkedIn and similar sites (such as Jobster or Plaxo) exist for the specific purpose of supporting professional networking and job hunting. These sites allow you to maintain an updated profile, resume, and list of professional references. You can also join professional groups; through these groups, you will receive postings of job openings and can connect with other people in your profession. For more on using professional networking sites for the job search, see Chapter 17, page 382.

GUIDELINES for Writing and Using Social Networks

- **Write with a friendly yet professional tone.** It's always nice to be friendly, but a professional tone will make your message more credible.
- **Keep ideas focused and specific.** Social networks let you narrow your message down to a targeted audience (say, customers who use a specific model of laptop).
- **If using photos or video, check the licensing agreement and other copyright information.** On photo sharing sites like Flickr, people typically list this information. Check to see if you need to request permission or if the photographer has granted some limited rights. See Chapter 12 for more about copyright and using visuals.
- **Be discreet about what you post.** When posting to your personal Facebook or other page, remember to omit private or potentially damaging information. It may be fun to tell your friends how many parties you've attended, but when you apply for a job, this information may come back to haunt you.
- **Keep global readers in mind.** Social networking pages can typically be viewed by readers from across many countries and cultures. Keep the content accessible to a wide audience (see Chapter 5 for more on global audiences).

Customer Review Sites

Use of Yelp and other customer review sites

For companies such as restaurants, hotels, and entertainment venues, word of mouth can be the most important—or the most damaging—form of advertising. Customer review sites (Yelp and TripAdvisor are two of the most popular) allow registered members to post feedback in the form of short reviews. People can also rate the business, using a number of stars. In some cases, companies are able to write a follow-up response, which can be especially important if the customer review is not favorable.

Twitter Feeds

Uses of Twitter

Twitter provides real-time postings and updates in a concise format. Individuals as well as companies, government agencies, and other organizations maintain Twitter feeds to keep friends, business associates, customers, and citizens informed and updated. Called "tweets," the form of writing on Twitter site is concise, with a limit of 140 characters. A tweet may contain a Web address, directing readers to a Web site for more information.

Twitter can be especially effective in situations that require a rapid response. For example, when major weather event (such as a hurricane or blizzard) interrupts air travel, airlines become inundated with calls from customers. A Twitter feed became an effective method for providing customers with up-to-date information, by the minute, on flight cancelations, contingency plans, and resources for more information. See Figure 26.2—note the short, compact, informational tweets that are written with a professional, friendly tone.

PineTree Airways	**PT Airways** @PTAirways @ LauraG Sorry you can't get through by phone. Blizzard has slowed things down. Please rebook online if you can bit.ly/LGjEcl/11 ^CF
PineTree Airways	**PT Airways** @PTAirways @ NitaR International connections are still being rebooked. Check with a gate agent when you get in. ^CF
PineTree Airways	**PT Airways** @PTAirways @ AnetaD Please call us again at the new 800 no. we just posted on the website. Have your confirmation no. handy. ^MC
PineTree Airways	**PT Airways** @PTAirways @ greg_s Greg, did you check your flight status on our website? Here's the link bit.ly/XYZGEx ^MC
PineTree Airways	**PT Airways** @PTAirways @ joan_kc MSP is providing meals and blankets if you are stranded. Please see a gate agent. Thank you for your patience. ^CF
PineTree Airways	**PT Airways** @PTAirways @ Geoff_travels Geoff, that flight is delayed two hours. Keep checking our website if you can bit.ly/LGjEcl/11 thank you. ^CF
PineTree Airways	**PT Airways** @PTAirways Dear customers, as storm conditions improve, we will be updating all flight statuses so please stay tuned to Twitter and our website.

FIGURE 26.2 **Twitter feed during a weather emergency.**

As Figure 26.2 shows, organizations recognize that Twitter can provide customers with real-time information and alleviate busy phone lines. This company is also using Twitter for marketing purposes by displaying its recognizable company logo. As well, many organizations are using Twitter to recruit new employees. See Chapter 17, page 382, for more information on Twitter and the job search.

ETHICAL AND LEGAL CONSIDERATIONS

Social media can be an effective way to reach customers, stay connected, and do research. But it also harbors potential for information abuse. One such example is "stealth marketing," in which bloggers who publish supposedly objective product reviews fail to disclose the free merchandise or cash payments they received for their flattering portrayals.

Social media and privacy

People need to be able to trust the information they receive. Furthermore, in workplace settings, coworkers need to have confidence in the discretion of their colleagues. As with email, any employee who discusses proprietary matters (see page 67) or who posts defamatory comments can face serious legal consequences—not to mention job termination. Also like email, blogs, wikis, and social networks carry the potential for violations of copyright or privacy (see page 340). To avoid such problems, corporate blogs often have a moderator who screens any comment before it is posted.

To reinforce ethical, legal, and privacy standards, companies such as IBM have established explicit policies that govern social media. See, for example, "IBM Social Computing Guidelines," at <www.ibm.com/blogs/zz/en/guidelines.html>.

Many companies view social media as an opportunity to reach thousands of potential customers—but not without risk. Employees assigned to work on social marketing may waste incredible amounts of time reading Facebook pages and looking at Twitter feeds. Also, if companies make a mistake (say, an inaccurate claim about a product) on a social network, those potential customers can turn the mistake into a public relations nightmare (Baker 48–50).

CHECKLIST: Social Media

(Numbers in parentheses refer to the first page of discussion)

- ☐ Is the information you post on social media written in a way that is appropriate for the audience and purpose? (634)
- ☐ Is the site organized, accessible, and current? (634)
- ☐ If the blog is internal, is the information appropriate for the organization? (636)
- ☐ If the blog is external, does it reflect positively on the organization? (636)
- ☐ If the wiki is internal, is the information current, accurate, and confidential? (637)

CHECKLIST: (*continued*)

- ☐ If the wiki is external, is there any editorial oversight? (637)
- ☐ Is the social network the most appropriate one for the intended readers (Facebook for a person or business, LinkedIn for job and career building)? (635)
- ☐ Does the site respect the privacy of its users? (641)
- ☐ Is the tone friendly, yet professional? If posting on Twitter, is the message clear in 140 characters or less? (639)
- ☐ If video, photographs, or other copyrighted information are included on a site, has permission been granted to use this material? (639)
- ☐ For personal sites (such as Facebook), does the information you've posted portray you in a way you would want a potential employer to see? (638)
- ☐ Does the posting satisfy ethical and legal standards? (641)

Projects

GENERAL

Locate a blog related to your major or an area where you've had an internship or job. Follow the discussion for a few days; then write a brief analysis of the blog and what you observed. Who is the audience? What topics are discussed? Is the blog suitable for professionals or is it more of a social hang-out? Assume you are applying for a job or internship. Using LinkedIn or another professional social networking site, make a list of the items you want to highlight about your education and skills. Review the entries of other professionals in your field to determine how you would set up your own entry. (See Chapter 17 for more on social networks and the job search process.)

TEAM

In teams of 3–4 students, pick an on-campus organization (a club, an athletic group, a professional society for students). What are some ways a social networking page, such as Facebook, could help the organization network with current members and reach out to potential new members? Discuss what information you would place on the site and what information you would omit. Review Guidelines for Writing and Using Social Networks in this chapter (page 639). Write an editorial policy with ground rules for the tone, style, and topics to be discussed.

DIGITAL AND SOCIAL MEDIA

Go to a customer review site and locate a customer complaint or bad review of a restaurant in your area. In groups of 2–3 students, discuss the appropriate tone, word choice, and approach you as the restaurant owner would take in response. Write your response, limiting the number of words to whatever the site allows. Now, imagine a similar situation on Twitter. Revise your response to fit Twitter's 140 character limit. (See Chapter 3 pages 53–55 for guidelines on persuasion and Chapter 11 page 233 for guidelines on professional tone and style.)

GLOBAL

Social media has global reach—you can use these tools to collaborate with team members from other countries. Locate a wiki related to your major (for science or engineering majors, the plastics wiki on page 637 is a good example). See if the wiki is available in languages other than English. Also, can you tell if contributors are from different countries? Write a memo to your instructor explaining what you found.

PART 5

Resources for Technical Writers

Appendix A: A Quick Guide to Documentation

Appendix B: A Quick Guide to Grammar, Usage, and Mechanics

Appendix

A A Quick Guide to Documentation

TAKING NOTES

Researchers take notes in many ways, including notecards or, increasingly, on a computer. You can take notes using citation software (such as *Ref Works* or *Zotero*) that allows notes to be filed, shuffled, and retrieved by author, title, topic, date, or key words. You can also just use a word-processing program. Whether you use a computer or notecards, your notes should be easy to organize and reorganize.

GUIDELINES for Recording Research Findings

- **Make a separate bibliography listing for each work you consult.** Record that work's complete entry (Figure QG.1), using the citation format that will appear in your document. (See pages 651–79 for sample entries.) Record the information accurately so that you won't have to relocate a source at the last minute.

Record each bibliographic citation exactly as it will appear in your final report

> Pinsky, Mark A. *The EMF Book: What You Should Know about Electromagnetic Fields, Electromagnetic Radiation, and Your Health.* New York: Warner, 1995. Print.

FIGURE QG.1 **Recording a Bibliographic Citation**

When searching online, you can often print out a work's full bibliographic record or save it to your computer, to ensure an accurate citation.

- **Skim the entire work to locate relevant material.** Look over the table of contents and the index. Check the introduction for an overview or thesis. Look for informative headings.
- **Go back and decide what to record.** Use a separate entry for each item.

- **Be selective.** Don't copy or paraphrase every word. (See the Guidelines for Summarizing, page 176.)
- **Record the item as a quotation or paraphrase.** When quoting others directly, be sure to record words and punctuation accurately. When restating material in your own words, preserve the original meaning and emphasis.
- **Highlight all quoted material.** Place quotation marks around all directly quoted material so that you don't lose track of exactly what is being quoted.

QUOTING THE WORK OF OTHERS

You must place quotation marks around all exact wording you borrow, whether the words were written, spoken (as in an interview or presentation), or appeared in electronic form. Even a single borrowed sentence or phrase, or a single word used in a special way, needs quotation marks, with the exact source properly cited. These sources include people with whom you collaborate.

Plagiarism is often unintentional

If your notes don't identify quoted material accurately, you might forget to credit the source. Even when this omission is unintentional, you face the charge of *plagiarism* (misrepresenting the words or ideas of someone else as your own). Possible consequences of plagiarism include expulsion from school, loss of a job, and a lawsuit.

The perils of buying plagiarized work online

It's no secret that any cheater can purchase reports, term papers, and other documents on the Web. But antiplagiarism Web sites, such as turnitin.com, now enable professors to cross-reference a suspicious paper against Web material as well as millions of student papers, flagging and identifying each plagiarized source.

GUIDELINES for Quoting the Work of Others

Expressions that warrant direct quotation

- **Use a direct quotation only when absolutely necessary.** Sometimes a direct quotation is the only way to do justice to the author's own words:

  > "Writing is a way to end up thinking something you couldn't have started out thinking" (Elbow 15).

  > Think of the topic sentence as "the one sentence you would keep if you could keep only one" (USAF Academy 11).

GUIDELINES *continued*

Consider quoting directly for these purposes:

Reasons for quoting directly

—to preserve special phrasing or emphasis
—to preserve precise meaning
—to preserve the original line of reasoning
—to preserve an especially striking or colorful example
—to convey the authority and complexity of expert opinion
—to convey the original's voice, sincerity, or emotional intensity

▸ **Ensure accuracy.** Copy the selection word for word; record the exact page numbers; and double-check that you haven't altered the original expression in any way (Figure QG.2).

Pinsky, Mark A. pp. 29–30.

Place quotation marks around all directly quoted material

"Neither electromagnetic fields nor electromagnetic radiation cause cancer per se, most researchers agree. What they may do is promote cancer. Cancer is a multistage process that requires an 'initiator' that makes a cell or group of cells abnormal. Everyone has cancerous cells in his or her body. Cancer—the disease as we think of it—occurs when these cancerous cells grow uncontrollably."

FIGURE QG.2 **Recording a Quotation**

▸ **Keep the quotation as brief as possible.** For conciseness and emphasis, use *ellipses:* Use three spaced periods (...) to indicate each omission within a single sentence. Add a fourth period to indicate each omission that includes the end of a sentence or multi-sentence sections of text.

Ellipsis within and between sentences

> Use three ... periods to indicate each omission within a single sentence. Add a fourth period to indicate ... the end of a sentence....

The elliptical passage must be grammatical and must not distort the original meaning. (For additional guidelines, see page 694.)

Brackets setting off the added words within a quotation

▸ **Use square brackets to insert your own clarifying comments or to add transitions between various parts of the original.**

> "Job stress [in aircraft ground control] can lead to disaster."

- **Embed quoted material in your sentences clearly and grammatically.** Introduce integrated quotations with phrases such as "Jones argues that," or "Gomez concludes that." More importantly, use a transitional phrase to show the relationship between the quoted idea and the sentence that precedes it:

> One investigation of age discrimination at select *Fortune* 500 companies found that " middle managers over age 45 are an endangered species" (Jablonski 69).

An introduction that unifies a quotation with the discussion

Your integrated sentence should be grammatical:

> "The present farming crisis," Marx argues, "is a direct result of rampant land speculation" (41).

Quoted material integrated grammatically with the writer's words

(For additional guidelines, see pages 693–94.)

- **Quote passages four lines or longer in block form.** Avoid relying on long quotations except in these instances:

—to provide an extended example, definition, or analogy (see page 231)
—to analyze or discuss an idea or concept (see page 515)

Reasons for quoting a long passage

Double-space a block quotation and indent the entire block ten spaces. Do not indent the first line of the passage, but do indent first lines of subsequent paragraphs three spaces. Do not use quotation marks.

- **Introduce the quotation and discuss its significance.**

> Here is a corporate executive's description of some audiences you can expect to address:

An introduction to quoted material

- **Cite the source of each quoted passage.**

Research writing is a process of independent thinking in which you work with the ideas of others in order to reach your own conclusions; unless the author's exact wording is essential, try to paraphrase, instead of quoting, borrowed material.

PARAPHRASING THE WORK OF OTHERS

Paraphrasing means more than changing or shuffling a few words; it means restating the original idea in your own words—sometimes in a clearer, more direct, and emphatic way—and giving full credit to the source.

Faulty paraphrasing is a form of plagiarism

To borrow or adapt someone else's ideas or reasoning without properly documenting the source is plagiarism. To offer as a paraphrase an original passage that is only slightly altered—even when you document the source—also is plagiarism. Equally unethical is offering a paraphrase, although documented, that distorts the original meaning.

GUIDELINES for Paraphrasing

- **Refer to the author early in the paraphrase,** to indicate the beginning of the borrowed passage.
- **Retain key words from the original,** to preserve its meaning.
- **Restructure and combine original sentences** for emphasis and fluency.
- **Delete needless words from the original,** for conciseness.
- **Use your own words and phrases** to clarify the author's ideas.
- **Cite (in parentheses) the exact source,** to mark the end of the borrowed passage and to give full credit.
- **Be sure to preserve the author's original intent** (Weinstein 3).

Figure QG.3 shows an entry paraphrased from Figure QG.2. Paraphrased material is not enclosed within quotation marks, but it is documented to acknowledge your debt to the source. The paraphrase in the figure is adapted from the quote on p. 646.

Signal the beginning of the paraphrase by citing the author, and the end by citing the source

Pinsky, Mark A.

Pinsky explains that electromagnetic waves probably do not directly cause cancer. However, they might contribute to the uncontrollable growth of those cancer cells normally present—but controlled—in the human body (29–30).

FIGURE QG.3 Recording a Paraphrase

WHAT YOU SHOULD DOCUMENT

Document any insight, assertion, fact, finding, interpretation, judgment, or other "appropriated material that readers might otherwise mistake for your own" (Gibaldi and Achtert 155). Whether the material appears in published form or not, you must document these sources:

Sources that require documentation

- any source from which you use exact wording
- any source from which you adapt material in your own words
- any visual illustration: charts, graphs, drawings, or the like (see Chapter 12 for documenting visuals)

How to document a confidential source

In some instances, you might have reason to preserve the anonymity of unpublished sources: for example, to allow people to respond candidly without fear of reprisal (as with employee criticism of the company), or to protect their privacy (as with certain material from email inquiries or electronic discussion groups). You must still document the fact that you are not the originator of this material. Do this by providing a general acknowledgment in the text such as "A number of employees expressed frustration with . . ." along with a general citation in your list of references or works cited such as "Interviews with Polex employees, May 2013."

Common knowledge need not be documented

You don't need to document anything considered *common knowledge:* material that appears repeatedly in general sources. In medicine, for instance, it has become common knowledge that foods containing animal fat contribute to higher blood cholesterol levels. So in a report on fatty diets and heart disease, you probably would not need to document that well-known fact. But you would document information about how the fat/cholesterol connection was discovered, what subsequent studies have found (say, the role of saturated versus unsaturated fats), and any information for which some other person could claim specific credit. If the borrowed material can be found in only one specific source, not in multiple sources, document it. When in doubt, document the source.

HOW YOU SHOULD DOCUMENT

Documentation practices vary widely, but all systems work almost identically: a brief reference in the text names the source and refers readers to the complete citation, which allows readers to retrieve the source.

Many disciplines, institutions, and organizations publish their own style guides or documentation manuals. This quick guide illustrates citations and entries for three styles widely used for documenting sources in their respective disciplines:

- Modern Language Association (MLA) style, for the humanities
- American Psychological Association (APA) style, for the social sciences
- Council of Science Editors (CSE) style, for the natural and applied sciences

Any of these three styles can be adapted to most research writing. Use one style consistently throughout the document.

MLA DOCUMENTATION STYLE

Cite a source briefly in text and fully at the end

Most writers in English and other humanities fields follow the *MLA Handbook for Writers of Research Papers, 7th ed.* New York: Modern Language Association, 2009. In MLA style, in-text parenthetical references briefly identify each source. Full documentation then appears in a Works Cited section at the end of the document. The parenthetical reference usually includes the author's surname and the exact page number where the borrowed material can be found:

Parenthetical reference in the text

> One notable study indicates an elevated risk of leukemia for children exposed to certain types of electromagnetic fields (Bowman et al. 59).

Readers seeking the complete citation for Bowman can refer easily to the Works Cited section, listed alphabetically by author:

Full citation at document's end

> Bowman, J. D., et al. "Hypothesis: The Risk of Childhood Leukemia Is Related to Combinations of Power-Frequency and Static Magnetic Fields." *Bioelectromagnetics* 16.1 (1995): 48-59. Print.

This complete citation includes page numbers for the entire article.

MLA Parenthetical References

For clear and informative parenthetical references, observe these rules:

How to cite briefly in text

- If your discussion names the author, do not repeat the name in your parenthetical reference; simply give the page number(s):

Citing page numbers only

> Bowman et al. explain how their study indicates an elevated risk of leukemia for children exposed to certain types of electromagnetic fields (59).

- If you cite two or more works in a single parenthetical reference, separate the citations with semicolons:

Three works in a single reference

> (Jones 32; Leduc 41; Gomez 293-94)

- If you cite two or more authors with the same surnames, include the first initial in your parenthetical reference to each author:

Two authors with identical surnames

> (R. Jones 32)

> (S. Jones 14-15)

- If you cite two or more works by the same author, include the first significant word from each work's title, or a shortened version:

(Lamont, *Biomedicine* 100–01)

Two works by one author

(Lamont, *Diagnostic Tests* 81)

- If the work is by an institutional or corporate author or if it is unsigned (author is unknown), use only the first few words of the institutional name or the work's title in your parenthetical reference:

(American Medical Assn. 2)

Institutional, corporate, or anonymous author

("Distribution Systems" 18)

Keep parenthetical references brief; when possible, name the source in your discussion and place only the page number(s) in parentheses.

Where to place a parenthetical reference

For a paraphrase, place the parenthetical reference *before* the closing punctuation mark. For a quotation that runs into the text, place the reference *between* the final quotation mark and the closing punctuation mark. For a quotation set off (indented) from the text, place the reference two spaces *after* the closing punctuation mark.

MLA Works Cited Entries

How to format the Works Cited list

The Works Cited list includes each source that you have paraphrased or quoted. Place your Works Cited list on a separate page at the end of the document. Arrange entries alphabetically by author's surname. When the author is unknown, list the title alphabetically according to its first word (excluding introductory articles such as *A*, *An*, *The*). For a title that begins with a numeral, alphabetize the entry as if the number were spelled out. In preparing the list, type the first line of each entry flush with the left margin. Indent the second and subsequent lines 1/2 inch (five spaces). Double-space within and between entries. Use one character space after all concluding punctuation marks (period, question mark).

How to cite fully at the document's end

Following are examples of complete citations as they would appear in the Works Cited section of your document. Shown below each citation is its corresponding parenthetical reference as it would appear in the text.

Index to Sample MLA Works Cited Entries

BOOKS

1. Book, single author
2. Book, two or three authors
3. Book, four or more authors
4. Book, anonymous author
5. Multiple books, same author
6. Book, one or more editors
7. Book, indirect source
8. Anthology selection or book chapter

PERIODICALS

9. Article, magazine
10. Article, journal with new pagination for each issue
11. Article, journal with continuous pagination
12. Article, newspaper

OTHER SOURCES

13. Encyclopedia, dictionary, other alphabetical reference
14. Report
15. Conference presentation
16. Interview, personally conducted
17. Interview, published
18. Letter or memo, unpublished
19. Questionnaire
20. Brochure or pamphlet
21. Lecture, speech, address, or reading
22. Government document
23. Document with corporate or foundation authorship
24. Map or other visual
25. Unpublished dissertation, report, or miscellaneous items

ELECTRONIC SOURCES

26. Online abstract
27. Print article posted online
28. Online scholarly journal
29. Online newspaper article
30. Reference database
31. Computer software
32. CD-ROM
33. Email discussion group
34. Personal email
35. Wiki
36. Blog
37. Podcast
38. Tweet
39. General reference to a Web site

What to include in an MLA citation for a book

MLA Works Cited Entries for Books. Any citation for a book should contain the following information: author, title, editor or translator, edition, volume number, and facts about publication (city, publisher, date, type of medium—"Print;" "Kindle file;" "PDF file;" "Nook file;" etc.).

1. Book, Single Author—MLA

Kerzin-Fontana, Jane B. *Technology Management: A Handbook*. 3rd ed. Delmar, NY: American Management Assn., 2013. Print.

Parenthetical reference: (Kerzin-Fontana 3-4)

Identify the state of publication by U.S. Postal Service abbreviations. For well-known U.S. cities, omit the state. If several cities are listed on the title page, give only the first. For unfamiliar cities in Canada, include the two-letter abbreviation for the province. For unfamiliar cities in other countries, include an abbreviation of the country name.

2. Book, Two or Three Authors—MLA

Aronson, Linda, Roger Katz, and Candide Moustafa. *Toxic Waste Disposal Methods*. New Haven: Yale UP, 2009. Print.

Parenthetical reference: (Aronson, Katz, and Moustafa 121-23)

Shorten publisher's names, as in "Simon" for Simon & Schuster, "GPO" for Government Printing Office, or "Yale UP" for Yale University Press. For page numbers with more than two digits, give only the final two digits for the second number when the preceding digits in the first number are identical.

3. Book, Four or More Authors—MLA

Santos, Ruth J., et al. *Environmental Crises in Developing Countries*. New York: Harper, 2006. Print.

Parenthetical reference: (Santos et al. 9)

The abbreviation "et al." is a shortened version of the Latin "et alia," meaning "and others."

4. Book, Anonymous Author—MLA

Structured Programming. Boston: Meredith, 2010. Print.

Parenthetical reference: (*Structured* 67)

5. Multiple Books, Same Author—MLA

Chang, John W. *Biophysics*. Boston: Little, 2010. Print.

---. *Diagnostic Techniques*. New York: Radon, 1997. Print.

Parenthetical references: (Chang, *Biophysics* 123-26), (Chang, *Diagnostic* 87)

When citing more than one work by the same author, do not repeat the author's name; simply type three hyphens followed by a period. List the works alphabetically.

6. Book, One or More Editors—MLA

Morris, A. J., and Louise B. Pardin-Walker, eds. *Handbook of New Information Technology*. New York: Harper, 2010. Print.

Parenthetical reference: (Morris and Pardin-Walker 34)

For more than three editors, name only the first, followed by "et al."

7. Book, Indirect Source—MLA

Kline, Thomas. *Automated Systems*. Boston: Rhodes, 2007. Print.

Stubbs, John. *White-Collar Productivity*. Miami: Harris, 2010. Print.

Parenthetical reference: (qtd. in Stubbs 116)

When your source (as in Stubbs, above) has quoted or cited another source, list each source in its alphabetical place on your Works Cited page. Use the name of the original source (here, Kline) in your text and precede your parenthetical reference with "qtd. in," or "cited in" for a paraphrase.

8. Anthology Selection or Book Chapter—MLA

Bowman, Joel P. "Electronic Conferencing." *Communication and Technology: Today and Tomorrow*. Ed. Al Williams. Denton, TX: Assn. for Business Communication, 1994, 123-42. Print.

Parenthetical reference: (Bowman 129)

The page numbers are for the selection cited from the anthology.

What to include in an MLA citation for a periodical

MLA Works Cited Entries for Periodicals. Give all available information in this order: author, article title, periodical title, volume or number (or both), date (day, month, year), and page numbers for the entire article—not just pages cited—along with medium: "Print."

9. Article, Magazine—MLA

DesMarteau, Kathleen. "Study Links Sewing Machine Use to Alzheimer's Disease." *Bobbin* Oct. 1994: 36-38. Print.

Parenthetical reference: (DesMarteau 36)

No punctuation separates the magazine title and date.

If no author is given, list all other information:

"Distribution Systems for the New Decade." *Power Technology Magazine* 16 Oct. 2007: 18+. Print.

Parenthetical reference: ("Distribution Systems" 18)

This article begins on page 18 and continues on page 21. When an article does not appear on consecutive pages, give only the number of the first page, followed immediately by a plus sign. Use a three-letter abbreviation for any month spelled with five or more letters.

10. Article, Journal with New Pagination for Each Issue—MLA

Thackman-White, Joan R. "Computer-Assisted Research." *American Librarian* 51.1 (2010): 3-9. Print.

Parenthetical reference: (Thackman-White 4-5)

Because each issue for a given year will have page numbers beginning with "1," readers need the number of this issue. The "51" denotes the volume number; "1" denotes the issue number. Omit "The," "A," or "An" if it is the first word in a journal or magazine title.

11. Article, Journal with Continuous Pagination—MLA

Barnstead, Marion H. "The Writing Crisis." *Journal of Writing Theory* 12.1 (2008): 415-33. Print.

Parenthetical reference: (Barnstead 415-16)

The "12" denotes the volume number; "1" denotes the issue number.

If, instead of the complete work, you are citing merely an abstract found in a bound collection of abstracts and not the full article, include the information on the abstracting service right after the information on the original article.

How to cite an abstract

Barnstead, Marion H. "The Writing Crisis." *Journal of Writing Theory* 12 (2008): 415-33. *Rhetoric Abstracts 67* (2009): item 1354. Print.

If citing an abstract that appears with the printed article, add "Abstract," followed by a period, immediately after the original work's page number(s).

12. Article, Newspaper—MLA

Baranski, Vida H. "Errors in Technology Assessment." *Boston Times* 15 Jan. 2010, evening ed., sec. 2: 3. Print.

Parenthetical reference: (Baranski 3)

When a daily newspaper has more than one edition, cite the edition after the date. Omit any introductory article in the newspaper's name (not *The Boston Times*). If no author is given, list all other information. If the newspaper's name does not include the city of publication, insert it, using brackets: *Sippican Sentinel* [Marion, MA].

MLA Works Cited Entries for Other Kinds of Materials. Miscellaneous sources range from unsigned encyclopedia entries to conference presentations to government publications. Give this information (as available): author, title, city, publisher, date, page numbers, and medium of publication (print, CD, Web site, etc.).

What to include in an MLA citation for a miscellaneous source

13. Encyclopedia, Dictionary, Other Alphabetical Reference—MLA

"Communication." *The Business Reference Book 2010*. Print.

Parenthetical reference: ("Communication")

Begin a signed entry with the author's name. For any work arranged alphabetically, omit page numbers in the citation and the parenthetical reference. For a well-known reference book, include only an edition (if stated) and a date. For other reference books, give the full publication information.

14. Report—MLA

Electrical Power Research Institute (EPRI). *Epidemiologic Studies of Electric Utility Employees*. (Report No. RP2964.5). Palo Alto, CA: EPRI, Nov. 1994. Print.

Parenthetical reference: (Electrical Power Research Institute [EPRI] 27)

If no author is given, begin with the organization that sponsored the report.

For any report or other document with group authorship, as above, include the group's abbreviated name (along with its full name) in your first parenthetical reference, and then use only that abbreviation in any subsequent reference.

15. Conference Presentation—MLA

Smith, Abelard A. "Radon Concentrations in Molded Concrete." *First British Symposium in Environmental Engineering. London, 11-13 Oct. 2009*. Ed. Anne Hodkins. London: Harrison, 2010. 106-21. Print.

Parenthetical reference: (Smith 109)

This citation is for a presentation that has been included in the published proceedings of a conference. For an unpublished presentation, include the presenter's name, the title of the presentation, and the conference title, and date, but do not italicize the conference information.

16. Interview, Personally Conducted—MLA

Nasser, Gamel. Chief Engineer for Northern Electric. Personal interview. 2 Apr. 2013.

Parenthetical reference: (Nasser)

17. Interview, Published—MLA

Lescault, James. "The Future of Graphics." *Executive Views of Automation*. Ed. Karen Prell. Miami: Haber, 2010. 216-31. Print.

Parenthetical reference: (Lescault 218)

The interviewee's name is placed in the entry's author slot.

18. Letter or Memo, Unpublished—MLA

Rogers, Leonard. Letter to the author. 15 May 2013. Print.

Parenthetical reference: (Rogers)

19. Questionnaire—MLA

Taylor, Lynne. Questionnaire sent to 612 Massachusetts business executives. 14 Feb. 2010. Print.

Parenthetical reference: (Taylor)

20. Brochure or Pamphlet—MLA

Investment Strategies for the 21st Century. San Francisco: Blount Economics Assn., 2010. Print.

Parenthetical reference: (*Investment*)

If the work is signed, begin with its author.

21. Lecture, Speech, Address, or Reading—MLA

Dumont, R. A. "Managing Natural Gas." UMASS Dartmouth, 15 Jan. 2010. Lecture.

Parenthetical reference: (Dumont)

If the lecture title is not known, write Address, Lecture, or Reading—without quotation marks. Include the sponsor and the location if available.

22. Government Document—MLA

Virginia Highway Dept. *Standards for Bridge Maintenance*. Richmond: Virginia Highway Dept., 2010. Print.

Parenthetical reference: (Virginia Highway Dept. 49)

If the author is unknown (as here), list the information in this order: name of the government organization, name of the issuing agency, document title, place, publisher, date, and medium.

For any congressional document, identify the house of Congress (Senate or House of Representatives) before the title, and the number and session of Congress after the title:

United States Cong. House, Armed Services Committee. *Funding for the Military Academies*. 108th Cong., 2nd sess. Washington: GPO, 2010. Print.

Parenthetical reference: (U.S. Cong. 41)

GPO is the abbreviation for the U.S. Government Printing Office.

For an entry from the *Congressional Record,* give only date and pages:

> *Cong. Rec.* 10 Mar. 2004: 2178-92. Print.

Parenthetical reference: (*Cong. Rec.* 2184)

23. Document with Corporate or Foundation Authorship—MLA

> Hermitage Foundation. *Global Warming Scenarios for the Year 2030.* Washington: Natl. Res. Council, 2005. Print.

Parenthetical reference: (Hermitage Foun. 123)

24. Map or Other Visual—MLA

> "Deaths Caused by Breast Cancer, by County." Map. *Scientific American* Oct. 1995: 32D. Print.

Parenthetical reference: (*"Deaths Caused"*)

If the creator of the visual is listed, give that name first. Identify the type of visual (Map, Graph, Table, Diagram) immediately following its title.

25. Unpublished Dissertation, Report, or Miscellaneous Items—MLA

> Author (if known). "Title." Sponsoring organization or publisher, date. Medium of publication.

For any work that has group authorship (corporation, committee, task force), cite the name of the group or agency in place of the author's name.

What to include in an MLA citation for an electronic source

MLA Works Cited Entries for Electronic Sources. Electronic sources include Internet sites, reference databases, CD-ROMs, computer software, email, and blogs. Any citation for an electronic source should allow readers to identify the original source (printed or electronic) and trace a clear path for retrieving the material. Provide all available information in the following order:

1. Name of author, editor, or producer of the work or site. If no author is given, begin with item 2. For works with multiple or anonymous authors, follow the guidelines for print sources.
2. Title of the work. For online postings such as email discussion lists, give the title of the posting. Italicize the title unless it is part of a larger work; in that case, enclose the title in quotation marks and italicize the larger work's title.
3. Title of the Web site (in italics) if this differs from item 2.
4. Version or edition of the site, if relevant.
5. Publisher or sponsor of the site (often listed at the bottom of the Web page). If this information is not given, use *n.p.* (for *no publisher*).

6. Publication date (day, month, and year, if available). If no date is given, use *n.d.*
7. Medium of publication that you accessed. For all online sources, this would be *Web.*
8. Date you accessed the source (day, month, and year).

> Kent, Maureen. "The Glass Ceiling." *Businessmorthlyonline.com.* n.d. Web. 4 Oct. 2013.

If the work you access electronically exists in a print or other version, include the publication information for that medium if readers would find it useful. Begin with (1) the citation format for the other medium, followed by (2) the title of the database or Web site (in italics) from which you retrieved the content, (3) the medium of publication (Web), and (4) your access date (day, month, year).

> Cayer, Kevin. "The Silent Depression." *Cashflow Magazine. Moneyline*, 1 June 2009. Web. 5 Apr. 2013.

Only include Web address in works-cited entries if your reader will have trouble locating the source without the Web address. This would be the citations's final item, enclosed in angle brackets (< >) and followed by a period. When a Web address continues from one line to the next, break it only after a slash or a period; do not insert a hyphen.

> "Filing Your Taxes Online." *IRS.gov*. Internal Revenue Service. June 2012. Web. Oct. 2013 <www.irs.gov/factsheets/online-filing.htm>.

Start the Web address with www. and not http://.

26. Online Abstract—MLA

> Lane, Amanda D., et al. "The Promise of Microcircuits." *Journal of Nanotechnology* 12.2 (2009): n.pag. Abstract. Web. 11 May 2010.

Parenthetical reference: (Lane et al.)

The *n. pag.* designates no page numbers.

27. Print Article Posted Online—MLA

> Jeffers, Anna D. "NAFTA's Effects on the U.S. Trade Deficit." *Sultana Business Quarterly* 3.4 (2004): 65-74. Web. 5 Apr. 2010.

Parenthetical reference: (Jeffers 66)

28. Online Scholarly Journal

For scholarly journal articles available only online (no print equivalent), use the citation format for an article from a print journal. Use *Web* as the publication medium, followed by date of access. If page numbers are not available, use *n. pag.*

Andres, Richard. "Public Accounting and the Legal Process." *Public Policy* 3.3 (2010): n. pag. Web. 28 May 2013.

Parenthetical reference: (Andres)

29. Online Newspaper Article

Rhode, Abbey. "Episodes of Oil Spills in the U.S. Mark a New Era in Accountability." *Star Tribune* 30 March 2009. *n. pag.* Web. 5 May 2013.

Parenthetical reference: (Rhode)

30. Reference Database—MLA

Sahl, J. D. "Power Lines, Viruses, and Childhood Leukemia." *Cancer Causes Control* 6.1 (Jan. 1995): 83-85. *MEDLINE.* Web. 7 Nov. 2013.

Parenthetical reference: (Sahl 83)

For entries with a print equivalent, begin with print publication information, then database title (italicized, as in *MEDLINE*, above), *Web* designation to indicate the medium, service provider, and date of access. Access date is important because frequent updatings of databases can produce different versions of the material.

For entries with no print equivalent, give the title and date of the work in quotation marks, followed by the electronic source information:

Argent, Roger R. "An Analysis of International Exchange Rates for 2009." *Accu-Data.* Dow Jones News Retrieval. Web. 10 Jan. 2013.

Parenthetical reference: (Argent)

If the author is not known, begin with the work's title. If the Web document has page numbers, include them in your entry and in your parenthetical reference.

31. Computer Software—MLA

Virtual Collaboration. Software. New York: Pearson, 2013.

Parenthetical reference: (*Virtual*)

Begin with the author's name, if known.

32. CD-ROM—MLA

Canalte, Henry A. "Violent Crime Statistics: Good News and Bad News." *Law Enforcement* Feb. 1995: 8. *ABI/INFORM.* CD-ROM. ProQuest. Sept. 2013 .

Parenthetical reference: (Canalte 8)

If the material is also available in print, begin with the information about the printed source, followed by the electronic source information: name of database (italicized), *CD-ROM* designation, vendor name, and electronic publication date. If the material has no print equivalent, list its author (if known) and its title (in quotation marks), followed by the electronic source information.

For CD-ROM reference works and other material that is not routinely updated, give the work title followed by the place, electronic publisher, date, and the *CD-ROM* designation:

Time Almanac. Washington: Compact, 2008. CD-ROM.

Parenthetical reference: (*Time Almanac* 74)

Begin with the author's name, if known.

33. Email Discussion Group—MLA

Kosten, A. "Major Update of the WWWVL Migration and Ethnic Relations." 7 Apr. 2013. *ERCOMER News*. E-mail.

Parenthetical reference: (Kosten)

Begin with the author's name (if known), followed by the title of the work (in quotation marks), date of message, title of discussion group (italicized), and medium. Do not include the date of your access.

34. Personal Email—MLA

Wallin, John Luther. "Frog Reveries." Message to the author. 12 Oct. 2013. E-mail.

Parenthetical reference: (Wallin)

Cite personal email as you would printed correspondence. If the document has a subject line or title, enclose it in quotation marks. For publicly posted email (say, a newsgroup or discussion list), include the address and the date of access.

Wikis, blogs, and podcasts, if needed as source material, should also be cited. Begin with the name of the communicator and topic title (in quotation marks), followed by the posting date, name of forum blog, wiki, or podcast (in italics), medium, and access date.

35. Wiki

"Printing Press." *Wikipedia*. Wikimedia Foundation, 2013. Web. 1 June 2013.

Parenthetical reference: ("Printing")

36. Blog

Hecht, Jeff. "How Galveston Weathered the Storm." *New Scientist Environment Blog*. www.newscientist/blog/environment, 15 Sept. 2008. Web. 22 Oct. 2013.

Parenthetical reference: (Hecht)

37. Podcast

"Countdown to Mars Touchdown." *NASA Solar System Audio Podcasts*. NASA, 16 May 2008. Web. 19 May 2013.

Parenthetical reference: ("Countdown")

38. Tweet

Gurak, Laura (ProfGurak). "Here's a good article on accuracy and relevance of crowd sourced content: http://goo.gl/Bs2Ah." 4 Dec. 2012, 6:48 p.m. Tweet.

Parenthetical reference: (Gurak)

39. General Reference to a Web Site—MLA

In referring to an entire site instead of a specific item, include the following information, as available. Follow this format to cite a Facebook posting, Google map, or other Web sournce not listed above.

Name of author, editor, or compiler; title of the site (in italics); site sponsor; date of publication or latest update; medium (Web); and your date of access.

MLA Sample Works Cited Pages

On a separate page at the document's end arrange entries alphabetically by author's surname. When the author is unknown, list the title alphabetically according to its first word (excluding introductory articles). For a title that begins with a digit ("5," "6," etc.), alphabetize the entry as if the digit were spelled out.

The list of works cited in Figure QG.4 accompanies the report on electromagnetic fields, pages 523–33. In the left margin, colored numbers refer to the elements discussed below. Bracketed labels identify different types of sources cited.

Discussion of Figure QG.4

1. Center Works Cited title at the page top. Double-space entries. Number the Works Cited pages consecutively with text pages.
2. Indent five spaces for the second and subsequent lines of an entry. Place quotation marks around article titles. Italicize periodical or book titles. Capitalize the first letter of key words in all titles. Also capitalize articles, prepositions, and

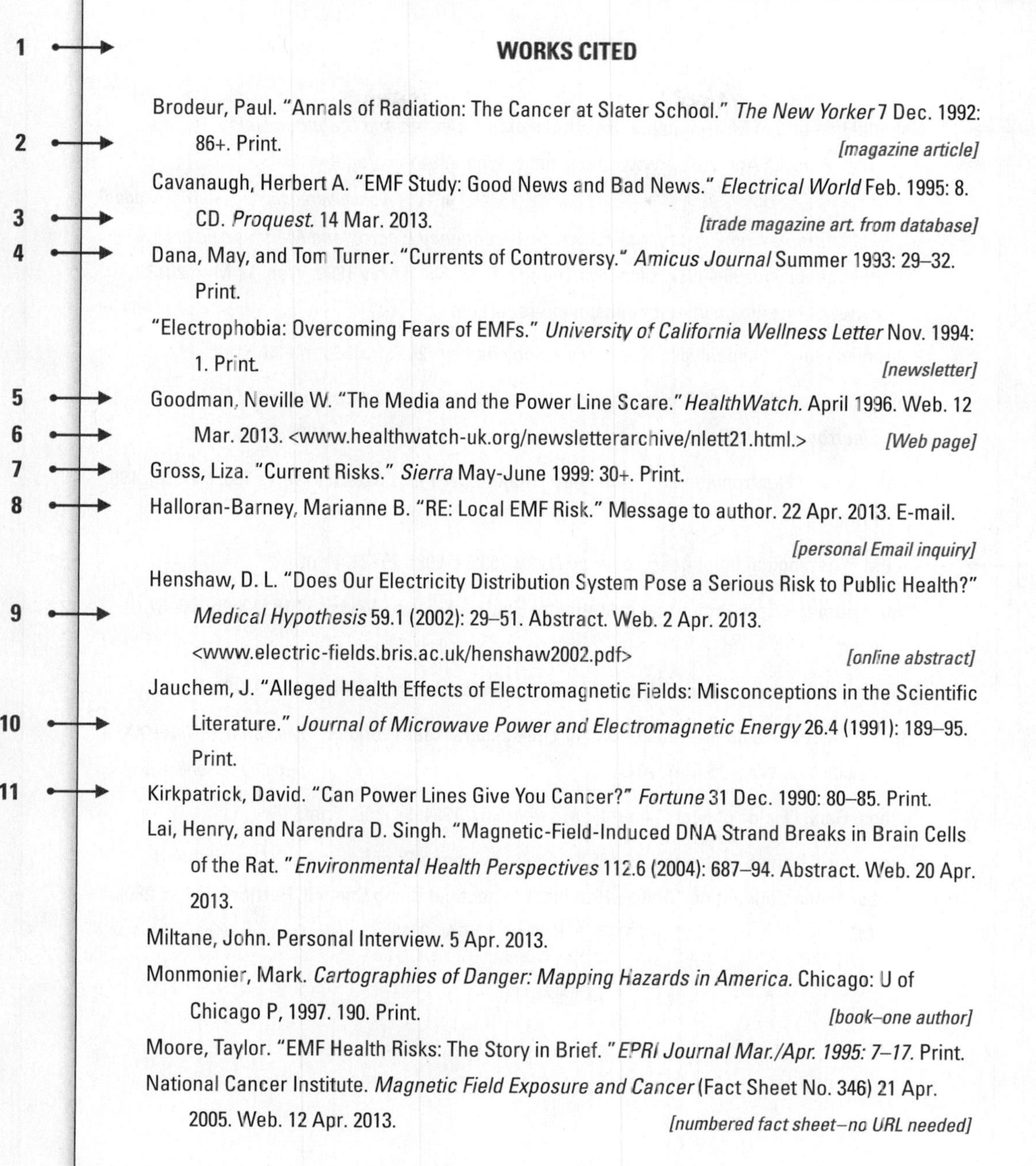

1 **WORKS CITED**

Brodeur, Paul. "Annals of Radiation: The Cancer at Slater School." *The New Yorker* 7 Dec. 1992:
2 86+. Print. *[magazine article]*

Cavanaugh, Herbert A. "EMF Study: Good News and Bad News." *Electrical World* Feb. 1995: 8.
3 CD. *Proquest.* 14 Mar. 2013. *[trade magazine art. from database]*

4 Dana, May, and Tom Turner. "Currents of Controversy." *Amicus Journal* Summer 1993: 29–32.
Print.

"Electrophobia: Overcoming Fears of EMFs." *University of California Wellness Letter* Nov. 1994:
1. Print. *[newsletter]*

5 Goodman, Neville W. "The Media and the Power Line Scare." *HealthWatch.* April 1996. Web. 12
6 Mar. 2013. <www.healthwatch-uk.org/newsletterarchive/nlett21.html.> *[Web page]*

7 Gross, Liza. "Current Risks." *Sierra* May-June 1999: 30+. Print.

8 Halloran-Barney, Marianne B. "RE: Local EMF Risk." Message to author. 22 Apr. 2013. E-mail.
[personal Email inquiry]

Henshaw, D. L. "Does Our Electricity Distribution System Pose a Serious Risk to Public Health?"
9 *Medical Hypothesis* 59.1 (2002): 29–51. Abstract. Web. 2 Apr. 2013.
<www.electric-fields.bris.ac.uk/henshaw2002.pdf> *[online abstract]*

Jauchem, J. "Alleged Health Effects of Electromagnetic Fields: Misconceptions in the Scientific
10 Literature." *Journal of Microwave Power and Electromagnetic Energy* 26.4 (1991): 189–95.
Print.

11 Kirkpatrick, David. "Can Power Lines Give You Cancer?" *Fortune* 31 Dec. 1990: 80–85. Print.

Lai, Henry, and Narendra D. Singh. "Magnetic-Field-Induced DNA Strand Breaks in Brain Cells of the Rat." *Environmental Health Perspectives* 112.6 (2004): 687–94. Abstract. Web. 20 Apr. 2013.

Miltane, John. Personal Interview. 5 Apr. 2013.

Monmonier, Mark. *Cartographies of Danger: Mapping Hazards in America.* Chicago: U of Chicago P, 1997. 190. Print. *[book–one author]*

Moore, Taylor. "EMF Health Risks: The Story in Brief." *EPRI Journal Mar./Apr. 1995: 7–17.* Print.

National Cancer Institute. *Magnetic Field Exposure and Cancer* (Fact Sheet No. 346) 21 Apr. 2005. Web. 12 Apr. 2013. *[numbered fact sheet–no URL needed]*

FIGURE QG.4 A List of Works Cited (MLA Style)

12 → National Institute of Environmental Health Sciences. *Electric and Magnetic Fields.* 14 Sept. 2009. Web. 24 Apr. 2013. <www.niehs.nih.gov/health/topics/agents/emf>. *[unnumbered fact sheet–URL needed]*

---. *Health Effects from Exposure to Power Line Frequency Electric and Magnetic Fields.* (NIH Publication No. 99-4493). Research Triangle Park, NC. 4 May 1999. Web. 11 Mar. 2013. <www.niehs.nih.gov/health/docs/niehs-report.pdf>. *[gov. report posted online]*

Palfreman, John. "Apocalypse Not." *Technology Review.* 24 Apr. 1996: 24–33. Print.

Pinsky, Mark. A. *The EMF Book: What You Should Know about Electromagnetic Fields, Electromagnetic Radiation, and Your Health.* New York: Warner, 1995. Print.

Raloff, Janet. "Electromagnetic Fields May Trigger Enzymes." *Science News* 153. 8 (1998): 199. Print.

13 → ---. EMFs' Biological Influences. *Science News* 153.2 (1998): 29–31. Print.

Sivitz, Laura B. "Cells Proliferate in Magnetic Fields." *Science News* 158.18 (2000): 196–97. Print.

Stix, Gary. "Are Power Lines a Dead Issue?" *Scientific American* Mar. 1998: 33–34. Print.

"Strong Electric Fields Indicated in Major Leukemia Risk for Workers." *Microwave News* XX. 3 (2000): 1–2. Web. 15 Mar. 2013. *[article from online journal]*

Taubes, Gary. "Fields of Fear." *Atlantic Monthly* Nov. 1994: 94–108. Print.

Wartenburg, Daniel. Testimony. "Solid Scientific Evidence Supporting an EMF-Childhood Leukemia Connection." Public Hearing, Connecticut Citing Council, Hartford. 9 Jan. 2007. *Microwave News* XXVII. 1 (2007): 5–6. Web. 10 Apr. 2013. *[online transcript of testimony]*

FIGURE QG.4 *(Continued)*

conjunctions only when they are the first or last word in a title. Do not cite a magazine's volume number, even if it is given. When an article skips pages in a publication, give only the first page number followed by a plus sign. Name the medium of publication (Print, CD, Web, and so on) for each source.

3. For a CD-ROM database that is updated often (such as *ProQuest*), conclude your citation with your date of access.
4. For additional perspective beyond "establishment" viewpoints, examine "alternative" publications (such as the *Amicus Journal* and *Mother Jones*).
5. In citing any online source, include your date of access (as in "12 Mar. 2013").
6. For a Web page that you think will be hard to locate, include the Web address. For a page that you think will be easy to locate (say by googling "National Cancer Society fact sheets"), omit the Web address.
7. Use a period and one space to separate a citation's three major items (author, title, publication data). Skip one space after a comma or colon. Use no punctuation to separate magazine title and date.
8. Alphabetize hyphenated surnames according to the name that appears first. When the privacy of the electronic source is not an issue (e.g., a library versus an email correspondent), include the electronic address in your entry.
9. When citing an abstract instead of the complete article, indicate this by inserting "Abstract" after the page numbers of the original.
10. For a journal, include the issue number after the volume number and separated by a period. For example, 26.4 would signify volume 26, issue 4. For page numbers of more than two digits, give only the final differing digits in the second number (but never less than two digits).
11. Use three-letter abbreviations for months with five or more letters.
12. For government reports, name the sponsoring agency and include all available information for retrieving the document.
13. When the same author is listed for two or more works, use three dashes to denote the author's name in any entries after the first one.

APA DOCUMENTATION STYLE

Another common citation style is one published in the *Publication Manual of the American Psychological Association*, 6th ed., Washington: American Psychological Association, 2009. Called APA for short, this method emphasizes the date. APA style (or some similar author-date style) is preferred in the sciences and social sciences, where information quickly becomes outdated. A parenthetical reference in the text briefly identifies the source, date, and page number(s):

> In one study, mice continuously exposed to an electromagnetic field tended to die earlier than mice in the control group (de Jager & de Bruyn, 1994, p. 224).

Reference cited in the text

The full citation then appears in the alphabetical listing of "References," at the report's end:

Full citation at document's end

> de Jager, L., & de Bruyn, L. (1994). Long-term effects of a 50 Hz electric field on the life-expectancy of mice. *Review of Environmental Health, 10*(3-4), 221-224.

APA Parenthetical References

How APA and MLA parenthetical references differ

APA's parenthetical references differ from MLA's (pages 650–62) as follows: The APA citation includes the publication date. A comma separates each item in the reference; and "p." or "pp." precedes the page number. When a subsequent reference to a work follows closely after the initial reference, the date need not be included. Here are specific guidelines:

- If your discussion names the author, do not repeat the name in your parenthetical reference; simply give the date and page numbers:

Author named in the text

> Researchers de Jager and de Bruyn (1994) explain that experimental mice exposed to an electromagnetic field tended to die earlier than mice in the control group (p. 224).

When two authors of a work are named in the text, their names are connected by "and," but in a parenthetical reference, their names are connected by an ampersand, "&."

- If you cite two or more works in a single reference, list the authors in alphabetical order and separate the citations with semicolons:

Two or more works in a single reference

> (Jones, 2007; Gomez, 2005; Leduc, 2002)

- If you cite a work with three to five authors, try to name them in your text, to avoid an excessively long parenthetical reference.

A work with three to five authors

> Franks, Oblesky, Ryan, Jablar, and Perkins (2008) studied the role of electromagnetic fields in tumor formation.

In any subsequent references to this work, name only the first author, followed by "et al." (Latin abbreviation for "and others").

- If you cite two or more works by the same author published in the same year, assign a different letter to each work:

Two or more works by the same author in the same year

> (Lamont, 2009a, p. 135)
>
> (Lamont, 2009b, pp. 67-68)

Other examples of parenthetical references appear with their corresponding entries in the following discussion of the reference list entries.

Index to Sample Entries for APA References

BOOKS

1. Book, single author
2. Book, two to seven authors
3. Book, eight or more authors
4. Book, anonymous author
5. Multiple books, same author
6. Book, one to five editors
7. Book, indirect source
8. Anthology selection or book chapter

PERIODICALS

9. Article, magazine
10. Article, journal with new pagination for each issue
11. Article, journal with continuous pagination
12. Article, newspaper

OTHER SOURCES

13. Encyclopedia, dictionary, alphabetical reference
14. Report
15. Conference presentation
16. Interview, personally conducted
17. Interview, published
18. Personal correspondence
19. Brochure or pamphlet
20. Lecture
21. Government document
22. Miscellaneous items

ELECTRONIC SOURCES

23. Online abstract
24. Print article posted online
25. Book or article available only online
26. Journal article with DOI
27. Online Encyclopedia, dictionary, or handbook
28. Personal email
29. Blog posting
30. Newsgroup, discussion list, or online forum
31. Wiki
32. Facebook and Twitter
33. Press Release
34. Technical or research report

APA Reference List Entries

The APA reference list includes each source you have cited in your document. Type the first line of each entry flush with the left margin. Indent the second and subsequent lines five character spaces (one-half inch). Skip one character space after any period, comma, or colon. Double-space within and between each entry.

How to space and indent entries

Following are examples of complete citations as they would appear in the References section of your document. Shown immediately below each entry is its corresponding parenthetical reference as it would appear in the text. Note the capitalization, abbreviation, spacing, and punctuation in the sample entries.

APA Entries for Books. Book citations should contain all applicable information in the following order: author, date, title, editor or translator, edition, volume number, and facts about publication (city, state, and publisher).

What to include in an APA citation for a book

1. Book, Single Author—APA

Kerzin-Fontana, J. B. (2013). *Technology management: A handbook* (3rd ed.). Delmar, NY: American Management Association.

Parenthetical reference: (Kerzin-Fontana, 2013, pp. 3-4)

Use only initials for an author's first and middle name. Capitalize only the first word of a book's title and subtitle and any proper names. Identify a later edition in parentheses between the title and the period.

2. Book, Two to Seven Authors—APA

Aronson, L., Katz, R., & Moustafa, C. (2009). *Toxic waste disposal methods*. New Haven, CT. Yale University Press.

Parenthetical reference: (Aronson, Katz, & Moustafa, 2009)

Use an ampersand (&) before the name of the final author listed in an entry. As an alternative parenthetical reference, name the authors in your text and include date (and page numbers, if appropriate) in parentheses.

Give the publisher's full name (as in "Yale University Press") but omit the words "Publisher," "Company," and "Inc."

3. Book, Eight or More Authors—APA

Fogle, S. T., Gates, R., Hanes, P., Johns, B., Nin, K., Sarkis, P.... Yale, B. (2009). *Hyperspace technology*. Boston, MA: Little, Brown.

Parenthetical reference: (Fogle et al., 2009, p. 34)

List the first six authors' names, insert an ellipsis, then add the last author's name. "Et al." is the Latin abbreviation for "et alia," meaning "and others."

4. Book, Anonymous Author—APA

Structured programming. (2010). Boston, MA: Meredith Press.

Parenthetical reference: (Structured Programming, 2010, p. 67)

In your list of references, place an anonymous work alphabetically by the first key word (not *The*, *A*, or *An*) in its title. In your parenthetical reference, capitalize all key words in a book, article, or journal title.

5. Multiple Books, Same Author—APA

Chang, J. W. (2010a). Biophysics. Boston, MA: Little, Brown.

Chang, J. W. (2010b). MindQuest. Chicago, IL: John Pressler.

Parenthetical references: (Chang, 2010a) (Chang, 2010b)

Two or more works by the same author not published in the same year are distinguished by their respective dates alone, without the added letter.

6. Book, One to Five Editors—APA

Morris, A. J., & Pardin-Walker, L. B. (Eds.). (2010). *Handbook of new information technology.* New York, NY: HarperCollins.

Parenthetical reference: (Morris & Pardin-Walker, 2010, p. 79)

For more than five editors, name only the first, followed by "et al."

7. Book, Indirect Source—APA

Stubbs, J. (2010). White-collar productivity. Miami, FL: Harris.

Parenthetical reference: (cited in Stubbs, 2010, p. 47)

When your source (as in Stubbs, above) has cited another source, list only your source in the References section, but name the original source in the text: "Kline's study (cited in Stubbs, 2010, p. 47) supports this conclusion."

8. Anthology Selection or Book Chapter—APA

Bowman, J. (1994). Electronic conferencing. In A. Williams (Ed.), *Communication and technology: Today and tomorrow* (pp. 123-142). Denton, TX: Association for Business Communication.

Parenthetical reference: (Bowman, 1994, p. 126)

The page numbers in the complete reference are for the selection cited from the anthology.

APA Entries for Periodicals. Give this information (as available), in order: author, publication date, article title (no quotation marks), periodical title, volume or number (or both), and page numbers for the entire article—not just page(s) cited.

What to include in an APA citation for a periodical

9. Article, Magazine—APA

DesMarteau, K. (1994, October). Study links sewing machine use to Alzheimer's disease. *Bobbin, 36,* 36-38.

Parenthetical reference: (DesMarteau, 1994, p. 36)

If no author is given, provide all other information. Capitalize the first word in an article's title and subtitle, and any proper nouns. Capitalize all key words in a periodical title. Italicize the periodical title, volume number, and commas (as shown above).

10. Article, Journal with New Pagination for Each Issue—APA

Thackman-White, J. R. (2010). Computer-assisted research. *American Library Journal, 51*(1), 3-9.

Parenthetical reference: (Thackman-White, 2010, pp. 4-5)

Because each issue for a given year has page numbers that begin at "1," readers need the issue number (in this instance, "1"). The "51" denotes the volume number, which is italicized.

11. Article, Journal with Continuous Pagination—APA

Barnstead, M. H. (2008). The writing crisis. *Journal of Writing Theory, 12*, 415-433.

Parenthetical reference: (Barnstead, 2008, pp. 415-416)

The "12" denotes the volume number. When page numbers continue from issue to issue for the full year, readers won't need the issue number. (You can include the issue number if you think it will help readers retrieve the article more easily.)

12. Article, Newspaper—APA

Baranski, V. H. (2010, January 15). Errors in technology assessment. *The Boston Times*, p. B3.

Parenthetical reference: (Baranski, 2010, p. B3)

In addition to year of publication, include month and day. If the newspaper's name begins with "The," include it. Include "p." or "pp." before page numbers. For an article on nonconsecutive pages, list each page, separated by a comma.

What to include in an APA citation for a miscellaneous source

APA Entries for Other Sources. Miscellaneous sources range from unsigned encyclopedia entries to conference presentations to government documents. Give this information (as available): author, publication date, work title (and report or series number), page numbers (if applicable), city, and publisher.

13. Encyclopedia, Dictionary, Alphabetical Reference—APA

Communication. (2010). In *The business reference book*. Boston, MA: Business Resources Press.

Parenthetical reference: ("Communication," 2010)

For an entry that is signed, begin with the author's name and publication date.

14. Report—APA

Electrical Power Research Institute. (1994). *Epidemiologic studies of electric utility employees* (Report No. RP2964.5). Palo Alto, CA: Author.

Parenthetical reference: (Electrical Power Research Institute [EPRI], 1994, p. 12)

If authors are named, list them first, followed by publication date. When citing a group author, as above, include the group's abbreviated name in your first parenthetical reference, and use only that abbreviation in subsequent references. When the organization and publisher are the same, list "Author" in the publisher's slot.

15. Conference Presentation—APA

Smith, A. A. (2009, March). Radon concentrations in molded concrete. In A. Hodkins (Ed.), *First British Symposium on Environmental Engineering* (pp. 106-121). London, UK: Harrison Press, 2010.

Parenthetical reference: (Smith, 2009, p. 109)

In parentheses is the date of the presentation. The symposium's name is proper and so is capitalized. Following the publisher's name is the date of publication.

For an unpublished presentation, include the presenter's name, year and month, presentation title (italicized), and all available information about the conference: "Symposium held at...." Do not italicize this last information.

16. Interview, Personally Conducted—APA

Parenthetical reference: (G. Nasser, personal interview, April 2, 2013)

This material is considered a nonrecoverable source, and so is cited in the text only, as a parenthetical reference. If you name the respondent in text, do not repeat the name in the citation.

17. Interview, Published—APA

Jable, C. K. (2009). The future of graphics [Interview with James Lescault]. In K. Prell (Ed.), *Executive views of automation* (pp. 216-231). Miami, FL: Haber Press, 2010.

Parenthetical reference: (Jable, 2009, pp. 218-223)

Begin with the interviewer's name, followed by interview date and title (if available), the designation (in brackets), and publication information, including the date.

18. Personal Correspondence—APA

Parenthetical reference: (L. Rogers, personal correspondence, May 15, 2013)

This material is considered nonrecoverable data, and so is cited in the text only, as a parenthetical reference. If you name the correspondent in your discussion, do not repeat the name in the citation.

19. Brochure or Pamphlet—APA

This material follows the citation format for a book entry (page 652). After the title of the work, include the designation "Brochure" in brackets.

20. Lecture—APA

Dumont, R. A. (2010, January 15). *Managing natural gas.* Lecture presented at the University of Massachusetts at Dartmouth.

Parenthetical reference: (Dumont, 2010)

If you name the lecturer in your discussion, do not repeat the name in the citation.

21. Government Document—APA

Virginia Highway Department. (2010). Standards for bridge maintenance. Richmond, VA: Author.

Parenthetical reference: (Virginia Highway Department, 2010, p. 49)

If the author is unknown, present the information in this order: name of the issuing agency, publication date, document title, place, and publisher. When the issuing agency is both author and publisher, list "Author" in the publisher's slot.

For any congressional document, identify the house of Congress (Senate or House of Representatives) before the date.

U.S. House Armed Services Committee. (2010). *Funding for the military academies*. Washington, DC: U.S. Government Printing Office.

Parenthetical reference: (U.S. House, 2010, p. 41)

22. Miscellaneous Items (Unpublished Manuscripts, Dissertations, and so on)—APA

Author (if known). (Date of publication.) *Title of work*. Sponsoring organization or publisher.

For any work that has group authorship (corporation, committee, and so on), cite the name of the group or agency in place of the author's name.

What to include in an APA citation for an electronic source

APA Entries for Electronic Sources. In 2009, the APA published the *Publication Manual of the American Psychological Association*, 6th edition. This manual provides instructions for citation of print and electronic sources. For electronic sources in particular, the APA notes that "in general . . . include the same elements, in the same order, as you would for a reference to a fixed-media source and add as much electronic retrieval information as needed for others to locate the sources you cited" (187). Including the Web address (Web address) is still recommended. However, one new feature is the use of digital object identifiers (DOIs). These are unique identifiers designed to last longer than Web addresses, which often disappear or get changed when Web pages are moved or renamed.

Identify the original source (printed or electronic) and give readers a path for retrieving the material. Provide all available information in the following order.

1. Author, editor, creator, or sponsoring organization.
2. Date the item was published or was created electronically. For magazines and newspapers, include the month and day as well as the year. If the date of an electronic publication is not available, use *n.d.* in place of the date.
3. Publication information of the original printed version (as in previous entries), if such a version exists. Follow this by designating the electronic medium [CD-ROM] or the type of work [Abstract], [Brochure]—unless this designation is named in the work's title (as in "Inpatient brochure").
4. Database names. Do not list database names (unless the database is obscure or the material hard to find), but do include the Web address (or DOI, discussed below).
5. Web addresses and DOIs. Provide the full electronic address. For Internet sources, only provide the Web address if the source would be impossible to locate without it. APA recommends only using home page Web address. For CD-ROM and database sources, give the document's retrieval number (see entry 23, below). Start the Web address with http://, but do not underline, italicize, use angle brackets, or add a period at the end of a Web address. When a Web address continues from one line to the next, break it only after a slash or other punctuation (except for http://, which should not be broken).

The APA now recommends using the DOI (Digital Object Identifier), when available, in place of a Web address in references to electronic texts. DOI numbers are found on some recent scholarly journals, especially in the sciences and social sciences. Here is a sample reference for a journal article with a DOI assigned:

Schmidt, D., et al. (2009). Advances in psychotropic medication. *Boston Journal of Psychotherapy, 81* (3), 398-413. doi: 10.1037/0555-9467.79.3.483

Parenthetical reference: (Schmidt, 2009)

23. Online Abstract—APA

Stevens, R. L. (2010). Cell phones and cancer rates. *Oncology Journal, 57*(2), 41-43. [Abstract]. Retrieved from http://nim.mh.gov/medlineplus. (MEDLINE Item: AY 24598).

Parenthetical reference: (Stevens, 2010)

Ordinarily an APA entry ends with a period. Entries with a DOI, however, omit the period at the end of the electronic address. If you are citing the entire article retrieved from a full-text database, delete [Abstract] from the citation.

24. Print Article Posted Online—APA

Alley, R. A. (2009, January). Ergonomic influences on worker satisfaction. *Industrial Psychology, 5*(12), 672-678. Retrieved from http://www.psycharchives

Parenthetical reference: (Alley, 2009)

If you were confident that the document's electronic and print versions were identical, you could omit the Web address and insert "[Electronic version]" between the end of the article title and the period.

25. Book or Article Available Only Online (no DOI)—APA

Kelly, W. (2013). *Early graveyards of New England.* Retrieved from http://www.onlinebooks.com

Parenthetical reference: (Kelly, 2013)

This source exists only in electronic format.

26. Journal Article with DOI

Tijen, D. (2009). Recent developments in understanding salinity tolerance. *Environmental & Experimental Botany. 67(1)*, 2-9. doi:10.1016/j.envexpbot.2009.05.008

Parenthetical reference: (Tijen, 2009)

27. Online Encyclopedia, Dictionary, or Handbook—APA

Ecoterrorism. (2009). *Ecological encyclopedia.* Washington, DC: Redwood. Retrieved May 1, 2010, from http://www.eco.floridastate.edu

Parenthetical reference: ("Ecoterrorism," 2009)

Include the retrieval date for works that are routinely updated. If a work on CD-ROM has a print equivalent, cite it in its printed form.

28. Personal Email—APA

Parenthetical reference: Fred Flynn (personal communication, May 10, 2013) provided these statistics.

Instead of being included in the list of references, personal email (considered a nonretrievable source) is cited fully in the text.

29. Blog Posting—APA

Owens, P. (2010, June 1). How to stabilize a large travel trailer. Message posted to http://rvblogs.com

Parenthetical reference: (Owens, 2010)

30. Newsgroup, Discussion List, or Online Forum—APA

LaBarge, V. S. (2013, October 20). A cure for computer viruses. Message posted to http://www.srb/forums

Parenthetical reference: (LaBarge, 2013)

Although email should not be included in the list of references, postings from blogs, newsgroups, and online forums, considered more retrievable, should be included.

31. Wiki—APA

Skull-base tumors. (n.d.). Retrieved June 10, 2009, from the Oncology Wiki: http://oncology.wikia.com

Parenthetical reference: ("Skull-Base," n.d.)

Notice the "n.d." ("no date") designation for this collaborative Web page that can be written or edited by anyone with access.

32. Facebook and Twitter

NASA. (2013, January 8). Astronomers have made a 3D weather map of a brown dwarf using NASA)s Spitzer and Hubble Space telescopes! [Facebook update]. Retrieved from www.facebock.com/NASA/posts/128611970637320

Parenthetical reference: (NASA, 2013)

APA Entries for Gray Literature. Gray literature is material that is not peer reviewed but according to the APA can play an important role in research and publication. Examples of gray literature include annual reports, fact sheets, consumer brochures, press releases, and technical reports (each type is so named in the title, in brackets, or elsewhere in the citation). In the sample citation in entry 32, the type of item is identified in brackets; in entry 33, it is part of the titling information.

What to include in an APA citation for gray literature

33. Press Release—APA

American Natural Foods Association. (2009, January 20). *Newest food additive poses special threat to children, according to the upcoming issue of* Eating for Health [Press release]. Retrieved from American Natural Foods Association Website: http://www.anfha.org

Parenthetical reference: (American Natural Foods Association, 2009)

34. Technical or Research Report—APA

Gunderson, H., et al. (2007). *Declining birthrates in rural areas: Results from the 2005 National Census Bureau Survey* (Report No. 7864 NCB 2005-171). Retrieved from the National Center for Population Statistics: http://ncps.gov

Parenthetical reference: (Gunderson, 2007)

Notice that the report number, if available, is given after the title.

APA Sample Reference List

APA's References section is an alphabetical listing (by author) equivalent to MLA's Works Cited section. Like Works Cited, the reference list includes only those works actually cited. (A bibliography usually would include background works or works consulted as well.) Unlike MLA style, APA style calls for only "recoverable" sources to appear in the reference list. Therefore, personal interviews, email messages, and other unpublished materials are cited in the text only.

The list of references in Figure QG.5 accompanies the report on a technical marketing career, pages 538–50. In the left margin, colored numbers denote elements of Figure QG.5 discussed below. Bracketed labels on the right identify different types of sources.

Discussion of Figure QG.5

1. Center the "References" title at the top of page. Use one-inch margins. Number reference pages consecutively with text pages. Include only recoverable data (material that readers could retrieve for themselves); cite personal interviews, email, and other personal correspondence parenthetically in the text only. See also item 7 in this list.
2. Double-space entries and order them alphabetically by author's last name (excluding *A, An,* or *The*). List initials only for authors' first and middle names. Write out names of all months. In student papers, indent the second and subsequent lines of an entry five spaces. In papers submitted for publication in an APA journal, the first line is indented instead.
3. Omit punctuation from the end of an electronic address.
4. Do not enclose article titles in quotation marks. Italicize periodical titles. Capitalize the first word in article or book titles and subtitles, and any proper nouns. Capitalize all key words in magazine or journal titles.
5. For more than one author or editor, use ampersands instead of spelling out "and."
6. Use italics for a journal's name, volume number, and the comma. Give the issue number in parentheses only if each issue begins on page 1. Do not include "p." or "pp." before journal page numbers (only before page numbers from a newspaper).
7. Treat an unpublished conference presentation as a "recoverable source"; include it in your list of references instead of only citing it parenthetically in your text.

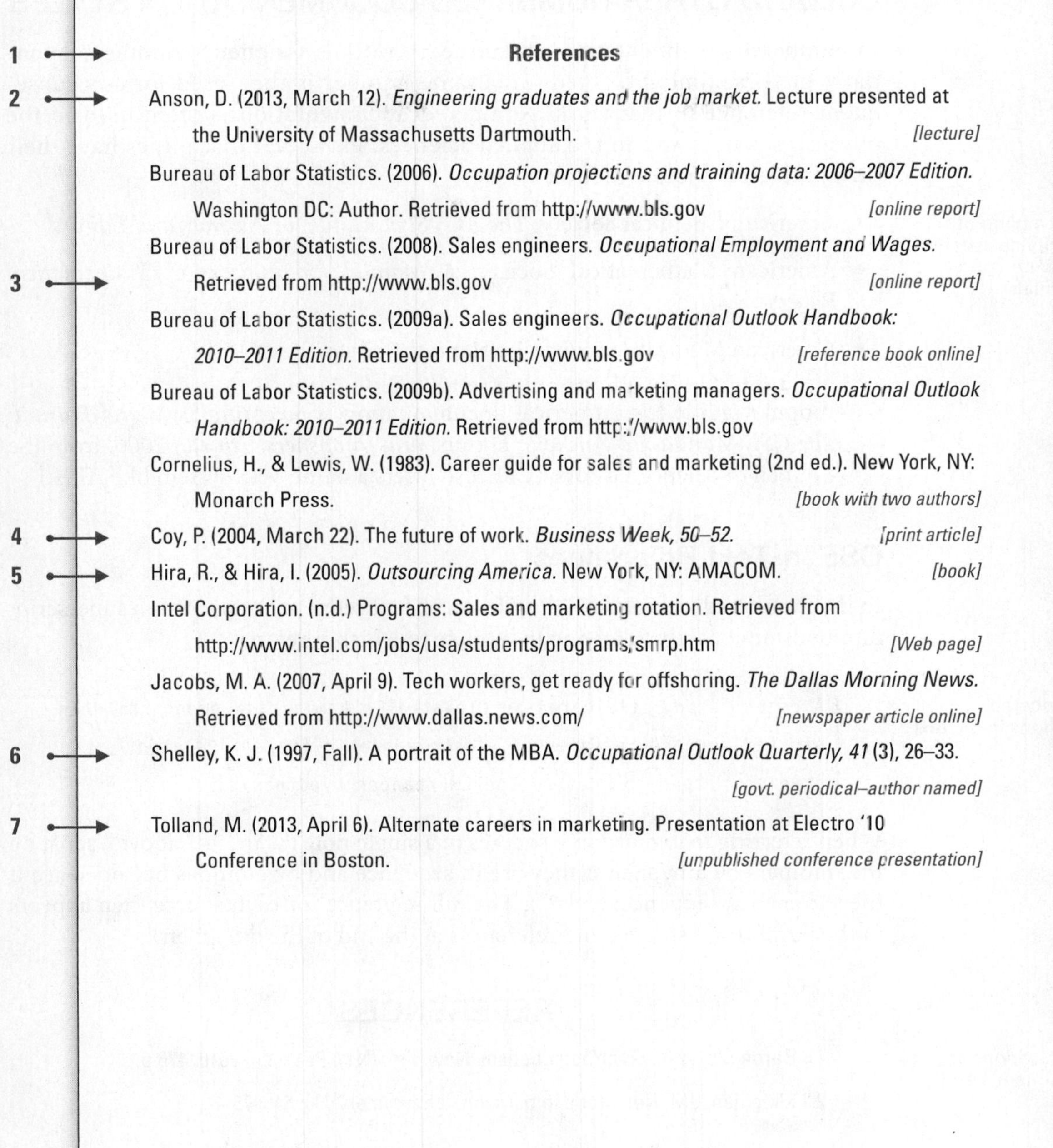

1 → **References**

2 → Anson, D. (2013, March 12). *Engineering graduates and the job market.* Lecture presented at the University of Massachusetts Dartmouth. *[lecture]*

Bureau of Labor Statistics. (2006). *Occupation projections and training data: 2006–2007 Edition.* Washington DC: Author. Retrieved from http://www.bls.gov *[online report]*

Bureau of Labor Statistics. (2008). Sales engineers. *Occupational Employment and Wages.*
3 → Retrieved from http://www.bls.gov *[online report]*

Bureau of Labor Statistics. (2009a). Sales engineers. *Occupational Outlook Handbook: 2010–2011 Edition.* Retrieved from http://www.bls.gov *[reference book online]*

Bureau of Labor Statistics. (2009b). Advertising and marketing managers. *Occupational Outlook Handbook: 2010–2011 Edition.* Retrieved from http://www.bls.gov

Cornelius, H., & Lewis, W. (1983). Career guide for sales and marketing (2nd ed.). New York, NY: Monarch Press. *[book with two authors]*

4 → Coy, P. (2004, March 22). The future of work. *Business Week, 50–52.* *[print article]*

5 → Hira, R., & Hira, I. (2005). *Outsourcing America.* New York, NY: AMACOM. *[book]*

Intel Corporation. (n.d.) Programs: Sales and marketing rotation. Retrieved from http://www.intel.com/jobs/usa/students/programs/smrp.htm *[Web page]*

Jacobs, M. A. (2007, April 9). Tech workers, get ready for offshoring. *The Dallas Morning News.* Retrieved from http://www.dallas.news.com/ *[newspaper article online]*

6 → Shelley, K. J. (1997, Fall). A portrait of the MBA. *Occupational Outlook Quarterly, 41* (3), 26–33. *[govt. periodical–author named]*

7 → Tolland, M. (2013, April 6). Alternate careers in marketing. Presentation at Electro '10 Conference in Boston. *[unpublished conference presentation]*

FIGURE QG.5

CSE AND OTHER NUMBERED DOCUMENTATION STYLES

In numbered documentation systems, each work is assigned a number sequentially the first time it is cited. This same number is then used for any subsequent reference to that work. Numbered documentation is often used in the physical sciences and in the applied sciences. Particular disciplines have their own preferred documentation styles:

A sampling of discipline-specific documentation manuals

- American Chemical Society, *The ACS Style Guide for Authors and Editors*
- American Mathematical Society, *A Manual for Authors of Mathematical Papers*
- American Medical Association, *Manual of Style*

One popular guide for numerical documentation is *Scientific Style and Format: The CSE Manual for Authors, Editors, and Publishers, 7th ed., 2006,* from the Council of Science Editors. (CSE also offers a name-year system like APA.)

CSE In-Text References

In the numbered version of CSE style, an in-text reference appears as a superscript number immediately following the source to which it refers:

Numbered citations in the text

> A recent study[1] indicates an elevated leukemia risk among children exposed to certain types of electromagnetic fields. Related studies[2-3] tend to confirm the EMF/cancer hypothesis.

When referring to two or more sources in a single note (as in "[2-3]" above), separate the numbers by a hyphen if they are in sequence and by commas but no space if they are not in sequence: ("[2,6,9]"). The full reference for each source then appears in the numerical listing of end references at the end of the document.

REFERENCES

Full citations at document's end

1. Baron, KL, et al. Electromagnetism. New York (NY): Pearson; 2010. 476 p.
2. Klingman, JM. Nematode infestation. J Entoymol 2006; 54: 475–8.

CSE Reference List Entries

List each source double-spaced, in the order in which it was first cited. Type the number flush with the left margin, followed by a period and a space. Align subsequent lines directly under the first word of the first line.

Index to Sample CSE Entries

1. Book, single author
2. Book, multiple authors
3. Article, magazine
4. Article, journal
5. Article, retrieved online

CSE Entries for Books. A book citation should provide all available information in this order: number assigned to the entry, author or editor, work title (and edition), facts about publication (place, publisher, date), and number of pages. Note capitalization, abbreviation, spacing, and punctuation in the sample entries.

1. Book, Single Author—CSE

```
1. Kerzin-Fontana JB. Technology management: A handbook. 3rd ed.
   Delmar (NY): American Management Assn Press; 2013. 356p.
```

2. Book, Multiple Authors—CSE

```
2. Aronson L, Katz R, Moustafa C. Toxic waste disposal methods. New
   Haven (CT): Yale Univ Press; 2009. 316p.
```

CSE Entries for Periodicals. An article citation should contain information in this order: number assigned to the entry, author, article title, periodical title, date (year, month), volume and issue number, and inclusive page numbers for the article. Note capitalization, abbreviation, spacing, and punctuation.

3. Article, Magazine—CSE

```
3. DesMarteau K. Study links sewing machine use to Alzheimer's
   disease. Bobbin 1994 Oct:36-8.
```

4. Article, Journal—CSE

```
4. Thackman-White JR. Computer-assisted research. Am Library J
   2010;51(1):3-9.
```

5. Article, Retrieved Online—CSE

```
5. Alley RA. Ergonomic Influences on worker satisfaction. Indust Psych
   [Internet]. 2009 [cited 2010 Feb 7]; 5(11): 17-23. Available from:
   www.pub/journals/industrialpsychology/2009.05055.pdf
```

For more on CSE, consult the *CSE Manual* or <www.lib.unc.edu/instruct/citations/css/csprint.html> or <www.lib.ohiostate.edu/guides/csegd.html>.

Appendix

B A Quick Guide to Grammar, Usage, and Mechanics

Page ii at the beginning of this book displays editing and revision symbols with corresponding page references. When your instructor marks a symbol on your paper, turn to the appropriate section in this appendix or in Chapters 10 or 11 for explanations and examples.

GRAMMAR

The following common grammatical errors are easy to repair.

frag Sentence Fragments

A sentence fragment is a grammatically incomplete sentence. A grammatically complete sentence consists of at least one subject-verb combination and expresses a complete thought. It might include more than one subject-verb combination, and it might include other words or phrases as well.

Complete sentences

- This book summarizes recent criminal psychology research.
- The smudge tool creates soft effects.
- My dog, Zorro, ate my paper.

Even though the following example contains a subject-verb combination, it doesn't express a complete thought:

Sentence fragment

- Although the report was not yet complete.

Although and other words like it, including *because, if, as, while, since, when,* and *unless* are called subordinating conjunctions. Any of these words combined with a subject-verb combination produces a subordinate clause (a clause that expresses an incomplete idea). Subordinating conjunctions leave readers waiting for something to complete the thought. The thought can be completed only if another subject-verb combination that does express a complete idea is added:

Additional subject-verb completes the thought

- Although the report was not yet complete, I began editing.

This next group of words is a fragment because it contains no verb:

- DesignPro, a new desktop publishing program.

Fragment with no verb

Simply add a verb to turn the fragment into a complete sentence:

- DesignPro, a new desktop publishing program, will be available soon.

or

- DesignPro is a new desktop publishing program.

Addition of verb corrects fragment

Avoid sentences that seem to contain a subject-verb combination but actually do not. Gerunds (verb forms ending in *-ing* that act like nouns, such as *being* in the first sentence below) and participles (verb forms ending in *-ing* that act like adjectives, such as *barking* in the second sentence below) look like verbs but actually are not:

- Dale being a document design expert
- The barking dog

Gerund and participle fragments

These fragments can be turned into complete sentences by substituting a verb for the gerund, or adding a verb to the participle:

- Dale is a document design expert.
- The barking dog finally stopped.

Verb substitution or new verb corrects fragment

Run-On Sentences

ro

A run-on sentence crams grammatically complete sentences together:

- For emergencies, we dial 911 for other questions, we dial 088

Run-on sentence

This sentence can be repaired by dividing it into two sentences:

- For emergencies, we dial 911. For other questions, we dial 088.

Division into two sentences corrects run-on

Another possibility is to join the two parts of the sentence with a semicolon. This option indicates a break that is not quite as strong as the period, and therefore signals to the reader that the two items are closely related:

- For emergencies, we dial 911; for other questions, we dial 088.

Added semicolon corrects run-on

Another possibility is to add a comma followed by a coordinating conjunction (*for, and, nor, but, or, yet, so*):

- For emergencies, we dial 911, but for other questions, we dial 088.

Coordinating conjunction corrects run-on

cs Comma Splices

In a comma splice, two complete ideas (independent clauses) that should be *separated* by a period or a semicolon are incorrectly *joined* by a comma:

Comma splice

- Sarah did a great job, she was promoted.

One option for correcting comma splices is to create two separate sentences:

Division into two sentences

- Sarah did a great job. She was promoted.

Another option is a semicolon to show a relationship between the two items:

Semicolon

- Sarah did a great job; she was promoted.

A third option is a semicolon with a conjunctive adverb (an adverb, ending in *-ly*, that shows a relationship between the items, such as *consequently*):

Semicolon with conjunctive adverb

- Sarah did a great job; consequently, she was promoted.

A fourth option is a coordinating conjunction: (*for, and, nor, but, or, yet, so*)—to create an equal relationship between items:

Coordinating conjunction

- Sarah did a great job and was promoted.

Finally, you can use a subordinating conjunction (a conjunction that creates an dependent relationship between items—see page 686):

Subordinating conjunction

- Because Sarah did a great job, she was promoted.

agr sv Faulty Agreement—Subject and Verb

The subject must agree in number with the verb. But when subject and verb are separated by other words, we might lose track of the subject-verb relationship:

Faulty subject-verb agreement

- The lion's share of diesels are sold in Europe.

Make the verb agree with its subject (*share*), not with a word that comes between the subject and the verb (in this case, the plural noun *diesels*):

Correct subject-verb agreement

- The lion's share of diesels is sold in Europe.

Treat compound subjects connected by *and* as plural:

Compound subject takes plural verb

- Terry and Julie enjoy collaborating on writing projects.

With compound subjects connected by *or* or *nor*, the verb is singular if both subjects are singular and plural if both subjects are plural. If one subject is singular and one is plural, the verb agrees with the one closer to the verb:

> Neither the professor nor the students were able to see what was going on.

Verb agrees with closer subject in compound subject

Also, treat most indefinite pronouns (*anybody, each, everybody*, etc.) as singular subjects:

> Almost everybody who registered for the class was there on the first day.

Indefinite pronoun agrees with singular verb

Treat collective subjects (*team, family, group, committee*, etc.) as singular unless the meaning is clearly plural. Both of the following sentences are correct. In the first sentence, the *group* is understood as a singular subject (the group is a single entity) and agrees with the singular verb *respects*, whereas in the second sentence, the *board* is understood as plural (as indicated by the plural word *authors*) and agrees with the plural verb *are*:

> The group respects its leader.
> The editorial board are all published authors.

Collective subjects agree with singular or plural verbs, depending on meaning

Faulty Agreement—Pronoun and Referent

agr p

A pronoun must refer to a specific noun (its *referent* or *antecedent*), with which it must agree in gender and number. Faulty pronoun-referent agreement is easy to spot when the gender and number clearly don't match (e.g., "He should proceed at their own pace"). However, when an indefinite pronoun such as *each, everyone, anybody, someone*, or *none* is the referent, the pronoun is always singular:

> Everybody should proceed at his or her own pace.
> None of the candidates described her career plans in detail.

Indefinite referents agree with singular pronouns

Dangling and Misplaced Modifiers

dgl

Problems with ambiguity occur when a modifying phrase has no word to modify.

> **Dialing the phone,** the cat ran out the open door.

Dangling modifier

The cat obviously did not dial the phone, but because the modifier **Dialing the phone** has no word to modify, the noun beginning the main clause (*cat*) seems to name the one who dialed the phone. Without any word to join itself to, the modifier *dangles*. Inserting a subject repairs this absurd message.

> As **Joe** dialed the phone, the cat ran out the open door.

Correct

A dangling modifier can also obscure your meaning.

Dangling modifier

> **After completing the student financial aid application form,** the Financial Aid Office will forward it to the appropriate state agency.

Who completes the form—the student or the financial aid office? Here are other dangling modifiers that obscure the message:

Dangling modifier

> **While walking,** a cold chill ran through my body.

Correct

> While **I** walked, a cold chill ran through my body.

Dangling modifier

> Impurities have entered our bodies **by eating chemically processed foods.**

Correct

> Impurities have entered our bodies by **our** eating chemically processed foods.

The order of adjectives and adverbs also affects meaning.

> I **often** remind myself of the need to balance my checkbook.

> I remind myself of the need to balance my checkbook **often.**

Position modifiers to reflect your meaning.

Misplaced modifier

> Joe typed another memo on our computer **that was useless.**

(Was the computer or the memo useless?)

Correct

> Joe typed another useless memo on our computer

or

> Joe typed another memo on our useless computer.

Misplaced modifier

> Mary volunteered **immediately** to deliver the radioactive shipment.

(Volunteering immediately, or delivering immediately?)

Correct

> Mary immediately volunteered to deliver . . .

or

> Mary volunteered to deliver immediately . . .

par Faulty Parallelism

To reflect relationships among items of equal importance, express them in identical grammatical form:

Correct

> We here highly resolve . . . that government **of the people, by the people, for the people** shall not perish from the earth.

Otherwise, the message would be garbled, like this:

> We here highly resolve . . . that government **of the people, which the people created and maintain, serving the people** shall not perish from the earth. — Faulty

If you begin the series with a noun, use nouns throughout the series; likewise for adjectives, adverbs, and specific types of clauses and phrases.

> The new apprentice is **enthusiastic, skilled,** and **you can depend on her.** — Faulty

> The new apprentice is **enthusiastic, skilled,** and **dependable.** — Correct

(all subjective complements)

> In his new job, he felt **lonely** and **without a friend.** — Faulty

> In his new job, he felt **lonely** and **friendless.** — Correct

(both adjectives)

> She plans **to study** all this month and **on scoring well** in her licensing examination. — Faulty

> She plans **to study** all this month and **to score well** in her licensing examination. — Correct

(both infinitive phrases)

> She **sleeps** well and **jogs** daily, **as well as eating** high-protein foods. — Faulty

> She **sleeps** well, **jogs** daily, and **eats** high-protein foods. — Correct

(all verbs)

Faulty Coordination

coord

Give equal emphasis to ideas of equal importance by joining them with coordinating conjunctions: **and, but, or, nor, for, so,** and **yet.**

> This course is difficult **but** worthwhile.

> My horse is old **and** gray.

> We must decide to support **or** reject the dean's proposal.

But do not confound your meaning by coordinating excessively.

> The climax in jogging comes after a few miles **and** I can no longer feel stride after stride **and** it seems as if I am floating **and** jogging becomes almost a reflex **and** my arms **and** legs continue to move **and** my mind no longer has to control their actions. — Excessive coordination

> The climax in jogging comes after a few miles when I can no longer feel stride after stride. By then I am jogging almost by reflex, nearly floating, my arms and legs still moving, my mind no longer having to control their actions. — Revised

Notice how the meaning becomes clear when the less important ideas (**nearly floating, arms and legs still moving, my mind no longer having**) are shown as dependent on, rather than equal to, the most important idea (**jogging almost by reflex**)—the idea that contains the lesser ones.

Avoid coordinating two or more ideas that cannot be sensibly connected:

Faulty

> John had a drinking problem **and** he dropped out of school.

Revised

> John's drinking problem depressed him so much that he couldn't study, and so he quit school.

Instead of *try and,* use *try to.*

Faulty

> I will try and help you.

Revised

> I will try to help you.

sub Faulty Subordination

Proper subordination shows that a less important idea is dependent on a more important idea. A dependent (or subordinate) clause in a sentence is signaled by a subordinating conjunction: **because, so, if, unless, after, until, since, while, as, and although.** Consider these complete ideas:

> Joe studies hard. He has severe math anxiety.

Because these ideas are expressed as simple sentences, they appear coordinate (equal in importance). But if you wanted to convey an opinion about Joe's chances of succeeding in math, you would need a third sentence: **His disability probably will prevent him from succeeding,** or **His willpower will help him succeed.** To communicate the intended meaning concisely, combine the two ideas. Subordinate the one that deserves less emphasis and place the idea you want emphasized in the independent (main) clause.

> Despite his severe math anxiety (*subordinate idea*), Joe studies hard (*independent idea*).

This first version suggests that Joe will succeed. Below, the subordination suggests the opposite meaning:

> Despite his diligent studying (*subordinate idea*), Joe has severe math anxiety (*independent idea*).

Do not coordinate when you should subordinate:

Weak

> Television viewers can relate to an athlete they idolize and they feel obliged to buy the product endorsed by their hero.

Of the two ideas in the sentence above, one is the cause, the other the effect. Emphasize this relationship through subordination:

> Because television viewers can relate to an athlete they idolize, they feel obliged to buy the product endorsed by their hero.

Revised

When combining several ideas within a sentence, decide which is most important, and subordinate the other ideas to it—do not merely coordinate:

> This employee is often late for work, and he writes illogical reports, and he is a poor manager, and he should be fired.

Faulty

> Because this employee is often late for work, writes illogical reports, and has poor management skills, **he should be fired**. (*This last clause is independent.*)

Revised

Faulty Pronoun Case

ca

A pronoun's case (nominative, objective, or possessive) is determined by its role in the sentence: as subject, object, or indicator of possession.

If the pronoun serves as the subject of a sentence (*I, we, you, she, he, it, they, who*), or follows a version of the linking verb *to be*, its case is *nominative*:

> She completed her graduate program in record time.
>
> Who broke the chair?
>
> The chemist who perfected this distillation process is he.

Nominative pronoun case

If the pronoun serves as the object of a verb or a preposition (*me, us, you, her, him, it, them, whom*), its case is *objective*:

> The employees gave her a parting gift.
>
> To whom do you wish to complain?

Objective pronoun case

If a pronoun indicates possession (*my, mine, our, ours, your, yours, his, her, hers, its, their, whose*), its case is *possessive*:

> The brown briefcase is mine.
>
> Whose opinion do you value most?

Possessive pronoun case

The incorrect sentences below are followed by corrected versions in parentheses.

> Whom is responsible to who? (Who is responsible to whom?)
>
> The debate was between Marsha and I. (The debate was between Marsha and me.)

Faulty pronoun case

PUNCTUATION

pct

Punctuation marks are like road signs and traffic signals. They govern reading speed and provide clues for navigation through a network of ideas. The three marks of end punctuation—period, question mark, and exclamation point—work like a red traffic light by signaling a complete stop.

./ Period

A period ends a declarative sentence.

Period ends declarative statement

I I see that you've all completed the essay.

It is also used as the final mark in some abbreviations, such as "Dr." and "Inc." and as a decimal point such as "$18.43" and "26.2%."

?/ Question Mark

A question mark follows a direct question:

Question mark ends direct question

I Have you all completed the essay?

Do not use a question mark to end an indirect question:

Incorrect

I Professor Grim asked if all students had completed the essay?

Period ends indirect question

I Professor Grim asked if all students had completed the essay.

!/ Exclamation Point

Use an exclamation point only when expression of strong feeling is appropriate:

Exclamation point provides emphasis

I I can't believe you finished the essay so fast!

;/ Semicolon

Like a blinking red traffic light at an intersection, a semicolon signals a brief but definite stop. Semicolons have several uses.

To Separate Independent Clauses. A semicolon can separate independent clauses (logically complete ideas) whose contents are closely related and are not already connected by a comma and a coordinating conjunction (*and, or, but*, etc.):

Semicolon separates independent clauses

I The project was finally completed; we had done a good week's work.

To Accompany Conjunctive Adverbs. A semicolon must accompany a conjunctive adverb such as *besides, otherwise, still, however, furthermore, moreover, consequently, therefore, on the other hand, in contrast*, or *in fact*:

Semicolon accompanies conjunctive adverbs

I The job is filled; however, we will keep your résumé on file.

I Your background is impressive; in fact, it is the best among our applicants.

To Separate Items in a Series. When items in a series contain internal commas, semicolons provide clear separation between items.

> I am applying for summer jobs in Santa Fe, New Mexico; Albany, New York; Montgomery, Alabama; and Moscow, Idaho.

Semicolon separates items in a series

Colon

:/

Like a flare in the road, a colon signals you to stop and then proceed, paying attention to the situation ahead. Colons have several uses.

To Signal a Follow-up Explanation. Use a colon when a complete introductory statement requires a follow-up explanation:

> She is an ideal colleague: honest, reliable, and competent.

Colon signals a follow-up explanation

Do not use a colon if the introductory statement is incomplete:

> My plans include: finishing college, traveling for two years, and settling down in Santa Fe.

Incorrect

To Replace a Semicolon. A colon can replace a semicolon between two related, complete statements when the second one explains or amplifies the first:

> Pam's reason for accepting the lowest-paying job offer was simple: she had always wanted to live in the Northwest.

Colon replaces a semicolon

To Introduce a Quotation. Colons can introduce quotations:

> The supervisor's message was clear enough: "You're fired."

Colon introduces a quotation

To Follow Salutations. Colons follow salutations in formal correspondence (e.g., Dear Ms. Jones:).

Comma

The comma is the most frequently used—and abused—punctuation mark. It works like a blinking yellow light, for which you slow down briefly without stopping. Never use a comma to signal a *break* between independent ideas, only a brief slow down. Use commas only in the following situations.

To Pause Between Complete Ideas. In a compound sentence in which a coordinating conjunction (*and, or, nor, for, but*) connects equal (independent) statements, a comma usually precedes the conjunction.

Comma to pause between complete ideas

> This is an excellent course, but the work is difficult.

To Pause Between an Incomplete and a Complete Idea. A comma is usually placed between a complete and an incomplete statement in a complex sentence when the incomplete statement comes first.

Comma between an incomplete and complete idea

> Because he is a fat cat, Jack diets often.

When the order is reversed (complete statement followed by an incomplete one), the comma is usually omitted:

No comma needed

> Jack diets often because he is a fat cat.

To Separate Items (Words, Phrases, or Clauses) in a Series. Use commas after items in a series, including the next-to-last item:

Comma separates items in a series

> Helen, Joe, Marsha, and John are joining us on the term project.

> The new employee complained that the hours were long, the pay was low, the work was boring, and the supervisor was paranoid.

Use no commas if *or* or *and* appears between all items in a series:

No commas needed if *or* or *and* appears between all items

> She is willing to study in San Francisco or Seattle or even in Anchorage.

To Set Off Introductory Phrases. Introductory phrases include infinitive phrases (*to* plus a simple form of the verb), prepositional phrases (beginning with *at, of, in, on,* etc.), participial phrases (beginning with an *-ing* or *-ed* form of a verb), and interjections (emotional words that have no connection with the rest of the sentence). These phrases are set off from the remainder of the sentence by a comma:

Commas to set off introductory phrases

> To be or not to be, that is the question. (infinitive phrase)

> In the event of an emergency, use the fire exit. (prepositional phrase)

> Being an old cat, Jack was slow at catching mice. (participial phrase)

> Oh, is that the verdict? (interjection)

To Set Off Nonrestrictive Phrases and Clauses. A *restrictive* phrase or clause modifies or defines the subject in such a way that deleting the modifier would change the meaning of the sentence. In the following sentence, "who have work experience" *restricts* the subject by limiting the category from all students to just those with work experience. Because this phrase is essential to the sentence's meaning, it is *not* set off by commas:

- All students who have work experience will receive preference.

Restrictive phrase (no comma)

A *nonrestrictive* phrase or clause could be deleted without changing the sentence's meaning ("Our new manager is highly competent") and *is* therefore set off by commas:

- Our new manager, who has only six weeks' experience, is highly competent.

Nonrestrictive phrase (use comma)

To Set Off Parenthetical Elements. Elements that interrupt the flow of a sentence (such as *of course, as a result, as I recall,* and *however*) are considered parenthetical and are enclosed by commas. These items may denote emphasis, afterthought, or clarification.

- This deluxe model, of course, is more expensive. (emphasis)
- Your essay, by the way, was excellent. (afterthought)
- The loss of my job was, in a way, a blessing. (clarification)

Commas to set off parenthetical elements

A direct address also interrupts a sentence and is set off by commas:

- Listen, my children, and you shall hear my story.

Commas to set off direct address

A parenthetical element at the beginning or the end of a sentence is also set off by a comma:

- Naturally, we will expect a full guarantee.
- You've done a good job, I think.

Commas to set off parenthetical elements at beginning and end

To Set Off Quoted Material. Quoted items within a sentence are set off by commas:

- The customer said, "I'll take it," as soon as he laid eyes on our new model.

Comma to set off quoted material

To Set Off Appositives. An *appositive*, a word or words explaining a noun and placed immediately after it, is set off by commas when the appositive is non-restrictive:

- Martha Jones, our new president, is overhauling all personnel policies.
- Alpha waves, the most prominent of the brain waves, are typically recorded in a waking subject whose eyes are closed.

Comma to set off appositives

Other Uses. Commas are used to set off the day of the month from the year in a date (May 10, 1989), to set off numbers in three-digit intervals (6,463,657), to separate city and state in an address (Albany, Iowa), to set off parts of an address in a sentence (J.B. Smith, 18 Sea Street, Albany, Iowa, 51642), to set off day and year in a sentence (June 15, 2013, is my graduation date), and to set off degrees and titles from proper names (Roger P. Cayer, M.D. or Gordon Browne, Jr.).

Commas Used Incorrectly. Avoid needless or inappropriate commas. Read a sentence aloud to identify inappropriate pauses.

Faulty

- The instructor told me, that I was late.

(separates the indirect from the direct object)

- The most universal symptom of the suicide impulse, is depression.

(separates the subject from its verb)

- This has been a long, difficult, semester.

(second comma separates the final adjective from its noun)

- John, Bill, and Sally, are joining us on the trip home.

(third comma separates the final subject from its verb)

- An employee, who expects rapid promotion, must quickly prove his or her worth.

(separates a modifier that should be restrictive)

- I spoke by phone with John, and Marsha.

(separates two nouns, linked by a coordinating conjunction)

- The room was, 18 feet long.

(separates the linking verb from the subjective complement)

- We painted the room, red.

(separates the object from its complement)

ap/ Apostrophe

Apostrophes indicate the possessive, a contraction, and the plural of numbers, letters, and figures.

To Indicate the Possessive. At the end of a singular word, or of a plural word that does not end in *-s*, add an apostrophe plus *-s* to indicate the possessive. Single-syllable nouns that end in *-s* take the apostrophe before an added *-s*:

Apostrophe to indicate possessives

- The people's candidate won.
- I borrowed Chris's book.

Do not add *-s* to words that already end in *-s* and have more than one syllable; add an apostrophe only:

- Aristophanes' death

Do not use an apostrophe to indicate the possessive form of either singular or plural pronouns:

- The book was hers.
- Ours is the best school in the county.

At the end of a plural word that ends in *-s*, add an apostrophe only.

- the cows' water supply
- the Jacksons' wine cellar

At the end of a compound noun, add an apostrophe plus *-s*:

- my father-in-law's false teeth

At the end of the last word in nouns of joint possession, add an apostrophe plus *-s* if both own one item:

- Joe and Sam's lakefront cottage

Add an apostrophe plus *-s* to both nouns if each owns specific items:

- Joe's and Sam's passports

To Indicate a Contraction. An apostrophe shows that you have omitted one or more letters in a phrase that is usually a combination of a pronoun and a verb:

cont

Apostrophes to show contractions

- I'm
- they're
- you'd

Faulty contractions

Avoid faulty contractions: For example, *they're* (short for "they are" and often confused with the possessive *their* and the adverb *there*); *it's* (short for "it is" and often confused with the possessive *its*); *who's* (short for "who is" and often confused with the possessive *whose*); and *you're* (short for "you are" and often confused with the possessive *your*). See Table B.1 (pages 699–700) for more examples.

To Indicate the Plurals of Numbers, Letters, and Figures. For example:

Apostrophes to pluralize numbers, letters, and figures

- The *6's* on this new printer look like smudged *G's*, *9's* are illegible, and the *%'s* are unclear.

Quotation Marks

""/

Quotation marks have a variety of uses:

To Set Off the Exact Words Borrowed from Another Speaker or Writer. The period or comma at the end is placed within the quotation marks:

Quotation marks to set off a speaker's exact words

- "Hurry up," Jack whispered.
- Jack told Felicia, "I'm depressed."

A colon or semicolon is always placed outside quotation marks:

> Our student handbook clearly defines "core requirements"; however, it does not list all the courses that fulfill the requirements.

When a question mark or exclamation point is part of a quotation, it belongs within the quotation marks, replacing the comma or period.

> "Help!" he screamed.
> Marsha asked John, "Can't we agree about anything?"

But if the question mark or exclamation point pertains to the attitude of the person quoting instead of the one being quoted, it belongs outside the quotation mark:

> Why did Boris wink and whisper, "It's a big secret"?

To Indicate Titles. Use quotation marks for titles of articles, paintings, book chapters, and poems (but italicize titles of books, journals, or newspapers instead):

Quotation marks to indicate titles

> The enclosed article, "The Job Market for College Graduates," should provide some helpful insights.

To Indicate Irony. Finally, use quotation marks (with restraint) to indicate irony.

Quotation marks to indicate irony

> She is some "friend"!

Ellipses

Three dots . . . indicate that you have omitted material from a quotation. If the omitted words include the end of a sentence, a fourth dot indicates the period. (Also see page 646.)

Ellipses to indicate omitted material from a quotation

> "Three dots . . . indicate . . . omitted . . . material . . . . A fourth dot indicates the period."

Brackets

Brackets are used within quotations to set off material that was not in the original quotation but is needed for clarification:

Brackets to indicate material added to a quotation

> "She [Amy] was the outstanding candidate for the scholarship."
> "It was in early spring [April 2, to be exact] that the tornado hit."

Use *sic* (Latin for "thus," or "so") in brackets when quoting an error from the original source:

Brackets to indicate an error in a quotation

> The assistant's comment was clear: "He don't [sic] want any."

Italics

ital

Use italics or underlining for titles of books, periodicals, films, newspapers, and plays; for the names of ships; and for foreign words or technical terms. Also, you may use italics *sparingly* for special emphasis.

Various uses of italics

> The *Oxford English Dictionary* is a handy reference tool.
>
> My only advice is *caveat emptor.*
>
> *Bacillus anthracis* is a highly virulent organism.
>
> *Do not* inhale these fumes under any circumstances!

Parentheses

( )/

Material between parentheses, like all other parenthetical material discussed earlier, can be deleted without harming the logical and grammatical structure of the sentence. Use parentheses to enclose material that defines or explains the statement that precedes it:

Parentheses to define or explain preceding material

> An anaerobic (airless) environment must be maintained for the cultivation of this organism.
>
> The cost of running our college has increased by 15 percent in one year (see Appendix A for full cost breakdown).

Dashes

—/

Dashes can be effective to set off parenthetical material if, like parentheses, they are not overused. Parentheses deemphasize the enclosed material, while dashes emphasize it:

Dashes to set off and emphasize material

> Have a good vacation—but watch out for sandfleas.
>
> Mary—a true friend—spent hours helping me rehearse.

On most word-processing programs, a dash is created by two hyphens, which the software will typically convert to a dash.

MECHANICS

The mechanical aspects of writing a document include abbreviation, hyphenation, capitalization, use of numbers, and spelling. (Keep in mind that not all of these rules are hard and fast; some may depend on style guides used in your field.)

ab Abbreviation

The following should *always* be abbreviated:

Always abbreviate

- Titles such as *Ms., Mr., Dr.*, and *Jr.*, when they are used before or after a proper name.
- Specific time designations (*400* b.c.e., *5:15* A.M.).

The following should *never* be abbreviated:

Never abbreviate

- Military, religious, academic, or political titles (*Reverend, President*).
- Nonspecific time designations (*Sarah arrived early in the morning*—not *early in the* A.M.).

Avoid abbreviations whose meanings might not be clear to all readers. Units of measurement (say, *mm.* for *millimeter*) can be abbreviated if they appear often in the document. However, spell out a unit of measurement the first time it is used. Avoid abbreviations in visual aids unless saving space is essential.

-/ Hyphenation

Hyphens divide words at line breaks, and join two or more words used as a single adjective if they precede the noun (but not if they follow it):

Correct use of hyphens

- Com-puter (*at a line break*)
- An all-too-human error (*but* "The error was all too human")

Other commonly hyphenated words include the following:

Other uses of hyphens

- Most words that begin with the prefix *self-* (*self-reliance, self-discipline*—see your dictionary for exceptions).
- Combinations that might be ambiguous (*re-creation* versus *recreation*).
- Words that begin with *ex* when *ex* means "past" (*ex-faculty member* but *excommunicate*).
- All fractions, along with ratios that are used as adjectives and that precede the noun, and compound numbers from twenty-one through ninety-nine (*a two-thirds majority, thirty-eight windows*).

cap Capitalization

Use capitalization in the following situations:

Uses of capitalization

- The first words of all sentences (*This is a good idea.*)
- Titles of people if the title precedes the person's name, but not after (*Senator Barbara Boxer* but *Barbara Boxer, U.S. senator*)

- Titles of books, films, magazines, newspapers, operas, and other longer works. In addition to capitalizing the first word, also capitalize all other words within the title (*A Long Day's Journey into Night*) except articles, short prepositions, and coordinating conjunctions (*and, but, for, or, nor, yet*).
- Parts of a longer work (*Chapter 25, Opus 23*)
- Languages (*French, Urdu*)
- Days of the week (*Saturday*)
- Months (*November*)
- Holidays (*Thanksgiving*)
- Names of organizations or groups (*World Health Organization*)
- Races and nationalities (*Asian American, Australian*)
- Historical events (*War of 1812*)
- Important documents (*Declaration of Independence*)
- Names of structures or vehicles (*Empire State Building*, the *Queen Mary*)
- Adjectives derived from proper nouns (*Chaucerian English*)
- Words such as *street, road, corporation, university*, and *college* only when they accompany a proper noun (*High Street, Rand Corporation, Stanford University*).
- The words *north, south, east*, and *west* when they denote specific regions (*the South, the Northwest*) but not when they are simply directions (*turn east at the light*)

Do not capitalize the seasons (*spring, winter*) or general groups (*the younger generation, the leisure class*).

Numbers and Numerals

#

Numbers expressed in one or two words can be written out or written as numerals. Use numerals to express larger numbers, decimals, fractions, precise technical figures, or any other exact measurements:

Uses of numerals

- 543
- 2,800,357
- 3.25
- 15 pounds of pressure
- 50 kilowatts
- 4,000 rpm

Use numerals for dates, census figures, addresses, page numbers, exact units of measurement, percentages, times with A.M. or P.M. designations, and monetary and mileage figures.

Additional uses of numerals

- page 14
- 1:15 P.M.
- 18.4 pounds
- 9 feet
- 12 gallons
- $15

Do not begin a sentence with a numeral. If the figure needs more than two words, revise your word order:

Uses of numbers in sentences

- Six hundred students applied for the 102 available jobs.
- The 102 available jobs attracted 600 applicants.

Do not use numerals to express approximate figures, time not designated as A.M. or P.M., or streets named by numbers less than 100:

When not to use numerals

- About seven hundred fifty
- Four fifteen
- 108 East Forty-Second Street

In contracts and other documents in which precision is vital, a number can be stated both in numerals and in words:

> The tenant agrees to pay a rental fee of eight hundred and seventy-five dollars ($875.00) monthly.

sp Spelling

Always use the spell-check function in your word-processing software. However, don't rely on it exclusively. Take the time to use a dictionary for all writing assignments. If you are a poor speller, ask someone else to proofread every document before you present the final version.

USAGE

Be aware of the pairs of words (and sometimes groups of three words) that are often confused. Refer to Table B.1 for a list of the most commonly confused words.

TABLE B.1 Commonly confused words

SIMILAR WORDS	USED CORRECTLY IN A SENTENCE
Accept means "to receive willingly."	She *accepted* his business proposal.
Except means "otherwise than."	They all agreed, *except* Bob.
Affect means "to have an influence on."	Meditation *affects* concentration in a positive way.
Affect can also mean "to pretend."	Boris likes to *affect* a French accent.
Effect used as a noun means "a result."	Meditation has a positive *effect* on concentration.
Effect used as a verb means "to make happen" or "to bring about."	Meditation can *effect* an improvement in concentration.
Already means "before this time."	Our new laptops are *already* sold out.
All ready means "prepared."	We are *all ready* for the summer tourist season.
Among refers to three or more.	The prize was divided *among* the four winners.
Between refers to two.	The prize was divided *between* the two winners.
Cite means "to document."	You must always *cite* your sources in research.
Sight means "vision."	Margarita seems to have the gift of second *sight*.
Site means "a location."	Have the surveyors inspected the *site* yet?
Continual means "repeated at intervals."	Our lower field floods *continually* during the rainy season.
Continuous means "without interruption."	His headache has been *continuous* for three days.
Council means "a body of elected people."	I plan to run for student *council*.
Counsel means "to offer advice."	Since you have experience, I suggest you *counsel* Jim on the project as it moves along.
Differ from refers to unlike things.	This plan *differs* greatly from our earlier one.
Differ with means "to disagree."	Mary *differs with* John about the plan.
Disinterested means "unbiased" or "impartial."	Good science calls for *disinterested* analysis of research findings.
Uninterested means "not caring."	Boris is *uninterested* in science.
Eminent means "famous" or "distinguished."	Dr. Ostroff, the *eminent* physicist, is lecturing today.
Imminent means "about to happen."	A nuclear meltdown seemed *imminent*.

(*Continued*)

TABLE B.1 (***Continued***)

SIMILAR WORDS	USED CORRECTLY IN A SENTENCE
Farther refers to physical distance (a measurable quantity).	The station is 20 miles *farther.*
Further refers to extent (not measurable).	*Further* discussion of this issue is vital.
Fewer refers to things that can be counted.	*Fewer* than fifty students responded to our survey.
Less refers to things that can't be counted.	This survey had *less* of a response than our earlier one.
Imply means "to insinuate."	This report *implies* that a crime occurred.
Infer means "to reason from evidence."	From this report, we can *infer* that a crime occurred.
It's stands for "it is."	*It's* a good time for a department meeting.
Its stands for "belonging to it."	The cost of the project has exceeded *its* budget.
Lay means "to set something down."	Please *lay* the blueprints on the desk.
Lie means "to recline." It takes no direct object.	This patient needs to *lie* on his right side all night.
(Note that the past tense of *lie* is *lay*.)	The patient *lay* on his right side all night.
Precede means "to come before."	Audience analysis should *precede* a written report.
Proceed means "to go forward."	If you must wake the cobra, *proceed* carefully.
Principle is always a noun that means "basic rule or standard."	Ethical *principles* should govern all our communications.
Principal, used as a noun, means "the major person(s)."	All *principals* in this purchase must sign the contract.
Principal, used as an adjective, means "leading."	Martha was the *principal* negotiator for this contract.
Stationary means "not moving."	The desk is *stationary.*
Stationery means "writing supplies."	The supply cabinet needs *stationery.*
Their means "belonging to them."	They all want to have *their* cake and eat it too.
There means "at that location."	The new copy machine is over *there.*
They're means "they are."	*They're* not the only ones who disagree.

TRANSITIONS

trans

You can choose from three techniques to achieve smooth transitions within and between paragraphs.

Use Transitional Expressions

Transitional expressions

Use words such as *again, furthermore, in addition, meanwhile, however, also, although, for example, specifically, in particular, as a result, in other words, certainly, accordingly, because*, and *therefore*. Such words serve as bridges between ideas.

Repeat Key Words and Phrases

To help link ideas, repeat key words or phrases or rephrase them in different ways, as in this next paragraph (emphasis added):

Repeated key words and phrases

> Whales are among the most *intelligent* of all mammals. Scientists rank whale *intelligence* with that of higher primates because of *whales' sophisticated* group behavior. These *bright creatures* have been seen teaching and disciplining *their* young, helping *their* wounded comrades, engaging in elaborate courtship rituals, and≈playing in definite *gamelike patterns. They* are able to coordinate such *complex cognitive activities* through *their* highly effective communication system of sonar clicks and pings. Such remarkable social organization apparently stems from the *humanlike* devotion that whales seem to display toward one another.

The key word *intelligent* in the above topic statement reappears as *intelligence* in the second sentence. Synonyms describing intelligent behavior (*sophisticated, bright, humanlike*) reinforce and advance the main idea throughout.

Use Forecasting Statements

Forecasting statements tell your readers where you are going next:

Forecasting statements

- The next step is to further examine the costs of this plan.
- Of course, we can also consider other options.
- This plan should be reconsidered for several reasons.

LISTS

Listed items can be presented in one of two ways: running in as part of the sentence (embedded lists) or displayed with each item on a new line (vertical lists).

Embedded Lists

An embedded list integrates a series of items into a sentence. To number an embedded list, use parentheses around the numerals and either commas or semicolons between the items, as in the following example:

Embedded list

> In order to complete express check-in for your outpatient surgery, you must (1) go to the registration office, (2) sign in and obtain your registration number, (3) receive and wear your red armband, and (4) give your check-in slip to the volunteer, who will escort you to your room.

Vertical Lists

Embedded lists are appropriate for listing only a few short items. Vertical lists are preferable for multiple items. If the items belong in a particular sequence, use numerals or letters; if the sequence of items is unimportant, use bullets.

There are a number of ways to introduce vertical lists. You can use a sentence that closes with "the following" or "as follows" and ends with a colon:

Vertical list using *following* and a colon

> All applicants for the design internship must submit the following:
>
> - Personal statement
> - Résumé
> - Three letters of reference
> - Portfolio

You can also use a sentence that closes with a noun and ends with a colon:

Vertical list using a noun and colon

> All applicants for the design internship must submit four items:
>
> 1. Personal statement
> 2. Résumé
> 3. Three letters of reference
> 4. Portfolio

Finally, you can introduce a vertical list with a sentence that is grammatically incomplete without the list items:

Vertical list using grammatical incompleteness

> To register as a new student:
>
> 1. Take the placement test at the Campus Test Center.
> 2. Attend a new student orientation.
> 3. Register for classes by Web or telephone.
> 4. Pay tuition and fees by the due date.

Do not use a colon with an introductory sentence that ends with a verb, a preposition, or an infinitive, as in the following incorrect examples:

> All applicants for the design internship must submit:
>
> - A personal statement
> - A résumé
> - Three letters of reference
> - A portfolio

Incorrect because the introductory sentence ends with a verb

> All applicants for the design internship need to:
>
> - Submit a personal statement and résumé.
> - Forward three letters of reference.
> - Provide a portfolio.

Incorrect because the introductory sentence ends with a preposition

> All applicants for the design internship need to submit:
>
> - A personal statement
> - A résumé
> - Three letters of reference
> - A portfolio

Incorrect because the introductory sentence ends with an infinitive

If the sentence that introduces the list is followed by another sentence, use periods after both sentences. Do not use a colon to introduce the list:

> The next step is to configure the following fields. Consult Chapter 3 for more information on each field.
>
> - Serial port
> - Baud rate
> - Data bits
> - Stop bits

Vertical list without a colon

Note that some of the preceding examples use a period after each list item and some do not. Use a period after each list item if any of the items contains a complete sentence. Otherwise do not use a period. Also note that items included in a list should be grammatically parallel. For more on parallelism, see page 684.

Works Cited

Abelman, Arthur F. "Legal Issues in Scholarly Publishing." *MLA Style Manual.* 2nd ed. New York: Modern Language Association, 1998: 30–57. Print.

Adams, Gerald R., and Jay D. Schvaneveldt. *Understanding Research Methods.* New York: Longman, 1985. Print.

The Aldus Guide to Basic Design. Aldus Corporation, 1988. Print.

Anson, Chris M., and Robert A. Schwegler. *The Longman Handbook for Writers and Readers,* 2nd ed. New York: Longman, 2000. Print.

"Any Alternative?" *The Economist* 1 Nov. 1997: 83–84. Print.

"Are We in the Middle of a Cancer Epidemic?" *University of California at Berkeley Wellness Letter* 10.9 (1994): 4–5. Print.

Armstrong, William H. "Learning to Listen." *American Educator* (Winter 1997–98): 24+. Print.

Author's Guide. New York: Addison Wesley Longman, 1998. Print.

Baker, Stephen. "Beware social media snake oil." *Bloomberg Businessweek.* 14 Dec. 2009: 48–50. Print.

Ball, Charles. "Figuring the Risks of Closer Runways." *Technology Review* Aug./Sept. 1996: 12–13. Print.

Barbour, Ian. *Ethics in an Age of Technology.* New York: Harper, 1993. Print.

Barnett, Arnold. "How Numbers Can Trick You." *Technology Review* Oct. 1994: 38–45. Print.

Baumann, K. E., et al. "Three Mass Media Campaigns to Prevent Adolescent Cigarette Smoking." *Preventive Medicine* 17 (1988): 510–30. Print.

Beamer, Linda. "Learning Intercultural Communication Competence." *Journal of Business Communication* 29.3 (1992): 285–303. Print.

Bedford, Marilyn S., and F. Cole Stearns. "The Technical Writer's Responsibility for Safety." *IEEE Transactions on Professional Communication* 30.3 (1987): 127–32. Print.

Begley, Sharon. "Is Science Censored?" *Newsweek* 14 Sept. 1992: 63. Print.

Bernstein, Peter L. *Against the Gods: The Remarkable Story of Risk.* New York: Wiley, 1998. Print.

Bjerklie, David. "E-Mail: The Boss Is Watching." *Technology Review* 14 Apr. 1993: 14–15. Print.

Bogert, Judith, and David Butt. "Opportunities Lost, Challenges Met: Understanding and Applying Group Dynamics in Writing Projects." *Bulletin of the Association for Business Communication* 53.2 (1990): 51–53. Print.

Bosley, Deborah. "International Graphics: A Search for Neutral Territory." *INTERCOM* Aug./Sept. 1996: 4–7. Print.

Brower, Vicki. "Ethics for Hire." *Technology Review* Mar./Apr. 1999: 25. Print.

Brownell, Judi, and Michael Fitzgerald. "Teaching Ethics in Business Communication: The Effective/Ethical Balancing Scale." *Bulletin of the Association for Business Communication* 55.3 (1992): 15–18. Print.

Bryan, John. "Down the Slippery Slope: Ethics and the Technical Writer as Marketer." *Technical Communication Quarterly* 1.1 (1992): 73–88. Print.

Burger, Katrina. "Righteousness Pays." *Forbes* 22 Sept. 2000: 11. Print.

Burghardt, M. David. *Introduction to the Engineering Profession.* New York: Harper, 1991. Print.

Byrd, Patricia, and Joy M. Reid. *Grammar in the Composition Classroom.* Boston: Heinle, 1998. Print.

Caher, John M. "Technical Documentation and Legal Liability." *Journal of Technical Writing and Communication* 25.1 (1995): 5–10. Print.

Carliner, Saul. "Demonstrating Effectiveness and Value: A Process for Evaluating Technical Communication Products and Services." *Technical Communication* 44.3 (1997): 252–65. Print.

Carr, David F. "How Social Media Changes Technical Communication." *The Brainyard,* 4 Jan. 2012. Web. 4 March 2013.

Caswell-Coward, Nancy. "Cross-Cultural Communication: Is It Greek to You?" *Technical Communication* 39.2 (1992): 264–66. Print.

Chauncey, C. "The Art of Typography in the Information Age." *Technology Review* Feb./Mar. (1986): 26+. Print.

Christians, C. G., et al. *Media Ethics: Cases and Moral Reasoning.* 2nd ed. White Plains, NY: Longman, 1978. Print.

Cialdini, Robert B. "The Science of Persuasion." *Scientific American* Feb. 2001: 76–81. Print.

Claiborne, Robert. "Our Marvelous Native Tongue: The Life and Times of the English Language." New York: *New York Times,* 1983. Print.

Clark, Gregory. "Ethics in Technical Communication: A Rhetorical Perspective." *IEEE Transactions on Professional Communication* 30.3 (1987): 190–95. Print.

Clark, Thomas. "Teaching students How to Write to Avoid Legal Liability. *Business Communication Quarterly* 60.3 (1997): 71–77.

Clement, David E. "Human Factors, Instructions and Warnings, and Product Liability." *IEEE Transactions on Professional Communication* 30.3 (1987): 149–56. Print.

Cochran, Jeffrey K., et al. "Guidelines for Evaluating Graphical Designs." *Technical Communication* 36.1 (1989): 25–32. Print.

Coe, Marlana. *Human Factors for Technical Communicators.* New York: Wiley, 1996. Print.

———. "Writing for Other Cultures: Ten Problem Areas." *INTERCOM* Jan. 1997: 17–19. Print.

Cohn, Victor. "Coping with Statistics." *A Field Guide for Science Writers.* Eds. Deborah Blum and Mary Knudson. New York: Oxford, 1997. 102–09. Print.

Cole-Gomolski B. "Users Loathe to Share Their Know-How." *Computerworld* 17 Nov. 1997: 6. Print.

Columbia Accident Investigation Board [NASA]. *Report,* Volume 1. Washington, DC: GPO, 2003. Print.

"Consequences of Whistle Blowing in Scientific Misconduct Reported." *Professional Ethics Report* [American Association for the Advancement of Science] IX.4 (Winter 1996): 2. Print.

Cooper, Lyn O. "Listening Competency in the Workplace: A Model for Training." *Business Communication Quarterly* 60.4 (Dec. 1997): 75–84. Print.

"Copyright Protection and Fair Use of Printed Information." *Addison Wesley Longman Author's Guide.* New York: Longman, 2006. Print.

Corbett, Edward P. J. *Classical Rhetoric for the Modern Student,* 3rd ed. New York: Oxford, 1990. Print.

Cotton, Robert, ed. *The New Guide to Graphic Design.* Secaucus, NJ: Chartwell, 1990. Print.

"Crime Spree." *Business Week* 9 Sept. 2002: 8. Print.

Crosby, Olivia. *Employment Interviewing.* Washington, DC: U.S. Department of Labor, 2000. Print.

———. *Résumés, Applications, and Cover Letters.* Washington, DC: U.S. Department of Labor, 1999. Print.

Cross, Mary. "Aristotle and Business Writing: Why We Need to Teach Persuasion." *Bulletin of the Association for Business Communication* 54.1 (1991): 3–6. Print.

Crossen, Cynthia. *Tainted Truth: The Manipulation of Fact in America.* New York: Simon, 1994. Print.

Crumpton, Amy. "Secrecy in Science." *Professional Ethics Report* [American Association for the Advancement of Science] XII.1 (Winter 1999): 1+. Print.

Davenport, Thomas H. *Information Ecology.* New York: Oxford, 1997. Print.

Debs, Mary Beth, "Collaborative Writing in Industry." In *Technical Writing: Theory and Practice.* Eds. Bertie E. Fearing and W. Keats Sparrow. New York: Modern Language Assn., 1989, 33–42. Print.

Devlin, Keith. *Infosense: Turning Information into Knowledge.* New York: W. H. Freeman, 1999. Print.

Dombrowski, Paul M. "*Challenger* and the Social Contingency of Meaning: Two Lessons for the Technical Communication Classroom." *Technical Communication Quarterly* 1.3 (1992): 73–86. Print.

Dorner, Dietrich. *The Logic of Failure.* Reading, MA: Addison, 1996. Print.

Doyle, Alison. "Twitter Job Search." About.com. 18 Mar. 2010. Web. 3 Mar. 2013.

Dumont, R.A., and J. M. Lannon. *Business Communications.* 3rd ed. Glenview, Il.: Scott, 1990.

Easton, Thomas, and Stephan Herrara. "J&J's Dirty Little Secret." *Forbes* 12 Jan. 1998: 42–44. Print.

Elbow, Peter. *Writing without Teachers.* New York: Oxford, 1973. Print.

Elias, Stephen. *Patent, Copyright, and Trademark.* Berkeley, CA: Nolo Press, 1997. Print.

Evans, James. "Legal Briefs." *Internet World* Feb. 1998: 22. Print.

Extejt, Marian M. "Teaching Students to Correspond Effectively Electronically." *Business Communication Quarterly* 61.2 (1998): 57–67. Print.

"Fair Use." 10 June 1993. Online. 2 pp. United States Copyright Office, Library of Congress. 10 June 2007. Web. 4 Mar. 2013.

Farnham, Alan. "How Safe Are Your Secrets?" *Fortune* 8 Sept. 1997: 114–20. Print.

Felker, Daniel B., et al. *Guidelines for Document Designers.* Washington: American Institutes for Research, 1981. Print.

Fineman, Howard. "The Power of Talk." *Newsweek* 8 Feb.1993: 24–28. Print.

Finkelstein, Leo, Jr. "The Social Implications of Computer Technology for the Technical Writer." *Technical Communication* 38.4 (1991): 466–73. Print.

Fisher, Anne. "Can I Stop Gay Bashing?" *Fortune* 7 July 1997: 205–06. Print.

———. "My Company Just Announced I May Be Laid Off. Now What?" *Fortune* 3 Mar. 2003. Print.

———. "My Team Leader Is a Plagiarist." *Fortune* 27 Oct. 1997: 291–92. Print.

———. "Truth and Consequences." *Fortune* 29 May 2000: 292. Print.

Foster, Edward. "Why Users Beef about Documentation." *INTERCOM* Nov. 1998: 10. Print.

Fox, Justin, " A Startling Notion—The Whole Truth." *Fortune* 24 Nov. 1997: 303. Print.

Freundlich, Naomi. "When the Cure May Make You Sicker." *Business Week* 16 Mar. 1998: 14. Print.

Friedland, Andrew J., and Carol L. Folt. *Writing Successful Science Proposals.* New Haven, CT: Yale UP, 2000. Print.

Garner, Rochelle. "IS Newbies: Eager, Motivated, Clueless." *Computerworld* 1 Dec. 1997: 85–86. Print.

Gartaganis, Arthur. "Lasers." *Occupational Outlook Quarterly* Winter 1984: 22–26. Print.

Gesteland, Richard R. "Cross-Cultural Compromises." *Sky* May 1993: 20+. Print.

Gibaldi, Joseph, and Walter S. Achtert. *MLA Handbook for Writers of Research Papers.* 3rd ed. New York: Modern Language Assn., 1988. Print.

Gibbs, W. Wayt. "Speech without Accountability." *Scientific American* Oct. 2000: 34+. Print.

Gilbert, Nick, "1-800-ETHIC." *Financial World* 16 Aug. 1994: 20+. Print.

Gilsdorf, Jeanette W. "Executives' and Academics' Perception of the Need for Instruction in Written Persuasion." *Journal of Business Communication* 23.4 (1986): 55–68. Print.

———. "Write Me Your Best Case for . . ." *Bulletin of the Association for Business Communication* 54.1 (1991): 7–12. Print.

Girill, T.R. "Technical Communication and Art." *Technical Communication* 31.2 (1984): 35. Print.

———. "Technical Communication and Law." *Technical Communication* 32.3 (1985): 37. Print.

Glidden, H. K. *Reports, Technical Writing and Specifications.* New York: McGraw, 1964. Print.

Goby, Valerie P., and Lewis Justus Helen. "The Key Role of Listening in Business: A Study of the Singapore Insurance Industry." *Business Communication Quarterly* 63.2 (June 2000): 41–51. Print.

Golen, Steven, et al. "How to Teach Ethics in a Basic Business Communications Class." *Journal of Business Communication* 22.1 (1985): 75–84. Print.

Goodall, H. Lloyd, Jr., and Christopher L. Waagen. *The Persuasive Presentation.* New York: Harper, 1986. Print.

Grant, Linda. "Where Did the Snap, Crackle, & Pop Go?" *Fortune* 4 Aug. 1997: 223+. Print.

Greenberg, Ilan. "Selling News Short." *Brill's Content* Mar. 2000: 64–65. Print.

Gribbons, William M. "Organization by Design: Some Implications for Structuring Information." *Journal of Technical Writing and Communication* 22.1 (1992): 57–74.

Grice, Roger A. "Focus on Usability: Shazam!" *Technical Communication* 42.1 (1995): 131–33. Print.

Griffin, Robert J. "Using Systematic Thinking to Choose and Evaluate Evidence." *Communicating uncertainty: Media Coverage of New and Controversial Science.* Eds. Sharon Friedman, Sharon Dunwoody, and Carol Rogers. Mahwah, NJ: Erlbaum, 1999. 225–48. Print.

Harcourt, Jules. "Teaching the Legal Aspects of Business Communication." *Bulletin of the Association for Business Communication* 53.3 (1990): 63–64. Print.

Harris, Richard F. "Toxics and Risk Reporting." *A Field Guide for Science Writers.* Eds. Deborah Blum and Mary Knudson. New York: Oxford, 1997. 166–72. Print.

Harrison, Bennett. "Don't Blame Technology This Time." *Technology Review* July 1997: 62. Print.

Hartley, James. *Designing Instructional Text.* 2nd ed. London: Kogan Page, 1985. Print.

in, David. "Meetings without Walls." *Internet World* Oct. 1997: 53–60. Print.

r, Gerald. *Introduction to Rhetorical Theory*. New York: Harper, 1986. Print.

kawa, S. I. *Language in Thought and Action*. 3rd ed. New York: Harcourt, 1972. Print.

, Robert. "Political Realities in Reader/Situation Analysis." *Technical Communication* 31.1 (1984): 16–20. Print.

n, Robert G. "Culture and Communication." *Technical Communication* 38.1 (1991): 125–26. Print.

l-Duin, Ann. "Terms and Tools: A Theory and Research-Based Approach to Collaborative Writing." *Bulletin of the Association for Business Communication* 53.2 (1990): 45–50. Print.

oft, Nancy L. *International Technical Communication: How to Export Information About High Technology*. New York: Wiley, 1995. Print.

Hollowitz, John C., and Donna Pawlowski. "The Development of an Ethical Integrity Interview for Pre-Employment Screening." *The Journal of Business Communication* 34.2 (1997): 203–19. Print.

Huff, Darrell. *How to Lie with Statistics*. New York: Norton, 1954. Print.

Hulbert, Jack E. "Developing Collaborative Insights and Skills." *Bulletin of the Association for Business Communication* 57.2 (1994): 53–56. Print.

———. "Overcoming Intercultural Communication Barriers." *Bulletin of the Association for Business Communication* 57.2 (1994): 41–44. Print.

"International Copyright." July 2002. Online. United States Copyright Office, Library of Congress. 21 Mar. 2006. Web. 4 Mar. 2013.

Isaacs, Arlene B. "Tact Can Seal a Global Deal." *New York Times* 26 July 1997, sec. B: 43. Print.

Jameson, Daphne A. "Using a Simulation to Teach Intercultural Communication in Business Communication Courses." *Bulletin of the Association for Business Communication* 56.1 (1993): 3–11. Print.

Janis, Irving L. *Victims of Groupthink: A Psychological Study of Foreign Policy Decisions and Fiascos*. Boston: Houghton, 1972. Print.

Johannesen, Richard L. *Ethics in Human Communication*. 2nd ed. Prospect Heights, IL: Waveland, 1983. Print.

Journet, Debra. Unpublished review of *Technical Writing*. 3rd ed. Print.

Kane, Kate. "Can You Perform under Pressure?" *Fast Company* Oct./Nov. 1997: 54+. Print.

Karaim, Reed. "The Invasion of Privacy." *Civilization* Oct./Nov. 1996: 70–77. Print.

Kelley-Reardon, Kathleen. *They Don't Get It Do They? Communication in the Workplace—Closing the Gap between Women and Men*. Boston: Little, 1995. Print.

Kelman, Herbert C. "Compliance, Identification, and Internalization: Three Processes of Attitude Change." *Journal of Conflict Resolution* 2 (1958): 51–60. Print.

Keyes, Elizabeth. "Typography, Color, and Information Structures." Technical Communication 40.4 (1993): 638–54. Print.

Kiely, Thomas. "The Idea Makers." *Technology Review* Jan. 1993: 33–40. Print.

King, Ralph T. "Medical Journals Rarely Disclose Researchers' Ties." *Wall Street Journal* 2 Feb. 1999: B1+. Print.

Kipnis, David, and Stuart Schmidt. "The Language of Persuasion." *Psychology Today* Apr. 1985: 40–46. Rpt. in Raymond S. Ross, *Understanding Persuasion*. 3rd ed. Englewood Cliffs: Prentice, 1990. Print.

Kohl, John R., et al. "The Impact of Language and Culture on Technical Communication in Japan." *Technical Communication* 40.1 (1993): 62–72. Print.

Kraft, Stephanie. "Whistleblower Bill's Holiday Adventures." *The Valley Advocate* [Northhampton, MA] 6 Jan. 1994: 5–6. Print.

Kremers, Marshall, "Teaching Ethical Thinking in a Technical Writing Course." *IEEE Transactions on Professional Communication* 32.2 (1989): 58–61. Print.

Lang, Thomas A., and Michelle Secic. *How to Report Statistics in Medicine*. Philadelphia: American College of Physicians, 1997. Print.

Larson, Charles U. *Persuasion: Perception and Responsibility*. 7th ed. Belmont, CA: Wadsworth: 1995. Print.

Lavin, Michael R. *Business Information: How to Find It, How to Use It*. 2nd ed. Phoenix, AZ: Oryx, 1992. Print.

Leki, Ilona. "The Technical Editor and the Non-native Speaker of English." *Technical Communication* 37.2 (1990): 148–52. Print.

Lemonick, Michael. "The Evils of Milk?" *Times* 15 June 1998: 85. Print.

Lenzer, Robert, and Carrie Shook. "Whose Rolodex Is It Anyway?" *Forbes* 23 Feb. 1998: 100–04. Print.

Lewis, Howard L. "Penetrating the Riddle of Heart Attack." *Technology Review* Aug./Sept. 1997: 39–44. Print.

Littlejohn, Stephen W., and David M. Jabusch. *Persuasive Transactions*. Glenview, IL: Scott, 1987. Print.

MacKenzie, Nancy. Unpublished review of *Technical Writing*. 5th ed. Print.

Mackin, John. "Surmounting the Barrier between Japanese and English Technical Documents." *Technical Communication* 36.4 (1989): 346–51. Print.

Maeglin, Thomas. Unpublished review of *Technical Writing*. 7th ed. Print.

Manning, Michael. "Hazard Communication 101." *INTERCOM* June 1998: 12–15. Print.

Martin, Jeanette S., and Lillian H. Chaney. "Determination of Content for a Collegiate Course in Intercultural Business Communication by Three Delphi Panels." *Journal of Business Communication* 29.3 (1992): 267–83. Print.

Martin, Justin. "So, You Want to Work for the Best . . ." *Fortune* 12 Jan. 1998: 77–78. Print.

Matson, Eric. "The Seven Sins of Deadly Meetings." *Fast Company* Oct./Nov. 1997: 27–31. Print.

McGuire, Gene. "Shared Minds: A Model of Collaboration." *Technical Communication* 39.3 (1992): 467–68. Print.

Merritt, Jennifer. "For MBAs, Soul-Searching 101." *Business Week* 16 Sept. 2002: 64–66. Print.

———. "You Mean Cheating Is Wrong?" *Business Week* 9 Dec. 2002: 8. Print.

Meyer, Benjamin D. "The ABCs of New-Look Publications." *Technical Communication* 33.1 (1986): 13–20. Print.

"Misconduct Scandal Shakes German Science." *Professional Ethics Report* [American Assoc. for the Advancement of Science] X3 (Summer 1997): 2. Print.

Monastersky, Richard. "Courting Reliable Science." *Science News* 153.16 (1998): 249–51. Print.

Monmonier, Mark. *Cartographies of Danger: Mapping Hazards in America*. Chicago: U of Chicago P, 1997. Print.

Monty, Scott. "The Social Media Marketing Blog." 30 June 2009. Web. 3 Mar. 2013.

Morgan, Meg. "Patterns of Composing: Connections between Classroom and Workplace Collaborations." *Technical Communication* 38.4 (1991): 540–42. Print.

Murphy, Kate. "Separating Ballyhoo from Breakthrough." *Business Week* 13 July 1998: 143. Print.

Nakache, Patricia. "Is It Time to Start Bragging about Yourself?" *Fortune* 27 Oct. 1997: 287–88. Print.

National Institutes of Health. "Study to Prove How Healthy Younger Adults Make Use of Genetic Tests." *NIH News*. 3 May 2007. Web. 4 May 2007 <www.nih.gov/news>.

Nelson, Sandra J., and Douglas C. Smith. "Maximizing Cohesion and Minimizing Conflict in Collaborative Writing Groups." *Bulletin of the Association for Business Communication* 53.2 (1990): 59–62. Print.

Nielsen, Jakob. "F-shaped pattern for reading web content." *Jakob Nielsen's Alertbox*. 17 Apr. 2006. Web. 3 Mar. 2013.

Nordenberg, Tamar. "Direct to You: TV Drug Ads That Make Sense." *FDA Consumer* Jan./Feb. 1998: 7–10. Print.

Notkins, Abner L. "New Predictors of Disease." *Scientific American* March 2007: 72–79. Print.

Nunberg, G. "The Trouble with PowerPoint." *Fortune* 20 Dec. 1999: 330–34. Print.

Nydell, Margaret K. *Understanding Arabs: A Guide for Westerners*. New York: Logan, 1987. Print.

Office of Technology Assessment. *Harmful Non-Indigenous Species in the United States*. Washington, DC: GPO, 1993. Print.

"On Line." *Chronicle of Higher Education* 21 Sept. 1992, sec. A: 29. Print.

Ornatowski, Cezar M. "Between Efficiency and Politics: Rhetoric and Ethics in Technical Writing." *Technical Communication Quarterly* 1.1 (1992): 91–103. Print.

Oxfeld, Jesse. "Analyze This." *Brill's Content* Mar. 2000: 105–06. Print.

Parrish, Deborah. "The Scientific Misconduct Definition and Falsification of Credentials." *Professional Ethics Report* [American Assoc. for the Advancement of Science] IX.4 (1996): 1+.

Pearce, C. Glenn, Iris W. Johnson, and Randolph T. Barker. "Enhancing the Student Listening Skills and Environment." *Business Communication Quarterly* 58.4 (Dec. 1995): 28–33. Print.

"People, Performance, Profits." *Forbes* 20 Oct. 1997: 57. Print.

"Performance Appraisal—Discrimination." *The Employee Problem Solver*. Ramsey, NJ: Alexander Hamilton Institute, 2000. Print.

Perloff, Richard M. *The Dynamics of Persuasion*. Hillsdale, NJ: Erlbaum, 1993. Print.

Peyser, Marc, and Steve Rhodes. "When E-Mail Is Oops-Mail." *Newsweek* 16 Oct. 1995: 82. Print.

Plumb, Carolyn, and Jan H. Spyridakis. "Survey Research in Technical Communication: Designing and Administering Questionnaires." *Technical Communication* 39.4 (1992): 625–38. Print.

Porter, James E. "Truth in Technical Advertising: A Case Study." *IEEE Transactions on Professional Communication* 33.3 (1987): 182–89. Print.

Powell, Corey S. "Science in Court." *Scientific American* October 1997: 32+. Print.

Privacy Rights Clearinghouse. "Fact Sheet 7: Workplace Privacy and Employee Monitoring." Feb. 2013. Web. 3 Mar. 2013.

Raeburn, Paul. "Warning: Biotech Is Hurting Itself." *Business Week* 20 Dec. 1999: 78. Print.

Raloff, Janet. "Chocolate Hearts: Yummy and Good Medicine?" *Science News* 157.12 (2000): 188–89. Print.

Read Me First!: A Style Guide for the Computer Industry. Palo Alto, CA: Sun Microsystems Press, 2003. Print.

Redish, Janice C., et al. "Making Information Accessible to Readers." *Writing in Nonacademic Settings*. Eds. Lee Odell and Dixie Goswami. New York: Guilford, 1985. Print.

Robinson, Edward A. "Beware—Job Seekers Have No Secrets." *Fortune* 29 Dec. 1997: 285. Print.

Rokeach, Milton. *The Nature of Human Values*. New York: Free, 1973. Print.

Rosman, Katherine. "Finding Drug Ties at a Medical Mag." *Brill's Content* Mar. 2000: 100. Print.

———. "Lies, Damned Lies, and Medical Statistics." *Forbes* 14 Aug. 1995: 130–35. Print.

Ross, Raymond S. *Understanding Persuasion*. 3rd ed. Englewood Cliffs: Prentice, 1990. Print.

Rottenberg, Annette T. *Elements of Argument*. 3rd ed. New York: St. Martin's, 1991. Print.

Rowland, D. *Japanese Business Etiquette: A Practical Guide to Success with the Japanese*. New York: Warner, 1985. Print.

Ruggiero, Vincent R. *The Art of Thinking*. 3rd ed. New York: Harper, 1991. Print.

Ruiz, Rebecca. "How the Internet Is Changing Health Care." Forbes.com. 30 Jul. 2009. Web. 3 Mar. 2013.

Sabath, Ann Marie. *Business Etiquette: 101 Ways to Conduct Business with Charm and Savvy*. Franklin Lakes, NJ: Career Press, 1998. Print.

Samuelson, Robert J. "Merchants of Mediocrity." *Newsweek* 1 Aug. 1994: 44. Print.

Schafer, Sarah. "Is Your Data Safe?" *Inc.* Feb. 1997: 93–97. Print.

Schein, Edgar H. "How Can Organizations Learn Faster? The Challenge of Entering the Green Room." *Strategies for Success: Core Capabilities for Today's Managers*. Boston: Sloan Management Review Assoc., 1996. 34–39. Print.

Schrage, Michael. "Time for Face Time." *Fast Company* Oct./Nov. 1997: 232. Print.

Scott, James C., and Diana J. Green. "British Perspectives on Organizing Bad-News Letters: Organizational Patterns Used by Major U.K. Companies." *Bulletin of the Association for Business Communication* 55.1 (1992): 17–19. Print.

Seglin, Jeffrey L. "Would You Lie to Save Your Company?" *Inc.* July 1998: 53+. Print.

Seligman, Dan. "Gender Mender." *Forbes* 6 Apr. 1998: 72+. Print.

Senge, Peter M. "The Leader's New York: Building Learning Organizations." *Sloan Management Review* 32.1 (Fall 1990): 1–17. Print.

Shedroff, Nathan. "Information Interaction Design: A Unified Field Theory of Design." *Information Design*. Ed. Robert Jacobson. Cambridge, MA: MIT Press, 2000. 267–92. Print.

Sherif, Muzapher, et al. *Attitude and Attitude Change: The Social Judgment-Involvement Approach*. Philadelphia: Saunders, 1965. Print.

Sittenfeld, Curtis. "Good Ways to Deliver Bad News." *Fast Company* Apr. 1999: 88+. Print.

Smith, Gary. "Eleven Commandments for Business Meeting Etiquette." *INTERCOM* Feb. 2000: 29. Print.

Sowell, Thomas. "Magic Numbers." *Forbes* 20 Oct. 1997: 120. Print.

Spencer, SueAnn. "Use Self-Help to Improve Document Usability." *Technical Communication* 43.1 (1996): 73–77. Print.

Sproull, Lee, and Sara Kiesler. *Connections: New Ways of Working in the Networked Organization*. Cambridge: MIT Press, 2001. Print.

Spyridakis, Jan H., and Michael J. Wenger. "Writing for Human Performance: Relating Reading Research to Document Design." *Technical Communication* 39.2 (1992): 202–15. Print.

Stanton, Mike. "Fiber Optics." *Occupational Outlook Quarterly* (Winter 1984): 27–30. Print.

Stepanek, Marcia. "When in Beijing, Mum's the Word." *Business Week* 13 July 1998: 4. Print.

Stevenson, Richard W. "Workers Who Turn in Bosses Use Law to Seek Big Rewards." *New York Times* 10 July 1989, sec. A: 7.

Stix, Gary. "Plant Matters: How Do You Regulate an Herb?" *Scientific American* Feb. 1998: 30+. Print.

Stonecipher, Harry. *Editorial and Persuasive Writing*. New York: Hastings, 1979. Print.

Sturges, David L. "Internationalizing the Business Communication Curriculum." *Bulletin of the Association for Business Communication* 55.1 (1992): 30–39. Print.

Taubes, Gary. "Telling Time by the Second Hand." *Technology Review* May/June 1998: 76–78. Print.

Thatcher, Barry. "Cultural and Rhetorical Adaptation for South American Audiences." *Technical Communication* 46.2 (1999): 177–95. Print.

Thrush, Emily A. "Bridging the Gap: Technical Communication in an Intercultural and Multicultural Society." *Technical Communication Quarterly* 2.3 (1993): 271–83. Print.

Timmerman, Peter D., and Wayne Harrison. "The Discretionary Use of Electronic Media: Four Considerations for Bad-News Bearers." *Journal of Business Communication* 42.4 (2005): 379–89. Print.

Trafford Abigail. "Critical Coverage of Public Health and Government." *A Field Guide for Science Writers*. Eds. Deborah Blum and Mary Knudson. New York: Oxford, 1997. 131–41. Print.

Tufte, Edward R. *The Cognitive Style of PowerPoint*. Cheshire, CT: Graphics Press, 2003. Print.

Unger, Stephen H. *Controlling Technology: Ethics and the Responsible Engineer*. New York: Holt, 1982. Print.

U.S. Air Force Academy. *Executive Writing Course*. Washington, DC: GPO, 1981. Print.

U.S. Bureau of Land Management. *Plain Language*. 10 April 2004. Web. 7 May 2007 <www.blm.gov/nhp/NPR>.

van der Meij, Hans, and John M. Carroll. "Principles and Heuristics for Designing Minimalist Instruction." *Technical Communication* 42.2 (1995): 243–61. Print.

Van Pelt, William. Unpublished review of *Technical Writing*. 3rd ed. Print.

Van Riper, Tom. "Text messaging generation entering workplace." Forbes.com, 22 August 2006. Web. 3 Mar. 2013.

Varchaver, Nicholas. "The Perils of E-mail." *Fortune* 17 Feb. 2003: 96–102.

Varner, Iris I., and Carson H. Varner. "Legal Issues in Business Communications." *Journal of the American Association for Business Communication* 46.3 (1983): 31–40. Print.

Victor, David A. *International Business Communication*. New York: Harper, 1992. Print.

"Walking to Health." *Harvard Men's Watch* 2.12 (1998): 3–4. Print.

Walter, Charles, and Thomas F. Marsteller. "Liability for the Dissemination of Defective Information." *IEEE Transactions on Professional Communication* 30.3 (1987): 164–67. Print.

Wandycz, Katarzyna. "Damn Yankees." *Forbes* 10 March 1997: 22–23. Print.

Wang, Linda. "Veggies Prevent Cancer through Key Protein." *Science News* 159.12 (2001): 182. Print.

Warshaw, Michael. "Have You Been House-Trained?" *Fast Company* Oct. 1998: 46+. Print.

Weimer, Maryellen. "Does PowerPoint Help or Hinder Learning?" *Faculty Focus*. Aug. 1 2012. Web. 4 Mar. 2013.

Weinstein, Edith K. Unpublished review of *Technical Writing*. 5th ed. Print.

Weymouth, L. C. "Establishing Quality Standards and Trade Regulations for Technical Writing in World Trade." *Technical Communication* 37.2 (1990): 143–47. Print.

White, Jan. *Color for the Electronic Age*. New York: Watson-Guptill, 1990. Print.

———. *Editing by Design*. 2nd ed. New York: Bowker, 1982. Print.

———. *Great Pages*. El Segundo, CA: Serif, 1990. Print.

———. *Visual Design for the Electronic Age*. New York: Watson-Guptill, 1988. Print.

"Why employers need a text messaging policy." Michael Best and Friedrich LLP. 20 Jan. 2010. Web. 4 Mar. 2013.

Wickens, Christopher D. *Engineering Psychology and Human Performance*. 3rd ed. New York: Pearson, 1999. Print.

Wight, Eleanor, "How Creativity Turns Facts into Usable Information." *Technical Communication* 32.1 (1985): 9–12. Print.

Williams, Robert I. "Playing with Format, Style, and Reader Assumptions." *Technical Communication* 30.3 (1983): 11–13.

Wojahn, Patricia G. "Computer-Mediated Communication: The Great Equalizer between Men and Women?" *Technical Communication* 41.4 (1994): 747–51. Print.

Writing User-Friendly Documents. Washington, DC: U.S. Bureau of Land Management, 2001. Print.

Yoos, George. "A Revision of the Concept of Ethical Appeal." *Philosophy and Rhetoric* 12.4 (1979): 41–58. Print.

Zibell, Kristin J. "Usable Information through User-Centered Design." *INTERCOM* Dec. 1999: 12–14. Print.

Index